THE
SALVATION ARMY
YEAR BOOK

2015

INTERNATIONAL
MISSION STATEMENT

The Salvation Army, an international movement, is an
evangelical part of the universal Christian Church.
Its message is based on the Bible. Its ministry is motivated by the
love of God. Its mission is to preach the gospel of Jesus Christ and
to meet human needs in his name without
discrimination.

THE SALVATION ARMY
INTERNATIONAL HEADQUARTERS
101 QUEEN VICTORIA STREET, LONDON EC4V 4EH, UNITED KINGDOM

**Dedicated to the glory of God
in whose name and by whose grace
the work described in this volume
has been accomplished**

Annual reports in this edition mostly cover the period 1 May 2013 to 30 April 2014.
Statistics are those recorded on 1 January 2014.
Staff lists and details of centres of work are generally accurate according to information published by 30 September 2014.

First published 2014

Copyright © 2014 The General of The Salvation Army

ISBN 978-0-85412-927-0
e-book ISBN 978-0-85412-928-7

Editor: Major Deslea Maxwell

Cover design and colour maps: Berni Georges
Photo design: Jooles Tostevin

Published by Salvation Books
The Salvation Army International Headquarters
101 Queen Victoria Street, London EC4V 4EH, United Kingdom

Printed in the United Kingdom by Page Bros Ltd, Norwich NR6 6SA
using paper from sustainable sources

Contents

Toward a Clearer, Open and more Transparent Future

Foreword by General André Cox
International Leader of The Salvation Army

General André Cox and World President of
Women's Ministries Commissioner Silvia Cox

2015 marks a significant milestone for The Salvation Army as we celebrate 150 years since William and Catherine Booth founded this movement that now officially works in 126 countries.

Such a landmark is not merely an opportunity to look back but also a vital springboard for the future. May Salvationists never forget that the primary purpose of our calling is to bring Jesus' message of hope, deliverance and salvation to the world! People, therefore, matter most in all that we think, plan and do.

It is the stories of individuals who found peace, change and transformation that have written Salvation Army history to date, and it is the real life-changing testimonies that write our story now and into the future.

If The Salvation Army is to be effective and fruitful in years to come then we will need to be an organisation that prioritises people. We need to solve problems, not just treat symptoms; we need to focus on helping people achieve lasting and real outcomes, not simply concentrate on outputs or activities.

In considering the issues currently facing The Salvation Army, a number link to two key questions which helpfully serve to focus our minds:

• How do we know what difference we are making in the world – can we improve our ways of measurement?

• How are we held to account for our actions – can we enhance our accountability?

I believe the answer to these questions is yes. It is critically important that we are clear about our God-given purpose, and can insightfully measure progress and impact as we journey together with the people we serve.

Any inconsistencies, weaknesses or failures in our programmes, or in the behaviour of our people have damaging consequences. Given that the world we live in demands ever-greater transparency and accountability, Salvationists must be people of utter integrity as we seek to be faithful to the call of God and to the divinely inspired vision of our Founders long ago.

It is the case, sadly, that many of the injustices seen by William and Catherine Booth remain a reality 150 years later in this 21st century. Within these pages Elise Belcher – Community Development Coordinator (Africa), IHQ – spotlights the realities of modern-day slavery and the evils of human trafficking. Dr Helen Cameron – Head of the Public Affairs Unit, United Kingdom Territory with the Republic of Ireland – astutely asks how The Salvation Army today can faithfully engage with the state, the market, non-governmental organisations and faith-based organisations, whilst Kevin Sims – Editor *All the World*, IHQ – whets our appetite as we anticipate exciting events when Salvationists from around the world gather in London during early July for the *Boundless* Congress.

This edition of *The Year Book* provides many facts and much information about the work of the worldwide Salvation Army. Most inspiring are the impact-filled stories of positive, lasting transformation, where God, through the mission and ministry of his faithful people, changes the lives of men, women, boys and girls for the present and into eternity. May these pages galvanise you to Christian prayer and service so that the world might be won for Jesus.

A Household of Faith

by Dr Helen Cameron

In March 2014 Dr Helen Cameron spoke at Global Conversation, the USA Salvation Army Conference for Social Work and Emergency Disaster Services considering how The Salvation Army can faithfully engage with the state, the market, NGOs and FBOs. The following article is a summary of the paper presented on that occasion.

A 'Household of Faith' describes the situation of Lydia, a trader in purple cloth whose story is told in Acts 16:11-15. Her husband Simon worked in Thyatira, dying the cloth which Lydia sold in Philippi. When Lydia became a Christian her household became the base for a growing church and part of a network of Christians across the Roman Empire. Lydia was the head of a complex operation which included a prosperous trade in textiles, an escape route for Christian slaves whose masters opposed their new religion, and a trusted means of conveying the apostle Paul's letters as they were passed from church to church. A large volume of people, goods, money and messages were dealt with by trusted household servants whose honesty was beyond question.

What is The Salvation Army?

Engagement starts with self-understanding. Lydia's household of faith is a useful model for The Salvation Army as it seeks to engage with other organisations, an engagement that starts with self-understanding. In founding The Salvation Army the Booths were clear that what they were starting was an expression of the church that was Christ-focused, based on missional principles of aggression and adaptation, Spirit-filled and eschatological. (Major (Dr) John Read provides a detailed study of this in chapter 5 of *Catherine Booth: Laying the Theological Foundation of a Radical Movement.*) In being adaptive and innovative the Booths devised a particular form of church government or polity based on the organisational innovation of their day – bureaucracy – which coordinated the efforts of many people towards a single aim. In his *In Darkest England and the Way Out* William Booth looked for a single organising intelligence to link up different agencies to deal with social problems at their roots

3

and holistically, rather than ameliorate them. Charity was only ever a step on the way to securing an adequate livelihood.

In each country where The Salvation Army is at work a legal form must be adopted as we move gradually to registration as a church. In many democratic countries we are obliged to adopt the legal forms of both charity and company. They then become a taken-for-granted part of our identity, shaping what we do and how we do it.

We have to decide what to do with the bureaucratic government we have inherited based upon a chain of command of appointed officers. Do we take the freedom Catherine offers us to find new means for new times? Or do we accept the Booths' legacy as giving us a distinctive polity that keeps us on the boundary between the church and the world? At its best the bureaucratic form delegates authority to the lowest level whilst retaining account-ability, it encourages activism and expansion whilst offering a level of consistency across different cultural contexts. At worst bureaucracy is seen as slow, open to corruption, self-perpetuating and prone to micromanagement, yet it is still the dominant form for any organisation seeking to deliver solutions.

If this is what we are, what is the scope for engagement?

Engagement with the state, the market, FBOs and NGOs gives us possibilities to tackle social problems in a more thorough-going way than we could if we acted alone. It also gives us the potential to set up entities that can work more fully with that partner as long as they remain connected to the chain of command.

The market operates by producing goods and services which are sold. When The Salvation Army partners with firms or trades in its own name it needs to ensure that it trades fairly, adds value through its goods and services and provides fair wages and working conditions for its employees.

The state operates by taxing its citizens in order to provide infra-structure and security. In some countries the state takes some responsibility for the welfare of its citizens. When The Salvation Army provides welfare services under contract to the state, we should ensure that the state does not offload its responsibility onto us. In countries where we provide education and health-care without any finance from the state, then these services must be accessible to the poorest citizens.

NGOs and FBOs take donor

funds and use them to deliver goods and services to people in line with their publicly stated purposes. The NGO mediates between the beneficiary and the donor, who may be very specific about the use of funding. The Salvation Army has the potential to be a confident partner, knowing it can span sector boundaries and rationales without losing its ecclesial identity as an overflowing of grace from the life of the Church into the world.

If there is scope for engagement, how do we do it faithfully?

If we are to be a credible church, faith-based organisation, faith-based enterprise and faith-based agent of the state, then we need to put those beliefs into a language the public can understand. Here are some suggestions:

• The equal dignity of all people lies at the heart of the production and consumption of goods and services.

• We serve people because they are of worth to God and not only as a means of enacting government policy.

• We seek donors that trust beneficiaries to understand how God wishes them to flourish.

The Salvation Army is part of the household of faith. All members of that household are in partnership in the divine economy – all are stewards, not one is an owners. The fact that we know Lydia's name suggests that she achieved some prominence in the network of churches that Paul established. She started with what she had, a household of faith, and adapted. We can do nothing less.

Dr Helen Cameron is Head of the Public Affairs Unit for the United Kingdom Territory with the Republic of Ireland.

A Formula for Freedom

Elise Belcher writes about bringing freedom to victims of human trafficking in Southern Africa

Groups of Salvationists have sung outside brothels all night. They've given hot chocolate to the women, and gone into the brothels in pairs to make friends with the sex workers. These women have now started attending the South Rand Community Church, Central Division. Margaret says: 'Faith becomes messy … how do you support all these different kinds of people who, as they are transforming and becoming more like Christ, worship on Sunday morning and return to "work" on Sunday evening? However, it is a fascinating journey of which to be a part! We will teach them about Jesus, tell them they are precious and go back to the gutter to show the love of our Salvationism.'

A lone little girl stands on the boardwalk. She represents millions around the world who are victims of human trafficking. It is the fastest growing international crime, only exceeded by drug smuggling as the largest source of illegal income. As millions are trafficked each year, nearly every country in the world is affected, as a point of origin, transit or destination.

Over 44,500 South Africans are enslaved. Women and children make up the vast majority of this number – whether for sexual exploitation or other forms of forced labour. This is a result of factors that are rooted in poverty, inequality and a lack of economic opportunity; provoking dangerous survival strategies amongst the most vulnerable.

The Southern African Territory is tackling this issue with a programme that is inspiring and involving young people across the country. Major Margaret Stafford, National Coordinator for the Anti-Human Trafficking programme* says: 'Our aim is to be an advocate for those who cannot advocate for themselves, to protect the innocent and the victim and to prevent the crime of human trafficking wherever possible.'

Advocacy

Advocacy stands up for lasting change. Not accepting the status quo, The Salvation Army partners with other organsations to act against injustice. The law, previously focused on domestic violence, took more than nine years to become more supportive of human trafficking victims. January 2014 saw the first prosecution of a man, sentenced to life imprisonment, for the forced marriage of a 14-year-old girl. Even with these vital changes, advocacy efforts in the territory continue to ensure the law is effectively implemented.

Protection

Protection meets the need directly.

The territory has set up a rescue hotline that has saved lives. Mary** called the hotline and realised her job offer in England was false because the Army proved the visa documents were fake and the job non-existent. Fachran's** call enabled The Salvation Army to trigger a police raid on a brothel that released his fiancée and several other women from across Asia. They had been tricked into coming to South Africa for work. 'I sincerely thank you who have helped me to locate my fiancée. I hope she can be back soon in Thailand. Our family is waiting for her return for a reunion. I sincerely hope that all sufferings in this world come to an end and there is peace. May you always be in good health, and all be smooth sailing. Let me know if there is anything I can do for the people, I will do my best to assist.'

Prevention

Prevention puts information into people's hands. In 2013, well over 8,500 people were taught how to protect themselves and others. From training workshops with major corporate businesses, to information stands at SEXPO and airports, radio interviews and dramatic 'flash mobs' at shopping centres, the message is building momentum. School assemblies teach the youngest not to accept gifts from strangers, whilst school leavers and first-time travellers receive luggage tags with information to keep them safe.

Youthful creativity and enthusiasm in this programme makes it relevant. Mutsa Mahwehwe, a young Salvationist, says: 'It is not always an easy task to understand another person's life or situation. To have been part of something that cries out to the good in humanity was a humbling experience. I enjoyed the time spent with friends all the while imagining never being able to see them again, a thought that could bring tears to my eyes. It emphasised the fact that freedom is a dream for others around us and the need for prayer within our communities and around the world.'

The girl on the boardwalk is given a balloon. Nothing changes. She is given another, but still with no result. When she has 25 helium balloons she gently starts to lift from the ground. It takes a huge amount of coordination, resources and time to free one victim. Just as the traffickers are organised, skilful and confident in their methods of abuse and exploitation, The Salvation Army in South Africa is using Christian innovation in mission to bring real freedom.

* The programme would not have been possible without the support of the Sweden and Latvia Territory

** Names changed for protection

Elise Belcher is the Community Development Coordinator (Africa) for International Projects and Development Services, IHQ.

Celebrating 150 Years

Kevin Sims anticipates the gathering of
16,000 Salvationists

It is not clear why the term 'congress' was chosen for a large gathering of Salvationists, especially considering the way that military terminology was grasped so strongly after The Christian Mission became The Salvation Army in 1878. Soldiers and officers could just have easily been summoned from their barracks and citadels to a muster, rally or assembly. But no – since the 1880s, gatherings of Salvationists have been known as congresses. And the greatest of these are international congresses!

The 2015 international congress, officially the eighth, can easily claim to be the most international ever, with delegates drawn from many of the 126 countries (and political entities/units) in which The Salvation Army works. This compares favourably with previous international congresses. According to the Army's official history the first, from 29 May to 4 June 1886, included representatives from 19 'countries and colonies'. By the time the 2000 International Millennial Congress was held in Atlanta, Georgia, USA – the only one to be held away from London –

the Army flag was flying in 19 countries fewer than today.

As well as the two mentioned above, previous international congresses were also held in 1894, 1904, 1914, 1978 and 1990. What many people think of as the centenary congress in 1965 was actually never called a congress – even though it served the same purpose!

Of the 16,000 delegates expected to gather in July 2015, well over 10,000 will travel to the UK from overseas. Among these will be 1,500 sponsored delegates, whose way to the congress has been made possible through donations to the 'Mind the Gap' fund-raising programme.

As well as being truly international, this year's 150th anniversary congress can also claim to have come back 'home', with the venue – the O2 Arena that was built to celebrate the new millennium – being only three miles from the east London streets where William and Catherine Booth began their ministry in 1865.

The congress theme, *Boundless – The Whole World Redeeming*, also strikes right at the heart of The Salvation Army. It's taken from what is known to Salvationists as the Founder's Song: 'O Boundless Salvation!'

The congress programme will cover three sub-themes – Commemorating the Past, Celebrating the Present and Innovating for the Future, ensuring there is a clear purpose for the gathering, not just looking back but looking forward to what the Salvation Army will become.

This sense of purpose in gathering together goes right back to the very first international congress, whose goals for the present were to 'better aquaint' the soldiers and leaders; and to increase 'brotherly love and mutual sympathy'. The official history book reports that the future was just as important, with 'new methods and plans of action' to be 'laid down, explained, understood and acted upon'. Today, this is neatly gathered under 'innovating', a word which would have been unfamiliar to most people in the late 19th century.

And, of course, just as the biblical apostle James reminds his readers that faith without works is dead, so any gathering of God's people – large or small – is pointless without what was sought at the 1886 congress: 'a great Pentecostal baptism of the fire of the Holy Spirit upon the multitudes purifying from sin and inflaming all with the pure love of God and pitying compassion for perishing men.'

Today, electronic communication and modern travel capacity can bring together an ever-growing Salvation Army more quickly than before. The 16,000 people at the O2 will be joined by thousands more through live-streaming and social media interaction.

The international congress isn't just for today, or the Army's special anniversary – it's for tomorrow, for next year, for the future days known only to God. The gathering of people from across this apparently 'boundless' movement will, no doubt, be a grand, even spectacular event. But the long-term value will be in the increase in 'brotherly love and mutual sympathy' that provides a Spirit-driven wave of prayer and loving support to the millions of people around the world who serve God through The Salvation Army and to those who feel his loving touch through its Christ-inspired ministry.

Kevin Sims works in the Programme Resources Department at IHQ as editor of All the World.

THE DOCTRINES OF THE SALVATION ARMY

We believe that the Scriptures of the Old and New Testaments were given by inspiration of God, and that they only constitute the Divine rule of Christian faith and practice.

We believe that there is only one God, who is infinitely perfect, the Creator, Preserver and Governor of all things, and who is the only proper object of religious worship.

We believe that there are three persons in the Godhead – the Father, the Son and the Holy Ghost, undivided in essence and co-equal in power and glory.

We believe that in the person of Jesus Christ the Divine and human natures are united, so that he is truly and properly God and truly and properly man.

We believe that our first parents were created in a state of innocency, but by their disobedience they lost their purity and happiness, and that in consequence of their fall all men have become sinners, totally depraved, and as such are justly exposed to the wrath of God.

We believe that the Lord Jesus Christ has by his suffering and death made an atonement for the whole world so that whosoever will may be saved.

We believe that repentance towards God, faith in our Lord Jesus Christ, and regeneration by the Holy Spirit, are necessary to salvation.

We believe that we are justified by grace through faith in our Lord Jesus Christ and that he that believeth hath the witness in himself.

We believe that continuance in a state of salvation depends upon continued obedient faith in Christ.

We believe that it is the privilege of all believers to be wholly sanctified, and that their whole spirit and soul and body may be preserved blameless unto the coming of our Lord Jesus Christ.

We believe in the immortality of the soul; in the resurrection of the body; in the general judgment at the end of the world; in the eternal happiness of the righteous; and in the endless punishment of the wicked.

FOUNDERS OF THE SALVATION ARMY

William Booth

The Founder of The Salvation Army and its first General was born in Nottingham on 10 April 1829 and promoted to Glory from Hadley Wood on 20 August 1912. He lived to establish Salvation Army work in 58 countries and colonies and travelled extensively, holding salvation meetings. In his later years he was received in audience by emperors, kings and presidents. Among his many books, *In Darkest England and the Way Out* was the most notable; it became the blueprint of all The Salvation Army's social schemes. It was reprinted in 1970.

Catherine Booth

The Army Mother was born in Ashbourne, Derbyshire, on 17 January 1829 and promoted to Glory from Clacton-on-Sea on 4 October 1890. As Catherine Mumford, she married William in 1855. A great teacher and preacher, she addressed large public meetings in Britain with far-reaching results, despite ill health. Her writings include *Female Ministry* and *Aggressive Christianity*.

William Bramwell Booth

The eldest son of the Founder, and his Chief of the Staff from 1880 to 1912, Bramwell (as he was known) was born on 8 March 1856. He was largely responsible for the development of The Salvation Army. His teaching of the doctrine of holiness and his councils with officers and young people were of incalculable value. In 1882 he married Captain Florence Soper (organiser of the Women's Social Work and inaugurator of the Home League), who was promoted to Glory on 10 June 1957. During his time as General (1912-1929), impetus was given to missionary work. Published books include *Echoes and Memories* and *These Fifty Years*. He was appointed a Companion of Honour shortly before his promotion to Glory from Hadley Wood on 16 June 1929.

THE HIGH COUNCIL

THE High Council was originally established by William Booth in 1904 as a safeguard to allow the removal from office of an incumbent General who had become, for whatever reason, unfit to continue to exercise oversight, direction and control of The Salvation Army. Should such an allegation be made and receive significant support from officers of the rank of commissioner, a High Council would be called to decide upon the matter and to elect a successor should the General be found unfit.

The Founder intended, however, that the normal method of succession would be for the General in office to select his or her successor, but only one General – Bramwell Booth in 1912 – was ever selected in this way.

By November 1928, Bramwell Booth had been absent from International Headquarters for seven months on account of illness, and a High Council was called. The 63 members, being all the commissioners on active service and certain territorial commanders, gathered at Sunbury Court near London on 8 January 1929 and eventually voted that the General, then aged 73, was 'unfit on the ground of ill-health' to continue in office. On 13 February 1929 the High Council elected Commissioner Edward Higgins as the Army's third General.

Subsequently, a commissioners' conference agreed to three major constitutional reforms later passed into law by the British Parliament as the Salvation Army Act 1931, namely:

i. the abolition of the General's right to nominate his or her successor, and the substitution of the election of every General by a High Council;

ii. the fixing of an age limit for the retirement of the General;

iii. the creation of a trustee company to hold the properties and other capital assets of the Army, in place of the sole trusteeship of the General.

The High Council is currently constituted under provisions of the Salvation Army Act 1980 as amended by deeds of variation executed in 1995, 2005 and 2010.

Since 1929, High Councils have been held in 1934 (electing General Evangeline Booth), 1939 (General Carpenter), 1946 (General Orsborn), 1954 (General Kitching), 1963 (General Coutts), 1969 (General Wickberg), 1974 (General Wiseman), 1977 (General Brown), 1981 (General Wahlström), 1986 (General Burrows), 1993 (General Tillsley), 1994 (General Rader), 1999 (General Gowans), 2002 (General Larsson), 2006 (General Clifton), 2011 (General Bond) and 2013 (General Cox).

High Councils are normally called by the Chief of the Staff and have usually met at Sunbury Court but can meet anywhere in the United Kingdom. Since 1995 the High Council has been composed of all active commissioners except the spouse of the General, and all territorial commanders. All TPWMs now attend.

GENERALS ELECTED BY A HIGH COUNCIL

Years in office are shown immediately below each General's name. The place and date at the beginning of an entry denote the corps and the year from which the General entered officer service.

Edward J. Higgins
1929-34

Reading, UK, 1882. General (1929-34). b 26 Nov 1864; pG 14 Dec 1947. Served in corps and divisional work, British Territory; at the International Training Garrison, as CS, USA; as Asst Foreign Secretary, IHQ; Brit Comr (1911-19); Chief of the Staff (1919-29). CBE. Author of *Stewards of God*, *Personal Holiness*, etc. m Capt Catherine Price, 1888; pG 1952.

Evangeline Booth
1934-39

b 25 Dec 1865; pG 17 Jul 1950. The fourth daughter of the Founder, at 21 years of age she commanded Marylebone Corps, its Great Western Hall being the centre of spectacular evangelistic work. As Field Commissioner this experience was used to advantage throughout Great Britain (1888-91). The Founder appointed her to train cadets in London (1891-96); then as TC, Canada (1896-1904); Commander of The Salvation Army in the United States of America (1904-34). Author of *Toward a Better World*; *Songs of the Evangel*, etc.

George L. Carpenter
1939-46

Raymond Terrace, Australia, 1892. b 20 Jun 1872; pG 9 Apr 1948. Appointments included 18 years in Australia in property, training and literary work; at IHQ (1911-27) for the most part with General Bramwell Booth as Literary Secretary; further service in Australia (1927-33), including CS, Australia Eastern; as TC, South America East (1933-37); TC, Canada (1937-39). Author of *Keep the Trumpets Sounding*; *Banners and Adventures*, etc. m Ens Minnie Rowell, 1899; pG 1960. Author of *Notable Officers of The Salvation Army*; *Women of the Flag*, etc.

Albert Orsborn
1946-54

Clapton, UK, 1905. b 4 Sep 1886; pG 4 Feb 1967. Served as corps officer and in divisional work in British Territory; as Chief Side Officer at ITC (1925-33); CS, New Zealand (1933-36); TC, Scotland & Ireland (1936-40); Brit Comr (1940-46). CBE, 1943. Writer of many well-known Army songs. Author of *The House of My Pilgrimage*, etc. m Capt Evalina Barker, 1909; pG 1942. m Maj Evelyn Berry, 1944; pG 1945. m Comr Mrs Phillis Taylor (née Higgins), 1947; pG 1986.

Wilfred Kitching
1954-63

New Barnet, UK, 1914. b 22 Aug 1893; pG 15 Dec 1977. Served in British Territory corps, divisional and NHQ appointments, then as CS, Australia Southern (1946-48); TC, Sweden (1948-51); Brit Comr (1951-54). Composer of many distinctively Salvationist musical works. Hon LLD (Yonsei, Seoul, Rep of Korea), 1961; CBE, 1964. Author of *Soldier of Salvation* (1963) and *A Goodly Heritage* (autobiography, 1967). m Adjt Kathleen Bristow (Penge, 1916), 1929; pG 1982.

Frederick Coutts
1963-69

Batley, UK, 1920. b 21 Sep 1899; pG 6 Feb 1986. Served in British Territory in divisional work (1921-25) and as corps officer (1925-35); for 18 years in Literary Dept, IHQ; writer of *International Company Orders* (1935-46); Editor of *The Officers' Review* (1947-53); Asst to Literary Secretary (1947-52); Literary Secretary (1952-53); Training Principal, ITC (1953-57); TC, Australia Eastern (1957-63). Author of *The Call to Holiness* (1957); *Essentials of Christian Experience* (1969); *The Better Fight* (1973); *No Discharge in this War* (1975), *Bread for My Neighbour* (1978); *The Splendour of Holiness* (1983), etc. Order of Cultural Merit (Rep of Korea), 1966; Hon Litt D (Chung Ang, Rep of Korea), 1966; CBE, 1967; Hon DD (Aberdeen), 1981. m Lt Bessie Lee, BSc, 1925; pG 1967. m Comr Olive Gatrall (Thornton Heath, 1925), 1970, pG 1997.

Erik Wickberg
1969-74

Bern 2, Switzerland, 1925. b 6 Jul 1904; pG 26 Apr 1996. Served as corps officer in Scotland; in Germany as Training (Education) Officer, and Private Secretary to CS and TC (1926-34); at IHQ as Private Secretary to IS and Asst to Under Secretary for Europe (1934-39); in Sweden as IHQ Liaison Officer (1939-46) and DC, Uppsala (1946-48); as CS, Switzerland, (1948-53); CS, Sweden (1953-57); TC, Germany (1957-61); Chief of the Staff (1961-69). Commander, Order of Vasa, 1970; Order of Moo Koong Wha (Rep of Korea), 1970; Hon LLD (Rep of Korea), 1970; Grand Cross of Merit, Fed Rep of Germany, 1971; King's Gold Medal (Grand Cross) (Sweden), 1980. Author of *Inkallad* (*Called Up*) (autobiography), Swedish, 1978; English, 2012) and *Uppdraget* (*The Charge – My Way to Preaching*) (1990).

m Ens Frieda de Groot (Berne 1, Switz, 1922), 1929; pG 1930. m Capt Margarete Dietrich (Hamburg 3, Ger, 1928), 1932; pG 1976. m Major Eivor Lindberg (Norrköping 1, Swdn, 1946), 1977.

Clarence Wiseman
1974-77

Guelph, Ont, Canada, 1927. b 19 Jun 1907; pG 4 May 1985. Served in Canada as corps officer and in editorial work; chaplain with Canadian forces overseas (1940-43); Senior Representative, Canadian Red Shield Services Overseas (1943-45); back in Canada as divisional commander (1945-54), Field Secretary (1954-57) and CS (1957-60); as TC, East Africa (1960-62); Training Principal, ITC (1962-67); TC, Canada & Bermuda (1967-74). Order of Canada, 1976, Hon LLD, Hon DD (Yonsei, Seoul, Rep of Korea). Author of *A Burning in My Bones* (1980) and *The Desert Road to Glory* (1980). m Capt Jane Kelly (Danforth, Ont, Can, 1927), 1932; pG 1993. Author of *Earth's Common Clay*; *Bridging the Year*; *Watching Daily*.

Arnold Brown
1977-81

Belleville, Canada, 1935. b 13 Dec 1913; pG 26 Jun 2002. Served in Canada in corps, editorial, public relations and youth work (1935-64); as Secretary for Public Relations at IHQ (1964-69); Chief of the Staff (1969-74); TC, Canada & Bermuda (1974-77). MIPR, Hon LDH (Asbury, USA); Freeman, City of London; Hon DD (Olivet, USA), 1981; Officer, Order of Canada, 1981. Author of *What Hath God Wrought?*; *The Gate and the Light* (1984); *Yin – The Mountain the Wind Blew Here* (1988); *With Christ at the Table* (1991); *Occupied Manger – Unoccupied Tomb* (1994). m Lt Jean Barclay (Montreal Cit, Can, 1938), 1939, pG 2012. Author of *Excursions in Thought* (1981).

Generals of The Salvation Army

Jarl Wahlström
1981-86

Helsinki 1, Finland, 1938. b 9 Jul 1918. pG 3 Dec 1999. Served in corps, youth and divisional work in Finland; as Second World War chaplain to Finnish armed forces; in Finland as a divisional commander (1960-63), Training Principal, Secretary of Music Dept (1963-68) and CS (1968-72); as CS, Canada & Bermuda (1972-76); TC, Finland (1976-81); TC, Sweden (1981); Knight, Order of the Lion of Finland, 1964; Order of Civil Merit, Mugunghwa Medal (Rep of Korea), 1983; Hon DHL (W Illinois), 1985; Paul Harris Fellow of Rotary International, 1987; Commander, Order of the White Rose of Finland, 1989. Author of *Pilgrimage Song* (autobiography, Finnish/ Swedish, 1989; English, 2012). m Lt Maire Nyberg (Helsinki 1, 1944).

Eva Burrows
1986-93

Fortitude Valley, Qld, Australia Eastern, 1951. b 15 Sep 1929. Appointed to corps in British Territory, before post-graduate studies; served at Howard Institute, Zimbabwe (1952-67), Head of Teacher Training (1965), Vice-Principal (1965-67); as Principal, Usher Institute (1967-70); Asst Principal, ICO (1970-74), Principal (1974-75); Leader, WSS (GBI) (1975-77); TC, Sri Lanka (1977-79); TC, Scotland (1979-82); TC, Australia Southern (1982-86). BA (Qld); M Ed (Sydney); Hon Dr of Liberal Arts (Ehwa Univ, Seoul, Rep of Korea), 1988; Hon LLD (Asbury, USA), 1988; Paul Harris Fellow of Rotary International, 1990; Hon DST (Houghton), 1992; Hon DD (Olivet Nazarene Univ), 1993; Hon Dr Philosophy (Qld), 1993; Hon Dr of University (Griffith Univ), 1994; Companion of Order of Australia, 1994; Living Legacy Award from Women's International Center, USA, 1996.

Bramwell Tillsley
1993-94

Kitchener, Ont, Canada, with wife née Maude Pitcher, 1956. b 18 Aug 1931. Served in Canada in corps, youth, training college and divisional appointments, including Training Principal USA E (1974-77), Provincial Commander in Newfoundland (1977-79) and DC, Metro Toronto (1979-81); as Training Principal, ITC (1981-85); CS, USA Southern (1985-89); TC, Australia Southern (1989-91); Chief of the Staff (1991-93). BA University of Western Ontario. Has written extensively for SA periodicals. Author of *Life in the Spirit*; *This Mind in You*; *Life More Abundant*; *Manpower for the Master*. Ww Mrs General Maude, pG 2014.

Paul Rader
1994-99

Cincinnati Cit, USA Eastern, with wife née Frances Kay Fuller, BA (Asbury), Hon DD (Asbury Theol Seminary) 1995, Hon LHD (Greenville) 1997, 1961. b 14 Mar 1934. Served in corps prior to transfer to Korea in 1962; in Korea in training work (1962-73), as Training Principal (1973), Education Secretary (1974-76), Asst Chief Secretary (1976-77) and CS (1977-84); in USA Eastern as Training Principal (1984-87), DC, Eastern Pennsylvania (1987-89) and CS (1989); as TC, USA Western (1989-94). BA, BD (Asbury); MTh (Southern Baptist Seminary); D Miss (Fuller Theological Seminary); Hon LLD (Asbury); 1984 elected to board of trustees of Asbury College; 1989 elected Paul Harris Fellow of Rotary International; Hon DD (Asbury Theol Seminary), 1995; Hon LHD (Greenville), 1997; Hon DD (Roberts Wesleyan), 1998.

John Gowans
1999-2002

Grangetown, UK, 1955. b 13 Nov 1934; pG 8 Dec 2012. Served in British Territory as corps officer, divisional youth secretary, National Stewardship Secretary and divisional commander; as Chief Secretary, France (1977-81); in USA Western as Programme Secretary (1981-85) and DC, Southern California (1985-86); TC, France (1986-93); TC, Australia Eastern and Papua New Guinea (1993-97); TC, UK (1997-99). Paul Harris Fellow of Rotary International; Hon DLitt (Yonsei, Seoul, Rep of Korea); Freedom of the City of London (2000). Songwriter. Author of *O Lord!* series of poetry books and *There's a Boy Here* (autobiography, 2002). Co-author with John Larsson of 10 musicals. m Lt Gisèle Bonhotal (Paris Central, France, 1955) 1957.

John Larsson
2002-2006

Upper Norwood, UK, 1957. b 2 Apr 38. Served in corps; at ITC; as TYS (Scotland Territory); NYS (British Territory); CS, South America West (1980-84); Principal, ITC (1984-88); Assistant to Chief of the Staff for UK Administrative Planning, IHQ (1988-1990); TC, UK (1990-93); TC, New Zealand and Fiji (1993-96); TC, Sweden and Latvia (1996-99); Chief of the Staff (1999-2002). BD (London). Author of *Doctrine without Tears* (1964); *Spiritual Breakthrough* (1983); *The Man Perfectly Filled with the Spirit* (1986); *How Your Corps Can Grow* (1989); *Saying Yes to Life* (autobiography, 2007); *Inside a High Council* (2013). Composer of music and co-author with John Gowans of 10 musicals. m Capt Freda Turner (Kingston-upon-Thames, UK, 1964) 1969.

Shaw Clifton
2006-2011

Edmonton, UK, with wife née Helen Ashman, 1973. b 21 Sep 45. Served as corps officer in British Territory; in Literary Department, IHQ (1974); in Zimbabwe as Vice Principal, Mazoe Secondary School (1975-77) and CO, Bulawayo Citadel (1977-79); in further BT corps appointments (1979-82, 1989-92); at IHQ as Legal and Parliamentary Secretary (1982-89); in UK as DC (1992-95); in USA Eastern as DC, Massachusetts (1995-97); as TC, Pakistan (1997-2002); TC, New Zealand, Fiji & Tonga (2002-04); TC, UK (2004-06). LLB (Hons), AKC (Theol), BD (Theol) (Hons), PhD. Freedom of the City of London (2007). Author of *What Does the Salvationist Say?* (1977); *Growing Together* (1984); *Strong Doctrine, Strong Mercy* (1985); *Never the Same Again* (1997); *Who are these Salvationists?* (1999); *New Love – Thinking Aloud About Practical Holiness* (2004); *Selected Writings, vols 1 and 2;* (2010); *'Something Better...' Autobiographical Essays* (2014). Ww Comr Helen Clifton, pG 2011; m Comr Birgitte Brekke (née Nielsen, Copenhagen Temple, 1980) 2013.

Linda Bond
2011-2013

St James, Winnipeg, Canada, 1968. b 22 Jun 46. Served as corps officer in Canada and Bermuda Territory (1969-78) (1987-89); at the Training College (1978-82) (1989-91), Secretary for Candidates (1982-87); Divisional Secretary (1991-93); divisional commander (1993-95) and Chief Secretary (1999-2002); in UK as divisional commander (1998-99); at IHQ as Under Secretary for Personnel (1995-98); Secretary for Spiritual Life Development and International External Relations (2005-08); TC/TPWM, USA Western (2002-04) and Australia Eastern (2008-11). B Relig Ed, MTS, Hon DD (Tyndale University College, Canada) 2012.

André Cox
2013-present

Geneva 1, Switzerland, with wife née Silvia Volet, 1979. b 12 Jul 54. Served as corps officer in Switzerland, Austria and Hungary Territory; in Zimbabwe as public relations secretary (1987-92) and financial secretary (1992-97); in Switzerland as business administrator at Bern THQ (2001-05); TC, Finland and Estonia (2005-08); TC, Southern Africa (2008-12); TC, United Kingdom with the Republic of Ireland (May 2012-Jan 2013); Chief of the Staff (Feb-Aug 2013).

SIGNIFICANT EVENTS 2013-2014

2013
October
IHQ: Salvation Army International Emergency Services team in **Jordan** assisted refugees from Syria.

Europe Zone: The Salvation Army's European anti-human trafficking response was launched in Budapest, **Hungary,** by personnel from 23 countries.

SPEA Zone: Salvation Army emergency service crews provided support as fires brought devastation in New South Wales, **Australia**. Salvation Army representatives attended the 10th Assembly of the World Council of Churches (WCC) in **Korea**.

Africa Zone: Salvationists in **Rwanda** provided emergency assistance to thousands of people fleeing ongoing conflict in the Democratic Republic of Congo.

November
SPEA Zone: Salvation Army emergency services personnel responded when Typhoon Haiyan caused devastation in the **Philippines.**

Americas Zone: Salvation Army emergency response teams met the needs of tornado survivors in Midwestern USA.

December
Europe Zone: In Thessaloniki, General André Cox made the first official visit to **Greece** by a General in office.

2014
February
Europe Zone: Russian Salvationists engaged in outreach at 2014 Winter Olympics held in Sochi and Krasnapolyna.

IHQ: Delegates from IHQ, Africa, Australia, Canada, The Netherlands, the United Kingdom and the United States attended the first International Communications Summit held at William Booth College, London.

IHQ: On 22 February at the **ICO** a valedictory service was held to mark the conclusion of 63 years of officer development at The Cedars, Sydenham Hill, London.

March
Americas Zone: The Global Conversation gathering took place in Orlando, Florida, USA.

April
IHQ: General André Cox reopened The Salvation Army's historic Sunbury Court, now home to the ICO and CSLD.

May
South Asia Zone: The first-ever visit of a Salvation Army General to **Kuwait,** Middle East Region, included a meeting between General André Cox and the Crown Prince of Kuwait.

IHQ: The first four units of the *One Army* multi-format teaching materials were released.

July
IHQ: The Salvation Army's International Conference of Leaders (ICL) took place in **Singapore** under the leadership of General André Cox.

COUNTRIES WHERE THE SALVATION ARMY IS AT WORK

THE Salvation Army is at work in 126 countries. A country in which the Army serves is defined in two ways:

(i) Politically - see a, b, c below.

(ii) Where the General has given approval to the work, thus officially recognising it, ensuring it has legal identity and a Deed Poll is published to acknowledge this.

As far as political status is concerned, for the Army's purposes, three categories are recognised:

(a) Independent countries, eg USA and New Zealand;

(b) Internally independent political entities which are under the protection of another country in matters of defence and foreign affairs, eg The Færoes, Isle of Man, Puerto Rico;

(c) Colonies and other dependent political units, eg Bermuda, French Guiana, Guernsey, Jersey.

Administrative subdivisions of a country such as Wales and Scotland in the UK are not recognised as separate countries for this purpose. The countries fulfilling the quoted criteria, with the date in brackets on which the work was officially recognised, are as follows:

Angola ....(1985)	Cambodia............(2012)	Dominican Republic
Antigua ....(1903)	Canada ....(1882)	............................(1995)
Argentina ....(1890)	Chile....................(1909)	
Australia..............(1881)	China ....(1916)	Ecuador ....(1985)
Austria ....(1927)	Colombia ....(1985)	El Salvador ....(1989)
	Congo, Republic of	Estonia ....(1927)
Bahamas..............(1931)	(Brazzaville) ....(1937)	............(reopened 1995)
Bangladesh...........(1971)	Congo, Democratic	
Barbados ....(1898)	Republic of (Kinshasa)	Færoes, The ....(1924)
Belgium ....(1889)	............................(1934)	Fiji ....(1973)
Belize ....(1915)	Costa Rica ....(1907)	Finland................(1889)
Bermuda..............(1896)	Cuba....................(1918)	France ....(1881)
Bolivia ....(1920)	Czech Republic ..(1919)	French Guiana ....(1980)
Botswana ....(1997)	............(reopened 1990)	
Brazil ....(1922)		Georgia ....(1993)
Burundi ....(2007)	Denmark ....(1887)	Germany ....(1886)

Countries where The Salvation Army is at work

Ghana.................(1922)
Greece ....(2007)
Greenland............(2012)
Grenada ....(1902)
Guam ....(1994)
Guatemala ....(1976)
Guernsey ....(1879)
Guyana...............(1895)

Haiti ....(1950)
Honduras ....(2000)
Hong Kong ....(1930)
Hungary ....(1924)
............(reopened 1990)

Iceland ....(1895)
India ....(1882)
Indonesia ....(1894)
Ireland, Republic of
  (Eire) ....(1880)
Isle of Man..........(1883)
Italy ....(1887)

Jamaica ....(1887)
Japan ....(1895)
Jersey ....(1879)

Kenya..................(1921)
Korea ....(1908)
Kuwait ....(2008)

Latvia..................(1923)
............(reopened 1990)
Lesotho ....(1969)
Liberia ....(1988)
Lithuania ....(2005)

Macau ....(2000)
Malawi................(1967)
Malaysia..............(1938)
Mali ....(2008)

Marshall Islands..(1985)
Mexico ....(1937)
Micronesia ....(1993)
Moldova..............(1994)
Mongolia.............(2008)
Mozambique ......(1916)
Myanmar ....(1915)

Namibia ....(1932)
............(reopened 2008)
Nepal ....(2009)
Netherlands, The (1887)
New Zealand ......(1883)
Nicaragua............(2010)
Nigeria ....(1920)
Norway ....(1888)

Pakistan ....(1883)
Panama................(1904)
Papua New Guinea
.............................(1956)
Paraguay ....(1910)
Peru ....(1910)
Philippines, The ..(1937)
Poland ....(2005)
Portugal ....(1971)
Puerto Rico ....(1962)

Romania..............(1999)
Russia..................(1913)
............(reopened 1991)
Rwanda ....(1995)

St Christopher Nevis
  (St Kitts) ....(1916)
St Helena ....(1884)
St Lucia ....(1902)
St Maarten ....(1999)
St Vincent ....(1905)
Sierra Leone........(2010)
Singapore............(1935)

Solomon Islands (2011)
South Africa........(1883)
Spain ....(1971)
Sri Lanka ....(1883)
Suriname ....(1924)
Swaziland............(1960)
Sweden................(1882)
Switzerland ....(1882)

Taiwan ....(1965)
Tanzania..............(1933)
Togo....................(2011)
Tonga ....(1986)
Trinidad and Tobago
.............................(1901)
Turks and Caicos
  Islands..............(2011)

Uganda................(1931)
Ukraine ....(1993)
United Arab Emirates
.............................(2010)
United Kingdom (1865)
United States of
  America ....(1880)
Uruguay ....(1890)

Venezuela ....(1972)
Virgin Islands ....(1917)

Zambia................(1922)
Zimbabwe ....(1891)

INTERNATIONAL STATISTICS
(as at 1 January 2014)

Countries and territories where SA serves *(at 31 October 2014, see pp 18-19)* 126

Corps, outposts, societies, new plants and recovery churches 15,636

Goodwill centres 223

Officers 26,497
    Active 17,193
    Retired 9,304

Auxiliary-captains 204

Envoys/sergeants/non officer personnel, full-time 1,126

Cadets 1,099

Employees 107,918

Senior soldiers 1,174,913

Adherent members 169,491

Junior soldiers 385,994

Corps cadets 38,022

Senior band musicians 30,151

Senior songsters 114,402

Other senior musical group members 106,342

Senior and young people's local officers 141,064

Women's Ministries (all groups) members 665,720

League of Mercy – members 150,917

SAMF – members 9,065

Over-60 clubs – members 119,394

Men's fellowships – members 79,843

Young people's bands – members 15,795

Young people's singing companies – members 96,221

Other young people's music groups – members 107,801

Sunday schools – members 630,060

Junior youth groups (scouts, guides, etc, and clubs) – members 378,106

Senior youth groups – members 145,495

Corps-based community development programmes 11,570

Beneficiaries/clients 1,891,877

Thrift stores/charity shops (corps/territorial) 2,071

Recycling centres 46

Social Programme
Residential

Hostels for the homeless 446
    Capacity 24,148

Emergency lodges 371
    Capacity 19,530

Children's homes 222
    Capacity 9,913

Homes for elderly persons 158
    Capacity 11,309

Homes for disabled persons 50
    Capacity 1,810

Homes for blind persons 7
    Capacity 174

Remand and probation homes 43
    Capacity 1,052

Homes for street children 24
    Capacity 471

Mother and baby homes 41
    Capacity 1,163

Training centres for families 13
    Capacity 513

Care homes for vulnerable people 43
    Capacity 1,518

Women's and men's refuge centres 65
    Capacity 2,140

Other residential care homes/hostels 119
    Capacity 4,455

Day Care

Community centres 603
    Capacity 148,339

Early childhood education centres 90
    Capacity 4,544

Day centres for the elderly 106
    Capacity 4,037

Play groups..64
    Capacity 878
Day centres for street children 19
    Capacity 805
Day nurseries 540
    Capacity 18,555
Drop-in centres for youth.................116
    Capacity 190,550
Other day care centres 420
Capacity 23,866

Addiction Dependency

Non-residential programmes 74
    Capacity 18,863
Residential programmes....................234
    Capacity 14,108
Harbour Light programmes 27
    Capacity 2,976
Other services for those with
    addictions 32
    Capacity 2,665

Service to the Armed Forces

Clubs and canteens..............................15
Mobile units for service personnel......16
Chaplains 31

Emergency Disaster Response

Disaster rehabilitation schemes 100
    Participants 102,725
Refugee programmes –
    host country 5
    Participants 3,386
Refugee rehabilitation programmes......6
    Participants 4,937
Other response programmes 22,138
    Participants 268,437

Services to the Community

Prisoners visited........................ 272,593
Prisoners helped on discharge....116,109
Police courts – people helped 214,954
Missing persons – applications......5,836
    Number traced..............................3,127
Night patrol/anti-suicide –
    number helped..........................517,341
Community youth programmes 3,251

Beneficiaries 291,680
Employment bureaux –
    applications 84,911
    initial referrals..........................65,720
Counselling – people helped......495,233
General relief – people
    helped................................14,354,328
Emergency relief (fire, flood,
    etc) – people helped 676,478
Emergency mobile units 4,431
Feeding centres 1,053
Restaurants and cafes........................152
Thrift stores/charity shops
    (social) 993
Apartments for elderly 467
    Capacity 8,973
Hostels for students, workers, etc.......64
    Capacity 2,109
Land settlements (SA villages,
    farms etc) 5
    Capacity 1,350
Social Services summer camps 396
    Participants 43,336
Other services to the community
    (unspecified)...................................590
    Beneficiaries 136,750

Health Programme

General hospitals 19
    Capacity 2,264
Hospice long term care 9
    Capacity 512
Maternity hospitals.............................26
    Capacity......................................1,325
Other specialist hospitals 12
    Capacity 2,849
Specialist clinics.................................42
    Capacity 796
General clinics/health centres 102
    Capacity 8,527
Mobile clinics/community health
    posts 140
Inpatients....................................431,528
Outpatients 1,528,053
Doctors/medics 3,539
Non medical staff...........................1,907
Invalid/convalescent homes 2

Capacity 142
Health education programmes
(HIV/Aids, etc)..............................89
Beneficiaries 587,023
Day care programmes 23

Education Programme
Kindergarten/sub primary 976
Primary schools............................1,241
Upper primary and middle schools 149
Secondary and high schools............323
Colleges and universities 11

Vocational training schools/centres 74
Pupils..686,166
Teachers 19,485
Schools for blind students (included in
above totals)..................................20
Schools for disabled students (included
in above totals)..............................26
Boarding schools (included in
above totals) 68
Staff training and development
centres 12
Distance learning centres 10

SALVATION ARMY PERIODICALS
by territory/command

International Headquarters: *All the World, Revive, The Officer*

Australia National: *Kidzone, Warcry*

Australia Eastern: *Creative Ministry, Pipeline, Venue, Women in Touch*

Australia Southern: *On Fire, Red*

Brazil: *Ministério Feminino – Devocionais* (Women's Ministries magazines) *O Oficial, Rumo*

Canada and Bermuda: *Edge for Kids, En Avant, Faith & Friends, Foi & Vie, Salvationist*

Caribbean: *The War Cry*

Congo (Brazzaville): *Le Salutiste*

Democratic Republic of Congo: *Echo d'Espoir*

Denmark: *Krigsråbet (The War Cry), Vision-Mission*

Eastern Europe: *Vestnik Spaseniya (The War Cry), The Officer* (both Russian)

Finland and Estonia: *Nappis, Sotahuuto* (both Finnish)

France and Belgium: *Avec Vous, Le Fil, Le Magazine, Le partenaire de prière*

Germany and Lithuania: *Danke, Heilsarmee-Forum, Heilsarmee-Magazin*

Ghana: *Salvationist Newsletter*

Hong Kong and Macau: *Army Scene, The War Cry*

India National: *The War Cry* (English)

India Central: *Home League Magazine, Udyogasthudu, Yovana Veerudu, Yudha Dwani*

India Eastern: *Sipai Tlangau (The War Cry), The Officer, Young Salvationist, Chunnunpar, Naupang Sipai* (all Mizo)

India Northern: *Home League Yearly* (Hindi and English), *Mukti Samachar* (Hindi and Punjabi), *The Officer, Yuva Sipai* (both Hindi)

India South Eastern: *Chiruveeran, Home League Quarterly, Poresathan, The Officer* (all Tamil)

India South Western: *Home League Quarterly* (English/Malayalam), *The Officer* (Malayalam), *Youdha Shabdan, Yuva Veeran* (Malayalam/Tamil)

India Western: *Home League Quarterly, The Officer, The War Cry, The Young Soldier* (all Gujarati and Marathi)

Indonesia: *Berita Keselamatan (The War Cry), Cakrawala (Waves of Hope), Medical Fellowship Bulletin, Oasis Fajar* (Daily Devotions)

Italy: *Il Bollettino delle Risorse – Dipartimento dei Ministeri Femminili, Il Grido di Guerra*

Japan: *Home League Quarterly, The Officer, The Sunday School Guide, Toki-no-Koe, Toki-no-Koe Junior*

Kenya East: *Sauti ya Vita* (English and Kiswahili)

Kenya West: *Sauti ya Vita* (English and Kiswahili)

Korea: *Home League Programme Helps, The Officer, The War Cry*

Latin America North: *Voz de Salvación (Salvation Voice), Arco Iris de Ideas (Rainbow of Ideas)*

Mexico: *El Grito de Guerra (The War Cry), El Eslabón (The Link)*

Mozambique: *Devocionias para Encontros da Liga do Lar* (Home League resource manual)

The Netherlands and Czech Republic: *Dag in Dag Uit, Heils-en Strijdzangen, InterCom, Strijdkreet, Kans* (all Dutch), *Prapor Spásy* (Czech)

New Zealand, Fiji and Tonga: *War Cry*

Nigeria: *Jesus Kids, Salvationist, The Shepherd, The War Cry*

Norway, Iceland and The Færoes: *Krigsropet,* (Norwegian), *Herópid* (Icelandic)

Pakistan: *Home League Annual, The War Cry* (in Urdu)

Papua New Guinea: *Tokaut*

The Philippines: *The War Cry*

Rwanda: *Salvationist News*

Singapore, Malaysia and Myanmar: *The War Cry*

South America East: *El Oficial, El Salvacionista*

South America West: *El Grito de Guerra, El Trébol* (for Women's Ministries)

Southern Africa: *Home League Resource Manual, The Reporter, The War Cry*

Spain and Portugal: *O Salvacionista, Ideias e Recursos* (for Women's Ministries)

Sri Lanka: *Mulaadeniya (The Officer) Yudha Handa (The War Cry)*

Sweden and Latvia: *Stridsropet, Tidningen*

Switzerland, Austria and Hungary: *Espoir, Dialogue, Just 4 U, Trampoline* (all French), *Dialog, Klecks, Trialog* (all German), *IN* (French and German)

Taiwan: *Regional News*

Uganda: *Voice of Hope* (quarterly)

United Kingdom with the Republic of Ireland: *Kids Alive!, Salvationist, The War Cry*

USA National: *The War Cry, Women's Ministries Resources, Word & Deed – A Journal of Theology and Ministry, Young Salvationist*

USA Central: *Central Connection*

USA Eastern: *¡Buenas Noticias!, Cristianos en Marcha* (both Spanish), *Good News!* (English and Korean), *Priority!, Ven a Cristo Hoy* (Spanish)

USA Southern: *Southern Spirit*

USA Western: *Caring, New Frontier Chronicle, Vida* (Spanish)

Zimbabwe: *Zimbabwe Salvationist, ZEST*

Books Published during 2013-14

International Headquarters:
Boundless – The International Bible Reading Challenge by Phil Layton with Rachael Castle and Tracey Davies; *One Army – In Calling; In Christ; In Covenant; In Prayer; In Purpose; In Truth* by Robert Street; *'Something Better...'* *Autobiographical Essays* by Shaw Clifton; *The Salvation Army Year Book 2014* ed. by Jayne Roberts; *Words of Life* by Beverly Ivany; Since 2012 many IHQ titles have been published as e-books via Amazon and Kobo

Books Published 2013-14

Australia Eastern:

Salvation Stories Vol 2 ed. by Miriam Gluyas and Fay Foster

Australia Southern:

Happy Birthday by Sally-Anne Allchin; *Heart Talk* by Harry Read; *I Love Salvos Stores* by Mavis Sanders; *Jemima's Lullaby* by Rachael Castle; *The People's General* ed. by Mal Davies and Dawn Volz; *Vision* by Cymon Brooks

Canada:

Glory! Hallelujah!: The Innovative Evangelism of Early Canadian Salvationists by R.G. Moyles; *When Justice is the Measure* by M. Christine MacMillan, Don Posterski and James E. Read; *Convictions Matter: The Function of Salvation Army Doctrines* by Ray Harris

Eastern Europe:

How to Pray by Anna Beek; *How to Read the Bible* by Olive Holbrook; *Helps to Holiness/The Soul-winner's Secret/The Way of Holiness* (one volume) by Samuel Logan Brengle; *The Salvation Army Handbook of Doctrine; The Salvation Army in the Body of Christ – An Ecclesiological Statement* (all Russian)

Germany:

Called to be God's People by Robert Street; *Jesus and Justice* by the International Social Justice Commission; *The Sacraments and the Bible* by Philip Layton

Hong Kong:

Community Support for Early Prevention of Youth Substance Abuse; Let Children have HOPES; Love@Decoupage; My Home – My Heart: A Home Décor Handbook; Night Fluorescence

India Eastern:

A History of the Motherless Babies' Home; A Territorial Evangelical Ministry Guide Book by Vanlalthanga

Japan:

Inochi-no Kotoba (Words of Life) by Yoshiya Shimura; *Life of Gunpei Yamamuro* by Mitaro Akimoto (reprint)

Korea:

A Centenary History of Yi Chon Corps;
Stories of the life of Herbert A. Lord; Officers Who Brought Honor to The Salvation Army in the Korea Territory

New Zealand:

Set Free: One Hundred Years of Salvation Army Addiction Treatment in New Zealand 1907-2006 by Don and Joan Hutson

Norway:

Suppe, såpe, frelse siden 1888 – Frelsesarmeen i Norge 125 år (Soup, Soap, Salvation since 1888 – The Salvation Army in Norway 125 years) by Anna Rebecca Solevåg; *Asia Raya – Walgjerd Midteides dagbok – Indonesia 1942-1946 (Asia Raya – the diary of Walgjerd Midteide – Indonesia 1942-1946)* A missionary's diary; *Alle dager (Always) by Synneva Vestheim; Frelsesarmeen – Håndbok i troslære (The Salvation Army – Handbook of doctrine); Det skjer jo ikke meg (It won't happen to me)* by Emil Skartveit; *En liten slumsøster lå og skulle dø …. (A tiny slum-sister lay on her deathbed…)* by Nils-Petter Enstad

Pakistan:

The Salvation Army Song Book (Urdu)

Sweden:

Army on its Knees by Janet Munn and Stephen Court (Swedish)

United Kingdom:

The Joystrings: The story of The Salvation Army Pop Group

USA National Headquarters:

Inside a High Council by John Larsson; *In The Balance: Christ Weighs The Hearts of 7 Churches* by Allen Satterlee; *Say Something* by Stephen Banfield and Donna Leedon; *When God Becomes Small* by Phil Needham

USA Western:

Walking in White by Comr Jolene Hodder; *Orsborn Again* by Maj Rob Birks

Zimbabwe:

The Sacred Marriage by Hope Mungate

Published with the assistance of grants from the International Literature Programme, IHQ

Eastern Europe:

30 Days with Catherine Booth; 30 Days with William Booth (Romanian and Russian); *From Mercy Seat to Spiritual Maturity* (Romanian); *Giving to God* by Earnest Yendell (Russian); *One Army* teaching resources (Georgian, Romanian and Russian)

India Central:

How Your Corps Can Grow (Telugu)

India Northern:

The Salvation Army Song Book (Hindi reprint)

Pakistan:

The Handbook of Doctrine (Urdu)

South America West:

It Seemed Like a Good Idea at the Time (Spanish)

Southern Africa:

The Salvation Army Song Book (Zulu)

Sweden and Latvia:

Servant Leadership by Robert Street (Latvian)

ILP grants have also facilitated the translation and publication of newsletters, resources for evangelism and training and teaching materials. These include study material for corps cadets, junior soldiers, Sunday schools, soldiers' meetings and women's ministries. The following territories have benefitted during the year under review:

Caribbean, Eastern Europe, India Central, India Northern, India South Western, Nigeria, Pakistan, Papua New Guinea, The Philippines, South America East, South America West, Southern Africa, Sweden and Latvia, and Tanzania.

MINISTRIES AND FELLOWSHIPS

WOMEN'S MINISTRIES

World President of Women's Ministries: Commissioner Silvia Cox
World Secretary for Women's Ministries: Commissioner Nancy L. Roberts

THE ideal basic unit of society is the home and family, where women play a vital and definitive role. Furthermore, as natural providers of hope, women play an important part in shaping society. Therefore, any fellowship of women in which Christian influence is exerted and practical help given benefits not only the individual and the family, but also the nation.

Women's Ministries provide a programme of meetings and other activities based on the fourfold aim of the Army's international women's organisation, the Home League, which was inaugurated in 1907. Those aims are worship, education, fellowship, service. The motto of the Home League is: 'I will live a pure life in my house' (Psalm 101:2 *Good News Bible*).

The mission of Women's Ministries is to bring women into a knowledge of Jesus Christ; encourage their full potential in influencing family, friends and community; equip them for growth in personal understanding and life skills; address issues which affect women and their families in the world.

THE LEAGUE OF MERCY AND COMMUNITY CARE MINISTRIES

THE League of Mercy began in 1892 in Canada and is made up of people of all ages whose mission is to engage in a caring ministry. The main objective of the League of Mercy is to respond to the spiritual and social needs of the community. The ministry is adapted according to the local situation, the size of its membership and the skill of its members, and endeavours to follow Christ's injunction, 'Inasmuch as ye have done it unto one of the least of these my brethren, ye have done it unto me' (Matthew 25:40 *Authorised Version*).

THE SALVATION ARMY MEDICAL FELLOWSHIP

THE Salvation Army Medical Fellowship, instituted in 1943 by Mrs General Minnie Carpenter, is an international fellowship of dedicated medical personnel. Physical suffering in our world today challenges both the medical and the physical and emotional resources of medical personnel. The fellowship encourages a Christian witness and application of Christian principles in professional life while at the same time being involved with practical application in hospitals, clinics and various other places of medical care. The motto of the Fellowship is: 'If we walk in the light, as he is in the light, we have fellowship one with another' (1 John 1:7 *Authorised Version*).

SALVATION ARMY HONOURS

ORDER OF THE FOUNDER

Instituted on 20 August 1917 by General Bramwell Booth, the Order of the Founder is the highest Salvation Army honour for distinguished service.

IN 1917, five years after the death of William Booth, his son, General Bramwell Booth, inaugurated the Order of the Founder 'to mark outstanding service rendered by officers and soldiers such as would in spirit or achievement have been specially commended by the Founder'.

The first awards were made in 1920 to 15 officers and one soldier. Three years later, seven officers and one soldier were honoured. To date, 162 officers and 98 lay Salvationists have been recognised with the Army's highest honour – a total of 266 in 95 years (1920-2014).

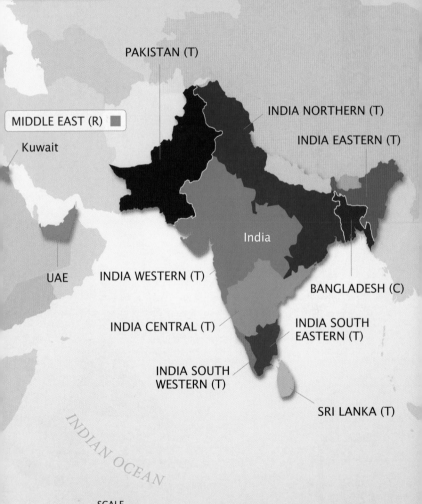

SOUTH ASIA ZONE

TERRITORIES (T)
COMMANDS (C)
REGIONS (R)

MIDDLE EAST (R)

PAKISTAN (T)

INDIA NORTHERN (T)

INDIA EASTERN (T)

Kuwait

India

UAE

INDIA WESTERN (T)

BANGLADESH (C)

INDIA CENTRAL (T)

INDIA SOUTH
EASTERN (T)

INDIA SOUTH
WESTERN (T)

SRI LANKA (T)

INDIAN OCEAN

SCALE

0 km   1000   2000   3000 km

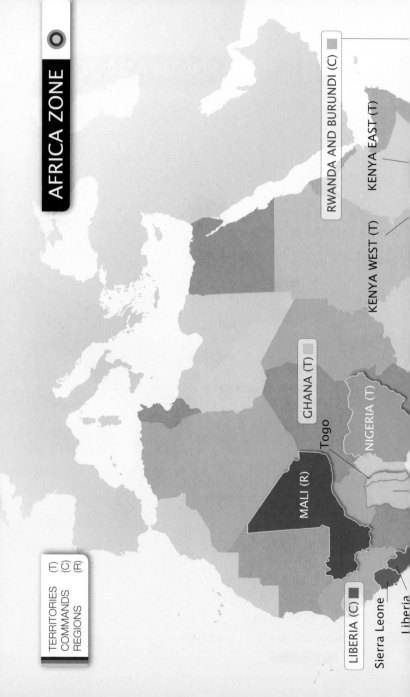

AFRICA ZONE

TERRITORIES (T)
COMMANDS (C)
REGIONS (R)

RWANDA AND BURUNDI (C)

KENYA EAST (T)

KENYA WEST (T)

GHANA (T)

NIGERIA (T)

Togo

MALI (R)

LIBERIA (C)

Sierra Leone

Liberia

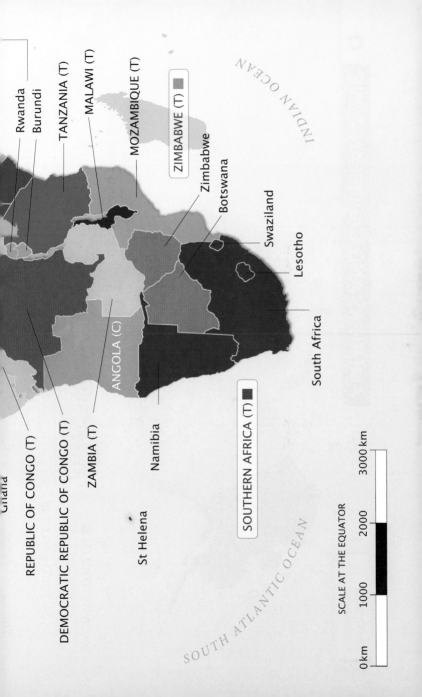

Rwanda
Burundi
TANZANIA (T)
MALAWI (T)
MOZAMBIQUE (T)

ZIMBABWE (T) ■

Ghana

REPUBLIC OF CONGO (T)

DEMOCRATIC REPUBLIC OF CONGO (T)

ZAMBIA (T)

ANGOLA (C)

Zimbabwe
Botswana

Swaziland

Lesotho

South Africa

Namibia

St Helena

SOUTHERN AFRICA (T) ■

INDIAN OCEAN

SOUTH ATLANTIC OCEAN

SCALE AT THE EQUATOR

0 km   1000   2000   3000 km

AMERICAS AND CARIBBEAN ZONE

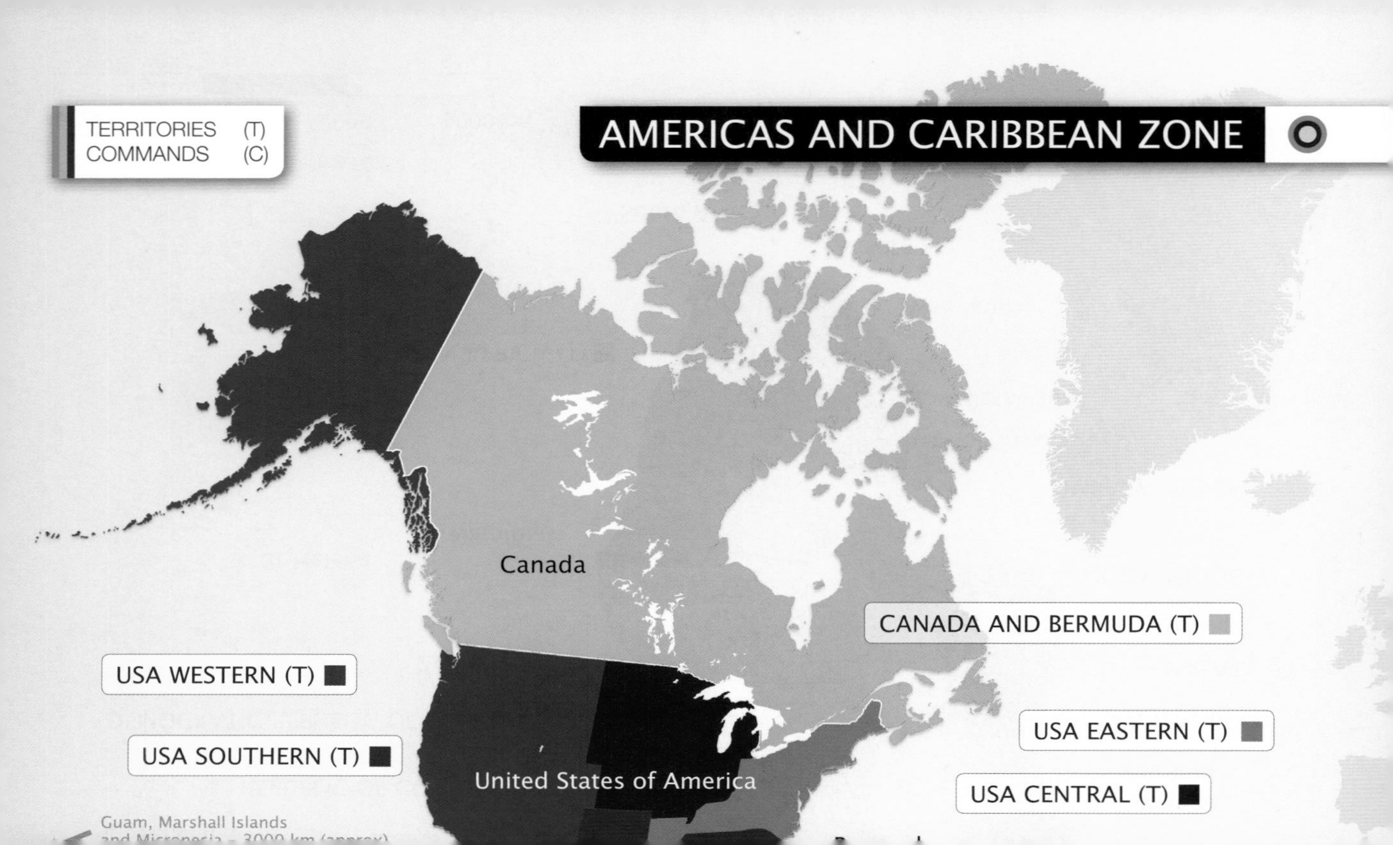

TERRITORIES (T)
COMMANDS (C)

CANADA AND BERMUDA (T)

USA EASTERN (T)

USA CENTRAL (T)

USA WESTERN (T)

USA SOUTHERN (T)

Canada

United States of America

Guam, Marshall Islands
and Micronesia 3000 km (approx)

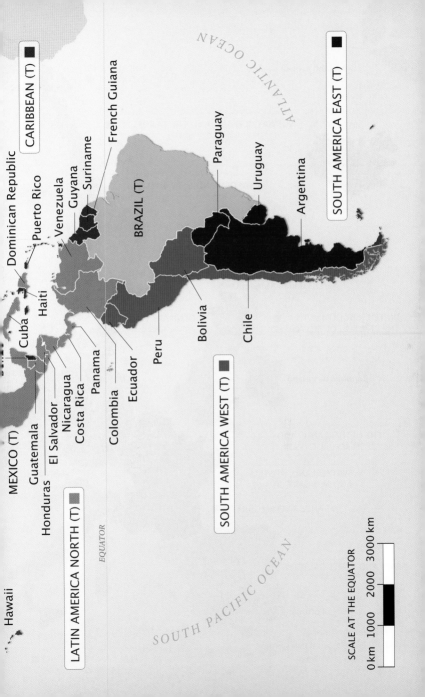

Hawaii

MEXICO (T)

Guatemala

Honduras

El Salvador

Nicaragua

Costa Rica

Panama

Colombia

Ecuador

Peru

Cuba

Haiti

Dominican Republic

Puerto Rico

Venezuela

Guyana

Suriname

French Guiana

BRAZIL (T)

Bolivia

Paraguay

Uruguay

Argentina

Chile

EQUATOR

LATIN AMERICA NORTH (T) ■

CARIBBEAN (T) ■

SOUTH AMERICA WEST (T) ■

SOUTH AMERICA EAST (T) ■

ATLANTIC OCEAN

SOUTH PACIFIC OCEAN

SCALE AT THE EQUATOR

0km 1000 2000 3000 km

Greenland (see small scale map)

NORWEGIAN SEA

FINLAND AND
ESTONIA (T ■

Iceland

NORWAY, ICELAND AND THE FÆROES (T) ■

Norway

SWEDEN AND LATVIA (T) ■

Sweden

The Færoes

NORTH SEA

GERMANY AND LITHUANIA (T) ■
(Includes Poland)

United Kingdom

Lithuania

UNITED KINGDOM WITH
THE REPUBLIC OF IRELAND (T) ■

DENMARK (T) ■
(Includes Greenland)

Netherlands

Poland

Republic of Ireland

Germany

Czech Republic

ATLANTIC OCEAN

THE NETHERLANDS AND
CZECH REPUBLIC (T) ■

Belgium

Austria

SWITZERLAND, AUSTRIA
AND HUNGARY (T) ■

France

Hunga

FRANCE AND BELGIUM (T) ■

Switzerland

Italy

SPAIN AND PORTUGAL (C) ■

Spain

Portugal

Canary Islands (part of Spain Command)

1000 km (approx)

ITALY AND GREECE (C) ■

land

onia

via

Russia
(see small scale map)

TERRITORIES   (T)
COMMANDS   (C)

EASTERN EUROPE (T) ■

Ukraine

Moldova

mania

Georgia

eece

SCALE

0 km   1000   2000 km

SOUTH PACIFIC AND EAST ASIA ZONE

Mongolia

China

KOREA (T) ■

Democratic People's Republic of Korea

Republic of Korea

JAPAN (T)

NORTH PACIFIC

HONG KONG AND MACAU (C) ■

TAIWAN (R)

Hong Kong

Myanmar

Macau

THE PHILIPPINES (T)

USA WESTERN (T) ■

Marshall Islands

SINGAPORE, MALAYSIA AND MYANMAR (T) ■

Guam

Singapore

Malaysia

Federated States of Micronesia

PAPUA NEW GUINEA (T)

EQUATOR

INDONESIA (T)

Solomon Islands

Fiji

INDIAN OCEAN

Tor

Australia

AUSTRALIA EASTERN (T)

NEW ZEALAND, FIJI AND TONGA (T) ■

AUSTRALIA SOUTHERN (T)

SOUTH PACIFIC

TERRITORIES (T)
COMMANDS (C)
REGIONS (R)

SCALE AT THE EQUATOR

0km 1000 2000 3000 km

Major Alfred Campbell Roberts
(New Zealand, Fiji And Tonga Territory)
  IN recognition of his contribution to New Zealand society, particularly his tireless advocacy and support for vulnerable New Zealanders. Major Roberts has demonstrated a wide knowledge of social justice issues and has become one of New Zealand's leading advocates for the poor. Admitted to the Order of the Founder on 20 September 2013.

Lieut-Colonel Ethne Mavis Flintoff
(New Zealand, Fiji And Tonga Territory)
  IN recognition of her years of service as an exemplary missionary in areas of great difficulty and challenge, her quality of Salvationism, and her intrepid and dedicated work primarily in the South Asia Zone including India, Pakistan and Bangladesh. Admitted to the Order of the Founder on 22 September 2013.

Dr Beatrice Holz
Dr Ronald W. Holz (USA Eastern Territory)
  IN recognition of each having given exemplary service through committed ministry in their corps (48 years), as members of the Asbury University faculty (33 years), and through influential leadership of the Salvation Army Student Fellowship, to the glory of God. Admitted to the Order of the Founder on 11 April 2014.

Commissioner James Osborne
Mrs Commissioner Ruth Osborne (USA Southern Territory)
  IN recognition of extraordinary leadership rendered to The Salvation Army in the United States of America. They have each continuously raised the standard of Army service by exhibiting a high degree of guidance, empowerment and clarity in mission, both as active officers and in retirement. Admitted to the Order of the Founder on 1 June 2014.

Bandmaster Noel Jones (Australia Southern Territory)
  IN recognition of faithfulness to God and The Salvation Army as a true example of Christlike holy living, and for exemplary service as a local officer, musician, composer and mentor for more than 53 years. Admitted to the Order of the Founder on 21 June 2014.

ORDER OF DISTINGUISHED AUXILIARY SERVICE

On 24 February 1941 General George Carpenter instituted this order to mark the Army's appreciation of distinguished service rendered by non-Salvationists who have helped to further its work in various ways.

Recipients of the Order of Distinguished Auxiliary Service 2013-14

Margot Birmingham Perot
(USA Southern Territory)

IN recognition of an extraordinary servant leader who has given decades of service through The Salvation Army. Margot Perot is a selfless, tireless, and visionary innovator, founder, mentor, benefactor and civic leader. She is a life member of the local and National Advisory Board. Admitted to the Order of Distinguished Auxiliary Service on 15 November 2013.

Gert Johansson
(South America West Territory)

THE Salvation Army wishes to record its deep gratitude to Mr Gert Johansson from Sweden for his generous financial support to build schools and daycare centres in Bolivia and Peru. He has also facilitated university studies for young people in Bolivia. Admitted to the Order of Distinguished Auxiliary Service on 1 December 2013.

Chief (Dr) Godswill Obot Akpabio
(Nigeria Territory)

THE life of Chief Godswill Akpabio is one of daring to be different; a story of compassion and service, of visionary and exemplary leadership and of extraordinary transformation. Admitted to the Order of Distinguished Auxiliary Service on 23 March 2014.

INTERNATIONAL HEADQUARTERS

The Salvation Army, 101 Queen Victoria Street, London EC4V 4EH, United Kingdom

Main entrance: Peter's Hill, London EC4

Tel: (020) 7332 0101 (national)
[44] (20) 7332 0101 (international);
email: websa@salvationarmy.org;
website: www.salvationarmy.org

General
ANDRÉ COX
(3 August 2013)

Chief of the Staff
COMMISSIONER WILLIAM A. ROBERTS
(1 October 2013)

INTERNATIONAL Headquarters exists to support the General as he leads The Salvation Army to accomplish its God-given worldwide mission to preach the gospel of Jesus Christ and meet human need in his name without discrimination. In so doing, it assists the General:

To give spiritual leadership, promote the development of spiritual life within the Army, and emphasise the Army's reliance on God for the achievement of its mission.

To provide overall strategic leadership and set international policies.

To direct and administer the Army's operations and protect its interests – by means of appointments and delegation of authority and responsibility with accountability.

To empower and support the territories and commands, encourage and pastorally care for their leaders, and inspire local vision and initiatives.

To strengthen the internationalism of the Army, preserve its unity, purposes, beliefs and spirit, and maintain its standards.

To promote the development, appropriate deployment and international sharing of personnel.

To promote the development and sharing of financial resources worldwide, and manage the Army's international funds.

To promote the development and international sharing of knowledge, expertise and experience.

To develop the Army's ecumenical and other relationships.

The General directs Salvation Army operations throughout the world through the administrative departments of International Headquarters, which are headed by international secretaries. The Chief of the Staff, a commissioner appointed by the

General to be second-in-command, is the Army's chief executive whose function is to implement the General's policy decisions and effect liaison between departments.

The Christian Mission Headquarters, Whitechapel Road, became the Army's first International Headquarters in 1880. However, the Founder soon decided that a move into the City of London would be beneficial and in 1881 IHQ was moved to 101 Queen Victoria Street. Sixty years after this move the IHQ building was destroyed by fire during the Second World War. The rebuilt International Headquarters was opened by Queen Elizabeth, the Queen Mother, in November 1963.

When it was decided to redevelop the Queen Victoria Street site, IHQ took up temporary residence at William Booth College, Denmark Hill, in 2001. Three years later IHQ returned to 101 Queen Victoria Street and the new building was opened by Her Royal Highness The Princess Royal in November 2004.

Website of the Office of the General: www.salvationarmy.org/thegeneral

INTERNATIONAL MANAGEMENT COUNCIL

The International Management Council (IMC), established in February 1991, sees to the efficiency and effectiveness of the Army's international administration in general. It considers in detail the formation of international policy and mission. It is composed of all London-based IHQ commissioners, and meets monthly with the General taking the chair.

Secretary: Lt-Col Rob Garrad
Asst Secretary: Capt Scott Linnett

GENERAL'S CONSULTATIVE COUNCIL

The General's Consultative Council (GCC), established in July 2001, advises the General on broad matters relating to the Army's mission strategy and policy. The GCC has no established membership but exists as a forum to which the General may invite any whose counsel he wishes to seek in relation to the matters under discussion. The council operates through a Lotus Notes database. Selected members also meet three times a year in London with the General taking the chair.

Secretary: Lt-Col Rob Garrad
Asst Secretary: Capt Scott Linnett

ADMINISTRATION DEPARTMENT

The Administration Department is responsible for all matters with which the Chief of the Staff deals; for the effective administration of IHQ; for IHQ personnel; for international external relations; for providing legal advice; and for ensuring that the strategic planning and monitoring process is implemented and used effectively. The department also facilitates the sharing and appropriate deployment of personnel resources on a global basis; assists in the identification of officers with

potential for future leadership; monitors training and development; registers and coordinates all offers for international service.

International Secretary to the Chief of the Staff

COMR WILLIAM COCHRANE (1 Jun 2009)

Under Sec for Administration: Maj Mark Watts
Under Sec for Administration (International Personnel and Leadership Development): Col Chris Webb
Executive Sec to the General: Lt-Col Rob Garrad
Private Sec to the General: Capt Scott Linnett
Private Sec to the Chief of the Staff: Maj Christine Clement
Sec for International Ecumenical Relations: Comr William Cochrane
Secretary for Spiritual Life Development: Lt-Col Deborah Cachelin
Director, International Social Justice Commission: Col Geanette Seymour Lt-Col Dean Pallant (from 1 Mar 2015)
International Theological Council: Chair: Lt-Col Karen Shakespeare
International Moral and Social Issues Council: Chair: Comr Robert Donaldson (from 1 Mar 2015)
IHQ Chaplain and City of London Liaison Officer: Maj Rosslyn Casey
Legal Sec: Maj Patrick Booth
Medical Sec for Personnel and International Statistician: Lt-Col Wendy Leavey
Project Coordinator, The Salvation Army Song Book: Maj Christine Clement
Youth and Children's Officer/One Army International Resource: Maj Janet Robson
2015 International Congress Coordinator: Lt-Col Eddie Hobgood

WOMEN'S MINISTRIES

World President of Women's Ministries

COMR SILVIA COX (1 Feb 2013)

World Secretary for Women's Ministries and World President of SA Scouts, Guides and Guards

COMR NANCY L. ROBERTS (1 Oct 2013)

Personal Assistant/Administrator to the World President of and the World Secretary for Women's Ministries: Maj Margaret Booth

BUSINESS ADMINISTRATION DEPARTMENT

The Business Administration Department is responsible for international accounting, auditing, banking, property and related matters. The International Secretary for Business Administration has the oversight of the finance functions in territories and commands.

International Secretary for Business Administration

COMR JOHN WAINWRIGHT (1 May 2013)

Company Sec: Dr Matthew Carpenter
Chief Accountant: Miss Karen Dare
Chief International Auditor: Col Knud David Welander
Auditors: Maj Wes Green, Maj Philip Maxwell, Maj Yusak Tampai, Capt Emerald Urbien, Maj Alan Milkins (part time)
Information Technology Manager: Mr Mark Calleran
Property Manager: Mr Howard Bowes
Travel Manager: Mr Mark Edwards

PROGRAMME RESOURCES DEPARTMENT

The mission of the Programme Resources Department is to participate with others in envisioning, coordinating, facilitating and raising awareness of programmes that advance the global mission of The Salvation Army.

International Secretary for Programme Resources

COMR CHARLES SWANSBURY (1 Jun 2014)

Under Sec: Col Lisbeth Welander
International Emergency Services Coordinator: Maj Alison Thompson
International Projects Officer: Capt Elizabeth Nelson
International Schools Coordinator: Mr Howard Dalziel

Mission Resources Secretary: Comr Denise Swansbury
Communications Sec and Literary Sec: Maj John Murray
  Editor-in-Chief and Editor *The Officer*: Maj Martin Gossauer
  Editorial Production Manager: Mr Paul Mortlock
  Editor *All the World*: Mr Kevin Sims
  Editor *Revive*: Maj Deslea Maxwell
  Editor *The Year Book*: Maj Deslea Maxwell
  International Literature Programme: Maj Martha Pawar
  Webmaster: Mr David Giles
  Writer *Words of Life*: Maj Beverly Ivany

ZONAL DEPARTMENTS

The zonal departments are the main administrative link with territories and commands. The international secretaries give oversight to and coordinate the Army's work in their respective geographical areas.

AFRICA
International Secretary

COMR JOASH MALABI (1 Jan 2013)

Under Secs: Lt-Col Margaret Wickings and Maj Daniel Kasuso
Zonal Sec WM: Comr Florence Malabi

AMERICAS AND CARIBBEAN
International Secretary

COMR BRIAN PEDDLE (1 Sep 2014)

Under Sec: Maj Deborah Sedlar
Zonal Sec WM: Comr Rosalie Peddle

EUROPE
International Secretary

COMR BIRGITTE BREKKE-CLIFTON (1 Mar 2013)

Under Sec: Col Neil Webb
Zonal Sec WM: Comr Dorita Wainwright (1 Mar 2013)

Officer for EU Affairs: Maj Mike Stannett

SOUTH ASIA
International Secretary

COMR LALZAMLOVA (1 Apr 2013)

Under Sec: Maj Suresh Pawar
Zonal Sec WM: Comr Nemkhanching (Nu-i)

31

SOUTH PACIFIC AND EAST ASIA
International Secretary
COMR GILLIAN DOWNER (1 Jun 2013)

Under Sec: Maj Barry Casey
Zonal Sec WM: Comr Denise Swansbury
(1 Jun 2014)

STATISTICS
Officers 58 Employees 66

International Social Justice Commission
221 East 52nd Street, New York, New York 10022, USA
Tel: [1] (212) 758-0763; website: www.salvationarmy.org/isjc
email: ihq-isjc@salvationarmy.org

Director: Colonel Geanette Seymour
Lieut-Colonel Dean Pallant (from 1 Mar 2015)

The International Social Justice Commission (ISJC) with its secretariat in New York, is attached to the Administration Department of IHQ. The ISJC advises the General and other senior leaders at IHQ in matters of social justice. The director and staff are the Army's principal international advocates and advisers on social, economic and political issues and events giving rise to the perpetuation of social injustice in the world. They assist the Army in addressing social injustice in a systemic, measured, proactive and Christian manner. The commission is also the secretariat to the work of the International Moral and Social Issues Council (IMASIC).

THE Salvation Army's mission has always been marked by love for God, service among the poor and an invitation to believe and follow Jesus Christ. The mandate of the ISJC is to challenge Salvationists to harmonize their historic mission with God's call to pursue justice in today's world.

The ISJC seeks to fulfil this mandate through the implementation of a strategic plan to:

• Raise strategic voices to advocate with the world's poor and oppressed.

• Be a recognised centre of research and critical thinking on issues of global social justice.

• Collaborate with like-minded organisations to advance the global cause of social justice.

• Exercise leadership in determining social justice policies and practices of The Salvation Army.

• Live by principles of justice and compassion and inspire others to do likewise.

The ISJC has an intentional and strategic approach to education, research and advocacy.

STATISTICS
Officers 5 Employees 5 (full-time 1 part-time 4)
Policy Interns 4

STAFF
Deputy Director: Lt-Col Eirwen Pallant
(from 1 Mar 2015)
Senior Policy Analyst: Capt Kathy Crombie
Senior Policy Analyst (IMASIC): Dr James E. Read
Senior UN Rep and Intern Trainer:
Maj Victoria Edmonds (New York)
UN Reps: Maj Sylvette Huguenin
(Geneva/Vienna);
Lt-Col Julius Mukonga (Nairobi);
Ms Christine Tursi (Geneva/Vienna)

International College for Officers and Centre for Spiritual Life Development

Sunbury Court, Lower Hampton Road, Sunbury-on-Thames, TW16 5PL, UK

Tel: [44] 01932 732250; website: www.salvationarmy.org/ico

Principal: Lieut-Colonel Hervé Cachelin (1 Sep 2014)

During the International Congress held at the Crystal Palace, Sydenham, London, in 1904, Commissioner Henry T. Howard voiced what he saw as the young Salvation Army's need for leaders inspired with the aggressive spirit of Salvationism. William Booth took up the idea and the International Staff Training Lodge was opened at Clapton on 11 May 1905.

Following the purchase of The Cedars in Sydenham, the International Staff College started in 1950. Four years later it became the International College for Officers (ICO), with General Albert Orsborn declaring it to be 'an investment in the great intangibles without which our cogs and wheels would soon be rusty and dead'. To date, more than 5,000 officers have attended the ICO, which Commissioner Alfred Gilliard (Principal 1954-60) described as 'one of the Army's most brilliant long-term investments'.

In July 2008 the mission of the college was broadened to include aspects of spiritual life development and the college was renamed International College for Officers and Centre for Spiritual Life Development (CSLD).

In March 2014 the ICO and CSLD relocated to the newly refurbished Sunbury Court Conference Centre in west London.

ICO MISSION STATEMENT
The Salvation Army's International College for Officers exists to further develop officers by:
- **nurturing personal holiness and spiritual leadership**
- **providing opportunity to experience the internationalism of the Army**
- **encouraging a renewed sense of mission and purpose as an officer**

CSLD MISSION STATEMENT
The international Centre for Spiritual Life Development exists to facilitate the development of the spiritual lives of Salvationists by:
- **offering conferences and events that are spiritually enriching and that help form people in Christlikeness**
- **providing resources to cultivate spiritual life development**
- **encouraging implementation of intentional and systematic opportunities for spiritual growth throughout the international Salvation Army**

DURING 2013-14 the ICO hosted more than 120 officers in four sessions (220-223) including French and Telegu translation sessions.

The final session to be held at The Cedars, Sydenham Hill, took place in early 2014. Delegates of Session 221 witnessed the official opening of the new ICO accommodation at Sunbury Court on 22 April, in the presence of General André Cox and the Chief of the Staff, Commissioner William A. Roberts.

ICO sessions currently include an exploration of items from the International Spiritual Life Commission. During each session the delegates create practical strategies to nourish Salvationist spirituality in their home contexts.

STATISTICS
Officers 4 Employees 6

STAFF
Secretary for Spiritual Life Development: Lt-Col Deborah Cachelin
Business Services Officer: Maj Graham Buckle
Programme Officer: Maj Widiawati Tampai

33

The Africa Development Centre

The Salvation Army Kabete Compound,
Karbarsiran Avenue, Nairobi, Kenya

On 17 April 2009, IHQ gave approval for the relocation of The Salvation Army Leadership Training College (SALT College) of Africa to Nairobi and the setting up of the Africa Development Centre, which was established on 1 January 2010.

The Centre was made up of three units: the SALT College of Africa, the Africa Programme Development Office and the Zonal Facilitation Resource Office. Later that year the Zonal Facilitation Resource Office and Africa Programme Development Office were combined, to form the Africa Development Office.

Since 1 July 2010 the Africa Development Centre has consisted of two units: the SALT College of Africa and the Africa Development Office, each unit a satellite office of the IHQ Africa Zone, reporting to the International Secretary for Africa.While each unit retains its individual identity and purpose, since August 2012 they have shared one building.

A comprehensive review of the Africa Development Office [ADO], conducted in 2012, confirmed some overlap with the programmes of other international departments. As a result, the community projects aspect of ADO was transferred to the IHQ projects office in October 2014. All other aspects of the ADO programme became part of a more varied programme for the SALT College of Africa, also from October 2014.

The Salvation Army Leadership Training College (SALT College) of Africa
Postal Address: PO Box 40575, Nairobi 00100 GPO, Kenya
tel: [254] (020) 221 2217

Prompted by the request of territorial leaders within Africa, The Salvation Army Leadership Training College of Africa was established in 1986. Its purpose is to coordinate in-service training for local leaders across Africa through the provision or recommendation of distance-learning courses and seminars, monitored by an extension training officer in each territory.

An IHQ-sponsored education and training facility, SALT College offers distance learning to 24 countries across the African continent. Its students include officers, envoys, candidates, local officers and soldiers.

An expanded programme is being designed, to assist the ongoing development of spiritual life, ministry and mission within Africa. This will include seminars, the provision of resource materials and consultative advice on a wide variety of matters. It will be introduced gradually, from the end of 2014.

Principal: Maj Bishow Samhika
Curriculum Development Officer: Maj Pamela Samhika
Director of Studies: Maj Julius Omukonyi
Office Administrator: Maj Gaudencia Omukonyi
   email: leadcoll_africa@salvationarmy.org

STATISTICS **Officers** 5 **Employees** 4

The Salvation Army International Trustee Company

Registered Office: 101 Queen Victoria Street, London EC4V 4EH

Registration No 2538134. Tel: (020) 7332 0101

Company Secretary: Dr Matthew Carpenter

DIRECTORS: Comr William A. Roberts (Chair), Comr John Wainwright (Managing Director and Vice Chair), Comr Birgitte Brekke-Clifton, Dr Matthew Carpenter, Comr William Cochrane, Comr Gillian Downer, Ms Elizabeth Edwards, Mr David Kidd, Mr Peter King, Comr Lalzamlova, Comr Joash Malabi, Mr David Mayes, Comr Brian Peddle, Comr Charles Swansbury.

The company is registered under the Companies Acts 1985 and 1989 as a company limited by guarantee, not having a share capital. It has no assets or liabilities, but as a trustee of The Salvation Army International Trusts it is the registered holder of Salvation Army property both real and personal including shares in some of the Army's commercial undertakings. The company is a trust corporation.

Reliance Bank Limited

Faith House, 23-24 Lovat Lane, London EC3R 8EB

Tel: (020) 7398 5400; fax: (020) 7398 5401; email: info@reliancebankltd.com; website: www.reliancebankltd.com

Chairman: Commissioner John Wainwright

Managing Director: Paul Underwood, ACIB

Finance Director: Kevin Dare, BA(Hons), CIMA

Banking Lending Manager and Company Secretary: Andrew Hunt, ACIB

Banking Services Manager: Lloyd Watkins, ACIB

Business Development Manager: Nichola Keating

DIRECTORS: Comr John Wainwright (Chairman), Comr William Cochrane, Lt-Col Alan Read, Col David Hinton, Maj John Warner, Miss Karen Dare, Mr Paul Underwood, Mr Kevin Dare, Mr Philip Deer, Mr Gerald Birkett, ACIB, Mr Ian Scott, ACIB.

Reliance Bank Limited is an authorised institution under the Banking Act 1987 and by the Prudential Regulation Authority. The bank is regulated by the Financial Conduct Authority and the Prudential Regulation Authority, and registered under the Companies and Consumer Credit Acts.

OWNED by The Salvation Army through its controlling shareholders – The Salvation Army International Trustee Company and The Salvation Army Trustee Company – Reliance Bank accepts sterling and foreign currency deposits, carries on general banking business, and provides finance for Salvation Army corporate customers and private and business customers.

The bank can grant residential and commercial mortgages, personal loans and overdrafts. It offers current accounts, together with a Reliance Bank Visa debit card, cheques, safe custody facilities, fixed deposits and savings accounts, including ISAs, and provides money transmission services both within the UK and abroad. Internet banking and telephone banking services are also offered.

The bank pays at least 75 per cent of its taxable profits by means of Gift Aid donation to its controlling shareholders.

Brochures are available on request, or visit www.reliancebankltd.com

STATISTICS Employees 22

OVERSEAS SERVICE FUNDS 2013–2014 INCOME

	International Self-Denial Contributions	International Self-Denial Special	Special Projects	Donations via IHQ	Total
	£	£	£	£	£
Angola	17,150	-	-	-	17,150
Australia Eastern	302,860		1,910,980	83,755	2,297,595
Australia Southern	781,821		1,370,322	464,204	2,616,347
Bangladesh	537		-	-	537
Brazil	22,749		-	-	22,749
Canada and Bermuda	1,261,651		1,485,406	402,566	3,149,623
Caribbean	50,728		-	-	50,728
Congo (Brazzaville)	83,895		-	-	83,895
Democratic Republic of Congo	60,376		-	-	60,376
Denmark	50,000		38,370	30,432	118,802
Eastern Europe	14,210		-	-	14,210
Finland and Estonia	50,813		34,052	22,542	107,407
France and Belgium	19,009		-	5,536	24,545
Germany and Lithuania	59,664		-	103,481	163,145
Ghana	18,902		-	-	18,902
Hong Kong and Macau	64,239		-	65,376	129,615
India Central	31,401		-	-	31,401
India Eastern	54,576		-	-	54,576
India Northern	16,085		-	-	16,085
India South Eastern	56,275		-	-	56,275
India South Western	25,302		-	-	25,302
India Western	22,182		-	-	22,182
Indonesia	39,045		-	13,069	52,114
Italy and Greece	8,890		-	6,168	15,058
Japan	59,422		136,463	30,554	226,439
Kenya East	105,127		-	-	105,127
Kenya West	77,976		-	1,580	79,556
Korea	65,464		-	-	65,464
Latin America North	13,750		-	-	13,750
Liberia	3,928		-	-	3,928
Malawi	3,130		-	-	3,130
Mexico	20,639		1,180	1,708	23,527
Middle East	4,176		-	-	4,176
Mozambique	3,783		-	-	3,783
Netherlands and Czech Republic	183,634		1,344,481	200,157	1,728,272
New Zealand, Fiji and Tonga	495,379		314,995	59,175	869,549
Nigeria	29,920		-	1,000	30,920
Norway, Iceland and The Faeroes	350,175		1,460,090	40,421	1,850,686
Pakistan	3,485		-	2,844	6,329
Papua New Guinea	6,387		-	-	6,387
Philippines	6,579		-	-	6,579
Rwanda and Burundi	1,891		-	-	1,891
Singapore, Malaysia and Myanmar	95,746		7,503	95,015	198,264
South America East	22,019		-	-	22,019
South America West	26,226		-	-	26,226
Southern Africa	41,139		-	-	41,139
Spain and Portugal	8,588		-	18,865	27,453
Sri Lanka	1,202		-	-	1,202
Sweden and Latvia	105,813		762,632	212,450	1,080,895
Switzerland, Austria and Hungary	698,567		1,297,658	261,795	2,258,020
Taiwan	5,952		-	8,925	14,877
Tanzania	6,306		-	-	6,306
Uganda	2,492		-	-	2,492
United Kingdom with the Republic of Ireland	1,849,806		595,786	563,195	3,008,787
USA Central	3,007,189	540,930	1,293,896	760,649	5,602,664
USA Eastern	3,019,864	135,624	1,835,692	1,095,170	6,086,350
USA Southern	3,302,981	328,079	1,294,559	773,804	5,699,423
USA Western	2,594,243	84,388	859,596	977,709	4,515,936
USA SAWSO	-		5,793,718	261,070	6,054,788
Zambia	52,793		-	-	52,793
Zimbabwe	415,282		-	1,243	416,525
	19,803,413	1,089,021	21,837,379	6,564,458	49,294,271

OVERSEAS SERVICE FUNDS 2013-2014 EXPENDITURE

	Support of Overseas Work	Special Projects	Donations via IHQ	Total
	£	£	£	£
Africa, General	(32,400)	36,529	-	4,129
Americas, General	-		21,552	21,552
Angola	64,652	441,849	6,117	512,618
Bangladesh	147,214	320,009	61,021	528,244
Brazil	661,971	497,192	29,044	1,188,207
Caribbean	713,458	5,029,619	54,187	5,797,264
Congo (Brazzaville)	531,126	149,782	18,688	699,596
Democratic Republic of Congo	617,917	445,100	17,005	1,080,022
Denmark	-		8,716	8,716
Eastern Europe	1,964,173	735,803	68,669	2,768,645
Europe, General	8,116		7,085	15,201
Finland and Estonia	127,936	66,049	7,033	201,018
France and Belgium	-	8,298	8,616	16,914
Germany, Lithuania and Poland	194,889	115,327	4,138	314,354
Ghana and Togo	223,537	232,737	19,831	476,105
Hong Kong and Macau	12,088	165,537	1,320	178,945
India National Secretariat	66,609	10,360	1,765	78,734
India Central	388,438	207,151	18,699	614,288
India Eastern	164,231	151,757	17,059	333,047
India Northern	366,321	367,008	14,290	747,619
India South Eastern	394,142	223,618	8,724	626,484
India South Western	396,795	170,774	8,627	576,196
India Western	308,919	417,228	35,293	761,440
Indonesia	89,508	863,630	28,037	981,175
Italy and Greece	220,874	268,137	2,555	491,566
Japan	-	484,130	76	484,206
Kenya East	401,551	732,746	29,378	1,163,675
Kenya West	545,288	950,758	258,023	1,754,069
Korea	491	99	27,265	27,855
Latin America North	664,105	525,040	4,585	1,193,730
Liberia and Sierra Leone	192,367	115,659	27,696	335,722
Malawi	131,612	346,791	21,854	500,257
Mali	67,292	982	31,561	99,835
Mexico	410,954	519,804	15,583	946,341
Middle East	151,019	3,437	95,816	250,272
Mozambique	199,714	57,590	734	258,038
Netherlands and Czech Republic	349,581	46,391	77	396,049
New Zealand, Fiji and Tonga	-	249,313	11,020	260,333
Nigeria	246,552	201,073	30,823	478,448
Norway, Iceland and The Faeroes	-	88,869	513	89,382
Pakistan	466,648	663,988	16,201	1,146,837
Papua New Guinea	429,671	336,332	31,208	797,211
Philippines	401,392	870,018	28,867	1,300,277
Rwanda and Burundi	177,663	364,423	28,029	570,115
SALT College	4,439		41	4,480
Singapore, Malaysia and Myanmar	137,923	540,163	38,299	716,385
South America East	596,358	299,439	32,022	927,819
South America West	504,061	522,206	52,195	1,078,462
South Asia, General	2,140		18,151	20,291
Southern Africa	222,763	155,414	22,881	401,058
Spain and Portugal	648,769	276,845	119,669	1,045,283
SPEA, General	9,229	109,518	4,334	123,081
Sri Lanka	73,909	212,575	103,282	389,766
Sweden and Latvia	119,360	76,855	21,783	217,998
Switzerland, Austria and Hungary	19,783	42,667	6,985	69,435
Taiwan	53,626	273,596	3,395	330,617
Tanzania	138,422	455,665	17,570	611,657
Uganda	123,011	254,992	16,116	394,119
USA Eastern	-	78,854	-	78,854
USA National	-	91,569	-	91,569
USA Southern	-	9,355	-	9,355
Zambia	452,810	292,668	15,892	761,370
Zimbabwe	599,783	664,061	25,918	1,289,762
Crisis Relief	-	-	2,367,485	2,367,485
Central Pension Scheme	-	-	100,000	100,000
International Congress 2015	-	-	1,037,530	1,037,530
Other International Operations	4,719,634	-	1,433,529	6,153,164
	20,892,434	21,837,379	6,564,458	49,294,271

COMMUNITY DEVELOPMENT PROJECTS

The Salvation Army thanks the donors listed below who, during **2013**, assisted in its ministry to some of the world's most vulnerable people. This was accomplished through community development projects monitored by the International Projects and Development Services (IPDS) at IHQ. The projects included:

Combatting the HIV/Aids pandemic; developing savings and loans groups; promoting healthy communities; supporting educational services; improving access to safe water and sanitation; supporting social service programmes to the aged, the marginalised and the young; responding to disaster-hit areas.

Country	Donor	US$
Australia	Eastern Territory (AusAID)	1,064,830
Germany	CBM (Christoffelblindmission)	42,147
Hong Kong	Gracious Glory Buddhism Foundation	22,195
	Government Grants	44,838
Netherlands	Dutch Government MFS2 Programme	386,616
	Goedkoop Legacy	140,368
	Hallers Fund	64,706
	ICCO Cooperation	106,298
	New Life Fund	13,770
	Spijker Trust	27,000
	Van de Neut - de Vos Trust	634,230
	Van Hoorn Legacy	92,597
	Wijnakker Legacy	37,518
New Zealand, Fiji and Tonga	New Zealand Foreign Affairs and Trade Aid Programme (MFAT)	294,177
Norway	NORAD - support to projects exclusive of administrative grant	1,383,940
	Administrative Grant	104,167
Sweden and Latvia	Swedish Mission Council (SMC)	44,594
Switzerland, Austria and Hungary	Bread for All	264,836
	Government Grants	761,713
	Government Grants in Kind	177,330
	Swiss Solidarity	122,487
	Unnamed Foundations	61,625
United Kingdom	Avalon	9,747
	Clifton Charitable Trust Legacy	19,717
	Constance Annie Inglish Legacy	15,578
	Constance Ellen Clark Legacy	6,808
	Crown Agents (DFID)	152,444
	Gwladys Bonsor Legacy	30,815
	J. Walker	8,080
	June Audrey Young Legacy	67,128
	M. Kimberley	8,391
	Marjorie Dorothy Harlow Legacy	9,487
	Sheila Martin Legacy	6,712
	Sidney Hamilton Legacy	15,740
	The Peter Vardy Foundation	8,391
USA	NHQ (SAWSO)	6,243,536
	USAID via SAWSO	1,074,794
TOTAL		US$ 13,624,200

Abbreviations used in *The Year Book*

A

(A) (active officer pG); Acc (Accommodation); Adj (Adjutant); Afr (Africa); Am (America); Ang (Angola); AO (Area Officer); Apt (Apartment); Appt (Appointment); ARC (Adult Rehabilitation Centre); Asst (Assistant); Aus (Australia); A/Capt, Aux-Capt (Auxiliary-Captain)

B

b (born); Ban (Bangladesh); Belg (Belgium); B/M (Bandmaster); Braz (Brazzaville); Brig (Brigadier); Brz (Brazil); BT (British Territory)

C

Can (Canada and Bermuda); Capt (Captain); Carib (Caribbean); CIDA (Canadian International Development Agency); CO (Commanding Officer); Col (Colonel); Comr (Commissioner); Con (Congo); Con [Braz] (Congo Brazzaville); CoS (Chief of the Staff); CPWM (Command President of Women's Ministries); Cze R (Czech Republic);CS (Chief Secretary); C/S (Corps Secretary); CSLD (Centre for Spiritual Life Development); CSM (Corps Sergeant-Major); C/T (Corps Treasurer)

D

DC (Divisional Commander); Den (Denmark); DO (Divisional Officer); DR Con (Democratic Republic of Congo)

E

E Afr (East Africa); E Eur/EET (Eastern Europe); Ens (Ensign); Env (Envoy); ESFOT (European School for Officers' Training)

F

Fin (Finland and Estonia); Frce (France and Belgium)

G

Ger (Germany and Lithuania); Gha (Ghana); Grce (Greece); GS (General Secretary)

H

HK (Hong Kong and Macau); HL (Home League); HLS (Home League Secretary); Hun (Hungary)

I

ICO (International College for Officers); IHQ (International Headquarters); IHS (International Health Services); ILP (International Literature Programme); Ind C, E, etc (India Central, Eastern, etc); Ind M&A (India Madras and Andhra); Indon (Indonesia); Intnl (International); IPDS (International Projects and Development Services); IS (International Secretary); ISJC (International Social Justice Commission); It (Italy and Greece); ITC (International Training College)

J

JHLS (Junior Home League Secretary); Jpn (Japan)

K

Ken (Kenya); Kin (Kinshasa); Kor (Korea)

L

L Am N (Latin America North); Lat (Latvia); Lib (Liberia); Lt, Lieut (Lieutenant); Lt-Col, Lieut-Colonel (Lieutenant-Colonel); LOM (League of Mercy)

Abbreviations used in *The Year Book*

M

m (married); Maj (Major); Mal (Malawi); Mid E (Middle East); Mli (Mali); Mlys (Malaysia); Mol (Moldova); Moz (Mozambique); My (Myanmar)

N

Nat (National); NC (National Commander); Neth (The Netherlands and Czech Republic); NHQ (National Headquarters); Nor (Norway, Iceland and The Færoes); NZ (New Zealand, Fiji and Tonga)

O

OC (Officer Commanding); ODAS (Order of Distinguished Auxiliary Service); OF (Order of the Founder); O&R (Orders and Regulations)

P

Pak (Pakistan); pG (promoted to Glory); Phil (The Philippines); PNG (Papua New Guinea); Port (Portugal)

R

RC (Regional Commander); RDWM (Regional Director of Women's Ministries); ret, (retired); RO (Regional Officer); ROS (Retired Officers Secretary); RPWM (Regional President of Women's Ministries); Rus (Russia/CIS); Rwa (Rwanda and Burundi)

S

S/, Snr (Senior); S Afr (Southern Africa); SALT (Salvation Army Leadership Training); S Am E (South America East); SAMF (Salvation Army Medical Fellowship); S Am W (South America West); SAWSO (Salvation Army World Service Office); Sec (Secretary); Sen (Senior); SFOT (School for Officers' Training); Sgt (Sergeant); Sing (Singapore, Malaysia and Myanmar); S/Ldr (Songster Leader); Soc S (Social Services); Sp (Spain); SP&S (Salvationist Publishing and Supplies); Sri Lan (Sri Lanka); Supt (Superintendent); Swdn (Sweden and Latvia); Switz (Switzerland, Austria and Hungary)

T

Tai (Taiwan); Tanz (Tanzania); tba (to be appointed); TC (Territorial Commander); TCCMS (Territorial Community Care Ministries Secretary); tel (telephone); THQ (Territorial Headquarters); TLWM, TPWM, TSWM, TSAFM (Territorial Leader of, President of, Secretary for Women's Ministries, Secretary for Adult and Family Ministries); TWMS (Territorial Women's Ministries Secretary)

U

Uga (Uganda); UK (United Kingdom); Uk (Ukraine); UKI (United Kingdom with the Republic of Ireland); USA (United States of America); USA Nat, USA C, etc (USA National, Central, etc)

W

WI (West Indies); WPWM WSWM (World President of, Secretary for Women's Ministries); Ww (Widow/Widower)

Z

Zai (Zaïre); Zam (Zambia); Zimb (Zimbabwe); ZSWM (Zonal Secretary for Women's Ministries)

ANGOLA COMMAND

Command leaders:
Lieut-Colonels Célestin and Véronique Pululu

Officer Commanding:
Lieut-Colonel Célestin Pululu (1 Jul 2012)

General Secretary:
Major Mario Nhacumba (1 Jun 2014)

**Command Headquarters: Igreja Exército de Salvação,
Rua Olympia Macueira, Comuna de Palanca, Luanda, Angola**
Postal address: Caixa Postal 1656-C, Luanda, Angola
Tel: [00244] 928-570 867; email: ang_leadership@ang.salvationarmy.org

Salvation Army work in Angola was officially established in 1985. Having been part of the Congo (Kinshasa) and Angola Territory, it became a separate command on 1 March 2008.

In 1974, two officers originally from Angola but trained and serving in Congo (Kinshasa) entered Angola by Uige Province to commence Salvation Army meetings in that part of the country. In 1978, other Salvationists from Kinshasa met in Angola's capital, Luanda, and 'opened fire'. The Salvation Army was officially recognised by the Angola Government on 14 February 1992.

Zone: Africa
Country included in the command: Angola
'The Salvation Army' in Portuguese: Exército de Salvação
Languages in which the gospel is preached: Humbundu, Kikongo, Kimbundu, Lingala, Nchokwe, Ngangela, Portuguese

THE COMMAND'S theme for the year under review was 'Evangelism and Discipleship'. Throughout the command events and campaigns were conducted to support the belief that Angola can be won for Jesus. In addition, each corps was encouraged to reach out beyond its immediate community and commence new openings.

The command conducted a three-day evangelistic campaign where testimonies, music and the Word of God were shared. The Army is on the move in Angola through evangelism, discipleship and church growth.

Following the opening and dedication of a new training college, the command's first Brengle Institute took place at the new college facilities.

Upon their return from out-training, the cadets were commissioned and ordained, marking another significant event for the command.

With the help of the band and timbrels, and led by corps flags, home league members took part in a march of witness to commemorate International Women's Day. Home league members also took part in a three-day evangelistic campaign in Benguela.

Practical training was a priority in the command. Training for local officers in youth, music and penitent form ministries was held. In addition, ongoing training in community development, community facilitation and understanding the need for the integration of community and corps ministries was also conducted.

The deepening of the officers' and soldiers' spiritual lives and the broadening of their witness has been an important part of Angola Command's strategy during the year.

STATISTICS
Officers 48 (active 44 retired 4) **Envoys** 5
  Employees 52
Corps 25 **Outposts** 13 **Schools** 3
Senior Soldiers 3,383 **Junior Soldiers** 826

STAFF
Women's Ministries: Lt-Col Véronique Pululu
  (CPWM) Maj Celeste Nhacumba (CSWM)
Extension Officer/SALT: Maj António Kupesa
Finance: Capt Laurindo Nombora
Projects: Capt Daniel Diantelo
Property: Capt Daniel Ngonga
Statistics: Maj António Kupesa
Training: tba
Youth: Capt Luisa Nombora
National BM: Sgt Raimundo Nkuansambu
National SL: Sgt Kinavuidi Álvaro

DISTRICTS
Luanda 1: Capt Antonio Nsingi;

tel: (00244) 923-003750
Luanda 2: Maj Domingo Makuntima;
  tel: (00244) 923-506986

SECTIONS
Benguela: Lt Matondo Nkomi
Cabinda: Lt Philip Mabanza;
  tel: (00244) 923-003750
Moxico: Lt Ricardo Bengui;
  tel: (00244) 923-242205
Uige: Capt Baptista Ndombele;
  tel: (00244) 924-118717
Zaire: Lt Emanuel Longui;
  tel: (00244) 934-657978

TRAINING COLLEGE
Colégio de Formação de Oficiais
Rua Olympia Macueira, Comuna de Palanca,
  Luanda, Angola
Postal address: Caixa Postal 1656-C, Luanda,
  tel: [00244] 928 570 867

SCHOOLS
Primary
William Booth Primary School of Petrangol
  Mr Paulo Mafuta (Director)
William Booth Primary School of Maquela do
  Zomba
  Lt Daniel Nkele

Secondary
Eng Afonso Nzoanene Secondary School
  Mr Diassonama Pedro (Director)

SOCIAL SERVICES
Development and Emergencies
Cabinda Corps (polio project)
Luau Corps (polio project and water/sanitation)
Luena Corps (polio project)
Moxico (vaccination, water and sanitation)

ANGOLA: Young Salvationists on the march

AUSTRALIA NATIONAL SECRETARIAT

Offices: 2 Brisbane Ave, Barton, Canberra, ACT 2600
Postal address: PO Box 4256, Manuka, ACT 2603, Australia
Tel: [61] (02) 6273 3055
email: Kelvin.Alley@aue.salvationarmy.org

Two Christian Mission converts, John Gore and Edward Saunders, pioneered Salvation Army operations on 5 September 1880 in Adelaide. These were officially established on 11 February 1881 by the appointment of Captain and Mrs Thomas Sutherland. In 1921 the work in Australia was organised into Eastern and Southern Territories with headquarters in Sydney and Melbourne.

A National Secretariat serving the whole of Australia and funded jointly by both territories was established in 1987.

Periodicals: *Kidzone, Warcry*

THE SALVATION Army's National Secretariat, strategically located in the capital Canberra, the centre of national political life, represents The Salvation Army to federal government and liaises with government ministers and officials. In turn, Major Kelvin Alley, National Secretary, provides information and advice to the leaders of the two Australian territories on developments and opportunities in current government activities, especially in relation to social welfare policy.

During the past year the national secretary consolidated strong relationships with parliament. Issues addressed included reforms in employment, charities and the not-for-profit sector, human trafficking and humanitarian support for asylum seekers.

The Army was also represented at a number of government discussions; with UNHCR (Refugee Agency) to facilitate consultation on the Army's work with asylum seekers and further discussion into reforms to gambling regulations.

In September 2013 Major Alley accompanied Commissioner Gillian Downer (International Secretary, South Pacific and East Asia Zone, IHQ) on her visit to Timor Leste to consider the possibility of The Salvation Army commencing work there.

Following the 2013 federal election, Major Alley focused on establishing good connections with the new government, particularly ministers whose offices impact on Salvation Army programmes.

National Secretary: Maj Kelvin Alley

National Editorial Department:
95-99 Railway Rd, Blackburn, Vic 3130
(PO Box 479); tel: 03 8878 2303
National Editor-in-Chief: Capt June Knop

Red Shield Defence Services National HQ:
32-54 Hayward Street, (PO Box 1422)
Stafford, QLD, 4053; tel: (07) 3356 8167

Chief Commissioner: Lt Lyndley Fabre

AUSTRALIA EASTERN TERRITORY

Territorial leaders:
Commissioners James and Jan Condon

Territorial Commander:
Commissioner James Condon
(2 Apr 2011)

Chief Secretary:
Colonel Richard Munn (1 Apr 2013)

Territorial Headquarters: 140 Elizabeth Street, Sydney, NSW 2000

Postal address: PO Box A435, Sydney South, NSW 1235, Australia

Tel: [61] (02) 9264 1711 (10 lines); website: www.salvos.org.au

Two Christian Mission converts having pioneered Salvation Army operations in Adelaide in September 1880, the work in Australia was organised into Eastern and Southern Territories in 1921, with headquarters for the Eastern Territory being set up in Sydney.

Zone: South Pacific and East Asia
States included in the territory: New South Wales, Queensland, The Australian Capital Territory (ACT)
Languages in which the gospel is preached: Cantonese, English, Korean, Mandarin
Periodicals: *Creative Ministry*, *Pipeline*, *Venue*, *Women in Touch*

MORE than 2,500 Salvationists and friends participated in the *Freedom Celebration* congress held at Sydney Olympic Park in September 2013. This was the first official overseas visit for General André Cox since being elected to the office of General. The General and Commissioner Silvia Cox (WPWM) were given an especially warm Australian welcome. The territory's missional energy and creativity was on full display, beginning with officers councils, a carnival of Salvation Army services and freedom celebration concert. Sunday's activities commenced with a young leaders' breakfast and continued with two meetings, characterised by prolonged seasons of prayer following the preaching of the General and Commissioner Cox.

Commissioner James Condon (TC) officially opened the state-of-the-art residential Elizabeth Jenkins Place (EJP) Aged Care Plus Centre at Collaroy in June 2013. EJP is made up of low-rise houses and communal areas for residents, including a putting green, freestanding chapel, cafe, shop, hairdresser and medical precinct.

Because 'Salvos' is a long-recognised and successful brand in Australia, a strategic rebranding of women's ministries as Salvos Women brought a more recognisable and interconnected role within the Mission Team Department. This adds to an established integrated ministry, one to the whole family and also speaking against injustices to women and children.

In September 2013, Emergency Services teams responded as bushfires ravaged the Blue Mountains in New South Wales destroying almost 200 homes. From a dedicated Emergency Services truck, Army personnel fed affected residents in evacuation centres as well as firefighters and other emergency service workers.

In October 2013 more than 200 women from across the territory and beyond attended the inaugural Women in Leadership Forum in Sydney. This forum addressed systemic issues of gender equality in leadership positions, as well as developing skills and self-awareness for such roles. Major Danielle Strickland (Canada and Bermuda Territory) was guest speaker.

The Australian national Royal Commission public hearing into institutional responses to child sexual abuse with a focus on historic cases in The Salvation Army, started in January 2014 and concluded in April. This was primarily a time for care leavers to share their experiences. The territory expressed profound regret for every instance of abuse experienced and reported, and recommendations from the Royal Commission on how to further protect children will be implemented.

In February the territory concluded its contract with the Department of Immigration and Border Protection that provided humanitarian mission services to adult asylum seekers at Manus Island and Nauru. This unique ministry placed the Army under a political spotlight and was clearly impactful, with certainty that the Kingdom of God was extended as a result of this commitment.

Major Val Mylechreest (United Kingdom Territory with the Republic of Ireland) was guest speaker for the *Captivated* conferences attended by over 600 women. This included the launch of the 2014 women's ministries project for education programmes and Bibles in Tanzania, with a goal of AUS$110,000.

STATISTICS

Officers 949 (active 532 retired 417)
   Cadets (1st Yr) 15 (2nd Yr) 19
   Employees 4,717
Corps 161 **Outposts/Plants/Missions** 13
   Social Centres/Programmes 320
   Community Welfare Services 149
   Thrift Stores/Charity Shops 229
Senior Soldiers 8,159
   Adherent Members 2,805
   Junior Soldiers 587
Personnel serving outside territory
   Officers 28 Layworkers 3

STAFF

Women's Ministries: Comr Jan Condon (TPWM)
Office of the TC:
   Sec for Education and Training: tba
Office of the CS:
   Booth College: Maj Peter Farthing
   International Development: Maj Julie Alley
   National Secretariat: Maj Kelvin Alley
   Spiritual Life Development: Maj Sharon
   Clanfield

Training Principal: Col Janet Munn
Business: Lt-Col Brian Hood
  Communications and Public Relations:
    Maj Bruce Harmer
  Finance: Mr Ian Minnett
  Information Technology: Mr Wayne Bajema
  Property: Mr Peter Alward
  Salvos Legal: Mr Luke Geary
  Salvos Stores: Mr Neville Barrett
  Territorial Legal Counsel: Maj Graeme Ross
  The Collaroy Centre: Mr Richard Javor
Personnel: Lt-Col David Godkin
  Candidates: Majs David and Shelley Soper
  Human Resources: Ms Ruth Hampton
  Pastoral Care and Officer Wellbeing: Majs
    David and Lea Palmer
Programme: Lt-Col Laurie Robertson
  Territorial Mission and Resource Directors
    Corps: Envoys Randall and Glenda Brown
    Recovery: Maj David Pullen
    Social: Maj Jeanette Stoltenberg
    Systems: Ms Nerys Hood
  Territorial Youth and Children's Ministry
    Secretaries: Maj Stephen Briggs (Strategy and
    Communications); Maj Tracy Briggs
    (Resources)
  Aged Care Plus: Ms Sharon Callister
  Emergency Services: Mr Norm Archer
  Red Shield Defence Services: Lt Lyndley
    Fabre
  Salvos Housing: Mr Robert Burnelek
  Sydney Staff Songsters: S/L Graham
    Ainsworth

DIVISIONS

Australian Capital Territory and South NSW:
2-4 Brisbane Ave, Barton, ACT 2600;
PO Box 4224, Kingston, ACT 2604;
tel: (02) 6273 2211;
Majs Howard and Robyn Smartt
Central and North Queensland: 54 Charles St,
North Rockhampton, QLD 4701; PO Box 5343,
Red Hill, Rockhampton, QLD 4701;
tel: (07) 4999 1999;
Majs Kelvin and Cheralynne Pethybridge
Newcastle and Central NSW: 94 Parry Street,
Newcastle West, NSW 2302, PO Box 684,
The Junction, NSW 2291; tel: (02) 4926 3466;
Majs Gavin and Wendy Watts
North NSW: 86 Beardy St, PO Box 1180,
Armidale, NSW 2350; tel: (02) 6771 1632;
Majs Earle and Christine Ivers
South Queensland: First Floor 97 School Street,
Spring Hill QLD 4004, GPO Box 2210,
Brisbane, QLD 4001; tel: (07) 3222 6666;
Majs Mark and Julie Campbell
Sydney East and Illawarra: 61-65 Kingsway,

Kingsgrove, NSW 2208; PO Box 740,
Kingsgrove, NSW 1480; tel: (02) 9336 3320;
Lt-Cols Peter and Jan Laws
The Greater West: 166-170 South Parade,
Auburn, NSW 2144; tel: (02) 8644 0110;
Majs Warren and Denise Parkinson

BOOTH COLLEGE
Bexley North, NSW 2207: 32a Barnsbury Grove,
PO Box 4063; tel: (02) 9502 0400

SCHOOL FOR OFFICER TRAINING
Bexley North, NSW 2207: 120 Kingsland Rd, PO
Box 4063; tel: (02) 9502 1777

SCHOOL FOR CHRISTIAN STUDIES
Bexley North, NSW 2207: 32a Barnsbury Grove,
PO Box 4063; tel: (02) 9502 0432

SCHOOL FOR LEADERSHIP TRAINING
Stanmore, NSW 2048: 97 Cambridge St;
tel: (02) 9557 1105

SCHOOL FOR MULTICULTURAL MINISTRY
c/o Auburn Corps, 166-170 Grand Parade,
Auburn

SCHOOL FOR YOUTH LEADERSHIP
Berkeley Vale, NSW 2261: 60 Berkeley Rd;
tel (02) 43882781

HERITAGE PRESERVATION CENTRE
Bexley North, NSW 2207: 120 Kingsland Rd,
PO Box 4063; tel: (02) 9502 0424;
email: AUEHeritage@aue.salvationarmy.org

CONFERENCE AND HOLIDAY HOUSES/UNITS
Collaroy: The Collaroy Centre, Homestead Ave,
Collaroy Beach, NSW 2097, PO Box 11;
tel: (02) 9982 9800 (office), 9982 6570 AH;
email: collaroy@collaroycentre.org.au
The folowing properties are booked through
The Collaroy Centre Reception:
Budgewoi, NSW 2262: 129 Sunrise Ave;
(cottage acc 6)
Caloundra, QLD 4551: 4 Michael St, Golden
Beach; (house/sleeps 8)
Main Beach, QLD 4217: Unit 23 Ocean Park
Towers, 3494 Main Beach Pde;
(apartment/sleeps 4)
Margate, QLD 4019: 2 Duffield Rd;
(3 units/sleeps 3x6; 1x4)
Monterey, NSW 2217: 1/60 Solander St (acc 6)

Tugan, QLD 4224: 3/15 Elizabeth St; (acc 4)
*The following property is booked through
DHQ Rockhampton;tel:(07) 4999 1999*
Cairns, QLD 4870: 281-289 Sheridan St;
(4 units)

EMPLOYMENT PLUS
National Support Office: Level 3, 10 Wesley Ct,
Burwood East, VIC 3151; tel: 136 123

SALVOS LEGAL
Level 2, 151 Castlereagh Street, Sydney
NSW 2000 Migration Agent Registration
Number 0635598; tel: (02) 8202 1500

SALVOS STORES
Head Office: 4 Archbold Rd, Minchinbury,
NSW 2770; tel: (02) 9834 9030
tel: 13 SALVOS (13 72 58)
ACT and Monaro Area: (8)
Brisbane Area: (18)
Central Coast: (5)
Eastern Sydney Area: (14)
Gold Coast: (12)
Illawarra Area: (8)
Newcastle Hunter Area: (9)
Townsville Area: (3)
Western Sydney Area: (21)

SOCIAL SERVICES
Residential Aged Care
Arncliffe, NSW (acc 139)
Balmain, NSW (acc hostel men 44)
Bass Hill, NSW (acc 104)
The Cairns Aged Care Centre, QLD
(acc 128)
Canowindra, NSW (acc 65)
Collary, NSW (acc 126)
Dee Why, NSW (acc 59)
Dulwich Hill, NSW (acc 38)
Erina, NSW (acc 169)
Goulburn, NSW (acc 103)
Merewether, NSW (acc 42)
Narrabundah, ACT (acc 67)
Parkes, NSW (acc 70)
Port Macquarie, NSW (acc 92)
Riverview, QLD (acc 167)
Rockhampton, QLD (acc hostel 50)

Independent Living Retirement Villages
Arncliffe, NSW (acc units 36)
Bass Hill, NSW (acc units 36)
Collaroy, NSW (acc units 108)
Erina, NSW (acc units 64)
Parkes, NSW (acc units 14)

Riverview, QLD (acc units 26)
Aged Care Respite and Day Care
Rivett, ACT (acc 15, plus respite day care)

Bridge Programme – Addiction Recovery (alcohol, other drugs and gambling)
Brisbane: Brisbane Recovery Services Centre
(acc men 58, women 26, detox unit 12,
halfway house 10)
Canberra: Canberra Recovery Services Centre
(acc men 38, halfway house 3); Nowra:
Shoalhaven Bridge Programme
Central Coast: Dooralong Transformation Centre:
Dual Diagnosis Bridge Program (acc 27 men);
Bridge Program (acc 78 men); Bridge Youth
and Family Drug and Alcohol Support
Program (halfway house acc 3 men); Women's
Bridge Programme (acc women 36,
halfway house 4)
Gold Coast: Recovery Services Centre
(acc men 40, detox unit 11, women 16)
Mount Isa Recovery Service (individuals, couples
and families 55 beds)
Sydney:William Booth House Recovery Services
Centre (acc men and women 131)
Alf Dawkins Detoxification Unit (acc 10 men)
Townsville: Recovery Services Centre
(acc men 30)
Women's out-Client Service: Grace Cottage

Chaplains
Rural: ACT and South NSW; Central and North
QLD; Newcastle and Central NSW; North
NSW; South Queensland
Statutory Authorities: fire and rescue, NSW;
rural fire service, NSW; fire and rescue, QLD
Other chaplaincy services: aged care plus,
courts and prisons, Employment Plus, hospitals,
Salvos stores, Sydney Airport and universities

Children's Services (Day Care and After School)
NSW: Macquarie Fields
QLD: Carina, Gladstone, Slacks Creek
Sydney: Young Hope Out of Home Care

Community Welfare Service
ACT and South NSW: 21; Central and North
QLD: 24; Newcastle and Central NSW: 22;
North NSW: 23; South QLD: 35; Sydney
East and Illawarra: 11; The Greater West: 21

Crisis and Supported Accommodation
Cairns North, QLD (acc men 29, women 20,
women with children 10, patient transfer

scheme men 5, women 5)
Carrington, NSW (acc men 22)
Faith Cottage, NSW (acc women and children 12)
Griffith, NSW (acc hostel 4, in community 6)
Leeton, NSW (acc family units 3)
Mount Isa, QLD (acc women and children 16)
Newcastle, NSW (acc single women, crisis hostel beds 8, community acc 24)
Oasis Youth Network, NSW
Southport, QLD (acc crisis beds women 20, women and children 7 units, single women 16)
Spring Hill, QLD (acc hostel 90 men, community units 9 men)
Spring Hill, QLD (acc 18 women)
Surry Hills, NSW 2010 (acc men's hostel 95 beds; IPU 30 beds; community housing 85) (acc women crisis hostel 10, medium-term beds 20, community units 10)
Tewantin, QLD (acc families, 16 places)
Toowoomba, QLD (acc men's crisis and family community places)

Youth Services (crisis and supported accommodation)

Bundaberg, QLD (acc 6)
Canberra, ACT: Oasis Support Services, Oasis Youth Residential Service (crisis acc 24)
Fortitude Valley, QLD
Newcastle, NSW (acc 20)
Surry Hills, NSW (crisis acc 13, medium-term 13, community 22)
Wyong, NSW

Domestic Violence Programme

Chatswood, NSW

The territory also has 5 women's refuge centres which include accommodation for mothers and children.

Employment Preparation and Skills Training

7 programmes

Family Tracing Service

Brisbane, QLD 4000: 342 Upper Roma St, GPO Box 2210, Brisbane 4000; tel: (07) 3222 6661
Sydney, NSW 2000: PO Box A435, Sydney South 1235; tel: (02) 9211 0277
Special Search, tel: (02) 9211 6491; 1300 667 366 (Australia wide)

Hostel for Students

Toowong, QLD (acc 66)

Intellectually Disabled Persons Services

Broken Hill, NSW
Toowong, QLD (acc in home community based lifestyle support 31 adults)
Toowoomba, QLD (acc 28)

Moneycare Financial Counselling and Salvos No Interest Loans

60 locations

Outback flying services

Flying Service Base: 4 Helen St, Mt Isa, QLD 4825; tel: (07) 4749 3875

Red Shield Defence Services

RSDS Administration: Queensland; tel: (07) 3356 8167; mob: 0407 830 488
Adelaide Edinburgh Defence Precinct, SA
Darwin Robertson Barracks, NT
Gallipoli Barracks, Brisbane, QLD
Holsworthy Military Camp, Sydney, NSW
Lavarack Barracks, Townsville, QLD
Puckapunyal Vic School of Armoured Trucks and Artillery
Royal Military College, Duntroon, ACT
Singleton Infantry Centre, NSW

Salvos Counselling

Head Office: Rhodes, NSW 2138: 15-17 Blaxland Rd, PO Box 3096; tel: (02) 9743 4535
Bayside, QLD; Cairns, QLD; Campbelltown, NSW; Canberra, ACT; Dalby/Toowoomba, QLD; Gold Coast, QLD; Goodna, QLD; Gosford, NSW; Penrith, NSW; Rhodes, NSW; Rockhampton, QLD; Stafford, QLD; Tuggeranong, ACT

Telephone Counselling Service

Salvo Care Line: Brisbane, QLD
Crisis Line: 1300 36 36 22 (Accessible across Australia)

Counselling Service and Crisis Intervention

24hr Telephone Counselling Service: tel: (02) 8736 3297
Salvo Youth Line and Crisis Intervention: tel: (02) 8736 3293
Suicide Prevention and Crisis Intervention: tel: (02) 8736 3295

AUSTRALIA SOUTHERN TERRITORY

Territorial leaders:
Commissioners Floyd and Tracey Tidd

Territorial Commander:
Commissioner Floyd Tidd
(1 Jun 2013)

Chief Secretary:
Colonel Peter Walker (1 Jul 2010)

Territorial Headquarters: 95-99 Railway Road, Blackburn, Victoria, 3130

Postal address: PO Box 479, Blackburn, Victoria, 3130, Australia

Tel: [61] (03) 8878 4500; email: Salvosaus@aus.salvationarmy.org

website: www.salvationarmy.org.au

Two Christian Mission converts having pioneered Salvation Army operations in Adelaide in September 1880, the work in Australia was organised into Eastern and Southern Territories in 1921, with headquarters for the Southern Territory being set up in Melbourne.

Zone: South Pacific and East Asia
States included in the territory: Northern Territory, South Australia, Tasmania, Victoria,
Western Australia
Languages in which the gospel is preached: Arabic, Cantonese, Dinka, English, Farsi, Kiswahili,
Mandarin, Nuer, Tagalog and local aboriginal languages
Periodicals: *On Fire, Red*

ON 6 June 2013, the Besen Centre in Melbourne was the venue chosen for the installation and territorial welcome to Commissioners Floyd and Tracey Tidd as Territorial Commander and Territorial President of Women's Ministries, respectively. This had been preceded in May by a salute to outgoing territorial leaders Commissioners Raymond and Aylene Finger, held at Waverley Temple.

A group of Salvationists manned a booth at the 'MindBodySpirit' festival in Melbourne in early June. Apart from praying with more than 300 people, many Bibles were handed out to festival goers.

In October a 'Composers' Symposium' was held at the Geelong Conference Centre, organised by the Territorial Creative Arts Department. This was a chance for writers of brass, vocal and worship music to hear from guest speakers, discuss composition and work on selections.

The Lord Mayor Robert Doyle named the corps officer from Melbourne's Project 614, Major Brendan Nottle, 'Melburnian of the Year'. Speaking of the work of the corps in the inner city, Mr Doyle said that Major Nottle's devotion to strengthening Melbourne's social fabric is an inspiration to all.

The territory celebrated the visit of General André Cox and Commissioner Silvia Cox (WPWM) early in December to lead the commissioning and ordination of the cadets of the Disciples of the Cross Session. This event commenced with officers councils where more than 400 officers were in attendance. The afternoon session included the launch of *The People's General*, a tribute book released to celebrate 20 years since the retirement from active officership of General Eva Burrows (Rtd). General Cox presented a copy of the book to General Burrows.

The Sunday meetings were conducted at the Melbourne Town Hall and included moments of great reverence and solemnity as well as joyous celebration. The weekend came to a close with the General leading a 'hallelujah wind-up' while waving the flag of the territory.

Summer saw the usual outbreak of bushfires across the territory and Salvation Army Emergency Services personnel were called on for support at multiple fires in Victoria, South Australia and Western Australia. Thousands of volunteer firefighters and others were fed, counselled and encouraged as life-threatening fires were confronted.

In March 2014, the 'GraceWorks' conference was organised by the Territorial Women's Ministries Department. Hundreds of women gathered to hear guest speaker Colonel Janet Munn (Australia Eastern Territory) and take part in electives and worship sessions.

STATISTICS

Officers 894 (active 493 retired 401) **Cadets** (1st Yr) 26 (2nd Yr) 18 **Employees** 5,137

Corps 163 **Outposts** 6

Social Centres/Programmes 207

Salvos Stores 210 **Community Support Centres** 126 **Outback Flying Service** 1

Senior Soldiers 7,121 **Adherent Members** 2,046 **Junior Soldiers** 1,186

Personnel serving outside territory Officers 14

STAFF

Women's Ministries: Comr Tracey Tidd (TPWM) Col Jennifer Walker (TSWM)

Asst Chief Secretary: Lt-Col Ian Callander

Catherine Booth College Chair/Training Principal: Maj Gregory Morgan

Communications: Maj Neil Venables

National Editor-in-Chief: Capt June Knop

Business Administration: Lt-Col Bruce Stevens

  Asst Sec for Business Admin: Maj Alan Milkins

  Asst Sec for Business Admin and Territorial Legal Secretary: Capt Malcolm Roberts

  Audit: Mr Cameron Duck

  Finance: Mr Gregory Stowe

  Information Technology: Mr Craig Tucker

  Overseas Development: Maj Ron Cochrane

  Property: Mr David Sinden

  Public Relations: Maj Paul Hateley

  Salvationist Supplies: Mrs Karen Newton

  Salvos Stores: Mr Allen Dewhirst

Personnel: Lt-Col Vivien Callander

  Asst Sec for Personnel: Maj Kelvin Merrett

  Candidates: Lt-Col Debra Stevens

  Human Resources: Mr Stephen Webb

  Officer Development: Lt-Col Karyn Rigley

  Overseas Personnel: Maj Dianne Main

  Pastoral Care: Maj Graeme Faragher

Programme: Lt-Col Graeme Rigley

  Chaplaincy: Maj Beth Roberts

  Family Tracing: Maj Sophia Gibb

  Melbourne Staff Band: B/M Ken Waterworth

  Melbourne Staff Songsters: S/L Brian Hogg

  Mission Resources: Maj Graham Roberts

  Social Justice: Maj Sandy Crowden

Social Programme: Ms Netty Horton
Spiritual Development: Maj Heather
Jenkins; Maj Marney Turner
Youth: Capt Craig Farrell

DIVISIONS

Eastern Victoria: 347-349 Mitcham Rd,
Mitcham, Vic 3132; tel: (03) 8872 6400;
Maj Winsome Merrett
Melbourne Central: 1/828 Sydney Rd,
North Coburg, Vic 3058; tel: (03) 9353 5200;
Majs Michael and Annette Coleman
Northern Victoria: 65-71 Mundy Street,
Bendigo, Vic 3550; tel: (03) 5440 8400;
Majs John and Wendy Freind
South Australia: 39 Florence St, Fullarton,
SA 5063; tel: (08) 8408 6900;
Lt-Cols Ronald and Robyn Clinch
Tasmania: 27 Pirie St, New Town, Tas 7008;
tel: (03) 6228 8400;
Majs Ritchie and Gail Watson
Western Australia: 333 William St,
Northbridge, WA 6003; tel: (08) 9260 9500;
Maj Wayne Pittaway
Western Victoria: 102 Eureka St, Ballarat,
Vic 3350; tel: (03) 5337 1300;
Majs Geoff and Kalie Webb

REGION

Northern Territory: Level 2, Suite C, Paspalis
Centrepoint, 48-50 Smith St, Darwin, NT
0800; tel: (08) 8944 6000;
Majs Darryl and Kaylene Robinson

CATHERINE BOOTH COLLEGE

Ringwood, Vic 3134: 100 Maidstone Street;
tel: tbc

SCHOOL FOR OFFICER TRAINING

Ringwood, Vic 3134: 100 Maidstone Street;
tel: tbc

SCHOOL FOR CHRISTIAN STUDIES

Ringwood, Vic 3134: 100 Maidstone Street;
tel: tbc

SCHOOL FOR LEARNING AND DEVELOPMENT

Ringwood, Vic 3134: 100 Maidstone Street;
tel: tbc

ARCHIVES AND HERITAGE CENTRES

Melbourne, Vic 3000: Territorial Archives and
Museum, 69 Bourke St; tel: (03) 9653 3270
Northbridge, WA 6003: Heritage Museum, 3rd
Floor, 333 William St; tel: (08) 9260 9552

CONFERENCE AND HOLIDAY CENTRES

Baldivis, WA 6171: New Heights Conference
Centre, 13 Fifty Rd; tel: (08) 9524 1181
Bicheno, Tas 7215: Holiday Home, 11 Banksia St
Cowes, Vic 3922: Holiday Unit,
2/28-30 McKenzie Rd; tel: (03) 5952 6497
Cullen Bay, NT 0820: Holiday Unit, 602/26
Marina Blvd
Daylesford, Vic 3460: Holiday Accommodation,
Unit 5/28 Camp St
East Geelong, Vic 3219: Geelong Conference
Centre, 20 Adams Court, Eastern Park
Gardens; tel: (03) 5226 2121
George Town, Tas, 7253: Holiday Home,
36 Low Head Rd
Ocean Grove, Vic 3226: Holiday Home,
4 Northcote Rd; tel (03) 5255 1784
Victor Harbor, SA 5211:
Encounters Conference Centre,
22 Bartel Blvd; tel: (08) 8552 2707
Weymouth, Tas 7252: Weymouth Holiday Camp,
1 Walden St

EMPLOYMENT PLUS

National Office: Level 3, 10 Wesley Court,
Burwood, Vic 3151; tel: (03) 9847 8700;
Mr Greg Moult
Service Delivery Centres: South Australia 3;
Tasmania 3; Victoria 15; Western Australia 7
Enquiries: tel: 136 123

FLYING PADRE AND OUTBACK SERVICES

PO Box 1460, Katherine, NT 0851;
tel: (08) 8972 3732; Capt Greg Howard

RED SHIELD DEFENCE SERVICES

Edinburgh Defence Precinct Representative;
tel: (08) 8251 3834
Puckapunyal Representative; tel: (03) 5793 1294
Robertson Barracks Representative;
tel: (08) 8983 1283

SALVOS STORES

Administration: 233-235 Blackburn Rd,
Mt Waverley, Vic 3149; tel: (03) 92105100
Stores: Northern Territory 7; South Australia
37; Tasmania 11; Victoria 105; Western
Australia 50

SOCIAL SERVICES
Aboriginal Ministry

Alice Springs, NT: Aboriginal Programme
Fullarton, SA: Divisional APY Lands Project
Geelong, Vic: Indigenous Money Management
Programme

Whittlesea, Vic: Indigenous Youth and Families Project

Aged Care Non-Residential Services
Modbury, SA: Healthlink: 6 programmes
Tasmania: Hobart; Ulverstone: Assistance with Care and Housing for the Aged/Community Aged Care Packages

Alcohol, Other Drugs and Corrections
Adelaide, SA: Towards Independence Sobering Up Unit; Supported Accommodation and Recovery Services; All Victorious; Tea Tree Gully (inc Police and Drug Court Diversion Initiative)
Alice Springs, NT: Men Taking Control – Comorbidity Recovery Programme
Bendigo, Vic: Intensive Rehabilitation Community Programme
Berrimah, NT: Drug and Alcohol Services
Burnie, Tas: Drug and Alcohol Day Programme with Outreach
Dandenong, Vic: Positive Lifestyle Counselling Services
Frankston, Vic: Positive Lifestyle Counselling Services
Geelong, Vic: SalvoConnect Alcohol and Other Drugs (inc Geelong Withdrawal Unit)
Highgate, WA: The Bridge Programme, WA
Launceston, Tas: Bridge Outreach Service; Drug and Alcohol Day Programme; Needle Syringe Programme
New Town, Tas: Bridge Programme; Drug and Alcohol Day Programme with Outreach; XCELL Prison Support Service; Transitional Housing Support for Prisoners
Preston, Vic: Bridgehaven
Ringwood, Vic: Positive Lifestyle Counselling Services
Stuart Park, NT: Drug and Alcohol Services
The Basin, Vic: The Basin Centre (residential rehabilitation)

Asylum Seeker Support
Brunswick, Vic

Bush Fire Outreach Programmes
Healesville, Vic; Seymour, Vic; Traralgon, Vic; Whittlesea, Vic

Chaplaincy
Melbourne, Vic: Melbourne hospitals
Perth, WA: FESA chaplain;
   tel: 0407 294 312
Tullamarine, Vic: Melbourne Airport chaplain;
   tel: (03) 9297 1488

Child Care and Family Services
Balga, WA: Early Learning Centre; Child Health
Ballarat, Vic: Karinya Occasional Childcare
Bendigo, Vic: Fairground Family Access Programme
Hobart, Tas: Communities for Children
Ingle Farm, SA: Communities for Children

Community Programmes
Adelaide, SA: Do Unto Others
Alice Springs, NT: The Waterhole
Ballarat, Vic: Community House
Bendigo, Vic: Gravel Hill Community Garden; Hillskills Workshop
Berri, SA: Riverland Community Services
Bordertown, SA: Thrift Shop
Corio, Vic: Northside Community Centre
Hawthorn, Vic: Hawthorn Project; Homeless Outreach Project; Community Connection Project; Equity; Access Project
Katherine, NT: Beacon
Mornington, Vic: Peninsula Youth and Family Services, Reconnect Programme
Rosebud, Vic: Peninsula Community Support
Shepparton, Vic: Work and Learning Centre

COMMUNITY SUPPORT SERVICES
Doorways Centres
Northern Territory Region
Alice Springs, Anula, Darwin, Katherine, Palmerston

South Australia Division
Adelaide, Berri, Campbelltown, Elizabeth East, Gawler, Ingle Farm, Kapunda, Kilkenny, Marion, Millicent, Modbury, Morphett Vale, Mount Barker, Mount Gambier, Murray Bridge, Norwood, Peterborough, Port Augusta, Port Lincoln, Seacombe Gardens, Tea Tree Gully, Victor Harbour, Whyalla Norrie, Wynn Vale

Tasmania Division
Burnie, Carlton, Clarence, Devonport, George Town, Hobart, Launceston, Moonah, New Norfolk, Scottsdale, Ulverstone

Victoria: Eastern Victoria Division
Bairnsdale, Bentleigh, Boronia, Box Hill, Camberwell, Cranbourne, Dingley Village, Doncaster, Doveton, Ferntree Gully, Frankston, Glen Waverley, Healesville, Leongatha, Mooroolbark, Morwell, Noble Park, Oakleigh, Pakenham, Ringwood, Rosebud, Sale, Warragul, Wonthaggi

Australia Southern Territory

Victoria: Melbourne Central Division
Altona, Brunswick, Coburg North, Craigieburn, Greensborough, Melbourne, Mill Park, Moonee Ponds, Preston, Richmond, St Kilda, Sunbury, Sunshine, Werribee

Victoria: Northern Victoria Division
Beechworth, Benalla, Bendigo, Broadford, Castlemaine, Echuca, Kyabram, Maryborough, Mildura, Red Cliffs, Rochester, Seymour, Shepparton, Swan Hill, Wangaratta, Wodonga

Victoria: Western Victoria Division
Ballarat, Colac, Geelong, Hamilton, Warrnambool

Western Australia Division
Albany, Armadale, Balga, Bentley, Bunbury, Busselton, Ellenbrook, Geraldton, Hamilton Hill, Heathridge, Inner City Vulnerable Persons, Kalgoorlie, Karratha, Kwinana, Mandurah, Merriwa, Morley, Narrogin, Northam, Northbridge, Perth, Rivervale, Rockingham Swan View Financial Counsellors: Balga, Morley, Perth, Rockingham

Court and Prison Services
Adelaide, SA; Alice Springs, NT; Ararat, Vic; Ballarat, Vic; Beechworth, Vic; Bendigo, Vic; Broadmeadows, Vic; Castlemaine, Vic; Colac, Vic; Dandenong, Vic; Deer Park, Vic; Frankston, Vic; Geelong, Vic; Hamilton, Vic; Heidelberg, Vic; Hobart, Tas; Horsham, Vic; Korumburra, Vic; Latrobe Valley, Vic; Launceston, Tas; Laverton North, Vic; Manningham, SA; Melbourne, Vic; Moorabbin, Vic; Mount Gambier, SA; Murray Bridge, SA; Northbridge, WA; Port Augusta, SA; Portland, Vic; Port Lincoln, SA; Ringwood, Vic; Riverland, SA; Sale, Vic; Sunshine, Vic; Tatura, Vic; Wangaratta, Vic; Warrnambool, Vic; West Melbourne, Vic; Wodonga, Vic; Yinnar, Vic

Crisis Services
Croydon, Vic: Gateways Crisis Services
Frankston, Vic: Peninsula Youth and Family Services Crisis Centre
Geelong, Vic: SalvoConnect
Geraldton, WA: Family Crisis Accommodation
Ingle Farm, SA: Community Services Programme
Leongatha, Vic: GippsCare Domestic Violence Outreach Service

New Town, Tas: SA Supported Housing
Northbridge, WA: Street to Home Programme
Perth, WA: Inner City Vulnerable Persons Programme
Rosebud, Vic: Crisis and Transitional Support
St Kilda, Vic: Access Health Service; Crisis Services, Crisis Accommodation Services

Doorways to Parenting
Tasmania: Clarence, Devonport, Kingborough, Moonah, New Norfolk

Emergency Accommodation
Alice Springs, NT (acc service, single men, dual diagnosis)
Balga, WA: Family Accommodation Programme
Ballarat, Vic: Karinya (acc women with children 8)
Berri, SA: Riverland Community Services (acc 30)
Bunbury, WA (acc family units 2)
Burnie, Tas: Oakleigh House (acc 61)
Croydon, Vic: Gateways
Geelong, Vic: SalvoConnect (accommodation cross target 18) SalvoConnect Women's Service (acc women with children 6)
Geraldton, WA (acc family units 3)
Hamilton, Vic (acc 2 units)
Horsham, Vic (acc family units 3, single 3)
Kalgoorlie, WA (acc family units 2)
New Town, Tas (acc 12)
Portland, Vic (acc 2 units)
Sale, Vic (acc 6)
Warrnambool, Vic (acc 3 units)

Emergency Family Accommodation
Ballarat, Vic: families (2); women and children transitional (4)
Berri SA: Riverland Community Services – Supported Accommodation for Families and Personal Support Programme
Geelong, Vic: SalvoConnect (acc cross target 48; motel units 14; male adults over 25 yrs, 8 crisis beds)
Horsham, Vic: (acc family units 3, single 3)
Port Augusta, SA: (acc 65)
St Kilda, Vic: (acc 20)

Emergency Services
Ballarat, Vic; Darwin, NT; Eltham, Vic; Hobart, Tas; Malaga, WA; Pooraka, SA

Family Outreach (Community Programme)
Port Augusta, SA

Family Tracing Service
Adelaide, SA; tel: (08) 8408 6900

Darwin, NT; tel: (08) 8927 6499
Hobart,Tas; tel: (03) 6228 8404
Perth, WA; tel: (08) 9260 9536
Victoria and Inter-Territorial enquiries only:
    Blackburn, Vic; tel: (03) 8878 4500

Family Violence Services
Burnie, Tas: (acc 17)
Darwin, NT: (acc 12)
Fullarton, SA: Bramwell House (acc 5)
Geelong, Vic: SalvoConnect Women's Services
Karratha, WA: (acc 16)
New Town, Tas: McCombe House (acc 12)
North Coburg, Vic: Crossroads (MAFVS)
Onslow, WA
Perth, WA: Graceville Centre (acc 43)
St Kilda, Vic: Crisis Services; Inner South
    Domestic Violence Services

Homeless or at Risk of Homelessness
Alice Springs, NT; Colac, Vic; Darwin, NT;
    Geelong, Vic; Hamilton, Vic; New Town, Tas;
    Portland, Vic; Shepparton, Vic; Wangaratta, Vic;
    Warrnambool, Vic; Wodonga, Vic

Hostels for Homeless Men
Adelaide, SA: Towards Independence (acc 75)
Alice Springs, NT (acc 27)
Darwin, NT: Sunrise Centre (acc 26)
Footscray, Vic: Foley House (acc 46)
Mount Lawley, WA: Tanderra Hostel (acc 27)
North Melbourne, Vic: The Open Door (acc 45)
Perth, WA: The Beacon (acc 102)
West Melbourne, Vic: Flagstaff Crisis
    Accommodation (acc 64)

Hostels/Housing for Homeless Youth
Altona North, Vic (hostels 2)
Fitzroy, Vic
Frankston, Vic (4 houses)
Hobart, Tas (4 houses)
Kadina, SA
Kalgoorlie, WA (acc 12)
Karratha, WA (acc 8)
Kealba, Vic (hostel)
Keilor Park, Vic (hostel)
Landsdale, WA (acc 8)
Leongatha, Vic: GippsCare Cross-target
    Transitional Support
Mirrabooka, WA: Oasis House (acc 8)
Plympton, SA: Muggy's
Pooraka, SA: Muggy's (acc 10)
Port Augusta, SA
Port Lincoln, SA
Port Pirie, SA: Muggy's Country
Reservoir, Vic (hostel)

Salisbury, SA: Burlendi (acc 8)
Shepparton, Vic
St Albans, Vic (hostels 2)
Sunshine, Vic (hostel)
Wallaroo, SA
Whyalla, SA

Hostels for Intellectually Disabled Persons
Manningham, SA: Red Shield Housing Network
    Services (properties 310)

Men's Shed and Support Service
Medina, WA

Mental Health Services
Geelong, Vic

Mobile Ministry
Katherine, NT Flying Padre

Positive Lifestyle Counselling Services
Dandenong, Vic; Hobart, Tas; Ringwood, Vic

Prison Support Programme
Hobart, Tas: XCELL Prison Support

Red Shield Hostel
Darwin, NT (acc 64)

Red Shield Housing Network Association
Hobart, Tas; Manningham, SA; North Coburg, Vic

Rehabilitation Services
Adelaide, SA:
    Towards Independence: 'IT' Futures Initiative
    (computer-based support programme) and
    Training Course; Sobering Up Unit; Supported
    Accommodation & Recovery Services (East);
    Supported Accommodation & Recovery
    Services (West); Comorbidity Project and
    Warrondi Engage and Link (WEL) initiative
Bendigo, Vic:
    Bendigo Bridge Intensive Community
    Rehabilitation Programme
Berrimah, NT: Drug and Alcohol Services (acc
    26); Sunrise Centre
Burnie, Tas: The Bridge Throughcare Programme
Corio, Vic: SalvoConnect Alcohol and Other
    Drugs (inc Geelong Withdrawal Unit)
Gosnells, WA: Harry Hunter Adult Rehabilitation
Hawthorn, Vic: Aurora Women's
    Accommodation Service, Drug and Alcohol
    Counselling Programmes
Highgate, WA: Bridge House (acc 27)
Launceston, Tas: The Bridge Throughcare
    Programme

New Town, Tas: The Bridge Throughcare
Programme
Northbridge, WA: Bridge Non Residential Services
Preston, Vic: Bridgehaven (acc 15)
Ringwood, Vic: Drug Diversion Programme
Swan Hill, Vic
The Basin, Vic: The Basin Centre

Rural Outreach
Bendigo, Vic; Horsham, Vic; New Town, Tas

Senior Citizens' Residences
Angle Park, SA Linsell Lodge
(acc single units 95)
Clarence Park, SA (acc single units 10, double 4)
Footscray, Vic: James Barker House (acc 120)
Gosnells, WA (acc hostel 61 , units 50)
Lenah Valley, Tas (acc units single 26)
New Town, Tas: Barrington Lodge Aged Care
(acc res beds 77)

Social Housing – SASHS
Alice Springs, NT: Towards Independence
Anula, NT: Towards Independence Top End
Geelong, Vic: SalvoConnect
Hawthorn, Vic: EastCare Housing Services
Leongatha, Vic: Gippsland Region
Manningham, SA: Red Shield Housing Network
Services

Morley, WA: Salvo Housing
New Town, Tas
Portland, Vic: SalvoConnect
Sunshine, Vic
Warragul, Vic
Warrnambool, Vic: SalvoConnect

Social Justice Advocacy
Adelaide, SA

Soup Run
Adelaide, SA
Marion, SA
Perth, WA

Telephone Counselling Service
Adelaide, SA: Financial Telephone Counselling;
tel: 1800 025 539

Youth and Family Services
Adelaide, SA; Alice Springs, NT; Ballarat, Vic;
Box Hill, Vic; Brunswick, Vic; Kew, Vic;
Leongatha, Vic; Melbourne, Vic; Melton
South, Vic; Mornington, Vic; Northbridge,
WA; North Coburg, Vic; Shepparton, Vic;
Sunshine, Vic

AUSTRALIA SOUTHERN: Major Brendan Nottle (Melbourne Project 614) receives his award as 'Melburnian of the Year' from Lord Mayor Robert Doyle

BANGLADESH COMMAND

Command leaders:
**Lieut-Colonels Alistair and
Marieke Venter**

Officer Commanding:
Lieut-Colonel Alistair Venter (1 Oct 2011)

General Secretary:
Lieut-Colonel Priscilla Nanlabi (1 Jun 2013)

**Command Headquarters: House 365/2, Lane 6 (West),
Baridhara DOHS, Dhaka 1216**
Postal address: GPO Box 985, Dhaka 1000, Bangladesh

Tel: [880] (2) 8411755/6

email: banleadership@ban.salvationarmy.org

Work in Bangladesh began immediately after the Liberation War with Pakistan in 1971. Thousands of people moved from refugee camps in Calcutta, where Salvationists had served them, and a team of Salvationists accompanied them. A year earlier, relief operations had been carried out by The Salvation Army in East Pakistan (later Bangladesh) following a severe cyclone. On 21 April 1980, The Salvation Army was incorporated under the Companies Act of 1913. Bangladesh was upgraded to command status on 1 January 1997.

Zone: South Asia
Country included in the command: Bangladesh
'The Salvation Army' in Bengali: Tran Sena
Languages in which the gospel is preached: Bengali, English

DURING 2013 the main focus within the command has been to live and share the gospel, to disciple believers and to address human need without discrimination. After much research, discussion and lengthy consultation, on 27 June 2013 The Salvation Army Church Trust registration document was signed. This means The Salvation Army can now take its place among the registered Christian churches in the country.

In October, the first officers' children's camp was held, where many experienced the first stirring of a personal call to officership. In November, 83 new junior soldiers were enrolled in the South Western District.

Due to the political unrest and instability within the country, in December many programmes, including Christmas celebrations, had to be cancelled or rescheduled. Salvationists were encouraged to pray for peace and they gave thanks to God when the political situation stabilised.

In February 2014 a Brengle Holiness Institute was held for officers. This was a time of rich fellowship, spiritual revival and growth.

Significant progress was made in March 2014 with the 'Umoja' workshop. Umoja means 'together-ness' in the Swahili language and is the preferred community engagement method of the command. Corps officers were encouraged to work together with the local community to bring about positive change, building on existing skills and resources.

Two corps in the north of Bangladesh have established a number of outreach centres to poor communities. The officers serve extensive areas where there is little or no Christian influence.

Salvation Army development projects continue to make a consider-able contribution to the lives of the people of Bangladesh. This includes education for visually and hearing impaired children. Efforts to eradicate leprosy are showing steady results, and the fight against tuberculosis continues. Disaster management projects, adult literacy and anti-human trafficking remain a priority. The Salvation Army provides awareness, training, education and practical support in the form of skills development to the human trafficking survivors.

STATISTICS
Officers 84 **Cadets** 8 **Employees** 200
Corps 32 **Outposts** 13 **Institution** 1 **Schools** 4
  Clinics 2 **HIV/Aids Counselling Centres** 2
Senior Soldiers 2,011 **Adherent Members** 857
  Junior Soldiers 341

STAFF
Women's Ministries: Lt-Col Marieke Venter (CPWM)
Business Administration: Maj Cornelis de Ligt
Information Technology Development: Mr Palash (Paul) Baidya
Projects: Maj Jacoba de Ligt-Oosterheerd
Training: Maj Tracey Palmer
Youth and Candidates: Capt Stephen Baroi

DISTRICTS
Dhaka: House 365/2, Lane 6 (West), Baridhara DOHS, Dhaka 1216; tel: (0171) 1546012; Capt Bibhudan Samadder
South Western: PO Box 3, By-Pass Rd, Karbala, Jessore 7400; tel: (0421) 68759; Maj Alfred Mir

TRAINING COLLEGE
Ganda, Savar, Dhaka; tel: (02) 7712614

COMMUNITY WORK
Disaster Risk Reduction and Climate Change Adaptation: South Western District
HIV/Aids Counselling Centres: Jessore, Old Dhaka
Income-generating Cooperatives: Jessore, Khulna
Training and Counselling Programme: Kalaroa, Satkhira

EDUCATIONAL WORK
Adult Education
Jessore, Khulna

Schools for the Hearing Impaired
Dhaka (acc 19); Jessore (acc 30)

Primary Schools: Jessore: Arenda, Bagdanga, Fatepur, Ghurulia, Kholadanga, Konejpur, Ramnagar, Sitarampur, Suro (total pupils 470)

Corps run Early Primary and Learning Centres
Gopalgonj: Bandhabari, Rajapur
Jessore: Arenda
Dinajpur: Shahargachchi
Joypurhat: Vanuikushalia, (total pupils 218)

Integrated Education for Sighted and Visually Impaired
Savar (pupils 382)

Vocational Training
Dhaka, Jessore, Khulna

MEDICAL AND DEVELOPMENT WORK
Urban Health and Development Project (UHDP)
Dhaka: Mirpur Clinic; Leprosy and TB Control Programmes

Community Health and Development Project (CHDP)
Khulna: Andulia Clinic

SOCIAL WORK
Integrated Children's Centre (ICC)
Savar (acc 42)

'SALLY ANN' PROGRAMME

'Sally Ann' Bangladesh Ltd (employees 15,
   production workers 934)
Managing Director: Lieut-Colonel Alistair Venter
   General Manager: Mr Utpal Halder
   Chair of Board: Lt-Col Priscilla Nanlabi

email: SallyAnn@ban.salvationarmy.com
website: www.sallyann.com
Shop: House 365/2, Lane 6 (West),
   Baridhara DOHS, Dhaka 1216;
Satu Barua (shop manager)

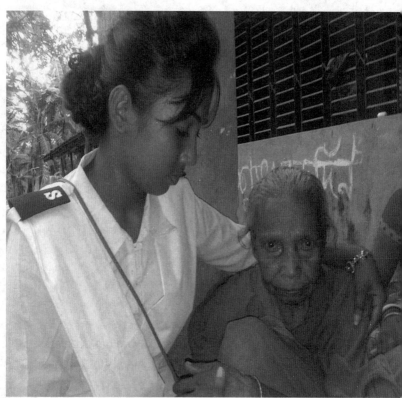

BANGLADESH: A Salvationist from the Spiritual Life Development Youth Team visiting community people

BRAZIL TERRITORY

Territorial leaders:
**Commissioners Oscar and
Ana Rosa Sánchez**

Territorial Commander:
Commissioner Oscar Sánchez
(1 Aug 2010)

Chief Secretary:
Lieut-Colonel Douglas Danielson (1 Feb 2014)

**Territorial Headquarters: Rua Juá, nº 264 - Bosque da Saúde,
04138-020, São Paulo-SP**

Postal address: Exército de Salvação; Caixa Postal 46036, Agência Saúde
04045-970 São Paulo-SP, Brazil

Tel: [55] (11) 5591 7070

email: BRA_Leadership@bra.salvationarmy.org;

website: www.exercitodesalvacao.org.br

Pioneer officers Lieut-Colonel and Mrs David Miche unfurled the Army flag in Rio de Janeiro on 1 August 1922. The Salvation Army operates as a national religious entity, Exército de Salvação, having been so registered by Presidential Decree 90.568 of 27 November 1984. All its social activities have been incorporated in APROSES (Assistência e Promoção Social Exército de Salvação) since 1974 and have had Federal Public Utility since 18 February 1991.

Zone: Americas and Caribbean
Country included in the territory: Brazil
'The Salvation Army' in Portuguese: Exército de Salvação
Language in which the gospel is preached: Portuguese
Periodicals: *O Oficial (The Officer), Ministério Feminino – Devocionais, Rumo with Revista Salvacionista*

IN NOVEMBER 2013 the territory held a national congress under the leadership of the Chief of the Staff, Commissioner William A. Roberts and Commissioner Nancy Roberts (World Secretary for Women's Ministries) with musical support given by Regent Hall Corps Band (United Kingdom Territory with the Republic of Ireland). Salvationists sang, danced and expressed Brazilian culture through many different expressions of worship.

One of the highlights of the congress was the commissioning and ordination of the Disciples of the Cross Session of cadets. The new generation of Salvation Army officers marched behind the flags of the most recently commissioned sessions.

The congress was a celebration of the past – with gratitude to God for the pioneering spirit and faithfulness – but also a celebration of the present with a commitment to keep the calling of The Salvation Army alive. Through the messages from God's Word, the Holy Spirit challenged those who gathered, and hundreds of Salvationists bowed in rededication and reconsecration.

In 1983 the Army's work began in the north-east region of Brazil. Thirty years later the Army is still fulfilling its mission in that beautiful part of the country and the corps in that area celebrated this occasion with praise and gratitude to God.

Earlier in the year, the women's ministries worship project 'Desperta Débora' ('Wake up Debora') was launched. 'Desperta Débora' encourages mothers to pray for each of their children for 15 minutes a day and this women's ministries initiative has been enthusiastically accepted throughout the territory.

STATISTICS
Officers 173 (active 129 retired 44)
 Cadets (1st Yr) 6 (2nd Yr) 3
 Employees 359
Corps 42 **Outposts** 10 **Social Institutions** 27
Senior Soldiers 1,984 **Adherent Members** 101
 Junior Soldiers 465
Personnel serving outside territory Officers 6

STAFF
Women's Ministries: Comr Ana Rosa Sánchez (TPWM) Lt-Col Verônica Danielson (TSWM)
Personnel: Lt-Col Verônica Danielson
Communications: Maj David Chadwick
Editor-in-Chief: Maj Paulo Soares
Education: Maj Maruilson M. de Souza
Finance: Capt Ricardo Iung
Legal/Property: Maj Giani Azevedo
Music: Maj David Chadwick
National Band: B/M João Carlos Cavalheiro
National Songsters: S/L Vera Sales

Projects: Maj Philippa Chagas
Social: Maj Mylka Santos
Training: Maj Maruilson M de Souza
Youth and Candidates: Maj Elisana Lemos

DIVISIONS
North East: Rua Carlos Gomes, nº 1016, Bonji, 50751-130, Recife – PE; tel: 3226-4032; Maj Joan Burton
Rio de Janeiro and Minas Gerais and Centre West Federal District: Rua Visconde de Santa Isabel nº 20, salas 712/713, 20560-120, Rio de Janeiro – RJ; tel: (21) 3879-5594
Rio Grande do Sul: Rua Machado de Assis nº 255, 97050-450, Santa Maria, RS; tel: (55) 3025-3769; Majs Wilson and Nara Strasse
São Paulo: Rua Taguá, nº 209, Liberdade, 01508-010, São Paulo – SP; tel: (11) 3275-0085; Majs Adão and Vilma Gonçalves

DISTRICT
Paraná and Santa Catarina: Rua Mamoré, nº 1191, 80810-080, Curitiba, PR; tel (41) 3336-8624; Maj Paulo Soares

TRAINING COLLEGE
Rua Juá, nº 264, Bosque da Saúde, 04138-020, São Paulo – SP; tel: (11) 5071-5041

SOCIAL WORK
Centre for Street Adults
São Paulo: Projeto Três Corações (acc 15)

Support Programmes for Socially Vulnerable Children and Young Adults
Carmo do Rio Claro: 'Recanto da Alegria' (acc 40)
Cubatão: 'Vila dos Pescadores' (acc 300)
Pelotas: Pelotas Integrated Centre (acc 40)
Prudente de Moraes: 'Arco Verde' Integrated Family Centre (acc 30)
Recife: Torre Integrated Community Centre (acc 250)
Rio de Janeiro:
 Socio-educational Centre 'Lar do Meier' (acc 50)
 Nova Divinéia Community Centre (acc 70)
Uruguaiana: Integrated Centre Uruguaiana (acc 50)

Early Childhood Education Centres and Crechés
Carmo do Rio Claro: 'Recanto da Alegria' (acc 90)
Petrolina: CEI Petrolina (acc 90)
São Paulo: 'Ranchinho do Senhor' (acc 72)

Suzano: 'Lar das Flores' (acc 404)

Home for Street Children
Curitiba: 'Casa de Apoio' (acc 11)

Vulnerable Women, Adolescents and Children
São Paulo: 'Rancho do Senhor' (acc 50)

Old People's Home
Campos do Jordão: (acc 20)

Prison Work
Piraí do Sul and Carmo do Rio Claro

Students' Residences
Brasília: (acc 14)
Santa Maria: (acc 8)

Territorial Camp
Suzano: Rua Manuel Casanova nº 1061,
   08664-000, Suzano – SP; tel: (11) 4746-3843

Thrift Stores
Rio de Janeiro: 1; São Paulo: 3

Vocational Training – Adolescents and Youth
Cubatão: 'Vila dos Pescadores' (acc 120)
Joinville: 'João de Paula' Integrated Centre
   (acc 90)

Work with Families
Paranaguá: Honorina Valente Integrated Centre
   (acc 50)
São Paulo: 'Três Corações' Project (acc 100)

BRAZIL: Enthusiastic Salvationists gather for the opening meeting of the congress

CANADA AND BERMUDA TERRITORY

Territorial Commander:
Commissioner Susan McMillan
(1 Sept 2014)

Chief Secretary:
Colonel Mark W. Tillsley (1 Jun 2013)

**Territorial Headquarters: 2 Overlea Blvd, Toronto,
Ontario M4H 1P4, Canada**

Tel: [1] (416) 425-2111; email: can_leadership@can.salvationarmy.org;

websites: www.salvationarmy.ca; www.salvationist.ca;

www.SendTheFire.ca; www.faithandfriends.ca

There are newspaper reports of organised Salvation Army activity in Toronto, Ontario, in January 1882, and five months later the Army was reported holding meetings in London, Ontario. On 15 July the same year, Major Thomas Moore, sent from USA headquarters, established official operations. In 1884 Canada became a separate command. The League of Mercy originated in Canada in 1892. An Act to incorporate the Governing Council of The Salvation Army in Canada received Royal Assent on 19 May 1909.

The work in Newfoundland was begun on 1 February 1886 by Divisional Officer Arthur Young. On 12 January 1896 Adjutant (later Colonel) Lutie Desbrisay and two assistant officers unfurled the flag in Bermuda.

Zone: Americas and Caribbean
Countries included in the territory: Bermuda, Canada
Languages in which the gospel is preached: Creole, English, French, First Nations languages (Gitxsan, Nisga'a, Tsimshian), Korean, Lao, Portuguese, Spanish, Thai
Periodicals: *Edge for Kids*, *Faith & Friends*, *Foi & Vie*, *Salvationist*

IN MAY 2013, 'Mission: Cuba', Ontario Central-East Division's five-year partnership with the Central Cuba Division, Latin America North Territory, concluded with the dedication of two new corps buildings. Over the five years, 150 Canadian volunteers, ranging in age from 14 to 81, completed 13 capital building projects to improve Army facilities in Cuba.

Twenty-three cadets from the Proclaimers of the Resurrection Session and graduates of the auxiliary-captains' programme were commissioned and ordained in Toronto, in June. Included were 14 cadets from the residential programme, four cadets from field-based training and five auxiliary-captains.

Emergency disaster services were called into action in June and July following extensive flooding in Alberta and a train derailment in Lac-Mégantic, Quebec, that resulted in significant casualties. Salvationists provided immediate and long-term practical and spiritual care to victims and relief workers.

Jackson's Point Conference Centre in Ontario welcomed 180 students plus faculty members in August 2013 for the National Music Camp. The week-long event featured band and choir instruction, worship and Bible studies, and included electives such as timbrels and drama.

In September, Booth University College recorded significant increases in the number of new students on the Winnipeg campus, including those undertaking distance education. Dr Marjory Kerr was welcomed as the new college vice-president.

For the first time in the territory's history, the Women's Ministries Department organised a leadership development live webcast in September. Under the theme 'Empowering Women to LOL (Live Out Loud)', 900 women viewed the four-hour event.

Living Hope Community Church was launched in September 2013 at the Barbara Mitchell Family Resource Centre in Winnipeg, Manitoba. Located in St Vital, a high-density neighbourhood with many younger families and a large immigrant population, the centre recognised a need for a spiritual component to its programmes. The partnership between the corps and its social ministry was successful as people seeking assistance were connected with the church.

In October, the territory's second Barbara Mitchell Family Resource Centre was opened in Calgary, Alberta. The building, formally known as The Salvation Army Children's Village, underwent a major renovation that included a new kitchen, entrance and reception area.

For the 2013 Christmas kettle campaign, the territory produced three short television commercials each in English, French, Cantonese, Mandarin and Punjabi. Featuring a soup kitchen, thrift store and shelter, they told a story of transformation and informed the public that: 'Your donation makes a difference.' Donors throughout Canada helped the Army exceed its goal, setting a new record for the annual campaign of more than CAN$21 million.

Salvationists in Bermuda gathered in November for the divisional congress under the theme *Declare His Glory* led by Colonels Mark and Sharon Tillsley (CS and TSWM). The event commemorated 117 years of ministry in Bermuda.

The then Territorial leaders Commissioners Brian and Rosalie Peddle visited Zimbabwe in March 2014 to observe the Army's work that is partly supported by the territory's world missions department and the Army's Partners in Mission Appeal.

In April, the newly-renovated Northern Centre of Hope was opened in Fort St John, British Columbia. Housing up to 64 people with both shelter and transitional accommodation, the centre provides support services, including addictions programming and a drop-in food line.

In May, an ensemble from the Canadian Staff Band visited Rimouski, Quebec, to mark the centenary of the sinking of the *Empress of Ireland* – a tragedy that took the lives of more than 1,000 people, including 124 Salvationists. The commemoration acknowledged this dark day, while honouring the memory and legacy of these faithful Salvationists.

STATISTICS

Officers 1,678 (active 766 retired 912) **Cadets** (1st Yr) 24 (2nd Yr) 14 **Employees** 8,315
Corps 314 **Outposts** 3 **Institutions** 128 **University College** 1
Senior Soldiers 17,329 **Adherent Members** 35,944 **Junior Soldiers** 2,395
Personnel serving outside territory Officers 27 Layworkers 3

STAFF

Women's Ministries: Comr Susan McMillan (TPWM) Col Sharon Tillsley (TSWM)
Spiritual Life Development: Lt-Col Ann Braund
Personnel: Lt-Col Jamie Braund
Programme: Lt-Col Junior Hynes
Business: Lt-Col Lee Graves
Communications: Lt-Col Jim Champ
Asst Chief Sec: Maj Wade Budgell
Asst Chief Sec – Special Events and Asst Sec for SLD: Maj Linda Budgell
Corps Ministries: Maj Fred Waters
Editor-in-Chief and Literary Sec: Mr Geoff Moulton
Employee Relations: Mrs Josie DelPriore
Finance: Mr Paul Goodyear
Information Technology: Mr Robert Plummer
Leadership Development: Maj Mona Moore
Legal: Mr Bryan Campbell
Music and Gospel Arts: Maj Kevin Metcalf
Officer Personnel Dept: Maj Eddie Vincent
Property: Mr Michael Gilbert
Public Relations and Development: Capt Les Marshall
Recycling Operations: Mr John Kershaw
Social: Mrs Mary Ellen Eberlin
Supplies/Purchasing: Maj Michael LeBlanc
College for Officer Training: Maj David Allen
Booth University College – Principal: Dr Donald Burke

Youth and Candidates: Majs Keith and Shona Pike

DIVISIONS

Alberta and Northern Territories: 9618 101A Ave NW, Edmonton, AB T5H OC7; tel: (780) 423-2111; Majs Ronald and Tonilea Cartmell
Bermuda: PO Box HM 2259, 76 Roberts Ave, Hamilton, HM JX Bermuda; tel: (441) 292-0601; Majs Frank and Rita Pittman
British Columbia: 103-3833 Henning Dr, Burnaby, BC V5C 6N5; tel: (604) 299-3908; Lt-Cols Larry and Velma Martin
Maritime: 330 Herring Cove Rd, Halifax, NS B3R 1V4; tel: (902) 455-1201; Maj Alison Cowling
Newfoundland and Labrador: 21 Adams Ave, St John's, NL A1C 4Z1; tel: (709) 579-2022/3; Lt-Cols Douglas and Jean Hefford
Ontario Central-East: 1645 Warden Ave, Scarborough, ON M1R 5B3; tel: (416) 321-2654; Lt-Col Sandra Rice
Ontario Great Lakes: 371 King St, London, ON N6B 1S4; tel: (519) 433-6106; Majs Morris and Wanda Vincent
Prairie: 204-290 Vaughan St, Winnipeg, MB R3B 2N8; tel: (204) 946-9101; Majs Shawn and Brenda Critch
Quebec: 625 President Kennedy Ave, Suite 1700, Montreal, QC H3A 1K2; tel: (514) 288-2848; Majs Brian and Anne Venables

COLLEGE FOR OFFICER TRAINING

100-290 Vaughan St, Winnipeg, MB R3B 2N8; tel: (204) 924-5606

BOOTH UNIVERSITY COLLEGE

447 Webb Pl, Winnipeg, MB R3B 2P2; tel: (204) 947-6701

ETHICS CENTRE

2 – 333 Vaughan St, Winnipeg, MB R3P 3J9; tel: (204) 957-2412; email: ethics_centre@can.salvationarmy.org;

SALVATION ARMY ARCHIVES

Archives: 26 Howden Rd, Scarborough, ON M1R 3E4
Museum: 2 Overlea Blvd, Toronto, ON M4H 1P4; tel: (416) 285-4344 email: Heritage_Centre@can.salvationarmy.org

NATIONAL RECYCLING OPERATIONS

2 Overlea Blvd, Toronto, ON M4H 1P4;
tel: (416) 425-2111

SOCIAL SERVICES (UNDER THQ)
Hospital (public)
Complex Continuing Care/ Rehabilitation/Palliative Care

Toronto, ON M4Y 2G5, Toronto Grace Health
Centre, 650 Church St; tel: (416) 925-2251

Family Tracing Services

2 Overlea Blvd, Toronto, ON M4H 1P4;
tel: (416) 422-6219

SOCIAL SERVICES (UNDER DIVISIONS)
Hospital Chaplaincy

Toronto, ON M1W 3W3 Scarborough Hospital,
3030 Birchmount Rd; tel: (416) 495-2536
St. John's, NL A1B 3V6 Health Sciences Centre,
300 Prince Phillip Drive; tel: (709) 777-6300

Hospices

Calgary, AB T2N 1B8, Agape Hospice,
1302 8th Ave NW; tel: (403) 282-6588 (acc 20)
Regina, SK S4R 8P6, Wascana Grace Hospice,
50 Angus Rd; tel: (306) 543-0655 (acc 10)
Richmond, BC V6Y 2S9, Rotary Hospice,
6460 No 4 Rd; tel: (604) 207-1212 (acc 10)

Adult Services to Developmentally Handicapped

Fort McMurray, AB T9H 1S7, 9919 MacDonald
Ave; tel: (780) 743-4135
Hamilton, ON L8M 1J1, Lawson Ministries, 533
Main St E; tel: (905) 527-6212 (acc 21)
Toronto, ON M4K 2S5, Broadview Village, 1132
Broadview Ave (Residential Living/Day
Programming for Developmentally
Handicapped Adults) ; tel: (416) 425-1052
(acc 160)
Winnipeg, MB R3A 0L5, Community Venture,
324 Logan Ave; tel: (204) 946-9418

Adult Services Mental Health

St John's, NL A1E 1C1, Wiseman Centre,
714 Water St; tel: (709) 739-8355/8 (acc 30)
Toronto, ON M8Z 6A4, Booth Support Services,
Unit 9A - 1020 Islington Ave,
tel: (416) 255-7070
Toronto, ON M5A 2R5, Maxwell Meighen
Centre Primary Support Unit, 135 Sherbourne
St, tel: (416) 366-2733

Sheltered Workshops

Toronto, ON M8Z 6A4, Booth Packaging and
Supportive Services, Unit 9A - 1020 Islington
Ave, tel: (416) 255-7070
Toronto, ON M3A 1A3, PLUS Program,
150 Railside Rd; tel: (416) 693-2116 (acc 44)

Addictions and Rehabilitation Centres (Alcohol/Drug Treatment)
Men

Calgary, AB T2G 0R9, 420 9th Ave SE;
tel: (403) 410-1150 (acc 34)
Chilliwack, BC V2P 2M3, Fireside Addiction
Services, #17 – 45966 Yale Road (Cascade
Centre); tel: (604) 702-9879
Edmonton, AB T5H 0E5, 9611 102 Ave NW;
tel: (780) 429-4274 (acc 158)
Glencairn, ON L0M 1K0, PO Box 100;
tel: (705) 466-3435/6 (acc 35)
Halifax, NS B3K 3A9, 2044 Gottingen St;
tel: (902) 422-2363 (acc 16)
Hamilton, Bermuda HM 12, 44 King St;
tel: (441) 292-2586 (acc 10)
Kingston, ON K7L 1C7, 562 Princess St;
tel: (613) 546-2333 (acc 24)
London, ON N6B 2L4, Withdrawal Management
Centre, 281 Wellington St, tel: (519) 432-7241
Montreal, QC H3J 1T4, 800 rue Guy;
tel: (514) 932-2214 (acc 55)
Ottawa, ON K1N 5W5, Booth Centre Anchorage,
171 George St; tel: (613) 241-1573
Moose Jaw, SK S6H 0Y9, Hope Inn
175 – 1st Avenue NE;
tel: (306) 692-2844 (acc 4)
Ottawa, ON K1N 5W5, 171 George St;
tel: (613) 241-1573 (acc 25)
Toronto, ON M5B 1E2, 160 Jarvis St;
tel: (416) 363-5496 (acc 85)
Toronto, ON M5A 2R5, Turning Point, 135
Sherbourne St; tel: (416) 366-2733
Vancouver, BC V6A 1K8, 119 East Cordova St;
tel: (604) 646-6800 (acc 70)
Victoria, BC V8W 1M2, 525 Johnson St;
tel: (250) 384-3396 (acc 109)
Williams Lake, BC V2G 1R3, Non-Residential
Substance Abuse Program, 267 Borland St,
tel: (250) 392-2429
Windsor, ON N9A 7G9, Community and
Rehabilitation Centre, 355 Church St;
tel: (519) 253-7473
Winnipeg, MB R3N 0J8, 180 Henry Avenue;
tel: (204) 946-9401 (acc 32)
Yellowknife, NT X1A 1K6, Community
Residential Services, 4925 45th St;
tel: (867) 920-4673

Canada and Bermuda Territory

Women

Hamilton, New Choices, ON L8S 2H6, 431
Whitney Ave; tel: (905) 522-5556 (acc 15)
Toronto, ON M5R 2L6, The Homestead,
78 Admiral Rd; tel: (416) 921-0953 (acc 18)
Vancouver, BC V6P 1S4, The Homestead, 975
57th Ave W; tel: (604) 266-9696 (acc 32)

Residential Services (Hostels, Emergency Shelters)

Men

Barrie, ON L4M 3A5, Bayside Mission Centre,
16 Bayfield St; tel: (705) 728-3737 (acc 32)
Brampton, ON L6T 4X1, Wilkinson Road
Shelter, 15 Wilkinson Rd; tel: (905) 452-1335
(acc 85)
Brantford, ON N3T 2J6, Booth Centre,
187 Dalhousie St; tel: (519) 753-4193 (acc 27)
Chilliwack, BC V2P 2N4, 45746 Yale Rd;
tel: (604) 792-0001 (acc 11)
Fort McMurray, AB T9H 1S7, 9919 MacDonald
Ave; tel: (780) 743-4135 (acc 32)
Halifax, NS B3K 3A9, 2044 Gottingen St;
tel: (902) 422-2363 (acc 49)
Hamilton, ON L8R 1R6, Booth Centre,
94 York Blvd; tel: (905) 527-1444 (acc 99)
Langley, BC V3A 0A9, Gateway of Hope,
5787 Langley-By-Pass; tel: (604) 514-7375
(acc 55)
Miramichi, NB E1V 1Y6, 231 Pleasant St;
tel: (506) 622-7826
Montreal, QC H3J 1T4, Booth Centre,
880 rue Guy; tel: (514) 932-2214 (acc 195)
Nanaimo, BC V9R 4S6, 19 Nicol St;
tel: (250) 754-2621 (acc 31)
New Westminster, BC V3L 2K1, 32 Elliot St; tel:
(604) 526-4783 (acc 33)
Ottawa, ON K1N 5W5, Booth Centre,
171 George St; tel: (613) 241-1573 (acc 213)
Pembroke, Bermuda HM 17, 5 Marsh Lane;
tel: (441) 295-5310 (acc 83)
Penticton, BC V2A 5J1, 2469 South Main St; tel:
(250) 492-6494 (acc 20)
Prince Rupert, BC V8J 1R3, 25 Grenville Court;
tel: (250) 624-6180 (acc 20)
Quebec City, QC G1R 4H8, Hotellerie,
14 Côte du Palais; tel: (418) 692-3956 (acc 60)
Regina, SK S4P 1W1, 1845 Osler St;
tel: (306) 569-6088 (acc 75)
Regina, SK S4P 1W1, Waterston Centre,
1865 Osler St; tel: (306) 566-6088 (acc 40)
Richmond, BC V6X 2P3, Richmond House
Emergency Shelter, 3111 Shell Rd;
tel: (604) 276-2490 (acc 10)
St Catharine's, ON L2R 3E7, Booth Centre,
184 Church St; tel: (905) 684-7813 (acc 21)

Saskatoon, SK S7M 1N5, 339 Avenue C South;
tel: (306) 244-6280 (acc 50)
Sudbury, ON P3E 1C2, 146 Larch St; tel: (705)
673-1175/6 (acc 45)
Thunder Bay, ON P7A 4S2, CARS,
545 Cumberland St N; tel: (807) 345-7319
(acc 46)
Toronto, ON M5T 1P7, Hope Shelter,
167 College St; tel: (416) 979-7058 (acc 108)
Toronto, ON M5C 2H4, The Gateway,
107 Jarvis St; tel: (416) 368-0324 (acc 100)
Toronto, ON M5A 2R5, Maxwell Meighen
Centre, 135 Sherbourne St; tel: (416) 366-2733
(acc 378)
Toronto, ON M5B 1E2, 160 Jarvis St;
tel: (416) 363-5496 (acc 98)
Vancouver, BC V6A 1K7, James McCready
Residence, 129 East Cordova St;
tel: (604) 646-6800 (acc 44)
Vancouver, BC V6A 1K7, The Haven,
128 East Cordova St; tel: (604) 646-6800
(acc 40)
Windsor, ON N9A 7G9, 355 Church St;
tel: (519) 253-7473 (acc 111)

Women

Brampton, ON L6X 3C9, The Honeychurch
Family Life Resource Center, 535 Main St N;
tel: (905) 451-4115 (acc 73)
Montreal, QC H3J 1M8, L'Abri d'Espoir,
2000 rue Notre-Dame oust;
tel: (514) 934-5615 (acc 36)
Quebec City, QC G1R 4H8, Maison Charlotte, 5
rue McMahon; ; tel: (418) 692-3956 (acc 25)
Toronto, ON M6P 1Y5, Evangeline Residence,
2808 Dundas St W; tel: (416) 762-9636
(acc 90)
Toronto, ON M6J 1E6, Florence Booth House,
723 Queen St W; tel: (416) 603-9800 (acc 60)
Vancouver, BC V5Z 4L9, Kate Booth House, PO
Box 38048 King Edward Mall;
tel: (604) 872-0772 (acc 12)

Mixed (male and female)

Abbotsford, BC V2S 2E8, 34081 Gladys Ave;
tel: (604) 852-9305 (acc 34)
Calgary, AB T2G 0R9, Centre of Hope,
420 9th Ave SE; tel: (403) 410-1111 (acc 295)
Courtney, BC V9N 2S2, 1580 Ftizgerald Ave
tel: (250) 338-5133 (acc 9)
Fort St John, BC, 10116 100th Ave;
tel: (250) 785-0506 (acc 20)
London, ON N6C 4L8, Centre of Hope,
281 Wellington St; tel: (519) 661-0343
(acc 253)
Maple Ridge, BC V2X 2S8, 22188 Lougheed
Hwy; tel: (604) 463-8296 (acc 43)

Medicine Hat, AB T1A 1M6, 737 8th St SE;
tel: (403) 526-9699 (acc 30)

Mississauga, ON L5A 2X3, Cawthra Road
Shelter, 2500 Cawthra Rd; tel: (905) 281-1272

Oakville, ON L6L 6X7, Lighthouse Shelter,
750 Redwood Sq; tel: (905) 339-2918
(acc 25)

Sudbury, ON P3A 1C2, 146 Larch St;
tel: (705) 673-1175 (acc 91)

Vancouver, BC V6A 4K9, Grace Mansion,
596 East Hastings St; tel: (778) 329-0674
(acc 85)

Vancouver, BC V6B 1K8, Belkin House,
555 Homer St; tel: (604) 681-3405 (acc 257)

Vancouver, BC V6B 1G8, The Crosswalk,
138-140 W Hastings St; tel: (604) 669-4349
(acc 35)

Winnipeg, MB R3B 0J8, Booth Centre Ministries,
180 Henry Ave; tel: (204) 946-9400 (acc 208)

Family

Mississauga, ON L5R 4J9, Angela's Place,
45 Glen Hawthorne Rd; tel: (905) 791-3887
(acc 80)

Mississauga, ON L4X 1L5, Peel Family Shelter,
1767 Dundas St. E; tel: (905) 272-7061

Montreal, QC H3J 1M8, L'Abri d'Espoir,
2000 rue Notre-Dame oust;
tel: (514) 934-5615 (acc 25)

Saskatoon, SK S7M 3A9, Mumford House,
341 Avenue T South; tel: (306) 986-2157

Youth

Moose Jaw, SK S6H 0Y9, Hope Inn
1st Avenue NE; tel: (306) 692-2894

Sutton, ON L0E 1R0, 20898 Dalton Rd;
tel: (905) 722-9076

Community and Family Services

Alberta: Calgary, Cranbrook, Drumheller,
Edmonton, Fort McMurray, Grande Prairie,
High River, Lethbridge, Lloydminster,
Medicine Hat, Peace River, Red Deer,
St Albert.

Bermuda: Hamilton.

British Columbia: Abbotsford, Campbell River,
Chilliwack, Courtenay, Dawson Creek, Duncan,
Fernie, Fort St John, Gibsons, Kamloops,
Kelowna, Maple Ridge, Nanaimo, Nelson,
New Westminster, North Vancouver, Parksville,
Penticton, Port Alberni, Powell River,
Prince George, Prince Rupert, Quesnel,
Richmond, Salmon Arm, Surrey, Terrace,
Trail, Vancouver, Vernon, Victoria,
White Rock, Williams Lake.

Manitoba: Brandon, Dauphin, Flin Flon,
Portage La Prairie, Thompson, Winnipeg (2).

New Brunswick: Bathurst, Campbelltown,
Fredericton, Miramichi, Moncton, Saint John,
Sussex.

Newfoundland and Labrador: Corner Brook,
Gander, Grand Falls-Windsor, Labrador City/
Wabush, Pasadena, Springdale, St Anthony,
St John's, Stephenville.

Nova Scotia: Bridgewater, Glace Bay, Halifax,
Kentville, New Glasgow, Sydney, Truro,
Westville, Yarmouth.

Ontario: Ajax, Belleville, Bowmanville,
Brampton, Brantford, Brockville, Burlington,
Cambridge, Chatham, Cobourg, Collingwood,
Cornwall, Essex, Etobicoke (2), Fenelon Falls,
Fort Frances, Gananoque, Georgetown,
Goderich, Gravenhurst, Guelph, Hamilton,
Huntsville, Ingersoll, Jackson's Point,
Kemptville, Kenora, Kingston, Kirkland Lake,
Kitchener, Leamington, Lindsay, Listowel,
London, Midland, Milton, Mississauga (3),
Napanee, New Liskeard, Newmarket,
Niagara Falls, North Bay, North York (2),
Oakville, Orillia, Oshawa, Ottawa, Owen Sound,
Pembroke, Perth, Peterborough, Renfrew,
Ridgetown, Sarnia, Sault Ste Marie,
Scarborough, Simcoe, Smiths Falls,
St Catharine's, St Mary's, St Thomas, Stratford,
Strathroy, Sudbury, Thunder Bay, Tillsonburg,
Toronto (3), Trenton, Wallaceburg, Welland,
Whitby, Windsor, Woodstock.

Prince Edward Island: Charlottetown,
Summerside.

Quebec: Montreal, Quebec City, Sherbrooke,
St-Hubert, Trois-Rivieres.

Saskatchewan: Moose Jaw, Prince Albert, Regina.

Yukon Territory: Whitehorse.

Correctional and Justice Services
Community Programme Centres

Barrie, ON L4M 5A1, 400 Bayfield St, Ste 255;
tel: (705) 737-4140

Chilliwack, BC V2P 2N4, 45742B Yale Rd;
tel: (604) 792-8581

Corner Brook, NL A2H 7T1, 124A Filatre Ave,
tel: (709) 639-1719

Guelph, ON N1L 1H3, 1320 Gordon St;
tel: (519) 836-9360

Hamilton, ON L7R 1Y9, 2090 Prospect St;
tel (905) 634-7977

Kingston, ON K7K 4B1, 472 Division St;
tel: (613) 549-2676

Kitchener, N2H 2M4, 1-657 King St. E
tel: (519) 744-4666

London, ON N6B 2L4, 281 Wellington St;
tel: (519) 432-9553

Maple Creek, SK, S0N 1N0, 203 Maple St;
tel: (306) 662-3871

Maple Ridge, BC V2X 2S8, Mountainview The
Caring Place, Lougheed Highway;
tel: (604) 463-8296

Medicine Hat, AB T1A 0E7, 874 2 St E;
tel: (403) 529-2111

Moncton, NB E1C 1M2, 68 Gordon St;
tel: (506) 853-8887

Ottawa, ON K1Y K1N, 171 George St;
tel: (613) 725-1733

Peterborough, ON K9H 2H6, 219 Simcoe St;
tel: (705) 742-4391

Prince Albert, SK S6V 4V3, 900 Central Ave;
tel: (306) 763-6078

Regina, SK S4P 3M7, 2240 13th Ave;
tel: (306) 757-4711

Smiths Falls, ON K7A 4T2 243 Brockville St
tel; (613) 283-3563

St Catharines, ON L2R 3E7, 184 Church St;
tel: (905) 684-7813

St John's, NL A1C 4Z1, 21 Adams Ave;
tel: (709) 726-0986

Swift Current, SK S9H 4M7, 780 1st Avenue;
tel: (306) 778-0515

Thunder Bay, ON P7A 4S2, 545 Cumberland St N;
tel: (807) 344-7300

Toronto, ON M5A 3P1, 77 River St;
tel: (416) 304-1974

Trois-Rivieres, QC G8Y 3N8,
3885 De Landerneau; tel: (819) 840-3420

Winnipeg, MB R3A 0L5, 324 Logan Ave,
2nd Floor; tel: (204) 949-2100

Windsor, ON N9A 7G9, 355 Church St;
tel: (519) 253-7473

Adult/Youth Residential Correctional Centres

Brampton, ON L6X 1C1, 44 Nelson St W;
tel: (905) 453-0988 (acc 12)

Brantford ON, N3T 2J6, 187 Dalhousie St,
tel: (519 753-4193

Calgary, AB T2G 0R9, 420-9 Ave SE,
(tel) (403) 410-1129

Dartmouth, NS B3A 1H5, 318 Windmill Rd;
tel: (902) 465-2690 (acc 20)

Dundas, ON L9H 2E8, 34 Hatt St;
tel: (905) 627-1632 (acc 10)

Kitchener, ON N2G 2M4, 657 King St E;
tel: (519) 744-4666 (acc 21)

Milton, ON L9P 2X9, 8465 Boston Church Rd;
tel: (905) 875-1775 (acc 10)

Moncton, NB E1C 8P6, 64 Gordon St,
PO Box 1121; tel: (506) 858-9486 (acc 22)

Nanaimo, BC V9R 4S6, 19 Nichol St;
tel: (250) 754-2621

Saskatoon, SK S7M 1N5, 339 Avenue C South;
tel: (306) 244-6280 (acc 15)

Sudbury, ON P3A 1C2, 146 Larch St;
tel: (705) 673-1175 (acc 4)

Toronto, ON M4X 1K2, 422 Sherbourne St;
tel: (416) 964-6316/967-6618 (acc 53)

Vancouver, BC V6B 1K8, Belkin House,
555 Homer St; tel: (604) 681-3405 (acc 30)

Victoria, BC V9A 7J6, Matson Sequoia
Residence, 554 Garrett Pl Ste 211;
tel: (250) 383-5821 (acc 30)

Whitehorse, YT Y1A 6E3, 91678 Alaska Hwy;
tel: (867) 667-2741 (acc 16)

Yellowknife, NWT X1A 1P4, 4927 45th St;
tel: (867) 920-4673 (acc 33)

Health Services
Long-Term Care/Seniors' Residences

Brandon, MB R7A 3N9, Dinsdale Personal
Care Home, 510 6th St; tel: (204) 727-3636
(acc 60)

Edmonton, AB T5X 6C4, Grace Manor,
12510 140 Ave; tel: (780) 454-5484 (acc 100)

Montreal, QC H4B 2J4, Montclair Residence,
4413 Montclair Ave; tel: (514) 481-5638
(acc 50)

New Westminster, BC V3L 4A4, Buchanan
Lodge, 409 Blair Ave; tel: (604) 522-7033
(acc 112)

Niagara Falls, ON L2E 1K5, The Honourable
Ray and Helen Lawson Eventide Home,
5050 Jepson St; tel: (905) 356-1221 (acc 100)

Ottawa, ON K1Y 2Z3, Ottawa Grace Manor,
1156 Wellington St; tel: (613) 722-8025
(acc 128)

Regina, SK S4R 8P6, William Booth Special
Care Home, 50 Angus Rd; tel: (306) 543-0655
(acc 81)

Riverview, NB E1B 4K6, Lakeview Manor,
50 Suffolk St; tel: (506) 387-2012/3/4 (acc 50)

St John's, NL A1A 2G9, Glenbrook Lodge,
105 Torbay Rd; tel: (709) 726-1575 (acc 114)

St John's, NL A1A 2G9, Glenbrook Villa,
107 Torbay Rd; tel: (709) 726-1575 (acc 20)

Toronto, ON M4S 1G1, Meighen Retirement
Residence, 84 Davisville Ave;
tel: (416) 481-5557 (acc 84)

Toronto, ON M4S 1J6, Meighen Manor,
155 Millwood Rd; tel: (416) 481-9449
(acc 168)

Vancouver, BC V5S 3T1, Southview Terrace,
3131 58th Ave E; tel: (604) 438-3367/8
(acc 57)

Vancouver, BC V5S 3V2, Southview Heights,
7252 Kerr St; tel: (604) 438-3367/8 (acc 47)

Victoria, BC V9A 4G7, Sunset Lodge,
952 Arm St; tel: (250) 385-3422 (acc 108)

Winnipeg, MB R2Y 0S8, Golden West
Centennial Lodge, 811 School Rd;
tel: (204) 888-3311 (acc 116)

Immigrant and Refugee Services

Toronto, ON M5B 1E2, 160 Jarvis St;
tel: (416) 360-6036

Women's Multi-Service Programmes (and unmarried mothers)

Hamilton, ON L8P 2H1, Grace Haven,
138 Herkimer St; tel: (905) 522-7336 (acc 12)
Ottawa, ON K2A 3V7, Bethany Hope Centre,
820 Woodroffe Ave; tel: (613) 725-1733
Regina, SK S4S 7A7, Gemma House,
2929 26th Ave; tel: (306) 352-1421 (acc 8)
Regina, SK S4S 7A7, Grace Haven,
2929 26th Ave; tel: (306) 352-1421 (acc 7)
Saskatoon, SK S7K 0N1, Bethany Home,
802 Queen St; tel: (306) 244-6758 (acc 15)

Child Day Care/Pre-schools

Brampton, ON L6S 4B7, Noah's Ark Day Care
Centre, 9395 Bramalea Rd N;
tel: (905) 793-5610 (acc 46)
Burnaby, BC V3N 4A6, Before and After School
Care Program, 7195 Cariboo Rd;
tel: (604) 525-7311
Chilliwack, BC V2P 1C5, Happy Hearts Day
Care, 46420 Brooks Ave; tel: (604) 792-5285
(acc 23)
Guelph, ON N1L 1H3, Salvation Army Nursery
School, 1320 Gordon St; tel: (519) 836-9360
(acc 121)
London, ON N5W 2B6, The Salvation Army
Village Day Nursery, 1340 Dundas St E;
tel: (519) 455-8155 ext 308 (acc 75)
Medicine Hat, AB T1B 3R3, Rise and Shine Day

Care, 164 Stratton Way SE;
tel: (403) 529-2003 (acc 58)
Mississauga, ON L5L 1V3, Erin Mills Day Care,
2460 The Collegeway;
tel: (905) 820-6500 (acc 32).
Mississauga, ON L5A 2X4, Mississauga Temple
Day Care, 3173 Cawthra Rd;
tel: (905) 275-8430 (acc 82)
Moncton, NB E1E 4E4, Small Blessings,
20 Centennial Dr; tel: (506) 857-0588 (acc 95)
New Westminster, BC V3L 3A9, Kids Place Day
Care, 325 6th St; tel: (604) 521-8223 (acc 20)
Peace River, AB T8S 1E1, School Readiness,
9710-74 Ave; tel: (780) 624-2370 (acc 43)
Scarborough, ON M1W 3K3, Agincourt Temple
Child Care, 3080 Birchmount Rd;
tel: (416) 497-0329 (acc 94)
Scarborough, ON M1R 2Z2, Scarborough Citadel
Child Care, 2021 Lawrence Ave E;
tel: 416-759-5340 (acc 36)
Windsor, ON N8T 2Z7, Learning Corner Day
Care Centre, 3199 Lauzon Rd;
tel: (519) 944-4918 (acc 111)
Winnipeg, MB R3E 1E6, Weston Child Care,
1390 Roy Ave; tel: (204) 786-5066 (acc 59)

Parent Child Resource Centres

Courtney, BC V9N 2S2, 1580 Fitzgerald Ave;
tel: (250) 338-6200
Hamilton, ON L8P 2H1, 138 Herkimer St;
tel: (905) 522-7336
Hamilton, ON L8S 2H6, 431 Whiteney Ave;
tel: (905) 522-5556
Kitchener, ON N2E 3T1, 75 Tillsley Dr;
tel: (519) 745-3351
Ottawa, ON K2A 3V7, 820 Woodroffe Ave;
tel: (613) 725-1733

CARIBBEAN TERRITORY

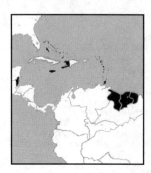

Territorial leaders:
Commissioners Gerrit and Eva Marseille

Territorial Commander:
Commissioner Gerrit Marseille
(1 Jun 2014)

Chief Secretary:
Lieut-Colonel Devon Haughton
(1 Jan 2015)

Territorial Headquarters: 3 Waterloo Rd, Kingston 10, Jamaica

Postal address: PO Box 378, Kingston 10, Jamaica, WI

Tel: [1876] 929 6190/91/92; email: car_leadership@car.salvationarmy.org;

website: www.salvationarmycarib.org

In 1887 The Salvation Army 'opened fire' in Kingston, and thence spread throughout the island of Jamaica and to Guyana (1895), Barbados (1898), Trinidad (1901), Grenada (1902), St Lucia (1902), Antigua (1903), St Vincent (1905), Belize (1915), St Kitts (1916), Suriname (1924), Bahamas (1931), Haiti (1950), French Guiana (1980), St Maarten (1999) and the Turks and Caicos Islands (2011). The General of The Salvation Army is a Corporation Sole in Jamaica (1914), Trinidad and Tobago (1915), Barbados (1917), Belize (1928), Guyana (1930), the Bahamas (1936) and Antigua (1981).

Zone: Americas and Caribbean
Countries included in the territory: Antigua, Bahamas, Barbados, Belize, French Guiana, Grenada, Guyana, Haiti, Jamaica, St Kitts, St Lucia, St Maarten, St Vincent, Suriname, Trinidad and Tobago and the Turks and Caicos Islands.
'The Salvation Army' in Dutch: Leger des Heils; in French: Armée du Salut
Languages in which the gospel is preached: Creole, Dutch, English, French, Surinamese
Periodical: *The War Cry*

IN MAY 2013 Salvationists of Antigua celebrated the 110th anniversary of the Army opening fire with events led by special guests Colonels Dennis and Sharon Strissel from the USA Central Territory. Self-Denial ingathering in June resulted in a contribution of US$102,793 to international mission.

The Proclaimers of the Resurrection Session of cadets was commissioned in June. This inlcuded the dedication of the new Training College facilities by Commissioners Torben and Deise

Eliasen (IS/ZSWM). Lieut-Colonels Vernon and Martha Jewett from the USA Southern Territory conducted the Brengle Memorial Institute in July.

Youth camps, sports ministries, music institutes, vacation Bible schools and youth councils were highlights of a year in which youth were encouraged to step up and be ready for action. Ten cadets representing Belize, Haiti, Jamaica and Suriname were welcomed into the Heralds of Grace Session.

Advisory boards continue to partner with the territory in its mission.

During December boards in Antigua, Guyana, and Eastern and Western Jamaica were instrumental in enhancing donor cultivation and guiding the Army's fund development plan.

Several development projects in the aftermath of the Haiti earthquake of 2010 were completed. Construction of 15 reservoirs and wells, the dedication of 19 renovated schools, and the opening of a new corps hall in Fond-des-Negres by the then territorial leaders Commissioners Onal and Edmane Castor were highlights. More than 473 young adults also graduated from vocational training classes.

In February 2014, the territory hosted an Intra Zonal Forum with representatives from Mexico, Latin America North and the Caribbean, followed by the territorial review conducted by Commissioners Torben and Deise Eliasen.

Women's ministries continues to play a vital role in the life of the territory. Seminars on domestic violence, child sexual abuse and marches against human trafficking and gender-based violence have been held. Fund-raising rallies have yielded over US$5,000 for the territorial Helping Hand project. Around the territory, self-help programmes are being developed to empower women in the drive for self-determination, dignity and self-reliance.

STATISTICS
Officers 313 (active 235 retired 78) Cadets (1st Yr) 10 (2nd Yr) 11 Employees 1,132
Corps 129 Outposts 42 Institutions 59 Schools 166 Senior Soldiers 11,167 Adherent Members 1,877 Junior Soldiers 3,717
Personnel serving outside territory Officers 11

STAFF
Women's Ministries: Comr Eva Marseille (TPWM) Lt-Col Verona Haughton (TSWM)
Personnel: Lt-Col Dewhurst Jonas
Programme: tba
Business: tba
Coordinator for Disaster Services: Maj Selbourne Oates
Ecumenical Relations: Maj Stanley Griffin
Editor: Lt-Col Vevene Jonas
Finance Secretary: Maj Brenda Greenidge
Leader Development: tba
Prayer Coordinator: Lt-Col Vevene Jonas
Projects/Sponsorship: Maj Bruce Carpenter
Property: Maj Stanley Griffin
Public Relations Director: Maj Bruce Carpenter
Spiritual Life Development: Lt-Col Vevene Jonas
Training: tba
Youth and Candidates: Maj Sherma Evelyn

DIVISIONS
Antigua: PO Box 2, 36 Long St, St John's; tel: [1268] 462-0115;
Majs Byron and Joycelyn Maxam
Bahamas: PO Box N 205, Nassau, NP; tel: [1242] 393-2340;
Maj Lester and Capt Beverley Ferguson
Barbados: PO Box 57, Reed St, Bridgetown; tel: [1246] 426-2467;
Maj Rosemarie Brown
Guyana: PO Box 10411, 237 Alexander St, Lacytown, Georgetown; tel: [592] 22 72619/54910;
Majs Emmerson and Carolinda Cumberbatch
Haiti: PO Box 301, 1342 Santo 6, Croix-des-Bouquets; tel: [509] 25 1036 71;
Majs Vilo and Yvrose Exantus
Jamaica Eastern: PO Box 153, Kingston; 153b Orange St, Kingston; tel: [1876] 922-6764/0287;
Majs Darrell and Joan Wilkinson
Jamaica Western: PO Box 44, Lot #949 West Green, Montego Bay, St James; tel: [876] 952-3778;
Majs Edward and Jennifer Lyons
Trinidad and Tobago: 154a Henry St, Port-of-Spain, Trinidad; PO Box 248, Port-of-Spain; tel: [1868] 625-4120;
Majs Emmanuel and Edeline Supre

REGIONS

Belize: PO Box 64, 41 Regent St, Belize City, Belize; tel: [501] 2273 365;
email: Belize HQ/BEL/CAR/SArmy;
Majs Joliker and Fidaliance Leandre

French Guiana: PO Box 329,97327 Cayenne Cedex, French Guyana; tel: [594] 31-5832;
Majs Alisthene and Souvenie Simeon

Suriname: PO Box 317, 126 A Henck Arron Straat, Paramaribo; tel: [597] 47-3310;
email: Suriname HQ/SUR/CAR/SArmy;
Majs Vilece and Joan Thomas

COUNTRIES NOT IN DIVISIONAL OR REGIONAL LISTS

Grenada: Grenville St, St George's, Grenada; tel: [1473] 440-3299

St Kitts: PO Box 56, Cayon Rd, Basseterre, St Kitts; tel: [1869] 465-2106

St Lucia: PO Box 6, High St, Castries, St Lucia; tel: [1758] 452-3108

St Maarten: 59 Union Rd, Cole Bay, PO Box 5184, St Maarten, Netherlands Antilles; tel: [5995] 445424

St Vincent: Hall Melville St, PO Box 498, Kingstown, St Vincent; tel: [1784] 456-1574

Turks and Caicos Islands
Discovery Bay: PO Box 1093, Providenciales, B.W.I.; tel: [649] 33-9711

TRAINING COLLEGE

57 Mannings Hill Road, PO Box 2779, Constant Spring, Kingston 8, Jamaica; tel: [1876] 924-2999

CITY WELFARE OFFICES

Bahamas: 31 Mackey St, Nassau NP
Jamaica: 57 Peter's Lane, Kingston

COMMUNITY CENTRES

Bahamas: Meadow and West Sts, Nassau
Barbados: Checker Hall, St Lucy; Wellington St, Bridgetown; Wotton, Christchurch
Jamaica: Rae Town Goodwill Centre, 24 Tower St, Kingston; tel: [1876] 928-5770/930-0028
Allman Town, 18-20 Prince of Wales St, Kingston 4; tel: [1876] 92-27279

FEEDING CENTRES

Antigua: Meals on wheels
Bahamas: Mackey St and Grantstown, Nassau
Barbados: Reed St, Bridgetown
Belize: 9 Glynn St, Belize City (acc 50)
Guyana:
237 Alexander St, Georgetown; Third Ave, Bartica; Rainbow City, Linden
Haiti: Port-au-Prince (Nutrition Centre)

Jamaica:
Peter's Lane, Kingston; Jones Town, Kingston; Spanish Town, St Catherine;
May Pen, Clarendon; St Ann's Bay, St Ann; Port Antonio, Portland; Montego Bay, St James; Savanna-La-Mar, Westmoreland
St Lucia: High St, Castries
Suriname: Gravenstraat 126, Paramaribo

For Children
Bahamas: Nassau, Mackey St
Grenada: St Georges
Guyana: Georgetown, Bartica, Linden
St Vincent: Kingstown

MEDICAL WORK

Haiti:
Bethel Maternity Home and Dispensary, Fond-des-Negres
Bethesda TB Centre, Fond-des-Negres
Primary Health Care Centre and Nutrition Centre, Port-au-Prince
Jamaica: Rae Town Clinic, 24 Tower St, Kingston; tel: (876) 928-1489/930-0028

PRISON, PROBATION AND AFTERCARE WORK

Antigua; Grenada; Guyana (Georgetown, Bartica, New Amsterdam); Jamaica; St Kitts; Suriname; Tobago; Trinidad

Prison Visitation Services
Belize: directed by Regional Commander

RETIRED OFFICERS' RESIDENCES

Barbados: Long Bay, St Phillip
Guyana: East La Penitence
Jamaica: Francis Ham Residence, 57 Mannings Hill Rd, Kingston 8; tel: (876) 924-1308 (acc 7)

SOCIAL SERVICES
Blind and Handicapped
Adults
Bahamas: Visually Handicapped Workshop, Ivanhoe Lane, PO Box N 1980, Nassau NP; tel: (242) 394-1107 (acc 19)
Jamaica: Francis Ham Residence (Home for Senior Citizens), 57 Mannings Hill Rd, Kingston 8; tel: (876) 924-1308 (acc 37)

Children (schools)
Bahamas: School for the Blind, 33 Mackay St, PO Box N 205, Nassau NP; tel: (242) 394-3197 (acc 15)
Jamaica: School for the Blind and Visually Impaired, 57 Mannings Hill Rd, PO Box 562,

Kingston 8; tel: (876) 925-1362
(residential acc 120)

Women (vocational training)
Jamaica: Evangeline Residence, Kingston;
Port Antonio, Portland

SOCIAL SERVICES
Children
Day Care Centres (nurseries)
Barbados: Wellington St, Bridgetown (acc 50)
Wotton, Christchurch (acc 50)
Grenada: St Georges (acc 25)
Jamaica: Allman Town, Kingston (acc 40)
Havendale, Kingston (acc 16) Lucea, Hanover
(acc 30) Montego Bay, St James (acc 40)
St Lucia: Castries (acc 50)
St Vincent: Kingstown (acc 20)
Trinidad: San Juan (acc 20)

Homes
Antigua: St John's Sunshine Home (acc 12)
Haiti: Bethany, Fond-des-Negres (acc 22)
Jamaica: Hanbury Home, PO Box 2, Shooter's
Hill PO, Manchester; tel: [1876] 603-3507
(acc 90)
The Nest, 57 Mannings Hill Rd, Kingston 8;
tel: [1876] 925-7711 (acc 45)
Windsor Lodge, PO Box 74,
Williamsfield PO, Manchester;
tel: [1876] 963-4222 (acc 80)
Suriname: Ramoth, Henck Arron Straat 172,
PO Box 317, Paramaribo; tel: [597] 47-3191
(acc 62)

Playgrounds
Jamaica: Rae Town, Kingston; Lucea, Hanover;
Montego Bay, St James
Suriname: Henck Arron Straat 126, Paramaribo

Schools
Basic (kindergartens)
Antigua: St John (acc 150)
Barbados: Checker Hall (acc 50)
Wellington St (acc 10)
Guyana: Bartica (acc 90)
Haiti:
Abraham (acc 63) Aquin (acc 112)
Arcahaie (acc 45) Balan (acc 30)
Bainet (acc 32) Bellamie (acc 35)
Bellegarde (acc 40) Belle Riviere (acc 24)
Bocolomond (acc 47) Bodoin (acc 17)
Brodequin (acc 64) Campeche (acc 43)
Cayot (acc 70) Couyot (acc 65)
Deruisseaux (acc 10) Dessources (acc 30)
Duverger (acc 77) Fond-des-Negres (acc 96)
Fort National (acc 26) Gardon (acc 40)

Gros-Morne (48) Guirand (acc 12)
Jacmel (acc 34) Kamass (acc 12)
L'Azile (acc 51) L'Homond (acc 75)
La Colline (acc 21) Laferonnay (acc 34)
Lafosse (acc 82) Lajovange (acc 35)
Le Blanc (acc 34) Lilette (acc 37)
Limbe (acc 20) Montrouis (30)
Moulin (acc 75) Perigny (acc 25)
Petit Goave (acc 53) Plaisance (acc 15)
Port-de-Paix (acc 14) Puit Laurent (acc 36)
Rossignol (acc 53) St Marc (acc 91)
Verena (acc 211) Vieux Bourg (acc 175)
Violette (acc 42)
Jamaica:
Bath (acc 25) Bluefields (acc 49)
Cave Mountain (acc 30) Cave Valley (acc 75)
Falmouth (acc 86) Great Bay (acc 40)
Kingston Allman Town (acc 150)
Kingston Havendale (acc 90)
Kingston Rae Town (acc 100)
Linstead (acc 65) Lucea (acc 200)
May Pen (acc 60) Montego Bay (acc 240)
Port Antonio (acc 50) St Ann's Bay (acc 36)
Savanna-la-mar (acc 110) Top Hill (acc 93)
St Kitts: Basseterre (acc 80)
St Lucia: Castries (acc 100)
Trinidad and Tobago: San Fernando (acc 80)
Scarborough, Tobago (acc 70)
Tragarete Rd, Port-of-Spain (acc 20)

Home Science
Barbados: Project Lighthouse (acc 12)
Haiti: Aquin; Carrefour; Desruisseaux;
Duverger; Fond-des-Negres, Gros Morne;
Vieux Bourg

Primary Schools
Belize: 12 Cemetery Road, Belize City;
tel: (501) 227-2156 (acc 250)
Haiti:
Abraham (acc 183) Aquin (acc 305)
Arcahaie (acc 212) Bainet (acc 150) Balan
(acc 178) Bas Fort National (acc 259)
Bellamy (acc 215) Bellegarde (acc 235) Belle
Riviere (acc 203) Boco Lomond (acc 255)
Bodoun (acc 76) Brodequin (acc 141)
Campeche (acc 130) Carrefour/Desruisseaux
(acc 250) Cayot (acc 273) College Verena (acc
486) Couyot (acc 375) Dessources (acc 160)
Duverger (acc 265) Fond-des-Negres (acc 574)
Fort National (acc 259) Gardon
(acc 166) Gros Morne (acc 325) Guirand
(acc 206) Jacmel (acc 97) Kamass (acc 21)
L'Azile (acc 174) L'Homond (acc 209)
La Colline (acc 125) La Fosse (acc 367)
La Jovange (acc 255) La Zandier (acc 170)
Laferonnay (acc 215) Lilette (acc 130) Limbe

Caribbean Territory

CARIBBEAN: Brengle Memorial Institute staff and participants

(acc 55) Luly (acc 182) Montrouis (acc 131)
Moulin (acc 180) Peirigny (acc 205) Petit Goave
(acc 165) Petite Riviere (acc118) Plaisance
(acc174) Port-de-Paix (acc 315)
Puits Laurent (acc 195) Rossignol (acc 239)
St Marc (acc 222) Vieux Bourg (acc 617)
Violette (acc 133)

Evening Schools
Guyana: Happy Heart Youth Centre, New
Amsterdam (acc 20)
Haiti: Port-au-Prince (acc 83)

Secondary School
Haiti: Port-au-Prince (acc 450) Gros-Morne
(acc 325)

SOCIAL SERVICES
Centre for Homeless
Belize: Raymond A. Parkes Home,
18 Cemetery Rd, Belize City;
tel: [501] 207-4309 (acc 12)

Eventide Home
Trinidad: Senior Citizens' Centre, 34 Duncan
St, Port-of-Spain; tel: [868] 624-5883 (acc 13)

Men
Guyana: MacKenzie Guest House, Rainbow
City, PO Box 67, Linden Co-op MacKenzie,
Guyana; tel: [592] 444-6406 (acc 10)

Hostels and Shelters
Guyana:
Men's Hostel, 6-7 Water St, Kingston,
Georgetown; tel: [592] 226-1235 (acc 40)

Drug Rehabilitation Centre,
6-7 Water St, Kingston, Georgetown;
tel: [592] 226-1235 (acc 18)
Jamaica:
Men's Hostel, 57 Peter's Lane, Kingston;
tel: [1876] 922-4030 (acc 25)
William Chamberlain Rehabilitation Centre,
57 Peter's Lane, Kingston (acc 25)
Suriname: Night Shelter, Ladesmastraat 2-6,
PO Box 317, Paramaribo; tel: [597] 4-75108
(acc 70)

Women
Eventide Homes
Belize: Ganns Rest Home, 60 East Canal St,
Belize City; tel: [501] 227 2973 (acc 12)
Guyana: 69 Bent and Haley Sts, Wortmanville,
Georgetown; tel: [592] 226-8846 (acc 22)
Suriname:
Elim Guest House, Henck Arron
Straat 126, PO Box 317, Paramaribo;
tel: [597] 48-4325 (acc 15)
Emma House, Dr Nassylaan 76, PO Box 2402,
Paramaribo; tel: [597] 47-3890 (acc 22)

Hostels and Shelters
Bahamas: Women and Children's Emergency
Residence, Grantstown, PO Box GT 2216,
Nassau NP; tel: [242] 323-5608 (acc 21)
Jamaica: Evangeline Residence, 153 Orange St,
Kingston; tel: 1 (876) 922-6398 (acc 50)
Trinidad:
Geddes Grant House, 22-24 Duncan St,
Port-of-Spain; tel: 1 (868) 623-5700 (acc 34)
Josephine Shaw House, 131-133 Henry St,
Port-of-Spain; tel: 1 (868) 623623-2547
(acc 106)

CONGO (BRAZZAVILLE) TERRITORY

Territorial leaders:
Commissioners Onal and Edmane Castor

Territorial Commander:
Commissioner Onal Castor (1 Jun 2014)

Chief Secretary:
Lieut-Colonel Eugene Bamanabio
(1 Jun 2014)

Territorial Headquarters: Rue de Reims, Brazzaville, République du Congo

Postal address: BP 20, Brazzaville, République du Congo

Tel: [242] 281 1144

In 1937 The Salvation Army spread from Léopoldville to Brazzaville, and in 1953 French Equatorial Africa (now Congo) became a separate command. Commissioner and Mrs Henri Becquet were the pioneers. The command was upgraded to a territory in December 1960.

Zone: Africa
Country included in the territory: The Republic of Congo
'The Salvation Army' in French: Armée du Salut; in Kikongo: Nkangu a Luvulusu; in Lingala: Basolda na Kobikisama; in Vili: Livita li Mavutsula
Languages in which the gospel is preached: French, Kikongo, Kituba, Lingala, Vili
Periodical: *Le Salutiste*

IN AUGUST 2013 the territory commemorated 75 years since The Salvation Army opened fire in Congo (Brazzaville).

The first ever territorial congress at Loua (Brazzaville 2 Division) conducted by the then territorial leaders Colonels Joseph and Angélique Lukau, saw more than 3,900 Salvationists and invited guests travel from all divisions and districts to mark this milestone.

Using the theme 'Salvationism and the future of the territory', Salvationists renewed their commitment to God and dedicated themselves to work for a better future for the Army. During this event, the territory was blessed to witness the commissioning and ordination of the 27 cadets of the Proclaimers of the Resurrection Session.

In September, 178 young people gathered for a divisional youth camp where they were encouraged to live 'A life of victory'. Fifty-six young people made a public decision to remain faithful to God. A territorial music camp saw Salvationists joining together for brass, vocal and timbrel workshops, and regional Scout camps were held throughout the territory in Tchitondi District, and Brazzaville 1 and Mbanza-Ndounga Divisions.

Commissioners Joash and Florence Malabi (IS/ZSWM) visited the territory in November to conduct the territorial review, during which time they also attended three rallies – men's fellowship, women's ministries and youth – and conducted a Sunday holiness meeting. During the women's rally a new women's ministries vehicle was dedicated to God. Commissioner Florence Malabi encouraged the women to persevere in obedience and in their prayer life.

In January 2014, the Social Secretary, Major Blaise Kombo, assisted by the International Emergency Services Department, distributed goods to Central African refugees.

STATISTICS

Officers 353 (active 295 retired 58)
  Employees 172
Corps 103 **Outposts** 70 **Maternity Units** 2
  Clinics 6 **Centres** 2 **Schools** 18
Senior Soldiers 22,376 **Adherent Members**
  1,526 **Junior Soldiers** 6,572
Personnel serving outside territory Officers 6

STAFF

Women's Ministries: Comr Edmane Castor (TPWM) Lt-Col Brigitte Bamanabio (TSWM) Lt-Col Angèle Taty (THLS) Lt-Col Marie Jeannette Sonda (TLOMS) Capt Marlene Christiane Mamona Madzou (TJLS)

Sec for Personnel: Lt-Col Daniel Taty
Sec for Programme: tba
Sec for Business Administration: Lt-Col Jean Pierre Sonda
Auditor: Capt Laurent Dibanssa
Editorial: Maj Blaise Kombo
Extension Training: Maj Prosper Komiena
Financial Administrator: Sgt Jean Mayandu
Health Services Coordinator: Maj Joseph Mavoungou
Information Technology: M'Passi Loukeba Richard
Music: Sgt Wilfrid Milandou
Projects: Sgt Edy Seraphin Kanda
Property: Maj Bonaventure Bibimbou
Public Relations: Maj Guy Bonaventure Conckot
Social: Maj Blaise Kombo
Territorial Bandmaster: Sgt Sensa Malanda
Territorial Songster Leader: Wilfrid Milandou
Training: Maj Dieudonné Louzolo
Youth and Candidates: Capt Edith Dibanssa

DIVISIONS

Brazzaville 1: c/o THQ; tel: 05 536 43 19;
  Majs Urbain and Judith Loubacky
Brazzaville 2: c/o THQ; tel: 05 547 12 86;
  Majs Gabin and Philomene Mbizi
Lekoumou: c/o THQ; tel: 05 556 38 72;
  Majs Patrick and Clémentine Tadi
Louingui: c/o THQ; tel: 05 568 11 85;
  Majs Jean-Pierre and Odile Douniama
Mbanza-Ndounga: c/o THQ; tel: 05 547 17 95;
  Majs Aristide and Nadege Stella Samba
Niari: BP 85, Dolisie; tel 05 558 41 36;
  Majs Victor and Emma Nzingoula
North: c/o THQ; tel: 05 528 35 87; Majs Jean Jacques Aimé And Véronique Massivi
Pointe Noire: BP 686, Pointe Noire;
  tel: 05 535 53 21;
  Majs Antoine and Marianne Massiélé
Yangui: BP 10, Kinkala; tel: 05 567 41 61;
  Majs Philippe and Rose Bonazebi

DISTRICTS

Bouenza: c/o THQ; tel: 05 553 83 75;
  Maj Alphonse Mayamba
Tchitondi: c/o THQ; tel: 05 558 37 14;
  Maj Gabriel Dimonékéné

TRAINING COLLEGE

Nzoko: c/o THQ; tel: 56 95 72

SOCIAL AND EDUCATIONAL CENTRES
Day Care Centre

Congo (Brazzaville) Territory

Ouenze Corps, Brazzaville
Guest Houses
Moungali: Auberge Makoumbou; (Brazzaville);
Pointe-Noire: Auberge Nottingham

Home for the Visually Impaired
Yenge, Nzoko; c/o THQ

Institute for the Blind
INAC, Mansimou Brazzaville; c/o THQ

Primary and Secondary Schools
Bouansa: François Mananga Primary School
Gamboma: Victor Makosso Primary School
Loua: John Swinfen Primary and Secondary School
Makelekele: Fred and Elaine Eardley Primary and
    Secondary School
Mfilou: Eugène Nsingani Primary School
Mpissa: Ime Akpan Nursery and Primary School
Moungali: Charles Houze Nursery, Primary and

Secondary School
Ouenze: John Larsson Nursery, Primary and
    Secondary School
Nzoko: Véronique Makoumbou Nursery, Primary
    and Secondary School

HEALTH SERVICES
Health Clinic and Eye Treatment Centre
Moukoundji-Ngouaka: c/o THQ

Health Clinics
Loua: BP 20, Brazzaville
Moungali: BP 20, Brazzaville
Nkayi: BP 229, Nkayi Nkouikou, Pointe Noire

Health Clinics and Maternity Units
Dolisie: BP 235, Dolisie
Yangui: c/o THQ

CONGO (BRAZZAVILLE): Newly commissioned and ordained cadets marching to receive their first appointment

DEMOCRATIC REPUBLIC OF CONGO TERRITORY

Territorial Commander:
Commissioner Madeleine Ngwanga
(1 Dec 2009)

Chief Secretary:
Lieut-Colonel Lucien Lamartiniere
(1 Dec 2011)

**Territorial Headquarters: Ave Ebea 23, Kinshasa-Gombe,
Democratic Republic of Congo**

Postal address: Armée du Salut 8636, Kinshasa 1, Democratic Republic of Congo

Tel: [243] 997-526050; email: kin_leadership@kin.salvationarmy.org

The first Salvation Army corps was established in Kinshasa in 1934 by Adjutant (later Commissioner) and Mrs Henri Becquet. By decree of Léopold III, Armée du Salut was given legal status, with powers set out in a Deed of Constitution, on 21 February 1936. Work spread to Congo in 1937 and 16 years later it became a separate command, later being elevated to territory status. Congo (Kinshasa) and Angola Territory was renamed on 1 March 2008 when Angola became a command, then became Democratic Republic of Congo Territory on 1 June 2008.

Zone: Africa
Countries included in the territory: Democratic Republic of Congo
'The Salvation Army' in French: Armée du Salut; in Kikongo: Nkangu a Luvulusu; in Lingala: Basolda na Kobikisa; in Swahili: Jeshi la Wokovu; in Tshiluba: Tshiluila Tsha Luhandu
Languages in which the gospel is preached: Chokwe, French, Kikongo, Lingala, Swahili, Tshiluba, Umbundu
Periodical: *Echo d'Espoir*

THE SALVATION Army in the Democratic Republic of Congo (DRC) embraced its mission of caring for the worst and the least, during the year under review. The situation for children within DRC worsened due to the lasting war in the eastern part of the country. Children were conscripted as soldiers by the militant forces, with many being raped or disabled. Those who became orphans had no choice but to live on the streets, begging to survive, with no hope for the future. Despite the limited resources, The

Salvation Army engaged in rescuing and feeding the children.

Because of the number of children who require care, The Salvation Army prepared a child protection document and distributed it throughout the territory, and the Army in DRC did not stay silent regarding social justice but engaged in the battle to stop using children and women as slaves of war.

By caring for others, The Salvation Army rescued many young women who were victims of sex trafficking. We rejoice that some have accepted

Christ as their Lord and Saviour, and two who had answered the call to officership have been commissioned and ordained as officers. There are others who are preparing to enter the training college as part of the next session of cadets.

The territorial emergency services, along with league of mercy workers, distributed food and other goods to the expelled Congolese from Congo (Brazzaville). The Army served 2,718 people with food kits as they were moving from the transitional camp to their home province, an intervention that made an effective social partnership for the Army with the government.

Well known in the country for its evangelical and social action, the Army runs a strong medical system with community health centres, hospitals, dental clinics, foot care clinics and maternity centres, serving those who cannot afford to access health care in the city. Competent staff made up of 27 physicians, 203 nurses, and 24 administrative staff, run the medical facilities and care for patients with diabetes, high blood pressure, tuberculosis, malaria, and dental and eye infections.

The HIV/Aids programme helped victims and conducted testing for those who are suspected of having HIV/Aids.

The Salvation Army is fulfilling its mission in DRC by maintaining a good balance between evangelisation and social service.

STATISTICS

Officers 453 (active 367 retired 86) **Cadets** (1st Yr) 10 (2nd Yr) 11 **Employees** 5,318
Corps 186 **Outposts** 116 **Health Centres** 29 **Maternity Hospitals/Clinics** 6 **Other specialist hospitals** 1 **Other specialist clinics** (inc HIV/Aids, dental) 6 **Institutions** 5 **Schools: Secondary** 180 **Primary** 253 **Boarding** 2 **Kindergarten** 9 **University** 1
Senior Soldiers 29,847 **Adherent Members** 4,774 **Junior Soldiers** 15,402
Personnel serving outside territory Officers 14

STAFF

Women's Ministries: Comr Madeleine Ngwanga (TPWM) Lt-Col Marie Lamartiniere (TSWM) Maj Bibisky Nzila (THLS) Lt-Col Celestine Ngoy (LOM, Literacy) Maj Marie-Thérèse Mabwidi (Women's Dev/Anti-sex Trafficking) Lt-Col Lydia Matondo (JHLS, Officers' Children, Retd Officers)
Sec for Business Administration: Lt-Col Gracia Matondo
Sec for Personnel: Lt-Col Hubert Ngoy
Sec for Programme: Lt-Col Jean-Baptiste Mata
Development and Emergency Services: Maj Dieudonné Tsilulu
Editorial/Literature: Maj Josué Leka
Extension Training: Maj Germain Luzolo
Finance: Maj Barthélemy Nzila
Information Technology: Sgt Mbumu Muba Jean-Marc
Medical: Dr David Nku Imbie
Music and Creative Arts: Maj Philippe Mabwidi **National Bandmaster:** Sgt Jean-Marc Mbumu **National Songster Leader:** Sgt Joseph Nsilulu **National Timbrel Leader:** Sgt Pauline Matanu
Property: Maj Léon Tubajiki
Public Relations: Capt André Mulenda
Schools Coordinator: Maj Norbert Makala
Social: Maj Philippe Mabwidi **HIV/Aids Section:** Mr Paul Kunzebiko **Sponsorship:** Maj Philippine Tsilulu
Training: Maj Sébastien Mbala
Youth: Maj Martin Buama **Candidates:** Maj Adolphe Masidiyaku

DIVISIONS

Bas-Fleuve/Océan: BP 123, Matadi; Majs Antoine et Bernadette Toni (mob: 0815107232)
Inkisi: Armée du Salut, Kavwaya, BP 45; Majs Isidore and Marthe Matondo (mob: 0990023962)

Kasaï-Occidental: BP 1404, Kananga;
Majs Esaïe and Marie-José Ntembi
(mob: 0991668909)
Kasangulu: BP 14, Kasangulu; Majs Emmanuel
and Madeleine Diakanwa
(mob: 0998336208)
Katanga: BP 2525, Lubumbashi; Majs Denis
and Modestine Mafuta (mob: 0994504967)
Kinshasa Central: BP 8636, Kinshasa;
Majs Alphonse and Bernadette Mayasi
(mob: 0998449971)
Kinshasa East: BP 8636, Kinshasa;
Maj Pascal Matsiona (mobile: 0998036399)
Kinshasa West: Lt-Cols Henri and Josephine
Nangi (mob: 0999371303)
Luozi: Armée du Salut, Luozi; Majs Clément and
Béatrice Ilunga (mob: 0998627937)
Mbanza-Ngungu: BP 160; tba
Orientale (Kisangani): BP 412, Kisangani;
Majs William and Rose-Marie Ntoya
(mob: 0998277857)

DISTRICTS
Bandundu: Armée du Salut, Bandundu;
Maj André Mobubu (mobile: 0811620092)
Isiro: BP 135 (under supervision of THQ)
Plateau: Majs Emmanuel and Albertine Mpanzu
(mob: 0995662729)
Tanganyika: (under supervision of Katanga)

SECTIONS
Bukavu: Maj Pierre Masundu
(mobile: 0993187354)
Kwilu: Maj Antoine Masaki
(mobile: 0998947602)

TRAINING COLLEGE
BP 8636, Kinshasa

UNIVERSITY
William Booth University: BP 8636, Kinshasa;
Rector: Dr Mpiutu ne Mbodi Gaston

ATTACHED TO THQ
Conference Centre:
Mbanza-Nzundu

MEDICAL WORK
Health Centres
Bas-Congo: Kasangulu, Boko-Mbuba, Kifuma,
Kingantoko, Kingudi, Kinzambi, Kintete,
Nkalama, Shefu, Kavwaya, Kimayala,
Mbanza-Nsundi, Mbanza-Nzundu
Kananga: Moyo

Kinshasa: Amba (Kisenso), Bakidi (Selembao),
Bomoi, Bopeto (Ndjili), Boyambi (Barumbu),
Elonga, Esengo (Masina), Kimia (Kintambo),
Molende (Kingasani)
Kisangani: Libota, Dengue

Clinic
Maj Leka (Maluku/Kinshasa)

Dental Clinics
Boyambi (Barumbu), Elonga (Masina),
Kasangulu (Bas-Congo)

Diabetic Clinic
Kananga

Foot Clinic
Boyambi

Ophthalmological Clinic
Boyambi (Barumbu)

Maternity Units
Bas-Congo (acc 13); Kavwaya, Bas-Congo
maternity and centre (acc 14); Bomoi
Kinshasa (acc 72); Kasangulu Maluku
Kinshasa (acc 12)

EDUCATION
Bandundu:
18 primary schools, 16 secondary schools
Bas-Congo:
80 primary schools, 60 secondary schools,
1 kindergarten
Equateur:
44 primary schools, 26 secondary schools,
5 kindergartens
Kasaï-Occidental (Kananga):
23 primary schools, 18 secondary schools
Kinshasa:
24 secondary schools, 39 primary schools
Province Orientale (Kisangani):
26 secondary schools, 33 primary schools,
1 kindergarten
Sud-Katanga (Lubumbashi):
2 secondary schools, 9 primary schools

SOCIAL SERVICES
Children's Home and Community Child Care
Children's home (acc 8)
Community placements (5)

Democratic Republic of Congo Territory

Development and Emergencies
Impini; Kasangulu; Kavwaya; Mato;
Mbanza-Nzundu

Elderly Care Home
Kinshasa-Kintambo (acc 18)

Vocational Training Centres
Bas-Fleuve: Boma (acc 15); Kinzau-Mvwete
(acc 12)
Inkisi: Kavwaya (acc 112)
Kasaï-Occidental: Kananga (acc 47)

Kasangulu: Centre Professionnel Kasangulu
(acc 11); Luila (acc 12); Matanda (acc 15);
Sona-Bata (acc 32)
Kinshasa Centre: Barumbu Kinshasa (acc 75);
Makala 2
Kinshasa East: Ndjili Kinshasa (acc 35)
Kinshasa West: Kimvula (acc 35); Kin 4
(acc 35);
Lubumbashi: Kisheko (acc 30)
Luozi: Kintete (acc 11)
Plateau: Maluku (acc 33)

Delegates to the Global Conversation held in Atlanta, USA, take part in
working groups

DENMARK TERRITORY

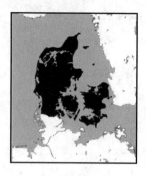

Territorial Commander:
Colonel Hannelise Tvedt
(1 Sept 2014)

Chief Secretary:
Lieut-Colonel Anthony Cotterill
(1 Sept 2014)

**Territorial Headquarters: Frederiksberg Allé 9,
1621 Copenhagen V, Denmark**

Tel: [45] 33 31 41 92; email: Frelsens@den.salvationarmy.org;
website: www.frelsens-haer.dk

The work of The Salvation Army in Denmark commenced in Copenhagen on 8 May 1887, pioneer officers being Majors (later Lieut-Colonels) Robert and Isabella Perry. Lieutenants Magnus and Petura Haraldsen were appointed to commence Army work in Greenland in August 2012.

Zone: Europe
Countries included in the territory: Denmark, Greenland
'The Salvation Army' in Danish: Frelsens Hær
Language in which the gospel is preached: Danish
Periodicals: *Krigsråbet (The War Cry), Vision-Mission*

GOD continues to bless the Denmark Territory. In May 2013, 30 years after the Army closed its doors in Sønderborg, a new facility was opened and dedicated to God. The rented facility was turned into a modern and suitable centre for the Army's growing work, and it was a cause for real celebration when four soldiers were enrolled and five adherent members welcomed – all with no connection to the Army prior to the relaunching of the work in the town.

In July, four lieutenants were commissioned and ordained in Oslo, having been cadets in the Norway, Iceland and The Færoes Territory, and in December a Danish lieutenant was commissioned in Australia Southern Territory, the first Danish officer to be trained outside Europe. These five new lieutenants represent an increase of more than 12 per cent in the number of active officers in the territory.

The work in Greenland is growing and developing in a positive way. The Army was accepted as part of the Greenlandic Society and was invited to speak at conferences and gatherings concerning the social challenges in the country. More importantly, more people are finding their way to the Army, as God works in their lives to bring about transformation and change.

In September 2013 a process toward developing a strategic framework for the future was launched, called 'Open doors of opportunity' (1 Corinthians

16:9). The title reflects the many opportunities the territory has experienced and its responsibility to seize the moments of opportunity in a wise and focused way.

Commuters and travellers were invited to stop and share a meal on the main concourse of the busy Copenhagen Central station in October. The event was used to launch a magazine highlighting the work of the Army and those who had received help and support. Volunteers from Army centres served soup and more than 500 people accepted the invitation not only to share a meal together, but also to share their story with clients from Salvation Army projects.

STATISTICS

Officers 75 (active 32 retired 43)
Cadets (2nd Yr) 3 **Employees** 207
Corps 29 **Outpost** 2 **Social Institutions** 11
Community Centres 11
Senior Soldiers 904 **Adherent Members** 295
Junior Soldiers 19
Personnel serving outside territory Officers 4

STAFF

Women's Ministries: Col Hannelise Tvedt
(TPWM) Lt-Col Gillian Cotterill (TSWM)
Sec for Spiritual Life Development: tba
Sec for Business Admin: Mr Lars Lydholm
Chief Accounting Officer: Ms Eva Haahr
Property: Maj Terje Tvedt
Public Relations: Mr Lars Lydholm
Technology: Mr Gert Pedersen
Sec for Personnel: tba
Sec for Programme: Maj John Wahl
HR Manager: Ms Anette Bøjstrup
Director of Social Institutions: Mr Kåre
Skarsholm
Family Work Coordinator: Ms Anne Jakshøj
Regional Pastoral and Development:
Funen: Majs Kurt and Helle Pedersen
North Jutland: Maj Kjell and Ann-Cathrin
Bergman
Sealand: Maj Kjell Olausson

South Jutland: Lts Magnus and Petura
Haraldsen
Child Sponsorship: Lt-Col Miriam
Frederiksen
Editor: Maj Levi Giversen
Missing Persons: Cols Jørn and Nina Lauridsen
Mission: Maj Ingrid Larsen
Over-60s: Sgt René Jamrath
Statistics: Lt-Col Miriam Frederiksen
Youth: Mr Gert Pedersen
Candidates: Capt Birgit Seier

SOCIAL INSTITUTIONS AND COMMUNITY CENTRES

Recycling Centres

Esbjerg: Ravnevej 2, 6705 Esbjerg Ø;
tel: [45] 75 14 24 22
Hadsund: Mariagervej 3, 9560 Hadsund;
tel: [45] 98 57 42 48
Nakskov: Narvikvej 15, 4900 Nakskov;
tel: [45] 54 95 12 05
Odense: Højvang 38-40, 5000 Odense C;
tel: [45] 66 11 25 21

Community Centres

Aalborg:
Møllepladscentret, Skipper Clementsgade 13,
9000 Aalborg; tel: [45] 98 11 50 62
Copenhagen:
Grundtvigsvej, Grundtvigsvej 17, 1864
Frederiksberg; tel: [45] 33 24 56 67
Nørrebro, Thorsgade 48 A, 2200
Copenhagen N; tel: [45] 35 85 00 87
Pakhuset, Wildersgade 66, 1408
Copenhagen K; tel: [45] 32 54 44 10
Nakskov:
Havnen, Niels Nielsengade 7,4900
tel (45) 5495 3006

Day Nurseries

Frederikshavn:
Humlebien, Knudensvej 1B, 9900
Frederikshavn; tel: [45] 98 42 33 27
(acc 40)
Copenhagen:
Melita, Mariendalsvej 4, 2000 Frederiksberg;
tel: [45] 38 87 01 48 (acc 74)
Kastanjehuset, Idrætsvej 65A, 2650 Hvidovre;
tel: [45] 36 78 40 23 (acc 33)
Solgården, Catherine Booths vej 22, 2650
Hvidovre; tel: [45] 36 78 07 71 (acc 128)

Emergency Shelters for Families

Copenhagen:

DENMARK: Two little girls wearing their backpacks from 'Others'

Svendebjerggård, Catherine Booths vej 20, 2650 Hvidovre; tel: [45] 36 49 65 77 (acc 25)
Den Åbne Dør, Hedebygade 30, 1754 Copenhagen V; tel: [45] 33 24 91 03 (acc 15)
Næstved:
  Krisecentret, Østergade 13, 4700 Næstved; tel: [45] 55 77 22 70 (acc 6)

Hostels
Copenhagen: Hørhuset, Hørhusvej 5, 2300 Copenhagen S; tel: [45] 32 55 56 22 (acc 64)
Nakskov: Havnen, Niels Nielsensgade 7, 4900 Nakskov; tel: [45] 54 95 30 06 (acc 7)

Project for Long-term Unemployed
Aalborg: Nørholmlejren, Oldenborrevej 2, 9000 Aalborg; tel: 98 34 18 10 (acc 10)

Eventide Nursing Centre
Copenhagen: Aftensol, Lundtoftegade 5, 2200 Copenhagen N; tel: 35 30 55 00 (acc 43)

Students Residence
Copenhagen: Kollegiet, Helgesengade 25, 2100 Copenhagen Ø; tel: [45] 35 37 74 32 (acc 41)

Summer Camps
Aalborg: Nørholmlejren, Oldenborrevej 2, 9000 Aalborg; tel: [45] 98 34 18 10 (acc 50)
Otterup: Rømhildsminde, Ferievej 11-13, Jørgensø, 5450 Otterup; tel: [45] 64 87 13 36

Holiday Home and Conference Centre
Copenhagen: Baggersminde, Fælledvej 132, 2791 Dragør; tel: [45] 32 53 70 18 (acc 80)
Funen: Lillebælt, Nørre Allé 47, Strib, 5500 Middelfart; tel: [45] 64 40 10 57 (acc 30)

EASTERN EUROPE TERRITORY

Territorial leaders:
Colonels Rodney and Wendy Walters

Territorial Commander:
Colonel Rodney Walters (1 Jul 2014)

Chief Secretary:
Lieut-Colonel Alexander Kharkov (1 Jul 2014)

Territorial Headquarters: Krestiansky Tupik 16/1, Moscow

Postal address: Russian Federation, 109044 Moscow, Krestiansky Tupik 16/1

Tel: [7] (495) 911 2600/2956 email: Russia@eet.salvationarmy.org;

website: www.thesalvationarmy.ru

Work was initiated in Russia in 1910 by Colonel Jens Povlsen of Denmark but circumstances necessitated his withdrawal after 18 months. Army operations then recommenced in St Petersburg in 1913 as an extension to the work in Finland. After the February 1917 revolution the work flourished, Russia became a distinct command and reinforcements arrived from Sweden. As a result of the October revolution they had, however, to be withdrawn at the end of 1918, leaving 40 Russian and Finnish officers to continue the work under extreme hardship until the Army was finally proscribed in 1923.

Salvation Army activities were officially recommenced in July 1991, overseen by the Norway, Iceland and The Færoes Territory with the arrival of Lieut-Colonels John and Bjorg Bjartveit. It became a distinct command in November 1992. Under the leadership of Commissioner Reinder J. Schurink, the work was extended to Ukraine (1993), Georgia (1993) and Moldova (1994). The Army commenced work in Romania in 1999. On 1 June 2001 the command was redesignated the Eastern Europe Command. It was elevated to territory status on 1 March 2005. The final stage of registering 'the Moscow Branch of The Salvation Army' was completed in April 2009.

Zone: Europe

Countries included in the territory: Georgia, Moldova, Romania, Russian Federation, Ukraine

'The Salvation Army' in Georgian: Khsnis Armia; in Moldovan/Romanian: Armata Salvarii; in Russian: Armiya Spaseniya; in Ukrainian: Armiya Spasinnya

Languages in which the gospel is preached: Georgian, Moldovan, Romanian, Russian, Ukrainian

Periodicals: *Vestnik Spaseniya* (*The War Cry*), *The Officer* (both Russian)

IT WAS the famous Russian writer Leo Tolstoy who once stated: 'If we would only testify to the truth as we see it, it would turn out that there are hundreds, thousands, even millions of other people just as we are, who see the truth as we do and are only waiting, again, as we are, for someone to proclaim it.' The Salvation Army

Eastern Europe Territory holds firm to the truth that Jesus is Lord. The desire to proclaim the gospel message has driven the mission of the territory with officers and soldiers committing themselves to share the good news and reach those ready to embrace the truth. God continues to bless the faithfulness of his people in Eastern Europe as they endeavour to fulfil the worldwide mission of The Salvation Army.

The Georgia Region and the Ukraine Division celebrated their 20-year anniversaries, these occasions proving to be a catalyst for revival and renewal.

In an effort to continue to equip officers for mission, a highlight of the year in review was the territorial officers development councils. Meeting in Chisinau, Moldova, the officers gathered for four days of intensive training on the practical aspects of mission and fund-raising.

One of the immediate goals was the further establishment and development of the Christmas fund-raising effort. This training proved to be successful.

Sports Ministries is a new outreach venture and is one of the focus points in the territory's Strategic Mission Plan. Corps recognise the potential in this area of outreach, especially to youth and children in their local communities. Ukraine, Georgia and Moldova have more than 12,000 people involved in this particular ministry.

With five countries making up the territory, the legal environment has been a major challenge. The political situation also created an uncertainty as to how The Salvation Army was to maintain its ministry, but the territory continues to believe for greater things.

STATISTICS

Officers 122 (active 116 retired 6) **Envoys** 3
  Cadets (2nd yr) 8 **Employees** 173
Corps 47 **Corps Plants** 4
Senior Soldiers 1,622 **Adherent Members** 877
  Junior Soldiers 355

STAFF

Women's Ministries: Col Wendy Walters
  (TPWM)
Sec for Business Admin: Lt-Col Gary Haupt
Sec for Personnel: Col Wendy Walters
Sec for Programme: tba
Candidates: Capt Inna Khurin
Editorial: Capt Elena Shulyanski
Education Secretary: Maj Judith Soeters
Legal: tba
Projects Officer: Lt-Col Suzanne Haupt
Property Secretary: Maj Mark Soeters
Public Relations and Director for Resources:
  Capt Elena Shulyanski
Youth and Children's Secretary: tba
Training Principal: Maj Judith Soeters

DIVISIONS

Russia: 105120 Russia, Moscow,
  Khlebnikov Pereulok, 7 bld, 2;
  tel: 495 678 03 51;
  Majs Alexander and Svetlana Sharov
Moldova: Chisinau, Petru Movila #19 ;
  Postal address: Armata Salvarii, Moldova:
  Chisinau, 2004, PO Box 412;
  tel: (37322) 237972;
  Majs Graham and Hélène Carey
Ukraine: 01033, Ukraine, Kiev,
  Shota Rustavely St 38, Suite 3;
  tel: (380 44) 287 4598, ;
  Majs Beat Rieder and Annette Rieder-Pell

REGIONS

Georgia: 16 Ikalto St, Tbilisi 0171, Georgia;
  tel: (995 32) 33 37 85/86;
Romania: 722212 Bucharest, Sector 2,
  Str Pargarilor Nr 2; tel: [10] (4037) 270 51 99;
  Majs Valery and Victoria Lalac

MISSION TRAINING AND EDUCATION CENTRE – INSTITUTE FOR OFFICER TRAINING

Russia, Moscow, 105120 Karl Larsson Centre,
  Khlebnikov Per 7/2; tel: (495) 678 55 14

SOCIAL SERVICES
Georgia
Children's After-School Programmes: Batumi,
  Didi Digomi, Lagodeki, Megobroba, Ponichala,
  Rustavi, Samgori, Tbilisi Central
Laundry Projects: Batumi, Didi Digomi; Rustavi,
  Samgori,
Senior Centres: Batumi, Megobroba, Samgori,
  Tbilisi Central
Various community aid programmes including:

baby song; back to school aid; computer class; feeding schemes; folk dance; library and literacy; medical services; mobile dental clinic, shower facilities

Moldova

After-School Centres: Beltsi, Cahul, Dubassari, Edinets, Ungheni;
Mobile medical clinic
Rusca Women's Prison project;
Work with invalids: Chimislia, Hincehsti
In addition: computer courses, HIV & Drug Prevention, humanitarian aid distribution, Sally Ann' programme, shoe project

Romania

Bucharest Roma School Children Outreach
Isasi: computer training and social canteen
In addition: laundry projects; after-school programmes; support for young families

Russia

Feeding Schemes: Moscow, Petrozavodsk, St Petersburg, Voronezh, Vyborg
Moscow: Karl Larsson Centre, Unified Homeless Services, Khlebnikov pereulok 7, bld 2; tel: (495) 678 03 51

Feeding programme; first aid; food and clothing distribution;
St Petersburg:Liteini Prospect # 44 B, 191104; tel: (812) 273-9297;
Project Hope: HIV/aids outreach and support; homeless feeding programme; food and clothing distribution; seniors' support group
Simferopol Children's Arts Centre: 95000 Crimea - Russia, Simferopol, ulitsa Nekrasova, 22 office 1

Ukraine

Kharkiv Corps Social Centre: Ukraine, Kharkiv, Moskovsky prospect 122, 'Kalibr club'; tel: (380-57) 759-42-48; email: Kharkiv_corps@ukr.net
Kirovograd Corps Social Centre: 25028 Ukraine, Kirovagrad, Volova St, #15, SPTU #8; tel: (380-52) 255-19-28; email: armiyas@rambler.ru
Programmes include: after school care; humanitarian aid; prison ministries; seniors' centres; sports ministry; work with families of disabled people

EASTERN EUROPE: A new initiative in EET – Christmas Kettle Outreach

FINLAND AND ESTONIA TERRITORY

Territorial leaders:
Colonels Johnny and Eva Kleman

Territorial Commander:
Colonel Johnny Kleman (1 Feb 2013)

Chief Secretary:
Lieut-Colonel Petter Kornilow (1 May 2013)

Territorial Headquarters: Uudenmaankatu 40, 00120 Helsinki

Postal address: Post Box 161, 00121 Helsinki, Finland

Tel: [358] (09) 6812300; email: finland@pelastusarmeija.fi;
website: www.pelastusarmeija.fi

Work in Finland was commenced on 8 November 1889 in Broholm's Riding School, Helsinki, by four aristocratic Finns – Captain and Mrs Constantin Boije with Lieutenants Hedvig von Haartman and Alva Forsius. Within six months Hedvig von Haartman was appointed leader of the work in the country.

Work in Estonia first commenced in 1927 and continued until 1940 when it was closed due to the Second World War. It recommenced in the autumn of 1995 when three Finnish officers were assigned to start the work in Tallinn.

Zone: Europe
Countries included in the territory: Estonia, Finland
'The Salvation Army' in Estonian: Päästearmee; in Finnish: Pelastusarmeija; in Swedish: Frälsningsarmén
Languages in which the gospel is preached: English, Estonian, Finnish, Russian, Swedish
Periodicals: *Nappis* (Finnish), *Sotahuuto* (Finnish)

THE SALVATION Army's mission has never been about making history, but about making a difference. Planning and launching the 'Vision 1-2-5' strategy to celebrate 125 years of service, was about finding new ways to continue to make a difference in society. This was not just a dream, but through prayer and active planning for the future, focusing on what kind of Salvation Army God wanted to see in these countries, the territory witnessed results. Several God-inspired initiatives confirmed that he is still doing something new in the territory.

In Finland, The Salvation Army has played a major role in the area of shelter, housing and accommodation for the needy. A new spiritual life development plan for social housing was implemented and Commissioner Birgitte Brekke-Clifton (IS) and Colonel Johnny Kleman (TC) opened two new housing units – one in Helsinki and another in Espoo.

To support the mission, the territory's recycling business opened two new stores. Permission was granted to introduce a Christmas kettle at every main ice hockey game. As ice hockey is 'the game' in Finland, this gave the territory a great opportunity to communicate and raise money.

In a number of corps new soldiers and members were enrolled. A new hall and day-care centre in Lahti was opened and in Kuopio the corps building was refurbished and reopened. After six years of waiting for renovations to take place, the oldest corps building in Finland – Helsinki Temple – was reopened.

In the Estonia Region, the new regional leaders Majors Cedric and Lyn Hills were welcomed. In the city of Narva a five-storey property was dedicated for the work of God. The Alpha Course has proved successful with the new hall being filled to capacity during each course. The Firewood Project, at Hope House social centre in Tallinn, gives meaningful work to people while raising much-needed finances for the mission. In order to become more effective the regional headquarters was relocated and the work restructured. However, the greatest blessing, and a historic turning point, took place in January 2014 when six cadets were welcomed as the first session to be trained in Estonia.

Celebrating 125 years has allowed the territory to acknowledge the way in which God has kept and guided his people. We dare to serve, grow and we see a bright future. It is not a dream. It is God's planned future.

STATISTICS

Officers 137 (active 46 retired 91) **Cadets** 2 **Employees** 431

Corps 29 **Outposts** 8 **Goodwill Centres** 2 **Institutions** 20

Senior Soldiers 782 **Adherent Members** 119 **Junior Soldiers** 32

STAFF

Women's Ministries: Col Eva Kleman (TPWM) Lt-Col Eija Kornilow (TSWM)

Programme: Maj Tella Puotiniemi
Asst for Programme and Youth: Capt Natalia Penttinen

Training and Education: Lt-Col Aino Muikku
School for Officer Training: Lt-Col Aino Muikku

Business Administration: Capt Rodrigo Miranda

Property: Mika Tiittanen
Recycling Industry: Harri Lehti
Information Technology: Tapani Saaristo
Personnel: Maj Pirjo Vallinsalo
Communications: Lt-Col Eija Kornilow
The War Cry: Toni Kaarttinen
Missing Persons: Maj Kirsti Reponen

SOCIAL CENTRES
Children's Day Care Centres

48100 Kotka, Korkeavuorenkatu 24; tel: 44 757 7866 (acc 25)

15200 Lahti, Teinintie 4; tel: 3 878680 (acc 94)

06100 Porvoo, Joonaksentie 1; tel: 45 635 8089 (acc 48)

28100 Pori, Mikonkatu 19; tel: 45 635 8088 (acc 83)

Clothing Industry (Recycling Centres)

90580 Oulu, Ratamotie 22; tel: 44 757 7945

33500 Tampere, Itsenäisyydenkatu 25-27; tel: 44 757 7943

20100 Turku, Yliopistonkatu 5; tel: 44 757 7965

01260 Vantaa, Itäinen Valkoisenlähteentie 15; tel: 9 877 0270

Finland and Estonia Territory

Eventide Home
02710 Espoo, Viherlaaksonranta 19;
   tel: 9 84938410 (acc 60)

Family Support Centre
00530 Helsinki, Hedvig House, Castréninkatu
   24-26 F; tel: 50 400 1708

Goodwill Centres
00530 Helsinki, Castréninkatu 24; tel: 44 757 7895
68600 Pietarsaari, Permontie 34; tel: 44 7577 897
33230 Tampere, Pyynikintori 3; tel: 44 757 7941
20540 Turku, Karjakuja 1; tel: 44 757 7940

Homes for Alcoholics and Homeless
68600 Pietarsaari, Permontie 34; tel: 44 757 7896
   (acc 10)
28120 Pori, Veturitallinkatu 3; tel: 45 139 3292
   (acc 24)
20500 Turku, Hämeenkatu 18; tel: 44 757 7984
   (acc 25)

Hostel for Women
00530 Helsinki, Castréninkatu 24-26 A 41;
   tel: 9 77431330 (acc 23)

Supported Housing Units
02710 Espoo, Kuusiniemi 5; tel: 45 7734 5379
   (acc 35)
00530 Helsinki, Alppikatu 25 tel: 044 757 7869
   (acc 85)

00380 Helsinki, Pitäjänmäentie 12; tel:44 757
   7999 (acc 111)

Reception Centre and Supported Living Unit
00550 Helsinki, Inarintie 8; tel: 44 756 2153
   (acc 52)

Senior Citizens' Unit
00760 Helsinki, Puistolantie 6 (acc 72)

Summer Camp Centre
03100 Nummela, Hiidenrannatie 22
   (acc 60)

Youth Camp
33480 Ylöjärvi, Sovelontie 91 (summer only)

ESTONIA REGION
Regional Headquarters: Narva mnt 38
   10152 Tallinn; tel: [372] 6413355

Regional Commander: Maj Cedric Hills
Corps 5

Centres
Hope House (Lootusemaja): Laevastiku 1a,
   10313 Tallinn; tel: 6561048
Camp: Ranna 24, Loksa; tel: 6031012

FINLAND: Captain Natalia Penttinen
distributing knitted clothes for babies

Canada: Children enthusiastically taking part in a programme at Kelowna, British Columbia (top); **Finland:** The opening of the Christmas Kettle campaign at an ice hockey game (below l); **Mexico:** Emergency services assisting the local community in Acapulco (below r)

(clockwise from I)
Nigeria: New soldiers enrolled by the General; Singapore: Commissioner Nancy Roberts receiving flowers during the welcome meeting at the International Conference for Leaders; Southern Africa: A little boy taking possession of goods provided by the Army; France and Belgium: Proclaimers of the Resurrection Session are commissioned as Salvation Army officers; Greenland: A soup kitchen established for the homeless in Nuuk

Sri Lanka: Commissioner Malcolm Induruwage greets His Royal Highness Prince Charles (above); USA Central: A newly commissioned officer excitedly receives her first appointment (below r); Scotland: The Chief of the Staff and Commissioner Nancy Roberts with the corps officers at Belshill Corps (below l); USA: A volunteer comforts a woman who lost her home during a tornado (above l)

(clockwise from top l) **Uganda:** Salvationists on the march; **Pakistan:** General André Cox greets a faith leader at the Badshahi Mosque; **Ghana:** Local children join The Salvation Army on the march; **India Eastern:** Children taking part in a march; **USA Eastern:** Commissioner Barry Swanson addressing the congregation during a commissioning weekend in his territory

Indonesia: The Palu choir greet the General and Commissioner Silvia Cox (above); **Pakistan: Commissioner Silvia Cox participating in a women's rally** (below r); **Philippines: A scene of devastation following a typhoon** (below l)

FRANCE AND BELGIUM TERRITORY

Territorial leaders:
Colonels Daniel and Eliane Naud

Territorial Commander:
Colonel Daniel Naud (1 Sept 2014)

Chief Secretary:
Lieut-Colonel Sylvie Arnal (1 Feb 2011)

**Territorial Headquarters: 60 rue des Frères Flavien
75976 Paris Cedex 20, France**

Tel: [33] (0) 43 62 25 00; website: www.armeedusalut.fr

Since 'La Maréchale' (eldest daughter of William and Catherine Booth) conducted The Salvation Army's first meeting in Paris on Sunday 13 March 1881, Salvationist influence has grown and remarkable social and spiritual results have been achieved. French officers commenced work in Algeria in 1934 and this work was maintained until 1970.

In Belgium, Salvation Army operations were pioneered on 5 May 1889 by Adjutant and Mrs Charles Rankin and Captains Velleema and Hass. Most of the work in Belgium operates within the Francophone part of the country so, from 1 January 2009, the former Belgium Command became a region linked administratively to France under the newly created France and Belgium Territory.

Zone: Europe
Countries included in the territory: Belgium, France
'The Salvation Army' in French: Armée du Salut; in Flemish: Leger des Heils
Languages in which the gospel is preached: French, Flemish
Periodicals: *Avec Vous*, *Le Bulletin de la Ligue du Foyer*, *Le Fil*, *Le Magazine*; *Le partenaire de prière*

DURING officers councils, the new territorial strategy for the next five years was prepared. The aim was to focus on growth, training and the wise use of resources. In the face of growing multiculturalism, the territory has found a new and relevant means of sharing the gospel. There is a strong desire to cultivate the essential character of an active church that is moving forward, living with passion and authenticity to announce the good news, in a clear, dynamic and pertinent

way, and loving unconditionally the people who make up society.

The youth met together during the summer for various camps. The 'Forever' camp held in August 2013, which trains youth in evangelism, took place on the beaches of Dunkirk, France, and in the streets of Mons, Belgium. This idea attracted different ages and gave up-to-date tools to spread the gospel throughout the territory.

Sixty-one scouts ('Porteurs de

Flambeau') had a positive experience as they took part in the Jamboree in London. A music camp was held with 60 young adults benefitting from the enriching and challenging spiritual time. A team of 10 from the Florida Division (USA Southern Territory) – one of the territory's Partners in Mission – participated and brought their musical expertise and spiritual support, as well as financial aid to the territory.

The commissioning and ordination of eight new cadets from the Proclaimers of the Resurrection Session was a great blessing, and the territory has witnessed a renewal within the youth with the enrolment of young soldiers, soldiers and people offering for officership.

During the winter months, the Foundation's (social services) goal for 2013-14 was to help 5,000 people each day. The opening of large social centres to provide emergency accommodation and individual flats for those who do not need constant supervision, is required.

In order to raise public awareness about the daily battles people encounter, an advertising campaign was launched using billboards and daily newspapers with the slogan 'Certain battles merit an Army'.

During the month of June, two centres for elderly dependent people were opened in the Sundgau region and the first foundation stone was laid for another centre in Mothe-St-Héray.

The theme 'Let's walk together with confidence!' based on Isaiah 30:15, was chosen for 2014.

Belgian Salvationists celebrated 125 years of the Army's presence and continue to trust in God, confident for the future.

STATISTICS
Officers 167 (active 66 retired 101)
   Employees 2,506
Corps 37 **Outposts** 2 **Institutions** 60
Senior Soldiers 1,174 **Adherent Members** 288
   Junior Soldiers 136
Personnel serving outside territory Officers 9

THE SALVATION ARMY CONGREGATION – FRANCE

BOARD OF THE CONGREGATION
Col Daniel Naud, Col Eliane Naud,
   Lt-Col Sylvie Arnal, Maj Bernard Fournel,
   Maj Ruth Moratto, Maj Patrick March

STAFF
Women's Ministries: Col Eliane Naud (TPWM)
   Maj Danièle César (TSWM)
Candidates: Col Eliane Naud
Education: Maj Anne Thöni
Field: Majs Bernard and Claire-Lise Fournel
Finance: Mr Alain Raoul
Retired Officers: Majs Christian and Joëlle
   Exbrayat
Territorial Band: B/M Mrs Arielle Mangeard
Trade: Maj Joëlle Exbrayat
Youth Coordinator: Maj David Vandebeulque

THE SALVATION ARMY FOUNDATION – FRANCE

BOARD OF DIRECTORS
President: Col Daniel Naud,
Secretary: Lt-Col Sylvie Arnal
Treasurer: Mr Olivier Ponsoye
Members: Mr Patrick Audebert, Mrs Catherine
   Bergeal, Maj Danièle César, Mr Bernard
   Westercamp

STAFF
Director General: Mr Alain Raoul
Director of Social Exclusion Programme:
   Mr Olivier Marguery
**Director of Care, Handicap and Dependence
   Programme:** Mr Eric Yapoudjian
Director of Youth Programme: Mr Samuel
   Coppens

Director of Projects and Property Programme:
Mr Bernard Guilhou

Director of Finance and Administration: Mrs
Martine Dumont

Director of Human Resources Mr François
Lelièvre

Communications: Mr David Germain

Information Technology: Mr Micha Karapetian

Spiritual Care: Capt Jean-Claude Ngimbi

Volunteers/Missing Persons: Maj Dominique
Glories

SOCIAL SERVICES

Centres for Men

57100 Thionville: L'Escale-C.H.R.S Florange,68
rte de Metz; tel: (0) 82 83 09 60 (acc 105)

59018 Lille Cedex: Les Moulins de l'Espoir,
48 rue de Valenciennes, BP 184;
tel: (0) 20 52 69 09 (acc 517)

75013 Paris: Palais du Peuple,
29 rue des Cordelières; tel: (0) 43 37 93 61
(acc 100)

Centres for Women (with or without children)

30900 Nîmes: Les Glycines (for victims of
domestic violence), 4 rue de l'Ancien
Vélodrome; tel: (0) 66 62 20 68 (acc 52)

75011 Paris: Le Palais de la Femme,
94 rue de Charonne; tel: (0) 46 59 30 00
(acc 374)

94320 Thiais: Résidence Sociale, 7 blvd de
Stalingrad; tel: (0) 48 53 57 15 (acc 57)

Centres for Men and/or Women (with or without children)

27400 Louviers: Residence Henri Durand,
51 ave Winston Churchill; tel: (0) 32 50 90 60
(acc 112)

13003 Marseille: Residence William Booth;
190 rue Félix Pyat; tel: (0) 91 02 49 37
(acc 152)

68100 Mulhouse: Le Bon Foyer,
24 rue de L'Ile Napoléon; tel: (0) 89 44 43 56
(acc 188)

69006 Lyon: La Cité de Lyon,
131 ave Thiers; tel: (0) 78 52 60 80 (acc 400)

74560 Monnetier-Mornex: Les Hutins;
3 chemin de la Vie de la Croix
tel: (0) 50 36 59 52 (acc 16)

75011 Paris: Résidence Catherine Booth,
15 rue Crespin du Gast; tel: (0) 43 14 70 90
(acc 108)

75013 Paris: La Cité de Refuge/Centre Espoir,
12 rue Cantagrel; tel: (0) 53 61 82 00
(acc 238)

75020 Paris: Résidence Albin Peyron,
60 rue des Frères Flavien; tel: (0) 48 97 54 50
(acc 273)

76600 Le Havre: Le Phare, 191 rue de la Vallée;
tel: (0) 35 24 22 11 (acc 463)

51100 Reims: Le Nouvel Horizon, 42 rue de
Taissy; tel: (0) 26 85 23 09 (acc 252)

76005 Rouen: Residence du Vieux Marché;
26 rue de Crosne; tel: (0) 35 70 38 00 (acc 241)

78100 St Germain en Laye: La Maison Verte,
14 rue de la Maison Verte;
tel: (0) 39 73 29 39 (acc 48)

81200 Aussillon: 23 blvd Albert Gaches;
tel: (0) 63 98 23 95 (acc 16)

90000 Belfort: 7 rue Jean-Baptiste Colbert;
tel: (0) 84 21 05 53 (acc 179)

81200 Mazamet 2 Avenue Maréchal Foch;
tel: (0) 63 61 73 73 (acc 91)

Work Rehabilitation and Recycling Centre

43400 Le Chambon sur Lignon: Pause Café,
Rte du Stade – La Levée Ferrier;
tel: (0) 71 65 84 78 (acc 16)

Emergency Accommodation

94260 Fontenay sous Bois: Fort de Nogent,
bld du 25 août 1944; (acc 160)

13015 Marseille: La Madrague, 110 chemin de
la Madrague Ville; tel: (0) 91 95 92 31
(acc 364)

92200 Neuilly sur Seine: L'Amirale Georgette
Gogibus, 14 quai du Général Koenig;
tel: (0) 55 62 02 95 (acc 50)

75019 Paris: Centre Mouzaïa , 66 Rue de la
Mouzaïa; tel: (0) 1 42 06 50 20 (acc 120)

Emergency Day Centres with orientation services

59140 Dunkerque Cedex 1: Au Cœur de
l'Espoir, 39 rue de la Verrerie, BP 130;
tel: (0) 3 28 29 09 37 (acc 100)

75003 Paris: ESI Saint-Martin, Face au 31 bld
St Martin; tel: (0) 40 27 80 07 (acc 200)

75019 Paris: La Maison du Partage,
32 rue Bouret; tel: (0) 53 38 41 30 (acc 200)

Mother and Baby Home

75019 Paris: Résidence Maternelle Les Lilas,
9 ave de la Porte des Lilas;
tel: (0) 48 03 81 90 (acc 77)

Children's Home

35400 Saint-Malo: Les enfants de
Rochebonne, 23 ave Paul Turpin,
tel: (0) 99 40 21 94 (acc 56)

Training Centres for Children and Young People

30000 Nîmes: La Villa Blanche Peyron, 122 Impasse Calmette; tel: (0) 66 04 99 40 (acc 44)

34093 Montpellier Cedex 5: Institut Nazareth, 13 rue de Nazareth; tel: (0) 4 99 58 21 21 (acc 94)

67100 Strasbourg: Le Foyer du Jeune Homme, 42 ave Jean Jaurès; tel: (0) 88 84 16 50 (acc 105)

68100 Mulhouse: Foyer Marie-Pascale Péan, 42 rue de Bâle; tel: (0) 89 42 14 77 (acc 43)

Centres for Children and Young People (Day Care)

69007 Lyon: L'Arche de Noé, 5 rue Félissent; tel: (0) 78 58 29 66 (acc 232)

Rehabilitation Centres for the Impaired

45410 Artenay: Château d'Auvilliers; tel: (0) 38 80 00 14 (acc 203)

13013 Marseille: Résidence Georges Flandre, 94 Chemin Notre-Dame de la Consolation; tel: (0) 91 61 81 10 (acc 42)

74560 Monnetier-Mornex: Résidence Leirens, Chemin St Georges; tel: (0) 50 31 23 12 (acc 62)

93370 Montfermeil: MAS Le Grand Saule, 2 ave des Tilleuls; tel: (0) 41 70 30 40 (acc 55)

Eventide Homes

35400 Saint-Malo: Résidence Boris Antonoff; tel: (0) 99 21 08 70 (acc 86)

42028 Saint-Etienne Cedex 01: La Sarrazinière; tel: (0) 77 62 17 92 (acc 157)

47400 Tonneins: Le Soleil d'Automne; tel: (0) 53 88 32 00 (acc 50)

60500 Chantilly: L'Arc-en-Ciel; tel: (0) 44 57 00 33 (acc 63)

67000 Strasbourg: Résidence Laury Munch; tel: (0) 88 22 83 60 (acc 144)

83230 Bormes les Mimosas: Res Olive et Germain Braquehais; tel: (0) 94 02 37 00 (acc 90)

68580 Seppois le Bas: Résidence Heimelig; tel: (0) 89 40 02 82 (acc 70)

68640 Waldighoffen: Résidence Heimelig; tel: (0) 89 40 03 34 (acc 70)

79800 La Mothe Saint-Héray: Notre Maison; tel: (0) 49 05 00 38 (acc 82)

Senior Housing

75014 Paris: 9 bis, Villa Cœur-de-Vey; tel: (0) 45 43 38 75

93230 Romainville: 2 rue Vassou

Short-term Care Home and Services

07800 St Georges-les-Bains: Le Château; tel: (0) 75 60 81 72 (acc 50)

Conference and Holiday Centre

30530 Chamborigaud: Chausse; tel/fax: (0) 66 61 47 08 (acc 100)

BELGIUM REGION

Regional Headquarters: Place du Nouveau Marché aux Grains, 34, 1000 Brussels; tel: [32] (0) 513 39 04; websites: www.armeedusalut.be; www.legerdesheils.be

Regional Officer: Maj Mike Stannett
Finance: Maj Marc Dawans

SOCIAL SERVICES
Hostels for Men

1000 Brussels, Foyer Georges Motte, bld d'Ypres 24; tel: (0) 217 61 36 (acc 75)

1000 Brussels, 'Le Foyer', Centre d'accueil, rue Bodeghem 27-29, 1000 Brussels; tel: (0) 512 17 92 (acc 70)

Family Aid (EU Food Distribution)

1000 Brussels, Service d'Aide aux familles: bld d'Ypres 26, tel: (0) 223 10 44

Guidance Centre (Housing Help and Debt Counselling)

1180 Brussels, 102 rue de l'Église Ste Anne; tel: (0) 414 19 16

Refugee Centre

1000 Brussels, 'Foyer Selah', bld d'Ypres 28, tel: (0) 219 01 77 (acc 90)

Mother and Children's Home

1180 Brussels, Maison de la Mère et de l'Enfant, Chaussée de Drogenbos 225, tel: (0) 376 17 01 (acc mothers 14, children 25)

Children's Home

1180 Uccle-Brussels, 'Clair Matin', rue des Trois Rois 88, tel: (0) 376 17 40 (acc 41)

SHOPS

2018 Antwerpen: Ballaerstraat 94;
  tel: (0)3/237 28 68
1000 Brussels, Foyer Georges Motte, bld
  d'Ypres 24 ; tel: (0)2/210 89 24
7390 Quaregnon: 81 rue Monsville;
  tel: (0)65/78 30 08

**CONFERENCE AND YOUTH
CENTRE**

4900 Spa, Villa Meyerbeer, rue de Barisart 256;
  tel: (0) 77 49 00

Members of the International Theological Council

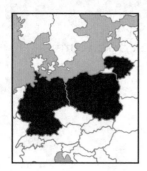

GERMANY AND LITHUANIA TERRITORY

Territorial leaders:
Colonels Patrick and Anne-Dore Naud

Territorial Commander:
Colonel Patrick Naud (1 June 2011)

Chief Secretary:
Lieut-Colonel Marsha-Jean Bowles (1 June 2011)

Territorial Headquarters: 50677 Köln, Salierring 23-27, Germany

Tel: [49] (221) 20 8190; email: thq@heilsarmee.de

website: www.thq@heilsarmee.de

Salvation Army work in Germany began in Stuttgart on 14 November 1886 through the persistent sale of the Swiss *Kriegsruf* by Staff-Captain Fritz Schaaff who, after being converted in New York, was stationed in Switzerland and could not resist the call to bring the message over the border into his fatherland.

The Salvation Army was first registered as a limited company in Berlin in 1897 and was recognised throughout Germany as a church and public corporation on 10 October 1967 by law in Nordrhein-Westfalen. It is recognised as a religious association with public rights in the states of Berlin, Hessen, Schleswig-Holstein and Baden-Württemberg.

Salvation Army work in Lithuania having begun in 1998, the Germany Territory was redesignated the Germany and Lithuania Territory in September 2005. That same month, 'Project Warsaw' was launched to begin the Army's work in Poland (under IHQ) and on 1 July 2008 the Germany and Lithuania Territory took responsibility for this work when a regional office for Poland was established in Dresden.

Zone: Europe
Countries included in the territory: Germany, Lithuania, Poland
'The Salvation Army' in German: Die Heilsarmee; in Lithuanian: Isganymo Armija; in Polish: Armia
    Zbawienia
Languages in which the gospel is preached: German, Lithuanian, Polish
Periodicals: *Danke*, *Heilsarmee-Forum, Heilsarmee-Magazin* (all German)

INSPIRATION was the theme of the 2013 territorial congress held in Siegen, under the leadership of the then world leader, General Linda Bond.

Commissioner Nancy Roberts (WSWM) visited the territory to lead a women's weekend and Commissioner Birgitte Brekke-Clifton (IS) was the special guest at the Territorial Leaders' Conference.

The territory held its first Brengle Institute for soldiers in conjunction with the Switzerland, Austria and Hungary Territory and a Design for Life weekend was held in Siegen. One hundred people joined at Plön for a music camp and several delegates from the territory attended the first European Anti-Human Trafficking Conference held in Budapest. The territory also conducted a Facebook campaign for victims of human trafficking.

The Communication and Marketing Department initiated a billboard campaign in eight German cities where posters depicting The Salvation Army's work with disadvantaged people were displayed for a month.

As part of the territorial 'Vision 2030', a new corps opening took place in Augsburg. The first meeting saw 15 people from the neighbourhood attending, along with 12 Salvationists from Munich Corps.

A Sports Ministry conference was held in Altenkirchen in November, with nearly 30 delegates from nine European territories participating. The European Territorial Children's and Youth Secretaries' Network and the European Scouts and Guides Network also met in Altenkirchen for meetings.

Staff and clients of the William Booth Centre in Munich participated in the European Homeless Cup where refreshments were distributed. Jakob Junker House Drop-In and Counselling Centre in Hamburg celebrated 20 years of ministry in September.

A highlight for 48 adults and children was the Patchwork Family Holiday for underprivileged families. The week included fun, practical learning and Bible teaching.

The year saw severe flooding in Germany, bringing distress and hardship to many. The corps in Meissen, Leipzig and Dresden assisted people with practical help and spiritual counselling during that period.

In Poland a new regional officer and a new leader for Warsaw Corps were appointed. One of the highlights in Poland was a holiness seminar attended by more than 20 people. A team from the USA Western Territory ministered in Warsaw, Starachowice and Malbork for six weeks.

In Lithuania more than 340 children attended a summer festival and 20 young people enjoyed a new year event held at Klaipeda Corps. The selling of second-hand clothing was very well received.

STATISTICS

Officers 132 (active 68 retired 64) **Aux-Capts** 8 **Cadets** 2 **Field Sergeants** 5 **Employees** 806 **Corps** 45 **Outposts** 10 **Institutions** 40 **Senior Soldiers** 880 **Adherent Members** 492 **Junior Soldiers** 73

STAFF

Women's Ministries: Col Anne-Dore Naud (TPWM) Lt-Col David Bowles (TSAFM with responsibility for Sports Ministries)
Seniors and Retired Officers Ministries: Majs Andrea and Stephan Weber
Family Ministries: Maj Stefanie Honsberg
Sec for Business Admin: Maj Hartmut Leisinger
Finance: Mr Hans-Joachim Bode
Property: Mr Rainer Wiebe
Trade: Mrs Margarete Olligschläger
Information Technology: Maj Hartmut Leisinger
Sec for Personnel: Maj Annette Preuss
Training and Cadets: Maj Annette Preuss
Sec for Programme: Maj Marianne Meyner
Spiritual Life Development: Maj Frank Honsberg
Children and Youth: Capts Oliver and Christiane Walz
Music and Gospel Arts: B/M Heinrich Schmidt
Sec for Communications and Marketing: Mr Andreas Quiring
Editorial: Mrs Romy Schneider
Fundraising: Mr Hans-Dieter Alzer
Public Relations: Mrs Rebekka Cuhls
Social Media: Mr Dave Naithani
German Staff Band: B/M Heinrich Schmidt
Projects Officer: Maj Philippa Smale

Germany and Lithuania Territory

DIVISIONS

North-East: 12159 Berlin, Fregestr 13/14;
tel: (0) 30-850 72980; email:
dhq-nordost@heilsarmee.de
Majs Reinhold and Ruth Walz
South-West: 45888 Gelsenkirchen,
Hohenzollernstr 83; tel: (0) 0209-14908 546;
email: dhq-suedwest@heilsarmee.de
Majs Paul-William and Margaret Saue Marti

INVESTIGATION

Heckerstr 85, 34121 Kassel;
tel: (0) 561 2889945; email:
suchdienst@heilsarmee.de

SENIOR CITIZENS' RESIDENCES

12159 Berlin, Dickhardtstr 52-53 (acc apts 42)
45127 Essen, Hoffnungsstr 23 (acc apts 25)
44623 Herne, Koppenbergshof 2 (acc apts 11)
50858 Köln, Rosenweg 1-5 (acc apts 42)
68159 Mannheim, G3, 1 + 20 (acc apts 31)
68165 Mannheim, Augartenstr 43, Haus Marie
Engelhardt (acc apts 19)
75175 Pforzheim, Pflügerstr 37-43 (acc apts 30)

SOCIAL SERVICES
Counselling

79110 Freiburg, Elsässer Str 7; tel: (0)761-89 44 92
20359 Hamburg, Counselling Centre, Talstr 11;
tel: (0) 40-31 65 43
21073 Hamburg, Counselling Centre for
Housing, Zur Seehafenbrücke 20;
tel: (0) 40 3095360
22117 Hamburg, Counselling Centre 'Park-In',
Oststeinbeckerweg 2 h; tel: (0) 40-713 65 64

Children's Day Nursery

12159 Berlin, Fregestr 13-14; (acc 55)

Drop-in Cafés

Freiburg; Hamburg; Lübeck; Nürnberg

Hostels

60314 Frankfurt, Windeckstr 58-60;
tel: (0) 69-49 74 33 (acc 36)
73033 Göppingen, Marktstr 58;
tel: (0) 7161-7 42 17; (acc 34)
37073 Göttingen, Untere-Maschstr-Str 13b;
tel: (0) 551-4 24 84 (acc 23)
23552 Lübeck, Engelsgrube 62-64;
tel: (0) 451-7 33 94 (acc 45)
81369 München, Steinerstr 20;
tel: (0) 89-26 71 49 (acc 44)
70176 Stuttgart, Silberburgstr 139;
tel: (0) 711-61 09 67/68 (acc 40)

65189 Wiesbaden, Schwarzenbergstr 7;
tel: (0) 611-70 12 68 (acc 210)

Nursing Homes

14163 Berlin, Goethestr 17-21; (acc 51)
47805 Krefeld, Voltastr 50; (acc 63)

Therapeutic Rehabilitation Institutions

14197 Berlin, Hanauer Str 63;
tel: (0) 30-8 20 08 40; (acc 45)
22453 Hamburg, Borsteler Chaussee 23;
tel: (0) 40-514 314 0 (acc 76)
34123 Kassel, Eisenacherstr 18 (acc 95)
50825 Köln, Marienstr 116/118;
tel: (0)221-955 6090 (acc 71)
90443 Nürnberg, Gostenhofer Hauptstr 47-49;
tel: (0) 911-28 730 (acc 232)

Therapeutic Workshops

22453 Hamburg, Borsteler Chaussee 23
90443 Nürnberg, Leonhardstr 17-21

Women's Hostels

34134 Kassel-Niederzwehren, Am Donarbrunnen
32; tel: (0) 561-43113 (acc 7)
90443 Nürnberg, Gostenhofer Hauptstr 65;
tel: (0) 911-272 3600 (acc 12)
65197 Wiesbaden, Königsteinerstr 24;
tel: (0) 611-80 67 58 (acc 45)

CONFERENCE AND HOLIDAY CENTRE

24306 Plön, Seehof, Steinberg 3-4;
tel: (0) 4522-5088200; email:
seehof@heilsarmee.de
Conference and Holiday Home (acc 72 + 36)
Youth Camp (acc 52) Camping Ground and
3 holiday chalets and flats

LITHUANIA

Officer-in-Charge:
Capt Susanne Kettler-Riutkenen

Isganymo Armija, Lietuvoje, Tiltu 18, LT 91246
Klaipeda; tel: [370] 46-310634;
email: klaipeda@isganymo-armija.org

POLAND

Regional Officer: Maj Joan Münch

Regional Office: Ul. Bialostocka 11, m. 21, 03-
748 Warszawa, Poland; tel: [48] 691 283 891;
email: joan.muench@armia-zbawienia.pl

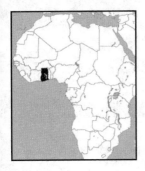

GHANA TERRITORY

Territorial leaders:
Colonels Joseph and Angélique Lukau

Territorial Commander:
Colonel Joseph Lukau (1 Jun 2014)

Chief Secretary:
Lieut-Colonel Samuel Kwao Oklah
(1 Jan 2011)

Territorial Headquarters: PO Box CT452 Cantonments, Accra, Ghana

Tel: [233] (21) 776 971; email: saghana@gha.salvationarmy.org

Salvation Army operations began in Ghana in 1922 when Lieutenant King Hudson was commissioned to 'open fire' in his home town of Duakwa. Ensign and Mrs Charles Roberts were also appointed to pioneer work in Accra. Work in neighbouring Togo was officially recognised on 1 April 2011

Zone: Africa
Countries included in the territory: Ghana, Togo
'The Salvation Army' in Ga: Yiwalaheremo Asrafoi Le; in Fante and Twi: Nkwagye Dom Asraafo; in Ewe: Agbexoxo Srafa Ha La
Languages in which the gospel is preached: Bassa, Builsa, Dangme, English, Ewe, Fante, Frafra, Ga, Gola, Grushia, Twi
Periodical: *Salvationist Newsletter*

IN RECOGNITION that the territory is moving toward the centenary of the Army's work in this part of west Africa, a series reflecting on its journey using the theme 'Walking in the light of God' was commenced.

Various achievements and milestones were marked, including a number of property improvements at the Begoro Health Centre and Begoro Rehabilitation Centre funded by projects, personal donations and internally-generated funds. Such improvements help affirm the status and credibility of the centres as well as improving the working environment.

A ground-breaking ceremony took place at the Duakwa Health Centre. This development – the first of its kind

in west Africa – will provide specialist care for children affected by cerebral palsy. Much of the funding is generated from within the country, sourced in partnership with various fund-raising agencies.

The territory continued its five-year project to improve facilities and infrastructure at 10 Salvation Army schools, funded by the Netherlands and Czech Republic Territory. A team from The Netherlands travelled to Tongo to assist with the construction of school classrooms. Team members also raised funds to plant mango trees around the perimeter of the school and rebuild the adjacent corps hall that had been seriously damaged in a storm.

The completion of a number of

toilet blocks at Salvation Army schools funded through the Sweden One-Day Project was also recognised.

In response to the challenge to generate an increasing proportion of its operational budget from within the country, a business forum was established. This saw Salvationists and businessmen join together to identify ways and means by which resources and funds might be generated to increase self-reliance and independence. As well as raising funds in response to specific needs, the group also considered other means of generating long-term funding sources.

In celebration of the role of women within the territory, a women's congress was held under the leadership of Commissioner Florence Malabi (ZSWM). More than 3,000 women gathered in Kumasi for a weekend of worship, fellowship and mutual encouragement. The meetings included a number of cultural expressions, including traditional dance and the presentation of crafts, fruit and vegetables.

The work undertaken at the Army's health centre at Ba was commended in a survey of medical work undertaken by religious organisations commissioned by the Christian Health Association of Ghana. It was noted that the number of people attending the centre was significantly higher than in previous years. This increase, together with the associated rise in the quality of service, was largely due to the management implementing a faith-based facilitation initiative.

STATISTICS

Officers 264 (active 212 retired 52) **Cadets** 17 **Employees** 1,911

Corps 115 **Societies** 142 **Schools** 201 **Health Centres** 9 **Social Centres** 8 **Day Care Centres** 73

Senior Soldiers 20,033 **Junior Soldiers** 4,616

Personnel serving outside territory Officers 8

STAFF

Women's Ministries: Col Angélique Lukau (TPWM) Lt-Col Philomina Oklah (TSWM) Lt- Col Beauty Zipingani (TDCM) Maj Jemima Amakye (TJHLS)

Business Administration: Lt-Col Langton Zipingani

 Audit: Major Francis Amakye

 Finance: Capt Stephen Adu-Gyan

Personnel: Lt-Col James Oduro

Programme: tba

Child Sponsorship: Maj Comfort Amankwah

Communications and External Relations: Mr Kofi Sakyiamah

Editor: Ag.Lt-Colonel James Oduro

Extension Training: Maj Samuel Agyei Dankwah

Human Resources: Lt-Col Elizabeth Oduro

Medical, Social and Community Services: Maj Heather Craig

Music: Capt Asare Bediako Tawiah

Projects: Maj Isaac Amankwah

Property: Maj Andrews Oyortey

Public Relations: Capt Bright Kumeto

Retired Officers: Lt-Col Elizabeth Oduro

Schools: Mr William Boateng

Spiritual Life Development: Maj Graeme Craig

Territorial Band: B/M Emmanuel Hackman

Territorial Songsters: S/L Titus Ofori Arkoh

Trade Manager: Maj Beatrice Oyortey

Training: Lt-Col Isaac Danso

Youth/Candidates: Maj Anthony Wiafe

Children Ministries Officer: Maj Gloria Wiafe

DIVISIONS

Accra: PO Box 166 Tema; tel: (022) 215 530; Majs Stephen and Cecilia Boadu

Akim Central: PO Box AS 283, Asamankese; tel: (081) 23 585; Majs Edward and Catherine Kyei

Ashanti Central: PO Box 15, Kumasi; tel: (051) 240 16; Majs Godfried and Felicia Oduro

Ashanti North: c/o PO Box 477, Mampong, Ashanti; Maj Christiana Oduraa

Central: PO Box 62, Agona Swedru; tel: (041) 20 285; Majs Peter and

Grace Oduro-Amoah

Nkawkaw: PO Box 3, Nkawkaw;
tel: (0842) 22 208; Maj Jonas and Capt
Constance Ampofo

Volta: PO Box 604, Ho, Volta Region;
Majs Edmund and Grace Abia

West Akim: PO Box 188, Akim Oda;
tel: (0882) 2 305; Maj Edward and Mercy
Addison

DISTRICTS

Brong Ahafo: PO Box 1454, Sunyani;
tel: (061) 23 513; Maj Alexander Siaw

East Akim: PO Box KF 1218, Koforidua E/R;
tel: (081) 22 580; Maj Modesto Kudedzi

Northern: PO Box 233, Bolgatanga;
tel: (072) 22 030; Maj Isaac Otsiwah

Western: PO Box 178, Sekondi, C/R;
tel: (031) 23 763; Maj Paul Asante

TRAINING COLLEGE

PO Box CE 11991, Tema; tel: (022) 306 252/253

EXTENSION TRAINING CENTRE

PO Box CT 452, Cantonments, Accra;
tel: (021) 776 971

HEALTH CENTRES

Accra Urban Aid: PO Box CT 452,
Cantonments, Accra; tel: (021) 230 918
(acc 11, including maternity)
Accra Urban Aid Outreach: PO Box CT 452,
Cantonments, Accra; tel: (021) 246 764
(mobile outreach for street children)
Adaklu-Sofa: PO Box 604, Ho, V/R
(acc 4, including maternity)
Anum: PO Box 17, Senchi, E/R
(acc 11, including maternity)
Ba: PO Box 8, Ba, C/R (acc 4, including
maternity)
Begoro: PO Box 10, Begoro, E/R (acc 10,
including maternity)
Duakwa: PO Box 2, Agona Duakwa, C/R
(acc 30, including maternity)
Wenchi: PO Box 5, Wenchi, Akim Oda
(acc 8, including maternity)
Wiamoase: PO Box 14, Wiamoase, Ashanti;
tel: (051) 32 613

EDUCATION

Sub-primary Schools 73, Primary Schools 78,
Junior Secondary Schools 44, Senior
Secondary Schools 3

SOCIAL WORK

Adaklu-Sofa Vocational Training Centre
Anidasofie Street Girls' Training Centre, Accra;
Begoro Rehabilitation Centre
Child Care Training Centre, Baa
Malnutrition Centre, Agona Duakwa
Rehabilitation Centre, Wiamoase, Ashanti
Voluntary Counselling and Testing Centre, Accra

TOGO (UNDER THQ)

Officer-in-Charge: Capt Godwin Kumeto

GHANA: Newly-enrolled soldiers 'sign' their
articles of war

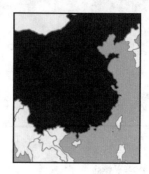

HONG KONG AND MACAU COMMAND

Command leaders:
Lieut-Colonels Ian and Wendy Swan

Officer Commanding:
Lieut-Colonel Ian Swan (1 Jul 2013)

General Secretary:
Major On Dieu-Quang (1 Oct 2012)

Command Headquarters: 11 Wing Sing Lane, Yaumatei, Kowloon, Hong Kong

Postal address: PO Box 70129, Kowloon Central Post Office, Kowloon, Hong Kong

Tel: [852] 2332 4531; email: Hongkong@hkt.salvationarmy.org;

website: www.salvation.org.hk

In March 1930, at a meeting held at Government House, Hong Kong, The Salvation Army was requested to undertake women's work in the crown colony, a work pioneered by Majors Dorothy Brazier and Doris Lemon. This work was directed from Peking until, in 1935, the South China Command was established in Canton to promote wide evangelistic and welfare operations. In 1939 Hong Kong became the Army's administrative centre. Later, the inclusion of the New Territories determined that the Command Headquarters move to Kowloon. Since 1951 the General of The Salvation Army has been recognised as a Corporation Sole. From 1993, disaster relief and community development projects have been carried out in mainland China. In 1999, a pioneer officer was appointed to the Special Administrative Region of Macau and Salvation Army work began there officially on 25 March 2000. In 2001, an officer was appointed to the North/North Eastern Project Office in Beijing.

Zone: South Pacific and East Asia

Regions included in the command: Hong Kong and Macau (Special Administrative Regions of the People's Republic of China) and Mainland China

'The Salvation Army' in Cantonese: Kau Sai Kwan; in Filipino: Hukbo ng Kaligtasan; in Putonghua: Jiu Shi Jun

Languages in which the gospel is preached: Cantonese, English, Filipino, Putonghua

Periodicals: *Army Scene, The War Cry*

ON 7 JULY 2013, the command Salvationists and friends expressed their joyous welcome and warm greetings to the new command leaders Lieut-Colonels Ian and Wendy Swan (OC/CPWM).

The Salvation Army Centaline Charity Fund Yau Tong Kindergarten was opened on 2 October providing pre-school educational services for up to 205 children aged between three and six years.

Three cadets entered the training college as part of the Heralds of Grace

Session to commence their in-house training in August.

The Salvation Army Joy Family Integrated Services Centre in Macau commenced services on 13 September, providing preventive, supportive and remedial assistance to drug and gambling addicts.

In October, Commissioner Gillian Downer (IS) visited the command and joined with Salvationists and friends at the united holiness meeting at the William Booth Secondary School hall. Lieut-Colonel Ian Swan introduced the theme 'You are loved' in his sermon and encouraged all comrades and friends to be ready to serve the Lord.

The Salvation Army flag day – a fund-raising activity – was held on 15 March 2014. More than 6,000 flag sellers from corps, The Salvation Army Educational and Social Services units, and other volunteers participated. In excess of HK$900,000 was raised for the units in Tung Chung, Kowloon City and Kwai Chung to help less fortunate families.

STATISTICS
Officers 55 (active 43 retired 12)
Employees 2,482
Corps 17 **Outpost** 1 **Institutions** 20 **Schools** 6
Kindergartens 7 **Nursery Schools** 17
Social Centres and Hotels 81
Senior Soldiers 2,461 **Adherent Members** 31
Junior Soldiers 343

STAFF
Women's Ministries: Lt-Col Wendy Swan (CPWM) Maj Ip Kan Ming-chun, Connie (CSWM)
Business Administration: Ms Deirdre Ashe
China Development: Capt Lam Yin-ming Jeremy
Community Relations: Envoy Simon Wong

Editor/Literary: Capt Chan Tsui Heung-Ying Minny
Educational Services: Dr Cheng Kai Yuen Carl
Emergency Services: Envoy Simon Wong
Human Resources: Ms Winnie Chui
Property: Envoy Daniel Hui Wah-lun
Sec for Personnel: Maj David Ip Kam-yuen
Sec for Programme: Capt Sara Tam Mei-shun
Social: Ms Irene Leung Pui Yiu
Trade: Mr Rico Lai
Training: Lt-Colonel Wendy Swan

DIVISION
1 Lung Chu St, Tai Hang Tung, Kowloon, HK; tel: 2195 0222; Maj Susan Siu-suen Wun

OFFICER TRAINING COLLEGE
1 Lung Chu St, Tai Hang Tung, Kln, PO Box 70129, Kowloon Central PO, Kln, HK; tel: 2783 2369/2195 0203

GLOBAL CHINESE MINISTRY TRAINING CENTRE
1 Lung Chu St, Tai Hang Tung, Kln, PO Box 70129, Kowloon Central PO, Kln, HK; tel: 2195 0205

CHINA DEVELOPMENT
Hong Kong Head Office: tel: (852) 2783 2288; China Development Sec: Capt Jeremy Lam Yin-ming; email: cdd@hkt.salvationarmy.org
North/Northeast Regional Project Office: Room 903, Unit 2, Block 8, Yang Guang Hua Yuan, Ma Jia Pu Dong Lu, 101 Hao Yuan, Feng Tai District, Beijing 100068, China tel: [86] (10) 5570 3907/3917;
Yunnan Project Office – China: 6D, Unit 1, Block 8, Yin Hai Hot Spring Garden, Northern District, 173 Guan Xing Rd, Guan Shang, Kunming 650200, Yunnan, China; tel: [86] (871) 67166 111/222;

EDUCATIONAL SERVICES
Kindergartens
Centaline Charity Fund: NT (acc 135)
Chan Kwan Tung: Kln (acc 316)
Fu Keung: NT (acc 300), nursery (acc 56)
Hing Yan: NT (acc 270) nursery (acc 108)
Ng Kwok Wai Memorial: NT (acc 360)
Ping Tin: Kln (acc 270) nursery (acc 42)
Tin Ka Ping: NT (acc 610)
Crèches (1 month-2 years)
North Point: HK (acc 28 full-day)
Pak Tin: Kln (acc 16 full-day)

Nursery Schools (2-6 years)
Catherine Booth: Kln (acc 110)
Hoi Fu: Kln (acc 118)
Jat Min: NT (acc 168)
Kam Tin: NT (acc 104)
Lai Chi Kok: Kln (acc 104)
Lei Muk Shue: NT (acc 116)
Lok Man: Kln (acc 145)
Ming Tak: Kln (acc 126)
North Point: HK (acc 28)
Pak Tin: Kln (acc 104)
Sam Shing: NT (acc 104)
Tai Wo Hau: NT (acc 126)
Tai Yuen: NT (acc 104)
Tin Ping: NT (acc 116)
Tsuen Wan: NT (acc 183)
Wah Fu: HK (acc 128)
Wo Che: NT (acc 168)

Primary Schools
Ann Wyllie Memorial School (acc 984)
Centaline Charity Fund School
   (acc 1,011)
Lam Butt Chung Memorial School
   (acc 1,290)
Tin Ka Ping School (acc 1,040)

Secondary School
William Booth Secondary School, Kln;
   (acc 1,120)

Special School
Shek Wu School, Sheung Shui, NT
   (acc 200)

GUEST ACCOMMODATION
Booth Lodge, 7/F, 11 Wing Sing Lane,
   Yaumatei, Kln; tel: (852) 2771 9266;
   email: boothlodge@salvationarmy.org.hk

RECYCLING PROGRAMME
Logistic Centre: 7/F Tat Ming Industrial
   Building, 44-52 Ta Chuen Ping St,
   Kwai Chung, NT; tel: 2332 4433
   email: Recycling@hkt.salvationarmy.org

Family Stores
Hong Kong; Aberdeen Store, Nam Cheong
   Store; North Point Store; Shau Kei Wan
   Store; Tin Hau Store; Wanchai Henessey
   Store; Western District Store; Yue Wan Store
Kowloon: Kwun Tong Store; Prince Edward
   Store; Tai Hang Tung Store; Whampoa Store;
   Yaumatei Store
Macau Store

SOCIAL SERVICES
Camp Service
Bradbury Camp: 6 Ming Fai Rd,
   Cheung Chau, HK; (acc 108)
Ma Wan Youth Camp: Ma Wan Island, HK; (acc 40)

Children and Youth Centres
Chuk Yuen: Kln
Lung Hang: Sin Sum House, Shatin, NT
Tai Wo Hau: Tai Wo Hau Community Centre,

Education and Employment Service
Education and Development Centre: 6 Salvation
   Army St, Wanchai, HK
The Integrated Employment Assistance
   Programme for Self-reliance (IEAPS): Flat 18,
   22/F, Tuen Mun Central Square, Tuen Mun

Integrated Services for Young People
Chaiwan: Podium Level Market Bldg, HK
Tai Po: Tai Man House, NT
Tuen Mun: Hing Ping House, NT
Tuen Mun East: Ancillary Facilities Block, NT
Yaumatei: Block 4, Prosperous Garden, Kln

School Social Work Services
Tuen Mun: G/F, 13-24 Hing Ping House,
   Tai Hing Estate, Tuen Mun, NT

Services for Young Night Drifters
Tuen Mun: 5/F Ancillary Facilities Block,
   Fu Tai Estate, 9 Tuen Kwai Rd,
   Tuen Mun, NT

Community Projects
Integrated Service for Street Sleepers: 1/F, GIC
   Bldg, 345A Shanghai St, Kln
Ngau Tam Mei Community Development
   Project: Kai Tak School, Wai Tsai Village,
   Yau Tam Mei, Yuen Long, NT
Sam Mun Tsai Community Development Project:
   31 Chim Uk Village, Shuen Wan, Tai Po, NT
Urban Renewal Social Service Team: G/F,
   Shop C, 182 Fuk Wa Street, Shamshuipo, Kln

Residential Care Service for Children and
   Youth
Tai Wo Hau Small Group Homes: NT:
   Home of Joy (acc 8)
   Home of Love (acc 8)
   Home of Peace (acc 8)
Ping Tin Small Group Homes: Kowloon:
   Home of Faithfulness (acc 8)
   Home of Goodness (acc 8)
   Home of Kindness (acc 8)

Hong Kong Island East Child Care Service:
Wan Tsui Home for Boys (acc 48)
Yue Wan Boys' Hostel (acc 15)

Family Support Centre
Tung Chung: No. 4, G/F. Ying Yat House,
Yat Tung Estate, Tung Chung, NT
Kowloon City: Flat C, 1/F. Po Shing Mansion,
157-159 Kowloon City Road, Tokwawan
Shamshuipo Family Support Networking Team:
Rm 69, 2/F Fuk Sing House,
63-69 Fuk Wing St, Shamshuipo, Kln

Temporary Shelter
Sunrise House: 323 Shun Ning Rd, Cheung Sha
Wan, Kln (acc 312)
Yee On Hostel: Unit 111-116, 1/F, Hoi Yu
House, Hoi Fu Court, Mongkok, Kln;
(acc 40)

Day Care Centres for Senior Citizens
Chuk Yuen: 141-150 Podium Level, Chui
Yuen House, Chuk Yuen (South) Estate, Kln
(acc 44)
Hoi Yu: G/F, Hoi Lam House, Hoi Fu Court, 2
Hoi Ting Rd, Mongkok, Kln (acc 44)
Tai Po: G/F. Wing B, Heng Yiu House, Fu Heng
Estate, Tai Po, NT (acc 64)

Rehabilitation Homes
Cheung Hong: 2/F & 3/F Hong Cheung Hse,
Cheung Hong Est, Tsing Yi, NT (acc 45)
Heng On Hostel: G/F, Heng Shan House, Heng
On Estate, Ma On Shan, NT (acc 62)
Lai King Home: 200-210 Lai King Hill Rd,
Kwai Chung, NT (acc 100)

Community Day Rehabilitation Services
Cheung Hong: 2/F & 3/F Hong Cheung Hse,
Cheung Hong Est, Tsing Yi, NT (acc 45)
Shaukeiwan: 456 Shaukeiwan Rd, Shaukeiwan,
HK (acc 40)
Tak Tin: G/F, Tak Yan House, Tak Tin Estate,
Lam Tin (acc 53)

Integrated Home Care Service Teams
Kwun Tong: Unit 1-2, Wing B, G/F, Tak Lung
House, Tak Tin Estate, Lam Tin, Kln
Sai Kung: 4/F, Po Kan House, Po Lam Estate,
Tseung Kwan O, Kln
Tai Po: G/F, Wing A, Heng Yiu House, Fu Heng
Estate, Tai Po, NT
Yau Tsim (Kowloon Central Office): G/F & 1/F,
Chee Sun Building, 161-165 Reclamation St,
Yaumatei
Yau Tsim (Yaumatei Office): 3/F, 11 Wing Sing
Lane, Yaumatei, Kln

Multi-service Centre for Senior Citizens
Yaumatei: 3/F 11 Wing Sing Lane, Yaumatei
Tai Po: 2/F - 3/F Tai Po Community Centre, 2
Heung Sze Wui Street, Tai Po Market, NT

Centres for Senior Citizens
Wai Fu: Unit 301-310, G/F Wah Kin House, Wah
Fu Est. Aberdeen, HK
Hoi Lam: 1/F, Hoi Yu Hse, Hoi Fu Court, 2 Hoi
Ting Road, MongKok
Nam Tai: G/F Nam Tai House, Nam Shan Estate,
ShamShuiPo
Chuk Yuen: 1-4/F Chuk Yuen (South) Est,
Community Centre, Kln
Tai Wo Hau: 1/F. 15 Tai Wo Hau Road, Tai Wo
Hau Community Centre, Kwai Chung

Elderly Special Projects
CDSMP: Rm 105, 6 Salvation Army Street, Wan
Chai, HK
Carer Project: 3/F, 11 Wing Sing Lane,
Yaumatei, Kln
Kwong Wah Hospital Integrated Discharge
Support Programme for Elderly Patients – The
Salvation Army Home Support Team:
161-165 Reclamation Street, Yaumatei, Kln
Palliative Care in Residential Care Homes for the
Elderly: Rm 105, 6 Salvation Army Street,
Wan Chai, HK
Promotional Scheme on Life and Death Journey:
Rm 105, 6 Salvation Army Street, Wan Chai, HK

Residences for Senior Citizens
Po Lam: 4/F Po Kan Hse, Po Lam Estate, Tseung
Kwan O, Kln (acc 105)
Tak Tin: 2/F Tak King Hse, Tak Tin Estate, Lam
Tin (acc 67)
Hoi Tai: 2/F, Hoi Tai Hse, Hoi Fu Crt, 2 Hoi
Ting Road, MongKok (acc 100)
Nam Ming: G/F Nam Ming House, Nam Shan
Estate, ShamShuiPo (acc 38)
Tai Wai: 16 Tung Lo Wan Hill Rd, Tai Wai,
Shatin, NT (acc 136)
Kam Tin: 103 Kam Tin Rd, Yuen Long, NT
(acc 150)
Lung Hang: 3 & 4/F Wing Sam Hse, Lung Hang
Estate, Shatin
Nam Shan: 1 & 2/F Nam Ming House, Nam Shan
Estate, ShamShuiPo (acc 102)

Rehabilitation Special Projects
Share-Care Project: 200-210 Lai King Hill Rd,
Kwai Chung, NT
SKY Family and Child Development Centre:
Room 403, 6 Salvation Army Street, Wanchai

Hong Kong and Macau Command

Integrated Service for Rehabilitation
Heng On Integrated Vocational Rehabilitation
Service: G/F, Heng Kong House,
Heng On Estate, Ma On Shan, Shatin (acc 304)
Talent Shop: G/F, Heng Sing House,
Heng On Estate, Ma On Shan, Shatin

Senior Citizens Talent Advancement Projects
Tung Tau Centre: Kln
Kwun Tong

Social Enterprises
Digital Plus: Kln
Fitness Box: NT
Shatin Family Store: NT
Shatin Park Food Kiosk: NT
Tuen Mun Family Store: NT

HONG KONG: Volunteers who took part in The Salvation Army
Flag Day fund-raising activity

INDIA NATIONAL SECRETARIAT

37 Lenin Sarani (1st Floor), Dharamtala St, PO Box 8994,
Kolkata – 700 013, West Bengal, India

Tel: [91] (0) 2249 7210
email:IND_Secretariat@ind.salvationarmy.org; website: www.salvationarmy.org/india

India is The Salvation Army's oldest mission field. Frederick St George de Latour Tucker, of the Indian Civil Service, read a copy of *The War Cry*, became a Salvationist and, as Major Tucker (later Commissioner Booth-Tucker), took the Indian name of Fakir Singh and commenced The Salvation Army's work in Bombay on 19 September 1882. The adoption of Indian food, dress, names and customs gave the pioneers ready access to the people, especially in the villages.

In addition to evangelistic work, various social programmes were inaugurated for the relief of distress from famine, flood and epidemic. Educational facilities such as elementary, secondary, higher secondary and industrial schools, cottage industries and settlements were provided for the disadvantaged classes. Medical work originated in Nagercoil in 1895 when Captain (Dr) Harry Andrews set up a dispensary at the headquarters there. The medical work has grown from this. Work among the then Criminal Tribes began in 1908 at government invitation.

The Salvation Army is registered as a Guarantee Company under the Indian Companies Act 1913.

Publication: *The War Cry* (English)

THE National Secretariat for India serves the six Salvation Army territories within the country.

The Conference of Indian Leaders (COIL), established in 1989, meets annually to coordinate national Salvation Army affairs and give direction to the National Secretariat.

Several national offices had been established in earlier years, including the Editorial and Literary Office and the Audit Office. Since the establishment of The Salvation Army Health Services Advisory Council (SAHSAC) in 1986, a regionally based National Secretariat evolved to provide support to many aspects of Salvation Army work in India.

An administrative reorganisation took place in 2008. This led to all the secretariat departments being brought together in one building under the leadership of the National Secretary with the result that the National Secretariat functions as a whole and not as separate departments.

THE SALVATION ARMY ASSOCIATION

Chairman: Comr Lalzamlova (IS, IHQ)
Secretary: Lt-Col Daniel Raju Dasari

NATIONAL SECRETARIAT

National Secretary: Lt-Col Daniel Raju Dasari
Administrator and Chaplain: Lt-Col Baby Sarojini Dasari
Business Administration: tba
Editorial and Communications: Maj Samraj Babu
Human Resources Development and Education: Maj Hnamte Lalramliana
Social, Health and Emergencies: Maj Raj Paul Thamalapakula
Women's Advisory Council: Maj C. Lalhriatpuii

THE SALVATION ARMY CHRISTIAN RETREAT CONFERENCE CENTRE

'Surrenden', 15-18 Orange Grove Rd, Coonoor – 643 101, Nilgiris Dt, Tamil Nadu, S India; tel: (0423) 2230242

INDIA CENTRAL TERRITORY

Territorial leaders:
Colonels Chelliah and Mallika Mony

Territorial Commander:
Colonel Chelliah Mony
(1 Jun 2014)

Chief Secretary:
Lieut-Colonel Jashwant Mahida
(1 Jul 2014)

**Territorial Headquarters: 31 (15) Ritherdon Road, Vepery,
Chennai 600 007**

Postal address: PO Box 453, Vepery, Chennai 600 007, India

Tel: [91] (044) 2532 3148; email: ICT_mail@ICT.salvationarmy.org;

website: www.salvationarmy.org/ind

The India Central Territory comprises three regions – North Tamil Nadu (Madras-Chennai), Karnataka and Andhra Pradesh. Salvation Army work was commenced at Vijayawada in Andhra Pradesh in 1895 by Staff Captain Abdul Aziz, a person of Muslim background, with his friend Mahanada. Captain Abdul attended a revival meeting led by Captain Henry Bullard in 1884 at Bangalore and subsequently dedicated himself to be a Salvation Army officer. The territory was named the India Central Territory in 1992, with its headquarters at Madras (Chennai).

Zone: South Asia

States included in the territory: Andhra Pradesh, Karnataka, Tamil Nadu

'The Salvation Army' in Tamil: Ratchania Senai; in Telugu: Rakshana Sinyamu

Languages in which the gospel is preached: English, Tamil, Telugu

Periodicals: *Home League Magazine, Udyogasthudu, Yovana Veerudu, Yudha Dwani*

DURING the year in review the territory experienced a great time of blessing with a new territorial headquarters being built and dedicated to the glory of God. Commissioners Paul R. and Carol Seiler (USA Central Territory) India Central's Partner in Mission, conducted the opening.

Five hundred and twenty-nine young people attended the territorial youth rally where the commissioners were the special guests. During the event the youth were encouraged to deepen their spiritual life and be motivated to lead a Christ-centred, Holy Spirit-filled life.

Twenty-four cadets from the Disciples of the Cross Session were commissioned and ordained and have successfully entered into the mission field with their respective tasks to fulfil.

The Women's Ministries Department conducted home league rallies in order to help the ladies understand their Christian purpose and to come closer to God. The 2013 women's ministries theme 'You are loved' assisted the women in understanding how much they are loved by God. Over 12,000 women took part in home league rallies throughout the territory, and raised finances to assist with the Helping Hand Project. The ongoing Community Empowerment Programme continued to support women in meeting their day-to-day needs.

The young people took part in a variety of programmes including sports ministries, a Bible reading contest, divisional youth rallies and young people's councils. The programmes encouraged the youth to be filled with the Spirit of the Lord. Besides the regular spiritual activities, the youth were also trained in capacity development and building a career.

As part of the mission, the health programmes conducted medical camps across the territory. Medical practitioners, as well as the Commissioner of Health and Medical Services (Tamil Nadu Government), who took part in a medical camp expressed admiration for the Army's dedicated services to the poor. Many of the poor and needy benefitted from various feeding programmes, and food and blanket distributions.

The Retired Officers Fellowship and the Officers' Children's Fellowship held events throughout the year. Women's ministry, finance, self-support, social and property seminars were also conducted.

Forty-three new soldiers were enrolled and spiritual programmes were conducted. These programmes helped to meet the needs of the soldiers and assisted them in growing stronger in the Lord.

Commissioners Lalzamlova and Nemkhanching (IS/ZSWM) conducted the installation of the new territorial leaders, Colonels Chelliah and Mallika Mony at the Central Corps, Bapatla.

STATISTICS
Officers 740 (active 572 retired 168) **Cadets** 31
Employees 520
Corps 281 **Outposts** 14 **Societies** 27 **Institutions** 14 **Schools and Colleges** 71
Day Care Centres 3 **Homes and Hostels** 20
Senior Soldiers 82,216 **Adherent Members** 15,328 **Junior Soldiers** 9,126

STAFF
Women's Ministries: Col Mallika Mony (TPWM) Lt-Col Ruth Mahida (TSWM) Lt-Col Gera Sion Kumari (THLS) Lt-Col A. Yesu Rajaswari (TLOMS) Maj Yesamma (S&GSS) Maj Mercy Manjula (TWDO)
Business Administration: Lt-Col Gera Thomas
Editor: Maj I.D. Ebenezer
Education: Maj T.C.H. Abraham
Emergencies: Maj M. Prakasha Rao
Finance: Maj K. Yesudas
Audit: Major K.Y. Dhana Kumar
Legal and Literature: Maj Abraham Lincoln
Personnel: Lt-Col A. Nathaniel
Human Resources Development: Maj G. Shanthi Babu
Programme: tba
Property and Projects: Maj B. Joseph
Public Relations Officer: A. Sundar Singh
Social: Maj Chella Wyclif
Sponsorship: Mr Jeevan Roy
Trade: Maj V. Yesupadam
Training: Maj S. Jayananda Rao
Candidates: Capt G. Shanthi Babu
Youth: Maj K. Prasad

DIVISIONS
Bapatla: Bapatla, Guntur District, 522 101; tel: (08643) 23931; tba
Chennai: 109 Gangadeeswara Koil St, Chennai 600 084; tel: (044) 2641 5021; Majs D. John Kumar & Mani Kumari

Eluru: Adivarapupet, Eluru, West Godavari
District, 534 005; tel: (08812) 2237484;
Majs D. Joshi & Leela Mani

Gudivada: Krishna District, 521 301;
tel: (08764) 4243524;
Majs K Suvarna Raju and Jhansi Bai

Hyderabad: 6D Walker Town, Padmarao Nagar,
Secunderabad, 500 025; tel: (040) 27502610;
tba

Nellore: Dargamitta, Nellore, 524 003;
tel: (0861) 2322 589;
Majs K. Sundara Rao and Dasaratna Kumari

Rajahmundry: Mallayapet, East Godavari
District, 533 105; tel: (0883) 6579200;
Majs K. Samuel Raju and Raja Kumari

Tanuku: West Godavari District, 534 211;
tel: 09989872902;
Majs O. Philip Raju and Lily

Tenali: Ithanagar, Tenali, Guntur District,
522 201; tel: (08644) 225949; Majs M.P.C.H.
Prasad and Krupamma

Vijayawada: nr Gymkhana Club,
Eastside H. No 26-191/2, Ghandi Nagar,
Vijayawada, 521 003; tel: (0866) 2575168;
Maj P. John William and Capt Ratna Sundari

DISTRICTS

Bangalore: Karnataka Main Rd, J.P. Nagar,
Bangalore, 560 078, Karnataka State;

Divi: PO Nagayalanka, Krishna District,
521 120; tel: (08671) 274991;
Maj G. Vijay Kumar

Machilipatnam: The Salvation Army,
Edepalli, Door No 15/344, Machilipatnam;
tel: (0867) 2224029; Maj J. Moshe

Mandavalli: Station Rd, Mandavalli, Krishna
District, 521 345; tel: (08677) 280503;
Maj D. Devadas

Prakasam: Stuartpuram, Guntur District, 522 317;
tel: (086432) 271131; Maj Chella Solomon Raju

EXTENSION AREAS
(under THQ)

Anantapur: The Salvation Army, H.No. 3616,
Jesus Nagar, Anantapur

Chittor: The Salvation Army, c/o Kamalamma
Samuel, D No 4 – 84, Balaji Nagar,
Greamspet, Chittor

Kadapa: The Salvation Army, c/o Mr M. Ajay
Kumar, D No 2/147 – 3, Balaji Nagar,
Kadapa, 515 003; tel: (098660) 77318

Khammam: The Salvation Army, c/o Ch.
Prabhakara Rao, D No 4-2-119, Sreenagar
Colony, nr Mamatha Medical College,
Khammam

Kurnool: The Salvation Army, c/o Y.A.

Evangeline, D No 40 – 448, A1A,
Gipson Colony, Kurnool; tel: (09391) 107852

Mahabub Nagar: The Salvation Army,
Venkateswara Colony, behind Jagadhamba
Temple, Laxmi Nager Colony, Mahabub Nagar
District

Medak: The Salvation Army, H. No. 4-7-
25/2/8/6, Plot No:64, Velugu Officer Rd,
Balajinagar Sangareddy, Medak

Nalgonda: The Salvation Army,
H No 7-1-155/D/19/4, Aruna Nilayam,
Srinagar Colony, Panagal Rd,
Nalgonda PO and District

Rangareddy: The Salvation Army, H No 20 – 45,
Madhuranagar, Shamshebad, Rangareddy
District

Srikakulam: The Salvation Army, H.No: 1-2-14,
Adivarapupet, Srikakulam Town,

Vizianagaram: The Salvation Army, H No: 103,
MIG -3, Phase - 3, Vuder Colony,
Vizianagaram - 535 003

Warangal: The Salvation Army, H No 7 – 91,
Gorry Kunta Crossroad, Labour Colony,
Warangal

TRAINING COLLEGE
Dargamitta, Nellore, 524 003;
tel: (0861) 2322687

EDUCATION
College (with hostel for boys and girls)
William Booth Junior College, Bapatla, Guntur
District, 522 101; tel: (0864) 3224259

Community College
Virugambakkam, Chennai

**High Schools (with hostels for boys
and girls)**
Bapatla: Guntur District, 522 101;
tel: (0864) 3224282 (acc 300)
Stuartpuram: Prakasam District, 522 317;
tel: (0864) 32271131 (acc 150)

Upper Primary Schools
Kondayapalem, Nellore, Nellore District

Elementary Schools (Telugu Medium)
Bapatla Division: Bethapudi, Chintayapalem,
Gudipudi, Kattivaripalem, Mallolapalem,
MR Nagar, Murukondapadu, Valluvaripalem,
Perlipadu, Pasumarthivaripalem, Pedapalli,
Parli Vadapalem, Yaramvaripalem, Yazali
Eluru Division: Bhogapuram, Dendulur,
Gopavaram, Gandivarigudem, Kovvali,

Musunur, Pathamupparru, Surappagudem,
Velpucharla
Gudivada Division: Chinaparupudi,
Edulamadalli, Guraza, Gajulapadu, Gudivada,
Kodur, Kancharlapalem, Kornipadu,
Mandavalli, Narasannapalem, Pedaparupudi,
Ramapuram
Nellore Division: Alluru, Buchireddipalem,
Chowkacherla, Iskapalli, Kakupalli,
Kanapartipadu, Mudivarthi, Modegunta,
North Mopur, Pallaprolu, Rebala
Tenali Division: Annavaram, Burripalem,
Chukkapallivaripalem, Duggirala,
Danthuluru, Emani, Ithanagar,
Kollipara, Kattivaram, Nambur, Nelapadu
Prakasam District: Cherukuru, Stuartpuram

Primary Schools (English Medium)
The Haven, 21 Thiru Narayanaguru Rd, Choolai,
Chennai 600 112; tel: (044) 26612784
Teachers' Colony, Vijayawada 500 008,
Krishna District; tel: (0866) 2479854
Hyderabad, 6D Walker Town, Padmarao
Nagar PO, Secunderabad 500 025
(with day care)

English Medium High School
Teachers' Colony, Vijayawada 500 008;
tel: (0866) 2479854

English Medium Matriculation School
The Haven, 21 Thiru Narayanaguru Rd, Choolai,
Chennai 600 112; tel: (044) 26612784

English Medium Upper Primary School
B.H. Puram, Mangalagir Post, Vijayawada

Residential School
Tissot Sunrise School, PB9 Bapatla, 522 101;
tel: (086432) 23336 (acc 125)

Vocational Training Centre
Adivarpet, Eluru, West Godivari District, 534 005
(with boys' hostel); tel: (08812) 550070

MEDICAL WORK
Evangeline Booth Hospital: Nidubrolu,
Guntur District, 522 123;
tel: (08643) 2522124 (acc 100)
Evangeline Booth Hospital (with home for the
aged), Bapatla, Guntur District, 522 101;
tel: (086432) 24134 (acc 75)

HIV/Aids Programme c/o THQ, Chennai

SOCIAL WORK
Children's Homes and Hostels

Boys' Hostels
Mallayyapet, Rajahmundry (acc 40)
Stuartpuram, Bapatla Mandal (acc 40)
Virugambakkam, Chennai (acc 80)

Girls' Hostels
Adivarpet, Eluru (acc 45)
Catherine Booth Girls' Hostel, Tenali (acc 30)
Dorcas Girls Hostel, Nagayalanka (acc 24)
Gudivada, Krishna District (acc 25)
'Haven', Virugambakkam, Chennai (acc 35)
'Home of Peace', Tanuku (acc 30)
Miriam Girls' Hostel, Kaikaluru, Mandavalli
(acc 30)
'Emma' Girls' Hostel, Nellore (acc 40)
'Stuart Girls Hostel', Stuartpuram, Bapatla
Mandal (acc 40)

Home for the Aged
Virugambakkam, Chennai; tel: (044) 23770400
(acc 70)

HRD and Social Centre
No 8, Perianna Maistry Street, Periamet
Chennai 600 003; tel: (044) 43033273

Working Women's Hostel
Catherine Booth Working Women's Hostel
No: 82, Nungambakkam High Road,
Chennai 600 034; tel: 30060325

Red Shield Guest House
15/31 Ritherdon Rd, Vepery, Chennai 600 007;
tel: (044) 2532 1821 (acc 60)

INDIA EASTERN TERRITORY

Territorial Commander:
Commissioner Lalngaihawmi (1 Jan 2011)
Chief Secretary:
Lieut-Colonel Davidson Varghese
(1 Jun 2014)

Territorial Headquarters: PO Box 5, Aizawl 796001, Mizoram, India

Tel: [91] 389 2322290 (EPABX) 2323755
email: IET_mail@IET.salvationarmy.org; website: www.salvationarmy.org/ind

Work in the region commenced on 26 April 1917 when Lieutenant Kawlkhuma, the first Mizo officer commissioned in India, returned to start the Army work. He was then joined by a group of earnest believers who shared his vision of an 'Army like a church, very much in line with The Salvation Army'. India Eastern became a separate command on 1 June 1991 and became a territory in 1993. Work was officially opened in Nepal on 26 April 2009.

Zone: South Asia
States included in the territory: Arunachal Pradesh, Assam, Manipur, Meghalaya, Mizoram, Nagaland, Sikkim, Tripura, West Bengal; also the Federal Democratic Republic of Nepal and Kingdom of Bhutan
'The Salvation Army' in Mizo: Chhandamna Sipai Pawl
Languages in which the gospel is preached: Adhibasi, Bengali, Bru, English, Hindi, Hmar, Manipuri (Meitei), Mizo, Nagamese, Nepali, Paite, Simte, Thadou, Vaiphai
Periodicals: *Sipai Tlangau* (Mizo *War Cry*), *The Officer* (Mizo), *Young Salvationist* (Mizo), *Chunnunpar* (Mizo Women's Ministries magazine), *Naupang Sipai* (Mizo *Young Soldier*)

IN JANUARY 2014 General André Cox and Commissioner Silvia Cox (WPWM) led a territorial congress in which the General testified to being a 'sinner saved by grace'. The General reminded his listeners that The Salvation Army is God's Army and therefore it should focus on Jesus alone. The General encouraged the territory to value 'One Army', to continue serving the lost by fulfilling the 'One Mission' as we proclaim 'One Message'. The leaders greatly inspired the Salvationists of the territory.

During the congress local officers attended a rally with the General where many gathered and rededicated their lives to the service of God and the Army. At every event, more than 200 seekers made their way to the place of prayer.

The territory gratefully acknowledges the assistance of the State Government in hosting the General and Commissioner Silvia Cox during their visit.

In March, 87 young people from 29 corps across the territory attended the first Brengle Institute for youth. The institute focused on 'Holiness – Body, Mind and Spirit' and the delegates were also given teaching on Salvation Army principles, the internationalism of the Army, and how to become useful for God and the community. From this event a group Facebook page was commenced, where the young people can keep in touch with each other, encourage one another and continue to build good relationships with the other delegates.

The territory endeavours to improve the economic status of marginalised families within local communities by forming self-help groups. Skills training was provided to members and loans were distributed in order to help participants commence their own income-generating businesses. More than 256 groups made up of 2,300 families have benefitted from the programme. The territory is grateful to the Sweden and Latvia Territory for its support of the project.

STATISTICS

Officers 316 (active 242 retired 74) **Cadets** 43
Employees 167
Corps 238 **Societies** 121 **Outposts** 16
Social Institutions 14 **Schools** 54
Senior Soldiers 39,566 **Adherent Members** 744
Junior Soldiers 10,271

STAFF

Women's Ministries: Comr Lalngaihawmi (TPWM) Lt-Col Mariamma Davidson (TSWM) Maj Sailo Hmunropuii (THLS)
Business Administration: Territorial Envoy Joseph Lalrintluanga
Editor and Literary Sec: Maj Lalrinawma Khawlhring
Education and Emergency: Maj Lalmuansanga Hnamte
Finance: Capt Ramdinthari Varte
Human Resources Development: Lt-Col Lalhlimpuii Chawngthu
Outreach: Maj Dawngliana Chhakchhuak

Personnel: Lt-Col Lalbulliana Tlau
Programme: Lt-Col Lalhmingliana Ngurte
Projects and Property: Maj Lalsangpuii Saza
Social: Capt Vanlaltluanga Pachuau
Sponsorship: Capt Rebek Lalrohnuni
Spiritual Life Development: Maj Vanlalthanga Hrahsel
Statistics: Lt-Col Lalnunhlui Khawlhring
Territorial Songsters: S/L K. Zohmingthanga
Territorial Band: B/M Territorial Envoy Joseph Lalrintluanga
Training: Maj Lalliankunga Ralte
Youth, Candidates and Public Relations: Reuben Lalnunthara Hnamte

DIVISIONS

Central North: PO Aizawl, 796 001, Mizoram; tel: (0389) 2317097; Majs Zothanmawia Khiangte and Vanlalnungi Thiak
Central South: PO Kulikawn, 796005, Aizawl – Mizoram; tel: (0389) 2300246; Majs Biakliana Sailo and Biakmawii Hrangkhawl
Himalayan: 8 Bylane Zoo Narengi Rd, nr SBI Geeta Nagar Branch, PO Box 65, Guwahati – 781021, Assam; tel/fax: (0361) 2413405; Majs Chawnghluna Chhangte and Lalchhuanmawii Khawlhring
Manipur: Salvation Rd, PO Churachanpur, 795 128, Manipur; tel: (3874) 233188; Majs Laithanmawia Ralte and Lalbiaktluangi Tochhawng
Southern: PO Lunglei, 796 701, Mizoram; tel: (95372) 2324027; Majs Sangchhunga Hauhnar and Vanlalauvi Fanai
Western: PO Kolasib, 796 081, Mizoram; tel: (3837) 220037; Majs Thanhranga Chhakchhuak and Lalruatsangi Fanai

UNDER THQ

Nepal: PO Box 8975, EPC-1677, Kathmandu, Nepal; tel: 00977-1-5537552; email: Lalsangliana/NEP/SArmy Majs Lalsangliana Vuite and Lalnunsangi Ralte
Kolkata: 72/3 SN Banerjee Road, 2nd Floor Suite No 17, Kolkata – 14; tel: 033-22654713; Capts Lalthlamuana Hauzel and Lalnunmawii Zote

TRAINING COLLEGE

Salem Mualpui, Aizawl - 796001, Mizoram; tel: (0389) 2322290

EDUCATION
Higher Secondary Schools
Children's Training Higher Secondary School: Churachandpur, Manipur; tel: (3874) 235097
Modern English Higher Secondary School: Aizawl, Mizoram; tel: (389) 2323248

High Schools
Blue Mount: Behliangchhip, Zampui, Tripura
Booth Tucker Memorial School: Gahrodpunjee, Cachar
Hermon Junior: Moreh, Manipur
School for the Blind (Junior High School): Kalimpong

Middle Schools
Booth Tucker: Thingkangphai, Manipur
Children's Education School: Zezaw, Manipur
Children's Training School: Singngat, Manipur
Hermon Junior: Moreh, Manipur
SA Middle School: Saikawt, Manipur
School for the Deaf: Darjeeling
Senior Captain Lalkaithanga Memorial School, Tuidam
Willow Mount: Durtlang, Mizoram

Primary School
Integrated Primary School: Kolasib

Outreach Schools: 20

Residential Schools for the Physically Challenged
Mary Scott Home for the Blind: Kalimpong, West Bengal;
email: sa_msh_kpg@yahoo.com (acc 65)
School for Deaf and Dumb Children: Darjeeling, West Bengal;
email: sadeaf80@gmail.com (acc 59)

CENTENARY PRESS
PO Box 5, Tuikal 'A', Aizawl, Mizoram; tel: (389) 2329626

SOCIAL WORK
Aged Care
Catherine Booth Home for the Aged, New Serchhip (acc 10)

Homes for Boys
Hostel for the Blind: Kolasib, Mizoram; (acc 25)
Enna In: Kolasib; (acc 30)
Kawlkhuma Home: Lunglei; (acc 25)
Muanna In: Mualpui, Aizawl;(acc 30)

Manipur Boys' Home: Mualvaiphei, Churachandpur; (acc 25)
Saiha Orphanage; (acc 15)
Silchar Home (acc 20)

Home for Girls
Hlimna In: Keifang, Mizoram; (acc 65)

Motherless Babies' Homes
Aizawl: Tuikal 'A', Aizawl, Mizoram; (acc 35)
Manipur: Mualvaiphei, Churachandpur, Manipur; (acc 10)

COMMUNITY DEVELOPMENT
Adult Education (literacy)
8 locations
Adult Rehabilitation Centres
3 locations
Community Empowerment
270 Self-Help Groups (Microcredit Loan for various trades)

Community Health Action Network (CHAN)
Kawlkhuma Bldg, Tuikal 'A', PO Box 5, Aizawl 796001; tel: (389) 2320202/2327609; email: chanaizawl@sancharnet.in

Community Health and Education
Guwahati

Deafness Reduction
Darjeeling, West Bengal

HIV/Aids Programme
Aizawl

Sanitation and Health Care
11 locations

Tailoring Centres
8 locations

INDIA NORTHERN TERRITORY

Territorial leaders:
Colonels Wilfred Varughese and Prema Wilfred

Territorial Commander:
Colonel Wilfred Varughese
(1 Dec 2013)

Chief Secretary:
Lieut-Colonel Daniel Raju Mathangi
(1 Oct 2011)

Territorial Headquarters: H-15, Green Park Extension, New Delhi 110 016, India

Tel: [91] (11) 26167764; email: INT_mail@INT.salvationarmy.org;

website: www.salvationarmy.org/ind

Shortly after arriving in India in 1882, Booth-Tucker visited major cities in northern India, including Allahabad, Delhi, Lucknow, Benares and Kolkata (Calcutta). Rural work was established later and operations were extended to Bihar and Odisha (Orissa). The boundaries of the India Northern Territory have changed over the years; there have been headquarters in Gurdaspur, Bareilly, Lucknow and Kolkata and, more recently, Delhi. In 1947, part of the territory became Pakistan. The present territory was established on 1 June 1991.

Zone: South Asia
States included in the territory: Bihar, Chattisgarh, Haryana, Himachal Pradesh, Jammu and Kashmir, Jharkhand, Odisha (Orissa), Punjab, Uttar Anchal, Uttar Pradesh, Uttara Khand, West Bengal; the Union Territories of Delhi, Chandigarh, and the Andaman and Nicobar Islands
'The Salvation Army' in Hindi, Punjabi and Urdu: Mukti Fauj
Languages in which the gospel is preached: Bengali, Burmese, English, Hindi, Kui, Nepali, Oriya, Punjabi, Santhali, Tamil, Urdu
Periodicals: *Home League Yearly* (Hindi and English), *Mukti Samachar* (Hindi and Punjabi), *The Officer* (Hindi), *Yuva Sipai* (Hindi)

THE YEAR 2013 concluded with the retirement of Commissioners Kashinath and Kusum Lahase and the installation of Colonels Wilfred and Prema Varughese as the new territorial leaders.

In January 2014, General André Cox and Commissioner Silvia Cox (WPWM) delighted Salvationists with their visit and encouraged them to keep themselves in God's love.

The ordination and commissioning of 18 cadets from the Disciples of the Cross Session was held at Central Corps, Bareilly, on 4 May.

Corps have been enrolling soldiers, and we give God all the praise for this new growth within the territory.

Seeing the need for Hindi songbooks

within the territory, 2,000 new books were printed with the assistance of the International Literature Programme.

The territory, with the help of International Emergency Services (IHQ) was able to supply food and other household items, such as blankets, tarpaulins, sweaters and shawls, for the fire victims at Patiala, and winter relief to more than 700 families in Moradabad and Bareilly Divisions. Goods were distributed to flash flood victims at Thatyur and Guptakashi in Uttarakhand and a tailoring and carpentry training centre has been established in order to assist with the construction of 23 houses for the victims. Winter relief material was also distributed to over 1,000 families in the Ganjam District in Odisha.

Veer Projects, which seek to assist street children, are operating in New Delhi and Kolkata.

The introduction of a Junior Miss Home League has helped to strengthen the women's ministries within the territory. Six hundred and sixteen self-help groups, as well as newly-established tailoring centres, are working well within the territory. These groups are creating awareness in the community regarding social, economic, spiritual and health issues for women and assisting them to earn a living. The overall growth and development of these types of centres provide the women with embroidery, sewing and tailoring skills in order to support themselves financially.

We thank God for his leading within the territory.

STATISTICS
Officers 499 (active 398 retired 101)
  Employees 302
Corps 172 **Outposts** 392 **Societies** 804
  Institutions 30 **Schools** 6 **College** 1
Senior Soldiers 69,271 **Adherent Members**
  3,004 **Junior Soldiers** 7,317

STAFF
Women's Ministries: Col Prema Wilfred
  (TPWM) Lt-Col Rachel Mathangi (TSWM)
  Lt-Col Mariam Parkash (THLS)
Editor: Maj Robin
Education and Emergency Response:
  Maj Tarsem Masih
Personnel: Lt-Col Parkash Masih
Business Administration: Lt-Col Yaqoob Masih
Human Resources: Maj Raj Kumar Gill
Music Ministry: Maj Swinder Masih
Programme: Lt-Col Robin Kumar Sahu
Projects: Maj Prakash Chandra Pradhan
Property: Maj Kashmir Masih
Public Relations/Fundraising: Maj George Patrick
Spiritual Life Development: Maj Vijayapal Singh
Training: Maj Manga Masih
  Candidates: Capt Lovely Thomson
Youth: Capt Thomson S. Masih

DIVISIONS
Amritsar: 25 Krishna Nagar, Lawrence Rd,
  Amritsar 143 001, Punjab; tel: 09872851593;
  Majs Manuel and Anita Masih
Angul: Sikhayak Pada, Angul Post, Angul District
  759 122, Odisha; tel: 06764-211271;
  Majs Dilip and Nivedita Singh
Bareilly: 220 Civil Lines, Bareilly 243 001, UP;
  tel: 05812-427081;
  Majs Ayoob and Reena Masih
Batala: Dera Baba Nanak Rd, Batala 143 505,
  Dist Gurdaspur, Punjab; tel: 01871-243038;
  Majs Makhan and Sunila Masih
Chandigarh: H. No. 303, Sector 38-A,
  Chandigarh-160036; tel: 0172-2685818;
  Majs Raj Kumar and Mohinder Kaur
Dera Baba Nanak: Dist Gurdaspur,
  PO Dera Baba Nanak 143 604, Punjab;
  tel: 01871-247262;
  Majs Sulakhan and Sheela Masih
Gurdaspur: Jail Rd, Dist Gurdaspur 143 521,
  Punjab; tel: 01874-220622;
  Majs Piara Lal and Madhu Lal
Jallandhar: Army Enclave, Phase III, Dheena,
  Jallandhar Cantt.144005, Punjab;
  tel: 9780888442
  Majs Piara and Grace Masih

Kolkata: 37 Lenin Sarani, Kolkata West Bengal
700 013; tel: 033-55101591;
Capts Philip and Nayami Nayak
Moradabad: Kanth Rd, nr Gandhi Ashram PAC,
Moradabad 244 001; tel: 09897268126;
Majs Samuel Ram and Sunila Lal
Mukerian: Rikhipura Mohalla,
Dist Hoshiyarpur, Mukerian – 144 211, Punjab;
tel: 01883-248733;
Majs Daniel and Parveen Gill

DISTRICTS

Jasidih: Deoghar Rd, Ramchanderpur, Jasidih,
Jharkand – 814 142; Maj Chotka Hembrom
Pathankot: Daulatpur Rd, Prem Nagar,
nr FCI Godown, Pathankot – 145001, Punjab;
tel: 09463-970566; Maj Salamat Masih

EXTENSION WORK

Bajpur: VIP Colony, H.No. 103, Opp. Jila
Parishad, Rampur - 244 901, UP;
tel: 09758635462; Maj Masih Dayal
Dehradun: c/o Mr Patwal, Kagri Wala,
PO Banjara Wala, Dehradun – 284001,
Uttrakhand; tel: 09758635462;
Maj Salamat Masih
Ferozpur: c/o Vedparkash, Near 33 K.V. Power
House, Gandhi Nagar, Ferozpur City-152002,
Punjab; tel: 09988086827;
Captain Yusaf Masih
Patiala: Near Railway Fatak N0. 16, H. No.
116, Gali No. 1, Rasulpur Saidan, Patiala -
147001, Punjab; tel: 09872-399215;
Maj Gurcharan Masih
Port Blair: Prothrapur, nr Atta Chakki,
PO Garacharma, Port Blair – 744105,
Andaman Nicobar Islands; Capt Jasbir Masih
Shahjahanpur and Lucknow: 43A Church Rd,
Vishnupuri, Aliganj, Lucknow – 226 022, UP;
tel: 0522-6540822 Maj Sanjay Robinson
Taran Taran: Sandhu Ave, nr Shota Kazi
Kot Rd, Ward 11, Taran Taran – 143401,
Dist Taran Taran, Punjab; Capt Victor Masih
Uttara Khand – Bajpur: Indira Colony, Baria
Rd, Bajpur Udham Singh Nagar – 261 401,
Uttara Khand; Maj John J. Loyal

TRAINING COLLEGE

Bareilly: 220 Civil Lines, Bareilly 243 001, UP;
tel: 0581-2423304

MEDICAL WORK
Hospital

MacRobert Hospital: Dhariwal,
Dist Gurdaspur 143 519, Punjab;
tel: 01874-275152/275274 (acc 50)

Clinics

Social Service Centre: 172 Acharya Jagdish
Chandra Bose Rd, Kolkata 700 014;
tel: 033-22840441
Community Health Centre: 192-A, Arjun Nager,
New Delhi 110 029; tel: 011-26168895

EDUCATION
Senior Secondary School

Batala: Aliwal Rd, Batala 143 505, Dist
Gurdaspur, Punjab; tel: 01871-242593
(acc 1,000)

High School

Gurdaspur: The Salvation Army DHQ
Compound, Jail Rd, Dist Gurdaspur,
Punjab; tel: 01874-20622

English Medium Schools

Andaman Nicobar Islands: Catherine Booth
Primary School, Prothrapur, PO Garacharma,
Port Blair – 744105 (acc 45)
Bareilly: William Booth Memorial School:
220 Civil Lines, Bareilly 243001, UP;
tel: 0581-2420007 (acc 200)
Batala: Aliwal Rd, Batala 143 505,
Dist Gurdaspur, Punjab; tel: 01871-242593
(acc 400)
Behala: 671 D.H. Rd, Hindustan Park, Behala,
Kolkata 700034; tel: 033-23972692
Moradabad: Kanth Rd, opp Gandhi Ashram PAC,
Moradabad 244 001, UP;
tel: 0591-2435438 (acc 400)

College

Batala: The Salvation Army College: Aliwal Rd,
Batala 143 505, Dist Gurdaspur, Punjab;
tel: 01871-242593 (acc 300)

Community Empowerment Programme

New Delhi: under THQ; tel: [91] (11) 26167764

Non-residential Tailoring Units

Batala: Punjab
Bhubaneswar : Angul
Dera Baba Nanak: Dist Gurdaspur, Punjab
Gurdaspur: Punjab
Kancharapada: West Bengal
New Delhi: H-15, Green Park Extn
Pathankot: Punjab
Patiala: Punjab
Port Blair: Port Blair, Andaman
Taran Taran: Punjab

Skill Training Centre

Training Centre for young men (Carpentry)
Shahpur Goraya, District Gurdaspur, Punjab

SOCIAL WORK
Free Feeding Programme
Kolkata: 172 Acharya Jagadish Chandra Bose Rd,
    Kolkata 700 014 (beneficiaries 250)

Homes for the Aged
Bareilly: 220 Civil Lines, Bareilly 243 001, UP;
    tel: 0581-2421432 (acc 20)
Dhariwal: MacRobert Hospital, Dhariwal,
    Dist Gurdaspur 143 519, Punjab;
    tel: 01874-275152/275274 (acc 20)
Kolkata: 172 Acharya Jagadish Chandra Bose Rd,
    Kolkata 700 014 (acc 15)

Homes for Boys
Angul: Angul 759 122, Odisha;
    tel: 06764-232829 (acc 25)
Batala: Aliwal Rd, Batala 143 505,
    Dist Gurdaspur (acc 60)
Kolkata: 37 Lenin Sarani, Kolkata 700 013;
    tel: 033-55124567 (acc 40)
Moradabad: Kanth Rd, Moradabad 244 001, UP;
    tel: 0591-2417351 (acc 40)
Simultala: Simultala 811 316, Dist Jamui, Bihar
    (acc 43)

Homes for Girls
Angul: Angul 759 122, Odisha; tel: 06764-232829
    (acc 40)
Bareilly: 220 Civil Lines, Bareilly 243 001, UP;
    tel: 0581-2421432 (acc 40)
Batala: Aliwal Rd, Batala 143505,
    Dist Gurdaspur (acc 100)
Behala: 671 D.H. Rd, Hindustan Park, Behala,
    Kolkata 700034; tel: 033-23972692 (acc 120)
Gurdaspur: Jail Rd, Dist Gurdaspur 143 521,
    Punjab (acc 100)

Hostels
Blind (Men)
1Kolkata: 72 Acharya Jagadish Chandra Bose Rd,
    Kolkata 700 014 (acc 30)

Working Men and Students
1Kolkata: 72 Acharya Jagdish Chandra Bose
    Rd, Kolkata 700 014; tel: 033-22840441
    (acc 200)

Young Women
Bareilly: 220 Civil Lines, Bareilly 243 001, UP;
    tel: 0581-2421432
Kolkata: 38 Lenin Sarani, Kolkata 700 013;
    tel: 033-22274281 (acc 50)
Ludhiana: 2230, ISA Nagari, Ludhiana – 141 008,
    Punjab

RED SHIELD GUEST HOUSE
Kolkata: 2 Saddar St, Kolkata 700 016;
    tel: 033-22861659
    (acc 80)

VEER PROJECT
Kolkata: 172 Acharya Jagadish Chandra Bose Rd,
    Kolkata 700 014
New Delhi: 6 Malik Bldg, Chunamandi Paharganj,
    New Delhi 110 055; tel: 011-2358 8433.

WASTE PAPER DEPARTMENT
New Delhi: 6 Malik Bldg, Chunamandi
    Paharganj, New Delhi 110 055; tel: 011-2358
    8433

INDIA SOUTH EASTERN TERRITORY

Territorial leaders:
Colonels Edwin and Sumita Masih

Territorial Commander:
Colonel Edwin Masih (1 Jul 2014)

Chief Secretary:
Lieut-Colonel Gabriel Christian (1 Aug 2011)

Territorial Headquarters: High Ground Road, Maharajanagar PO, Tirunelveli – 627 011, Tamil Nadu, India

Tel: [91] (462) 2574331/2574313; email: ISE_mail@ISE.salvationarmy.org;

website: www.salvationarmy.org/ind

The Salvation Army commenced operations in south-east India on 27 May 1892 as a result of the vision received by Major Deva Sundaram at Medicine Hill, while praying and fasting with three officers when the persecution in Southern Tamil Nadu was at its height. On 1 October 1970 the Tamil-speaking part of the Southern India Territory became a separate entity as the Army experienced rapid growth.

Zone: South Asia
States included in the territory: Pondicherry, Tamil Nadu
'The Salvation Army' in Tamil: Ratchaniya Senai; in Malayalam: Raksha Sainyam
Languages in which the gospel is preached: English, Malayalam, Tamil
Periodicals: *Chiruveeran* (Tamil), *Home League Quarterly*, *Poresatham* (Tamil), *The Officer* (Tamil)

THE 122nd commemoration of the commencement of The Salvation Army's work in Tamil Nadu was celebrated at the historical Booth Tucker Memorial Church in Nagercoil. Commissioners Lalzamlova and Nemkhanching (IS/ZSWM) were the guests for the celebration. The then territorial leaders Commissioners M.C. and Susamma James raised the flag to commence the celebration and 800 officers and soldiers attended, giving thanks for the sacrificial service rendered by Major Deva Sundaram and the pioneer officers in the region.

During the celebration, 421 young people attended a youth festival. Drama, dance and mime, inspirational songs, lectures, Bible study, testimonies and a devotional time all paved the way for more than 100 young people to dedicate their lives to God. This event saw more than 300 young Salvationists proudly wearing their uniforms for the first time, with over 40 giving testimony to God's leading in their lives.

Commissioner Lalzamlova conducted

the launch of the new Tamil song book and a book written by Commissioner M.C. James. Officers and soldiers each received a copy of the books.

Two girls reared in The Salvation Army's motherless babies home were both recently married. In order to fulfil the Tamil Nadu culture, officers and soldiers gave generously to support the girls during this special event. Two cabinet secretaries conducted the weddings and the girls appreciated the way in which The Salvation Army fulfilled the role of their 'mothers', in providing for them and preparing them for the ceremonies.

STATISTICS

Officers 639 (active 459 retired 180)
   Employees 514
Corps 318 **Outposts** 81 **Societies** 67
   Schools 19 **Institutions** 39
Senior Soldiers 51,304 **Adherent Members** 17,975 **Junior Soldiers** 4,786
Personnel serving outside territory
   Officers 16

STAFF

Women's Ministries: Col Sumita Masih (TPWM) Lt-Col Indumati G. Christian (TSWM)
Sec for Business Administration: tba
   Finance and Audit: Maj Masilamony Stalin
   Legal: Maj Swamidhas Nalladhas
   Property and Projects: Maj Yesuvadian Ponnappan
Sponsorship: Maj Kezial
   Supplies: Maj Geetha Nathan
Sec for Personnel: Lt-Col Perinbanayagam Suthananthadhas
   HRD: Maj Job William
   Training: Maj Yesuvadian Manoharan
Sec for Programme:
   Lt-Col Tharmar Alfred
   Health: Maj Jeeva Ratnam Darse
   Editorial: Lt-Col Esther Evangeline
   Projects and Development: Mr Gnanadhas Benjamin Dhaya
   Social: Maj Retnam Aruldhas
   Youth: Maj Yesuvadian Joseph

DIVISIONS

Azhagiapandipuram: KK Dist PO, 629 852; tel: (04652) 281952; Lt-Cols Arulappan Paramadhas and Retnam
Kanyakumari: Kadaigramam, Suchindram PO, KK Dist 629 704; tel: (04652) 243955; Majs Jeyaraj Daniel Jebasingh Raj and Rajam
Kulasekharam: Kulasekharam PO, 629 161 KK Dist; tel: (04651) 279446; Majs Nallathambi Edwin Sathyadhas and Gnana Jessy Bell
Marthandam: Pammam, Marthandam PO, 629 165; tel: (04651) 272492; Majs James Saharidas and Daizy
Nagercoil: Vetturnimadam PO, Nagercoil 629 003; tel: (04652) 272787; Majs Jebamony Jayaseelan and Gnanaselvi
Palayamcottai: 28 Bell Amorses Colony, Palayamcottai 627 002; tel: (0462) 2580093; Majs Majs Jeyaraj Samraj and Jessie
Radhapuram: Radhapuram PO, 627 111; tel: (04637) 254318; Majs Geevanantham Kumaradhas and Kala Siromony
Tenkasi: Tenkasi PO, 627 811; tel: (04633) 280774; Majs Grey F Singh Christopher Selvanath and Retnabai
Thuckalay: Mettukadai, Thuckalay PO, 629 175; tel: (04651) 252443; Majs Devasundaram Samuel Raj and Kanagamony
Valliyoor: Valliyoor PO, 627 117; tel: (04637) 221454; Majs Chelliah Swamidhas and Joicebai

DISTRICTS

Coimbatore: Dr Daniel Ngr, K. Vadamaduai PO, 641 017; tel: (0422) 2461277; Maj Ponniah Ashok Sundar
Erode: 9 Sakthivinayagar Koil St, Thengapattakarar Lane, Railway Colony Post, Poondurai Road, Erode 638 002; tel: (0424) 2283909; Maj Yacob Selvam
Madurai: TPK Rd, Palanganatham PO, 625 003; tel: (0452) 2370169; Maj Gnanamony Swamydhas
Trichy: New Town, Malakovil, Thiruvarumbur 620 013; tel: (0431) 2510464; Maj Abel Yesudhas
Tuticorin: 5/254 G, Caldwell Colony, Tuticorin 628 008; tel: (0461) 2376841; Maj Gnanabaranam Sam Singh

EXTENSION AREAS

Bhavani: No.770, Kalingarayan Palayam, Bhavani – 638301;

Katpady:13, Selvam Nagar, Old Katpady, Vellore Dist; Capt Anbaiah Makesh

Pondicherry: opp Mahatma Dental College, Kamaraj Ngr, Goremedu Check Post, Pondicherry 605 006; tel: (0413) 2271933; Maj Gnanamony Moses

Salem: Near AVS College, Ramalingapuram, Salem -636 106; Maj Jacob Vethamano

TRAINING COLLEGE
WCC Rd, Nagercoil 629 001; tel: (04652) 231471

MEDICAL WORK
Catherine Booth Hospital: Nagercoil 629 001; tel: (04652) 275516/7

The Salvation Army Community Health and Development Programme
Catherine Booth Hospital Campus, tel: 04652 272068; email: benny@sachdp.com
Director: Mr G. Benjamin Dhaya, Community Health Centre; comprehensive HIV/Aids care and support; District Resource Centre; Housing Project; microcredit scheme; spirulina farm; The Salvation Army integrated community empowerment programme

The Catherine Booth College of Nursing
Principal: Mrs T. Angel Priya
tel: 04652 272068
email: salvationarmycon@gmail.com
website: www.sacbcn.org

EDUCATION
Higher Secondary School (mixed)
Nagercoil 629003; tel: (04652) 272647

Matriculation Higher Secondary School
Nagercoil; tel: (04652) 272534

Middle School (mixed)
Nambithoppu Middle School

Noble Memorial High School
Valliyoor; tel: (04637) 220380
Village Primary Schools: 9

Nursery and English Medium Primary Schools: 4

RED SHIELD HOUSE AND RETREAT CENTRE
Muttom, via Nagercoil 629 202; tel: (04651) 238321

SOCIAL SERVICES
Boys' and Girls' Homes
Boys' Home: Nagercoil (acc 72)
Noble Memorial Boys' Home: Valliyoor (acc 70)
Tucker Girls' Home: Nagercoil (acc 135)
Girls' Home: Thuckalay (acc 100)

Children's Home
Palayamcottai

Child Development Centres
Chemparuthivilai, Chemponvilai, Kadaigramam, Madurai, Nagercoil, Pondicherry, Thuckalay, Valliyoor

Vocational Training Centre for the Physically Disabled (Men and Boys)
Aramboly 629 003; tel: (04652) 263133

Vocational Training Centre for Women and Home League Retreat Centre
Nagercoil 629 003; tel: (04652) 232348

Vocational Training Centres
Chemparuthivilai 629 166
tel: (04651) 253292
Kilkothagiri Junction, 643 216 Nilgris

Industrial Training School
Aramboly; tel: (04652) 262198

RETIRED OFFICERS' HOME
Catherine Booth Hospital, Nagercoil 629 001

INDIA SOUTH WESTERN TERRITORY

Territorial leaders:
Commissioners Samuel and Bimla Charan

Territorial Commander:
Commissioner Samuel Charan (1 Jan 2011)

Chief Secretary:
Lieut-Colonel Chawnghlut Vanlalfela (1 Jun 2014)

**Territorial Headquarters: The Salvation Army, Kowdiar,
Thiruvananthapuram, Kerala**

Postal address: PO Box 802, Kowdiar, Thiruvananthapuram 695 003, Kerala State, India

Tel: [91] (471) 2314626/2723238

email: ISW_mail@ISW.salvationarmy.org; website: www.salvationarmy.org/ind

Salvation Army work was commenced in the old Travancore State on 8 March 1896 by Captain Yesudasen Sanjivi, who was a high-caste Brahmin before his conversion. His son, Colonel Donald A. Sanjivi, became the first territorial commander from Kerala. The work spread to other parts of the state through the dedication of pioneer officers, including Commissioner P.E. George. The India South Western Territory came into being on 1 October 1970 when the Southern India Territory divided into two. The territory has its headquarters at Thiruvananthapuram (Trivandrum) and comprises the entire Malayalam-speaking area known as Kerala State.

Zone: South Asia
State included in the territory: Kerala
'The Salvation Army' in Malayalam: Raksha Sainyam; in Tamil: Ratchania Senai
Languages in which the gospel is preached: English, Malayalam, Tamil
Periodicals: *Home League Quarterly* (Malayalam/English), *The Officer* (Malayalam), *Youdha Shabdam* (Malayalam/Tamil), *Yuva Veeran* (Malayalam/Tamil)

LANGUAGE should never be a constraint for social work; it is all about accepting, sympathising and reacting to the right feelings and emotions of the isolated and down-trodden. Due to the assistance of the government and The Salvation Army's experience in caring for HIV-infected people and others impacted throughout Kerala, gone are the days of insecurity and other issues.

With more than two million migrants in that area, The Salvation Army commenced working with a holistic approach addressing the issues of HIV/Aids and justice for the poor.

Under the theme 'We are the sons' more than 1,000 children, including Hindus and Muslims, attended a vacation Bible school in April.

In March 2014 a colourful rally was organised by the community empowerment team at Thiruvananthapuram for the members of the 150 self-help groups from around the territory. More than 2,000 women from various places and a mix of cultural backgrounds gathered to register their disapproval of the violence and abuse against women and children. The meeting was arranged in connection with a women's day at Kowdiar, Thiruvananthapuram.

Annual conventions and special meetings were organised in divisions and corps as a part of the spiritual development of the people based on the theme 'Walk in the light of the Lord'. People from other denominations also attended.

The Women's Ministries Department arranged a spiritual life development seminar to promote women leaders in church ministry. A Bible camp was arranged for the women officers in the territory with the objective of promoting spiritual enrichment through the Scriptures.

The CSLD arranged a territorial seminar for officers and selected prayer cell leaders throughout the territory. This was a Spirit-filled experience.

In order to further develop the territory's educational facilities, new classrooms were opened and dedicated at Kurumkutty, Parassala. The regional medium school has been upgraded to an English medium school by the state Government.

The territory is excited to have commissioned and ordained another session of cadets.

STATISTICS

Officers 676 (active 407 retired 269) **Cadets** 10 **Employees** 83
Corps 333 **Societies and Outposts** 461 **Schools** 16 **Institutions** 20
Senior Soldiers 41,191 **Adherent Members** 15,223 **Junior Soldiers** 3,637
Personnel serving outside territory Officers 6

STAFF

Women's Ministries: Comr Bimla Charan (TPWM) Lt-Col Khupchawng Ropari (TSWM) Lt-Col Elizabeth Solomon (THLS) Maj Shylaja Babu (TLOMS)
Business Administration: Lt-Col K.M. Gabriel
Personnel: Lt-Col John Suseelkumar
Programme: Lt-Col K.M. Solomon
Editor and Literary Sec: Maj Roy Joseph
Education: Maj Simson Samuelkutty
Finance and Projects: Maj C.J. Bennymon
HRD and Education: Maj Saju Daniel
Property: Major P.S. Johnson
Social: Maj S.P Simon
Territorial Auditor: Capt Shaijuraj
Territorial Evangelist, Church Growth and Sec for Spiritual Life Development: Maj Jacob George
Training: Maj John Samuel
Youth and Candidates: Maj O.P. John

DIVISIONS

Adoor: Adoor 691 523; tel: 0473-4229648; Majs Rajan K. John and Susamma Rajan
Cochin: Erumathala PO, Alwaye 683 105; tel: 0484-2638429; Majs T.J. Simon and Ammini Simon
Kangazha: Edayirikapuzha PO, Kangazha 686 541; tel: 0481-2494773; Majs C.S. Yohannan and L. Rachel Yohannan
Kattakada: Kattakada 695 572; tel: 0471-2290484; Majs D. Israel and Rosamma Israel
Kottarakara: Kottarakara 691 506; tel: 452650; Majs Charles V. John and Florence Charles
Malabar: Veliyamthode, Chandakunnu PO, Nilambur 679 342; tel: 2222824; Majs V.D. Samuel and O.T. Rachel Samuel
Mavelikara: Thazhakara, Mavelikara 690 102; tel: 2303284; Majs Rajamani Christuraj and Mary Christuraj
Nedumangadu: Nedumangadu 695 541; tel: 2800352; Majs D. Gnanadasan and D.I. Sosamma Gnanadasan
Neyyattinkara: Neyyattinkara 695 121; tel: 2222916; Majs S. Samuelkutty and Lillybai Samuelkutty

Peermade: Kuttikanam PO, Peermade 685 501;
tel: 232816; Majs Sam Immanuel and Rachel
Immanuel
Tiruvella: Tiruvella 689 101; tel: 2602657;
Majs N.J. George and M.C. Ruth George
Thiruvananthapuram: Parambuconam,
Kowdiar PO, Thiruvananthapuram 695 003;
tel: 2433215; Majs Davidson Daniel and
M.V. Estherbai Davidson

DISTRICTS
Kottayam: Manganam PO, Kottayam 686 018;
tel: 0481-2577481; Maj Yohannan Joseph
Punalur: The Salvation Army, PPM PO,
Punalur; tel: 0475-2229218; Maj John Rose

TRAINING COLLEGE
Kowdiar, Thiruvananthapuram 695 003;
tel: 2315313

TERRITORIAL PRAYER CENTRE FOR SPIRITUAL EMPOWERMENT
Kowdiar PO, Thiruvanathapuram 695 003;
tel: 0471-2723237

MEDICAL WORK
Hospitals
Evangeline Booth Community Hospital:
Puthencruz 682 308; tel: Ernakulam 2731056
Evangeline Booth Leprosarium: Puthencruz
682 308; tel: Ernakulam 2730054 (acc 200)
Administrator: Maj P.V. Stanley Babu
General Hospital: Kulathummel, Kattakada
695 572, Thiruvananthapuram Dist;
tel: Kattakada 2290485 (acc 60)

Medical Centre
Kanghaza (acc 12)

EDUCATION
Higher Secondary School (mixed)
Thiruvananthapuram (acc 1,371)

Primary Schools:
15 (acc 2,640)

SOCIAL WORK
Boys' Homes
Kangazha (acc 30)
Kottarakara (acc 30)
Kowdiar, Thiruvananthapuram (acc 20)
Mavelikara (acc 25)

Community Development Centres
North: Trikkakara, Cochin
South: Konchira, Thiruvananthapuram

HIV/Aids Faith-Based Facilitation Community Development Office
Kowdiar, Thiruvananthapuram, 695 003,
tel: 0471- 2318668

Girls' Homes
Adoor (acc 25)
Kowdiar, Thiruvananthapuram (acc 24)
Nedumangad (acc 30)
Peermade, Kuttikanam (acc 30)
Thiruvalla (acc 25)

Microcredit Service Centre/Self-Help Group Office
Kowdiar, Thiruvananthapuram, 695 003;
tel: 0471- 2721540

Vocational Training Centre for Women
Nedumangad (acc 25)

Young Men's Training Centre
Thiruvananthapuram

Printing Press
Kowdiar, Thiruvananthapuram 695 003;
tel: 0471 2725358

Tailoring Centres
Adoor, Cochin, Kangazha, Kattakada,
Kottarakara, Malabar, Neyyattinkara,
Peermade

Working Women's Hostels
Thiruvananthapuram (acc 20)
Thrikkakara, B.M.C. PO, Ernakulam

Youth Centre
Kowdiar, Thiruvananthapuram

RED SHIELD GUEST HOUSES
Kowdiar, Thiruvananthapuram 695 003;
tel: 0471-2319926
Kovalam, Thiruvananthapuram; tel: 0471
2485895

INDIA WESTERN TERRITORY

Territorial leaders:
Commissioners M.C. and Susamma James

Territorial Commander:
Commissioner M.C. James (1 Jul 2014)

Chief Secretary:
Lieut-Colonel Joginder Masih
(1 Jun 2014)

Territorial Headquarters: Sheikh Hafizuddin Marg, Byculla, Mumbai 400 008

Postal address: PO Box 4510, Mumbai 400 008, India

Tel: [91] (022) 2308 4705/2307 1140;

email: IWT_mail@iwt.salvationarmy.org; website: www.salvationarmy.org/ind

The Salvation Army began its work in Bombay (later Mumbai) in 1882 as a pioneer party led by Major Frederick Tucker and including Veerasoriya, a Sri Lankan convert, who invaded India with the love and compassion of Jesus. Bombay (Mumbai) was the capital of Bombay Province, which included Gujarat and Maharashtra, and the first headquarters in India was in a rented building at Khetwadi. From these beginnings the work of God grew in Bombay Province. Various models of administration were tried for the work in Gujarat and Maharashtra until the India Western Territory was established in 1921.

Zone: South Asia
States included in the territory: Gujarat, Maharashtra, Madhya Pradesh, Rajasthan
'The Salvation Army' in Gujarati and Marathi: Muktifauj
Languages in which the gospel is preached: Gujarati, Hindi, Marathi, Tamil
Periodicals: *Home League Quarterly* (Gujarati and Marathi), *The Officer* (Gujarati and Marathi), *The War Cry* (Gujarati and Marathi), *The Young Soldier* (Gujarati and Marathi)

THE TERRITORY gives thanks to God for the continued prayer support from throughout the Army world that it has received. Through this support the territory has 'Become one in spirit and purpose' (Philippians 2:2), which has been the theme for 2013.

Evangelical campaigns were conducted throughout the territory at corps and these brought inspiration and encouragement to Salvationists and others to be one in spirit and purpose.

With the support of women's ministries funds, four new church halls have been built in south Gujarat. These centres have given people a place to gather and encounter the presence and fellowship of God.

Prayer cell groups and fasting and prayer have been a catalyst for spiritual growth within the territory.

When there was heavy rain in the tribal areas within the Vansda region, more than 1,200 families were helped with food and other materials.

Territorial youth camps were conducted in Gujarat and Maharashtra with 800 young people participating. The camps culminated with a total of 206 young people kneeling before God, dedicating their lives for future service in The Salvation Army.

With the continued technical and financial support from International Health Services (IHQ), the territory was able to continue its health and hospital ministry, an outreach that has continued for 75 years.

Salvationists give praise and glory to God for his goodness, grace and leading within the territory and our prayer for the territory is for: 'Greater things! Greater things! Give us faith, O Lord, we pray, Faith for greater things' (*SASB* 769).

STATISTICS
Officers 591 (active 375 retired 216) **Cadets** 16 **Employees** 301
Corps 271 **Outposts** 275 **Institutions** 20 **Day Schools** 12
Senior Soldiers 42,788 **Adherent Members** 3,864 **Junior Soldiers** 10,303

STAFF
Women's Ministries: Comr Susamma James (TPWM) Lt-Col Shanti Masih (TSWM)
Lt-Col Flora Damor (THLS - Gujarati)
Lt-Col Leela R. Kale (THLS/LOM – Marathi)
Lt-Col Eunice Parmar (LOMS – G)
Lt-Col Ratnamala Randive (WDO – M)
Maj Sunita J. Macwan (SSM – G)
Sec for Business Administration: tba
  Finance: Maj Emmanuel Masih
  Property: Maj Jashwant T. Macwan (G)
  Property: Maj J.P. Salve (M)
Sec for Personnel:
  Lt-Col K.K. Parmar – G;
  Lt-Col Ratnakar D. Kale – M
Human Resources: Maj Yusuf D. Christian (G); Maj Pramod Kamble (M)

Sec for Programme:
  Lt-Col Nicholas Damor – G;
  Lt-Col Benjamin Randive – M
Editors: Maj Harish Katarnavre (M); Maj Jashiben D. Khristie (G)
Projects: Maj Ashok Dushing
Training: Maj Yakub Macwan (G); Maj Vijay Dalvi (M)
Youth: Maj Yusuf Daud (G) Capt Ravindra Kharat (M)

DIVISIONS
Gujarat
Ahmedabad: Behrampura, Ahmedabad 380 022; tel: (079) 2539 4258;
  Majs Rasik and Ramila Paul
Anand: Amul Dairy Rd, Anand 388 001; tel: (02692) 240638;
  Majs Jashwant and Indira Chauhan
Matar: Behind Civil Court, Matar District, Kheda 387 530; tel: (02694) 285482;
  Majs Prabhudas and Persis Christian
Nadiad: Nadiad, District Kheda 387 002; tel: (0268) 2558856;
  Majs Viajy and Pushpa Mahida
Panchmahal: Dohad, Panchmahal 389 151; tel: (02673) 221771;
  Majs Ranmal and Ambabai Charel
Petlad: Sunav Rd, Post Petlad, District Anand 388 450; tel: (02679) 221527;
  Majs Kantilal and Elishaben Parmar
South Gujarat: Khambla Zampa, PO Vansda, 396 580 District Navsari;
  Majs Samuel and Gunwanti Parmar

Maharashtra
Ahmednagar: Fariabagh, Sholapur Rd, 414 001; tel: (95241) 2358194;
  Majs Ivor Salve and Meena Salve
Mumbai: Sankli St, Byculla, Mumbai 400 008; tel: (022) 2300 3990;
  Majs Jagannath and Kusum Tribhuwan
Pathardi: Pathardi, District Ahmednagar 414 102; tel: (952428) 223116;
  Majs Ashok and Sheela Mandgule
Pune: 19 Napier Rd, 411 040; tel: (9520) 2636 3198;
  Majs Gulab and Meena Pathare
Satara: Satara, District Satara 415 001; tel: (952162) 234006;
  Majs Sunil and Sunita Waghmare
Shevgaon: Shevgaon, District Ahmednagar 414 502; tel: (952429) 223191;
  Majs Bapusaheb Salvi and Vinodini Salvi
Shrirampur: District Ahmednagar 413 709, Tal Shrirampur; Majs Chabu and Sunita Salve

EXTENSION AREAS

Aurangabad: Maj Philip Jadhav
Dharampur: Maj Ramesh Dhanji
Kaprada: Maj Prakash K. Macwan
Madhya Pradesh: Capt Savsing Bhabhor
Rajasthan: tba
Sangli: Maj Bhausaheb Thombe

TRAINING COLLEGES

Gujarat: Anand 388 001, District Anand,
    Amul Dairy Rd; tel: (02692) 254801
Maharashtra: Fariabagh,
    Ahmednagar 414 001; tel: (95241) 2355950

EDUCATION
Boarding Schools (Boys and Girls)

William Booth Memorial Children's Home
    and Hostel: Anand 388 001, District Anand,
    Gujarat; tel: (2692) 255580 (acc 226)
William Booth Memorial Primary and High
    Schools: Farlabagh, District Ahmednagar
    414 001, Maharashtra;
    tel: (022) 95241 2324267 (acc 513)

Day Schools

Anand:
    William Booth Memorial High School,
        Amul Dairy Rd; tel: (2692) 254901 (acc 276)
    English Medium Primary and High
    School Anand (acc 1,260)
    William Booth Primary School (acc 476)
Ashakiran: Primary School, Satara;
    under DHQ (acc 130)
Dahod: English Medium School (acc 210)
Muktipur: PO Bareja 382 425, District
    Ahmednabad; tel: 02718 233318 (acc 93)
Mumbai: Tucker English Medium School,
    Sankli St, Byculla, Mumbai 400 008;
    tel: (022) 307 7062 (acc 652)
Pune: English Medium School, Vishrantwadi,
    Pune 411 015; tel: (9520) 2669 2761 (acc 25)
Vadodara: English Medium School:
    Chhani Rd, Vadodra; tel: (0265) 277 5361
    (acc 150)

MEDICAL WORK

Emery Hospital: Amul Dairy Rd, Anand 388 001,
    District Anand, Gujarat; tel: (2692) 253737
    (acc 160)
Evangeline Booth Hospital: Ahmednagar 414 001,
    Maharashtra; tel: (022) 95241 2325976 (acc 100)

HUMAN RESOURCES
   DEVELOPMENT CENTRES

Anand (Gujarat):

Faujabad Comp, Anand 388 001
Ahmednagar (Maharashtra):
    tel: (022) 95241 2358489

SOCIAL WORK
CARE Programme Centre

Byculla, Mumbai: Community-based aids
    programme; confidential aids counselling
    clinic; Aruna children's shelter; Jeevan Asha
    centre and night shelter

Farm Colony

Muktipur 382 425, Post Bareja,
    District Ahmedabad; tel: (02718) 33318

Feeding Programme

Mumbai (under King Edward Home) and street
    children programme

Homes
Children

Mumbai: Sion Children's Home (acc 100)
Pune: Hope House (acc 50)

Elderly Men

Mumbai 400 008: 122 Maulana Azad Rd,
    Byculla; tel: (022) 23071346 (acc 15)

Industrial

King Edward Home: 122 Maulana Azad Rd,
    Byculla, Mumbai 400 008

Physically Handicapped Children

Joyland, Anand 388 001, District Anand,
    Gujarat; tel: (02692) 251891 (acc 20)

'Ray of Hope' Home

Vansda: under DHQ (acc 63)

Hostels
Blind Working Men

Ahmedabad: Locoshed, Rajpur-Hirpur,
    Ahmedabad, Gujarat; tel: (079) 2294 1217;
    (acc 15)
Mumbai 400 008: Sankli St, Byculla;
    tel: (022) 2305 1573 (acc 50)

Young Women

Anand: Gujarat (acc 90)
Mumbai: Concord House (acc 80)
Pune: c/o DHQ, Pune 411 040 (acc 20)

RED SHIELD HOTEL

30 Mereweather Rd, Fort, Mumbai 400 039;
    tel: (022) 2284 1824 (acc 450)

INDIA WESTERN: (above) The territory's youth kneel to dedicate themselves for future service

INDONESIA: (below) Members of the Bamboo Band taking part in the territorial congress

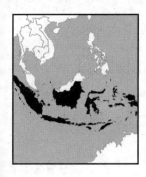

INDONESIA TERRITORY

Territorial leaders:
Commissioners Michael and Joan Parker

Territorial Commander:
Commissioner Michael Parker
(1 Jan 2013)

Chief Secretary:
Lieut-Colonel Jones Kasaedja (1 Jan 2013)

Territorial Headquarters: Jalan Jawa 20, Bandung 40117

Postal address: Post Box 1640, Bandung 40016, Indonesia

Tel: [62] (22) 4207029/4205056

website: www.salvationarmy.or.id

The Salvation Army commenced in Indonesia (Java) in 1894. Operations were extended to Ambon, Bali, East Kalimantan, Sulawesi (Central, North and South), Sumatra (North and South) Nias and East Nusa Tenggara and Papua. A network of educational, medical and social services began.

Zone: South Pacific and East Asia

Country included in the territory: Indonesia

'The Salvation Army' in all Indonesian languages: Bala Keselamatan

Languages in which the gospel is preached: Indonesian with various dialects such as Batak, Daa, Dayak, Javanese, Ledo, Makassarese, Moma, Niasnese, Tado and Uma

Periodicals: *Berita Keselamatan* (*The War Cry*), *Cakrawala* (*Waves of Hope*), *Medical Fellowship Bulletin, Oasis Fajar* (Daily Devotions)

'HARVEST of Souls' has been the theme and focus for the year in review and the significant growth seen in many areas is a cause for celebration. The net growth in soldiership of over 2,000 is exciting. In September, to mark the 100 years of ministry in Central Sulawesi, General André Cox and Commissioner Silvia Cox (WPWM) enrolled more than 200 new soldiers. Prior to this event, 30 cadets, making up the Heralds of Grace Session, were welcomed.

The territory has celebrated 119 years of ministry in Indonesia and in preparation for the future focused on the theme 'I'll Fight'.

To raise awareness for World AIDS Day, the youth of the territory held musical celebrations.

To assist with leadership development throughout the territory, risk management and change management workshops were held.

Indonesia continues to be impacted by natural disasters, with volcanic eruptions and severe flooding causing death and damage. Thousands of refugees were served by the territory's Compassion in Action teams with food, clothing, sleeping pads and blankets being distributed. Clinics offering counselling and children's activities also assisted those in need. The territory remains deeply grateful to its partners throughout the world who enable them to respond effectively to disasters, yet also invest in programmes that lead to both spiritual and numerical growth within the territory.

Commissioner Michael Parker (TC) opened a 24-hour general medical clinic which has 10 beds available for in-patients, in addition to its heavy use of out-patient services.

Ecumenical participation remains strong between the Christian churches.

Home league seminars and rallies using the international theme 'You are Loved' were held. These events included teaching modules on nutrition to help alleviate poverty and malnutrition, and safe motherhood to help deal with the high rate of infant mortality within the country.

On the island of Nias a ground-breaking ceremony took place for the new Salvation Army children's home that is to be built. The Pearl of Love home will be a safe refuge for approximately 50 children who are in need of shelter and adequate education.

The territory rejoices in the continued growth of its programmes and membership, and the impact it has within the communities where each centre serves. We give thanks to God for his blessing on the ministry taking place within the territory.

STATISTICS

Officers 746 (active 605 retired 141) **Cadets** (1st Yr) 29 (2nd Yr) 17 **Employees** 2,438
Corps 278 **Outposts** 110 **Schools** 98
Theological College 1 **Hospitals** 6 **Clinics** 18
Social Institutions 20 **Day Care Centre** 1
Senior Soldiers 32, 041 **Adherents** 15.055
Junior Soldiers 7,281 **Officers serving outside territory** 2

STAFF

Women's Ministries: Comr Joan Parker (TPWM) Lt-Col Mariyam Kasaedja (TSWM)
Sec for Business Admin: Lt-Col Dina Ismael
Legal and Parliament: Lt Olwin Sumampouw
Finance Sec: Lt-Col Herlina Widyanoadi
Chief Auditor: Maj Sinur Supardi
Property: Maj Immanuel Supardi
Information Technology: Kadek White
Sec for Programme: Lt-Col I. Made Petrus
Literature and Editorial: Maj Bambang White
Projects: Maj James Cocker
Corps Growth: Maj Hany Tuhumury
Youth and Children's Ministries: Maj Erwin Tampubolon
Sec for Personnel: Lt-Col I. Wayan Widyanoadi
Spiritual Life Sec: Maj Santi White
Candidates: Maj Murgiati Mardiyudi
Social Services: Maj Ernie Lasut
Training Principal: Maj Gidion Rangi

DIVISIONS

East Kalimantan: Jl. A.M. Sangaji No. 2 RT 10, Kel. Bandara - Kec. Samarinda Utara, Kalimantan Timur; tel. (0541) 201 594; Majs Sasmoko and Dumasari Hertjahjo
Jawa and Bali: Jalan Dr Cipto 64b, Kelurahan Bugangan, Semarang 50126, Jateng; tel: (024) 355 1361; Majs Pilemon and Christien Ngkale
Kulawi: Bala Keselamatan Post Office, Kulawi 94363, Sulteng; tel: (0451) 811 017; Majs Indra and Helly Mangiwa
Manggala (West Palu, Central Sulawesi): c/o Jalan Miangas 1-3, Palu 94112; Majs Imanuel and Henny Duhu
Palu Timur (East Palu): Jalan Miangas 1, Kantor Pos Palu 94112; tel: (0451) 426 821; Lt-Cols Selly and Anastasia Poa
Palu Barat (West Palu): Jalan Miangas 1-3, Palu 94112, Sulteng; mobile: 0816 4304498; Majs I. Made Sadia and Syastiel Lempid
Regional East Indonesia: Jl Dr Sutomo No 10, Makasar; tel: (0411) 312 919; Majs Spener and Rai Tetenaung

Sulawesi Utara (North Sulawesi): Jalan A.
Yani 15, Manado 95114; tel: (0431) 864 052;
Majs Ezra and Marisa Mangela

Sumatera Utara: Jl. Sei Kera 186 Medan 20232,
Sumatera Utara; tel: (061) 4510284;
Majs Marthen and Yulin Pandorante

DISTRICTS
Under Jawa and Bali Division
Central Java: Maj Janes Thenu
East Java: Capt Andreas Kasmun
Jadetabek: Maj Erik Kape
West Java: Maj Nicolas Lengkong
Under East Palu Division
Berdikari: Maj Sakius Salogi
Maranatha: Maj Immanuel Sabadi
Napu-Besoa: Capt Alfinus Rue
Nokilalaki: Maj Sunarto Suparmo
Parimo: Maj Argus Lago
Palu: Maj Benyamin Ruku
Under West Palu Division
Dombu: Capt Bambang Tadewatu
Pakawa: Maj William Kaligis
Porame: Capt Datkita Ginting
Rowiga: Maj Bambang Supriyanto
Wawugaga: Capt Johnmboge Rusadama
Under Manggala Division
Lalundu: Capt Gunawan Mantaely
Malino: Capt Elfan Yago
North Mamuju: Capt Albert Silinawa
Under Kulawi Division
Gimpu: Maj Normawati Biro
Kantewu: Maj Wartono
Karangana: Maj Yusuf Tarusu
Kulawi: Maj Elias Sale
Lindu: Maj Arsan Sukarmin
Tobaku: Maj Derens Lodju
Under North Sumatera Division
Nias: Maj Sopani Laia

OFFICER TRAINING COLLEGE
Jalan Kramat Raya 55, Jakarta 10450, PO Box
3203, Jakarta 10002; tel: (021) 310 8148

EDUCATION
Central Sulawesi: 75 schools (acc 7,118)
1 theological university (acc 223)
East Kalimantan: 2 schools (acc 52)
Jawa: 13 schools (acc 1,110)
Kalawara: 3 schools (acc 400)
North Sumatra: 2 schools (acc 62)
South Sulawesi: 3 schools (acc 106)

MEDICAL WORK
General Hospitals (Jawa)
Bandung: Bungsu Hospital (acc 49)

Palu: Woodward Hospital (acc 101)
Semarang: William Booth Hospital (acc 50)
Surabaya: William Booth Hospital (acc 144)
Turen: Bokor Hospital (acc 85)

Maternity Hospital
Makassar, Sulawesi Selatan: Catherine Booth
Mother and Child Hospital (acc 53)

Clinics
Bandung (1) Central Java (1) Central Sulawesi
(7) East Kalimantan (5) North Sulawesi (3)
Regional East Indonesia (1)

Academy for Nurses' Training
Palu: under Woodward Hospital (acc 345)

William Booth Medical College
Surabaya: under William Booth Hospital
(acc 155)

SOCIAL WORK
Babies' and Toddlers' Home
Surabaya: (acc 60)

Boys' Homes
Bandung: Maranatha (acc 80)
Denpasar, Bali: William Booth Home (acc 200)
Kalawara: Bahagia (acc 60)
Medan: William Booth Home (acc 90)
Semarang: Betlehem (acc 80)
Tompaso: Wisma Anugerah (acc 80)
Yogyakarta: Tunas Harapan (acc 40)

Children's Homes
Ambon: William Booth (acc 24)
Bandung: William Booth Home (acc 90)
Denpasar: Anugerah (acc 60)
Jakarta: Catherine Booth Home (acc 90)
Malang: Elim (acc 80)
Manado: Bukit Harapan (acc 60)
Medan: Evangeline Booth Home (acc 80)
Palu: Sejahtera (acc 80)

Eventide Homes
Bandung: Senjarawi (acc 100)
Semarang: Bethany (acc 60)
Turen: Tresno Mukti (acc 50)

Students' Hostels
Bandung:(acc 34)
Bandung: (acc 32)
Medan: (acc 30)
Palu: (acc 24)
Surabaya: (acc 24)

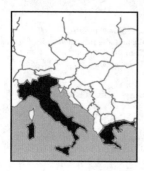

ITALY AND GREECE COMMAND

Command leaders:
Lieut-Colonels Massimo and Anne-Florence Tursi

Officer Commanding:
Lieut-Colonel Massimo Tursi (1 Sep 2014)

General Secretary:
Major David Cavanagh (1 Sep 2011)

Command Headquarters: Via degli Apuli 39, 00185 Rome, Italy

Tel: [39] 06 44740630

email: Italy_Command@ity.salvationarmy.org; website: www.esercitodellasalvezza.org

The Salvation Army flag was unfurled in Italy on 20 February 1887 by Major and Mrs James Vint and Lieutenant Fanny Hack, though subsequent difficulties necessitated withdrawal. In 1890 Fritz Malan (later lieut-colonel) began meetings in his native village in the Waldensian Valleys. In 1893 Army work was re-established. In a decree of the President on 1 April 1965, The Salvation Army was recognised as a philanthropic organisation competent to acquire and hold properties and to receive donations and legacies. It received legal status as a religious body/church on 20 March 2009.

On 8 October 2007 The Salvation Army began operations in Greece, the work being linked to the Italy Command. Captains Polis Pantelidis and Maria Konti-Galinou, UK officers of Greek nationality, launched the Army's mission in their home country. Greece was recognised as part of the command on 2 February 2011.

Zone: Europe
Countries included in the command: Greece, Italy
'The Salvation Army' in Italian: Esercito della Salvezza; in Greek: O Stratos Tis Sotirias
Languages in which the gospel is preached: Greek, Italian
Periodicals: *Il Bollettino delle Risorse – Dipartimento dei Ministeri Femminili, Il Grido di Guerra*

FOUR cadets from the Proclaimers of the Resurrection Session were commissioned and ordained on 4 May 2013 in the presence of more than 300 people who gathered in the Methodist Church in Rome. The ceremony that marked the end of the session was led by the then Chief of the Staff, Commissioner André Cox and Commissioner Silvia Cox (WPWM).

Some months later, Thessaloniki corps officers and their nine recently

enrolled soldiers, were blessed by the visit of General André Cox. This was the first visit of the Army's international leader to Greece. During the visit the General, accompanied by Commissioner Silvia Cox, enrolled four new soldiers in Athens.

Commissioners William and Marilyn Francis (USA Eastern Territory) conducted officers councils for both active and retired officers. The commissioner also led a series of six

Bible study sessions. At the closing meeting officers within the command assembled together with Rome Corps personnel to attend a holiness meeting that concluded with a significant number of seekers.

Baby Song activities, funded partly by the Helping Hand project, had a positive response with new families attending corps within the command. A summer youth camp, adult Bible study camp, 360° expression and various workshops, including social justice, continue to show growing interest year after year.

STATISTICS
Officers 49 (active 28 retired 21) **Auxiliary-Captains** 1 **Envoys** 2 **Employees** 28
Corps 17 **Outposts** 17 **Institutions** 7
Senior Soldiers 248 **Adherent Members** 116
Junior Soldiers 33

STAFF
Women's Ministries: Lt-Col Anne-Florence Tursi (CPWM) Maj Elaine Cavanagh (CSWM)
Coordinator for Anti-Human Trafficking: Maj Estelle Blake
Spiritual Life Development: Maj Elaine Cavanagh
Finance: Capt Emmanuel Gau
Property: Maj David Cavanagh
Social and PR Coordinator: Major Paolo Longo
Training: Maj David Cavanagh
Family Tracing: Maj Angela Dentico
Candidates: Maj Lidia Bruno

SOCIAL WORK
Centre for the Homeless
Centro Virgilio Paglieri, Via degli Apuli 41, 00185 Roma; tel: 0039 06 44740622/23 (acc 200)

Workers' Lodge
Villa Speranza, Contrada Serra 57a, 85100 Potenza; tel: 0971 51245 (acc 6)

Holiday Centres
Le Casermette, Via Pellice 4, 10060 Bobbio Pellice (To); tel: 0121 957728 email: lecasermette@esercitodellasalvezza.org; www.centrovacanzebobbio.com (acc 206)

Concordia, Via Casa di Majo 36, 80075 Forio d'Ischia (Na); tel: 081 997324 email: concordia@esercitodellasalvezza.org
L'Uliveto, Via Stretta della Croce 20, 84030 Atena Lucana (Sa); tel: 0975 76321 (acc 80) email: uliveto@esercitodellasalvezza.org

Guest Houses
Florence: Villa delle Rose, Via Aretina 91, 50136 Firenze; tel/fax: 055 660445 email: villadellerose@esercitodellasalvezza.org (acc 13)
Rome: Foresteria, Via degli Apuli 41, 00185 Roma; tel: 06 44740622/23; email: foresteriaroma@esercitodellasalvezza.org (acc 70)

GREECE
Regional Officer: Maj Polycarpos Pantelidis
P.O. Box 23069
11210 Athens, Greece; email: athens@salvationarmy.gr
tel : 0030/2111 821 846; www.salvationarmy.gr

JAPAN TERRITORY

Territorial leaders:
Commissioners Jiro and Keiko Katsuchi

Territorial Commander:
Commissioner Jiro Katsuchi (1 Jan 2013)

Chief Secretary:
Lieut-Colonel Kenji Fujii (1 Jan 2013)

**Territorial Headquarters: 2-17 Kanda-Jimbocho,
Chiyoda-ku, Tokyo 101-0051, Japan**

Tel: [81] (03) 3237 0881; website: www.salvationarmy.or.jp

In 1895 a small group of pioneer officers from Britain arrived in Japan at Yokohama to start operations. In spite of great difficulties, work was soon established. Of several outstanding Japanese who were attracted to The Salvation Army, the most distinguished was Commissioner Gunpei Yamamuro OF, prominent evangelist and author, whose book *The Common People's Gospel* has been reprinted more than 500 times.

Zone: South Pacific and East Asia
Country included in the territory: Japan
Language in which the gospel is preached: Japanese
Periodicals: *Home League Quarterly*, *The Officer*, *The Sunday School Guide*, *Toki-no-Koe*, *Toki-no-Koe Junior*

THE THEME for the young people of the territory was 'Feed My Sheep', based on John 21:17 with the aim of revitalising the youth evangelism programme that has been challenged by Japan's hyper-aging and diminishing child demographics.

The territorial youth councils, under the theme 'One Army, One Mission, One Message', held in May, saw youth enjoy creative workshops of worship, music and visual arts. The event culminated in a creative arts night that showcased the talents of the young people. During the concluding meeting, Territorial Commander Commissioner

Jiro Katsuchi challenged the youth, with many responding at the mercy seat.

Baby and mother clubs, junior soldier rallies, and many other activities took place in the year. The rebuilt Kiekoryo children's home was dedicated to God in November 2013 and the Sano day nursery was rebuilt and dedicated to God in March 2014. Both these centres will assist in meeting community needs.

The newly-opened Megumi-no-Ie home for the aged was awarded the Best Town Design award from local government for its architectural design. The home collaborates with the neighbouring Salvation Army hospital and centres to provide medical and nursing care to the community.

Over-60s clubs have become a regular aspect of corps ministry, providing fellowship and spiritual care through lunchtime gatherings.

Disaster relief has continued since the tsunami of 11 March 2011. A large tent theatre was built in Minamisanriku in August 2013 and was used for various events and exhibitions. The territory's emergency service office was established in November 2013 and a branch office was opened in Sendai. The aim is to open a new corps community centre in the disaster area through aiding various projects.

Wellington Citadel Band (New Zealand, Fiji and Tonga Territory) visited Japan in November for its fourth tour of the territory. The band brought encouragement to many through its music performances including in schools and temporary commercial towns in the disaster area.

The 2014 territorial theme is 'Hold the Vision' and the territory seeks a continuing vision for The Salvation Army in the 21st century. 'Whoever believes in me will do the works I have been doing and they will do even greater things' (John 14:12) is the promise for the territory as it marches forward.

STATISTICS
Officers 173 (active 77 retired 96) **Cadets** (2nd Yr) 2 **Employees** 1,135
Corps 45 **Outposts** 12 **Institutions** 21 **Hospitals** 2
Senior Soldiers 2,530 **Adherent Members** 25 **Junior Soldiers** 92

STAFF
Women's Ministries: Comr Keiko Katsuchi (TPWM) Lt-Col Chiaki Fujii (TSWM)
Business Administration: Maj Teiichi Tanaka
Candidates: Maj Shinji Ishizaka
Editor: Ms Keiko Saito
Literary: Maj Kazumitsu Higuchi
Medical: Comr Makoto Yoshida (R)
Music: S/L Mikako Ebara
Personnel: Maj Chieko Tanaka
Programme: Maj Kazumitsu Higuchi
Social: Maj Tamotsu Nishimura
Staff Band: B/M Masaki Hikichi
Staff Songsters: S/L Mikako Ebara
Training: Lt-Col Kenji Fuji
Youth: Maj Shinji Ishizaka

DIVISIONS
Hokkaido: 5-1-5, Kita-22-jo-Nishi, Kita-ku, Sapporo-shi, Hokkaido 001-0022; tel: (011) 788 5352; Majs Nobuhiro and Yasuko Hiramoto
Kanto-Tohoku: 5 Yoriai-cho, Takasaki-shi, Gunma Ken 370-0822; tel: (027) 323 1337; Majs Tsukasa and Kyoko Yoshida
Nishi Nihon: 3-6-20 Tenjinbashi, Kita-ku, Osaka-shi 530-0041; tel: (06) 6351 0084; Majs Haruhisa and Hiromi Ota
Tokyo-Tokaido: 4-11-3 Taihei, Sumida-ku, Tokyo 130-0012; tel: (03) 5819 1460; Majs Kazuyuki and Yoshiko Ishikawa

TRAINING COLLEGE
1-39-5 Wada Suginami-ku, Tokyo 166-0012; tel: (03) 3381 9837

MEDICAL WORK
Booth Memorial Hospital: 1-40-5 Wada, Suginami-ku, Tokyo 166-0012; tel: (03) 3381 7236 (acc hospital 179, hospice 20)
Kiyose Hospital: 1-17-9 Takeoka, Kiyose-shi, Tokyo, 204-0023; tel: (042) 491 1411/3 (acc hospital 117, hospice 25)

SOCIAL WORK
Alcoholic Rehabilitation Centre
Tokyo: Jiseikan (acc 50)

Rehabilitation Centre (Men)
Tokyo (acc 15)

Social Service Centre (Men) (Bazaar)
Tokyo

Working Men's Homes
Tokyo:
  Jijokan (acc 35)
  Shinkokan (acc 37)

Women's Homes
Tokyo:
  Fujinryo (acc 40)
  Shinseiryo (acc 70)

Children's Homes
Hiroshima:
  Aikoen (acc 30); Toyohama-Gakury (acc 44)
Osaka:
  Kibokan (acc 65)
Tokyo:
  Kiekoryo (acc 42)
  Sekoryo (acc 56)

Day Nurseries
Kure-shi: Kure Hoikusho (acc 60)
Sapporo-shi:
  Kikusui Kamimachi Hoikuen (acc 90)

Shiseikan Hoikuen (acc 120)
Soen Hoikusho (acc 90)
Sano-shi: Sano Hoikuen (acc 110)

Homes for the Aged
Tokyo: Keisen Home (acc 50)
      Megumi-no-Ie (acc 80)

Hostel
Kyoto: Kyoto Hostel (acc 6)

**Senior Citizens' Housing and
  Care Centre**
Tokyo: Grace (acc 100)

Care House
Tokyo: Izumi (acc 32)

RETIRED OFFICERS' APARTMENTS
Olive House: 1-39-12 Wada, Suginami-ku, Tokyo
  166-0012
Osaka Central Hall 5F: 3-6-20 Tenjinbashi,
  Kita-ku, Osaka 530-0041
Tokiwa House: 1-17-12 Takeoka, Kiyose-shi,
  Tokyo 204-0023

JAPAN: The Nishiarai Corps Over Sixties Club

KENYA EAST TERRITORY

Territorial Commander:
Commissioner Vinece Chigariro
(1 Jan 2013)

Chief Secretary:
Lieut-Colonel Nahashon Njiru
(1 Jan 2013)

Territorial Headquarters: Marist Lane, Karen, Nairobi, Kenya

Postal address: Box 24927, Karen 00502, Nairobi, Kenya

Tel: [254] (020) 240-3260

In 1896 three Salvationists went to Kenya to work on the building of a new railway and made their witness while based at the Taru Camp. The first official meetings were held in Nairobi in April 1921, led by Lieut-Colonel and Mrs James Allister Smith. The first cadets were trained in 1923. On 1 March 2008, the Kenya Territory was divided into two and Kenya East Territory and Kenya West Territory were created.

Zone: Africa
Country included in the territory: Kenya
'The Salvation Army' in Kiswahili: Jeshi La Wokovu
Languages in which the gospel is preached: English, Kiswahili and a number of regional languages
Periodicals: *Sauti ya Vita* (*The War Cry,* English and Kiswahili)

'FAN THE Flame' was the theme that continued to inspire Kenya East Territory during the year under review. The visit of General André Cox and Commissioner Silvia Cox (WPWM) inspired a spiritual revival among the more than 8,000 Salvationists who attended the gatherings, and children in the social institutions were also blessed by the presence of the international leaders. At the event more than US$244,000 was raised for the Self-Denial appeal and a number of musicians were commissioned.

Commissioner Vinece Chigariro (TC/TPWM) conducted the commissioning and ordination of 36 cadets.

The Women's Ministries Department purchased a vehicle that enabled the women to visit Lang'ata Women's Prison and share God's Word with the inmates and present personal items and clothes for the babies, and Njoro Special School where 75 mattresses, bedding and food were distributed.

The Salvation Army Disaster Response Group provided assistance to security personnel, blood donors and the rescuers at the Westgate shopping mall terrorist attack in Nairobi. They also offered pastoral care to the family members of the hostages.

Official opening ceremonies for Salvation Army halls and officers' quarters took place. A new dormitory is being built at the Njoro Special School.

'Rekindle the fire in Marriage' was the theme of the first-ever officer couples' seminar held and attended by 20 couples. Community conferences, men's, women's and youth rallies, and health and spiritual life seminars were held.

The first four-day officers councils was conducted, during which spiritual nourishment was received and information about child protection issues and the Territorial Strategic Plan, were shared. Kenya East has been represented in international forums such as the International Communications Summit and Chaplain's Conference in London, International Social Justice Conference in New York, the Writers Conference in St Louis and the Global Conversation Conference in Florida, USA.

A team from Aberdeen Corps (United Kingdom Territory with the Republic of Ireland) visited centres where projects are being undertaken and painted a dormitory at Kabete Children's Home. Students from Jeløy Salvation Army School (Norway, Iceland and The Færoes Territory) visited Thika School for the Blind and two corps. They also set up a computer laboratory and painted the Variety Village Vocational Training Centre. Our Partners in Mission, USA Central

Territory, also visited some of the territory's projects.

Two physiotherapy facilities were officially opened; one in Likoni School for the Blind, and the other at Joytown Primary School.

STATISTICS

Officers 598 (active 526 retired 72) **Cadets** 72
  Employees 112
Corps 394 **Outposts** 353
  Pre-primary Schools 159 **Primary Schools**
  162 **Secondary Schools** 44 **Institutions** 13
Senior Soldiers 79,714
  Junior Soldiers 61,023
  Personnel serving outside the territory:
  Officers 8

STAFF

Women's Ministries: Comr Vinece Chigariro
  (TPWM) Lt-Col Zipporah Njiru (TSWM)
Asst Chief Sec: Lt-Col Julius Mukonga
Business Administration: Lt-Col John Kumar
Personnel: Lt-Col Isaac Kivindyo
Programme: Lt-Col Herman Mbakaya
Audit: Maj Matthew Wangubo
Candidates: Capt James Kilonzo
Finance: Maj Joshua Kitonyi
Editorial: Maj Jane Musyoki
Education: Maj Thomas Musyoki
Extension Training: Capt Juliana Musilia
Information Technology: Capt Samson Maweu
Projects: Cadet Richard Bradbury
Property Sec: Capt John Kilonzo
Public Relations: Capt Benjamin Musila
Social: Maj Bilhah M'rewa
Spiritual Life Development: Lt-Col Lucia
  Mbakaya
Territorial Band: B/M Jason Kinyua
Territorial Songsters: S/L Fanuel Misango
Trade: Mr Joshua Mugera
Training Principal: Maj John Mutune
Youth: Capt James Kilonzo
  Children: Capt Agnes Kilonzo

DIVISIONS

Coast: PO Box 98277, Mombasa; tel: 041-490629;
  Majs Immanuel and Beatrice Mtepe
Embu: PO Box 74, Embu; tel: 068-20107;
  Majs Lucas and Agnes Kithome

Kangundo: PO Box 324, Kangundo; tel: 044-21049;
Majs Peter and Anna Mutuku
Kathiani: PO Box 2, Kathiani;
Majs Ibrahim and Ann Lorot
Machakos: PO Box 160, Machakos;
tel: 044-21660; Majs Simon and
Zippora Mbuthu
Nairobi: PO Box 31205, Nairobi;
tel: 020-767208; Majs Richard and Eunice
Mweemba
Nakuru: PO Box 672, Nakuru; tel: 051-212455;
Capts Titus and Damaris Kyengo
Sulutani: PO Box 842 Sultan Hamud;
Capts Pheneas and Evangeline Karanja
Thika: PO Box 809, Thika; tel: 067-22056;
Maj Joyce Mbungu
Westlands: PO Box 25240, Nairobi;
Maj Sarah M'tetu
Yatta: PO Box 29 Kithimani;
Majs Daniel and Ann Kiama

DISTRICTS

Eastlands: PO Box 2, Kathiani;
Maj Ibrahim Lorot
Kibwezi: PO Box 230, Ngwata via Kibwezi;
Maj Julius Sengete
Kilome: PO Box 85, Nunguni;
Capt Joseph Muindi
Kirinyaga: PO Box 21, Kerugoya;
Capt Kenneth Muriithi
Kitui / Mwingi: PO Box 89, Migwani;
Maj Gideon Nako
Makueni: PO Box 40, Wote; tel: 044-77 Makueni;
Capt Phineas Karanja
Matungulu: PO Box 422, Tala;
Capt Newton Madegwa
Mbooni: PO Box160, Machakos;
Maj Simon Wambua
Meru: PO Box 465, Nkubu, Meru; tel: 064-51207;
Maj Samson Mwangi
Mwala: PO Box 19, Mwala; Maj Wellington
Ongaya
Mwea: PO Box 80, Karaba; Capt Anubi

TRAINING COLLEGE

PO Box 4467, Thika; tel: 0733-629411

EDUCATIONAL WORK

SA Sponsored Primary Schools: 15
**SA Sponsored and Managed Secondary
Schools:** 26
Special Schools: 8

Schools for the Visually Handicapped

Thika High School (acc 163)
Likoni Primary School (acc 120)
Thika Primary School (acc 297)

Schools for the Physically Disabled

Joytown Primary School (acc 215)
Joytown Secondary School (acc 110)

Special Units for the Multi-Handicapped

Joytown: (acc 22)
Njoro Special School
Thika Primary School

SOCIAL SERVICES
Children's Homes

Kabete: Sarit Centre (acc 114)
Mombasa (acc 40)
Thika: Karibu Children's Centre

Community Centre

Kibera: Nairobi
Dandora Phase V: Nairobi

Lions Girls' Hostel

Nairobi: PO Box 31354, Nairobi;
tel: 020-765750

Health Clinic

Kithituni: PO Box 482, Sultan Hamud 90132;
tel: 020-136492

Vocational Training Centres

Variety Village: Thika
Nairobi Girls' Centre (acc 60)

KENYA WEST TERRITORY

Territorial leaders:
**Commissioners Kenneth G. and
Jolene K. Hodder**

Territorial Commander:
Commissioner Kenneth G. Hodder
(1 Jan 2013)

Chief Secretary:
Colonel Stephen Chepkurui
(1 Aug 2014)

Territorial Headquarters: Kisumu – Kakamega Highway, Kakamega, Kenya
Postal address: PO Box 660, Kakamega 50100, Kenya

Tel: [254] (020) 249-3210

In 1896 three Salvationists went to Kenya to work on the building of a new railway and made their witness while based at the Taru Camp. The first official meetings were held in Nairobi in April 1921, led by Lieut-Colonel and Mrs James Allister Smith. The first cadets were trained in 1923. On 1 March 2008, the Kenya Territory was divided into two and Kenya East Territory and Kenya West Territory were created.

Zone: Africa
Country included in the territory: Kenya
'The Salvation Army' in Kiswahili: Jeshi La Wokovu
Languages in which the gospel is preached: English, Kiswahili and a number of regional languages
Periodicals: *Sauti ya Vita* (English and Kiswahili)

UNDER the theme 'Living in God's Power', Salvation Army ministry in the Kenya West Territory continues to grow with significant increases reported in the number of converts, recruits, and senior and junior soldiers. In the past year, the territory has opened 51 new corps, a division and a district. An active scouting programme and the first annual Junior Miss Congress, which brought together more than 4,000 girls and young women for three days of worship and celebration, was the catalyst for this growth.

The territory has implemented its Strategic Training Initiative. This is a flexible plan under which 190 envoys and sergeants-in-charge will be commissioned as officers by the end of 2016.

There was also dramatic growth in the territory's programmes and institutions for children with special needs. These improvements, which included both the upgrading of current facilities and the founding of additional special units, culminated in the first International Disabilities Day celebration at Joyland Primary School.

The musical development of the territory was boosted through a territorial music school under the leadership of

Envoy Ken Clarke (United Kingdom Territory with the Republic of Ireland) and his team from the Kenya Trust.

Working in close cooperation with the Kenya East Territory, the territory had the privilege of hosting the annual Brengle Holiness Institute where the special guests were Lieut-Colonels Vern and Martha Jewett (USA Southern Territory).

To guide its development, the territory established Territorial and Retired Leaders' Advisory Councils, and an Investment Advisory Committee.

During the year, the territory assisted all corps in opening their own bank accounts. This has improved accountability and transparency at the local level, eliminated the need for corps trust accounts, and allowed the electronic transfer of funds directly from THQ to local units. In addition, thanks to the generous support of the USA Western Territory, Kenya West established satellite trade shops at four divisional headquarters. These shops provide Salvationists with easier access to uniform items, soldier training materials and related products. The increased sales volume is helping to move the territory closer to financial self-sufficiency. Payment for purchases is made directly to THQ through the purchaser's mobile phone.

In November General André Cox and Commissioner Silvia Cox (WPWM) honoured the territory by their visit, during which the General dedicated the site for the territory's new officer training college, laid the foundation stone for the new Kakamega Central

Corps, and presided over the official opening of the Shikulu Corps, which he had inaugurated as an outpost only eight months before. More than 12,000 people attended the final holiness meeting at Bukhungu Stadium.

At the end of April 2014, the territory held its annual Self-Denial ingathering that raised more than KES13.8 million.

STATISTICS

Officers 770 (active 541 retired 229) **Cadets** 31
  Envoys/Employees 211
Corps 415 **Outposts** 973
  Pre-Primary Schools 407 **Primary Schools**
  406 **Secondary Schools** 55 **Institutions** 3
Senior Soldiers 121,752
  Junior Soldiers 119,195

STAFF

Women's Ministries: Comr Jolene K. Hodder
  (TPWM) Col Grace Chepkurui (TSWM)
Business Administration: Lt-Col Fanuel Maube
Personnel: Lt-Col Stephen Moriasi
Programme: Lt-Col Enock Lufumbu
Audit: Capt Celestin Ayabagabo
Editor: Ms Hellen Obimbo
Education: Maj Wycliffe Ambuga
Finance: Maj Jacob Olubwayo
Information Technology: Ms Naum Juma
Projects: Capt Geoffrey Muyoma
Property: Maj Fredrick Omuzee
Public Relations: Capt Timothy Kwalanda
Social and Sponsorships: Maj Eleanor Haddic
Statistics: Capt Elizabeth Muyoma
Training Principal: Maj Fredrick Khamalishi
Youth: Capt Pelegi Wanyama
Candidates: Capt Catherine Alemba

DIVISIONS

Bungoma: PO Box 1106, Bungoma;
  tel: 055-30589; Lt-Col Sarah Wanyama
Eldoret: PO Box 125, Eldoret; tel: 053-22266;
  Lt-Cols Tirus and Mebo Mbaja
Elgon: PO Box 274, Malakisi; tel: 055-20443;
  Majs Henry and Grace Changalwa
Kakamega: PO Box 660, Kakamega;
  tel: 331-20344; Majs Moses and Gladys
  Shavanga
Kitale: PO Box 548, Kitale; tel:054-30259;
  Lt-Cols Edward and Florence Shavanga

141

Mbale: PO Box 80, Maragoli; tel: 056-51076;
Majs Harun and Beatrice Chepsiri

Musudzuu: PO Box 278, Seremi;
tel: 056-45055;
Lt-Cols Peter and Jessica Dali

Shigomere: PO Box 125, Khwisero;
tel: 056-20260; Majs Isaack and
Rose Liviala

Tongaren: PO Box 127, Tongaren; Majs John
and Mary Olewa

DISTRICTS

Bunyore: PO Box 81, Bunyore; Maj Isaac
Siundu

Kapsabet: PO Box 409, Kapsabet; Maj James
Mukubwa

Kimilili: PO Box 220, Kimilili; Maj Nathan
Musieni

Kisumu: PO Box 288, Kisumu; tel: 057-2025632;
Maj Meshack Wanjia

Lugari: PO Box 15, Matete; Maj Reuben
Malaba

Madzuu: PO Box 381, Vihiga; Capt Patrick
Kimaswoch

Migori: PO Box 59, Suna, Migori; Capt Paul
Kyalo

Sabatia: PO Box102, Wodanga; Capt Amos
Malabi

Sirisia: PO Box 50, Sirisia; Maj Joseph Mwanga

Turkana: PO Box 118-30500, Lodwar;
tel: 054-21010; Maj Peter Masaka

Webuye: PO Box 484, Webuye; Capt Samson
Maweu

EDUCATIONAL WORK

SA Sponsored Kindergartens: 407
SA Sponsored Primary Schools: 406
**SA Sponsored and Managed Secondary
Schools:** 52

Special Schools
Schools for Visually Impaired Pupils
Kibos Primary School: PO Box 477, Kisumu
(acc 230)
Kibos Secondary School: PO Box 77, Kisumu
tel: 057-43135

Schools for Physically Impaired Pupils
Joyland Primary School: PO Box 1790, Kisumu;
tel: 057-41864/50574 (acc 230)
Joyland Secondary School: PO Box 19494,
Kisumu (acc 174)

School for Hearing Impaired Pupils
Chekombero Primary School: PO Box 93,
Wodanga via Maragoli (60 pupils)

School for Mentally Challenged Pupils
Madegwa Primary School: PO Box 52,
Maragoli (55 pupils)

Inclusive School
Joy Valley Primary School – Kimatuni:
PO Box 1293, Bungoma (236 pupils)

SOCIAL SERVICES
Feeding Programmes for Destitute
Persons
Kisumu: PO Box 288, Kisumu; tel: 057-4151
Shinoyi Community Centre

Health Centre
Kolanya: PO Box 88, Malakisi via Bungoma

Workshop
Kibos: PO Box 477, Kisumu (acc 12)

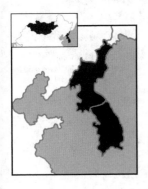

KOREA TERRITORY

Territorial leaders:
**Commissioner Park, Chong-duk and
Commissioner Yoon, Eun-sook**

Territorial Commander:
Commissioner Park, Chong-duk
(1 Oct 2013)

Chief Secretary:
Colonel Kim, Pil-soo (1 Oct 2013)

**Territorial Headquarters: The Salvation Army Central Hall
130 Deoksugung-gil (Jeong-dong), Jung-gu,
Seoul 100-120, Republic of Korea**

Postal address: The Salvation Army, Central PO Box 1192, Seoul 100-709, Republic of Korea

Tel: [82] (2) 6364 4000

email: korea@kor.salvationarmy.org; website: www.salvationarmy.or.kr

Responding to a request while visiting Japan in 1907, the Founder despatched Commissioner George Scott Railton to survey prospects on the Korean peninsula. As a result, in October 1908 Colonel and Mrs Robert Hoggard (née Annie Johns) arrived with a group of officers to 'open fire' in Seoul.

During the Korean conflict, which took place from 1950 to 1953, one Korean officer and one corps sergeant-major were martyred. Three further Salvationists were believed martyred and all five names are registered as matyrs of the Korean church.

Outreach work in Mongolia was officially commenced in October 2008 and in the Kingdom of Cambodia in November 2012.

Zone: South Pacific and East Asia
Countries included in the territory: Cambodia, Republic of Korea (South Korea), Democratic People's
  Republic of Korea (North Korea), Mongolia
'The Salvation Army' in Korean: (pronounced) 'Koo Sei Goon'
Languages in which the gospel is preached: Khmer, Korean, Mongolian
Periodicals: *Home League Programme Helps*, *The Officer*, *The War Cry*

THE THEME for the year in review was 'Living as Christ's Disciples'.

Along with a change in the territorial leadership of the Korea Territory, the 10th assembly of the World Council of Churches was held in Busan in November 2013. Territorial Commander Commissioner Park, Chong-duk was elected as the 62nd President of the National Council of Churches in Korea.

In August, the South Pacific and East Asia College for Officers (SPEACO) was held within the territory. Twenty-five delegates from 11 territories and commands, two translators and three administrative staff attended. Commissioner Lynette Pearce Australia Eastern Territory) was the principal,

Major Kim, Dong-jin served as the assistant principal and Major Kaylene Fyfe (Australia Southern Territory) was the secretary.

To provide for the communities in remote areas, 12 libraries have been established so that people can join in fellowship as they read. The opening ceremony for these was held in October 2013 at Yi Chon Corps, Kyung Buk Division. The territorial commander, along with Commissioner Yoon, Eun-sook (TPWM), the president of the Educational Broadcasting System, the head of the Arts Council of Korea, the divisional commander from the Kyung Buk Division and a member from the local assembly, all participated in the official opening ceremony.

'Sympathy and Hope' was the theme for the territorial officers councils held in October. During the councils, the territorial commander unpacked the new territorial vision to 600 officers. In his presentation, he outlined the further five-year strategic plan phase II, with the emphasis being on the expansion of national mission fields, the strength of corps growth and the specialisation of social welfare programmes.

STATISTICS

Officers 798 (active 629 retired 169) **Cadets** (1st Yr) 8 (2nd Yr) 16 **Employees** 1,214
Corps 254 **Outposts and Societies** 24
Residential Institutions 31
Senior Soldiers 44,997 **Adherent Members** 8,240 **Junior Soldiers** 7,328
Personnel serving outside territory Officers 24

STAFF

Women's Ministries: Comr Yoon, Eun-sook

(TPWM) Col Choi, Sun-hee (TSWM)
Lt-Col Lee, Mi-hwa (THLS)
Sec for Personnel: Lt-Col Kim, Dong-jin
  Editor and Education: Maj Cho, Hyo-jung
  Literary and Publishing Sec: Capt Kim, Byung-yoon
  Development Ministries Sec: Capt Kim, Kyu-han
  Overseas Service Bureau: Capt Kim, Byung-yoon
Sec for Programme/Church Growth: Lt-Col Shin, Jae-kook
  Social Sec: Maj Kwak, Chang-hee
  Spiritual Life Development Sec: Maj Han, Sea-jong
  Music: Capt Kim, Hai-du
  Youth: Capt Han, Seung-ho
Sec for Business: Lt-Col Kim, Young-tae, MBA
  Financial Sec: Capt Hwang, Kyu-hong
  Information Technology: Maj Lee, Hyun-hee
  Property: Capt Lee, Sung-jae
  Public Relations: Capt Kim, Kyu-han
  Sponsorship: Maj Park, Eun-young
  Trade: Capt Kim, Sook-yung
Director, Territorial Heritage Centre: Lt-Col Hwang, Sun-yup
Training: Lt-Col Lim, Hun-taek

DIVISIONS

Choong Buk: 704 Doosan Hansol 1 cha Apartments 101 dong, 447-15 Kaeshin Dong, Heungduk Ku, Chung Ju, Choong Book 361-746; tel: (043) 276 1634;
  Maj Lee, Choong-ho and Maj Kim, Sook-ja
Choong Chung: 603 Oosung Apartments 126 dong,162-15 Jeonglim suh Ro Suh ku, Taejon, Choong Nam Do 302-795; tel: (042) 584 2891;
  Maj Kim, Jong-koo and Maj Kim, Kye-suk
Choong Saw: 401 Hyundai Apartments 3-cha 302 dong, 208 Choongmoo Ro (Ssangyong dong), Suh Buk Ku, Chonan, Choong Nam Do 330-091; tel: (041) 572 0855;
  Lt-Col Kim, Nam-sun
Chulla: 117-30 Song San Il Kil, Chung Eup, Chun Buk 580-200; tel: (063) 536 1190;
  Maj Ahn, Guhn-shik and Maj Yang, Shin-kyong
Kyung Buk: #901 Doosan We've Apartments 102 dong, Dang San Ro 82, Dahl suh ku, Taegu 704-082; tel: (053) 322 3695;
  Maj Lee, Jae-seup and Major Kim, Keum-hee
Kyung Nam: #1306 Green Core Apartments 301 dong, Deok Cheon Ro 234, Buk ku, Pusan, Kyung Sang Nam Do 616-782; tel: (051) 337 0789;

144

Maj Son, Suk-young and Maj Park, Chung-hee
Seoul: The Salvation Army Office Building,
#705, 69 Saemoonan Gil Chongno gu,
Seoul 110-061; tel: (02) 720 9543;
Lt-Col Choo, Seung-chan and Lt-Col Lee, Oh-hee
Seoul South: 602, Soojung Hanyang Apartments
235-dong, 1086 Sunboo 3-dong, Danwon Ku,
Ansan, Kyunggi-do 425-765; tel: (031) 413 7811;
Lt-Col Kim, Un-ho and Lt-Col Lee, Ok-kyung
Suh Hae: 301 Dongshin Apartments 204 dong,
(Eupnae Dong Daelim Dongshin), 47 Buk
Choon 2 Ro, Sosan, Choong Nam 356-758;
tel: (041) 667 2580;
Maj Lee, Ki-yong and Maj Kim, Sun-ho

MONGOLIA OFFICE
District 22, Bayanzurkh, Ulaanbaatar, Mongolia;
tel: (976) 7016 7260; mobile: (976) 9191 7261;
Maj Lee, Jong-woo and Maj Kim, Hoe-gyeong

KINGDOM OF CAMBODIA OFFICE
#503, ST 90 BT, Boeung TumPun, Mean Chey,
Phnom Penh, Kingdom of Cambodia;
tel: (855) 077 907 500;
Capt Shin, Jin-kyun and Capt Lim, Hyang

CONFERENCE CENTRES
Territorial Retreat and Conference Centre:
Paekhwasan (Mount Paekhwa) (acc 1,000)
Choong Chung Div: Taejon Central Corps,
Taejon (acc 400)
Seoul Div: Ah Hyun Corps, Kangwondo (acc 300)
Seoul Div: Youngwol Corps (acc 50)

OFFICER TRAINING COLLEGE
83-2 Chungang-dong, Kwachun, Kyunggi-do
427-010; tel: (02) 502 9505/2927

RETIRED OFFICERS' RESIDENCE
'Victory Lodge' Silver Nursing Home
(acc 50)

SCHOOL
Inpyung Technical High School (acc 1,340)

TERRITORIAL HERITAGE CENTRE
1st and 2nd floors A, The Salvation Army
Central Hall, 130 Deoksugung-gil
(Jeong dong), Jung-gu, Seoul 100-120

THE SALVATION ARMY BUILDING
476 Choong Chung Ro 3-ga, Sudaemun Gu,
Seoul 120-837

THE SALVATION ARMY OFFICE BUILDING (THE SAOB)
69 Saemoonan Gil, Chongno Ku, Seoul 110-061

SOCIAL MINISTRIES
Adult Rehabilitation Centre (ARC)
Iljook (acc 36)

Bridge Centre (drop-in centre)
Seoul (acc 891)

Centres for the Handicapped
Kunsan: Catherine Centre (acc 60)
Day Care Centre (acc 21)
Suwon: Support Centre (acc 5)
Rehabilitation Centre (acc 20)
Day Care Centre (acc 15)

Children's Homes
Kunsan (acc 75)
Seoul Broadview (acc 100)
Taegu (acc 61)
Taejon No 1 (acc 50)
Taejon No 2 (acc 75)
Sarangsaem (acc 7)

Community Centres
Community Centres: Hapchong, Hongeun,
Kang Buk, Myung Chun, Non Hyun
(Incheon city) Samyang Dong, Suh San Suklim,
Youngwol
Corps Welfare Centres: An Sung Gongdo,
Booyuh, Cheju, Mosan, Najoo, Seogwipo,
Taegu, Suh An Sung Home Helper Centre
for the Elderly, Taegu Chil Kok Centre for
the Elderly, Yoju
Self-Support Training Centres: Asan, Bohryung,
Nonsan, Sosan, Tai An

Corps Day Care Centres
Bahnyawol, Boo Nam, Chin Chang, Chun Kok,
Hap Duk, Kang Buk, Keumbit Namoo
(Hongeun), Kim Chon, Kwachun, Masan
(Moonwha), Mindalae, Mosan, Myung Chun,
Osan Saetbyeol (Star), San Kok, Sharon,
Sok Cho, Sudaemun, Suh Taegu, Suh San
Suk Lim, Taegu, Wonju, Yul Mok

Counselling and Friendship Centres
Chonan Counselling Centre for Women
Donui-dong
Suh Taejon
Taegu
Taejon
Tong Taegu

Family Welfare Centres
Bohryung Multicultural Family Support Centre

Food Banks, Food Markets and Distribution Centres
Asan, Bohryung, Cheju, Chun An, Kwachun, Mapo #1, Mapo #2 Nonsan, Seogwipo, Song Dong, Sosan, Sudaemun #1, Sudaemun #2, Suh Chung Ju, Taejon, Taian, Yea San, Yeoju

HIV/Aids Care and Prevention Programme Units
Pusan Shelter; Red Ribbon Centre, Seoul

Oori Jip (transitional housing for those leaving children's homes)
Choongdong (Seoul Broadview Children's Home) (acc 2),
Chun Yun (acc 3)

Sarangbang Centres (hostels for the homeless)
Heemang Hostel of Hope (acc 55)
Iljook (acc 36),
Mangu Dong (acc 75)
Sudaemun (acc 50)

Self-Support Training Centres
Boryung, Nonsan, Taian

Senior Citizens' Services
Residential
Ansung Nursing Home (acc 60)
Ansung Peace Village Nursing Home (acc 70)
Kwachun Home for the Elderly (acc 60)
Kwachun Nursing Home (acc 20)
Namdong Peace Village Nursing Home (acc 60)
Pusan Home for the Elderly (acc 71)
Sooyong, Sun Chang Welfare Centre for the Elderly (acc 30)
'Victory Lodge' Silver Nursing Home, Kwachun (acc 58)
Sun Chang Welfare Centre for the Elderly (acc 30)

Day Care Centres
Hapjung Day Centre for the Elderly (acc 20)
Hongjae Dong Day Care Centre for the Elderly (acc 34)
Mooan 'Silver Centre' for the Elderly (acc 5)
Najoo Day Centre for the Elderly (acc 10)

Namdong Day Centre for the Elderly (acc 119)
Suh Ansung Day Centre for the Elderly (acc 15)
Suwon Day Care Centre for the Elderly (acc 15)
Wolsung Day Care Centre for the Elderly (acc 18)

Long-term Care Centres
Boryeong Multicultural Family Support Centre
Tongnae, Muloori (acc 20)

Welfare Centres for Seniors
Ansung, Balggeun, Chung Sung, Dan Chun, Sunchang, Taian

Special Service and Relief Services
9 programmes, 5 vehicles

Students' Study Centres (and after-school programmes)
1318 Happy Zone (Cheju), 1318 Happy Zone (Onyang), Asan, Baesan, Buk Choon Chun, Buk Gumi, Cheonju, Chew Kok, Chin Hae, Chisan, Chun An, Daniel (Eonyak), Doriwon, Eden, Hongjae, Huimang (Uijeongbu), Kang Buk, Keumsan, Leewon, Majeon, Mil Yang, Oh Ka, Sae Chung Ju, Sae Sungnam, Sak Sun, Seogwipo, Seoul Broadview, Shim Chon, Shinchang, Soyang, Taegu, Taegu Chil Kok, Wadong, Yea San, Yong Dong, Yoju, Youngwol

Student Accommodation
Taejon (university students, acc 25)

Thrift Stores and Sally's Coffee
Ah Hyun, Seoul; Buk Ahyun, Seoul; Changdong, Seoul; Daehangno, Seoul; Sookmyung Women's University Shop, Seoul; Suhdaemun, Seoul

Vocational Training and Support Centres
Chung Daoon House, Taejon (acc 20)
Sally Home, Pusan (acc 22)

Women's Homes
Chonan House of Hope (acc 24)
Didimdol (acc 16)
Doori Home, Seoul (acc 35)
Taejon Women's Refuge Shelter (acc 35)

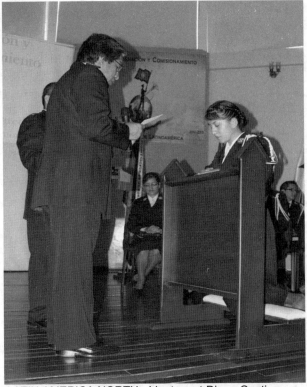

LATIN AMERICA NORTH: Lieutenant Diana Gantiva
kneels in prayer prior to her commissioning and ordination
as a Salvation Army officer

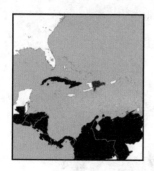

LATIN AMERICA NORTH TERRITORY

Territorial leaders:
Colonels Tito and Martha Paredes

Territorial Commander:
Colonel Tito Paredes (1 Aug 2010)

Chief Secretary:
Lieut-Colonel David Alarcón (1 Feb 2014)

Territorial Headquarters: Avenida 11, Calle 20, San José, Costa Rica

Postal address: Apartado Postal 125-1005, Barrio México, San José, Costa Rica

Tel: [506] 2257-7535; fax: [506] 2257-5291; email: lan_leadership@lan.salvationarmy.org

The Salvation Army's work commenced in the Isthmus of Panama (1904), Costa Rica (1907), Cuba (1918), Venezuela (1972), Guatemala (1976), Colombia (1985), El Salvador (1989), Dominican Republic (1995), Honduras (2000) and Nicaragua (2010).

Legal recognition was given to El Ejército de Salvación by the Republic of Panama (1946), Costa Rica (1975), Guatemala (1978), Colombia (1988), Dominican Republic (1995), El Salvador (1996) and Honduras (2001). The territory was formed on 1 October 1976, then reformed on 1 September 1998, when Mexico became a command.

Zone: Americas and Caribbean
Countries included in the territory: Colombia, Costa Rica, Cuba, Dominican Republic, El Salvador, Guatemala, Honduras, Nicaragua, Panama, Venezuela
'The Salvation Army' in Spanish: Ejército de Salvación
Languages in which the gospel is preached: English, Kaqchikel, Spanish
Publications: *Voz de Salvación (Salvation Voice), Arco Iris de Ideas (Rainbow of Ideas)*

THE YEAR in review has been a very exciting one for the youth in the Latin America North Territory. With continued innovation, the youth programmes have motivated the young people to have a stronger relationship with Jesus that has resulted in an increase in the number of programmes being held throughout the territory.

The first-ever territorial Bible Bowl competition – where students challenge each other over their knowledge of Scripture – was held. This exciting programme has been instrumental in seeing an increase in Sunday school attendance of some 80 per cent.

Thirty-five young people answered God's call to officership and, as a result, the territory accepted 21 cadets for the Heralds of Grace Session.

The youth of the territory joined together in October for a territorial youth congress. The theme for the congress was *Shine* and over 400 young people from nine countries   gathered under the leadership of Lieut-Colonels Guy and Henrietta Klemanski (USA Eastern Territory), assisted by the Greater New York Youth Band. The young people participated in   folkloric dance and a reflection of   different cultures and customs. During the meetings the youth were challenged to be involved in the service to God. The movement of the Spirit during the congress will live on in the hearts of all who attended.

Commissioners Brian and Rosalie Peddle (then TC/TPWM, Canada and Bermuda Territory) were the special guests for the commissioning and ordination of 11 cadets from the Proclaimers of the Resurrection Session. Along with the territorial leaders, Colonels Tito and Martha Paredes, more than 450 Salvationists from Colombia came together to celebrate this event. The commissioners spoke powerfully from God's Word, resulting in many kneeling in dedication to God.

STATISTICS

Officers 148 (active 131 retired 17) **Cadets** (1st year) 21 (2nd year) 16 **Employees** 200 **Corps** 64 **Outposts** 12 **Institutions** 6 **Schools** 8 **Day Care Centres** 5 **Children's Development Centres** 8 **Vocational Training Centres** 4 **Feeding Centres** 13 **Camps** 2 **Senior Soldiers** 3,401 **Adherent Members** 977 **Junior Soldiers** 1,561

STAFF

Women's Ministries: Col Martha Paredes (TPWM) Lt-Col María Alarcón (TSWM)
Business Administration: Lt-Col María Alarcón
Personnel: Maj Esteban Calvo
Programme: Maj Agripina Gochez
Editorial: Maj Agripina Góchez
Education: Maj Ileana Calvo
Finance/Property: Capt Flor Canto

Public Relations/Fundraising: Maj Gerardo Gochez
Sponsorship: Ms Beatriz Villegas
Social: Maj Agripina Gochez
Training: Maj Betzabé Moya
Youth and Candidates: Capt Alexander Díaz

DIVISIONS

Colombia: Apartado Aéreo 17756 Santa Fe de Bogotá, Colombia; tel: (571) 263 2633;
Majs Guillermo and Martha Portela
Costa Rica: Apartado Postal 6227-1000, San José, Costa Rica; tel: (506) 2221 8266;
Majs Faber and Taura Palacio
Central Cuba: Calle 96 Nª 5513 entre 55 Y 57, Marianao CP 11400, Ciudad de la Habana, Cuba; tel: (53) 7260-2171;
Capts Julio and Leyanis Moreno
Guatemala: Apartado Postal 1881, Guatemala CA; 2a Avenida 3-10, Sector A4 San Cristóbal 1, Zona 8 de Mixco, Guatemala; tel: (502) 2472-4868;
Capt Quelvin Cañas
Panama: Apartado Postal 0843-01134 Balboa, Ancón Panamá, República de Panamá, Balboa Calle La Boca, Calle Julio Linares Edificio 0792, República de Panamá; tel: (507) 228-0146;
Majs Elicio and Darlan Marquez

REGIONS

Dominican Republic: Residencial Antares casa N° B11, Ensanche Isabelita Sector Los Mameyes, Santo Domingo; tel: 1(809) 335 2678;
Capts Marcos and Kenia Piña
El Salvador: Apartado Postal No 7, Centro de Gobierno, Calle 15 de Septiembre, N° 119 y N° 121 Barrio Candelaria, San Salvador; tel: (503) 2237-0269;
Majs Walter and Lidia Gutierrez
Honduras (under THQ): Colonia Miraflores Norte, Portón #1, atrás de las bodegas Lipol; tel: (504) 2230-6982/2230-7131;
Lt Saraí Almendares
Venezuela: Calle 71 # 14 A63, Juana de Avila, Apdo Postal 1464 Maracaibo 4001; Estado de Zulia, Venezuela; tel: (058) 416 498-3375;
Lts Juan and Ignabel Soteldo
Nicaragua: Reparto Miraflores de donde fue el Restaurante Munich, 1 cuadra al Sur, 2 cuadras arriba y media cuadra al Sur tel: (505) 2250 2527
Lts Alvaro and Ingrid Vargas

DISTRICT
Cuba East: Calle Rastro # 62 entre Frexes, Holguín, CP 80.100, Holguín, Cuba; tel: (53) 2442-4674; Capt Alberto Pereira

TRAINING COLLEGES
Costa Rica: Calle Puente de Piedra, Barrio Los Angeles, San Rafael de Heredia, Costa Rica; Postal address: Apartado 173-3015 San Rafael de Heredia, Costa Rica; tel: (506) 2262 0061; Maj Betzabé Moya
Cuba: Calle Reinaldo Perez #14209 e/ Santos y Caraballo, San Francisco de Paula San Miguel de Padrón, CP 191180, Ciudad de la Habana, Cuba; Capts David and Niurka Ramírez

CONFERENCE CENTRE
Costa Rica: Calle Puente de Piedra, 1 km norte del Puente de Piedra, Barrio Los Angeles, San Rafael de Heredia, Costa Rica; Postal address: Apartado 173-3015 San Rafael de Heredia, Costa Rica; tel: (506) 2262 0061;

SOCIAL SERVICES
Centre for Homeless
Costa Rica: Refugio de Esperanza: Avenida 9 Zona Roja, San José; tel: (506) 2233-2059 (acc 30)

Residential Home for Disabled People
Costa Rica: Hogar Sustituto 'Tierra Prometida', Carretera Interamericana 100 metros sur de Autos Mundiales, Pérez Zeledón; tel: (506) 2771-2517 (acc 13)

Residential Homes for the Elderly
Cuba: William Booth Home, Calle 84 No 5525 e/55 y Lindero, Marianao, CP 11400, Ciudad de la Habana; tel: (537) 260-1118
Panama: Hogar Jackson Home, Avenida Amador Guerrero y Calle 3 No 201, Colón; tel: (507) 441-3371 (acc 30)

Residential Homes for Children
Panama: Hogar Dr Eno (Girls), Transísmica, Sabanitas, Colón; tel: (507) 442-0371 (acc 20)
Venezuela: Hogar Nido Alegre, Calle 71 # 14 A63, Juana de Avila, Apdo Postal 1464 Maracaibo 4001; Estado de Zulia, Venezuela; tel: (58) 261 798-3761 (acc 50)

Adult Rehabilitation Centres
Costa Rica:
Centro Modelo: Calle Naranjo, Concepción de Tres Ríos, Cartago; tel: (506) 2273-6307

Cuba: Centro de Rehabilitación de Alcoholicos: Carretera de Vertienes Km 3 #335, Reparto Río Verde Camagüey CP 71200; tel: (53) 3220-1908

EDUCATIONAL WORK
Kindergartens
Dominican Republic: Moca, Prolongación Sánchez #12, Moca; tel: (1809) 578-9712 (acc 20)
Panama: Panamá Templo: Calle 25 y Avenida Cuba-Este; tel: (507) 262-2545 (acc 30)

Kindergartens and Schools
Dominican Republic:
Cotui: Calle Duarte 62, Sector La Gallera Provincia Sánchez Ramírez; tel: (1809) 240-4031 (acc 40)
Tres Brazos: Tres Brazos, Santo Domingo, República Dominicana (acc 20)
Guatemala:
Chimaltenango: 7a Avenida y 1a Calle, Zona 1, Villas del Pilar; tel: (502) 7839-6585 (acc 150)
Maya: Manzana #2, Lote 262, Zona 18, Colonia Maya; tel: (502) 2260 1519
Mezquital: 4a Calle 3-99, Zona 12, Colonia Mezquital; tel: (502) 2479-8443 (acc 150)
Tierra Nueva: Sector B-1, Manzana D, Lote 3, Colonia Tierra Nueva 1, Chinautla; tel: (502) 2484-1255 (acc 150)
Honduras: San Pedro Sula: Colonia Residencial Monte Bello, Casa 56, bloque 39; tel (504) 565 6488
Panama: Calle 11 y 1/2, La Pulida, Río Abajo; tel: (507) 224-7480 (acc 40)

Kindergarten, Primary and Secondary School
Guatemala: Limón: Colegio William Booth, Centro Communal 'El Limón' Costado Derecho, Zona 18; tel: (502) 2260-0723 (acc 395)

Health Education in Hospitals
Honduras:
Cuerpo de Tegucigalpa: Escuela en Hospital Materno Infantil (4 classrooms); tel: (504) 2230-6982
Cuerpo San Pedro Sula: Escuela en Hospital Mario Catarino Rivas (2 classrooms); tel (504) 565-6488

Day Care Centres
Colombia:
San Cristóbal Sur, Bogotá: Calle 12 Sur # 11-71 Este, Barrio San Cristóbal Sur, Santa Fe de Bogotá; tel: (571) 280-3905

Latin America North Territory

Costa Rica:
Central Corps: Avenida 16, Entre Calle 5 y
7 San José; tel: (506) 2233-6850 (acc 35)
León XIII: Ciudadela León XIII, Detrás de la
Escuela de León XIII, San José;
tel: (506) 2524-1748 (acc 80)
Limón Central: Av 4 entre Calles 7 y 9;
tel: (506) 2758-0657 (acc 75)
Pavas: Villa Esperanza de Pavas, Contiguo
Al Instituto Nacional de Aprendizaje,
San José; tel: (506) 2290-6220 (acc 80)

El Salvador:
Gualache Outpost:
Merliot Corps: Jardines del Volcán, call
ElJabalí #36, Ciudad Merliot, La Libertad
tel: (503) 2278 7071
Usulután Corps: 6ta Avenida y 7a calle
Oriente, Barrio El Calvario, Departamento de
Usulután. tel: (503) 2624 9653

Panama:
Templo Central: Calle 25 y Av Cuba-Este;
tel: (507) 262-2545 (acc 20)
Río Abajo: Calle 11 y 1/2 y la Pulida;
tel: (507) 224-7480 (acc 25)

Children's Development Centres

Colombia:
Armenia Outpost: Carrera 11 # 14-19 Barrio
Guayaquil; tel: (576) 313 232-6688
Nuevo Kennedy: Avda Calle 43 Sur #79 B47,
Barrio Nuevo Kennedy, Santa Fe de Bogotá,
Colombia; tel: (57) 1 264 9161
Ibague, Tolima: Carrera 5ta Sur # 20A-34,
Barrio Yuldaima, Apartado Aéreo 792;
tel: (578) 260-8070
Robledo, Medellín: Carrera 84B # 63-73,
Barrio Robledo, Medellín, Antioquía;
tel: (574) 234-8250
San Cristóbal Sur, Bogotá: Calle 12 Sur # 11-71
Este, Barrio San Cristóbal Sur, Santa Fe de
Bogotá; tel: (571) 280-3905

El Salvador:
Cuerpo Central: Calle 15 de Septiembre # 199
y # 121, Barrio Candelaria, San Salvador;
tel: (503) 2237-0269 (acc 246)

Venezuela:
Maracaibo: Calle 10 (99E) #62-09, Barrio
Simón Bolivar, Apartado postal 322,
Maracaibo 4001, Estado Zulia

Vocational Training Centres

Cuba:
Cuerpo Central: Computer Centre, Calle 96
Nª 5513 entre 55 y 57, Marianao 11400,
La Habana; tel: (53) 260-2171

Diezmero: Calle 3ra Nª 25304
entre 2da y Martí Diezmero San Miguel
del Padrón, CP 130000 Guevara, La Habana
Venezuela: Centro Vocacional – Carpenteria y
Costura, Calle 71 # 14 A-63, Cuartel Juana
de Avila, Apartado Postal 1464;
tel: (58) 261 798-3761

Feeding Centres

Costa Rica: Liberia: 500 mts Norte Estación de
Bomberos 100 Este y 50 Norte,
Barrio San Roque; tel: (506) 2666-4691
(acc 100)
Limón 2000: Barrio Limón 2000 frente al
Predio El Aragón, Alameda # 4;
tel: (506) 2797-1602 (acc 30)
Nicoya: Escuela de San Martín 900 al Oeste,
Barrio San Martín; tel: (506) 2685-5531 (acc
100)
Sagrada Familia: Costado Este de la Escuela
Carolina Dent, Barrio Sangrada Familia
Salitrillos: Salitrillos de Aserri, de las
Prestaciones, 300 metros al sur;
tel: (506) 2230-4668 (acc 80)
San Isidro del General: Barrio Los Angeles,
Apartado Postal 7-8000;
tel: (506) 2770-6756 (acc 150)
Santa Cruz: Barrio Tulita Sandino,
300 este del IDA Guanacaste;
tel: (506) 2680-0724 (acc 100)
Colombia: Comedor de Ancianos, Carrera 5ta
Sur # 20A-34, Barrio Yuldaima, Ibague,
Tolima
Cuba: Comedor William Booth: Calle 96
No 5513 entre 55 y 57
Panama:
Colon: Avenida Amador Guerrero 14201,
Apartado 1163; tel: (507) 441-4570 (acc 75)
Chilibre: Transistmica, Lote No 175,
Chilibre; tel: (507) 216-2501 (acc 100)
Venezuela: Simón Bolívar, Calle 10 (99E) #62-
09, Barrio Simón Bolivar, Apartado postal 322,
Maracaibo 4001, Estado Zulia

Camps

El Salvador: Km 50, Carretera a la Herradura,
Caserio los Novios, Hacienda del Cauca;
tel: (503) 2354-4530 (acc 150)
Guatemala: Tecpán: Calle Tte Coronel Jack
Waters, Barrio Poromá, Colonia Iximché;
tel: (502) 2237 0269 (acc 100)

151

LIBERIA COMMAND

Command Leaders:
Colonels Gabriel and Monica Kathuri

Officer Commanding:
Colonel Gabriel Kathuri
(1 Jun 2014

General Secretary:
Major Samuel Amponsah (1 Sep 2013)

Command Headquarters: 17th Street, Sinkor, Monrovia

Postal address: PO Box 20/5792, Monrovia, Liberia

The Salvation Army opened fire in Liberia in May 1988 as part of the Ghana and Liberia Territory, with Major and Mrs Leonard Millar as pioneer officers. This happened after more than 10 years of letters being written to International Headquarters by church pastors asking that they become part of the movement. Liberia was given separate command status on 1 January 1997. Neighbouring Sierra Leone became part of the command on 1 January 2010, with Captains John and Rosaline Bundu as pioneer officers.

Zone: Africa
Countries included in the command: Liberia, Sierra Leone
Languages in which the gospel is preached: Bassa, English, Gola, Krahn, Lorma

IN DECEMBER 2013 the command celebrated its 25th anniversary. The Chief of the Staff Commissioner William A. Roberts and Commissioner Nancy Roberts (WSWM) were the special guests. His Excellency Joseph Boakai, Vice President of the Republic of Liberia, also attended as the local guest. Some Salvationists from Sierra Leone also attended the celebration.

Liberia has come through the devastating effects of the 14-year civil war and as the government seeks to reorganise the infrastructure and put reconciliation processes in place, the command has been vigorously pursuing its mission as a pillar of the Church. As such evangelical outreach, social activities, educating the youth and showing concern for humanity in the communities, have been priorities.

The strategic plan was a major focus during the command retreat. All heads of department were given the opportunity to unpack their plans for the next three years. The territory's faith-based facilitation coordinator attended a one-week retreat in Kenya where 17 coordinators, representing their respective territories, commands and regions, were in attendance.

The command mobile clinic operates through a medical team of committed workers and volunteers who have a passion for helping those who live in rural Liberia. The teams remains fully committed to providing social and medical services to all without discrimination.

The William Booth Clinic located in

Paynesville provides both in-patient and out-patient services for mothers and their children. Laboratory facilities and vaccinations for mothers and children under five years old, are available.

The schools system continues to run smoothly in the midst of many national challenges and supervision is being reinforced to maintain the standards and core values within it.

During August, the field department, in association with the command youth and candidates secretary, conducted a local officers' seminar at Margibi Section. The seminar was a four-day event during which 15 local officers from all centres were trained in their respective responsibilities.

STATISTICS

Officers 57 **Auxiliary-Captains** 7 **Envoys** 1
Corps Leaders 14 **Cadets** 14 **Employees** 238
Corps 23 **Outposts** 27 **Schools** 12 (pupils 2,992)
Child Day Care Centres 6
Clinic 1 **Mobile Clinic** 1
Senior Soldiers 3,209 **Adherent Members** 155
Junior Soldiers 690

STAFF

Women's Ministries: Col Monica Kathuri (CPWM) Maj Hagar Amponsah (CSWM) Maj Martha Zogar (LOMS) Lt Georgina Snogba (JHLS/YWFS)
Education Secretariat: Mr David Massaquoi (Dir Education) Mr Elijah Sowen (Dep Dir Education) Mr Julius Fayiah, Mr Christian Smith (Education Officers)
Field: Maj Anthony Sio
Finance: Maj Wilson Chiwoya
Information Technology: Lt Lincoln Stewart
Projects: Capt John Bundu
Property: Maj William Zogar
Protocol and Communications: Mr Momo Douwee
Sponsorship: Maj Besnat Chiwoya
Trade: Lt Lincoln Stewart
Training/ETO: Maj Richmond Obeng Appau
Youth and Candidates: Lt Edwin Snogba

DISTRICT

Grand Bassa: c/o CHQ, PO Box 20/5792, Monrovia; Maj Amos Diah

SECTIONS

(c/o CHQ, PO Box 20/5792, Monrovia)
Bomi: Capt George Morris
Bong: Capt Jerry Duwar
Bushrod Island: Capt Philip Boweh
Grand Gedeh: Capt Abraham Collins
Margibi: Capt Edwin Kpadebah
Monrovia City: Maj Muna Sio
Mount Coffee: Capt Jonah Roberts
Paynesville: Capt John Bundu
Sinoe: Capt Broton Weah

TRAINING COLLEGE

17th Street, Sinkor, Monrovia

SCHOOLS AND COLLEGES

(c/o CHQ, PO Box 20/5792, Monrovia)
Salvation Army Vocational Technical and Training College; Programme Coordinator: Mr Tweh Wesseh BSc, LLB; Programme Consultant: Mr Taweh Johnson MSc
William Booth High School; Principal: Mr Levi S. Nyumah
John Gowans Junior and Senior High School; Principal: Mr Morris Sargba BSc
Bill Norris Primary, Elementary and Junior High School; Principal: Mr Joshua Jackson
Albert Orsborn Primary and Elementary School; Principal: Mr Moses Garnet
Bramwell Booth Primary and Elementary School; Principal: Mr Davison Paye
Len Millar Primary and Elementary School; Mr Amu Q Roberts BTh
Len Millar Junior and High School; Mr Amadu Roberts, BTh, AA
Paul A. Rader Primary and Elementary School; Principal: Mr Arthur Gbartolmah
William Booth Primary and Elementary School; Principal: Mr Richard Zekor

CLINIC

William Booth Clinic: c/o CHQ, PO Box 20/5792, Monrovia; Administrator: Mrs Korlu Smoke Geh; Physician Asst: Mr Johannson David

SIERRA LEONE (under CHQ)

Officer-in-charge: Maj Ben Gaymo
The Salvation Army, 92 Soldier St, Freetown, Sierra Leone
Senior Soldiers 184 **Adherent Members** 3
Junior Soldiers 46

MALAWI TERRITORY

Territorial leaders:
**Colonels Moses and
Sarah Wandulu**

Territorial Commander:
Colonel Moses Wandulu (1 Jan 2013)

Chief Secretary:
Lieut-Colonel Chatonda Theu (1 Sep 2013)

Territorial Headquarters: PO Box 51140, Limbe, Malawi

tel: [265] 1 917073 / 981142 email: MAL_Leadership@mal.salvationarmy.org

The Salvation Army began operations in Malawi on 13 November 1967 and was granted official government recognition on 2 October 1973. The Malawi Division was part of the Zimbabwe Territory until 1988, when it was integrated into the Zambia Command, which was given territorial status and became known as the Zambia and Malawi Territory. The Army's work in Malawi has grown and developed and on 1 October 2002 it became a separate region. Further growth and expansion of the work in Malawi resulted in the region being elevated to command status on 1 February 2004. The Malawi Command was elevated to territorial status on 1 March 2011.

Zone: Africa
Country included in the territory: Malawi
'The Salvation Army' in Chichewa: Nkhondo ya Chipulumutso
Languages in which the gospel is preached: Chichewa, English, Lomwe, Sena, Tumbuka

THE YEAR began with a number of events to enhance the growth and development of the territory. In August 2013, more than 600 youth from Zambia and Malawi joined together for youth councils. In November, 13 cadets of the Proclaimers of the Resurrection Session were commissioned and ordained by Colonel Moses Wandulu (TC) and the calendar year concluded with officers councils

In February 2014, 14 cadets entered the Messengers of Light Session and the territory embarked on a soul-winning campaign. Held in four divisions, the

campaign resulted in people being won for the Lord and centres opening.

Captain Lena Wanyonyi (Africa Development Office, Nairobi) visited the territory with the aim of reviewing the faith-based facilitation work being undertaken by the territory and to visit farming communities.

Due to the amount of rain in the country, floods have occurred with many farms and houses being destroyed. The Army responded with assistance and supplies.

Community development projects conducted during 2014 provided safe and clean water to communities, promoted sanitation and good hygiene and farming practices. Women empowerment and adult literacy projects, introduced by the Women's Ministries Department, assisted women with both literacy and business skills, and 70 women officers attended the territorial Naomi Project seminar.

Major Mark Bearcroft (Middle East Region) was the special guest for the territorial music school.

To combat the spread of malaria, women's ministries distributed mosquito nets to expectant and nursing mothers with the aim of reducing infant mortality and improving safe motherhood.

The territorial Self-Denial appeal ingathering was well attended and the appeal itself saw an increase of 62.5 per cent.

The territory is progressing under the theme 'Moving forward together in action for growth'.

STATISTICS

Officers 109 (active 101 retired 8) **Cadets** 15 **Employees** 78
Corps 50 **Outposts** 19 **Outreach Units and New Openings** 64
Senior Soldiers 7,351 **Junior Soldiers** 2,411 **Personnel serving outside the territory** Officers 4

STAFF

Women's Ministries: Col Sarah Wandul (TPWM) Lt-Col Joyce Theu (TSWM)
Finance: Capt David Mysoki
Development Services: Narelle Gurney
Extension Training: Capt Richard Mahata
Field: Maj Gerald Chimimba
Information Technology: Mr Aleck Chikopa
Projects and Public Relations: Capt Dyson Chifudzeni
Property: Capt Stanley Phiri
Sponsorship: Capt Aida Chifudzeni
Youth and Candidates: Capt Grace Mysoki

DIVISIONS

Blantyre: PO Box 51749, Limbe; tel: 01 655 901
Central: PO Box 40058, Kanengo, Lilongwe; tel: 01 716 869; Capts Oker and Gladys Ntomba
Phalombe: PO Box 99, Migowi; tel: 01 481 216; Capts Paul and Doreen Kholowa
Shire Valley: PO Box 48, Chiromo; Capts Luke and Stella Msikita

DISTRICTS

Northern: PO Box 1129, Mzuzu: Capt Lanken Phiri
Upper Shire: P/Bag 8, Ntcheu CDSS, Ntcheu; Capt Andson Namathanga

OFFICER TRAINING COLLEGE AND EXTENSION TRAINING CENTRE

Ndirande Ring Rd, Chinseu, Blantyre; PO Box 51140, Limbe

COMMUNITY DEVELOPMENT PROGRAMMES

Adult Literacy
Blantyre, Central, Phalombe and Shire Valley Divisions, Northern District
Agriculture, Irrigation, Food Security Programme
Shire Valley Division; Northern District Foundation for Farming
Anti-Child Trafficking Project
Central Division
HIV/Aids Home-based Care
Bangwe, Migowi, Nguludi, Nsanje, Phalombe
Rural Women Empowerment
Blantyre, Central and Shire Valley Divisions
School Feeding Programme
Chikwawa, Migowi, Nguludi, Nsanje
Solar Power (Small Business) Enterprise
Blantyre Division

All divisions and districts are involved in programmes and projects including:
Adult literacy; bush ambulances; livestock income generation; microcredit schemes orphans and vulnerable children; water, sanitation and hygiene promotion

Mission Projects: Faith-based Facilitation; Home League Health Education; Spiritual Life Development

SOCIAL SERVICES

Hans Andersen Memorial Youth Centre for Child Anti-Trafficking: PO Box 167, Mchinji
Administrator: Maj Dorica Tulombolombo

MALI REGION

Regional leaders:
Majors Kapela and Rose-Nicole Ntoya

Regional Commander:
Major Kapela Ntoya (1 Nov 2011)

Regional Headquarters: Armée du Salut,
Quartier Général Régional, Rue 360 (vers Place CAN),
Hamdallaye, ACI 2000 Bamako, Mali
Postal address: Armée du Salut Quartier Général, B.P. E 5249, Bamako, Mali
Tel. [223] 20-238315 – Email: MLI_Leadership@mli.salvationarmy.org

Following an invitation for the Army to establish a presence in Mali, registration was given on 29 November 2007. Work began under local leadership with oversight from Nigeria. In February 2008 officers were appointed. Mali was officially declared a separate region on 1 April 2011.

Zone: Africa
Country included in the region: Mali
'The Salvation Army' in Bambara: Kisili Kelebolo; in French: Armée du Salut
Languages in which the gospel is preached: Bambara and French,

THE REGIONAL theme, 'Giving to God', encouraged Mali Salvationists to improve their tithes and offerings in order to contribute to the building of the Army's work in the region during 2013-14.

Youth Bible camps were held in Mali and neighbouring Burkina Faso, resulting in many young people deepening their relationship with God.

Army personnel were deployed in the capital Bamako to attend to the needs of those who were displaced due to the outbreak of war. Several hundred families were given assistance.

Two training seminars were organised throughout the region. The first seminar, on how to win souls for Christ using the four spiritual laws, was organised with the assistance of personnel from Campus Crusade for Christ, and a three-day training session was conducted on how to evangelise through the Internet.

Winning souls has been a challenge in this Muslim-dominated society. Many activities were organised, such as movie sessions at public places and radio broadcast programmes. These proved successful and helped to promote the visibility of the Army.

STATISTICS
Officers 6 **Cadets** 2 (training elsewhere)
Corps 3 **Outpost** 2
Senior Soldiers 104 **Adherent Members** 41
Junior Soldiers 43
Vocational Training Centre 1

STAFF
Women's Ministries: Maj Rose-Nicole Ntoya (RPWM)
Projects Coordinator: Mr Falo Tounkara

156

MEXICO: Joyful moments during the commissioning weekend for the Proclaimers of the Resurrection Session of cadets (above); Future officers fellowship conference delegates (below)

MEXICO TERRITORY

Territorial leaders:
Colonels Ricardo and Sonia Bouzigues

Territorial Commander:
Colonel Ricardo Bouzigues (1 Jul 2012)

Chief Secretary:
Lieut-Colonel Edgar Chagas (1 Jul 2013)

Territorial Headquarters: San Borja No 1456, Colonia Vértiz Narvarte, Delegación Benito Juárez, México 03600, DF

Postal address: Apartado Postal 12-668, México 03020, DF

Tel: [52-55] 5575-1042; 5559-5244/9625

email: mexico@mexsalvationarmy.org;

website: www.ejercitodesalvacion.org.mx

In 1934, a group known as the Salvation Patrol was commenced in Mexico by Alejandro Guzmán. In October 1937, he was presented with a flag by General Evangeline Booth at the USA Southern Territory Congress in Atlanta, Georgia. The Salvation Patrol then became absorbed into the international Salvation Army, operating under the supervision of DHQ in Dallas, Texas, later becoming part of Latin America North Territory. On 1 September 1998 it was made a command and, on 1 October 2001, it became a territory.

Zone: Americas and Caribbean
Country included in the territory: Mexico
'The Salvation Army' in Spanish: Ejército de Salvación
Language in which the gospel is preached: Spanish
Publications: *El Grito de Guerra (The War Cry), El Eslabón (The Link)*

THE COMMISSIONING and ordination of eight cadets of the Proclaimers of the Resurrection Session was full of joy and was a stimulus for the territory. Under the leadership of territorial leaders Colonels Ricardo (TC) and Sonia Bouzigues (TPWM), a great number of Salvationists joined together to see the outpouring of God's Holy Spirit upon all who gathered.

During July and August 2013, divisional youth councils were held where the young people eagerly learned,

shared and surrendered themselves to the Lord.

During the welcome to the cadets of the Heralds of Grace Session, Lieut-Colonels Edgar and Sara Chagas (CS/TSWM) were welcomed to the territory.

A territorial strategic plan for the next three years has been implemented under the initiative 'Forward Together – One Army, One Mission, One Message'.

The Future Officers Fellowship met in

January 2014 with 69 delegates. This event gives hope for the growth in the number of officers in the territory over the next few years.

The Women's Ministries Department conducted two events under the international theme 'You are loved' and home league camps in two divisions were excellent opportunities for the participants to engage in Bible studies and workshops, with the women learning about the wonderful love of God for all.

A territorial music institute, with special guests from the South America East Territory, saw 120 delegates engage in brass band, singing, percussion and dance electives.

Territorial Commander Colonel Ricardo Bouzigues conducted the opening of a new building at Mazatlán Corps and the opening of the La Gloria Kindergarten and outpost in Tijuana.

In April 2014, a community training seminar was held. Territorial and divisional leaders and staff participated and learned new ways to assist those within the community.

The territory is grateful to God for his leading and the empowering of his Holy Spirit upon the officers and soldiers as they endeavour to preach the good news and move 'Forward Together'.

STATISTICS

Officers 171 (active 131 retired 40) **Sergeants** 2 **Cadets** (1st Yr) 8 (2nd Yr) 11 **Employees** 75 **Corps** 52 **Outposts** 3 **Institutions** 27 **Senior Soldiers** 2,014 **Adherent Members** 606 **Junior Soldiers** 924 **Officers serving outside territory** 1

STAFF

Women's Ministries: Col Sonia Bouzigues (TPWM) Lt-Col Sara Chagas (TSWM)

Personnel: Maj Víctor Valdés
Programme: Maj Martín Gutiérrez
Education and Editorial: Maj Ruth Ruiz
Finance: Maj Jannette Sáenz
Information Technology: Capt Omar Venegas
Legal: Maj Víctor Valdés
Music: B/M David Camargo
Projects: Mrs. Alva Catalán
Property: Maj Marcos Tavares
Public Relations: Capt Miguel Rodriguez
Social: Lt-Col Sara Chagas
Trade: Maj Alva Vargas
Training: Maj Maj Ofelia Valdés
Youth and Candidates: Capt Moisés Cerezo

DIVISIONS

Capital: Alicante No 88, Colonia Alamos Delegación Benito Juárez, México 03400, DF; Apartado Postal 13-013, México, 03501 DF; tel: [52-55] 5590-9220 Majs Manuel and Ana Campos
Noroeste: Tamborel No 601, Colonia Santa Rosa, Chihuahua 31050, tel: [52-614] (614) 435-5968 Maj Margarita Alemán (Rtd)
Río Bravo: Lombardo Toledano No 2709, Colonia Alta Vista Sur, Monterrey 64740, Nuevo León; tel: [52-81] (81) 8359-5711 Majs Gilberto and Lorena Martínez
Sureste: Calle 19 No 116 x 22 y 24, Colonia México, Mérida, 97128 Yucatán; tel: [52-999] 944-6415; Lt-Cols Josué and Ruth Cerezo

TRAINING COLLEGE

Calle Monte Albán No 510, Colonia Independencia, México 03630, DF; tel: [52-55] 5672-7986

SOCIAL SERVICES
Adult Educational Support Programme
San Juan Ixhuatepec, Estado de México (acc 40)

Children's Day Care Centres
Ciudad Juárez, Chihuahua (acc 60)
Culiacán, Sinaloa (acc 27)
La Gloria, (Tijuana, Baja California) (acc 30)
México, DF Corps #1 (acc 30)
Nuevo Laredo, Tamaulipas (acc 20)
Reynosa, Tamaulipas (acc 25
San Luís Potosí (acc 30)
Tampico, Tamaulipas (acc 30)
Torreón, Coahuila (acc 20)

Children's Educational Support Programmes
Ciudad Victoria, Tamaulipas (acc 40)
Genaro Vázquez, Monterrey (acc 40)
Mexicali, Baja California (acc 40)
Monclova, Coahuila (acc 40)
Nogales, Sonora (acc 50)

Mexico Territory

Nueva Atzacoalco (México, DF) (acc 20)
Puerto Vallarta, Jalisco (acc 30)
Sabinitas, (Guadalupe, Nuevo León) (acc 60)
San Juan Ixhuatepec, Estado de México (acc 40)
Tuxtla Gutiérrez, Chiapas (acc 20)
Villahermosa, Tabasco (acc 15)

Children's Homes
Acapulco, Guerrero (acc 90)
Chihuahua, Chihuahua (acc 70)
Coatzacoalcos, Veracruz (acc 30)
Cuernavaca, Morelos (acc 45)
Culiacán, Sinaloa (acc 25)
Guadalajara, Jalisco (acc 100)
Matamoros, Tamaulipas (acc 35)
Mazatlán, Sinaloa (acc 40)
Mérida, Yucatán (acc 30)
México, DF (acc 120)
Nuevo Laredo, Tamaulipas (acc 40)
Puebla, Puebla (acc 35)
Reynosa, Tamaulipas (acc 45)
Saltillo, Coahuila (acc 35)
San Luis Potosí, San Luís Potosí (acc 30)
Tampico, Tamaulipas (acc 55)
Torreón, Coahuila (acc 50)
Veracruz, Veracruz (acc 50)
Villahermosa, Tabasco (acc 30)

Clinic and Dispensary
México DF: Clínica de Salud Mental

Feeding Centres
(Senior Citizens and Children)
Alvarado, Veracruz (acc 160)
Can Cún, Quintana Roo (acc 50)
Ciudad Madero, Tamaulipas (acc 40)
Ciudad Victoria, Tamaulipas (acc 40)
Cocotitlán, Estado de México (acc 25)
Durango, Durango (acc 100)
El Paso Texas, Mérida, Yucatán (acc 50)
Genaro Vázquez, Monterrey (acc 40)
Hermosillo, Sonora (acc 50)
Mazatlán, Sinaloa (acc 40)
Mexicali, Baja California (acc 40)
México, DF Corps #3 (acc 20)
México, DF Corps #6 (acc 30)
Monclova, Coahuila (acc 40)
Monterrey, Nuevo León (acc 15)
Piedras Negras (acc 50)
Puerto Vallarta, Jalisco (acc 60)
Querétaro, Querétaro (acc 25)
Sabinitas, (Guadalupe, Nuevo León) (acc 60)
Saltillo, Coahuila (acc 35)
San Juan Ixhuatepec, Estado de México (acc 80)
Tapachula, Chiapas (acc 35)
Toluca, Estado de México (acc 25)

Tuxtla Gutiérrez, Chiapas (acc 20)
Xochitepec, Morelos (acc 40)

(Men)
Mexicali, Baja California (acc 50)
Nogales, Sonora (acc 50)

Night Shelters (Men)
México, DF La Esperanza (acc 125)
Monterrey, Nuevo León (acc 80)
Piedras Negras, Coahuila (acc 50)
Tijuana, Baja California (acc 150)

Vocational Training Centre
Cocotitlán: Estado de México (acc 6)

Street Children's Programme
Tapachula, Chiapas (acc 40)

Refuge from Domestic Abuse (women with children)
Ensenada, Baja California (acc 20)
Mexico, DF - Cuerpo #5 (acc 20)

Thrift Stores
México City: 2

MIDDLE EAST REGION

Regional leaders:
Majors Stewart and Heather Grinsted

Regional Commander:
Major Stewart Grinsted (1 January 2011)

**Regional Headquarters: The Salvation Army,
Ishbiliya, Block 4, Street 418, Villa 27, Flat 2**

Postal address; c/o The Lighthouse Church
National Evangelical Church Of Kuwait (Neck)
PO Box: 80 Safat 13001 Kuwait

The Salvation Army in the Middle East began with meetings held by ex-patriot Salvationists from South Asia who had moved to the Gulf coast countries for employment. After years of independent effort by local leaders, requests for official recognition were sent to IHQ. In August 2008 General Shaw Clifton appointed the first officers to Kuwait. Expansion continued from 2010 and onwards into neighbouring countries, the United Arab Emirates, Bahrain and Oman, and became a region officially on 1 April 2011.

Zone: South Asia
Countries included in the region: Kuwait, United Arab Emirates
Languages in which the gospel is preached: Arabic, Amharic, English, French, Hindi, Nepali, Oromo, Tamil

DURING 2013 the regional officer team continued to serve around the region to enable, encourage, equip and challenge Salvationists to confront the obstacles, consolidate what has already been achieved and participate in building an enthusiastic Salvation Army presence in the region.

In the United Arab Emirates (UAE), Oman, Bahrain and Kuwait, steady growth has been witnessed in the lives of the people, resulting in house group fellowships commencing and corps witnessing new people attending.

Many people have been helped through the Booth House social care programme, with many Kuwaitis and expatriates generously donating to its work.

In May 2014, General André Cox and Commissioner Silvia Cox (WPWM) visited the region for what proved to be a time of challenge and encouragement to Salvationists. The visit included a praise celebration featuring the youth praise band, brass band and youth drama, and a lunchtime reception saw embassy staff, senior church leaders, lawyers and other representatives join together to greet the General.

His Highness Sheikh Nawaf Al-Ahmad Al-Jaber Al-Sabah, Crown Prince of Kuwait, welcomed the international leaders to the Seif Palace.

The General told the Crown Prince that Christians are grateful for the freedom they have to worship in Kuwait, and assured him that The Salvation Army seeks to be of assistance to the state and the people. The Crown Prince assured the General of his support for the Army.

Salvationists in the Middle East Region continue to worship, witness and serve the people in the name of Christ.

STATISTICS
Officers 4 **Senior Soldiers** 319 **Junior Soldiers** 67 **Congregations** 10 **Employees** 4 **Volunteers** 15

STAFF
Women's Ministries:
  Maj Heather Grinsted (RPWM)
Finance: Maj Heather Grinsted
Assistant Regional Officers:
  Majs Mark and Tracy Bearcroft

Residential Social Care Centre
 Kuwait: Booth House (acc women)

Outreach Care Centres
Kuwait: 2

MIDDLE EAST: The General addressing a lunchtime reception

MOZAMBIQUE TERRITORY

Territorial leaders:
Colonels Daniel and Arschette Moukoko

Territorial Commander:
Colonel Daniel Moukoko
(1 Jun 2014)

Chief Secretary:
Lieut-Colonel Manuel Nhelenhele
(1 Jul 2012)

Territorial Headquarters: Avenue Filipe Samuel Magaia, 860, Maputo, Mozambique

Postal address: PO Box 4099, Maputo, Mozambique

Tel: 843007490

The Salvation Army's evangelistic endeavours in Mozambique were pioneered in 1916 by Mozambican converts returning from South Africa. The work was recognised by the Mozambique government in 1986 and officially registered in June 2005. Previously part of the Southern Africa Territory, Mozambique became a separate command on 1 March 2008. It was elevated to a territory on 1 March 2011.

Zone: Africa
Country included in the territory: Mozambique
'The Salvation Army' in Portuguese (the official language): Exército de Salvação
Languages in which the gospel is preached: Chona, Chopi, Gitonga, Makhuwa, Ndau, Portuguese, Sena, Tchewa, Tsonga, Tswa
Periodicals: *Devocionias para Encontros da Liga do Lar* (Home League resource manual in Portuguese)

THE MOZAMBIQUE Territory gives thanks to God for what has been accomplished during the year in review. Despite the political situation in the country, officers and Salvationists continue to work to extend God's Kingdom.

The Women's Ministries programmes were enhanced through seminars conducted in the three divisions.

During the year in review, the territorial leaders have focused on evangelism, candidates for officership and working toward the territory becoming self-sufficient. The territory is grateful for its reinforcement officers who work alongside local Salvationists to spread the gospel and help the needy.

The new territorial leaders, Colonels Daniel and Arschette Moukoko

(TC/TPWM), along with the territorial headquarters staff, encourage Salvationists to continue to move forward, to develop established work, and build God's Kingdom in this part of Africa.

STATISTICS

Officers 63 **Cadets** 13 **Employees** 20
Corps 57 **Outposts** 39 **Day Care Centres** 5 **HIV Home-based Care and OVC Projects** 4 **Adult Literacy Projects** 75
Senior Soldiers 4,391 **Junior Soldiers** 1,720

STAFF

Women's Ministries: Col Arschette Moukoko (TPWM) Lt-Col Irene Nhelenhele (TSWM)
Education: Maj Elias António Nhanez
Finance: Capt Sérgio Tsumbu
Development and Projects: Maj Peter White
Property: Maj Peter White
Public Relations: Manuel Alioso Daimone
Social: Maj Gail White
Sponsorship: Maj Gail White

Training: Capt José Nharugue
Youth and Candidates: Capt Ana Tsumbu

TRAINING COLLEGE

Rua no 5514 (do Hospital), 1360 Bagamoio, Maputo; tel: (258) 843986476

DIVISIONS

Capital
Province and City of Maputo
Rua no 5514 (do Hospital), 1360
Bagamoio, Maputo; tel: (258) 843012023
Capt Luisa Augusto Agostinho
Central-North
Provinces of Nampula, Zambezia, Tete, Manica and Sofala
Rua Dom António Barroso, 3272
Pioneiros, Beira: tel: (258) 843986478
Capts Félix and Amélia Nhaduate
South
Provinces of Inhambane and Gaza
Rua Ngungunhane, talhão 100
Chambone, Maxixe; tel: (258) 843986491
Capts Alípio and Leonor Zualo

MOZAMBIQUE: Cadets spend a moment in reflection prior to their commissioning and ordination

THE NETHERLANDS AND CZECH REPUBLIC TERRITORY

Territorial leaders:
Commissioners Hans and Marja van Vliet

Territorial Commander:
Commissioner Hans van Vliet (1 Jun 2010)

Chief Secretary:
Colonel Henrik Andersen (1 Sep 2014)

**Territorial Headquarters: Spoordreef 10, 1315 GN Almere,
The Netherlands**

Tel: [31] (36) 5398111; fax: [31] (36) 5331458; email: ldhnl@legerdesheils.nl;
websites: www.legerdesheils.nl; www.armadaspasy.cz

Captain and Mrs Joseph K. Tyler, English officers, and Lieutenant Gerrit J. Govaars, a gifted Dutch teacher, commenced Salvation Army work in the Gerard Doustraat, Amsterdam, on 8 May 1887. Operations soon spread throughout the country and reached Indonesia (then The Netherlands East Indies) in 1894. Further advances were made in 1926 in Surinam and in 1927 in Curaçao.

Salvation Army operations in Czechoslovakia commenced in 1919, the pioneer being Colonel Karl Larsson. Evangelistic and social activities were maintained until suppressed in June 1950. After the opening of the central European borders, The Salvation Army's work was re-established and The Netherlands Territory was asked to take charge of the redevelopment. By the end of 1990 centres were reopened in Havirov, Prague, Brno and Ostrava and the work has grown steadily since then.

On 1 February 2002 the territory was renamed The Netherlands and Czech Republic Territory.

Zone: Europe
Countries included in the territory: Czech Republic, The Netherlands
'The Salvation Army' in Dutch: Leger des Heils; in Czech: Armáda Spásy
Languages in which the gospel is preached: Czech, Dutch
Periodicals: *Dag In Dag Uit*, *Heils-en Strijdzangen*, *InterCom*, *Strijdkreet*, *Kans,* (all Dutch), *Prapor Spásy* (Czech)

THE NETHERLANDS and Czech Republic Territory's focus on prayer for new officers resulted in an increase of applicants. Four officers, three auxiliary-captains and nine cadets were commissioned and ordained, two from the Czech Republic.

The restructuring programme for corps commenced in 2009, resulting in three outposts being elevated to corps status. The Salvation Army's work at these centres, in Delfzijl and Elburg in the Northern Division and Maassluis in the Southern Division, keeps growing.

Television programmes focusing on the work of The Salvation Army, particularly with regards to health and welfare, received wide acclaim.

In October 2013 an outpost was opened in Bratislava. Two soldiers have been enrolled and others are undertaking recruits' classes. The outpost serves the local homeless community and holds regular Sunday worship.

In December 2013, more than 2,000 people gathered at Dam Square, Amsterdam, to witness the recording of *Kerst op de Dam* (*Christmas on Dam Square*) for Dutch television. Along with famous Dutch artists, the Amsterdam Staff Songsters and Staff Band performed live on stage. In the weeks prior to the television programme being aired, the artists visited Salvation Army corps and social services centres.

A number of years ago, Commissioner Marja van Vliet (TPWM) commenced a 'Fit to Knit' programme in which volunteers from all over The Netherlands knit socks and sweaters for the homeless. The territory is grateful that the programme has gained momentum. Commissioner van Vliet and her team tour The Netherlands distributing the knitted garments to shelters and centres for the homeless.

In northern Bohemia two new projects were opened, extending the work of the Army into that region. Mother and child projects commenced in Jirkov and a second-hand shop with social activities and training for the unemployed was established in Chodov.

The officers and soldiers give thanks to God for what he is doing in the territory.

STATISTICS
Officers 303 (active 104 retired 199) **Cadets** (1st Yr) 1 (2nd Yr) 4 **Employees** 5,973
Corps 48 **Outposts** 10 **Business Units** 10 (251 institutions and programmes)
Senior Soldiers 3,881 **Adherent Members** 1,176 **Junior Soldiers** 356

STAFF
The Salvation Army Church
Women's Ministries: Comr Marja van Vliet (TPWM) Col Lisbeth Andersen (TSWM)
Field: Lt-Col Johannes den Hollander
Mission Development: Mr Adiel Vader
Field Programme Support (inc Youth and Adult Ministries): Mr Alex van Zoeren
Candidates: Maj Ingeborg M. Keijzer
Education/Training: Maj Ingeborg M. Keijzer
Family Tracing: Maj Gerda van Schaik
Business Administration: Maj Stuart Evans
Data processing/Accounting: Mr Bert Barink
International Projects: Mr Hans de Graaf
Communications: Maj Robert Paul Fennema
Literary: Maj Simon M. van der Vlugt
Music: Mr Roel van Kesteren

DIVISIONS
Northern: Esdoornstraat 7, 3434 CD Nieuwegein; tel: (30) 6017535; Maj Ben Keijzer
Southern: Piccolostraat 13, 1312 RC Almere; tel: (036) 5365106; Maj Ans Wimmers

THE SALVATION ARMY MAIN FOUNDATION
Board of Administration
Chairman: Comr Hans van Vliet (TC)

Staff
Secretary: Col Henrik Andersen (CS)
Financial Sec and Managing Director: Maj Stuart Evans

THE SALVATION ARMY SERVICES FOUNDATION
Board of Administration
Chairman: Comr Hans van Vliet (TC)
Vice-Chairman: Col Henrik Andersen (CS)
Official (non-voting) Sec: Maj Stuart Evans
Members: Mr R. Heijboer, Mr P. Visser, Mr H.G. Vollmuller

Staff
Managing Director: Envoy Ed Bosma
Policy Worker: Mrs Martine Sloezarwij
Central Purchasing: Mr Egbert Oostra
Communications: Maj Robert Paul Fennema

Finance and Accounting: Mr Reinier Klunder
Fundraising and Marketing:
  Mr Will van Heugten
Human Resources: Maj Richard de Vree
Information Technology: Mr Friso van den Berg

Leger des Heils ReSHARE
(Recycling Services)
Koopvaardijweg 15, 4906 CV Oosterhout;
tel: (0900) 9900099
  Depot: Hattem
  Director Operations: Mr Simon Smedinga

THE SALVATION ARMY
FUNDRAISING FOUNDATION
Board of Administration
Chairman: Comr Hans van Vliet (TC)
Vice-Chairman: Col Henrik Andersen (CS)
Official Sec: Maj Stuart Evans
Members: Mrs J.W. Immink, Mrs N.C. de Waard,
  Mr. A.G.C. van de Haar, Mr. P. Stigter

Staff
Managing Director: Envoy Ed Bosma
Director Operations: Mr Will van Heugten
All activities of the Foundation are to be executed
by The Salvation Army Services Foundation.

THE SALVATION ARMY
FOUNDATION FOR WELFARE AND
HEALTH CARE
Care for the Homeless (total acc 3,740):
  emergency lodges (acc 440); drop in /day
  centres (acc 535); homes for addicts
  (acc 1,165); homes for street children (acc
  287); hostels for homeless people (acc 1,270);
  mother and baby homes (acc 50); preventative
  homelessness projects, ambulatory programmes
  (286 FTE)
Substance Misuse Services (total acc 42):
  residential (acc 30); specialist hospital (12);
  ambulatory programmes (5 FTE)
Probation Services: ambulatory programmes
  (259 FTE); day training centres (acc 56)
Health Care and Care for the Elderly (total
  capacity 882): permanent stay (acc 371); hospice care (acc 20); temporary stay (inc medical
  care of homeless) (acc 151); day care (acc 30);
  ambulatory programmes (inc home care) (78
  FTE); supervised living (acc 200); psychiatric
  clinic (acc 110)
Custody Care (total pupils 2,609): ambulatory
  programmes (225 FTE)
Care for Children and Young People
  residential care (acc 410); day care (acc 70)

Prevention and Social Rehabilitation Services
  (total acc 1,029): community centres (675);
  ambulatory programmes (acc 474 FTE);
  occupational rehabilitation projects (acc 354)

Supervisory Council
Chairman: Comr Hans van Vliet (TC)
Vice-Chairman: Col Henrik Andersen (CS)
Official Sec: Mrs Marianne Trompetter
Treasurer: Maj Stuart Evans
Members:
  Mr A. Lock, Mr D.J. Rutgers,
  Mrs M. Trompetter, Mrs M.F.D. Waling-
  Huijsen, Mr J. Wienen, Mr. P.W.D. Venhoeven

Board of Management
Envoy Cornel Vader
Mr Hermanus M. van Teijlingen

Staff
Executive Sec: Mr Jeroen Hoogteijling
Business Administration: Mr Ruud de Vries
Risk Management and Internal Control:
  Mr Piet van Keulen
Main Office: Spoordreef 10, 1315 GN Almere;
  tel: (36) 539 82 50

CENTRES FOR LIVING, CARE AND
WELFARE
Central Region
Managing director: Mr Jan Jans
  Information: Aïdadreef 8, 3561 GE Utrecht;
  tel: (30) 274 91 21
Northern Region
Managing director: Mr Elzo Edens
  Information: Kwinkenplein 10-A, 9712 GZ,
  Groningen; tel: (50) 317 26 70
South-Western Region
Managing director: Mrs Joanne Blaak-van de
    Lagemaat
  Information: Kromhout 110, 3311 RH
  Dordrecht; tel: (78) 632 07 00
Gelderland
Managing director: Mr Harry de Heer
  Information: Hoenderloseweg 108, 7339 GK
  Ugchelen; tel: (55) 538 03 33
Flevoland
Managing director: Mr Christiaan Sleurink
  Information: Spoordreef 12, 1315 GN Almere;
  tel: (36) 549 68 00
Northern Holland
Managing director: Mr Evert Pater
  Information: Mariettahof 25, 2033 WS
  Haarlem; tel: (23) 553 39 33
Overijssel
Managing director: Mr Dik van den Hoek

167

Information: Eiffelstraat 1 – 117, 8013 RT
Zwolle; tel: (38) 467 19 40
Limburg/Brabant
Managing director: Mr Hans Martin Don
Information: Kolonel Millerstraat 67, 6224 XM
Maastricht; tel: (43) 350 33 84
Amsterdam Goodwill Centres
Managing director: Envoy Henk Dijkstra
Information: Rode Kruisstraat 24b, 1025 KN
Amsterdam; tel: (20) 630 11 11
The Hague Goodwill Work
Managing director: Mr Bert Sprokkereef
Information: St Barbaraweg 4, 2516 BT
Den Haag; tel: (70) 311 55 40
Rotterdam Centres for Social Services
Managing director: Mr Johan Koeman
Information: Kooikerweg 28, 3069 WP
Rotterdam; tel: (10) 222 98 88
Probation Services and Leger des Heils
Youthcare
Managing director: Mr Peter Palsma
Central Office: Zeehaenkade 30, 3526 LC
Utrecht; tel: (88) 090 10 00

HOTEL AND CONFERENCE CENTRE
'Belmont', Goorsteeg 66, 6718 TB Ede;
tel: (31) 848 23 65 (50 twin-bedded rooms;
14 conference rooms acc varying 12-350)
(96 additional beds available in summer)

CZECH REPUBLIC
Officer-in-charge: Maj Maj Teunis Scholtens
National Headquarters: Armáda Spásy
Petrzilkova 2565/23, 158 00 Praha 5;
tel: (00420) 251 106 424;
email: ustredi@armadaspasy.cz;
website: www.armadaspasy.cz

STATISTICS
Officers 20 (active 18 retired 2) **Envoys** 5
Employees 547
Corps 9 **Outposts** 5 **Community Centres** 18
Institutions 21
Senior Soldiers 67 **Adherent Members** 68
Junior Soldiers 11

STAFF
Asst Officer-in-charge: Maj Ria Scholtens
Personal Assistant: Mrs Marta Kopečkova
Business Administration Manager:
Envoy Pavla Vopeláková
Nat Director Residential Social Services:
Mr Jan Krupa
Nat Director for Corps and Community

Centres: Maj Rein van Wagtendonk
Editorial: Maj Attie van Wagtendonk
Finance: Mr Jan Benda
Fundraising: Envoy Jakub Vopelak

CENTRES
Hostels for Men and Women/Night Shelters
Brno: Dům Josef Korbel Mlýnská 25,
602 00 Brno; tel: 543 212 530 (acc 136)
Karlovy Vary: Nákladní 7, 360 05 Karlovy Vary;
tel: 353 569 267 (acc 60)
Krnov: Csl armády 837 bcd, Opavské předměstí,
794 01 Krnov; tel: 554 612 296
(acc 85, includes mothers and children)
Prague: Dům Bohuslava Bureš, Tusarova 60,
170 00 Praha 7; tel: 220 184 000 (acc 220)

Hostels for Men and Night Shelters
Havířov: Hostel, Na spojce 2, 736 01 Havířov;
tel: 596 810 197 (acc 53)
Ostrava: U Novych Válcoven 9,
709 00 Ostrava-Mariánské Hory;
tel: 596 620 650 (acc 114)
Šumperk: Vikyrovicka 1495, Šumperk-Luže;
tel: 583 224 634 (acc 35)

Homes for Mothers and Children
Havířov: Dvorákova 21/235, 736 01 Havířov;
tel: 596 810 221 (acc 18 mothers plus children)
Jírkov: Studentská 1242, 431 11 Jirkov
tel: 773 770 285 (acc mothers 7, children 33)
Krnov: Csl armády 837 bcd, Opavské předměstí,
794 01 Krnov; tel: 554 612 296 (acc 85,
includes hostel for men and women)
Ostrava: Gen Píky 25, Ostrava-Fifejdy 702 00;
tel: 596 611 962 (acc women 30, mothers 10,
children 15-20)
Opava: Rybárská 86, 746 01 Opava;
tel: 553 714 509 (acc mothers 11, children 33)
Přerov: 9 kvetna 2481/107, 750 02 Přerov;
tel: 581 210 769 (acc 60)

Alternative Punishment Programme
Opava: Nákladní 24, 746 01 Opava

Azylovy Dům for Families
Stankova 4, 602 00, Brno; tel: 543 212 530
(acc 12 flats)

Elderly Persons Project (for handicapped and elderly homeless)
Přistav I: Holvekova 38, 718 00, Ostrava-Kunčičky;
tel: 596 238 163 (acc 40)
Přístav II: Zukalova 1401/3, Ostrava;
tel: 773 770 267 (acc 29)

The Netherlands and Czech Republic Territory

Farm Rehabilitation Project
Strahovice č.16, 747 24 pošta, Chuchelná;
  mobile: 773 770 251 (acc 4)

Follow-up Care (for alcoholics)
Dům pod svahem, Pod Svahem 1, 736 01,
  Havířov-Šumbark; tel: 596 881 007
  mob: 773 770 271 (acc 15 in men's programme; acc 8 in 'Na Vyhlídce' women's programme)

Prevention Project (against homelessness)
Palackeho 25, 702 00 Ostrava – Přívoz;
  tel: 596 133 417 (32 units)

Prison Work
Šumperk: Štefánikova 1, 787 01, Šumperk;
  tel: 737 215 396

Youth Centre
Jonaš: Brno-Bystrc: Kubickova 23,
  635 00 Brno-Bystrc; tel: 773 770 235

NEW ZEALAND: General André Cox and Commissioner Silvia Cox dressed in traditional Maori attire

NEW ZEALAND, FIJI AND TONGA TERRITORY

Territorial leaders:
Commissioners Robert W. and Janine Donaldson

Territorial Commander:
Commissioner Robert W. Donaldson
(1 Nov 2013)

Chief Secretary:
Colonel Willis Howell (1 Sep 2014)

Territorial Headquarters: 204 Cuba Street, Wellington, New Zealand

Postal address: PO Box 6015, Wellington 6141, New Zealand

Tel: [64] (04) 384 5649; website: www.salvationarmy.org.nz

On 1 April 1883 Salvation Army activities were commenced at Dunedin by Captain George Pollard and Lieutenant Edward Wright. Social work began in 1884 with a home for ex-prisoners. Work was begun officially in Fiji on 14 November 1973 by Captain Brian and Mrs Beverley McStay, and in Tonga on 9 January 1986 by Captain Tifare and Mrs Rebecca Inia.

Zone: South Pacific and East Asia
Countries included in the territory: Fiji, New Zealand, Tonga
'The Salvation Army' in Maori: Te Ope Whakaora
Languages in which the gospel is preached: English, Fijian, Hindi, Korean, Maori, Rotuman, Samoan, Tongan and Vietnamese
Periodical: *War Cry*

FOR THE first time in its history, each country within the territory has its own indigenous Salvation Army leaders.

In September 2013 a new mission goal – developing leaders – was added to the territory's already established goals of making disciples, increasing the number of soldiers and fighting injustice. The desire to have each goal realised in all Salvation Army programmes – working together in a mission-focused, connected and streamlined way – is the aim for all Army activities.

The territory hosted General André Cox and Commissioner Silvia Cox (WPWM) at a territorial congress in September. More than 2,500 delegates heard the Army's international leaders call for greater spiritual depth. The General admitted New Zealanders Lieut-Colonel Ethne Flintoff and Major Campbell Roberts to the Order of the Founder. Both officers stated that Micah 6:8, with its focus on acting justly, showing mercy and walking humbly with God, had strongly influenced their officer service.

The Fiji Division celebrated its 40th anniversary at the end of 2013. Over the period since the work commenced, The Salvation Army has been successful in turning troubled lives around and introducing people to Jesus. A number of children in Fiji and Tonga benefit from Salvation Army child sponsors.

In Tonga, the Alcohol and Drug Awareness Centre endeavours to limit the growing problem of substance abuse through tobacco, alcohol and illicit drugs. The centre has been operating for 16 years and is the only alcohol and drug service in the Kingdom of Tonga. It enjoys strong support from the Tongan royal family, government, other churches and the wider community.

In February 2014 the Army's Social Policy and Parliamentary Unit delivered its annual State of the Nation report. The review highlighted a lack of progress in reducing child poverty, family violence, the harmful use of alcohol, the failure to address criminals reoffending and serious crime.

The Salvation Army community ministries centres and a number of corps are seeing success through the Positive Lifestyle Programme. This 10-week course has helped people develop self-esteem and problem-solving skills as they are encouraged and supported to face life's challenges. The Department of Corrections, New Zealand, refer recently-released prisoners to The Salvation Army to undertake the course.

As rebuilding continues after the Christchurch earthquakes of September 2010 and February 2011, The Salvation Army is helping to bring cohesion to people in quake-affected areas. One corps has developed DALTA (Deliberate Acts of Love To All), a programme that uses volunteers to assist property owners who are struggling to meet the cost of rebuilding. The Salvation Army's education and employment training programme has been running a series of six-week courses to help trainees find work in infrastructure industries. With a 98 per cent attendance rate, 83 per cent of trainees have secured employment as a result of the course.

STATISTICS
Officers 524 (active 263 retired 261) **Cadets** (1st Yr) 28 (2nd Yr) 8 **Employees** 2,793
Corps 93 **Plants** 6 **Outposts** 5 **Recovery Churches** 13 **Institutions** 84
Senior Soldiers 5,502 **Adherent Members** 1,445 **Junior Soldiers** 830
Personnel serving outside territory Officers 9

STAFF
Women's Ministries: Comr Janine Donaldson (TPWM) Col Barbara Howell (TSWM)
Asst Chief Secretary: Lt-Col Yousaf Ghulam
Business Administration: Lt-Col Lynette Hutson
  Audit: Mr Graeme Tongs
  Finance: Maj David Bateman
  Information Technology: Mr Mark Bennett
  Property: Mr Ian McLaren
  Public Relations: Mr Shane Chisholm
  Trade: Emma Buckingham
  Communications: Maj Christina Tyson
Personnel: Capt Gerald Walker
  Asst (Officer Resources): Maj Lorraine LePine
  Human Resources: Mr Paul Geoghegan
Candidates: Lt Pauleen Richards
Spiritual Life Development: Maj Heather Rodwell
Programme: Lt-Col Rod Carey
  Asst: Lt-Col Jenny Carey

Social Services/Community Ministries:
Maj Pam Waugh
Creative Ministries: Mr Jim Downey
National Youth B/M: Mr Duncan Horton
Youth: Maj Joanne Wardle
Planned Giving: Majs Rex and Geraldine
Johnson
SpiritSong: Vocal Leader Marie Downey
Children's Ministries: Maj Bronwyn Malcolm
Book Production: Maj Christina Tyson
Moral and Social Issues Council: Maj Garth
Stevenson
Overseas Development Consultant:
Maj Vyvyenne Noakes
Social Policy and Parliamentary Unit: Maj
Campbell Roberts
Territorial Events Co-ordinator: Mrs Selena
Thomson

DIVISIONS

Central: 204 Cuba St, Wellington 6011,
PO Box 6421, Wellington 6141;
tel: (04) 384 4713;
email: cdhq@nzf.salvationarmy.org;
Lt-Colonel Ian Hutson
Midland: 12 Vialou St, PO Box 500,
Hamilton 3240; tel: (07) 839 2242;
email: Midland_dhq@nzf.salvationarmy.org;
Majs Garth and Suzanne Stevenson
Northern: 691A Mt Albert Road, Royal Oak,
Auckland, 1023, PO Box 24306,
Royal Oak, Auckland 1345; tel: (09) 639 1103
email: ndhq@nzf.salvationarmy.org;
Majs Stephen and Sheryl Jarvis
Southern: 1st Floor, 119 Wrights Road,
Addington, Christchurch 8024, PO Box 25207,
Victoria Street, Christchurch 8144;
Majs Majs Ivan and Glenda Bezzant

FIJI

PO Box 14412, Suva, Fiji; tel: [679] 331 5177;
email: dhq_fiji@nzf.salvationarmy.org
Divisional leaders: Majs Iliesa and Litiana Cola;
Corps 11 **Outposts** 4

TONGA REGION
Regional Headquarters:
Mosimani Building, cnr Hala Fatafehi and
Mateialona, Nuku'alofa, PO Box 1035,
Nuku'alofa, Tonga; tel: (676) 23-760
email: rhq_tga@nzf.salvationarmy.org
Regional leaders: Capts Sila and Malia Siufanga
Corps 4 **Outpost** 1

BOOTH COLLEGE OF MISSION (BCM)
20 William Booth Grove, Upper Hutt 5018;
PO Box 40-542, Upper Hutt, 5140;
tel: (04) 528 8628

Principal, BCM and SFOT: Maj David Noakes
School for Officer Training (SFOT)
School for Officer Training, Fiji
School for Bible and Mission
Centre for Leadership Development
Leadership Development, Fiji
Plowman Resource Centre: (Library, Archives
and Heritage Centre)

FARM
Jeff Memorial Farm, Kaiwera RD 2, Gore;
tel: (03) 205 3572

FAMILY TRACING SERVICE
tel: (04) 382 0710; fax: (04) 802 6257;
email: familytracing@nzf.salvationarmy.org

INDEPENDENT LIVING UNITS
Ashburton: Wilson Court, 251-255 Tancred St
(units 3)
Auckland: Denver Avenue, Sunnyvale (units
10);353 Blockhouse Bay Rd Blockhouse Bay
(units 26);
425 West Coast Road Glen Eden (units 14);
Roy Douglas Place Mangere (units 11);
Dewhurst Place Mangere (units 2);
Ceasar Place Mangere (units 2)
New Plymouth: Bingham Court, 46 Murray St,
Bell Block (units 10)
Blenheim: 35 George St (units 7)
Carterton: 204 High St South (units 8)
Christchurch: 794 Main North Rd, Belfast
(units 10)
Gisborne: Edward Murphy Village,
481 Aberdeen Rd (units 30)
Hamilton: Nawton Village, 57 Enfield St
(units 40)
Kapiti: 41 Bluegum Rd, Paraparaumu Beach
(units 18)
Mosgiel: Elmwood Retirement Village,
22 Elmwood Dr (units 30); 17 Cedar Cres
(units 30)
Oamaru: Glenside, 9 Arthur St (units 12)
Papakura: 91 Clevedon Rd (units 6)
Wellington: Summerset Units, Newtown: 182a
Owen St (units 11); 210, 212, 214 Owen St
(units 3)

RETIRED OFFICERS' ACCOMMODATION (under THQ)

Auckland: Lang Court, 9 Willcott St (units 6);
14 Clyde Street, Epsom, Auckland (unit 1);
19 Splendour Cl, Henderson (unit 1)
Wellington: 176, 176a, 178, 178a Queens Dr,
Lyall Bay (units 4)

YOUTH CAMPS AND CONFERENCE CENTRES

Blue Mountain Adventure Centre: RD 1,
Owhango 3989; tel: (07) 892 2630;
website: www.bluemountainadventure.co.nz

SOCIAL SERVICES (under THQ)
Addiction and Supportive Accommodation Services

National Office: Level 1, 691a Mt Albert Road,
Royal Oak, Auckland 1023, PO Box 24073,
Royal Oak, Auckland 1345; tel: (09) 639 1135
National Director: Comr Alistair Herring;
email: Alistair_Herring@nzf.salvationarmy.org

Addiction Centres: Community and Residential Programmes (Treatment of Alcohol and Drug Dependency)

Auckland: (acc 32 treatment 22 day clients 10);
Christchurch: (acc 26); Dunedin: (acc 7);
Hamilton: Midland Regional Residential and
Detox Centre; Invercargill; Manukau;
Waikato; Waitakere; Wellington (acc 24);
Whangarei

Oasis Centres: Treatment Centres for Gambling

Auckland; Christchurch; Dunedin; Hamilton;
Tauranga; Wellington

Community Addictions Programme

Invercargill; Kaitaia; Kaikohe: New Plymouth;
Palmerston North; Tauranga

Supportive Accommodation Services

Auckland: Epsom Lodge (acc men 90)
Christchurch: Addington Supportive
Accommodation Services Social Services
Centre (acc 70)
Wellington: (Intellectual Disability) (acc 12)

Reintegration Services

Christchurch; Hawkes Bay; Wellington

Education and Employment

National Office: 204 Cuba St, PO Box 6015,

Wellington 6141; tel: (04) 382 0714;
toll free: 0800 437 587
Chief Executive: Mr Gregory Fortuin; email:
gregory_fortuin@nzf.salvationarmy.org

Regions
Auckland, Lower Central, Northern, Southern,
Upper Central

Home Care Services

National Office: 71 Seddon Rd, Hamilton 3204;
PO Box 9417, Hamilton 3240; tel: (07) 848 2157
National Director: Mr Ross Smith;
email: homecare.hamilton@xtra.co.nz
Service Centres: Auckland, Hamilton, Paeroa,
Rotorua, Tauranga

SOCIAL SERVICES (under DHQ)
Community Ministries

Aranui; Auckland City; Blenheim; Christchurch
City; Dunedin; Gisborne; Gore; Hamilton:
Community Ministries (The Nest); Hastings;
Hornby; Hutt City; Invercargill; Levin;
Linwood; Napier; Nelson Tasman Bays; New
Plymouth; North Shore City; Palmerston
North; Porirua; Queenstown; Rotorua; South
Auckland; Sydenham; Tauranga; Timaru;
Tokoroa; Upper Hutt; Waitakere Central;
Wellington; Whangarei;

Early Childhood Education Centres

Gisborne: 'Noah's Young Ones' (24 places)
Hamilton: The Nest Educare (50 places)
Upper Hutt: William Booth Educare (roll 25)
Waitakere: Kidz Matter 2US (25 places)
Wellington: Britomart ECEC (roll 28)
Wellington Bridge – Te Matua Tamariki
Home-based ECE Service

COURT AND PRISON SERVICE

Alexandra; Ashburton; Auckland; Blenheim;
Christchurch; Dunedin; Gore; Hamilton;
Invercargill; Kaitaia; Manukau; North Shore;
Lower Hutt/Upper Hutt; Palmerston North;
Porirua; Rimutaka; Tauranga; Thames; Timaru;
Waitakere; Wellington; Westport; Whangarei

FIJI DIVISION SOCIAL SERVICES
Family Care Centres
Labasa: (acc 12); Lautoka: (acc 16); Suva: (acc 18)

Court and Diversion Officers
Lautoka; Suva

173

Farm Project
Farm 80, Lomaivuna; (acc 10)

Raiwai Hostel
Hostel for young male tertiary students,
    Grantham Rd, Suva (acc 20)

Red Shield House
Suva Hostel; tel: (679) 338 1347 (acc 9)

Sewing Skills Programmes
Labasa; Suva

Tiny Tots Kindergartens
Ba (acc 15); Labasa (acc 47); Lautoka (acc 50);
Lomaivuna (acc 15); Nadi (acc 15);
Nasinu (acc 64); Suva Central (acc 30)

TONGA REGION
Social Services based at Regional Headquarters
Community Ministries
Court and Prison Work: Nuku'alofa
Addiction Programme (ADAC)
Heath Team (incl. Mobile Health Clinic:
    Patangata, Popua and Sopu communities)
Farming project: Kolovai Corps

Kindergartens:
Sopu, Nuku'alofa (acc 30)
Kolovai (acc 25)

**NEW ZEALAND: Enthusiastic children taking part in one of the Army's
programmes**

NIGERIA TERRITORY

Territorial leaders:
Colonels Victor and Rose-Marie Leslie

Territorial Commander:
Colonel Victor Leslie
(1 Jan 2015)

Chief Secretary:
Lieut-Colonel Friday Ayanam (1 Aug 2014)

Territorial Headquarters: 6 Shipeolu St, Onipanu, Shomolu, Lagos

Postal address: Box 3025, Shomolu, Lagos, Nigeria

Tel/fax: [234] (1) 774 9125;

email: nig_leadership@nig.salvationarmy.org; thq.nigeria@gmail.com

Salvation Army operations began in Nigeria in 1920 when Lieut-Colonel and Mrs George H. Souter landed in Lagos, to be followed later by Staff-Captain and Mrs Charles Smith with 10 West Indian officers. Following an invitation for the Army to establish a presence in Mali, with registration being given on 29 November 2007, a response was undertaken under local leadership. In February 2008 officers were appointed and Mali became a separate region on 1 April 2011.

Zone: Africa
Country included in the territory: Nigeria
'The Salvation Army' in Yoruba: Ogun Igbala Na; in Ibo: Igwe Agha Nzoputa; in Efik: Nka Erinyana; in Edo: Iyo Kuo Imienfan; in Urhobo: Ofovwi re Arhc Na; in Hausa: Soldiogi Cheta
Languages in which the gospel is preached: Calabari, Edo, Efik/Ibibio, English, Hausa, Ibo, Ijaw, Tiv, Urhobo, Yoruba
Periodicals: *Jesus Kids, Salvationist, The Shepherd, The War Cry*

NIGERIA Territory held a number of major events during the year, as well as some significant workshops that helped move the territory forward. Soldiers' rallies were held in June 2013 with different territorial cabinet members responsible for each rally and using the same material that was jointly prepared. These proved to be well attended and are considered worth replicating in the future.

Other events included a Brengle Institute for officers, led by Majors Julius and Gaudencia Omukonyi (Nairobi SALT Centre), a 15-year review conference for officers, and the first territorial conference for the Students and Graduates Fellowship in Port Harcourt. Workshops for improving financial management were held, and a helpful 'PREPARE' workshop for west African delegates was held in September in Lagos by International Emergency Services (IHQ).

In November, Commissioner Sue Swanson (TPWM, USA Eastern Territory) and Major Soo Jung Kim (USA Eastern Territory) were the special guests for a women officers' retreat held at Onitsha Central Corps. The weekend incorporated teaching and many opportunities to demonstrate cultural dance. Major Kim instructed the women on how dance can be set to music and can assist in worship.

In March 2014, General André Cox and Commissioner Silvia Cox (WPWM) visited Nigeria. During the visit they met government officials as well as the president of the Christian Association of Nigeria, and had the opportunity to tour the ecumenical church in the capital city. From there they led a congress weekend that included officers councils, rallies and worship services. During the youth rally more than 500 junior soldiers were enrolled and in the final holiness meeting, with 7,000 people in attendance, more than 700 senior soldiers were sworn in. During the congress, the Order of Distinguished Auxiliary Service award was given to the Governor of Akwa Ibom State, Chief (Dr) Godswill Akpabio.

At the conclusion of their visit, the General opened a new hall at Ejigbo Corps as well as dedicating a new accommodation block at THQ, both in Lagos.

The territory's work with HIV/Aids victims has continued, supported by USA funding. Territorial leadership and Salvationists throughout the territory are grateful for the interest shown in this work, and thank those who enable its various social and awareness programmes to continue and thrive through their generous donations.

STATISTICS

Officers 381 (active 321 retired 60) **Cadets** 32 **Employees** 284
Corps 169 **Societies and Outposts** 168 **Institutions** 11 **Schools** 28 **Hospitals** 2 **Clinics** 4
Senior Soldiers 17,460 **Adherent Members** 863 **Junior Soldiers** 6,936
Personnel serving outside territory Officers 1

STAFF

Women's Ministries: Col Rose-Marie Leslie (TPWM) Lt-Col Glory Ayanam (TSWM) Lt-Col Patience Akpan (THLS) Lt-Col Edinah Onyekwere (Junior Miss and Young Women's Sec) Lt-Col Definah Kamambo (LOMS)
Auditor/Finance Trainer: Maj Benjamin Udoh
Business Administration: Lt-Col Clever Kamambo
Editorial/Literary: Capt Ifesinachi Ijioma
Extension Training: Capt Ekebike Ijioma
Finance: Capt Loveth Onuorah
Programme: Lt-Col Gabriel Adepoju
Personnel: Lt-Col Paul Onyekwere
Prison and Hospitals: Maj Raphael Ogundahunsi
Property: Lazarus Akpadiaha
Social: Maj Udo Uwak
HIV/Aids: Maj Bessie Udoh
Spiritual Life Development: Maj Josep Mbagwu
Sponsorship: Maj Esther Uwak
Training: Maj Emmanuel Ohaeri
Youth and Candidates: Maj John U. Okpalaihedi

DIVISIONS

Akwa Ibom Central: PO Box 8, Afia Nsit Urua Nko, Nsit Ibom LGA, Akwa Ibom State; Majs Maurice and Mercy Akpabio
Akwa Ibom East: PO Box 20, Ikot Ubo, via Eket, Akwa Ibom State; Majs Samuel and Glory Edung
Akwa Ibom South West: c/o Abak PO Box 23, Abak; Majs Ezekiel and Eno Akpan
Akwa Ibom West: PO Box 47, Etinan, via Uyo, Akwa Ibom State; Majs Godpower and Christiana Sampson
Anambra East: PO Box 16, Umuchu, Anambra State; Majs Ebenezer and Comfort Abayomi
Anambra West: PO Box 1168, Boundary Road Housing Estate, Onitsha, Anambra State; Majs Patrick and Blessing Orasibe
Ibadan: PO Box 261, Ekotedo, Ibadan, Oyo State; Majs Simon and Eva Ekpendu
Imo Central: c/o Orogwe PO, Owerri, Imo State; Majs Obed and Violet Mgbebuihe

Lagos City: 41 Ajao Road, PO Box 2640,
Surulere, Lagos State;
Majs Benson and Celine Mgbebuihe
Northern: PO Box 617, Garki, Area 1, Abuja,
Federal Capital Territory; Lt-Col Joseph and
Patience Akpan
Ondo/Ekiti: 34 Odokoyo Street, PO Box 51,
Akure, Ondo State;
Majs Michael and Comfort Sijuade
Rivers-Bayelsa: PO Box 1161, Port Harcourt,
Rivers State; Maj Silas and Capt Ifeyinwa
Olebunne

DISTRICTS
Abia: 2-8 Market Rd, PO Box 812, Aba,
Abia State; Maj Michael Oyesanya
Cross River: 32 Goldie Street, PO Box 11,
Calabar, Cross River State;
tel: (087) 220284; Maj Friday Ekpo
Edo/Delta: 20 First Circular Road, PO Box 108,
Benin City, Edo State; Maj Alpheous Nwafor
Imo North: PO Box 15, Akokwa, Imo State;
Maj Michael Olatunde
Lagos West: Mission Street, PO Box 28,
Badagry, Lagos State
Ogun: PO Box 64, Ado Odo, Ogun State

SECTIONS
Akwa Ibom South East: PO Box 25,
Ikot Abasi; Maj Iko Moses Oduok
Egbe: PO Box 37, Oke Egbe, via Ilorin,
Kogi State; Maj Vincent Adejoro
Enugu/Ebonyi: PO Box 1454, Enugu;
4 Moorehouse St, Ogui, Enugu State;
Maj Martins Ujari

TRAINING COLLEGE
4 Shipeolu St, PO Box 17, Shomolu, Igbobi,
Lagos; tel: (01) 774 9125

SOCIAL SERVICES
THQ-based Prison Ministry
Badagry Prison, Ikoyi Prison, Kirikiri Maximum
Security, Kirikiri Minimum Security, Kirikiri
Women's Prison

Corps-based Prison Ministry
Afaha Eket, Agbor, Badagry, Benin Central,
Enugu, Ibadan Central, Port Harcourt Corps

HIV/Aids Facilitation Teams:
Lagos (based at THQ)
Oyo State (based at Ibadan)

HIV/Aids Action Centre and Voluntary Counselling and Testing Centre
11 Odunlami St, PO Box 125, Lagos

Medical Centres
Gbethromey Hospital: Lagos State (acc 10)
Nda Nsit Clinic/Maternity: Akwa Ibom State
Oji River Hospital (Eye Clinic and
Rehabilitation Centre): Enugu State (acc 65)
Uga Corps Eye Clinic
Umucheke Corps Clinic: Imo State (acc 4)

Social Centres/Institutions/Programmes
Akai Children's Home: Akwa Ibom State
(acc 35)
Benin Rehabilitation Centre: Edo State
(acc 21)
Gbethromey Hospital: Lagos Stte (acc 10)
Oji River Hospital/Rehabilitation Centre: Enugu
State (acc 65)
Orphans/Vulnerable Children Centre/Orphans
Psycho-Social Centre – Akai: Akwa Ibom State

SCHOOLS
Nursery
Catherine Booth School, Lagos;
and at Aba Corps, Agbor Corps, Akai Corps,
Akokwa Corps, Amauzari Corps, Benin Corps,
Ibughubu Corps, Ikot Inyang Eti, Ile Ife Corps,
Ivue Corps, Jos Corps, Mpape Corps, Onitsha
Corps, Osumenyi Corps, Somorika Corps,
Suleja, Umucheke Corps, Umuchu Corps,
Umudike Corps

Primary
Catherine Booth School, 4 Shipeolu Street,
Shomolu, Lagos
Also at: Aba Corps, Akai, Amauzari Corps,
Benin Corps, Ile Ife, Ikot Inyang Eti,
Ivue Corps, Jos Corps, Mpape Corps,
Onitsha Corps, Somorika Corps, Suleja

Secondary
Akai Ubium, Ilesha Corps, Ile-Ife, Orogwe

VOCATIONAL TRAINING CENTRES
Afia Nsit-Nsit: Akwa Ibom State (acc 8)
Enugu: Enugu State (acc 6)
Ikot Okobo Training Centre: Akwa Ibom State
(acc 20)

NORWAY, ICELAND AND THE FÆROES TERRITORY

Territorial leaders:
Commissioners Dick and Vibeke Krommenhoek

Territorial Commander:
Commissioner Dick Krommenhoek
(1 Feb 2013)

Chief Secretary:
Colonel Jan Peder Fosen (1 Dec 2010)

Territorial Headquarters: Kommandør T I Øgrims plass 4, 0165 Oslo, Norway

Postal address: Box 6866, St Olavs Plass, 0130 Oslo, Norway

Tel: [47] 22 99 85 00; fax: [47] 22 20 84 49; email: nor.leadership@frelsesarmeen.no;
website: www.frelsesarmeen.no

Commissioners Hanna Ouchterlony and George Scott Railton with Staff-Captain and Mrs Albert Orsborn 'opened fire' in Oslo (Kristiania) on 22 January 1888. Work began in Iceland on 12 May 1895, pioneered by Adjutant Christian Eriksen, Captain Thorstein Davidsson and Lieutenant Lange, and spread to The Færoes in 1924.

Zone: Europe
Countries included in the territory: Iceland, Norway, The Færoes
'The Salvation Army' in Norwegian: Frelsesarmeen; in Icelandic: Hjálpraedisherinn; in Færoese: Frelsunarherurin
Languages in which the gospel is preached: English, Færoese, Icelandic, Norwegian
Periodicals: *Krigsropet,* (Norwegian), *Herópid* (Icelandic)

IN 2013 The Salvation Army celebrated 125 years since it opened fire in Norway. To create a good foundation for the territorial congress and celebration weekend, a 3,000 hour-long prayer relay, involving the whole territory, was undertaken.

The territorial leaders Commissioners Dick and Vibeke Krommenhoek (TC/TPWM) oversaw the congress which was a great celebration and time of visitation by the Holy Spirit. The congress concluded with an open-air meeting on the roof of the National Opera House, Oslo, featuring the International Staff Songsters and the Territorial Band.

To enhance the level of effectiveness and quality in the distribution of donated food, a centre was opened in a Salvation Army property in September 2013. Several supermarket chains

178

supplied good quality food for the benefit of the needy.

'Jobben' ('The Job') provides work for people who are on social benefits and struggle to remain in permanent employment. This project has been so successful that Her Royal Highness Queen Sonja visited 'Jobben' in December 2013.

Prior to Christmas, The Salvation Army was featured in four Advent programmes on national television. Under the title *Hope in a Kettle*, a presentation of the multifaceted ministry of the Army was linked to the Christmas kettle.

A large tent was erected in one of the central marketplaces in Oslo to run a 125-hour non-stop programme as a finale for the anniversary year.

People suffering under poor conditions in a cold Nordic climate remain a challenge. The Salvation Army endeavours to alleviate the immediate need of some of these individuals through providing food, a hot shower and a place to sleep on cold nights.

'Others' (previously the 'Sally Ann' Trading Programme) held a photo exhibition at IHQ in March 2014 and continues to seek new ways to make its fair-trade initiative sustainable.

'Fretex' (recycling programme) has made it possible for people to donate clothes through the national mail. This initiative provides The Salvation Army with good visibility in all post offices throughout Norway.

However, the main focus of everything remains the salvation of souls. The territory rejoices that more than 200 young people joined together at Jeløy Resource Centre for a new year conference and new soldiers have been enrolled throughout the territory, with several offering for full-time service.

STATISTICS

Officers 377 (active 156 retired 221) **Cadets** 12 **Employees** 1,288
Corps 104 **Outposts** 293 **Institutions** 22 **Industrial Centres/Second-hand Shops** 40
Senior Soldiers 4,780 **Adherent Members** 1,606 **Junior Soldiers** 40
Personnel serving outside territory Officers 18

STAFF

Women's Ministries: Comr Vibeke Krommenhoek (TPWM) Col Birgit T. Fosen (TSWM) Maj Helen Stangeland (Home and Family)
Asst Chief Secretary: Maj Jan Risan
Sec for Business Administration: Lt-Col Thorgeir Nybo
Financial Sec: Maj Eli Nodland Hagen
  Chief Accountant: Vegar Thorsen
  Missionary Projects: Maj Tone Gjeruldsen
  Property: Dag Tellefsen
  IT: Reidar Myre
Under Leadership Office:
  Information: Andrew Hannevik
  Editor: Hilde Dagfinrud Valen
Sec for Personnel: Maj Lise O. Luther
  Asst Sec for Personnel: Maj Bjørn Ove Frøyseth
Sec for Field and Programme: Maj Frank Gjeruldsen
  Asst Sec for Field and Programme: Maj Frank Gjeruldsen
  Music: Maj Jan Harald Hagen
    Territorial Band: B/M Espen Ødegaard
  Over 60s: Maj Leif-Erling Fagermo
  Youth and Children: Maj Anders Skoland
Special Efforts: Lt-Col Jan Øystein Knedal
Sec for Social Services: Lindis Evja
  Alcohol and Drug Rehabilitation: Maj Knut Haugsvær
  Children and Family Services: Anne Hernæs Hjelle (pro tem)
  Day Care Centres for Children: Anne-Dorthe Nodland Aasen
  Family Tracing: Maj Inger Marit Nygård

Welfare and Development: Elin Herikstad
Work Rehabilitation and Recycling (Fretex):
Trond Ivar Vestre

JELØY RESOURCE CENTRE:
1516 Moss, Strandpromenaden 171;
tel: 69 91 10 60; Maj Jan Risan (Chair of the
Board)
Training College: Strandpromenaden 179, 1516
Moss tel: 69 91 10 80
Lt-Col Odd Berg (Training Principal)
Jeløy Folk High School: 1516 Moss,
Strandpromenaden 173; tel: 69 91 10 70;
Maj Wenche Walderhaug Midjord (Principal)
Co-worker School: Strandpromenaden 179;
Rune Isegran (Principal)

DIVISIONS
Central: Nordregt, 25 A, 0551 Oslo;
tel: 23 24 49 20; Lt-Col Elisabeth Henne
Eastern: Brendsrudtoppen 40, 1385 Asker;
Maj Solfrid Bakken
Iceland and The Færoes: Kirkjurstræti 2,
IS 121 Reykjavik; tel: (00354) 552 0788;
Majs Gunnar and Ida Karin Eide
Northern: Bjørkvn 12, PO Box 8255 Jakobsli,
7458 Trondheim; tel: 73 57 14 20;
Majs Per Arne and Lillian Pettersen
North Norway: Skolegt 6, PO Box 177,
9252 Tromsø; tel: 77 68 83 70;
Maj Gro-Merete Berg
Western: Kongsgt 50, PO Box 553,
4003 Stavanger; tel: 51 56 41 60;
Majs Jostein and Magna Våje Nielsen

SOCIAL SERVICES
Head Office: 0165 Oslo, Kommandør T.I.
Øgrims plass 4; tel: 22 99 85 00

**Accommodation and Welfare Centre for
Elderly People**
0661 Oslo, Malerhaugvn 10b; tel: 22 57 66 30

Children's and Youths' Homes
3028 Drammen, Bolstadhagen 61; tel: 32 20 45 80
1441 Drøbak, Nils Carlsensgt 31; tel: 64 90 51 30
2021 Skedsmokorset, Flesvigs vei 4;
tel: 63 83 67 10
4011 Stavanger, Vidarsgt 4; tel: 51 52 11 49
7037 Trondheim, Øystein Møylas veg 20 B;
tel: 73 95 44 33,
1540 Vestby, Soldammen, Gjølstadveien 73;
tel: 64 98 04 70

Day Care Centres for Children
1385 Asker, Brendsrudtoppen 60; tel: 66 78 74 86
5011 Bergen, Skottegaten 16; tel: 55 23 08 83
1441 Drøbak, Niels Carlsensgt 31; tel: 64931509
0664 Oslo, Regnbuevn. 2C; tel: 23 03 93 30
4017 Stavanger, Auglendsdalen 62; tel: 51 88 68 80

Home-Start Family Contact
Drammen: 3007 Drammen, Rådhusgt 19,
tel: 478 93 800
Gamle Oslo: 0561 Oslo, Heimdalsgt 14 B;
tel: 90 61 76 74
Kristiansand: Dronningensgt. 23, 4610
Østensjø: 0686 Oslo, Vetlandsveien 99/100;
tel: 23 43 89 10
Nordre Aker: 0487 Oslo, Kapellveien 61;
tel: 922 28 158

Slum and Goodwill Centres
6005 Ålesund, Giskegt 27; tel: 70 12 18 05
5808 Bergen, Hans Haugesgt 1; tel: 55 62 75 10
0566 Oslo, Gøteborggt 4; tel: 22 80 93 30

Temporary Accommodation for Families
0487 Oslo, Kapellvn 61; tel: 22 09 86 20

SERVICES AND CENTRES FOR
ALCOHOL AND DRUG ADDICTS
Day Care Centres
0187 Oslo, Urtegaten 16 A/C; tel: 23 03 66 80
1301 Sandvika, Kinoveien 4; tlf: 67 54 38 99
7012 Trondheim, Hvedingsveita 3; tel: 73 52 0900
8001 Bodø, Kongensgt 16
2208 Kongsvinger, Sofiesgate 2; tel: 23 69 19 84
Færøe Islands: FO-100 Torshavn, Dalavegur 1;
tel: (00298) 31 73 93

Hospital and Health Clinic
0650 Oslo, Borggt 2, tel: 22 08 36 70
0187 Oslo, Urtegt 16 A/C; tel: 22 67 43 45

Rehabilitation Homes
5812 Bergen, Bakkegt 7; tel: 55 30 22 85,
8001 Bodø, Kongensgt 16; tel: 75 52 23 38
5501 Haugesund, Sørhauggt 215; tel: 52 73 95 50
0561 Oslo, Heimen, Heimdalsgt 27 A;
tel: 23 21 09 60
0656 Oslo, Den °Apne Dør,Schweigaardsgt 70;
tel: 23 24 39 00
0354 Oslo, Fagerborg Sporveisgt 33; tel: 22 957350
3111 Tønsberg, Farmannsvn 26; tel: 33 31 54 09
7041 Trondheim, Furulund, Lade Allè 84;
tel: 73 90 70 30

Norway, Iceland and The Færoes Territory

Færoe Islands: FO-100 Torshavn, N Winthersgt
  3; tel: (00298) 31 73 93

Self-catering Accommodation for Women
8000 Bodø, Prinsensgate 151B; tel: 75 52 39 90

Supervised Residence
0561 Oslo, Heimdalsgt 25; tel: 23 21 09 73

Treatment Centres
4017 Stavanger, Auglendsdalen 64;
  tel: 51 82 87 00
1900 Fetsund, Falldalsveien 411; tel: 915 97 363

Work-rehabilitation Programme ('The Job')
2208 Kongsvinger, Sofiesgate 2; tel: 23 69 19 84
2609 Lillehammer, Morterudveien 15;
  tel: 61 60 06 84
4514 Mandal, Torjusheigata 1A; 38 60 01 26
0192 Oslo, Arupsgt 5; tel: 22 68 90 68
1301 Sandvika, Kinoveien 4; tel 67 54 38 99

Prison Work
5032 Bergen; tel: 474 63 122
0666 Oslo, Ole Deviksv 20; tel: 23 06 92 35
0561 Oslo, Grønlandsleiret 30;
  tel: 474 63 122
4002 Stavanger, Kongensgt 50
Projects: Safe Way Home (repatriation of foreign
  prisoners) and
Trafficking 4002 Stavanger, Kongensgt 50;
  tel: 51 56 41 66

Rehabilitation Home for Convicts
0666 Oslo, Ole Deviksv 20; tel: 23 06 92 35

Work Rehabilitation and Recycling
  Centres (FRETEX)
  (including 40 second-hand shops)
9008 Tromsø, Fretex Nord-Norge AS,
  Strandgata 5/7; tel 47 78 01 15 00
7080 Heimdal, Fretex Midt-Norge AS,
  Heggstadmyra 2; tel 47 72 59 59 00
4315 Sandnes, Fretex Vest-Norge AS,
  Torneroseveien 7; tel 47 51 95 13 00
0668 Oslo, Fretex Øst-Norge AS,
  Ole Deviksvei 50; tel 47 23 06 92 00
3036 Drammen, Fretex Øst-Norge AS,
  Kobbervikdalen 71; tel 47 32 20 83 50
0668 Oslo, Fretex International AS,
  Ole Deviksvei 50; tel 47 23 06 92 00

Second-hand Shops
Ålesund , Bergen (4), Bodø, Bryne, Drammen,
  Fredrikstad, Gol, Harstad, Haugesund,
  Jessheim, Jørpeland, Kirkenes, Kristiansand,
  Lillehammer, Lillestrøm, Lyngdal, Mandal,
  Molde, Moss, Oslo (5), Sandnes (2), Sandvika,
  Skien, Stavanger (3), Tromsø, Trondheim (4),
  Tønsberg, Voss

Art Gallery
Bergen

ICELAND
Convalescent Home: Skólabraut 10, PO Box 115,
  IS-172 Seltjarnarnes; tel: [354] 561 2090
Guest Home: PO Box 866, IS-121 Reykjavik;
  tel: [354] 561 3203

PAKISTAN TERRITORY

Territorial leaders:
Colonels Ivor and Carol Telfer

Territorial Commander:
Colonel Ivor Telfer (1 May 2014)

Chief Secretary:
Lieut-Colonel Washington Daniel (1 Mar 2013)

Territorial Headquarters: 35 Shahrah-e-Fatima Jinnah, Lahore

Postal address: PO Box 242, Lahore 54000, Pakistan

Tel: [92] (042) 3758 1644/3756 9940

website:www.salvationarmy.org/pakistan

The Salvation Army began work in Lahore in 1883 and was eventually incorporated under the Companies Act of 1913 on 9 October 1968.

Zone: South Asia
Country included in the territory: Pakistan
Languages in which the gospel is preached: English, Pashto, Punjabi, Urdu
Periodicals: *Home League Annual, The War Cry* (in Urdu)

A HIGHLIGHT for officers and soldiers of the territory was the visit of General André Cox and Commissioner Silvia Cox (WPWM) during March 2014. Everyone who attended both the public meetings and officers councils were not only spiritually renewed, but also challenged and encouraged.

The General visited the training college and a village corps, as well as meeting the Governor of Punjab, His Excellency Chaudhry Mohammad Sarwar, who told of his desire for the people to have clean drinking water.

The governor was overjoyed to learn that The Salvation Army had already commenced working on the issue.

The General also visited Maulana Abdul Khabir Azad, from the Badshahi Mosque, and Sardar Bishan Singh, president of the Sikh community. These visits helped to promote interfaith relations and emphasised the need to live in harmony and peace with each other.

Colonel Sylvia Hinton (TSWM) and Lieut-Colonel Marion Drew (Secretary for Communications), both from the

United Kingdom Territory with the Republic of Ireland, met with divisional leaders and visited Joyland Girls' Home, Lahore. The UK Territory is one of the territory's Partners in Mission and the Pakistan Territory is grateful for its support and generosity.

In May 2014, Colonels Ivor and Carol Telfer (TC/TPWM) commenced their appointments as the new territorial leaders.

Following much discussion, the territory has developed its vision for the coming years, highlighting seven priorities encompassing spiritual development, leadership, property, relationships, stewardship, youth and children, and education and development.

We pray that the Holy Spirit will continue to guide and lead the Pakistan Territory.

STATISTICS
Officers 418 (active 321 retired 97)
Cadets 29 **Employees** 166
Corps 133 **Societies** 459 **Institutions** 7 **Schools** 3
Senior Soldiers 45,410 **Adherent Members** 5,688 **Junior Soldiers** 12,308

STAFF
Women's Ministries: Col Carol Telfer (TPWM)
  Lt-Col Azra Washington (TSWM)
Projects: Maj Winsome Mason
  National Project Director: Mr Asher David
  'Sally Ann': Mr Faysal Yacoob
Secretary for Business Administration:
  Maj Sandra Maunder
  Finance: Capt Amjad Sardar
Communications: tba
Property: Maj Yaqub Sardar
Secretary for Personnel: tba
  Asst Sec for Personnel: Capt Diana MacDonald
  Candidates: Maj Aneela Fahim
  Mission Training and Education

Coordinator: tba
Training Principal: Maj Arif Masih
Secretary for Programme: Maj Winsome
  Mason
  Prayer Coordinator: Maj Victoria Khuram
  Social Services and Sponsorship:
    Lt-Col Zarina Veru
  Youth: Maj Fahim Asghar
Emergency Services and Public Relations:
  Capt MacDonald Chandi

DIVISIONS
Faisalabad: Jamilabad Jamia Salfia Rd, Faisalabad; tel: (041) 8783472; Majs Raja Azeem Zia and Nasreen Raja
Islamabad: House No 4, Street 8, Raja Iqbal Town, Rawalpindi ; mobile: 00300- 8431704; Majs Imran Ali Sabir and Nighat Imran
Jaranwala: Water Works Rd, nr Telephone Exchange, Jaranwala; tel: (041) 4312423; Majs Michael Gabriel and Shamim Michael
Jhang: Yousaf Shah Rd, Jhang Saddar; tel: (047) 7611589; Majs Samuel John and Rebecca Samuel
Karachi: 78 NI Lines, Frere St, Saddar, Karachi 74400; tel: (021) 3225460; Majs Javid Yousaf and Surriya Javid
Khanewal: Chak Shahana Rd, Khanewal 58150; tel: (065) 2553860; Majs Haroon Ghulam and Jennifer Haroon
Lahore: The Salvation Army, Bahar Colony, Kot Lakhpat, Lahore; tel: (042) 35834568; Majs Salamat Masih and Grace Salamat
Sahiwal: Karbala Rd, Sahiwal; tel: (040) 4466383; Majs Safdar Iqbal and Asia Safdar
Sheikhupura: 16 Civil Lines Rd, Qila, Sheikhupura; tel: (056) 3786521; Majs Samuel Barkat and Margaret Samuel

DISTRICT
Hyderabad: Bungalow No 9, 'E' Block, Unit No 11, Latifabad 11, Hyderabad; tel: (022) 3813445; Majs Michael Paul and Samina Michael

TRAINING COLLEGE
Ali Bridge, Canal Bank Rd North, Tulspura, Lahore; tel: (042) 36582450;

CONFERENCE CENTRE
Lahore: 35 Shahrah-e-Fatima Jinnah, PO Box 242, Lahore 54000; tel: (042) 37581644/37569940

MISSION TRAINING AND EDUCATION CENTRE

35 Shahrah-e-Fatima Jinnah, PO Box 242, Lahore
54000; tel: (042) 37581644/37569940

SOCIAL SERVICES
Boarding Hostels
Boys: Jhang (acc 50)
Karachi (acc 50)
Girls: Sheikhupura (acc 50)

Children's Home
Joyland Children's Home: Lahore (acc 50)

EDUCATION
Schools
Azam Town Secondary School
Shantinagar Educational Institute
Tibba Coaching Centre: Shantinagar, Khanewal

REHABILITATION CENTRES FOR DISABLED PERSONS

Karachi: Manzil-e-Umead, PO Box 10735,
Site Metroville, Karachi 75700;
tel: (021) 36650434
Lahore: Manzil-e-Shifa, 35 Shahrah-e-Fatima
Jinnah, PO Box 242, Lahore 54000;
tel: (042) 37569940/37581644

COMMUNITY DEVELOPMENT PROGRAMMES

Faisalabad; Hyderabad; Islamabad; Jaranwala;
Jhang; Karachi; Khanewal; Lahore; Peshawar;
Sahiwal; Sheikhupura

PAKISTAN: The General signs an autograph following the congress meeting (above); Dancers greet the General (below)

PAPUA NEW GUINEA TERRITORY

Territorial leaders:
Colonels Andrew and Yvonne Westrupp

Territorial Commander:
Colonel Andrew Westrupp (1 Apr 2014)

Chief Secretary:
Lieut-Colonel Miriam Gluyas (1 Feb 2013)

Territorial Headquarters: Angau Dr, Boroko, National Capital District

Postal address: PO Box 1323, Boroko, NCD, Papua New Guinea

Tel: [675] 325-5522/5507; fax: [675] 323 3282; website: www.png.salvationarmy.org

The Salvation Army officially commenced in Papua New Guinea on 31 August 1956 and the first meeting was conducted on Sunday 21 October at the Royal Police Constabulary Barracks in Port Moresby. The first officers appointed there were Major Keith Baker, Mrs Major Edna Baker and Lieutenant Ian Cutmore. On 4 July 1994, after 38 years as part of the Australia Eastern Territory, Papua New Guinea became an independent command and on 9 December 2000 was elevated to territory status. Work began in The Solomon Islands in 2010 and was officially recognised on 1 February 2011.

Zone: South Pacific and East Asia
Countries included in the territory: Papua New Guinea, Solomon Islands
Languages in which the gospel is preached: English, Hiri Motu, Pidgin and many local languages
Periodicals: *Tokaut*

GOD IS at work in the Papua New Guinea Territory. The emphasis on saving souls, growing saints, serving suffering humanity, transforming society, prayer and discipleship has meant that mission priorities have been developed and implemented. This has resulted in an increase in soldiership and new fellowships being established.

The territory's young people attended a prayer weekend where they learned of the importance of prayer. A new initiative aimed at young adults, called '12@4', has gathered momentum over the year in review. Young people join together 12 times a year at 4 p.m. on a Sunday to learn about discipleship.

A leadership development framework has been implemented for every officer in the territory. Each officer undertakes four modules and completes practical assignments related to their ministry, with the focus being on spiritual and missional effectivness.

The territory continues to be blessed with mission team support from the

Australia Eastern Territory and with the assistance of the Hong Kong and Macau Command, has explored the possibility of every corps having a 'school under the mango tree'.

Two young Salvationists from the territory are interns at the International Social Justice Commission in New York, and another is at ALOVE in the United Kingdom. Others have had the opportunity to travel to Australia to undertake educational and leadership opportunities, run marathons and take part in a basketball carnival.

The territory continues to provide excellent holistic services in the areas of health, education, community development, literacy, restorative justice and water projects.

The Papua New Guinea Territory's prayer is that 'We see a God-raised, Spirit-filled Army for the 21st century – convinced of our calling, moving forward together into the world of the hurting, broken, lonely, dispossessed and lost, reaching them in love by all means with the transforming message of Jesus, bringing freedom, hope and life' (The Salvation Army One Army International Vision).

STATISTICS
Officers 320 (active 258 retired 62) **Cadets** (1st Yr) 10 (2nd Yr) 10 **Employees** 366 **Corps** 61 **Outposts** 82 **Institution** 1 **Motels** 2 **Schools** 10 **Health Centre and Sub Centres** 5 **Community Health Posts** 18 **Counselling Centres** 4 **Staff Clinic** 1 **Senior Soldiers** 4,798 **Adherent Members** 3,999 **Junior Soldiers** 1,123

STAFF
Women's Ministries: Col Yvonne Westrupp (TPWM) Lt-Col Miriam Gluyas (TSWM)

Business Administration: tba
Personnel: Maj Iveme Yanderave
Programme: Maj Kevin Unicomb
Leadership Development: Maj Bugave Kada
Editorial/Literature: Maj Gwenda Pratt
Property: Mr Kei Gabi
Projects: tba
Public Relations and Planned Giving:
  Maj David Vele
SALT: Maj Kabona Rotona
Training: Maj Tilitah Goa
Youth: Capt Kila Apa

DIVISIONS
North Coastal: PO Box 667, Lae, Morobe Province; tel: 472 0905; fax: 472 0897; Majs George and Georgina Karogo
North Eastern: PO Box 343, Kainantu, Eastern Highlands Province; tel: 537 1220; tel/fax: 537 1482; Capts Jackson and Lennie Suave
North Western: PO Box 365, Goroka, Eastern Highlands Province; tel: 532 1382; fax: 532 1218; Majs Lapu and Araga Rawali
Sepik: PO Box 184, Wewak, East Sepik Province; tel/fax: 456 1641; Majs David and Doreen Temine
South Central: PO Box 4227, Boroko, National Capital District; mobile: 7285 0568; fax: 321 6008; Majs Michael and Giam Dengi
South Eastern: PO Box 49, Kwikila, Central Province; 2-way Radio Cell call no: 8564; tel: 329 5008; Majs Vari and Captain Nellie Burava

DISTRICT
Gulf District Office: PO Box 132, Kerema, Gulf Province; tel/fax: 648 1384; Capt Saini and Judith Gari

OFFICER TRAINING COLLEGE
PO Box 5355, Boroko, National Capital District; tel: 323 0553; fax: 325 6668

SALT COLLEGE
PO Box 343, Kainantu, Eastern Highlands Province; tel/fax: 537 1125

EDUCATION SERVICES
Mary and Martha Child Care Centre, Koki (acc 40)
Boroko Primary School (acc 800)
Lae Primary School (acc 689)
Goroka Elementary School (acc 197)
Kainantu Elementary School (acc 190)

Kerowagi Elementary School (acc 94)
Tamba Elementary School (acc 91)
Koki Secondary School (acc 440)
Boroko FODE Centre (inc Boroko Driving
School) (acc 700)
Kimbe Computer School (acc 31)
Tent City Elementary School (acc 45)

Community Health Workers
Training School
Private Mail Bag 3, Kainantu, Eastern Highlands
Province; tel/fax: 537 1404 (acc 52)

SOCIAL PROGRAMME
Community Services and HIV/Aids
Courts and Prison Ministry, Missing Persons,
Welfare Feeding Projects
House of Hope: Ela Beach Care and
Counselling Centre; tel: 320 0389
Jim Jacobsen Centre: PO Box 901, Lae,
Morobe Province; tel/fax: 472 1117

DEVELOPMENT SERVICES
Onamuga Development Project:
Private Mail Bag 3, Kainantu,
Eastern Highlands Province
Literacy Programmes: each division

HEALTH SERVICES PROGRAMMES
Gulf District: PO Box 132, Kerema, Gulf
Province; tel/fax: 648 1384 Community Health
Posts (acc 2)

North Coastal: PO Box 667 Lae, Morobe
Province; tel: 472 0905, fax 472 0897
Community Health Posts (acc 3)
North Eastern: Private Mail Bag 3, Kainantu,
Eastern Highlands Province; tel/fax: 537 1279
Community Health Centres (acc 35)
North Western: PO Box 365, Goroka, Eastern
Highlands Province; tel: 532 1382; fax: 532 1218
Community Health Centres (acc 4)
South Central: PO Box 4227, Boroko,
National Capital District; tel: 321 6000;
fax: 321 6008 Community Health
Centres (acc 5)
South Eastern: PO Box 49, Kwikila,
Central Province Community Health
Centres: (acc 11)

MOTELS
Goroka: PO Box 365, Goroka, Eastern Highlands
Province; tel: 532 1382; fax: 732 1218
(family units 2, double units 4, house 1)
The Elphick: PO Box 637, Lae,
Morobe Province; tel: 472 2487;
(double rooms 22)

THE PHILIPPINES TERRITORY

Territorial leaders:
Colonels Wayne and Robyn Maxwell

Territorial Commander:
Colonel Wayne Maxwell (1 Apr 2013)

Chief Secretary:
Lieut-Colonel Bob Lee (1 Feb 2013)

Territorial Headquarters: 1843 Leon Guinto Sr St, 1004 Malate, Manila

Postal address: PO Box 3830, Manila 1099, The Philippines

Tel: [63] (2) 524 0086/88; (2) 524-2550

email: saphl1@phl.salvationarmy.org

The first Protestant preaching of the gospel in The Philippines was done by Major John Milsaps, a chaplain appointed to accompany US troops from San Francisco to Manila in July 1898. Major Milsaps conducted open-air and regular meetings and led many into a saving knowledge of Jesus Christ.

The advance of The Salvation Army in The Philippines came at the initiative of Filipinos who had been converted through contact with The Salvation Army in Hawaii, returned to their homeland and commenced meetings in Panay, Luzon, Cebu and Mindanao Islands during the period 1933-37. On 6 June 1937 Colonel and Mrs Alfred Lindvall officially inaugurated this widespread work.

The Salvation Army Philippines was incorporated in 1963 as a religious and charitable corporation under Company Registration No 24211. The Salvation Army Social Services was incorporated in 1977 as a social welfare and development corporation under Company Registration No 73979 and The Salvation Army Educational Services was incorporated in 2001 as an educational corporation under Company Registration No A200009937.

Zone: South Pacific and East Asia
Country included in the territory: The Philippines
'The Salvation Army' in Filipino: Hukbo ng Kaligtasan; in Ilocano: Buyot ti Salakan
Languages in which the gospel is preached: Antiqueño (Kinaray-a), Bagobo, Bicolano, Cebuano, English, Filipino (Tagalog), Hiligaynon (Ilonggo), Ilocano, Korean, Pangasinan, T'boli, Waray
Periodical: *The War Cry*

THE TERRITORIAL theme of 'Fixing our eyes on Jesus' set a relevant challenge to every Salvationist to reach out and make a difference in their communities, by allowing Jesus to take them deeper in faith and service.

With the ongoing recovery work throughout the country following Typhoon Haiyan, Salvationists have been providing food, water, medical care, comfort and hope to those who have lost family members or had their homes destroyed. The Army has concentrated on the island of Leyte, and in particular the city of Tacloban and the municipality of Dulag. The overwhelming support of local and international communities enabled the territory to continue its recovery and rehabilitation programmes for survivors. Roofing materials, agricultural goods, stress debriefing retreats, repairs to school buildings, and the supply of school equipment, were distributed and gratefully received. A partnership conference between the territory and international donors was held in February 2014 for the purpose of developing long-term strategic recovery and rehabilitation plans.

Aside from natural calamities, officers and soldiers also provided help for the victims of man-made disasters. In Mindanao, where many child trafficking cases were recorded, a seminar on 'Combat and Care' was conducted to train the officers to identify and help victims of trafficking.

While serving suffering humanity, the territory continues to work toward its mission priorities. In June 2013, 19 cadets of the Heralds of Grace Session were welcomed.

There is an evident growth in corps ministries with two centres being upgraded to outpost status, two outposts to society status and an outpost to corps status.

In May 2013, a ground-breaking ceremony was held for Tanay Corps, Rizal. Through the generous giving of Salvationists from Australia and the USA Central Territory, in December the corps was completed and dedicated to God.

STATISTICS

Officers 230 (active 176 retired 54) **Cadets** 15 **Envoys/Field Sgts** 6 **Employees** 58
Corps 81 **Societies, Outposts and Outreaches** 67 **Institutions** 2 **Social Programmes** 26
Senior Soldiers 7,476 **Adherent Members** 4,788 **Junior Soldiers** 991
Personnel serving outside territory
Officers 5 Layworker 2

STAFF

Women's Ministries: Colonel Robyn Maxwell (TPWM) Lt-Col Wendy Lee (TSWM)
Sec for Business Administration:
Lt-Col Beverley Woodland
Finance: Maj Allain Nietes
Property: Mr Alfredo Agpaoa Jr
Sec for Personnel Administration:
Lt-Col Virgilio Menia
Youth Sec/Candidates: Maj Nelia Almenario
Sec for Programme Administration:
Lt-Col Alexander Genabe
Social Programme: Lt-Col Jocelyn Genabe
Corps Programme: Maj David Casimero
Training Principal: Maj Linda Manhardt
Training and Development/Education Services: Maj Ruby Casimero
Gospel Arts Coordinator: Mr Nicanor Bagasol
Editor and Literary Sec: Maj Elsa Oalang
Legal Consultant: Mr Paul Stephen Salegumba
Projects: Maj Susan Tandayag
Public Relations Sec: Maj Miguel Tandayag
Territorial Planned Giving Director: Maj Miguel Tandayag

DIVISIONS

Central Philippines: 20 Senatorial Dr, Congressional Village, Project 8, Quezon City; tel: (02) 929 6312; email: Central@phl.salvationarmy.org; Majs Joel and Susan Ceneciro
Mindanao Island: 344 NLSA Rd, Purok Bayanihan, San Isidro, Lagao 9500 General Santos City; tel: (083) 302 3798; email: Mid@phl.salvationarmy.org; Majs Rodolfo and Josalie Salcedo
Northern Luzon: Doña Loleng Subd., Nancayasan 2428 Urdaneta Pangasinan City; tel: (075) 656 2383; email: Northern@phl.salvationarmy.org; Majs Gerardo and Cristina Lopez

Visayas Islands: 731 M. J. Cuenco Ave,
Cebu City; tel: (032) 505 6972/6054;
email: Vid@phl.salvationarmy.org;
Majs Edward and Arlene Manulat

TRAINING COLLEGE
Pantay Rd, Sitio Bukal Brgy, Tandang Kutyo,
Tanay, Rizal; tel: (02) 654 2909

UNDER THQ
Sponsorship/Scholarship Programme;
Missing Persons/Family Tracing Service;
Emergency Disaster Relief

SOCIAL SERVICES
Residential Social Centres
Abused girls/children
Bethany Home: Quezon City (acc 25)

Street children in need of protection
Joyville Home: Rizal
(acc 30-40)

Schools
Asingan: Pangasinan;
Caloocan: Metro, Manila
Cebu City: Cebu
Laoag: Ilocos Norte
Mariveles: Bataan
Tondo: Manila

Child Care Learning Centres
La Paz: Ilo-Ilo City; Olongapo; Quezon City;

Nutrition, Feeding
Acala Corps: Pangasinan
Antipolo Outreach: Sitio San Lorenzo Ruiz
Bacolod: Bacolod City
Bagong Silang: Bagong Silang Tala
Bautista Corps: Pangasinan
Lamsine Corps: Surallah South Cotabato
Manila Central Corps: Ermita, Manila
Palhi: Leyte
Polomolok Corps Plant: South Cotabato

Programmes for Minorities
Bulalacao: Bulalacao, 5214 Oriental Mindoro
Lake Sebu: 9512 Poblacion, Lake Sebu South
Cotabato
Lamsine: Lamsine, T'boli town South Cotabato
Palawan: Tabun, Quezon, Puerto Princesa
Wali: Bo Wali, Maitum, Saranggani Province

Skills Training
Lapu-lapu City

Livelihood Support
Bayanihan; Camanggaan; Cantamuak; Maiting;
Manila (2 programmes); Nasucob; Pahanocoy

Agricultural Assistance
Bella Luz; Cabayaoasan; Camanggaan;
Nasukob; Palili; Santa Wali

Microcredit Enterprise Projects
Ansiray: Bulalacao; Caguray; Dagupan;
Magsaysay; Malingao; Nasukob; Ozamis;
Palili; Patnongon

Combat & Care Anti-Human Trafficking Projects
Bansalan; Davao; Fatima; General Santos; Lake
Sebu; Lamsine; Lebe, Kiamba; Midsayap;
Polomolok; Wali;

After-School Feeding Programme
Alcala: Pangasinan; Antipolo: Rizal; Bacolod
City: Bacolod; Bautista: Pangasinan;
Lamsine: South Cotabato; Pasay: Metro
Manila; Palhi: Leyte; Polomolok: South
Cotabato

Drop-in Centre for Trafficking Survivors
Davao

Health
Pandanan: Real Street, 5702 Patnongon, Antique

RWANDA AND BURUNDI COMMAND

Command leaders:
Lieut-Colonels Seth and Janet Appeateng

Officer Commanding:
Lieut-Colonel Seth Appeateng (1 Sept 2013)

General Secretary:
Major Jean Laurore Clénat (1 Apr 2010)

Command Headquarters: Plot 11737, Kibagabaga Road, Kimironko, Kimironko Sector, Kigali

Postal address: PO Box 812, Kigali, Rwanda

Tel: 250 252587639; email: Rwanda@rwa.salvationarmy.org

As a result of civil war and genocide in Rwanda, The Salvation Army became actively involved in relief work in September 1994. Operations were concentrated in Kayenzi Commune, part of the Gitarama Prefecture. Following mission work by officers from Zaïre, Uganda and Tanzania in 1995, officers were appointed from Congo (Brazzaville) to develop corps and mission work in Kayenzi Commune. Kayenzi Corps officially began its ministry on 5 November 1995. The Salvation Army was officially registered as a church in Rwanda on 15 September 2008.

In 1983, Justin Lusombo-Musese (a Congolese born in Burundi) was introduced by a friend to some of William Booth's writings and learned about The Salvation Army's early history. Justin and the friend were so enthused they decided to become members of the Army. Over the ensuing years they persistently requested International Headquarters to start Army operations in Burundi, and on 5 August 2007 the work was officially recognised with the warranting of Justin Lusombo-Musese and his wife Justine Fatouma as auxiliary-captains. The Rwanda Region was redesignated Rwanda and Burundi Region in October 2008 and upgraded to command status on 1 April 2010.

Zone: Africa
Countries included in the command: Burundi, Rwanda
The Salvation Army in Kinyarwanda: Ingabo Z'Agakiza
Languages in which the gospel is preached: English, French, Kinyarwanda, Kirundi, Kiswahili
Periodical: *Salvationist News*

THE THEME for 2013, 'Forgetting what is behind and pressing on toward the goal', has helped to empower and focus the work undertaken by officers and soldiers in the Rwanda and Burundi Command.

Training seminars were conducted on a variety of subjects and the command has been blessed to receive donations from the Norway, Iceland and The Færoes Territory to purchase new equipment for the officer training college.

In October 2013, 547 Salvationists

witnessed the installation of the new command leaders Lieut-Colonels Seth and Janet Appeateng (OC/CPWM) by Commissioners Joash and Florence Malabi (IS/ZSWM).

In December 2013, 350 young people joined together for youth councils and two outposts were upgraded to corps status in Burundi. New halls were dedicated to the glory of God by Lieut-Colonel Appeateng at Rwimiyaga (funded by Australia Southern Territory) and at Gatumba (funded by USA Eastern Territory).

The command Executive Council met in February 2014 to discuss the strategic plan for the next four years. Copies of the Dickson Teacher's Bible were received from the Protestant Council of Rwanda and in April many Salvationists attended the 20th commemoration of the genocide in Rwanda.

More than 180 junior home league and young women's fellowship members enjoyed spiritual blessings and support during a three-day rally in Burundi, conducted by the command leaders.

Accountant: Albine Batamuliza
Education and Extension Training: Capt Dancille Mukafuraha Ndagijimana
Finance: Capt Leonard Nyongesa
Projects: tba
Public Relations/Candidates: Capt Emmanuel Ndagijimana
Social: tba
Sponsorship: Capt Violet Nyongesa
Training: Maj Bente Gundersen
Youth: Capt Obed Tungo

DIVISION
Kamonyi: PO Box 812, Kigali;
Majs Annet and George Musamali

SECTIONS
all c/o PO Box 812, Kigali
Kayenzi: Capt Jean Damascene Turikumana
Kigali: Capt Obed Tungo
Muhanga: Capt Theobald Kabagema
Nyagatare: Capt André Nsengiyaremye
Rukoma: Lt Jean Damascène Mudengei

BURUNDI
Rohero II. Otto route Road. Butusi Avenue 010 08 13 3329 Bujumbura Burundi;
Majs Japhet and Maureen Agusiomah

STATISTICS
Officers 29 Cadets 8 Corps Leaders 7
Employees 24
Corps 14 Outposts 20 Societies 3
Pre-School Facilities 9 (acc 595)
Senior Soldiers 2,368 Adherent Members 892
Junior Soldiers 1,012
Personnel serving outside command:
Officers: 2

STAFF
Women's Ministries: Lt-Col Janet Appeateng (CPWM) Maj Elianise Clénat (CSWM) Capt Dyna Namugisha Tungo (JHLS)

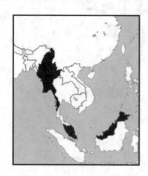

SINGAPORE, MALAYSIA AND MYANMAR TERRITORY

Territorial leaders:
Colonels Lyndon and Bronwyn Buckingham

Territorial Commander:
Colonel Lyndon Buckingham (1 Jun 2013)

Chief Secretary:
Lieut-Colonel Leopoldo Posadas (1 Jun 2013)

Territorial Headquarters: 20 Bishan St 22, Singapore 579768

Postal address: Ang Mo Kio Central, PO Box 640, Singapore 915605

Tel: [65] 6555 0188; website: www.salvationarmy.org.sg

In May 1935 Salvation Army work began in Singapore. It spread to Penang (1938), Melaka and Ipoh (1940), Kuching (Sarawak) (1950), Kuala Lumpur (1966) and Kota Kinabalu (Sabah) (1996).

'The General of The Salvation Army' is a 'corporation sole' by The Salvation Army Ordinance 1939 in the Straits Settlements; by The Salvation Army (Incorporation) Ordinance 1956 in the Federation of Malaya; and by the Missionary Societies Order 1957 in the Colony of Sarawak.

Adjutant Taran Das (Reuben Moss), who was attached to the Lahore headquarters in India, was appointed to open the work in Burma (now Myanmar) by Commissioner Booth Tucker in January 1915. Myanmar Salvationists have, since 1966, developed their witness and service despite the restriction on reinforcements from overseas. In 1994 Myanmar was joined to the Singapore and Malaysia Command. The command was elevated to territory status on 1 March 2005.

Zone: South Pacific and East Asia

Countries included in the territory: Malaysia, Myanmar, Singapore

'The Salvation Army' in Chinese: (Mandarin) Chiu Shi Chen, (Cantonese) Kau Shai Kwan, (Amoy, Hokkien) Kiu Se Kun; Bahasa: Bala Keselamatan; Myanmar: Kae Tin Chin Tat; Tamil: Retchania Senai

Languages in which the gospel is preached: Bahasa, Burmese, Chinese (Amoy, Cantonese, Hokkien, Mandarin), English, Falam, Hakah, Karen, Matu, Mindat, Mizo, Paoh, Tamil, Tedim, Telegu, Thado, Zarngeit)

Periodical: *The War Cry*

THE Singapore, Malaysia and Myanmar Territory saw a significant change in leadership with the installation of new territorial leaders, Colonels Lyndon and Bronwyn Buckingham (TC/TPWM) and the

welcome to Lieut-Colonels Leopoldo and Evelyn Posadas (CS/TSWM).

The territorial theme for 2014, 'The Name of Jesus', brought great blessing through many opportunities.

In May 2013, under the leadership

of the then General Linda Bond, a congress was held in Yangon with more than 1,000 delegates in attendance. During the event junior soldiers were enrolled, senior soldiers sworn in and seven Salvation Army officers commissioned and ordained.

One of the highlights of the year in review was the welcome of nine cadets – six from Singapore and Malaysia and three from Myanmar – making up the Heralds of Grace Session. In March 2014, 10 cadets from the Proclaimers of Salvation Session were commissioned and ordained, making a total of 93 commissioned officers in the Myanmar Region.

There have been new corps buildings opened at Bisham Chinese Corps, Singapore and Banting Corps and Tamil Corps and Community Centre, West Malaysia. Redevelopment work has also commenced in Melaka, West Malaysia, on the site where the Army's current work is located.

Penang Corps in Malaysia celebrated 75 years with a weekend led by the territorial leaders and supported by Singapore Central Band. During the celebration the corps held a fund-raising dinner and on Sunday nine senior soldiers were sworn in.

The Women's Ministries Department's Helping Hand Project raised funds for musical instruments to support The Philippines Territory. Colonel Bronwyn Buckingham said, 'To place almost S$27,000 into The Philippines Territory's bank account will be the answer to many prayers.'

The officers and soldiers in Myanmar distributed water during the Southeast Asian Games. During this time The Salvation Army was very visible and many contacts were made.

The annual Red Shield Appeal luncheon featured a peer-mentoring scheme under Prison Support Services. This unique programme continues to bring joy to the lives of many children whose parents are in prison.

STATISTICS

Officers 148 (active 129 retired 19)
Cadets 15 **Employees** 771
Corps 58 **Outposts** 17 **Institutions** 18
Kindergartens 3 **Day Care Centres** 9
Senior Soldiers 2,681 **Adherent Members** 461
Junior Soldiers 526

STAFF

Women's Ministries: Col Bronwyn Buckingham (TPWM) Lt-Col Evelyn Posadas (TSWM)
Finance: Mdm Koh Guek Eng
Human Resources: Mrs Toh-Chia Lai Ying
Literary Sec: tba
Programme: tba
  Asst Programme Sec: tba
Property: Mr John Ng
Public Relations: Angeline Tan
Projects: tba
Training: Col Lyndon Buckingham
Youth: Capt Lalrindiki
Candidates: Maj Irene Chang

SCHOOL FOR OFFICER TRAINING (Singapore and Malaysia)

500 Upper Bukit Timah Rd, Singapore 678106; tel: 6349 5333

SINGAPORE
Children's Homes

Gracehaven: 3 Lorong Napiri (off Yio Chu Kang Rd), Singapore 547528; tel: 6488 1510 (acc 160)
The Haven: 350 Pasir Panjang Rd, Singapore 118692; tel: 6774 9588/9 (acc 50), Interim Placement and Assessment Centre (The Haven) (acc 15)

Day Care Centres for Children

Ang Mo Kio Child Care Centre: Blk 610 Ang Mo
Kio Ave 4, #01-1227 Singapore 560610;
tel: 6452 4862 (acc 89)

Bukit Batok East Child Care Centre: Blk 247
Bukit Batok East Ave 5, #01-86 Singapore
650247; tel: 6562 4976 (acc 73)

Bukit Panjang Child Care Centre: Blk 402
Fajar Rd, #01-217 Singapore 670402;
tel: 6760 2624 (acc 82)

Tampines Child Care Centre: Blk 159
Tampines St 12, #01-95 Singapore 521159;
tel: 6785 2976 (acc 90)

Day Care Centres for the Elderly

Peacehaven Bedok Multi Service Centre
Blk 121, #01-161/163 Bedok North Rd,
Singapore 460121; tel: 6445 1630 (acc 50)

Peacehaven Nursing Home (SPICE)Programme,
9 Upper Changi Road North, Singapore 507706
(acc 50)

Family Support Services

Blk 42, Beo Cresc, #01-95 Singapore 160042;
tel: 6273 7207

Hostel

Peacehaven Nurses' Hostel: 9 Upper Changi Rd
North, Singapore 507706; tel: 6546 5678
(acc 100)

Retreat Centre

Praisehaven, 500 Upper Bukit Timah Rd,
Singapore 678106; tel: 6349 5302 (acc 210)

Nursing Home

Peacehaven, 9 Upper Changi Rd North,
Singapore 507706; tel: 6546 5678 (acc 401)

Prison Support Services – Kids In Play

7 Upper Changi Rd North,
Singapore 507706;
tel 6546 5868 (130 families)

Red Shield Industries

309 Upper Serangoon Rd, Singapore 347693;
tel: 6288 5438

Youth Development Centres

William Booth Corps at Bukit Panjang: Fajar Rd,
#01-267 Singapore 670404; tel: 6763 0837
(acc 70)

Riverpoint Youth Development Centre: Blk 65
Kallang Bahru, #01-305 Singapore 330065;
tel: 6291 6303; under Balestier Corps

EAST MALAYSIA

Boys' Home

Kuching Boys' Home: Jalan Ban Hock,
93100 Kuching; PO Box 547, 93700 Kuching,
Sarawak, Malaysia; tel: (082) 24 2623
(acc 30)

Children's Home

Kuching Children's Home: 138 Jalan Upland,
93200 Kuching; PO Box 106, 93700 Kuching,
Sarawak, Malaysia; tel: (082) 24 8234 (acc 60)

Home School (Learning Centre)

Jalan Ban Hock: 93100 Kuching; PO Box 547,
93700 Kuching, Sarawak, Malaysia;
tel: (082) 24 2623 (acc 30)

Kindergarten

Kuching Kindergarten: Sekama Rd,
93300 Kuching, Sarawak, Malaysia;
PO Box 44, 93700 Kuching, Sarawak,
Malaysia; tel: (082) 333981 (acc 100)

Corps Community Services

Bintulu; Kota Kinabalu; Kuching

WEST MALAYSIA

Liaison and Public Relations Office:
26-1 Jalan Puteri, 4/2 Bandar Puteri,
47100 Puchong, Selangor Darul Ehsan,
Malaysia; tel: (06) 8061 4929

Boys' Home

Ipoh Boys' Home: 4367 Jalan Tambun,
31400 Ipoh; PO Box 221, 30720 Ipoh, Perak,
Malaysia; tel: [60] (05) 545 7819 (acc 60)

Centre for Special Children

Hopehaven Centre for Special Children:
321 Jalan Parameswara, 75000 Melaka,
Malaysia; tel: [60] (06) 283 2101 (acc 100)

Children's Homes

Ipoh Children's Home: 255 Kampar Rd,
30250 Ipoh, Perak, Malaysia;
tel: (05) 254 9767; fax: (05) 242 9630 (acc 50)

Melaka Lighthouse Children's Home:
404 Taman Sinn, Jalan Semabok 75050,
Melaka, Malaysia; tel: (06) 283 2101 (acc 25)

Penang Children's Home: 8A Logan Rd,
10400 Penang, Malaysia; tel: (04) 227 0162
(acc 60)

Day Care Centre for Children

Banting Day Care Centre: 1 Jalan Emas 2,
Bandar Sungai Emas, Banting 47200 (acc 50)

Kindergartens

Batang Melaka Kindergarten: J7702 Main Rd,
Batang Melaka 77500, Selandar, Malaysia;
tel: (06) 446 1601 (acc 50)

Kuala Lumpur Kindergarten: 1 Lingkungan
Hujan, Overseas Union Garden, 58200 KL,
Malaysia; tel: (03) 7782 4766 (acc 60)

Homes for the Aged

Joyhaven Home for the Elderly: 1 Jalan 12/17,
Seksyen 12, 46200 Petaling Jaya, Selangor,
Malaysia; tel: (03) 7958 6257 (acc 25)

Perak Home for the Aged: Jalan Bersatu,
Jelapang, 30020 Ipoh, Perak, Malaysia;
tel: (05) 526 2108 (acc 50)

Corps Community Services

Banting Corps Community Services:
2 Jalan Emas 2, Bandar Sungai Emas, Banting
47200 (acc 50)

Kuala Lumpur Community Services: 26-1 Jalan
Puteri 4/2, Bandar Puteri 47100, Puchong,
Selangor, Malaysia; tel: (03) 8061 4929
(acc 50)

Penang Corps Community Services: 53 Perak Rd,
10150 Penang, West Malaysia;
tel: (04) 2290921

Social/Community Services

Melaka State Community Services: 321 Jalan
Parameswara, 75000 Melaka, Malaysia;
tel: (06) 283 1203

MYANMAR REGION

Headquarters: 176-178 Anawrahta St,
Botahtaung, East Yangon 11161, Myanmar;
Postal address: GPO Box 394, Yangon,
Myanmar; tel: [95] (1) 294267/293307;
Regional Officer: tba

DISTRICTS

Central, Phyu; Maj Tint Tae
Kalay: Capt Lalbiakdika
Tamu, Khampat: Capt Kyaw Kyaw Oo
Southern, Yangon; Capt Lalsangliana

COLLEGE FOR OFFICER TRAINING

50 Byaing Ye O Zin St, Tarmway, Yangon,
Myanmar; tel: [95] (1) 543694;
Training: Maj Nay Lin Tun.

Day Care Centres for Children

Letpanchaung; Letpanchaung North Corps.
(acc 30)

Myauk Chhaw Taw; Myauk Chhaw Taw Corps.
(acc 30)

Phyu; Phyu Corps. (acc 20 children)

Yangon; Tarmway Corps. (acc 35)

Yeni; Yeni Corps Plant. (acc 35)

SOCIAL CENTRES:
Children's Homes

Phyu Children's Home: 50 Bago Rd, Pyu,
Myanmar (acc 50)

Yangon Boy's Home: 406 Banyadala Rd,
Tarmway, Yangon, Myanmar; (acc 50)

Yangon Girls' Home: 50 Byaing Ye O Zin St,
Tarmway, Yangon, Myanmar; tel: (acc 50)

Student Hostel

Taunggyi Hope Centre: 94-95, Ward (5)
Naung In Street, Aye Thar Yar, Taunggyi.
(acc 40)

SOUTH AMERICA EAST TERRITORY

Territorial Leaders
Commissioners Jorge A. and Adelina Ferreira

Territorial Commander:
Commissioner Jorge A. Ferreira
(1 Sept 2014)

Chief Secretary:
Lieut-Colonel Ricardo Fernández
(1 Jul 2012)

Territorial Headquarters: Avda Rivadavia 3257 (C1203AAE), Buenos Aires, Argentina

Postal address: Casilla de Correo 2240 (C1000WAW) Buenos Aires, Argentina

Tel/fax: [54] (11) 4864-9321/9348/9491/1075; email: .sae.secretaria@sae.salvationarmy.org
websites: www.ejercitodesalvacion.org.ar; www.ejercitodesalvacion.org.py;
www.ejercitodesalvacion.org.uy

Four officers, who knew no Spanish, established The Salvation Army in Buenos Aires in 1890. Operations spread to other South American nations, of which Paraguay (1910), Uruguay (1890) and Argentina now comprise the South America East Territory.

The Salvation Army was recognised as a juridical person in Argentina by the Government Decree of 26 February 1914 (No A 54/909); in Uruguay by the Ministry of the Interior on 17 January 1917 (No 366537); and in Paraguay by Presidential Decree of 28 May 1928 (No 30217).

Zone: Americas and Caribbean
Countries included in the territory: Argentina, Paraguay, Uruguay
'The Salvation Army' in Spanish: Ejército de Salvación
Languages in which the gospel is preached: Guaraní, Korean, Spanish
Periodicals: *El Oficial*, *El Salvacionista* (both Spanish)

THE LORD has been faithful showing his love, mercy and grace once again to the South America East Territory with the De Viso Outpost, Buenos Aires Division, being elevated to corps status, Sunday school teachers commissioned and a new multipurpose room located in Mendoza City, Central West Argentina District, being opened.

The Dorcas group (League of Mercy) has been working during the year taking winter clothes to many hospitals and nursing homes and giving heart-shaped pillows to each person who was receiving treatment for breast cancer. The pillows were especially designed to ease pain following surgery.

Many families in Rosario City lost

their possessions due to a gas explosion that levelled an apartment building. In keeping with the mission of The Salvation Army, Salvationists provided emotional and spiritual support, and food for the residents and workers.

As part of the continued assistance to women, a new centre was opened, which has increased the number of shelters and support given to women.

Territorial youth councils were held in January 2014, with many young people expressing the desire to deepen their commitment to God, his Word and their ministry as leaders within their local corps. A territorial music institute enabled the young people to develop their musical skills and artistic abilities and worship the Lord with their talents.

During Holy Week the Territorial Band and Songsters travelled to the USA Eastern Territory for a 10-day tour. The territory is grateful for this opportunity and the evidence of God's presence during the tour.

STATISTICS
Officers 157 (active 127 retired 30) Cadets 6
    Employees 178
Corps 45 Outposts 9 Institutions 28
Senior Soldiers 1,835 Adherent Members 330
    Junior Soldiers 540

STAFF
Women's Ministries: Comr Adelina Ferreira
    (TPWM) Lt-Col Mirtha Fernández (TSWM)
Personnel: Maj Raúl Bernao
Programme: Maj Danton Moya
Business Administration: Maj Miguel Del Bello
Education: Maj Karina Giusti
Finance: Mr Sergio Cerezo (Chief Accountant)
Legal: Mr Rene Menares
Literature and Editor: Maj Alicia Gauchat
Music and Gospel Arts: B/M Omar Pérez
Projects/Sponsorship/Missing Persons:
    Mrs Claudia Franchetti

Property: tba
Red Shield/Thrift Store Operations:
    Maj Daniel Barth
Spiritual Formation: Maj Bartolo Aguirre
Training: Maj Eduardo Baigorria
Youth: Maj Rafael Giusti
Candidates: Maj Karina Giusti

DIVISIONS
Buenos Aires: Avda Rivadavia 3257 – Piso 2
    (C1203AAE), Buenos Aires, Argentina;
    tel: (011) 4861 1930/9499;
    Majs Roberto and María Juárez
Central Argentina: Urquiza 2142, (S2000AOD)
    Rosario Pcia de Santa Fe, Argentina;
    tel: (0341) 425 6739;
    Majs Marcio and Jurema Mendes
Uruguay: Avda Agraciada 3567 (11700)
    Montevideo, Uruguay;
    tel: (00598) (2) 409 7581; Majs Hugo and
    María del Luján Ramos

DISTRICTS
Central West Argentina: Felix Frías 434/6,
    (X5004AHJ) Córdoba, Argentina;
    tel: (351) 423-3228; Maj Osvaldo Corazza
Paraguay and NEA: Héroes de la Independencia
    y Vietnam, Casilla 2008, (CP 2160) San
    Lorenzo, Paraguay; tel/fax: 595 (21) 577 082;
    Maj Pablo Nicolasa
Southern Argentina: Moreno 759 (B8000FWO),
    Bahía Blanca, Pcia de Buenos Aires;
    tel/fax: (291) 4533 642; Maj Diego Barth

TRAINING COLLEGE
Avda Tte Gral Donato Álvarez 465/67,
    (C1406BOC) Buenos Aires;
    tel/fax: (011) 4631 4815

CONFERENCE CENTRES AND YOUTH CAMP
Argentina
    Parque General Jorge L. Carpenter, Avda
        Benavídez 115, (Paraguay y Uruguay)
        (B1621) Benavídez, Pcia de Buenos Aires;
        tel: (03488) 458644
    Parque El Oasis, Ruta 14 Km 1 Camino a
        Soldini – Zona Rural– Perez (Santa Fe);
        tel: (341) 495 0003

COMMUNITY AND DAY CARE CENTRES
Argentina
    Buenos Aires: Nueva Chicago (acc 30)

Carlos Pellegrini 376: (acc 20)
Quilmes: 'Evangelina Espacio Verde' (acc 30)
Paraguay
Capiatá: Cerrito c/ Fidel Maís (acc 30)
Posadas: School Support Class (acc 15)
Rayito de Luz: Perú y Artigas Bº San Vicente
(acc 25)
Viñas Cue: (acc 25)
Uruguay
Montevideo Central Corps School Support
Class (acc 10)
Sarandí 1573, (60,000) Paysandú (acc 84)
Tres Arroyos 'Aprendamos Jugando' (acc 30)

SOCIAL SERVICES
Counselling and Labour Exchange
Argentina
Loria 190, (C1173ACD)
Buenos Aires; tel: (11) 4865 0074
Central Division: Rosario, Av. Juan Bautista
Alberdi 773 (S2002EOC) tel : (0341) 438-6750

Children's Homes (mixed)
Paraguay
El Redil, Dr Hassler 4402 y MacArthur,
Asunción; tel: [595] (21) 600 291 (acc 40)
Uruguay
El Lucero, J.M. Blanes 62, (50,000) Salto;
tel: (00598732) 32740 (acc 30)

Eventide Homes
Argentina
Catalina Higgins Home, Calle Mitre, 54 No 2749,
(1650) Villa Maipú, San Martín, Pcia de
Buenos Aires; tel: (11) 4753 4117 (acc 35)
Eliasen Home, Primera Junta 750, (B1878IPP)
Quilmes, Pcia de Buenos Aires;
tel: (011) 4254 5897 (acc 40)
Uruguay
El Atardecer, Avda Agraciada 3567,
(11800) Montevideo;
tel: (00598) (2) 308 5227 (acc 75)

Recycling Operations
Argentina
Avda Hipólito Irigoyen 4750, (B1814ABQ)
Lanús Oeste, Buenos Aires; tel: (11) 42414756
Avda Sáenz 580, (C1437DNS) Buenos Aires;
tel: (11) 4911 7561/0781/7585
Avda Sánchez de Bustamante Gerli,
Lanús Este, Buenos Aires
Calle 93 # 883 Barrio Aeropuerto, Villa Elvira,
La Plata, Buenos Aires;
tel: (0221) 486 6654
Calle 4 Nº 711, (B1900) La Plata, Buenos Aires;
tel: (0221) 483-6152

Cañada de Gómez 2322, (1440EGV) Buenos
Aires
Gral Juan O'Brien 1260, (1137ABD)
Buenos Aires; tel: (011) 4305-5021
(B1688DBO) Villa Santos Tesei,
Buenos Aires; tel: (011) 4450-3606
Barrio ULM, Cnel Bogado Nº 5, (H3730QA)
Charata, Chaco; tel: (03731) 421-292
Salta 3197, Barrio San Javier, (H3500BOF)
Resistencia, Chaco; tel: (03722) 466 529
Godoy Cruz 348, (M5500GOQ) Mendoza,
tel: (0261) 429-6113
Amenábar 581, (S20000QK) Rosario;
tel: (0341) 482 0155
Pérez: Ruta 14 Km, 1 Soldini;
tel: (0341) 45-0003
Rosario: Avda Alberdi 773 (S200EOC);
tel: (0341) 438-6750
Mendoza: Zone 'Las Tortugas' Barcala 1570
(ex Chililicoy); tel: (0261) 4296113

Uruguay
Félix Laborde 2577, (12000) Montevideo;
tel: (00598-2) 508-7766
Brasil 1946, esq Blanes; tel (00598 4732047)

Night Shelters (Men)
Argentina
Buenos Aires (acc 86)

Night Shelters (Women and Children)
Argentina
O'Brien 1272, Buenos Aires: 'El Amparo'
(acc 38)
O'Brien 1274: 'Betania' (acc 50)

Students' Homes
Argentina–7 homes
(total acc 241)
Paraguay–2 homes
(total acc 22),
Uruguay–1 home
(acc 8)

Women's Residence
Argentina
Esparza 93, (C1171ACA)
Buenos Aires; tel: (11) 4861 3119 (acc 56)

Primary School
Argentina
EEGB No 1027 Federico Held, Barrio ULM,
(H3730BQA) Charata,
Pcia del Chaco; tel: (3731) 421 292 (acc 450)

Health Centre
Argentina
Pcia del Chaco, Coronel Bogado 4, Barrio ULM,
  (H3730BQA) Charata;
  tel: (3731) 421 292

Medical Clinic
Paraguay: Héroes de la Independencia y
  Vietnam, Villa Laurelty, San Lorenzo;
  tel: [595] 21 577 082

SOUTH AMERICA EAST: Captain Leonardo Fernandez providing support for relief workers following a gas explosion in the city of Rosario, Argentina

SOUTH AMERICA WEST TERRITORY

Territorial leaders:
Commissioners Torben and Deise Eliasen

Territorial Commander:
Commissioner Torben Eliasen
(1 Sep 2014)

Chief Secretary:
Lieut-Colonel Alex Nesterenko (1 Feb 2014)

Territorial Headquarters: Avenida España No 44, Santiago, Chile

Postal address: Casilla 3225, Santiago, Chile (parcels/courier service: Avenida España No 44, Santiago Centro, Santiago, Chile)

Tel: [56] (2) 671 8237/695 7005; email: saw_leadership@saw.salvationarmy.org

Salvation Army operations were commenced in Chile soon after the arrival of Brigadier and Mrs William T. Bonnet to Valparaíso on 1 October 1909. The first corps was opened in Santiago on 28 November, with Captain David Arn and Lieutenant Alfred Danielson as officers. Adjutant and Mrs David Thomas, with Lieutenant Zacarías Ribeiro, pioneered the work in Peru in March 1910. The work in Bolivia, started in December 1920, was planned by Brigadier Chas Hauswirth and established by Adjutant and Mrs Oscar E. Ahlm. Quito was the location of the Army's arrival in Ecuador on 30 October 1985 under the command of Captain and Mrs Eliseo Flores Morales.

Zone: Americas and Caribbean
Countries included in the territory: Bolivia, Chile, Ecuador, Peru
'The Salvation Army' in Aymara: Ejercitunaca Salvaciananaca; in Quechua: Ejercituman Salvacionman; in Spanish: Ejército de Salvación
Languages in which the gospel is preached: Aymara, Quechua, Spanish
Publications: *El Grito de Guerra* (*The War Cry*), *El Trébol*

WITH 'One Army, One Mission, One Message' as the theme, blessing upon blessing was showered down through the ministry of special guests General André Cox and Commissioner Silvia Cox (WPWM) at the territorial congress celebration in the South America West Territory in 2013.

With the joy and spirit that define South American Salvationists, the congress was celebrated in the city of Arica, Chile. During the congress the General called everyone to reflect on the reality that, 'it is good to be together and celebrate, but let's not forget that out there, there is a world that needs us'.

Having travelled from all over the territory, 1,600 Salvationists met for three days of celebration and renewal. Personal testimonies brought great blessing and encouragement as we heard how the Lord is working in the lives of his people.

During the congress weekend, Salvationists from Chile, Peru, Bolivia and Ecuador impacted the local community with a Salvationist fair. The fair consisted of folkloric dances, an exhibition representing many of the handicrafts created by women's ministries from the divisions and district, and the distribution of evangelistic materials. Salvationists also provided spiritual support when necessary.

The then TC Commissioner Jorge Ferreira challenged Salvationists to read the entire Bible in one year. Two hundred and seventy-two soldiers and officers rose to the challenge and reached their goal, while others were encouraged to accept the same challenge in the coming year.

Men's and women's rallies brought spiritual challenge and the youth took part in a 'Batucada' – a street ministry programme – that included a parade with percussion, juggling, dance and music.

A 'Celebration of Mission' focused on the beginnings of The Salvation Army in the countries that make up our territory. God has been moving throughout the territory, no matter the culture, country or language (Spanish, Quechua, Aymara and Quichua) in which the message is preached.

Many young people have answered the call for full-time ministry as officers within The Salvation Army. God truly has greater things in store for the South America West Territory

STATISTICS

Officers 289 (active 241 retired 48) **Cadets** (1st Yr) 8 (2nd Yr) 12 **Employees** 1,122 **Corps** 89 **Outposts** 18 **Schools and Vocational Institutes** 13 **Day Nurseries** 34 **Community Centres** 41 **Hospital** 1 **Health Centre** 1 **Mobile Clinic** 1 **Community Health** 1 **Pre-Primary Schools** 28 **Institutions** 38 **Senior Soldiers** 4,716 **Adherent Members** 541 **Junior Soldiers** 2,006

STAFF

Women's Ministries: Comr Deise Eliasen (TPWM) Lt-Col Luz H. Nesterenko (TSWM)
Business Administration (Legal): Maj Manuel Márquez
Personnel: Lt-Col Cecilia Bahamonde
Programme: Maj Paulina Márquez
Editor, Lit and Communication: Maj Eduardo Almendras
Education: Maj Eliseo Flores
Enterprise Development: Maj Jaime Herrera
Finance: Maj Alberto Serém
League of Mercy/Golden Age: Maj Paulina Márquez
Property and Public Relations: Maj Manuel Márquez
Social: Maj Maria José Serém
Sponsorship: Maj Maria José Serém
Trade: Maj Alberto Serém
Training: Maj Eliseo Flores
Candidates: Maj Paulina Márquez

DIVISIONS

Bolivia Altiplano: Calle Cañada Strongest 1888, Zona San Pedro, Casilla 926, La Paz, Bolivia; tel: 591 (2) 249 1560; Majs Sixto and Aída Alí
Bolivia Central: Calle Rico Toro 773 Zona Queru Queru, Casilla 3594, Cochabamba, Bolivia; tel: 591 (4) 445 4281/468 1147; Majs Javier and Maria Obando
Chile Central: Agustinas 3020, Casilla 3225, Santiago, Chile; tel: 56 (2) 681 4992/5277; Majs Hernán and Glenda Espinoza
Chile South: Av Caupolicán 990, Casilla 1064, Temuco, Chile; tel: 56 (45) 215 850; Majs Antonio and Lilian Arguedas
Ecuador: Tomás Chariove 149-144 y Manuel Valdivieso, El Pinar Bajo, Casilla 17.10.7179, Quito, Ecuador; tel: 593 (2) 243 5422/ 244 7829; Majs Pedro and Raquel Sánchez
Peru: Calle Zaragoza 215, Urbanización Parque San Martín, Pueblo Libre, Lima 21, Apartado 690, Lima 100; tel: 51 (1) 653 4965/6; Maj Deisy Costas

DISTRICT
Chile North: Sucre 872, Casilla 310, Antofagasta,
Chile; tel: 56 (55) 280 668/224 094;
Maj Maria Flores

TRAINING COLLEGE
Coronel Souper 4564, Estación Central,
Casilla 3225, Santiago, Chile;
tel: 56 (2) 776 2425/5153

SALVATION ARMY CAMP GROUNDS
Bolivia
'Chapare', Población Chimoré, Chapare;
tel: 591 7642 8777
'Eben-Ezer', Puente Villa, Comunidad Tarila,
Provincia Nor Yungas
Chile
Complejo Angostura, Panamericana Sur km 55,
Paine, Región Metropolitana, Casila 3225,
Santiago; tel: 591 (2) 825 0398
Villa Frontera, Parcela 16, Calle San Martín,
Villa la Frontera, Arica

EDUCATIONAL WORK
Vocational Institutes
Bolivia
'Lindgren' Murillo 4364, Barrio Central Viacha,
La Paz; tel: 591 (2) 280 0969 (acc 200)
'William Booth' – Oruro, Sucre 909, Oruro;
tel: 591 (2) 525 1369

Aymara Bible Institute
Bolivia
La Paz, Prolongación Illampu 1888, Zona San Pedro

Schools
Bolivia
'William Booth' – Villa Cosmos: Uraciri
Patica 2064, Barrio Cosmos 79, Unidad
Vecinal C, La Paz; tel: 591 (2) 288 0118
'William Booth' – Oruro: Sucre 909, Oruro;
tel: 591 (2) 525–1369; (acc 800)
'William Booth' – Viacha: Murillo 4364, Barrio
Central, Viacha; tel: 591 (2) 280 0969 (acc 200)
Chile
Arica: Av Cancha Rayada 3839, Segunda Etapa
Población Cardenal Silva Henríquez,
Casilla 203; tel: 56 (58) 211 100 (acc 678)
Calama:
Anibal Pinto 2121, Casilla 62, Calama;
tel: 56 (55) 311 216/345 802
Catalina Booth – Calama, Irene Frei 2875,
Villa Esmeralda, Casilla 347, Calama;
tel: 56 (55) 360 458 (acc 800)
Osorno: William Booth, Zenteno 1015,

Casilla 317, Osorno; tel: 56 (64) 247 449;
(acc 879)
Puerto Montt: Naciones Unidas – Antuhue,
Presidente Ibáñez 272, Casilla 277;
tel: 56 (65) 286 236 (acc 1,207)
Ejército de Salvación, Séptimo de Línea 148,
Población Libertad, Casilla 277;
tel: 56 (65) 254 047/251 918 (acc 363)
Santiago: Ejército de Salvación, Herrera 185,
Santiago; tel: 56 (2) 681 7097 (acc 400)
Peru
Eduardo Palací, Av Progreso 1032, Urb San
Gregorio, Vitarte, Lima; tel/fax: 51 (1) 356 0461
(acc 500)
Miguel Grau, Av 29 de Diciembre 127, Trujillo;
tel/fax: 51 (44) 255 571 (acc 300)
Ecuador
Ejército de Salvación – Cayambe, Calle H 1
393 Morales, Urbanización Las Orquídeas,
Cayambe, Casilla 17.10.7179, Quito;
tel: 593 (2) 211 0196 (acc 150)
Ejército de Salvación – Manta, Avenida 201,
entre Calles 116 y 117, Barrio, La Paz;
tel: 593 (5) 292 0147 (acc 40)

Pre-Primary Schools
Chile
Santiago:
El Bosque, Las Vizcachas 858, Población
Las Acacias, Comuna de El Bosque;
tel: 56 (2) 529 4242 (acc 45)
Ejército de Salvación N°1619, Pudahuel
(and Initial Grades of Primary) Mapocho
9047, Comuna de Pudahuel, Santiago;
tel: 56 (2) 643 1875 (acc 160)

MEDICAL WORK
Bolivia
Harry Williams Hospital: Av Suecia 1038-1058,
Zona Huayra K'assa, Casilla 4099,
Cochabamba; tel: 591 (4) 422 7778/474 5329/
447 45612 (30 beds)
Community Extension Programme: Av Suecia
1038-1058, Zona Huayra K'assa, Casilla 4099,
Cochabamba; tel: 591 (4) 422 7778/
474 5329/447 45612

SOCIAL WORK
Emergency and Social Welfare Office:
Chile Central, Mapocho 4130, Comuna de
Quinta Normal, Casilla 3225 Santiago;
tel: 56 (2) 775 1566

Men's Shelters
Bolivia
Calle Prolongación Illampu 1888,

South America West Territory

Zona San Pedro, Casilla 926, La Paz;
tel: 591 (2) 231 1189 (acc 100)
Chile
Villagrán 9, Casilla 1887, Valparasío;
tel: 56 (32) 221 4946 (acc 170)
Peru
Calle Colón 138/142, Apartado 139, Callao;
tel: 51 (1) 429 3128 (acc 24)

Transit House (Women)
Chile: Calle Zenteno 1499, Casilla 3225,
Santiago; tel: 56 (2) 554 1767 (acc 15)

Student Residence Halls
Bolivia
Cochabamba: 'Tte - Coronel Rosa de Nery' (Girls),
Calle Lanza S-0555, Casilla 3198,
Cochabamba; tel: 591 (4) 422 6553 (acc 30)
La Paz: 'Remedios Asín' (Girls), Cañada
Strongest 1888, Casilla 926, La Paz;
tel: 591 (2) 248 0502 (acc 20)
Oruro: 'Tte - Coronel Jorge Nery Torrico' (Boys),
Calle Junin 459, entre 6 de Octubre y Potosí;
Casilla 86, Oruro; tel: 591 (2) 528 6885 (acc 24)
Peru
Lima: 'Catalina Booth' (Girls), Jirón Huancayo
245, Apartado 690, Lima 100; tel: 51 (1) 433
8747 (acc 20)
San Martín: 'Las Palmeras' – Tarapoto, Jirón
Amoraca 212, Distrito Morales, Apartado 88,
Tarapoto, San Martín; tel: 51 (42) 527 540
(acc 20)

Children's Homes
Bolivia
Cochabamba:
'Evangelina Booth' (Girls), Francisco
Viedma 1054, Villa Montenegro, Casilla 542;
tel: 591 (4) 424 1560 (acc 60)
'Oscar Ahlms' (Boys), Km 19.5 Carretera a
Oruro cruce San Jorge, Calle Boliviar s/n,
Comunidad de San Jorge, Vinto, Casilla 542;
tel: 591 (4) 435 6264 (acc 48)
La Paz: 'María Remedios Asín' (Boys),
Murillo 434, Barrio Central Viacha,
Casilla 15084; tel: 591 (2) 280 0404 (acc 50)
Potosi: Hogar de Ninos (AS) Wasinchej
'Cerca del Cielo' Zona Villa Canteria,
Calle Final Canada Strongest
tel: 591 (7)063 3659 (acc 48)
Chile
Llo Lleo: 'El Redil' (Boys), Arzobispo
Valdivieso 410, Casilla 61, Llo Lleo;
tel: 56 (35) 282 054 (acc 52)

Eventide Home
Chile
'Otoño Dorado', Av La Florida 9995, La Florida,
Casilla 3225, Santiago; tel: 56 (2) 287 5280;
tel/fax: 56 (2) 287 1869 (acc 48)

Day Care Centres for the Aged
Chile
'Los Lagos', Berlín 818, Población Los Lagos,
Angol; tel: 56 (45) 712 583 (acc 20)
Ecuador
Cayambe, Calle Montalvo 220, Las Orquideas,
Cayambe; tel: 593 (2) 236 1273 (acc 60)

Day Nurseries
Bolivia
Cochabamba:
'Catalina Booth', Lanza S-0555, Zona Central,
Casilla 542; tel: 591 (4) 422 7123 (acc 150)
La Chimba, Av Cañada Cochabamba 2572,
Zona La Chimba, Casilla 542;
tel: 591 (4) 428 3079 (acc 75)
'Mi Casita' – El Temporal, Calle J. Mostajo s/n,
Zona El Temporal,Casilla 542;
tel: 591 (4) 445 0809 (acc 70)
'Wawasninchej' – Huayra K'assa,
Av Suecia 1083, Zona Huayra K'assa,
Casilla 542; tel: 591 (4) 422 4808 (acc 50)
La Paz: 'Refugio de Amor', Villa 8 de Diciembre,
Calle Rosendo Gutiérrez 120, Barrio Alto
Sopocachi, Casilla 926; tel 591 (2) 241 0470
Santa Cruz:
'Gotitas de Amor', Calle Corumba 2360
(esq Calle Cañada Larga), Barrio Lazareto,
Casilla 2576; tel: 591 (3) 346 3531 (acc 40)
'La Roca', Calicanto, Comunidad La Serena
Calicanto, Kilómetro 8, Carretera antigua a
Santa Cruz, Casilla 542; tel: 591 (4) 433 8338
(acc 35)
Chile
Antofagasta: Lautarito, Castro 5193, Población
Lautaro, Casilla 581; tel: 56 (55) 380 719
(acc 70)
Concepción: Catalina Booth, Hipólito Salas 760;
tel: 56 (41) 223 0447 (acc 24)
Copiapó: Gotitas, Av Carlos Condell 1535,
Los Salares, Casilla 436; tel: 56 (52) 216 099
(acc 32)
Iquique: Las Estrellitas, Esmeralda 862,
Casilla 134; tel: 56 (57) 421 325 (acc 38)
Rancagua: Hijitos de Dios, Iquique 24
(esquina Bolivia), Población San Francisco;
tel: 56 (72) 239 028 (acc 20)
Santiago:
Arca de Noé, El Fundador 13678, Población

Santiago de la Nueva Extremadura,
La Pintana, Casilla 3225; tel: 56 (2) 542 4523
(acc 58)
La Estrellita, Maipú 284, Maipú, Casilla 3225;
tel: 56 (2) 531 2638 (acc 40)
Las Acacias, Las Vizcachas 858, Población
Las Acacias, El Bosque, Casilla 3225;
tel: 56 (2) 529 4242 (acc 52)
Marta Brunet, Montaña Adentro 01650,
Puente Alto, Casilla 3225,
tel: 56 (2) 572 9340 (acc 50)
Neptuno, Los Aromos 833, Lo Prado,
Casilla 3225; tel: 56 (2) 773 5154 (acc 40)
Puente Alto, Soldaditos de Jesús, Santo
Domingo 90, Puente Alto, Casilla 3225;
tel: 56 (2) 419 0110/850 3331 (acc 86)
Rayitos de Sol, Av Brasil 73, Casilla 3225;
tel: 56 (2) 699 3595; (acc 90)
Temuco: Padre Las Casas, Los Misioneros 1354,
Comuna de Padre Las Casas, (acc 20)
Valdivia: Rayito de Luz, Picarte 1894;
tel: 56 (63) 214 404 (acc 120)
Valparaíso: Faro de Ángeles, Calle Santa
Martha 443, Cerro Playa Ancha, Casilla 1887;
tel: 56 (32) 228 1160 (acc 76)
Ecuador
Guayaquil: Nueva Esperanza, Av Martha de
Roldós km 5½, Vía Daule, Casilla
09.01.10478; tel: 593 (4) 383 0351 (acc 60)
Manta: Arca de Noé, Av 201, entre calles
116 y 117, Barrio La Paz, Casilla 13-05-149;
tel: 593 (5) 292 0147 (acc 30)
Quito: El Ranchito Manzana 44, Lote 801-802,
Rancho Alto, Casilla 7110.7179;
tel 593 (2) 338 2408/9 (acc 50)
Gotitas de Miel: Montalvo 220, Cayambe,
Casilla 17.10.7179; tel: 593 (2) 236 1273
(acc 100)
La Colmena:Calle Pomasqui 955 y Pedro Andrade,
La Colmena, Casilla17.01.1120;
tel: 593 (2) 258 1081/228 4776 (acc 60)
Mi Casita: Apuela S 25-182 y Malimpia,
Santa Rita, Casilla 17.107179;
tel: 593 (2) 284 5529 (acc 40)
Mi Hermoso Redil: Urbanización Sierra
Hermosa, Calle 5, lotes 237-239, Parroquia de
Carapungo; tel: 593 (2) 282 6835 (acc 100)

Food Aid Programmes
Chile
Calle Ejército casa 721, Pobl Oscar Bonilla 2,
Ancud; tel: 56 (65) 622 045 (acc 80)
Avanzada Bonilla, Río Lauca 1162, Pobl Bonilla,
Antofagasta; tel: 56 (55) 761 312
Peru
Chiclayo: PP.JJ. Sto Toribibio de Mogrovejo

MZ A Lote 17, Chiclayo;
tel: 51 (74) 208 216 (neighbour) (acc 100)
El Porvenir: Calle Synneva Vestheim 583,
Cacerío El Porvenir, Provincia Rioja,
Dpto San Martín (acc 50)

Development Integral Centres and Nutritional Centres
Bolivia
Achachicala, La Paz (acc 150)
Corqueamaya, La Paz (acc 70)
El Tejar, La Paz (acc 245)
Lacaya, La Paz (acc 75)
Nueva Vida, Santa Cruz (acc 250)
Potosí (acc 30)
Tiahuanacu, La Paz (acc 200)
Yaurichambi, La Paz (acc 75)
Villa Cantería, Potosí (acc 50)
Villa Cosmos, La Paz (acc 250)
Villa Fátima, La Paz (acc 50)
Villa 8 de Diciembre, La Paz (acc 90)
Viacha, La Paz (acc 250)
Zona Este de Oruro, Oruro (acc 150)
Ecuador
Bastión Popular, Guayaquil (acc 100)
El Rancho, Quito (acc 100)
Mi Casita, Quito Sur (acc 120)
Nido Alegre, La Colmena, Quito (acc 150)
Nueva Esperanza, Guayaquil (acc 160)
Pedacito de Cielo, Esmeraldas (acc 200)
William Booth, Cayambe (acc 150)
Peru
Moquegua (acc 60)

Day Care Centre (without corps/outposts)
Chile
Nido Alegre, Santiago (acc 40)

Community Day Centres/School-age Day Care Centres (attached to corps/outposts)
Bolivia
Batallón Colorados, Sucre (acc 60)
El Temporal, Cochabamba (acc 75)
'El Vergel', Chapare (acc 60)
Fortín del Niño, Uspha Ushpha, Santa Cruz
(acc 100)
Huayra K'assa, Cochabamba (acc 50)
La Chimba, Cochabamba (acc 80)
La Roca, Calicanto, Santa Cruz (acc 25)
Pacata, Cochabamba (acc 200)
Parotani, Cochabamba (acc 60)
Pockonas, Sucre (acc 50)
Primero de Mayo, Santa Cruz (acc 300)
Tarija (acc 50)

Peru
Buenos Aires, Trujillo (acc 50)
La Esperanza, Trujillo (acc 40)
San Martín de Porras, Lima (acc 40)
Tacna (acc 60)
Vitarte, Lima (acc 80)

Enterprise Development
Warehouse: Coronel Souper 4564,
   Estación Central, Casilla 3225, Santiago,
   Chile; tel: 56 (2) 764 1917

SOUTH AMERICA WEST: The General presents an Others Award to the Santiago Rotary Club

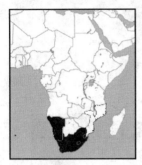

SOUTHERN AFRICA TERRITORY

Territorial leaders:
Commissioners William and Thalitha Langa

Territorial Commander:
Commissioner William Langa (1 May 2012)

Chief Secretary:
Lieut-Colonel Keith Conrad (1 Nov 2013)

Territorial Headquarters: 119-121 Rissik Street, Braamfontein, Johannesburg 2001

Postal address: PO Box 1018, Johannesburg 2000, South Africa

Tel: [27] (011) 718 6700

email: CS_SouthernAfrica@SAF.salvationarmy.org; website: www.salvationarmy.co.za

On 4 March 1883 Major and Mrs Francis Simmonds with Lieutenant Alice Teager 'opened fire' in Cape Town. Other officers were sent to the island of St Helena in 1886 to consolidate work commenced (in 1884) by Salvationist 'Bluejackets'. Social services began in 1886. The Salvation Army's first organised ministry among the African people was established in 1888 in Natal and, in 1891, in Zululand. Work in Swaziland was commenced in 1960. Having previously been in Namibia from 1932 to 1939, the Army re-established a presence in the country in January 2008 and was given official recognition on 11 March 2008.

Zone: Africa

Countries included in the territory: Lesotho, Namibia, Island of St Helena, South Africa, Swaziland

'The Salvation Army' in Afrikaans: Die Heilsleër; in IsiXhosa: Umkhosi wo Sindiso; in IsiZulu: Impi yo Sindiso; in SeSotho: Mokhosi oa Poloko; in SiPedi: Mogosi wa Pholoso; in Tshivenda: Mbi ya u Tshidza; in Tsonga: Nyi Moi Yoponisa

Languages in which the gospel is preached: Afrikaans, English, IsiXhosa, IsiZulu, SeSotho, Shangaan, SiPedi, Tshivenda, Tsonga, Tswana

Periodicals: *Home League Resource Manual*, *The Reporter*, *The War Cry*

THE TERRITORY continued to experience momentum as the Territorial Strategic Plan entered its fourth year, giving impetus to youth and children, leadership development, Salvation Army community life, community engagement and business practice.

Through regular monitoring, evaluation and review, the overarching vision of 'The Salvation Army is a vibrant movement with people of integrity, coming alongside communities, enabling growth and transformation of the whole person through the gospel of

Jesus Christ', will continue to be achieved.

With the implemetation of the Territorial Strategic Plan focusing on children and youth ministries, new crèches that were in poor and remote areas were upgraded through overseas funding. This has resulted in an increase in children attending.

A tri-territorial music school, sponsored by the Swiss Capacity Building Project, was held in Zimbabwe, comprising of participants from the Southern Africa, Zimbabwe and Zambia Territories. A territorial social conference, funded by the Sweden and Latvia Territory, our Partners in Mission, saw 40 officers from around the territory receive training.

Anti-human trafficking work continued to expand throughout the territory with more divisions becoming involved and creating awareness about the issue. In September 2013, the Public Relations Department was present at Sexpo South Africa. As people became aware of the motive behind the Army's presence – creating awareness of the dangers of sex trafficking – people had the highest praise and appreciation for the Army and its mission. It was said: 'It was refreshing to see The Salvation Army doing what they were birthed to do!'

STATISTICS

Officers 251 (active 160 retired 91) **Auxiliary-Captains** 9 **Cadets** 5 **Employees** 630
Corps 88 **Societies and Outposts** 128 **Hospitals** 2 **Institutions** 15 **Day Care Centres** 17
Senior Soldiers 18,176 **Adherent Members** 1,914 **Junior Soldiers** 3,962

STAFF

Women's Ministries: Comr Thalitha Langa (TPWM) Lt-Col Yvonne Conrad (TSWM)
Business Administration: Capt Garth Niemand
  Chief Financial Officer: Mr Leon Viljoen
  Financial Consultant: Mr John Pugsley
  Information Technology: Capt Brendan Browski
  Property and Projects: Mr Handre du Toit
  Public Relations: Maj Carin Holmes
  Trade: Mr Gavin Blackwood
Personnel: Lt-Col Jabulani Khoza
  Asst Personnel Sec: Maj Rasoa Khayumbi
  Human Resources: Mr Leon Schmahl
  Retired Officers: Comr William Mabena
Programme: Maj Luka Khayumbi
  Anti-Human Trafficking: Maj Lenah Jwili
  Child Sponsorship: Capt Magdeline Phore
  Editorial and Literary: Maj Lenah Jwili
  Family Tracing: Maj Margaret Strydom
  Statistician: Maj Naomi Malinga
  Candidates: Capt Darren Huke
  Youth: Capt Ananias Nhandara
  Social Programme: Capt Patti Niemand
  Community Care Ministries: Lt-Col Fikile Khoza
  Medical Ministries: Capt (Dr) Felicia Christians
Training Principal: Maj Kervin Harry
Extension Training Officer: Capt Colleen Huke

DIVISIONS

Central: PO Box 756, Rosettenville, Johannesburg 2130; tel: (011) 408-6400; Majs Shadrack and Rosannah Ntshangase
Eastern Cape: PO Box 12514, Centralhill, Port Elizabeth 6006; tel: (041) 585-5363; Capts Themba and Nokuthula Mahlobo
Eastern Kwa Zulu/Natal: PO Box 1267, Eshowe 3815; tel: (035) 474-1132; Majs Albert and Peggy Shekwa
Limpopo: PO Box 3549, Makhado 0920; tel/fax: (015) 516-6658; Majs Thomas and Doris Dlamini
Mid Kwa Zulu/Natal: PO Box 100061, Scottsville, Pietermaritzburg 3209; tel: (033) 386-3881; Majs Solomon and Mercy Mahlangu
Mpumalanga/Swaziland: PO Box 1571, Nelspruit 1200; tel: (013) 741-2869; Majs Herbert and Elizabeth Ngcobo
Northern Kwa Zulu/Natal: PO Box 923, Vryheid 3100; tel: (034) 982-3113; Capts Thataetsile and Noluntu Semeno
Western Cape: PO Box 18179, Wynberg,

Cape Town 7824; tel: (021) 761-8530/6;
Majs Stephen and Theresa Malins

St Helena: The Salvation Army, Jamestown,
Island of St Helena, South Atlantic Ocean;
tel: 09 (290) 2703;
email: salvationarmy@cwimail.sh;
Envoy Coral Yon

THQ OUTREACH – NAMIBIA
The Salvation Army, PO Box 26820,
Windhoek, Namibia; tel: [00] (264) 61223881;
mobile: 264 813087518;
email: salvationarmy@iway.na;
Capts Robert and Felicia Hendricks

COLLEGE FOR OFFICER TRAINING
PO Box 32902, Braamfontein 2017,
Johannesburg; tel: (011) 718 6762

CHILD AND YOUTH DAY CARE CENTRES
Central: Benoni, Bridgman Jabavu Crèche, Carl
Sithole Crèche, Galashewe, Katlehong,
Lethlabile, Mangaung
Eastern Kwa Zulu Natal: Inkonisa
Limpopo: Thohoyandou
Mpumalanga/Swaziland: Barberton, Pienaar
Mid Kwa Zulu/Natal: Hammarsdale, Kwa Mashu,
Umlazi
Northern Kwa Zulu/Natal: Gwegwede,
Nongoma, Ulundi
Western Cape: Bonteheuwel, Mitchells Plein,
Manenburg

DAY CARE CENTRE FOR SENIOR CITIZENS
Central: Benoni

GOODWILL CENTRES
Benoni: PO Box 17299, Benoni West 1503
Family Mission Centre: PO Box 351,
Krugersdorp 1740

HEALTH SERVICES
Booth Hospital: 32 Prince St, Oranjezicht, Cape
Town 8001; tel: (021) 465-4896/46 (acc 84)
Mountain View Hospital: PO Box 1827
Vryheid, KZN; tel: (034) 982-6014
(acc 88) (with Mountain View Mobile Clinic)
Msunduza Community and Primary Health Care
Centre and Mbuluzi Clinic: Box 2543, Mbabane,
Swaziland; tel: (268) 404-5243/404 7365

RETIRED OFFICERS RESIDENCES
Citadel Court: Vrede St Gardens, Cape Town 8001
Emmarentia Flats: PO Box 85214, Emmarentia
2029, Johannesburg; tel: (011) 646-2126
Ephraim Zulu Flats: PO Box 49, Orlando 1804,
Soweto; tel: (011) 982-1084

SOCIAL SERVICES
Crèches
Central: Benoni Day Care, 77 Mowbray Ave,
PO Box 17299, Benoni West, 1503;
tel: (011) 422 4417
Bridgman Jabavu Crèche, 883b White City,
PO Box 62, Kwaxuma, 1867;
tel: (011) 982 5574
Carl Sithole Crèche, PO Box 180, Orlando,
Soweto 1804; tel: (011) 527 1109
Galashewe, 1526 Kekane St. PO Box 8025,
Galeshewe, 8330; tel: (053) 871 1119
Katlehong, PO Box 12002, Katlehong, 1432;
tel: (011) 909 8423
Lethlabile, 22-25 Plot A, Letlhabile, 0264,
PO Box 40, Brits 0250;
tel: 079 028 8468
Limpopo: Thohoyandou, PO Box 2015,
Thohoyandou, 0950
Mangaung, PO Box 4432, Bloemfontein 9300;
tel: (051) 432 0064Mpumalanga/Swaziland:
Barberton, PO Box 202, Barberton, 1300;
tel (079) 193 1741
Pienaar, PO Box 232, Kanyamazane, 1214;
tel: (013) 794 7304
Mid Kwa Zulu/Natal: Hammarsdale,
PO Box 327, Hammarsdale, 3700;
tel: (031) 771 1194
Kwa Mashu, PO Box 2019, Durban, 4000;
tel: (031) 503 5150
Umlazi, PO Box 54780, Umlazi, 4031;
tel: (031) 907 1944
Northern Kwa Zulu/Natal: Gwegwede,
PO Box 2295, Nongoma, 3950;
tel: (083) 230 2957
Nongoma, PO Box 2295, Nongoma, 3950;
tel: (035) 831 0292
Ulundi, PO Box 613, Ulundi, 3838;
tel: (035) 877 1723
Western Cape: Bonteheuwel, PO Box 208,
Eppindut, Cape Town, 7475;
tel: (021) 694 7250
Mitchells Plein, PO Box 19625, Lantegeur, 7786;
tel: (021) 374 2782
Manenburg, PO Box 537, Gatesville, 7766;
tel: (021) 691 0405

Child and Youth Care Centres

Bethany: Carl Sithole Centre, Klipspruit,
PO Box 180, Orlando 1804;
tel: (011) 572 1109 (acc 85 children 6-18 yrs)

Bethesda: Zodwa's House, Carl Sithole Centre,
PO Box 180, Orlando 1804, Soweto (acc 32
children 2-6 yrs)

Ethembeni (Place of Hope): 84 Davies St,
Doornfontein, Johannesburg 2094;
tel: (011) 402-8101/401 4011
(acc 60 children 0-3 yrs)

Firlands: Fourth Ave & 11th St, PO Box 44291,
Linden 2195; tel: (011) 782-5556/7
(011) 888 9188 (acc 60 children 3-18 yrs)

Joseph Baynes House: 89 Trelawney Rd,
Pentrich, PO Box 212275, Oribi 3205, Natal;
tel: (033) 386-2266 (acc 82 children 0-18 yrs)

Strathyre: Eleventh Ave, Dewetshof,
PO Box 28501, Kensington 2101,
Johannesburg; tel: (011) 615-7327/7344
(acc 60 children 3-18 yrs)

Community Programme

Msunduza: Orphans/Vulnerable Children and
Home-based Community Care Programme,
Swaziland

Eventide Home (men)

Beth Rogelim: 22 Alfred St, Roggebbai,
Cape Town 8005, 22 Alfred St;
tel: (021) 425-2138 (acc 88)

Eventide Homes (men and women)

Emmarentia: Johannesburg, PO Box 85214,
Emmarentia 2029, 113 Komatie Rd;
tel: (011) 646-2126 (acc 40)

Ephraim Zulu Senior Citizen Centre: PO Box 49,
Orlando 1804; tel: (011) 982-1084 (acc 100)

Thembela: 68 Montpelier Place, Durban 4001;
PO Box 47117, Greyville, 4023;
tel: (031) 321-6360 (acc 50)

Homes for Abused Women

Beth Shan, Pretoria (acc 15)

Care Haven: Cape Town;
email: careaid@iafrica.co.za
(acc 28 women, 45 children)

Men's Hostel

Beth Rogelim: 22 Alfred St, Cape Town 8005;
tel: (021) 425-2138 (acc 100)

Rehabilitation Centre

Hesketh King Treatment Centre: PO Box 5,
Elsenburg 7607, Cape; tel: (021) 884-4600
(acc 60)

Residential Psychiatric Care

Mountain Lodge: PO Box 168, Magaliesburg
2805; tel: (+27) 82 855 0382 (acc 60)

SOUTHERN AFRICA: A young Salvationist sharing during a
teaching class in Namibia.

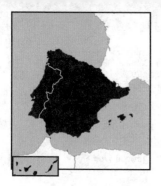

SPAIN AND PORTUGAL COMMAND

Command leaders:
Lieut-Colonels Gordon and Susan Daly

Officer Commanding:
Lieut-Colonel Gordon Daly
(1 Feb 2013)

Command Headquarters:
Ejército de Salvación, Vereda del Alquitón 9. 28500 Arganda del Rey, Madrid, Spain

Tel: [34] 91 871 9099; email: Spain_Command@SAP.salvationarmy.org;

websites: www.ejercitodesalvacion.es www.exercitodesalvacao.pt

The Salvation Army in Spain commenced in May 1971 when Captain and Mrs Enrique Rey were appointed to La Coruña. By December 1971 The Salvation Army had been granted the status of a Legal Person and permitted to carry on its work without let or hindrance.

In July 1971 work in Portugal commenced in Porto. On 28 January 1972, Major and Mrs Carl S. Eliasen arrived in Lisbon and on 4 July 1974 The Salvation Army was recognised by the Ministry of Justice as a religious and philanthropic organisation. All social activities were incorporated in Centro Social do Exército de Salvação in March 1981. On 10 September 2009 The Salvation Army became an Established Collective Religious Person (church) by decree from the Minister of Justice.

Salvation Army work in Spain and Portugal became a united command on 1 February 2013.

Zone: Europe
Countries and autonomous communities included in the command: Balearic Islands, Canary Islands, Portugal, Spain
'The Salvation Army' in Portuguese: Exército de Salvação; in Spanish: Ejército de Salvación
Languages in which the gospel is preached: English, Filipino, Portuguese, Spanish
Periodicals: *O Salvacionista, Ideias & Recursos* (for Women's Ministries) [both Portuguese]

THE WORK of The Salvation Army in the newly-united Spain and Portugal Command has continued to bear fruit for the Kingdom of God. Corps and social services in both countries have faced increasing demands for assistance but also added opportunities to reach out to people with the gospel.

In September 2013, Lausanne Band (Switzerland, Austria and Hungary Territory) visited Madrid Central Corps and in February 2014 Yorkshire Divisional Youth Band from the United Kingdom Territory visited Denia Corps.

The command has been blessed to receive two recently-commissioned and ordained Spanish officers who were trained in the USA Eastern Territory, and an officer who has recently been reinstated. One candidate is preparing for distance training in Spain and another, from Portugal is preparing to enter training in Brazil.

A very helpful and well-attended local officers' seminar was held in

March 2014, and a sports ministry seminar for Salvationists from Spain and Portugal was held in April.

Summer camps in both Spain and Portugal gave many opportunities for ministry to women, children and young people. For the first time in some years a men's retreat was held in Spain and this proved to be a time of spiritual refreshment and growth. The annual music school in Portugal was again a highlight of the year for young people. Officers' retreats held in Spain in September 2013 and in Portugal in January 2014 included a focus on The Salvation Army's response to human trafficking in Europe.

STATISTICS
Officers 40 (active 38 retired 2) **Employees** 113
Corps 16 **Outposts** 2 **Thrift Shops** 13 **Institutions** 6
Senior Soldiers 418 **Adherent Members** 90
Junior Soldiers 106
Personnel serving outside command Officers 6

STAFF - SPAIN
Women's Ministries: Lt-Col Susan Daly (CPWM)
Finance: tba
Programme/Evangelism: Maj Miguel Aguilera
Training: Maj Angélica Aguilera
Youth: Capt Jenniffer Beltrán

STAFF - PORTUGAL
Finance: Rui Kunzika
Social Services Director: Sandra Martins Lopes

SOCIAL SERVICES - SPAIN
Food and/or Clothing Distribution Centres
Alicante; Barcelona; Carrer General Riera 77; Denia;La Coruña; Las Palmas; Lateral del Norte;Madrid (2 locations); Mallorca (4 locations);Palomeras,Tenerife; Valdemoro-Madrid

Emergency Feeding Kitchens
Barcelona 08024: c/ del Rubí 18
La Coruña 15010: c/ Francisco Añón 9

Homeless Day Care Centres
La Coruña 15010: 'Sen Teito' (acc 25)
Madrid 28028: c/ Hermosilla, 126, Local 4

Social Emergency Apartments
La Coruña 15010: c/ Francisco Añón 9

CONFERENCE, RETREAT AND HOLIDAY CENTRE
Camp Sarón, Partida Torre Carrals 64, 03700 Denia, Alicante; tel: 96 578 2152; website: www.campsaron.com (acc 60)

PORTUGAL
Portugal office:
Rua Capitao Roby 19, 1900-111 Lisboa
tel: 217 802 930

SOCIAL SERVICES
Children's Home
Centro de Acolhimento Novo Mundo, tel: 219 244 239; (acc 14)

Clothing and Food Distribution Centre
Rua Escola do Exército, 11-B, 1150-143 Lisboa; tel: 213 528 137

Day Centres for the Elderly and Home Help Services
Colares: Av dos Bombeiros Voluntários, Várzea de Colares, 2705-180 Colares; tel: 219 288 450
Porto: Av Vasco da Gama, 645, Lojas 1 e 2, Ramalde, 4100-491 Porto; tel: 226 172 769

Employment Skills Centre
Rua Capitâo Roby 17, 1900-111 Lisboa

Eventide Homes
Nosso Lar: Av dos Bombeiros Voluntários, Várzea de Colares, 2705-180 Colares; tel: 219 288 450; (acc 30)
Lar Marinel: Rua das Marinhas, 13, Tomadia, Praia das Maçãs, 2705-313 Colares; tel: 219 288 480; (acc 50)

Night Shelter for the Homeless
Rua da Manutenção, 7 (Xabregas) – 1900-318 Lisboa; tel: 218 680 908; (acc 75)

Thrift Shops
Chelas: Rua Rui de Sousa, Lote 65-A Loja C, 1900-802 Lisboa
Porto: Rua D Jerónimo de Azevedo, 640-Loja, 4550-241 Porto

HOLIDAY AND CONFERENCE CENTRES
Casa Marinel, Colares
Vivenda Boa Nova, Colares; tel: 214 095 738 (Information and holiday bookings: Portugal office)

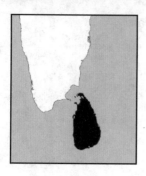

SRI LANKA TERRITORY

Territorial leaders:
Commissioners Malcolm and Irene Induruwage

Territorial Commander:
Commissioner Malcolm Induruwage
(1 April 2011)

Chief Secretary:
Lieut-Colonel Nihal Hettiarachchi
(1 Nov 2013)

Territorial Headquarters: 53 Sir James Peiris Mawatha, Colombo 2

Postal address: PO Box 193, Colombo, Sri Lanka

Tel: [94] (11) 232 4660/232 2159; website: www.sri.salvationarmy.org

Salvation Army work began in Ceylon (now Sri Lanka) on 26 January 1883 under the leadership of Captain William Gladwin. 'The General of The Salvation Army' is a corporation Sole by Ordinance No 11 of 1924.

Zone: South Asia
Country included in the territory: Sri Lanka
'The Salvation Army' in Sinhala: Gelaveeme Hamudaava; in Tamil: Ratchaniya Senai
Languages in which the gospel is preached: English, Sinhala, Tamil
Periodical: *Mulaadeniya (The Officer) Yudha Handa (The War Cry)*

THE SALVATION Army Sri Lanka Territory moves forward with the intention of seeing more lives transformed through its varied ministries. Ten cadets from the Heralds of Grace Session who commenced training in April 2013 add to the team of officers currently ministering throughout the island of Sri Lanka.

In August, 188 children attended a Christian education camp with the theme 'One Army – Come join our Army' and 197 young people attended two youth camps under the theme 'One Mission and One Message'.

The territory was delighted to welcome Lieut-Colonels Nihal and Rohini Hettiarachchi, who have taken up the positions of CS and TSWM respectively.

The territorial leaders conducted successful pastoral interviews with all officers at divisions, districts and sections.

In January 2014 the Women's Ministries Department conducted a two-day training seminar and the Sri Lanka Territory proudly hosted the 2014 South Asia College for Officers. Forty teachers participated in the

Sunday school teachers' empowerment training workshop, conducted in collaboration with the Ceylon Bible Society, and in September 42 officers participated in the second evangelism seminar conducted by the Campus Crusade for Christ. Officers and social institution employees have also taken part in a Social Care Diploma Course conducted by the National Institute of Social Training and Development of Sri Lanka.

Service within the community continues. The Salvation Army commenced a Safe Water and Livelihood Project and a mobile medical clinic in Polonnaruwa. The project, fully supported by the government of Sri Lanka, and staffed by qualified personnel, commenced because of the increasing number of kidney patients in the area.

A foster child care programme continues to provide financial assistance to 100 children affected by the tsunami and war, and more than 200 people, including children, receive dry rations and cooked food through the Newman Feeding Programme.

For 131 years the territory has been serving the needy. We are grateful for the prayers and support given over these years which are a result of God's grace.

STATISTICS

Officers 144 (active 95 retired 49) **Cadets** 10 **Employees** 90
Corps 45 **Corps Plants** 13 **Social Homes and Hostels** 13 **Community Centres** 2 **Day Care Centres** 2 **Corps-based Child Care Centres** 4 **Health Centre** 1 **Camp Centres** 2
Senior Soldiers 4,295 **Adherent Members** 913 **Junior Soldiers** 688

STAFF

Women's Ministries: Comr Irene Induruwage (TPWM) Lt-Col Rohini Hettiarachchi (TSWM)
Business Administration: Lt-Col Alister Philip
Candidates: Maj Ranjith Senaratne
Editorial: Maj Chandra Jayaratnasingham
Finance: Capt Felix Kumaravel
Information Technology: Mr T.Gajaruban
Personnel: Maj Packianathan Jayaratnasingham
Programme: tba
Projects: Mrs Pamela Hunter
Property: Mr Stuart Hunter
Training: Lt-Col Nilanthi Philip
Youth and Chidren: Maj Ranjith Senaratne

DIVISIONS

Rambukkana: Mawanella Rd, Rambukkana; tel: (35) 226 5179; Majs Vitharamalage and Nalani Gunadasa
Western: 11 Sir James Peiris Mawatha, Colombo 2; tel: (11) 232 4660 ext 214; Majs Newton and Ajantha Fernando

DISTRICTS

Kandy: 26 Srimath Bennet Soysa Veediya, Kandy; tel: (81) 223 4804; Maj Newton Jacob
Northern: 55, Bankshall Street, Jaffna; tel: (21) 321 7450; tba

SECTIONS

Eastern: 135 Trincomalee St, Batticaloa; tel: (65) 222 4558; tba
Southern: Weerasooriya Watte, Patuwatha-Dodanduwa; tel: (91) 227 7146; Capt Solomon John Christopher

TRAINING COLLEGE

77 Ananda Rajakaruna Mawatha, Colombo 10; tel: (11) 268 6116; email: sritraining.college@sri.salvationarmy.org

SOCIAL SERVICES
The Salvation Army Child Development Centres / Remand Homes

Batticoloa: 135 Trincomalee St, Batticaloa; tel: (65) 222 4558 (acc 16)
Dehiwela: 12 School Ave, Dehiwela; tel: (11) 271 7049 (acc 50)
Rajagiriya: Obeysekera Rd, Rajagiriya; tel: (11) 286 2301 (acc 30)
Shalom: Kandy Rd, Kaithady, Jaffna; tel: (21) 3 210779 (acc boys 6, girls 12, remandees 17)

Sunshine Home: 127 E. W. Perera Mawatha,
Colombo 10 (acc remandees 50)
SwedLanka: South Pallansena Jaya Mawatha,
Kochchikade; tel: (31) 227 7964 (acc 22)
The Haven: 127, E. W. Perera Mawatha,
Colombo 10; tel: (11) 269 5275
(acc babies 13, children 10)

Hostels

Dehiwela Eventide Home for Women: 8 School
Ave, Dehiwela; tel: (11) 272 8542 (acc 34)
Home for Employed Disabled Men:
Obeysekera Rd, Rajagiriya;
tel: (11) 286 2301 (acc 5)
Ladies' Hostel (1): 18 Sri Saugathodaya
Mawatha, Colombo 2; tel: (11) 311 7783
(acc 84)
Ladies' Hostel (2): 30 Union Pl, Colombo 2;
tel: (11) 311 7735 (acc 84)
Rajagiriya Elders' Home and Iris Perera Home:
1700 Cotta Rd, Rajagiriya; tel: (11) 288 5947
(acc men 20, women 24)
Rajagiriya Young Men's Hostel: Obeysekera Rd,
Rajagiriya; tel: (11) 286 2301 (acc 10)
Rawathawatte Hostel for Women: 14 Charles Pl,
Rawathawatte, Moratuwa; tel: (11) 264 7209
(acc working girls 24)
The Haven: 127 E. W. Perera Mawatha,
Colombo 10; tel: (11) 269 5275
(acc unwed mothers 13, elderly women 10,
rehabilitation 8)

Community Centres

Hope House: 11 Sir James Peiris Mawatha,
Colombo 2; tel: (11) 232 4660 ext 200

Rambukkana: Mawanella Rd, Rambukkana;
tel: (35) 226 5179

Child Day Care Centres

Kudagama: Kudagama, Dombemada;
tel: (35) 3950 261
Hewadiwela: Halwatte, Hewadiwela;
tel: (35) 226 6785
Talampitiya: Talampitiya, Mahagama,
Kohilagedera; tel: (37) 223 8278
Wattegama: 34 Nuwaratenne Rd, Wattegama; tel:
(81) 380 3319

Guest Accommodation

Hope House: The Salvation Army,
53 Sir James Peiris Mawatha, Colombo 2,
Sri Lanka tel: (11) 232 4660 Ext 138 or 275
Hikkaduwa: The Salvation Army, Weerasooriya
Watte, Patuwatha-Dodanduwa;
tel: (91) 227 7146

HEALTH SERVICES

Physiotherapy Unit: Colombo; tel [11] 232 4660
ext 204

CAMP CENTRES

Rambukkana: Mawanella Rd, Rambukkana;
tel: (35) 2265179
Kalutara: The Salvation Army, Mudagamuwa,
Galapatha, Kalutara; tel: (78) 6883475

KALUTARA RUBBER ESTATE:

The Salvation Army, Mudagamuwa, Galapatha,
Kalutara; tel: (34) 3944041

SWEDEN AND LATVIA TERRITORY

Territorial Commander:
Commissioner Marie Willermark
(1 Feb 2011)

Chief Secretary:
Lieut-Colonel João Paulo Ramos
(1 Feb 2013)

Territorial Headquarters: Nybrogatan 79B, 114 41, Stockholm, Sweden

Postal address: Box 5090, SE 102 42 Stockholm, Sweden

Tel: [46] (08) 562 282 00; email: fralsningsarmen@fralsningsarmen.se;

website: www.fralsningsarmen.se

Commissioner Hanna Ouchterlony, inspired by the first Army meeting held on Swedish soil in Värnamo in 1878 led by the young Chief of the Staff, Bramwell Booth, began Salvation Army work in a Stockholm theatre on 28 December 1882. The first women's home and a men's shelter were opened in 1890. Work among deaf and blind people was inaugurated in 1895. The Salvation Army was re-established in Latvia on 18 November 1990 and two months later, on 23 January 1991, The Salvation Army in Latvia became a juridical person. On 15 November 1994 the Sweden Territory was renamed the Sweden and Latvia Territory.

Zone: Europe
Countries included in the territory: Latvia, Sweden
'The Salvation Army' in Swedish: Frälsningsarmén; in Latvian: Pestīšanas Armija; in Russian:
  Armiya Spaseniya Армии Спасения
Languages in which the gospel is preached: English, Latvian, Russian, Swedish
Periodical: *Stridsropet, Tidningen*

VISION 2020 'Jesus to everyone' was launched with territorial cabinet members introducing the vision to corps throughout the territory. The theme focused on our identity and mission for the next seven years.

Through dedicated local officers, a number of corps that were struggling to continue have been renewed through service to their local community and the enrolment of new soldiers and recognition of adherent members.

A prayer network called 'The Flame'

was developed during a conference in August 2013 with many young people attending. The need for more national prayer became clear and the idea of 'The Flame – Youth edition' was born.

In mid-October five youngsters travelled to Zimbabwe as part of the 'Check-In' course organised by Ågesta People's High School. The goal of the course was to see how involvement through The Salvation Army con-tributes to social justice.

In November a day centre for

homeless European migrants opened in Gothenburg, the special target group being the Romani people who are increasing in number in our cities. The day centre is part of a larger project in cooperation with Gothenburg City Mission and local authorities.

Norrbotten county in the far north of Sweden has been one focus area. The Norrbotten project consists of four parts. In cooperation with corps the project leader has done research and mapping of spiritual, historical, demographic and social areas. This has united corps as well as contributed to local ecumenical cooperation.

In Latvia the first soldiers were sworn in at the corps plant in Saldus and work in the community continues to expand. Another corps plant was started in a building formerly used to house a children's home in Riga. This plant is the focus for reaching children, youth and families.

After a year of building a relationship with the fire department, we faced our biggest challenge when tragedy struck with the collapse of a large supermarket in Riga in November. The Army was there throughout, providing refreshments to all the emergency workers on site, as well as a listening ear.

Training for local officership has been a big emphasis and has been greatly aided by the course 'Equipping for Mission' which has had a growing attendance throughout the year. We are praying this will ensure a good future for The Salvation Army in Latvia.

STATISTICS
Officers 321 (active 137 retired 184)
Cadets (1st Yr) 4 (2nd Yr) 8
Employees 1,158 **Envoys/Sergeants** 24
Corps 97 **Outposts** 9 **Community Centres** 32
Senior Soldiers 3,900 **Adherent Members** 864
Junior Soldiers 166
Personnel serving outside territory Officers 12

STAFF
Women's Ministries: Comr Marie Willermark (TPWM) Lt-Col Karin Ramos (TSWM)
Sec for Business Administration: Capt Elisabeth Beckman
Editor-in-Chief: Maj Bert Åberg
Fundraising: Mr Mats Wiberg
Legacies: Maj Margaretha Andersson
Sec for Personnel: Maj Sonja Blomberg
Training College: Maj Mattias Nordenberg
Candidates Sec: Maj Anna-Lena Paulsson
People's High School: Mr Magnus Wetterberg
Sec for Programme: Maj Henrik Bååth
Development Officers: Maj Per-Olof Larsson, Maj Christel Lindgren, Maj Gunilla Olausson, Maj Christian Paulsson, Maj Leif Öberg
Area Support: tba
Corps Development: Maj Marianne Ljungholm
Pioneer work: Maj Kjell Karlsten, Maj Mattias Nordenberg
Home and Family: Maj Lisbeth Månsson
Institutions: Maj Leif Öberg
Social Work: Maj Ywonne Eklund
Social Justice: Ms Madeleine Sundell
Spiritual Life Development: Maj Michael Hjerpe
Youth: Lt Hanna Smedjegård
International Development: Mr Christian Lerne
Child Sponsorship: Mrs Anna-Carin Wiberg Löw
Missing Persons: Mrs Kristine Falk

Training College
Frälsningsarméns Officersskola, Ågestagården, Bonäsvägen, 5, 123 52 Farsta; tel: (08) 562 281 50

People's High Schools
Ågesta Folkhögskola: Bonäsvägen 5, 123 52 Farsta; tel: (08) 562 281 00
Älvsjö Bransch: Älvsjö Gårdsväg 9, 125 30 Älvsjö; tel: (08) 647 52 77

SOCIAL SERVICES
Work Among Alcoholics
Treatment Centre for Substance Abusers
'Kurön', 178 92 Adelsö; tel: (08) 560 518 80; (acc 63)

Sweden and Latvia Territory

Rehabilitation Centres
Göteborg: 'Lilla Bommen' (acc 63)
Göteborg: 'Nylösegården' (acc 21)
Örebro: 'Gnistan' (acc 10)
Stockholm: 'Midsommarkransen' (acc 6)
Stockholm Tyresö: 'Källan' (acc 12)
Stockholm: 'Värtahemmet' (acc 42)
Sundsvall: 'Klippangården' (acc 13)
Uppsala: 'Sagahemmet' (acc 27)

Night Shelters
Örebro: 'Gnistan' (acc 10)
Stockholm: 'Midsommarkransen' (acc 24)
Stockholm: 'Källan' (acc 10)
Sundsvall: 'Klippangården' (acc 6)
Uppsala: 'Sagahemmet' (acc 10)

Drop-in Centres
Stockholm: 'Social Centre'
Göteborg: 'Hisingskåren'

Advisory Services
Stockholm: 'Eken' Counselling Centre,
  Hornsgatan 98, 118 21 Stockholm;
  tel: (08) 55 60 80 76
Uppsala: 'Brobygget', S: t Persgatan 20,
  753 20 Uppsala; tel: (018) 71 05 44

Work Among Children and Families
Pre-Schools
Jönköping: 'Vårsol' (acc 30)
Skövde 'Solstrålen' (acc 20)
Umeå: 'Krubban' (acc 30)
Västra Frölunda: 'Morgonsol' (acc 34)

School and Treatment Centre for Adolescents
Svartsjö: 'Sundsgården' (acc 16)

Treatment Centre for Families
Fristad 'FAM-Huset' (acc 12)

Emergency Diagnostic and Short-term Treatment Centre
Jönköping: 'Vårsol' (acc 6)

Group Home for Adolescents
Stockholm: 'Locus' (acc 10)

Family Centres with Advisory Service
Göteborg: Majorna Family Centre
Jönköping: Vårsols Family Centre
Mölndal: Family Centre
Nässjö: Family Centre
Stockholm: 393: Family Centre

Refugee Aid
Jönköping SARA väster: V:a Storgatan 21;
  tel: (036) 17 32 75 (acc 23)
Jönköping SARA söder: S:t Larsgatan 16;
  tel: (036) 17 32 55 (acc 22)

Vacation Centres for Children
Gävle: 'Rörberg', Hedesundavägen 89,
  818 91 Valbo; tel: (026) 330 19 (acc 15)
Luleå: 'Sunderbyn', Sunderbynvägen 323,
  954 42 Södra Sunderbyn (acc 15)
Malmö: 'Kotten', Klockarevägen 20,
  236 36 Höllviken; tel: (040) 45 05 24 (acc 15)

Centre for Elderly People
'Dalen', Kapellgatan 14, 571 31 Nässjö;
  tel: (0380) 188 11 (acc 20)

Recreation Centre for Elderly People
Stockholm: Elisabetgården, Observatoriegatan 4,
  113 29 Stockholm

Multicultural Ministries
'Akalla', Sibeliusgången 6, 164 73 Kista;
  tel: (08) 750 62 16

Women's Emergency Residence
Stockholm: 'Skogsbo', Box 112,
  132 23 Saltsjö Boo; tel: (08) 21 47 92 (acc 17)

Second-hand Shops
Head office: Partihandlarvägen 47, 120 44 Årsta;
  tel (08) 120 198 81
Shops: Borås, Eskilstuna, Falun, Gävle,
  Göteborg, Halmstad, Jönköping, Karlstad,
  Linköping, Luleå, Malmö (3), Norrköping,
  Örebro, Skellefteå, Skövde, Stockholm (10),
  Sundbyberg, Sundsvall, Trollhättan, Umeå,
  Uppsala (3), Västerås

LATVIA REGION (under THQ)
Regional Headquarters: Bruninieku iela 10A,
LV 1001 Riga; tel: [371] 673 10036;
email: info@pestisanasarmija.lv;
website: www.pestisanasarmija.lv

Regional Leader: Maj Christine Bailey
Asst Regional Leader: Capt Sarah Ilsters

STATISTICS
Officers 21 (active 20 retired 1)
  Envoys 1 **Employees** 55
Corps 9 **Outposts** 4 **Social Institutions** 4
Senior Soldiers 178 **Adherent Members** 216
  Junior Soldiers 35

TRAINING COLLEGE

Virsnieku apmācības skola, Āgenskalna iela 3a,
  Riga, LV-1007
  tel: 676 01700

SOCIAL SERVICES

Riga Social Centre:
  Avotu iela 41, LV-1009; tel 673 11 463

Day Care Centre for Children
'Patverums' Bruninieku iela 10 A, LV 1001
  Riga; tel: [371] 6731 14 63

Work among Children and Families
Salvation Army Music School, Bruņinieku iela
  10a, Riga, LV-1001; tel: [371] 265 43 905

Children Support and Social Care Centre:
  Skangale Manor
'Skangaļi', Liepas pag., Priekuļu novads,
  LV-4128

Crisis Centre for Mothers with Children
'Skangaļi'; tel: 254 26 037

Guest House
'Skangaļi'; tel: 641 72 000

Camp Site
'Ģirti', Bernāti,Nīcas novads, LV-3473

SWEDEN AND LATVIA: Cadets from the Disciples of the Cross Session
enjoying life in the training school

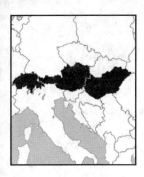

SWITZERLAND, AUSTRIA AND HUNGARY TERRITORY

Territorial leaders:
Commissioners Massimo and Jane Paone

Territorial Commander:
Commissioner Massimo Paone
(1 Sep 2014)

Chief Secretary:
Lieut-Colonel Allan Hofer
(1 Sep 2014)

Territorial Headquarters: Laupenstrasse 5, Bern, Switzerland

Postal address: Die Heilsarmee, Postfach 6575, 3001 Bern, Switzerland

Tel: [41] (31) 388 05 91; email: info@swi.salvationarmy.org

websites: www.heilsarmee.ch; www.armeedusalut.ch; www.salvationarmy.ch

On 10 December 1882 Salvation Army operations were commenced in the Salle de la Réformation, Geneva, by the Maréchale, Catherine Booth, and Colonel Arthur S. Clibborn. Bitter opposition was encountered but now the Army is recognised as an evangelical and social force throughout the Confederation. The Salvation Army's constitution consists of Foundation Salvation Army Switzerland; Cooperative Salvation Army Social Organisation; Salvation Army Immo Ltd.

Work first commenced in Austria on 27 May 1927 in Vienna. Unofficial meetings had been held earlier, but the official opening was conducted by Lieut-Commissioner Bruno Friedrich and Captain Lydia Saak was the officer-in-charge. 'Verein der Heilsarmee' was legally recognised by the Austrian Federal Ministry on 8 May 1952.

The Salvation Army's operations in Hungary were commenced on 26 April 1924 by Colonel Rothstein with two German female officers. The evangelistic and social activities were maintained until suppressed in 1950. After the opening of the central European borders, The Salvation Army was officially re-established on 3 November 1990 by General Eva Burrows. In 2013 The Salvation Army in Hungary successfully campaigned to retain its legal status as a church.

Zone: Europe

Countries included in the territory: Austria, Hungary, Switzerland

'The Salvation Army' in German: Die Heilsarmee; in French: Armée du Salut; in Hungarian:
Üdvhadsereg; in Spanish: Ejército de Salvación

Languages in which the gospel is preached: French, German, Hungarian, Spanish

Periodicals: *Espoir* (French), *Dialog* (German), *Dialogue* (French), *IN* (French and German), *Just 4 U* (French), *Klecks* (German), *Trampoline* (French), *Trialog* (German)

IN APRIL 2014, the Switzerland, Austria and Hungary Territory celebrated 90 years since it opened fire in Hungary.

A major highlight of the year in review was the territorial congress held in Bulle, Switzerland, with a varied programme for all ages. The weekend brought together more than 1,200 participants from all over the territory to celebrate our faith. This included the commissioning and ordination of the cadets of the Proclaimers of the Resurrection Session and the welcome to the cadets of the Heralds of Grace Session. During the congress many young people accepted Christ as Saviour and Lord.

The local government in Vienna, Austria, has praised the work carried out by The Salvation Army and appreciates all we are doing to assist local communities.

A new line of clothing including uniforms, accessories and other products, has been launched at the trade shop. This initiative to include a modern and timeless style and improve product quality and service has proved successful. Salvationists can now purchase goods including uniforms from three centres – Zurich, Geneva and Berne.

During 2014 a new communications strategy was initiated throughout the territory. This strategy focused on both present and future officers' service. We believe for greater things in the future for the Switzerland, Austria and Hungary Territory and anticipate an exciting period of growth ahead.

STATISTICS *(Switzerland and Austria)*
Officers 389 (active 164 retired 225) **Cadets** 7 **Employees** 1,781
Corps 61 **Outposts** 25 **Institutions** 40 **Thrift Stores** 22
Senior Soldiers 2,558 **Adherent Members** 1,266 **Junior Soldiers** 337
Personnel serving outside territory Officers 14 Layworkers 2

STAFF
Dept of Evangelisation: Maj Jacques Donzé
  Society and Family: Comr Jane Paone (TPWM) Lt-Col Fiona Hofer (TSWM) Maj Brigitta Heiniger (Women's Ministries and Seniors Sec)
  Family Work/Candidates: Maj Barbara Bösch
  Music and Gospel Arts: Mr Micael Dikantsa
  Youth: Maj Thomas Bösch
Dept of Social Work: Mr Daniel Röthlisberger
  Social French Part: Mr Didier Rochat
  Social German Part: Mr Christian Rohrbach; Mr Marco Innocente
  Family Tracing: Maj Regula Kurilin
  Pastoral Care Unit: Maj Christine Volet
  Refugees: Mr Paul Mori
  Thrift Stores: Mr Jakob Amstutz
Dept of Personnel: Maj Daniela Zurbürgg-Jäggi
  Training: Maj Jean-Marc Flückiger
  Personnel Administration: Mr Mathias Hofstetter
Dept of Finance and Business Administration: Sgt Andreas Stettler
  Finance Controlling Evangelisation: Maj Peter Zurbrügg
  Finance Controlling Social: Mr Michael Lippuner
  Finance Controlling THQ: Mrs Karin Haldimann
  Property: Mr Marc Hendry
  Mission and Development: Mr Jacques Miaglia
Dept of Communication: Sgt Philipp Steiner
  Editor-in-Chief: Maj Jacques Tschanz
  Fundraising: Sgt Christoph Bitter
  Information Technology: Mr Mathias Haller
  Trade Shop: Ms Martina Meyner

DIVISIONS
Mitte-Division: Gartenstrasse 8, 3007 Bern; tel: (031) 380 75 45; Majs Bernhard and Regina Wittwer

Division Romande: Rue de l'Ecluse 16,
2000 Neuchâtel; tel: (032) 729 20 81;
Maj Sylvette Huguenin
Ost-Division: Eidmattstrasse 16, 8032 Zürich;
tel: (044) 383 69 70;
Majs Markus and Renée Zünd

SCHOOL FOR OFFICER TRAINING
4012 Basel, Habsburgerstrasse 15, Postfach 54,
CH-4012 Basel; tel: (061) 387 91 11

SOCIAL WORK
Social Services Advice Bureaux
4053 Basel: Frobenstrasse20A;
tel: (061) 270 25 00
3007 Bern: Gartenstrasse 8;
tel: (031) 380 75 40
2503 Biel-Bienne: Kontrollstrasse 22;
tel: (032) 322 53 66
1018 Lausanne: Rue de la Borde 22;
tel: (021) 646 46 10
8400 Winterthur: CASA, Wartstrasse 9;
tel: 052 202 77 80
8032 Zürich: Eidmattstrasse 16; Postfach 1610;
tel: 044 383 69 70
8005 Zürich: Luisenstrasse 23; tel: 044 273 90 01

Adult Rehabilitation Centres
1201 Genève: Centre-Espoir, Rue Jean-Dassier
10; tel: (022) 338 22 00 (acc 109)
3098 Köniz: Buchseegut, Buchseeweg 15;
tel: (031) 970 63 63 (acc 48)
(with gardening and workshop)
1003 Lausanne: Foyer Féminin,
Ave Ruchonnet 49; tel: (021) 310 40 40 (acc 22)
1005 Lausanne: La Résidence, Place du Vallon 1A;
tel: (021) 320 48 55 (acc 32)
5022 Rombach (Aarau): Obstgarten,
Bibersteinstrasse 54; tel: (062) 839 80 80 (acc 34)
2024 St-Aubin: Le Devens, Alcoholic Home;
tel: (032) 836 27 29 (acc 34)
9205 Waldkirch: Hasenberg; tel: (071) 434 61 61
(acc 48) (agriculture and workshop)

'At Home' Psychiatric Support
9424 Rheineck: Psychiatrische Spitex Rheintal,
Thalerstrasse 61; tel: (071) 888 25 26

Community Centres
Hochfeld, Bern; Eidmattegge, Zürich; Open
Heart, Zürich; Genève.

Crèches
2024 St-Aubin: La Bergerie, rue de la Poste 5A;
tel (032) 835 39 55 (acc 31)

8008 Zürich: Kinderkrippe der Heilsarmee,
Neumünsterallee 17; tel (044) 383 47 00 (acc 50)

Emergency Shelters
1201 Genève: Accueil de Nuit, Chemin Galiffe 4;
tel: (022) 388 22 00 (acc 40)
1005 Lausanne: La Marmotte, Rue du Vallon 17;
tel: (021) 311 79 12 (acc 30)

Holiday Flats
3715 Adelboden: Chalet Bethel;
tel: (033) 673 21 62 (acc 20)

Homes for the Aged
3013 Bern: Lorrainehof, Lorrainestrasse 34;
tel: (031) 330 16 16 (acc 39 + 21 studios)
1814 La Tour-de-Peilz: Le Phare-Elim,
Ave de la Paix 11, case postale 444;
tel: (021) 977 33 33 (acc 44)
1201 Genève: Résidence Amitié, Rue Baudit 1;
tel: (022) 919 95 95 (acc 52)
2000 Neuchâtel: Le Foyer, Rue de l'Ecluse 18;
tel: (032) 729 20 20 (acc 30)

Homes for Children
4054 Basel: Kinderhaus Holee, Nenzlingerstrasse
2; tel: (061) 301 24 50 (acc 26)
8932 Mettmenstetten: Wohnheim für Kinder und
Jugendliche Paradies; Paradiesstrasse;
tel: (044) 768 58 00 (acc 24)
3110 Münsingen: Kinderheim Sonnhalde,
Standweg 7; tel: (031) 721 08 06 (acc 24)

Home for Physically Disabled Children
8344 Bäretswil: Sunnemätteli, Entlastungsheim
Für behinderte Kinder Rüeggenthalstrasse 71;
tel: (044) 939 99 80 (acc 16)

Hostels for Men
4058 Basel: Wohnen für Männer, Rheingasse 80;
tel: (061) 666 66 77 (acc 50)
8004 Zürich: Dienerstrasse 76; tel: (044) 298 90 80
(acc 24)
8005 Zürich: Geroldstrasse 27;
tel: (043) 204 10 20 (acc 24)

Hostels for Men and Women
3006 Bern: Passantenheim, Muristrasse 6;
tel: (031) 351 80 27 (acc 50)
2504 Biel: Passantenheim, Jakob-Strasse 58;
tel: (032) 322 68 38 (acc 25)
3600 Thun: Passantenheim, Waisenhausstrasse
26; tel: (033) 222 69 20 (acc 17)
8400 Winterthur: Durchgangsheim,
Habsburgstrasse 29, tel: (052) 226 01 61 (acc 12)

Switzerland, Austria and Hungary Territory

8400 Winterthur: Wohnheim Wartstrasse 42;
tel: (052) 208 90 50 (acc 34)
8026 Zürich: Wohnheim Molkenstrasse 6;
Postfach 1669; tel: (044) 298 90 00 (acc 85)

Hostel for Women
4058 Basel: Wohnen für Frauen,
Alemannengasse 7; tel: (061) 681 34 70
(acc 37)

Social Flats
8580 Amriswil: Begleitetes Wohnen (acc 8)
4058 Basel: Begleitetes Wohnen (acc 10 flats)
3012 Bern: Begleitetes Wohnen (acc 45 flats)

Thrift stores (22 stores)

Young Women's Residence
4059 Basel: Schlössli, Eichhornstrasse 21;
tel: (061) 335 31 10 (acc 14)

Social Justice
3008 Bern: Effingerstrasse 53; email:
socialjustice@swi.salvationarmy.org
tel: (031) 388 05 70

Refugee Work
Main Office: 3008 Bern, Effingerstrasse 67;
tel: (031) 380 18 80 (6 centres, 5 offices)

Work Integration Programmes
(Travailplus/Arbeitsintegration)
3008 Bern: travailPLUS, Effingerstrasse 53;
tel: (031) 388 06 06
4950 Huttwil: Leuchtturm, Langenthalstrasse 17;
tel:(062) 962 06 34
3414 Oberburg: Facility management,
Krauchthalstrasse 16; tel:(034) 426 20 50
4056 Basel: Sewing studio, Schönbeinstrasse 13;
tel: (061) 261 34 01

HOTELS
4055 Basel: Alegria B&B, Habsburgerstrasse
15; tel: (061) 387 91 10
1204 Genève: Bel' Espérance, Rue de la Vallée
1; tel: (022) 818 37 37; (acc 39 beds)
3852 Ringgenberg: Guesthouse, Hauptstrasse
125; tel: (033) 822 70 25 (acc 22 beds)

YOUTH CENTRES
Under THQ
3715 Adelboden (acc 75)

Under DHQ
Nordwestschweiz: 4462 Rickenbach, Waldegg
(acc 100)

Division Romande: 1451 Les Rasses (acc 150)
Ost-Division: 8712 Stäfa (acc 55)

AUSTRIA
City Command: AT-1020 Vienna
Salztor-Zentrum, Grosse Schiffgasse 3;
tel: [43] (1) 890 3282 2266;
City Commander: Maj Hans-Marcel Leber
www.heilsarmee.at

Hostel for Men
SalztorZentrum, AT-1020 Vienna:
Grosse Schiffgasse 3; tel: [43] (1) 214 48 30 27
(acc 54)

Residential Home for Men
Haus Erna, AT-1210
Vienna Moritz-Dreger-Gasse 19 tel: [43] (1) 890
3282 2017 (acc 60)

Prison Chaplaincy
Missing Persons Bureau
at above address; tel: 890 3282 2264
Vienna Corps:at above address (entrance in
Oswald-Redlich-Strasse 11a)
mobile tel: [43] (664) 163 67 23

HUNGARY REGION
Regional Headquarters: Bajnok utca 25,
1063 Budapest, Hungary; tel: 36-1-332-3324;
email: kozponti@swi.salvationarmy.org;
website: www.udvhadsereg.org
Regional Officer: Maj Andrew Morgan

STATISTICS
Officers 15 (active 12 retired 3) **Employees** 55
Corps 4 **Outpost** 2 **Institutions** 3
Senior Soldiers 59 **Adherent Members** 11
Junior Soldiers 13

STAFF
Asst Regional Officer: Maj Darlene Morgan
Finance: Zsuzsa Kübler

SOCIAL WORK
Hostel for Men
'Új Remenység Háza', 1086 Budapest,
Dobozi utca 29; tel: +36-1-314-2775 '(acc 98)
Rehabilitation Home for Women
'Válaszút Háza', 1171 Budapest,
Lemberg utca 38-42; tel: +36-1-259-1095
(acc 24)

Refuge for Women and Children
'Fény Hazá', Budapest
(acc 40, inc mothers with children)

Adult Day Drop-In Centre
1171 Budapest, Lemberg utca 38-42; tel: +36-1-259-1095 (acc 50)

Day Nursery
1086 Budapest, Dobozi utca 31; tel: +36-20-572-9656 (acc 7)

Feeding Programmes
1086 Budapest, Dobozi utca 29; tel: +36-1-314-2775 (250 meals daily)
1171 Budapest, Lemberg utca 38-42; tel: +36-1-259-1095 (150 meals daily)
4034 Debrecen, Ruyter utca 23; tel: +36-52-534-616 (200 meals daily)

SWITZERLAND: Music sections supporting the territorial congress

TAIWAN REGION

Regional Commander:
Lieut-Colonel Jennifer Groves
(1 Apr 2013)

Regional Headquarters: 3/F, 273 Dun Hua South Road, Section 2, Da-An District, Taipei 106

Postal address: PO Box 44-100, Taipei, Taiwan

Tel: [886] (02) 2738 1079/1171

email: TAW_Leadership@taw.salvationarmy.org: website: www.salvationarmy.org.tw

Pioneered in 1928 by Colonel Yasowo Segawa, Salvation Army work in Taiwan was curtailed by the Second World War. Following initiatives by an American serviceman, operations were officially re-established in October 1965 by Colonel and Mrs George Lancashire. Taiwan has been a separate region since 1997.

Zone: South Pacific and East Asia
Country included in the region: Taiwan
'The Salvation Army' in Taiwanese (Hokkien): Kiu Se Kuen; in Mandarin: Chiu Shih Chun
Languages in which the gospel is preached: English, Mandarin, Taiwanese (Hokkien)
Periodicals: *Regional News*

TAIWAN Region has experienced a year of new beginnings. In her welcome meeting the Regional Commander, Lieut-Colonel Jennifer Groves, encouraged those gathered to be people of purpose, power and prayer. This became the focus throughout the year.

The officers met together in July 2013 for their annual officers' fellowship using the theme 'Right at the Heart – Soul Care'. A women's camp with the theme 'Lovely Lady' was held in October – the first for a number of years – and a regional dream was realised in December with the purchase of a building designated to

meet the needs of young men in Taiwan. A new outpost was opened at Yuchi in April 2014 with significant links being made with those in the local community.

The need to raise up leaders is imperative and therefore specific focus has been given to developing both pre- and post-commissioning courses for candidates and officers, as well as enabling senior soldiers and local officers to receive leadership development training.

The officers and soldiers give thanks to the Lord for his refreshment, renewal and encourgement through these events.

STATISTICS
Officers 19 (active 17 retired 2)
Corps with Community Centres 5 **Outposts** 1
   Social Services Centres 3
   University Outreach Mission 1
Senior Soldiers 184 **Adherent Members** 110
   Junior Soldiers 35

STAFF
Women's Ministries: Lt-Col Jennifer Groves
   (RPWM) Maj Mary Tsou (WMO)
Administration Officer: Maj Stephen Tsou
Training and Development Officers:
   Majs Norm and Isabel Beckett
Finance: Mr Fred Lee

SOCIAL SERVICES
Homeless
Taipei Homeless Caring Centre: c/o 1/F, No 42,
   Lane 65, Jin Si St, Taipei 103

Youth
Puli Youth Services Centre: No 192 Pei Hwang
   Rd, Puli Town, Nantou County 545
   (acc 60)

COMMUNITY SERVICES
Puli Community Development Centre:
   c/o No 62-1, Shueitou Rd, Puli Town,
   Nantou County 545

TANZANIA TERRITORY

Territorial leaders:
Colonels S. Edward and Deborah Horwood

Territorial Commander:
Colonel S. Edward Horwood (1 June 2014)

Chief Secretary:
Lieut-Colonel Samuel Mkami (1 Sep 2013)

Territorial Headquarters: Kilwa Road, Dar es Salaam

Postal address: PO Box 1273, Dar es Salaam, Tanzania

Tel/fax: [255] (22) 2850468/2850542

Adjutant and Mrs Francis Dare began Salvation Army work in Tabora, Tanzania (formerly known as Tanganyika), in November 1933, as part of the East Africa Territory. In 1950, at the request for assistance from the Colonial Governor, The Salvation Army set up Mgulani Camp, where the Tanzania Headquarters is now located. Tanzania became a separate command on 1 October 1998 and was elevated to territory status on 1 February 2008.

Zone: Africa
Country included in the territory: Tanzania
'The Salvation Army' in Kiswahili: Jeshi la Wokovu
Languages in which the gospel is preached: Kiswahili and various tribal languages

MEETING contemporary challenges with contemporary ministries has been a hallmark of the year. Issues of child exploitation, forced labour and trafficking have prompted the territory to develop programmes in order to address needs. The government and police have referred more than 100 rescued girls to Mbagala and Kwetu centres where they have been provided with safety, recovery, education and skills training.

This year the territory supported more than 2,000 people with direct relief due to drought conditions which ruined the harvest. The Army's ministry in Dar es Salaam has increased because many people either send their children to work or seek work themselves in the city, as life in many rural villages continues to suffer from chronic natural disasters. Strengthening the connection between the ministries that take place in corps and communities continued to be reinforced throughout the country. With the support of partners, donors and friends, seminars and training were conducted, keeping the Army's distinctive character prominently seen and effectively implemented through corps and institutions.

In June 2013, the territory welcomed Commissioners Joash and Florence Malabi (IS and ZSWM) who visited to offer encouragement and spiritual support, and in September the territory welcomed home Lieut-

Colonels Samuel and Mary Mkami as CS and TSWM respectively.

In October, the Tanzania Territory celebrated 80 years of ministry by holding a worship service that gave gratitude to the Lord and commemorated the founding officers in the District of Tabora – the original location of the inception of the Army. Soldiers and friends look forward to many more years of ministry and service.

Under the banner of 'Forward Together', the work continues as the territory strives to preach the gospel of Jesus Christ and meet human need throughout the country.

STATISTICS
Officers 151 (active 146 retired 5) Cadets (2nd Yr) 13 Employees 152
Corps 76 Outposts 75 Schools 2 Day Care Centres 17 Hostel 1
Senior Soldiers 6,822 Junior Soldiers 4,242

STAFF
Women's Ministries: Col Deborah Horwood (TPWM) Lt-Col Mary Mkami (TSWM) Maj Enacy Gitonga (LOMS/ SAMF)
Candidates: Capt Lucas Chacha
Education and Officer Development: Capt Elisabeth Gainsford
Editor: Maj Daniel Simwali
Field: Maj Isaac Gitonga
Finance: Maj Francis Amakye
Projects: Mr Frederick Urembo
Property: Capt Julius Mwita
Public Relations: Maj Daniel Simwali
Social Services: Capt Josephat Nyerere
Sponsorship: Capt Anna Gibson
Training: Capt Ian Gainsford
Youth and Children: Capt Lucas Chacha

DIVISIONS
Coastal: PO Box 7622, Dar es Salaam; tel: (022) 2860365;
   Majs Christopher and Mary Ighoty
Ilembo: PO Box 2545, tel: (0255) 0752 820045;
   Majs Japhael and Aliyinza Madoki

Mbeya: PO Box 1214, Mbeya; tel: (025) 2560009;
   Majs James and Yustina Gitang'ita
Tarime: PO Box 37, Tarime; tel: (028) 2690095
   Majs Wilson and Tamali Mwalukani
Serengeti: PO Box 28, Mugumu; tel: (028) 2621434;
   Majs Musa and Esther Magaigwa

DISTRICTS
Bukine: Capt Juliana Kusyetela
Mwanza: PO Box 11267, Mwanza; tel: (028) 40123; Maj Fanuel Ndabila
Tabora: PO Box 1, Tabora tel: (026) 2604728) Maj Daniel Simwali

TRAINING COLLEGE
PO Box 1273, Dar es Salaam

AGRICULTURE DEVELOPMENT PROGRAMME
PO Box 1273, Dar es Salaam

EDUCATIONAL WORK
College for Business Management and Administration
Shukrani International College for Business Management and Administration, PO Box 535, Mbeya; tel: (00255) (0)25 2504404
Primary School for Disabled Children
Matumaini School, PO Box 1273, Dar es Salaam; tel: (022) 2851861 (acc 175)
Secondary School
Itundu School, PO Box 2994, Mbeya

SOCIAL SERVICES
Postal address PO Box 1273, Dar es Salaam;
   Kwetu Counselling and Psycho-Social Support Services
   Mbagala Girls' Home: Mgulani Hostel and Conference Centre: tel: (022) 2851467 (acc 110)
   Vocational Training Workshop

Anti-Human Trafficking Programmes

Rehabilitation and Reunification Services for Orphans and Vulnerable Children

PROJECTS
Community counselling, Gardening and farming activities, Goat banks schemes, Home-based care services, Literacy classes, Microcredit schemes, Nutrition programmes, Primary health care, Training and economic empowerment for rural women, Water and sanitation programmes

UGANDA TERRITORY

Territorial leaders:
Colonels Benjamin and Grace Mnyampi

Territorial Commander:
Colonel Benjamin Mnyampi (1 Jan 2013)

Chief Secretary:
Lieut-Colonel Eliud Nabiswa (1 Jun 2014)

Territorial Headquarters: Plot 78-82 Lugogo Bypass, Kampala

Postal address: PO Box 11776, Kampala, Uganda

Tel: [256] 41 533901; Kampala mobile: [256] 752 375782

The Salvation Army opened fire in Uganda in 1931 when Captain and Mrs Edward Osborne unfurled the flag in Mbale, as part of the East Africa Territory. In September 1977 the Army's religious teaching was banned and in June 1978 its ministry, including social work, was proscribed. In 1980 Majors Leonard and Dorothy Millar began work with the persecuted Salvationists to re-establish The Salvation Army. Uganda became a separate command on 1 November 2005 and was elevated to territorial status on 1 March 2011.

Zone: Africa
Country included in the territory: Uganda
'The Salvation Army' in Kiswahili: Jeshi La Wokovu; in Luganda: Ejje Elyobulokozi
Languages in which the gospel is preached: English, Kiswahili, Luganda and a number of tribal languages
Periodicals: *Voice of Hope* (quarterly)

THE UGANDA Territory is progressing well.

The visit of the Army's international leaders, General André Cox and Commissioner Silvia Cox (WPWM) to the territory was a remarkable event. Officers, soldiers, youth and children, and friends of the Army gathered to welcome the General and were blessed by the Bible messages given.

The territory acknowledges wonderful achievements and growth during the year in review. We have officially launched a men's fellowship programme, planted a new outreach centre at Ishongororo, implemented the Territorial Strategic Plan, undergone a territorial review and conducted corps inspections, all indicating a growing of the Army in Uganda.

The Easter campaign conducted by Colonels Benjamin and Grace Mnyampi (TC and TPWM) at the newly-created Mulimani District and the official opening of a new church hall at Soono were a blessing to many.

The territory has been involved in supporting the government in implementing projects that help vulnerable children and households in many communities. Through the 'Score', STAR – E (assisting vulnerable children and families), EPFOSE (providing skills in food security and economical empowerment) and faith-based facilitation projects, the Army has been able to help people acknowledge the challenges affecting their communities and families and assist them to find a way forward.

Utilising the passion brought about through 'One Army, One Mission, One Message', the Army, led by the Holy Spirit, is moving forward.

STATISTICS

Officers 102 (active 96 retired 6) **Envoys** 2
Corps Leaders 91 **Cadets** 20 **Employees** 86
Corps 84 **Outposts** 28 **Outreach Centres** 1
Pre-primary Schools 4 **Day Care Centre** 1
Primary Schools 12 **Vocational Centres** 2
Senior Soldiers 12,669 **Junior Soldiers** 7,300
Personnel serving outside the territory
Officers 4

STAFF

Women's Ministries: Col Grace Mnyampi
(TPWM) Lt-Col Aidah Nabiswa (TSWM)
Maj Nolega Imbiakha (CCMS/Ret Officers Sec)
Field: Maj Daniel Imbiakha
Finance: Maj William Mutungi
Projects: Maj Emmanuel Sichibona
Property: Maj Moses Ndeke
Social Services: Maj Rose Ndeke
Sponsorship Sec: Maj Florence Mutungi
Statistics: Maj Fred Walukano
Training: Maj Alfred Banda
Youth/Candidates: Maj Grace Walukano

DIVISIONS

Central: PO Box 11776, Kampala;
Majs Jamin and Topista Wasilwa
Eastern: PO Box 168, Tororo;
Majs Peter and Elizabeth Soita
Mbale: PO Box 2214, Mbale;
Majs Bramwell and Magret Simiyu
Southern: PO Box 2012, Busia;
Majs Joseph and Alice Wandulu
West: PO Box 73, Kigumba via Masindi;
Majs Esau and Margaret Wekalao

DISTRICTS

Busulwa: PO Box 33, Magale via Mbale;
Maj Vincent and Apolonia Nazeba
Lwakhakha: PO Box 33, Magale via Mbale;
Maj Augustus Webaale
Mulimani: PO Box 33, Magale via Mbale;
Majs Vincent and Appolonia Natseba
Sebei: PO Box 2214, Mbale; Maj David Wangatia

TRAINING COLLEGE
Jinja: PO Box 133, Jinja

SOCIAL SERVICES
Children's Home
Tororo: PO Box 48, Tororo; tel: 045-45244
(acc 54)

Community Centre
Kampala: PO Box 11776; tel: 041-532517

**Home for Children with Physical
Disabilities**
Home of Joy, PO Box 1186, Kampala;
tel: 041-542409 (acc 30)

Vocational Training Workshops
Kampala (carpentry, catering, tailoring):
PO Box 11776, Kampala
Kigumba Agrigultural Farm Project: PO Box 73,
Kigumba via Masindi
Lira (carpentry, tailoring, building): PO Box 13,
Lira
Mbalala: Kasenge Vocational Training
(carpentry, tailoring): PO Box 11776, Mbalala

EPFOSE Project
Providing skills in food preparation and economical empowerment PO Box 11776, Kampala

STAR - E Project
Empowering families and vulneralbe children PO
Box 11776, Kampala

**Score' Project for vulnerable children and
their households**
PO Box 11776, Kampala; tel: 041-533113

Reproductive Health Project
Family planning, PO Box 11776, Kampala

WORTH Programme
Income Generation for Women: PO Box 2214,
Mbale; tel: 045-79295

UNITED KINGDOM TERRITORY WITH THE REPUBLIC OF IRELAND

Territorial leaders:
Commissioners Clive and Marianne Adams

Territorial Commander:
Commissioner Clive Adams (1 Feb 2013)

Chief Secretary:
Colonel David Hinton (1 Jul 2011)

Territorial Headquarters: 101 Newington Causeway, London SE1 6BN, UK

Tel: [44] 20 7367 4500; email: thq@salvationarmy.org.uk;
website: www.salvationarmy.org.uk

The foundation of the territory dates from the earliest formation of The Salvation Army – prior to the adoption of that title in 1878 – when in July 1865 the Founder, William Booth, took charge of a mission to the East End of London. Certain UK corps were first established as Christian Mission stations.

Throughout the Army's history its work in this geographical area has been organised in a variety of forms and territories, but before 1990 these were all part of International Headquarters administration. However, on 1 November 1990 a restructuring occurred so that now the United Kingdom Territory is separate from International Headquarters and under a single command similar to that of the Army's other territories.

Zone: Europe
Countries included in the territory: Channel Islands, Isle of Man, Republic of Ireland, United Kingdom of
   Great Britain and Northern Ireland
Languages in which the gospel is preached: Czech, English, Korean, Urdu, Welsh
'The Salvation Army' in Welsh: Byddin Yr Iachawdwriaeth; in Czech: Armáda Spásy
Periodicals: *Kids Alive!*, *Salvationist*, *The War Cry*

THE UNITED Kingdom Territory with the Republic of Ireland faces a time of societal transition due to welfare reforms, economic recession and moral challenges that bring into question the place of faith-based organisations. The introduction of harsher sanctions to the welfare benefits system has resulted in a greater number of people in financial crisis approaching frontline centres for support. Increasingly 'suffering humanity' is looking to The Salvation Army for practical help. The Army is speaking for those who find themselves marginalised by poverty, the addictive nature of online gambling and alcohol abuse as well as providing valuable support to the most vulnerable in our society, including adult victims of trafficking.

The territory faces the need to adapt when mission opportunities shift, and so with the change in practice by the armed forces relating to service personnel, the Army provided full-time military chaplains when the opportunity was given.

The final Roots Conference took place in May 2013 with the theme 'Changing Minds'. A capacity congregation participated in worship and Bible study before listening to speakers on issues of social justice and how communities and individuals can become empowered to improve the lives of disadvantaged people.

Spring Harvest, an ecumenical Christian gathering in the UK, shared the event with The Salvation Army in April, and in August, Chingford, London, was the setting for Ignite – the centenary celebration of Salvation Army scouting and guiding. Scouts, guides and their leaders attended the camp with 10 Salvation Army countries represented. During the opening ceremony the delegates were challenged to 'change the world' – that challenge was met with enthusiasm.

A spirit of renewal and refreshment has caused Salvationists to deepen spiritually by allowing our theology to shape our practice. A Mission Symposium held at William Booth College, and the appointment of senior leaders to the position of Spiritual Life Development officers, has enabled our people to be resourced for our primary focus.

The process of review and discernment known as Fit for Mission, which began in 2012, is ongoing and has gained breadth and momentum as mission development plans have been analysed. Wide consultation, a culture of openness, collaboration and creative thinking has been invited during a 'listening' to the territory initiative, in order to discern how best to move forward.

Conversations based around the question, 'How can The Salvation Army ensure it remains relevant in a changing world with so many needs and opportunities?', was held through-out the territory. This 'conversation' encouraged Salvationists to unite behind one vision, as well as affirm the mission and development of a sustainable and mission-driven strategy as we journey into the future.

The territory's strategic mission priorities include transformation, integration, discipleship and effective-ness. Every expression of Salvation Army mission was encouraged to have a mission development plan in order to focus and shape the Army's impact in the local community.

THE SALVATION ARMY TRUSTEE COMPANY
Registered Office: 101 Newington Causeway, London SE1 6BN

THE SALVATION ARMY (REPUBLIC OF IRELAND)
Registered Office: 114 Marlborough St, Dublin 1, Republic of Ireland

STATISTICS
Officers 2,434 (active 1,033 retired 1,401 **Cadets** (1st Yr) 25 (2nd Yr) 24 (+ 10 distance learning cadets) **Employees** 4,800

United Kingdom Territory with the Republic of Ireland

Corps/Outreach Centres/New Plants 706
  Social Services Centres 99 **Red Shield
  Defence Services Clubs** 7 **Mobile Units for
  Service Personnel** 4
Senior Soldiers 27,183 **Adherent Members**
  9,083 **Junior Soldiers** 3,624
Personnel serving outside territory Officers 86
  Layworkers 6

STAFF

Women's Ministries: Comr Marianne Adams
  (TPWM) Col Sylvia Hinton (TSWM)
Asst Chief Secs: Maj Darrell Thomas, Maj John
  Warner
  International Staff Band: B/M Dr Stephen
    Cobb
  International Staff Songsters: S/L Mrs
    Dorothy Nancekievill
Sec for Business Admin: Lt-Col Alan Read
  **Asst Sec for Business Admin (Risk and
    Research):** Mr David Rice
  Company Sec: Maj John Warner
  Finance: Maj Richard Welch
  Internal Audit: Mr John Galbraith
  Property: Mr Keith Manners
  SAGIC: Mr Gordon Dewar
  Strategic Information: Mr Martyn Croft
  Trade: Mr Trevor Caffull
Sec for Communications: Lt-Col Melvyn Fincham
  Assistant Sec for Communications:
    Mr Julius Wolff-Ingham
  Editor-in-Chief and Publishing Sec:
    Maj Martin Hill
    Editors: *Salvationist*: Maj Jane Kimberley
    The War Cry: Maj Nigel Bovey
    Kids Alive!: Mr Justin Reeves
  Head of Media: Joanna Inskip
  Head of Public Affairs Unit: Dr Helen
    Cameron
  Territorial Ecumenical Officer: Maj John
    Read
  International Heritage Centre: Maj Stephen
    Grinsted (Director)
  Schools and Colleges Unit: Maj Stephen
    Grinsted (Director)
  Marketing and Fundraising: Mr Julius
    Wolff-Ingham
Sec for Personnel: Col Sylvia Hinton
  Asst Sec for Personnel: Maj Colin Cowdrey
  **Asst Sec for Personnel (Leadership
    Development):** Maj Judith Payne
  Human Resources (Employees): Mr Ian
    Hammond
  Overseas Services Sec: Maj Pam Cameron
  Pastoral Care Unit: tba
  Retired Officers Sec: Maj James Williams

Safeguarding: Mr Dean Juster
Sec for Programme: Lt-Col George Pilkington
  Asst Sec for Programme: Maj Mark Herbert
  Anti-Trafficking Response: Maj Anne Read
  Employment Plus: Maj Julian Watchorn
  Evangelism: Maj Noel Wright
    Adult and Family Ministries: Maj Valerie
      Mylechreest
    Children's and Youth Ministries:
      Maj Denise Cooper; Maj Mike Lloyd-Jones
    Music Ministries: B/M Dr Stephen Cobb
  International Development: Maj Heather
    Poxon
  Family Tracing: Maj Paul Hardy
  Research and Development: Mrs Jacqui King
Social Services: Soc S Sec: Maj Paul Kingscott
  Homelessness Services: Mr Mitch Menagh;
  Older People's Services: Mrs Elaine Cobb
  Red Shield Defence and Emergency Services:
    tba
Special Events: Mr Melvin Hart

WILLIAM BOOTH COLLEGE

Denmark Hill, London SE5 8BQ;
  tel: (020) 7326 2700
Principal: Lt-Col Mike Caffull
  Asst Principal: Lt-Col Wendy Caffull
  Directors of School for Officer Training:
    Training Programme: Maj Malcolm Martin
    Spiritual Programme: Capt David Alton
  **Director of School for In-Service Training
    and Development:** Maj Gillian Jackson
  Territorial Candidates Director: Maj David
    Kinsey

INTERNATIONAL HERITAGE CENTRE (including The William Booth Birthplace Museum, Nottingham) AND SCHOOLS AND COLLEGES UNIT

Denmark Hill, London SE5 8BQ;
  tel: (020) 7326 7801;
  email: heritage@salvationarmy.org.uk;
  Director: Maj Stephen Grinsted

SCOTLAND SECRETARIAT

12a Dryden Rd, Loanhead, Midlothian
  EH20 9LZ; tel: (0131) 440 9100;
  Scotland Sec: Lt-Col Carol Bailey

DIVISIONS

Anglia: 2 Barton Way, Norwich NR1 1DL;
  tel: (01603) 724 400; Maj David Jackson (DC)
  Lt-Col Mary Capsey (DDWM)
Central North: 80 Eccles New Rd, Salford,
  Gtr Manchester M5 4DU; tel: (0161) 743 3900;

Majs Alan and Linda Watters
Central South: 16c Cowley Rd, Uxbridge,
UB8 2LT; tel: (01895) 208800;
Majs Paul and Jenine Main
East Midlands: Paisley Grove, Chilwell,
Nottingham NG9 6DJ; tel: (0115) 983 5000;
Majs Wayne and Deborah Bungay
East Scotland: 12a Dryden Rd, Loanhead,
Midlothian EH20 9LZ;
tel: (0131) 440 9100;
Lt-Col Carol Bailey
Ireland: 12 Station Mews, Sydenham,
Belfast BT4 1TL; tel: (028) 9067 5000;
Majs Elwyn and Carole Harries
London Central: 1 Tiverton St, London SE1 6NT;
tel: (020) 7378 1021;
Lt-Col Suzanne Fincham
London North-East: Maldon Rd, Hatfield
Peverel, Chelmsford CM3 2HL;
tel: (01245) 383000;
Majs Norman and Margaret Ord
London South-East: 1 East Court, Enterprise Rd,
Maidstone ME15 6JF;
tel: (01622) 775000;
Lt-Cols Ray and Angela Irving
North Scotland: Deer Rd, Woodside,
Aberdeen AB24 2BL;
tel: (01224) 496000;
Majs Brian Slinn and Liv Raegevik-Slinn
North-Western: 16 Faraday Rd, Wavertree
Technology Park, Liverpool L13 1EH;
tel: (0151) 252 6100;
Majs Drew and BeverleyMcCombe
Northern: Unit 4, Hedley Court, Orion Business
Park, Newcastle upon Tyne NE29 7TS;
tel: (0191) 293 1300;
Majs Denis and Olive Lomax
South and Mid Wales: East Moors Rd,
Ocean Park, Cardiff CF24 5SA;
tel: (029) 2044 0600;
Majs Derek and Susan Jones
South-Western: 6 Marlborough Court,
Manaton Close, Matford Business Park,
Exeter EX2 8PF; tel: (01392) 822100;
Majs Ian and Jean Harris
Southern: 6-8 Little Park Farm Rd, Segensworth,
Fareham PO15 5TD; tel: (01489) 566800;
Lt-Cols Karen and David Shakespeare
West Midlands: 102 Unett St North, Hockley,
Birmingham B19 3BZ; tel: (0121) 507 8500;
Majs Peter and Julie Forrest
West Scotland: 4 Buchanan Court, Cumbernauld
Rd, Stepps, Glasgow G33 6HZ;
tel: (0141) 779 5000;
Majs Russell and Catherine Wyles
Yorkshire: Millshaw Business Living,
Global Avenue, Leeds LS11 8PR;

tel: (0113) 387 7600;
Lt-Cols Michael and Lynn Highton

FAMILY TRACING SERVICE
101 Newington Causeway, London SE1 6BN; tel:
(020) 7367 4747

FARM
Hadleigh: Castle Lane, Hadleigh, Benfleet, Essex;
tel: (01702) 558550

INSURANCE CORPORATION
The Salvation Army General Insurance
Corporation Ltd, Faith House,
23-24 Lovat Lane, London EC3R 8EB;
tel: 0845 634 0260

PASTORAL CARE UNIT
Counselling Services: 1 Water Lane, Stratford,
London E15 4LU; tel: (020) 8536 5480

TRADE (SP&S)
Head Office (and shop): 66-78 Denington Rd,
Denington Industrial Estate, Wellingborough,
Northants NN8 2QH; tel: (01933) 445445
(mail order); fax: (01933) 445415
Shop: 1 Tiverton St, London SE1 6NT

TRADING (SA TRADING CO LTD)
66-78 Denington Rd, Denington Industrial Estate,
Wellingborough, Northants NN8 2QH
Textile Recycling Division: tel: (01933) 441086
email: paul.ozanne@satradingco.org
Charity Shops Division: el: (01933) 441807
email: reception@satradingco.org

SOCIAL SERVICES DEPARTMENT
Centres for Older People
Bath: Smallcombe House (acc men and
women 32, sheltered flat 1)
Buxton: The Hawthorns (acc 34)
Coventry: Youell Court (acc 40)
Edinburgh: Davidson House (acc 40)
Eagle Lodge (acc 33)
Glasgow: Eva Burrows Day Centre (places 112)
Hassocks: Villa Adastra (acc 40, day centre 20)
Holywood: The Sir Samuel Kelly Memorial
Home (acc 39)
London:Alver Bank, Clapham (acc 30)
Morton House, Lewisham (acc 27)
North Walsham: Furze Hill House (acc 40, day
centre 22)
Prestwich: Holt House, (acc 31)
Sandridge: Lyndon, (acc 32)
Southend-on-Sea: Bradbury Home (acc 34)
Weston-super-Mare: Dewdown House (acc 40)

United Kingdom Territory with the Republic of Ireland

Centres for Families (Residential)
Belfast:
  Belfast:Glen Alva (acc family units 20,
  max 77 residents)
  Thorndale Parenting Assessment/Family
  Centre, (acc family units 34, single bedsits 4,
  max 125 residents)
Portsmouth: Catherine Booth House
  (acc family units 21, max 40 residents)

Refuge from Domestic Abuse (women with children)
Birmingham: Shepherd's Green House;
  contact via West Midlands DHQ (acc 16
  families, 4 single women, max 44 residents)

Centre for Employment and Training:
Hadleigh (Essex): Hadleigh Farm

Centre for People with Learning Difficulties
Kilbirnie: George Steven Centre

Centres for the Single Homeless
Accrington: (acc 11)
Belfast: Centenary House (acc direct access 80)
  Calder Fountain (attached to Centenary
  House) (registered care 28, resettlement 12)
Birmingham: William Booth Centre (acc 74)
Blackburn: Bramwell House (acc 55)
Braintree: New Direction Centre,
  David Blackwell House (acc 14)
Bridgend: (acc 16)
Bristol: Logos House (acc 69)
Cardiff: Crichton House Outreach Services,
  Dowlais Court
  Northlands (acc 26)
Coventry: Harnall (acc 80)
Dublin: Granby Centre (acc units 101)
Dundee: Strathmore Lodge (acc 25)
  Burnside Mill (acc 20)
Edinburgh: Ashbrook (acc 30)
  The Pleasance (acc 37)
Glasgow: Eva Burrows 1st Stop Project, Eva
  Burrows Centre (acc 32)
  Hunters Hill Court (acc 10)
  Wallace of Campsie House (acc 52)
  William Hunter House (acc 43)
Grimsby: The Booth Lifehouse (acc 35)
Hull: William Booth House (acc 113)
Huntingdon: Kings Ripton Court (acc 36)
Ipswich: Lyndon House (acc 39)
Isle of Man: David Gray House (acc 13)
Isle of Wight: Fellowship House (acc 27)
Leamington Spa: Eden Villa (acc 11)
Liverpool: Ann Fowler House (acc 38)

Darbyshire House (acc 45)
  Green Lane Lifehouse (acc 23)
London: Booth House (acc 150)
  Cambria House (acc 48)
  Edward Alsop Court (acc 108)
  Springfield Lodge (acc 35)
Manchester: Discovery House (10)
  Endeavour House (15)
  Independence House (15)
Newcastle upon Tyne: Cedar House
  (acc direct access 18, resettlement flats 6)
Perth: Skinnergate (acc 30)
Plymouth: Devonport House and Zion House
  (acc 72)
Portsmouth: Mill House (acc 24)
Reading: Willow House (acc 38)
St Helens: Salisbury House (acc 68)
Salford: Abbot Lodge (acc 20)
Sheffield: Charter Row (acc 56)
Skegness: Witham Lodge (acc 30)
Southampton: The Booth Centre (acc 46)
Stoke-on-Trent: Vale St
  (acc 60 + 4 training flats)
Sunderland: Swan Lodge (acc 65)
Swindon: Booth House (acc 50)
Warrington: James Lee House (acc 54)

Children's Homes/Centres (Residential)
Dublin: Lefroy Night Light (acc 7 overnight
  emergency beds)
  Lefroy Support Flats (acc 7)
Leeds: Spring Grove (acc 6 female care leavers)

Day Care, Early Years Education and Contact Centres for Children
Birmingham: Sally Ann's Pre-School and Out of
  School Club (registered for 64 total)
Leeds: Copper Beech Day Nursery and Rainbow
  After-School Club (registered for 62 total)
Nottingham: Sunshine Corner Playgroup
  (pre-school) and Out of School Club
Central North: Sunbeams Playgroup (pre-school)
Failsworth: Out of School Club
Droitwich Spa: Pre-School Playgroup
Heckmondwike: Playgroup (pre-school)
York: Salvation Army Playgroup (pre-school)
Croydon: Little Pandas Pre-School
Staines: Rainbow Playgroup (pre-school)
William Booth College: Humpty Dumpty
  Nursery and Out of School Club
Bridgwater: Salvation Army Pre-School
Gillingham: Salvation Army Pre-School
Clacton-on-Sea: Salvation Army Pre-School
Leigh-on-Sea: Smiley Centre for Children
Wood Green: Salvation Army Playgroup
Portsmouth: The Haven Nursery

United Kingdom Territory with the Republic of Ireland

Southsea: The Lighthouse Out of School Club
Worthing: Welcome In Pre-School
Southsea: The Salvation Army Noah's Ark
  Nursery
Ringwood: Sally Anne's Pre-School

Registered Settings (Non-OFSTED) -
Douglas (Isle of Man): Pre-School

*There are a further 6 Day Nurseries, 24
Pre-schools/Playgroups, 2 Crèches, 9 Out-of-
School Clubs and 8 Child Contact Centres
attached to social centres and corps.*

Domiciliary Care (elderly)
Community Care Service (Angus) Forfar

Drop-in Centres
Edinburgh: Regener8+
London: No 10 Drop In
Norwich: Pottergate Arc
Southampton: H2O Project

Employment Training Centre
Norwich, Norfolk

Outreach Teams
Bristol: Logos House, Bridge Project (acc 24)
Cardiff: Bus Project, Ty Gobaith
London: Faith House, King's Cross
York: Homeless Prevention/Resettlement,
  Gillygate

Prison Ministries
Prison Ministries Officer, THQ,
  101 Newington Causeway,
  London SE1 6BN; tel: (020) 7367 4866

Probation Hostel
Isle of Man: David Gray House (acc 9)

Red Shield Services
UK THQ: 101 Newington Causeway,
  London SE1 6BN; tel: (020) 7367 4851

Germany Regional Office: Arndt Strasse,
  Paderborn BFPO 22; tel: [49] (5251) 55763

Sheltered Housing
London: Alver Bank (acc single 6, double 2)
Tunbridge Wells: Charles Court (acc single 9,
  double 8)

Addiction Service
Bristol: Bridge Project (acc 24)
Cardiff: Bridge Project, Ty Gobiath, (acc 23)

Dublin: York House, Alcohol Recovery Unit
  (inc short-term intervention) (acc 80)
Highworth: Gloucester House (Residential
  Rehabilitation Centre), Swindon
  (acc 12, halfway house 3, day programme 5)
London: Greig House (acc 36)
  Riverside House 'Specialist' Homeless Centre
    for People with Addiction Issues
    (acc 31)
  Riverside House Harbour Recovery
    Project (inc detoxification)
    (acc 40)
Stirling: Harm Reduction Service,
  SA Hall, Drip Rd, FK8 1RA;
  tel: (01786) 448923

Offering Hope to Trafficked Women
The Jarrett Community c/o THQ

Biomedical Services
Biomedical Support Services are
  provided across social work disciplines in
  partnership with the University of Kent,
  Canterbury

THE UNITED STATES OF AMERICA

National leaders:
Commissioners David E. and Barbara Jeffrey

National Commander:
Commissioner David E. Jeffrey (14 Oct 2013)

National Chief Secretary:
Colonel Merle Heatwole (1 Oct 2014)

**National Headquarters: 615 Slaters Lane, PO Box 269,
Alexandria, VA 22313-0269, USA**

Tel: [1] (703) 684 5500

website: www.salvationarmyusa.org

The Salvation Army began its ministry in the United States in October 1879. Lieutenant Eliza Shirley left England to join her parents who had migrated to America in search of work. She held meetings that were so successful that General William Booth sent Commissioner George Scott Railton and seven women officers to the United States in March 1880 to formalise the effort. Their initial street meeting was held on the dockside at Battery Park in New York City the day they arrived.

In only three years, operations had expanded into California, Connecticut, Indiana, Kentucky, Maryland, Massachusetts, Michigan, Missouri, New Jersey, New York, Ohio and Pennsylvania. By 1902 The Salvation Army was operating throughout the United States. Family services, youth, elderly and disaster services are among the many programmes offered in local communities throughout the United States, in Puerto Rico, the Virgin Islands, the Marshall Islands and Guam.

The National Headquarters was incorporated as a religious and charitable corporation in the State of New Jersey in 1982 as 'The Salvation Army National Corporation' and is qualified to conduct its affairs in the Commonwealth of Virginia.

Zone: Americas and Caribbean
Periodicals: *The War Cry, Women's Ministries Resources, Word & Deed – A Journal of Theology and Ministry, Young Salvationist*

SALVATION Army services and programmes nationally reached more than 30 million Americans in 2013.

The new national leaders, Commissioners David and Barbara Jeffrey, were installed in October 2013.

Among the ways The Salvation Army National Headquarters serves a vital coordinating and supporting role in the USA is through the organisation and facilitation of key training and networking opportunities. During the year in review, five major seminars and conferences were conducted to strengthen the ministries across America and to provide a strong network of support among officers, employees and programmes.

The 65th National Brengle Institute was held in June 2013 with officers from partnering territories joining with national officers for study, prayer and meditation guided by the principals of the four USA training colleges and additional staff.

In summer 2013 The Salvation Army equipped thousands of children with essential school supplies. Additionally, The Salvation Army has several highly successful corporate partnerships.

Salvation Army Emergency Disaster Services teams served families, individuals and first responders at the scene of wildfires, floods, tornadoes and man-made disasters. In Oklahoma, The Salvation Army continues to provide long-term recovery for tornado survivors with food, financial assistance, emotional care and rebuilding efforts. Corporate and private supporters entrusted US$12 million in donations to Oklahoma relief efforts, some of which has been designated for recovery with a focus on permanent housing.

The 44th National Seminar on Evangelism was held in August in Colorado and continues to inspire soldiers and officers in the mission of saving souls and seeing them grow as saints through a personal commitment of shared faith and life.

In October a National Writers Conference inspired and guided a number of Salvationist writers, including participants from 12 other countries.

The Salvation Army's 123rd Red Kettle Campaign raised US$526.5 million and at the Dallas Cowboys' Thanksgiving Day game, National Advisory Board chairperson, Charlotte Jones Anderson, again promoted the Army's annual Red Kettle Kick-Off halftime show.

Walmart facilitated the collection of more than 135,000 toys and 10,000 coats from shoppers during the company's second annual 'Fill the Truck' event, benefiting The Salvation Army's toyshops.

In March 2014 the National Social Services Conference and Global Conversation was host to more than 850 delegates. Delegates were challenged to consider 'One Army' comprehensive solutions to international problems, how to serve suffering humanity on limited resources, and the transformation of people as disciples.

The National Community Relations and Development Conference in Indianapolis in April saw more than 600 officers and employees discuss public relations, fund-raising and community engagement.

2014 marks the 10th anniversary of the late Mrs Joan Kroc's historic donation to The Salvation Army of US$1.5 billion for the construction of 27 community centres around the nation. In April 2014, the 26th Kroc Corps Community Center was opened.

The Salvation Army is thankful for every Salvationist, employee, board member and partner in mission committed to 'Doing the Most Good' in the name of Jesus Christ.

NATIONAL STATISTICS
(incorporating all USA territories)

Officers 5,409 (active 3,398 retired 2,011)
  Cadets (1st Yr) 178 (2nd Yr) 165
  Employees 60,559
Corps 1,216 **Outposts** 16 **Institutions** 812
  Senior Soldiers 84,539 **Adherent Members** 16,748 **Junior Soldiers** 24,169

STATISTICS
(National Headquarters)
Officers (active) 21 **Employees** 82

STAFF

Women's Ministries: Comr Barbara Jeffrey (NPWM); tel: (703) 684 5503; Col Dawn Heatwole (NSWM, NRVAVS); tel: (703) 684 5514

Asst Nat Chief Sec: Maj Raymond Cooper III; tel: (703) 684 5514

Nat Treasurer and Nat Sec for Business Administration: Lt-Col Walter J. Fuge; tel: (703) 684 5507

Nat Sec for Personnel: Lt-Col Naomi R. Kelly; tel: (703) 684 5512

Nat Sec for Programme: Lt-Col David E. Kelly; tel: (703) 684 5527

Nat Social Services Sec: Lt-Col Ardis Fuge; tel: (703) 684 5521

Nat Community Relations and Development Sec: Lt-Col Ronald Busroe; tel: (703) 684 5526

Nat Director for White House Relations and Liaison for Emergency Disaster Services: Lt-Col Carol Busroe; tel: (703) 684 5508

Editor-in-Chief and Nat Literary Sec: Lt-Col Allen Satterlee; tel: (703) 684 5523;

The Salvation Army World Service Office (SAWSO): Lt-Col William Mockabee; tel: (703) 684 5510; Lt-Col Debra Mockabee; tel: (703) 299 5547

ARCHIVES AND RESEARCH CENTRE
Email: Archives@usn.salvationarmy.org

SALVATION ARMY STUDENT FELLOWSHIP/ASBURY UNIVERSITY
The Salvation Army Moulton Memorial Student Center, 402 West College Street, Wilmore, KY, 40390-1059; tel: (859) 858-3734

USA NATIONAL:Delegates to the National Seminar on Evangelism spend time in prayer

USA CENTRAL TERRITORY

Territorial leaders:
Commissioners Paul R. and Carol Seiler

Territorial Commander:
Commissioner Paul R. Seiler (1 May 2010)

Chief Secretary:
Colonel Jeffrey Smith (1 Oct 2014)

**Territorial Headquarters: 10 W Algonquin Rd, Des Plaines,
IL 60016-6006, USA**

Tel: [1] (847) 294-2000; website: www.usc.salvationarmy.org

The Salvation Army was incorporated as a religious and charitable corporation in the State of Illinois in 1913 as 'The Salvation Army' and is qualified to conduct its affairs in all of the states of the territory.

Zone: Americas and Caribbean
USA states included in the territory: Illinois, Indiana, Iowa, Kansas, Michigan, Minnesota, Missouri, Nebraska, North Dakota, South Dakota, Wisconsin
'The Salvation Army' in Spanish: Ejército de Salvación; in Swedish: Frälsningsarmén
Languages in which the gospel is preached: English, Korean, Laotian, Russian, Spanish, Swedish
Periodical: *Central Connection*

AS SALVATIONISTS focused on mission effectiveness, encouraging outcomes emerged from new initiatives such as 'STEP' (Strategic Tool to Engage Potential) – an initiative that involves more people in each corps' evaluation and planning process to identify the goals each year that will make the most difference

The territory was awarded US$4.8 million from Lilly Endowment Incorporated to further implement 'Pathway of Hope' – an initiative to break the cycle of intergenerational poverty – with the desire of doubling the impact of basic emergency social service assistance. As of April 2014,

this approach was being utilised in 145 corps with more than 455 families.

US$1.2 million in incentive grants was awarded through the Thomas Lyle Williams Fund to six programmes ranging from helping children with healthy nutrition choices to preparing inmates for successful assimilation back into society.

More than 3,600 Salvationists gathered in June 2013 for a family congress where the then General Linda Bond unpacked the International Vision Statement. Highlights included a massed singing company, the commissioning and ordination of 32 cadets, the participation of four young adult summer mission teams and the announcement of a record $8.1 million raised for World Services/Self-Denial.

In February 2014 the territory engaged the Lewis Pastoral Leadership Inventory to develop officers' leadership skills. To better recognise and promote the work of married women officers, the territory began pursuing policy changes from recommendations by the Married Women in Leadership committee. The territorial commander created the position of Ambassadors for Holiness and appointed Lieut-Colonels Daniel and Rebecca Sjögren to this new ministry.

The Ray and Joan Kroc Corps Community Center in Chicago received three National Phoenix Awards from the US Environmental Protection Agency for changing a brownfield site to a residential standard. The territory's five Kroc Centers used creative programmes and outreach to impact their communities and the Youth Assessment Development Initiative used by the Kroc Centers began to be used in corps.

'Safe from Harm' – a safety programme and territorial policy to protect children and vulnerable adults – introduced a new centralised structure, reporting process and training module for emergency disaster relief. Disaster Services also introduced a new training course in emotional and spiritual care. After the devastating typhoon in The Philippines, the territory initially sent US$100,000 and three relief personnel, one of whom taught Salvationists and members of other churches effective chaplaincy in disasters.

The USA Central Territory marked its largest Child Sponsorship giving year with sponsors contributing $131,762 in 2013 to more than 90 Salvation Army homes, schools and centres.

More than 1,000 men were encouraged to take a stand for Christ by Commissioner Israel L. Gaither at a conference in April 2014. Women's ministries continued to develop its social media presence with an updated website, Facebook and Pinterest pages and online video Bible studies.

STATISTICS

Officers 1,143 (active 709 retired 434) **Cadets** (1st Yr) 21 (2nd Yr) 14 **Employees** 11,965 **Corps** 257 **Institutions** 174 **Senior Soldiers** 16,271 **Adherent Members** 2,115 **Junior Soldiers** 3,469 **Personnel serving outside territory** Officers 27

STAFF

Women's Ministries: Comr Carol Seiler (TPWM) Col Dorothy R.Smith (TSWM) Lt-Col Rebecca Sjögren (TSWA)
Personnel: Lt-Col Ralph Bukiewicz
Programme: Lt-Col Paul D. Smith
Business: Lt-Col Richard Amick
Territorial Ambassador for Holiness: Lt-Col Daniel Sjögren
Adult Rehabilitation Centres: Maj Graham Allan
Audit: Maj Joyce M. Shiels
Candidates: Maj Patricia E. Taube
Community Care Ministries/Corps Mission and Adult Ministries: Maj Carol J. Wurtz
Community Relations and Development: Mr Douglas McDaniel
Corps Mission and Adult Ministries: Maj Carol J. Wurtz
Evangelism and Corps Growth: Ma Marie C. Poff
Finance: Maj E. Randall Polsley
Human Resources: Mr Eric Van Cleven
Information Technology: Mr Ronald E. Shoults

Legal: Mr Bramwell Higgins
Multicultural Ministries: Capt Enrique P.
Azuaje
Music and Gospel Arts: B/M William F.
Himes Jr, OF
Pastoral Care Officers: Majs Larry and Margo
Thorson
Property: Maj Cheryl Lawry
Resource Officer and Development:
Lt-Col Susan Bukiewicz
Resource Connection Dept: Mr Robert Jones
Retired Officers: Lt-Col Vicki Amick
Risk Management: Mr Wesley Carter
Social Services: Mrs Maribeth Velasquez
Swanson
Training: Maj Charmaine Hobbins
Volunteer Services: Mr Robert Bonesteel
World Missions: Mrs Chris Shay
Youth: Maj Monty B. Wandling

DIVISIONS
Eastern Michigan: 16130 Northland Dr,
Southfield, MI 48075-5218;
tel: (248) 443-5500; Lt-Cols John and Theresa
Turner
Heartland: 401 NE Adams St, Peoria,
IL 61603-4201; tel: (309) 655-7220;
Maj Kelly Collins
Indiana: 3100 N Meridian St, Indianapolis,
IN 46208-4718; tel: (317) 937-7000;
Majs Robert and Collette Webster
Kansas and Western Missouri: 3637 Broadway,
Kansas City, MO 64111-2503;
tel: (816) 756-1455;
Maj Evelyn Diaz
Metropolitan: 5040 N Pulaski Rd, Chicago,
IL 60630-2788; tel: (773) 725-1100;
Lt-Cols Charles and Sharon Smith
Midland: 1130 Hampton Ave, St Louis, MO
63139-3147; tel: (314) 646-3000;
Majs Lonneal and Patty Richardson
Northern: 2445 Prior Ave, Roseville,
MN 55113-2714; tel: (651) 746-3400;
Lt-Cols Robert E. and Nancy Thomson, Jr
Western: 3612 Cuming St, Omaha,
NE 68131-1900; tel: (402) 898-5900;
Majs W. Paul and Paula Fleeman
Western Michigan and Northern Indiana:
1215 E Fulton, Grand Rapids, MI 49503-3849;
tel: (616) 459-3433;
Majs Thomas and Jacalyn Bowers
Wisconsin and Upper Michigan: 11315 W
Watertown Plank Rd, Wauwatosa, WI
53226-0019; tel: (414) 302-4300;
Majs Dan and Dorene Jennings

COLLEGE FOR OFFICER TRAINING
700 W Brompton Ave, Chicago, IL 60657-1831;
tel: (773) 524-2000

UNDER THQ
Conference Centre
10 W Algonquin, Des Plaines, IL 60016-6006

SOCIAL SERVICES
Adult Rehabilitation Centres
Chicago (Central), IL 60654: 506 N Desplaines
St; tel: (312) 738-4367 (acc 206)
Chicago (North Side), IL 60614: 2258 N
Clybourn Ave; tel: (773) 477-1771 (acc 140)
Davenport (River Valley), IA 52809: 4001 N
Brady St; tel: (563) 323-2748 (acc 91)
Des Moines, IA 50309-4897: 133 E 2nd St;
tel: (515) 243-4277 (acc 58)
Flint, MI 48506: 2200 N Dort Highway;
tel: (810) 234-2678 (acc 121)
Fort Wayne, IN 46802: 427 W Washington Blvd;
tel: (260) 424-1655 (acc 80)
Gary, IN 46402: 1351 W 11th Ave;
tel: (219) 882-9377 (acc 110)
Grand Rapids, MI 49507-1601: 1491 S Division
Ave; tel: (616) 452-3133 (acc 115)
Indianapolis, IN 46202-3915: 711 E Washington
St; tel: (317) 638-6585 (acc 114)
Kansas City, MO 64106: 1351 E 10th St;
tel: (816) 421-5434 (acc 132)
Milwaukee, WI 53202-5904: 324 N Jackson St;
tel: (414) 276-4316 (acc 100)
Minneapolis, MN 55401-1039: 900 N 4th St;
tel: (612) 332-5855 (acc 125)
Omaha, NE 68131-2642: 2551 Dodge St;
tel: (402) 342-4135 (acc 95)
Rockford, IL 61104-7385: 1706 18th Ave;
tel: (815) 397-0440 (acc 72)
St Louis, MO 63108-3211: 3949 Forest Park
Ave; tel: (314) 535-0057 (acc 101)
South Bend, IN 46601-2226: 510-18 S Main St;
tel: (574) 288-2539 (acc 60)
Southeast, MI 1627: W Fort St, Detroit,
MI 48216; tel: (313) 965-7760; toll-free: 1-(800)
SA Truck (acc 360 men, 95 women)
Springfield, IL 62703-1003: 221 N 11th St;
tel: (217) 528-7573 (acc 85)
Waukegan, IL 60085-6511: 431 S Genesee St;
tel: (847) 662-7730 (acc 100)

UNDER DIVISIONS
Emergency Lodges
Alton, IL 62002: 525 Alby
Alton, IL 62002: 14-16 E 5th St

USA Central Territory

Ann Arbor, MI 48108: 3660 Packard Rd
Benton Harbor, MI 49022: 645 Pipestone St
Bloomington, IL 61701: 601 W Washington St
Champaign, IL 61820: 2212 N Market St
Chicago, IL 60640: 800 W Lawrence
Columbia, MO 65203: 602 N Ann St
Davenport, IA 52803-5101: 301-307 W 6th St
Decatur, IL 62523: 137 Church St
Detroit, MI 48208-2517: 3737 Lawton
Detroit, MI 48219: 20775 Pembroke
Grand Island, NE 68801-5828: 818 W 3rd St
Independence, MO 64050-2664: 14704 E Truman Rd
Indianapolis, IN 46204: 540 N Alabama St
Jefferson City, MO 65101: 907 Jefferson St
Kankakee, IL 60901: 148 N Harrison
Kankakee, IL 60901: 541 E Court Ave
LaCrosse, WI 54601: 223 N 8th St
Lafayette, IN 47904-1934: 1110 Union St
Madison, WI 53703: E 630 Washington Ave E
Mankato, MN 56001-2338: 700 S Riverfront Dr
Milwaukee, WI 53205: 1730 N 7th St
Monroe, MI 48161: 815 E 1st St
O'Fallon, MO 63366-2938: 1 William Booth Dr
Olathe, KS 66061: 400-402 E Santa Fe
Omaha, NE 68131: 3612 Cuming St
Peoria, IL 61603: 417 NE Adams St
Peoria, IL 61603: 414 NE Jefferson St
Quincy, IL 62301: 501 Broadway
Rockford, IL 61104: 1706 18th Ave E
St Cloud, MN 56304: 400 US Highway 10 W
St Joseph, MO 64501: 618 S 6th St
St Louis, MO 63132: 10740 W Page Ave
Sheboygan, WI 53081: 710 Pennsylvania Ave
Sioux Falls, SD 57103-0128: 800 N Cliff Ave
Somerset, WI 54025: 203 Church Hill Rd
Springfield, IL 62701: 100 N 9th St
Springfield, MO 65802: 636 N Boonville
Steven's Point, WI 54481: 824 Fremont
Warren, MI 48091: 24140 Mound Rd
Waterloo, IA 50703: 218 Logan Ave
Waterloo, IA 50703: 229 Logan Ave
Waterloo, IA 50703: 603 S Hanchett Rd
Waukesha, WI 53188: 445 Madison St
Wausau, WI 54401-4630: 113 S Second St

Senior Citizens' Residences

Chicago, IL 60607: 1500 W Madison
Columbus, IN 47201: 300 Gladstone Ave
Grandview, MO 64030: 6111 E 129th St
Indianapolis, IN 46254-2738: 4390 N High
  School Rd
Kansas City, KS 66112: 1331 N 75th St
Minneapolis, MN 55403-2116: 1421 Yale Pl
Oak Creek, WI 53154: 150 W Centennial Dr
Oak Creek, WI 53154: 180 W Centennial Dr

Omaha, NE 68131: 923 N 38th St
St Louis, MO 63118: 3133 Iowa St

Harbour Light Centres

Chicago, IL 60607: 1515 W Monroe St;
  tel: (312) 421-5753
Clinton Township, MI 48043: 42590 Stepnitz
Detroit, MI 48201: 3737 Lawton;
  tel. (313) 361-6136
Indianapolis, IN 46222: 2400 N Tibbs Ave;
  tel: (317) 972-1450
Kansas City, KS 66102: 6721 State Ave;
  tel: (913) 232-5400
Minneapolis, MN 55403: 1010 Currie Ave;
  tel: (612) 767-3100
Monroe, MI 48162: 3250 N Monroe
St Louis, MO 63188: 3010 Washington Ave

Substance Abuse Centres

Clinton Township, MI 48043: 42590 Stepnitz
Detroit, MI 48216: 3737 Lawton
Grand Rapids, MI 49503: 72 Sheldon Blvd SE
Kansas City, MO 64127: 5100 E 24th
Minneapolis, MN 55403: 1010 Currie Ave
Monroe, MI 48162: 3250 N Monroe

Transitional Housing

Appleton, WI 54914: 105 S Badger Ave
Champaign, IL 61820: 502 N Prospect
Cheboygan, MI 49712: 444 S Main St
Clinton Township, MI 48043: 42590 Stepnitz
Detroit, MI 48216: 3737 Lawton
Detroit, MI 48219: 20775 Pembroke
Duluth, MN 55806: 215 S 27th Ave W
Grand Haven, MI 49417: 310 N Despelder St.
Grand Island, NE 68801-5828: 818 W 3rd St.
Grand Rapids, MI 49503: 1215 E Fulton St
Green Bay, WI 54301: 626 Union Ct
Jefferson City, MO 65101: 907 Jefferson St
Joplin, MO 64801: 320 E 8th St
Kansas City, KS 66102: 6723 State Ave
Kansas City, MO 64111: 101 W Linwood Blvd
Minneapolis, MN 55403: 1010 Currie
Monroe, MI 48162: 3250 N Monroe
New Albany, IN 47151: 2300 Green Valley Rd
Olathe, KS 66061: 400 E Santa Fe
Omaha, NE 68131: 3612 Cuming St
Pekin, IL 61554: 243 Derby St
Pine Lawn, MO 63120: 4210 Peyton Ln
Rochester, MN 55906: 20 First Ave NE
Rockford, IL 61104: 416 S Madison
St Louis, MO 63132: 10740 Page Ave
St Paul, MN 55108: 1471 Como Ave W
Sioux Falls, SD 57103-0128; 800 N Cliff Ave
Springfield, MO 65802: 10740 W Chestnut Expy

Waterloo, IA 50703: 149 Argyle St
Wichita, KS 67202-2010: 350 Market

Child Day Care
Benton Harbor, MI; Chicago, IL (6 centres);
Kansas City, MO; Lansing, MI; Manitowoc,
WI; Maplewood, MN; Menasha, WI; Oak
Creek, WI; Olathe, KS; Pekin, IL; Peoria, IL;
Plymouth, MI; Sheboygan, WI; St. Paul, MN;
Topeka, KS

Emergency Shelter Care of Children
Kansas City, MO 64111: 101 W Linwood Blvd
North Platte, NE 69101: 704 S Welch Ave
Oak Park, IL 60302-1713: 924 N Austin
Wichita, KS 67202-2010: 350 N Market

Emergency Shelter of Young Adults
St Paul, MN 55108-2542: 1471 Como Ave W
Wichita, KS 67202-2010: 350 Market St

Head Start Programmes
Chicago, IL 60651: 4255 W Division
Chicago, IL 60651: 1345 N Karlov
Chicago, IL 60607: 1 N Ogden
Chicago, IL 60621: 945 W 69th St

Early Head Start
Chicago, IL 60608: 1321 S Paulina
Chicago, IL 60647: 5317 W Chicago Ave
Chicago, IL 60621: 945 W 69th St
Omaha, NE 68131: 3612 Cuming St.

Home (with facilities for unmarried mothers)
Grand Rapids, MI 49503: 1215 E Fulton St;
tel: (616) 459-9468 (teen-parent centre)

Latchkey Programmes
DeKalb, IL (2); Evanston, IL; Fort Wayne, IN;
Gary-Merrillville, IN; Huntington, IN; Huron,
SD; Indianapolis, IN; Jacksonville, IL; Newton,
IA; North Platte, NE; Pekin, IL; Royal Oak, MI;
Springfield, MO; Wyandotte, MI

Residential Services for Mentally Ill
Kansas City, MO 64111: 101 W Linwood Blvd
Omaha, NE 68108: 819 Dorcas St
Omaha, NE 68108: 415 South 25th St

Permanent and/or Supportive Housing
Coon Rapids, MN 55433: 10347 Ibis Ave
Indianapolis, IN 46204: Barton Center,
210 E Michigan St

Indianapolis, IN 46204: Carpenter Apartments,
222 E Michigan St
Jefferson City, MO 65101: 907 Jefferson St
Joplin, MO 64801: 320 E 8th St
Kansas City, KS 66102: 6723 State Ave
Kansas City, MO 64111: 101 W Linwood
Mankato, MN 56001: 324 Maxfield Place
Milwaukee, WI 53208: 3120 W Wisconsin Ave
Minneapolis, MN 55403: 53 Glenwood Ave
Omaha, NE: 3612 Cuming St
Rochester, MN 55906: 120 N Broadway
Somerset, WI 54025: 203 Church Hill Rd
St Louis, MO 63103: 205 N 18th St
St Louis, MO 63132: 10740 W Page Ave
St Paul, MN 55108: 1471 Como Ave W

Foster Care
Wichita, KS 67202: Koch Center, 350 N Marat

Medical/Dental Clinics
Grand Rapids, MI 49503: 1215 E Fulton St
Manitowoc, WI 54220: 411-415 N 6th St
Rochester, MN 55906: 120 N Broadway
Sheboygan, WI 53081: 710 Pennsylvania Ave

Legal Aid Clinic
Detroit, MI 48201: 3737 Lawton

In addition, fresh-air camps, youth centres, community centres, red shield clubs, day nurseries, family service and emergency relief bureaux are attached to corps and divisions. Veterans' services, including residential/transitional housing and supportive services are available in 8 centres including some Harbour Light facilities.

USA EASTERN TERRITORY

Territorial leaders:
**Commissioners Barry C. and
E. Sue Swanson**

Territorial Commander:
Commissioner Barry C. Swanson
(1 Feb 2013)

Chief Secretary:
Colonel William Bamford (1 Feb 2014)

**Territorial Headquarters: 440 West Nyack Road, PO Box C-635,
West Nyack, New York 10994-1739, USA**

Tel: [1] (845) 620-7200; website: www.salvationarmy-usaeast.org

The Salvation Army was incorporated as a religious and charitable corporation in the State of New York in 1899 as 'The Salvation Army' and is qualified to conduct its affairs in all of the states of the territory.

Zone: Americas and Caribbean

USA states included in the territory: Connecticut, Delaware, Kentucky, Maine, Massachusetts, New Hampshire, New Jersey, New York, Ohio, Pennsylvania, Rhode Island, Vermont

Other countries included in the territory: Puerto Rico, Virgin Islands

'The Salvation Army' in Korean: Koo Sei Kun; in Norwegian: Frelsesarmeen; in Spanish: Ejército de Salvación; in Swedish: Frälsningsarmén

Languages in which the gospel is preached: Creole, English, Korean, Laotian, Portuguese, Russian, Spanish, Swedish

Periodicals: *¡Buenas Noticias!* (Spanish), *Cristianos en Marcha* (Spanish), *Good News!* (English and Korean), *Priority!* (English), *Ven a Cristo Hoy* (Spanish)

IN APRIL 2013, the territory reached its 'Come Join Our Army' goal of 31,463 senior/junior soldiers.

The territory joined forces with Asbury University to provide laser focused learning for new officers pursuing a Bachelor of Science degree in ministry management with an emphasis on non-profit administration. In addition, in June 42 cadets from the Proclaimers of the Resurrection Session were commissioned and ordained, and in September 53 cadets were welcomed into the Heralds of Grace Session.

Commissioner Barry C. Swanson (TC) created a new Communications Department at territorial headquarters, combining the skills of dedicated employees from the former Literary Department (print) and Media Ministries Bureau (video and live events). A Social Media section has been added in order to connect people to the Lord through SAConnects.org, a new website, and Facebook and Twitter pages. This new initiative provides online readers with easy access to the territory's print, video and social media messages. The territorial leaders also launched their own Twitter and blog sites in an effort to establish wider and younger audiences. Commissioner Swanson used these technologies to share his vision for the territory, presented in the form of four strike points – deeper discipleship, skilled leadership, integrated urban–focused mission, and young adult empowerment. The commissioning weekend served as the launch for the multi-component ministry training initiative designed to equip and support officers and soldiers in developing themselves as leaders.

A conference organised by the Women's Ministries Department saw 2,000 women Salvationists come together to worship.

In March 2014, a gas–leak explosion levelled two buildings in East Harlem. The Manhattan Citadel Community Center was transformed into an official resident service centre and emergency shelter.

Good News! the territory's award-winning 'paper of record', celebrated 30 years of publication. Since 1984, it has reached over 31,000 readers monthly and many more online via its official website, Facebook and Twitter pages, and through its Spanish- and Korean-language versions.

Author and pastor Max Lucado

appeared at Centennial Memorial Temple in a programme that attracted 1,000 people and featured the ministries of The Salvation Army's Greater New York Youth Band and Chorus. Lucado partnered with National Headquarters, Thomas Nelson publishers and the Association of Christian Retail to reach one million disaster survivors through his book *You'll Get Through This: Hope and Help for Your Turbulent Times*

STATISTICS
Officers 1,650 (active 1,012 retired 638)
    Cadets 115 **Employees** 10,389
Corps 356 **Outposts** 2 **Institutions** 61
Senior Soldiers 22,471
    Adherent Members 8,454
    Junior Soldiers 9,212
Personnel serving outside territory Officers 31
    Layworker 1

STAFF
Women's Ministries: Comr Sue Swanson
    (TPWM) Col Lorraine Bamford (TSWM)
    Maj June Carver (TCCM, TWAS)
    Maj Inger Furman (OCS)
Asst Chief Sec: Col Janice Howard
Personnel: Col Steven M. Howard
Programme: Lt-Col Kenneth W. Maynor
Business: Lt-Col James W. Reynolds
Territorial Ambassador for Holiness:
    Maj Young Sung Kim
ARC Commander: Lt-Col Hubert S. Steele III
Audit: Maj Billie-Jeanne Whitaker
Candidates: Maj Thomas M. Lyle
Community Relations/Development:
    Maj George Polarek
Education: Maj Robin R. Lyle
Finance: Maj Glenn C. Bloomfield
Information Technology: Mr Paul Kelly
Legal: Maj Thomas A. Schenk
Literary: Mr Warren Maye
Mission and Culture: Maj Betty Pate
Music: B/M Ronald Waiksnoris
    New York Staff Band: B/M Ronald Waiksnoris
    Territorial Songsters: S/L Gavin Whitehouse
Officers' Services/Records: Maj Deborah K.
    Goforth
Pastoral Care: Maj David E. Antill
Property/Mission Expansion: Maj Jorge E. Diaz

Risk Management: Alastair Bate
Social Services: Maj James Foley
Supplies/Purchasing: Maj Ronald Lugiano
Training: Maj Ronald R. Foreman
Youth: Maj Philip Lloyd

DIVISIONS
Eastern Pennsylvania and Delaware:
701 N Broad St, Philadelphia, PA 19123;
tel: (215) 787-2800;
Lt-Cols Stephen and Janet Banfield
Empire State: 200 Twin Oaks Dr, PO Box 148,
Syracuse, NY 13206-0148; tel: (315) 434-1300;
Majs Donald D. and Arvilla Hostetler
Greater New York: 120 West 14th St, New
York, NY 10011-7393; tel: (212) 337-7200;
Lt-Cols Guy D. and Henrietta Klemanski
Massachusetts: 25 Shawmut Rd, Canton,
MA 02021; tel: (339) 502-5934;
Majs David B. and Margaret W. Davis
New Jersey: 4 Gary Rd, Union, NJ 07083-5598,
PO Box 3170, 07083; tel: (908) 851-9300;
Majs Donald and Vicki Berry
Northeast Ohio: 2507 E 22nd St, Cleveland, OH
44115-3202, PO Box 5847, 44101-0847;
tel: (216) 861-8185;
Majs Evan P. and Suzanne R. Hickman
Northern New England: 297 Cumberland Ave,
Portland, ME 04101, PO Box 3647, 04104;
tel: (207) 774-6304;
Majs James and Patricia LaBossiere
Puerto Rico and Virgin Islands: 1679 Ave
Ponce de León, San Juan PR 00909-1802,
PO Box 71523, 00936-8623; tel: (787) 999-7000;
Maj Jorge L. and Capt Limaris Marzan
Southern New England: 855 Asylum Ave,
Hartford, CT 06105, PO Box 628, 06142-0628;
tel: (860) 543-8400;
Majs David A. and Eunice M. Champlin
Southwest Ohio and Northeast Kentucky:
114 E Central Parkway, Cincinnati, OH 45202,
PO Box 596, 45201; tel: (513) 762-5600;
Majs Larry and Janet Ashcraft
Western Pennsylvania: 700 N Bell Ave,
PO Box 742, Carnegie, PA 15106;
tel: (412) 446-1500;
Majs William H. and Joan I. Bode

COLLEGE FOR OFFICER TRAINING
201 Lafayette Ave, Suffern, NY 10901-4798;
tel: (845) 357-3501

THE SALVATION ARMY
RETIREMENT COMMUNITY
1400 Webb St, Asbury Park, NJ 07712;
tel: (732) 775-2200; John Coolican
(Residence Manager) (acc 32)

SOCIAL SERVICES
Adult Rehabilitation Centres*
Akron, OH 44311: 1006 Grant St, PO Box 1743;
tel: (330) 773-3331 (acc 83)
Albany, NY 12206: 452 Clinton Ave,
tel: (518) 465-2416 (acc 90)
Altoona, PA 16602: 200 7th Ave,
PO Box 1405, 16603;
tel: (814) 946-3645 (acc 39)
Binghamton, NY 13904: 3-5 Griswold St;
tel: (607) 723-5381 (acc 62)
Boston (Saugus), MA 01906: 209 Broadway
Rte 1; tel: (781) 231-0803 (acc 125*)
Bridgeport CT 06607: 1313 Connecticut Ave; tel:
(203) 367-8621 (acc 50)
Brockton, MA 02301: 281 N Main St;
tel: (508) 586-1187 (acc 56)
Brooklyn, NY 11217: 62 Hanson Pl;
tel: (718) 622-7166 (acc 136)
Buffalo, NY 14217-2587: 1080 Military Rd,
PO Box 36, 14217-0036; tel: (716) 875-2533
(acc 90)
Cincinnati, OH 45212: 2250 Park Ave,
PO Box 12546, Norwood, OH 45212-0546;
tel: (513) 351-3457 (acc 150)
Cleveland, OH 44103: 5005 Euclid Ave;
tel: (216) 881-2625 (acc 159)
Columbus, OH 43207: 1675 S High St;
tel: (614) 221-4269 (acc 122)
Dayton, OH 45402: 913 S Patterson Blvd;
tel: (937) 461-2769 (acc 74*)
Erie, PA 16501: 1209 Sassafras St, PO Box 6176,
16512; tel: (814) 456-4237 (acc 50)
Harrisburg, PA 17110: 3650 Vartan Way,
PO Box 60095, 17106-0095;
tel: (717) 541-0203 (acc 100*)
Hartford, CT 06132: 333 Homestead Ave,
tel: (860) 527-8106 (acc 110*)
Hempstead, NY 11550: 194 Front St;
tel: (516) 481-7600 (acc 100)
Jersey City, NJ 07302: 248 Erie St; PO Box 261
07310; tel: (201) 653-3071 (acc 75)
Mount Vernon, NY 10550: 745 S Third Ave;
tel: (914) 664-0800 (acc 80)
Newark, NJ 07101: 65 Pennington St, PO Box 815;
tel: (973) 589-0370 (acc 125)
New Haven, CT 06511: 301 George St; tel: (203)
865-0511 (acc 45)
New York, NY 10036: 535 W 48th St;
tel: (212) 757-7745 (acc 140*)
Paterson, NJ 07505: 31 Van Houten St,
PO Box 1976, 07509; tel: (973) 742-1126 (acc 89)
Philadelphia, PA 19128: 4555 Pechin St;
PO Box 26099, tel: (215) 483-3340 (acc 138*)
Pittsburgh, PA 15203: 44 S 9th St;
tel: (412) 481-7900 (acc 127)

Portland, ME 04101: 30 Warren Ave, PO Box
1298, 04104; tel: (207) 878-8555 (acc 70)
Poughkeepsie, NY 12601: 570 Main St;
tel: (845) 471-1730 (acc 50)
Providence, RI 02906: 201 Pitman St;
tel: (401) 421-5270 (acc 129*)
Rochester, NY 14611: 745 West Ave;
tel: (585) 235-0020 (acc 135*)
San Juan, PR 00903: ARC, Fernández Juncos Ave,
cnr of Valdés #104, Puerta de Tierra,
PO Box 13814, 00908; tel: (787) 724-2525 (acc 36)
Scranton, PA 18505: 610 S Washington Ave,
PO Box 3064; tel: (570) 346-0007 (acc 62)
Springfield, MA 01104: 327 Liberty St,
PO Box 1569, 01101-1569;
tel: (413) 785-1921 (acc 70)
Syracuse, NY 13224: 2433 Erie Blvd East;
tel: (315) 445-0520 (acc 100*)
Toledo, OH 43602: 27 Moorish Ave,
PO Box 355 43697; tel: (419) 241-8231 (acc 60)
Trenton, NJ 08638: 436 Mulberry St,
PO Box 5011; tel: (609) 599-9801 (acc 86)
Wilkes-Barre, PA 18702: PO Box 728,
18703-0728; tel: (570) 822-4248 (acc 60)
Wilmington, DE 19801: 107 S Market St;
tel: (302) 654-8808 (acc 81*)
Worcester, MA 01603: 72 Cambridge St;
tel: (508) 799-0520 (acc 115*)

includes facilities for women

ATTACHED TO DIVISIONS
Adult Day Care
Buffalo, NY 14202: Golden Age Centre,
Day Program for Senior Citizens,
960 Main St; tel: (716) 883-9800
Lancaster, OH 43130: 228 W. Hubert Ave,
tel: (740) 687-1921, ext 111 (acc 50)
Syracuse, NY 13202: 749 S Warren St;
tel: (315) 479-1309

Extended In-home Service for the Elderly
Syracuse, NY 13202: 749 S Warren St;
tel: (315) 479-1309

Anti-Human Trafficking
Cincinnati, OH 45202: 131 E 12th St. PO Box
238 hotline tel: (513) 800-1863
Columbus, OH 45206: 966 Main St
hotline tel: (614) 285-4357
Philadelphia, PA 19131: 4050 Conshohocken
Ave; tel: (215) 717-1195
Portland, ME 04104: 297 Cumberland Ave;
tel: (207) 774-4172

Day Care Centres
Akron, OH 44303: 135 Hall St;
tel: (330) 762-8177 (acc 74)

Boston, MA 02124: 26 Wales St;
tel: (617) 436-2480 (acc 70)
Bronx, NY 10451: 425 E 159th St;
tel: (718) 742-2346 (acc 45)
Bronx, NY 10457: 2121 Washington Ave;
tel: (718) 563-1530 (acc 69)
Brooklyn, NY 11212: 280 Riverdale Ave;
tel: (718) 345-2488 (acc 100)
Brooklyn, NY 11216: 110 Kosciusko St;
tel: (718) 857-7264 (acc 39)
Brooklyn, NY 11221: 1151 Bushwick Ave;
tel: (718) 455-0100 (acc 55)
Cambridge, MA 02139: 402 Massachusetts Ave,
PO Box 390647; tel: (617) 547-3400 (acc 46)
Cincinnati, OH 45202: 3501 Warsaw Ave;
tel: (513) 251-1451 (acc 112)
Danbury, CT 06813-0826: 15 Foster St,
PO Box 826; tel: (203) 792-7505 (acc 30)
Hartford, CT 06105: 121-123 Sigourney St;
tel: (860) 543-8488
Hartford, CT 06120: 100 Nelson St;
tel: (860) 543-8419
Jersey City, NJ 07034: 562 Bergen Ave,
PO Box 4237, Bergen Stn;
tel: (201) 435-7355 (acc 70)
Lexington, KY 40508: 736 W Main St;
tel: (859) 252-7709 (acc 80)
Meriden, CT 06450-0234: 23 St Casimir Dr,
PO Box 234; tel: (203) 235-6532 (acc 27)
Morristown, NJ 07960: 95 Spring St,
PO Box 9150; tel: (973) 538-0543 (acc 95)
Philadelphia (Kroc), PA 19129: 4200
Wissahickon Ave; tel: (215) 717-1200 (acc 78)
Syracuse, NY 13202:
677 S Salina St; Cab Horse Commons,
tel: (315) 479-1113
South Salina Street Infant Care Center,
tel: (315) 479-1329;
749 S Warren St; School Age Day Care,
Cab Horse Commons, tel: (315) 479-1334
Wilmington, DE 19899: 107 W 4th St;
tel: (302) 472-0712 (acc 110)

Family Centres
Dorchester, MA 02125: The Salvation Army
Ray and Joan Kroc Corps Community Center,
650 Dudley Street; tel: (617) 318-6900
Johnstown, PA 15901: The Salvation Army
Dental Center, 647 Main Street;
tel: (814) 262-8500
Newark, NJ 07102: Newark Area Services
45 Central Ave Kinship Care and Legal
Guardianship, Grand Family Success Center,
tel: (973) 375-5933
Oil City, PA 16301: The Salvation Army
Dental Center, 217 Sycamore St;
tel: (814) 677-4056

Development Disabilities Services

Beaver Falls, PA 15010: Friendship Homes
Program for Developmentally Disabled,
414 16th St; tel: (724) 846-2330

Bronx, NY 10457: Topping Ave Residence,
1638-1640 Topping Ave; tel: (718) 466-1567
(acc 8)

Brooklyn, NY 11220: Centennial House,
426 56th St; tel: (718) 492-4415 (acc 9)

Brooklyn, NY 11237: Decade House,
315 Covert St; tel: (718) 417-1583 (acc 10)

Brooklyn, NY 11206: Millennium House,
13 Pulaski St; tel: (718) 222-0736 (acc 8)

Glendale, NY 11385: Glendale House,
71-29 70th St; tel: (718) 381-7329 (acc 10)

Jamaica, NY 11423: Family Care,
90-23 161st St; tel: (718) 206-9171 (acc 16)

Philadelphia, PA 19123: Developmental
Disabilities Program, 701 N Broad St,
Administrative Offices; tel: (215) 787-2804
(community homes 45, acc 101)

South Ozone Park, NY 11420: Hope House, 115-
37 133rd St; tel: (718) 322-1616 (acc 9)

Springfield, OH 45501: Hand N'Hand Activity
Center for Adults with Disabilities,
15 S Plum St; tel: (937) 322-3434

St Albans, NY 11412: Pioneer House, 104-14
186th St; tel: (718) 264-8350 (acc 12)

Evangeline Residence

New York, NY 10011: 123 W 13th St (Markle
Memorial Residence); tel: (212) 242-2400

Family Counselling

Buffalo, NY 14202: Emergency Family Assistance,
Supervised Visitation Program; Conflict
Resolution/Anger Management Program;
960 Main St; tel: (716) 883-9800

Pittsburgh, PA 15206: Family Caring Center,
6017 Broad St; tel: (412) 362-0891

Rochester, NY 14604-4310: Rochester
Emergency and Family Services, 70 Liberty
Pole Way, PO Box 41210;
tel: (585) 987-9540

San Juan, PR 00921-2118: Family Services for
Victims of Crime, 1679 Ave Ponce de León,
00909-1802, PO Box 10601, 00922-0601;
tel: (787) 919-0701

Syracuse, NY 13202: Family Services,
749 S Warren St; tel: (315) 479-1369
Family Place Visitation Center, 350 Rich St;
tel: (315) 474-2931

Foster Home Services

Allentown, PA 18109: Foster Care In-Home
Placement Services, Adoption Services and
Administrative Services, 425 Allentown Dr,
Suite 1; tel: (610) 821-7706

Group Home for Adolescents

Fall River, MA 02720: Gentle Arms of Jesus Teen
Living Center, 429 Winter St;
tel: (508) 324-4558 (acc 15)

Harbour Light Centres

Cleveland, OH 44115-2376: Harbor Light
Complex, 1710 Prospect Ave;
tel: (216) 781-3773 (acc 221)

Pittsburgh, PA 15233: 865 W North Ave;
tel: (412) 231-0500 (acc 50)

Hotels, Lodges, Emergency Homes

Akron, OH 44302: Booth Manor Emergency
Lodge, 216 S Maple St; tel: (330) 762-8481 ext
1113 (acc 62)

Allentown, PA 18102: Hospitality House,
344 N 7th St; tel: (610) 432-0128 (acc 65)

Bellaire, OH 43906: 315 37th St;
tel: (740) 676-6810 (acc 40)

Brooklyn, NY 11203: Kingsboro Men's Shelter,
681 Clarkson Ave; tel: (718) 363-7738 (acc 126)

Bronx, NY 10456: Franklin Women's Shelter and
Referral, 1122 Franklin Ave;
tel: (347) 417-8240 (acc 200)

Buffalo, NY 14202: 960 Main St, Emergency
Family Shelter; tel: (716) 884-4798 (acc 77)

Cambridge, MA 02139-0008: Day Drop-in Shelter
for Men and Women/Night Shelter for Men,
402 Mass Ave, PO Box 390647;
tel: (617) 547-3400 (acc 200/50)

Carlisle, PA 17013: Genesis House (Men's
Emergency Housing), 24 E Pomfret St;
tel: (717) 249-1411

Chester, PA 19013: Warming Center,
151 W 15th St; tel: (610) 874-0423 (acc 35)

Cincinnati, OH 45210: Emergency Shelter,
131 E 12th St, PO Box 238;
tel: (513) 762-5655 (acc 24)

Cleveland, OH 44115: Zelma George Family
Shelter, 1710 Prospect Ave;
tel: (216) 641-3712 (acc 110)

Concord, NH 03301: McKenna House (Adult
Shelter), 100 S Fruit St; tel: (603) 228-3505
(acc 26)

East Stroudsburg, PA 18301: 226 Washington St;
tel: (570) 421-3050

Elizabeth, NJ 07201: 1018 E Grand St;
tel: (908) 352-2886 (acc 45)

Elmira, NY 14902: 414 Lake St;
tel: (607) 732-0314 (24-hour Domestic
Violence Hotline); Victims of Domestic
Violence Safe House (acc 25)

Australia: Help is offered following the devastation by bushfires in New South Wales (above); **Moldova:** Another day of service and ministry for a corps officer (below)

(clockwise from l) **USA Western: Commissioner James Knaggs addressing the congregation during a commissioning weekend; Japan: Mother and baby group in Tohoku Division; Australia: General André Cox ar Commissioner Silvia Cox with General Eva Burrows (R); Norway: Queen Sonja of Norway visits Jobben, a place that provides work training for those who have been addicted to drugs; Finland: Young Salvationists take part ir 'Museum Day', part of the 125 anniversary celebrations**

(clockwise from top l) **Chile:** General André Cox and Commissioner Silvia Cox are greeted at the airport; **Tanzania:** Salvationists take part in a march of witness; **Tanzania:** Officers conducting an open-air meeting at the Jerusalem Outpost, Tarime; **India:** Women taking part in a rally for women's day; **Rwanda and Burundi:** Junior home league members and youth following rallies

(clockwise from top l) **Philippines: Help is offered following a typhoon; Tonga: Children being cared for by the Army following a cyclone; Kenya: Commissioner Silvia Cox planting a tree; Papua New Guinea: World Day of Prayer participants; Jordan: Syrian refugee relief programme**

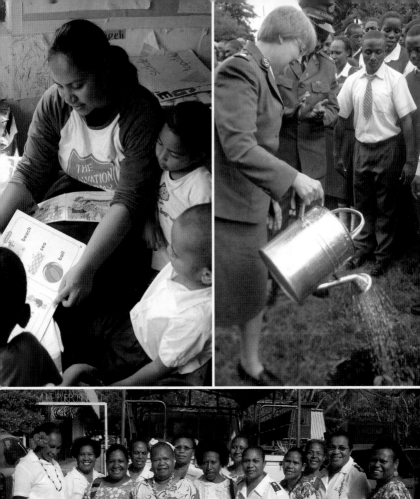

(above) **Southern Africa: Joyful Salvationists on the march; Singapore: Salvationists praying for their new leaders during the installation** (above l); **Sri Lanka: Ja___ Safe Water and Livelihood Project in Polonnaruwa District** (above r)

Hartford, CT 06105: 225 S Marshall St;
Family Shelter; tel: (860) 543-8423
Emergency Shelter; tel: (860) 543-8430

Jamaica, NY 11434: Springfield Family
Residence, 145-80 Guy R. Brewer Blvd;
tel: (718) 521-5090 (acc families 82)

Jamestown, NY 14702: Anew Center: Domestic
and Rape Crisis Programs, PO Box 368;
tel: (716) 661-3894;
24-hour Hotline tel: (800) 252-8748 (acc 13)

Laconia, NH 03246: The Carey House,
6 Spring St; tel: (603) 528-8086 (acc 30)

Lexington, KY 40508: W. Arnold Hanger
Emergency Lodge, 736 W Main St;
tel: (859) 252-7706 (acc 129)

Montclair, NJ 07042-2776: 68 N Fullerton Ave;
tel: (973) 744-8666 (acc 18)

Newark, OH 43055: 250 E Main St;
tel: (740) 345-3289 (acc 60)

New Britain, CT 06050: 78 Franklin Sq;
tel: (860) 225-8491 (acc 25 men)

Norristown, PA 19404: 533 Swede St;
tel: (610) 275-9225 (acc 41)

Northport, NY 11768-0039: Northport Veterans'
Residence, 79 Middleville Rd, Bldg 11,
PO Box 300; tel: (631) 262-0601 (acc 41)

Perth Amboy, NJ 08862-0613:
Seasonal Shelter for Men, 433 State St;
tel: (732) 826-7040 (acc 20)

Philadelphia, PA 19107: Eliza Shirley House,
1320 Arch St; tel: (215) 568-5111 (acc 125)

Philadelphia, PA 19123: Red Shield Family
Residence, 715 N Broad St;
tel: (215) 787-2887 (acc 100)

Pittsburgh, PA 15206: Family Caring Center,
6017 Broad St; tel: (412) 362-0891 (acc 40)

Pottstown, PA 19464: Lessig-Booth Family
Residence, 137 King St; tel: (610) 327-0836
(acc 32)

Queens (Jamaica), NY 11435: Briarwood Family
Residence, 80-20 134th St; tel: (718) 268-3395
(acc 91)

Rochester, NY 14604-4310: Booth Haven Men's
Emergency Shelter, 84 Liberty Pole Way,
PO Box 41210; tel: (585) 987-9540 (acc 39)
Hope House Women's Emergency Shelter,
100 West Ave, PO Box 41210; Rochester, NY
14611
tel: (585) 697-3430 (acc 24)
Safe Haven Shelter for Chronically Homeless
Men, 60 Liberty Pole Way, PO Box 41210;
tel: (585) 987-9540 (acc 54)

San Juan, PR 00903: Homeless Shelter, Proyecto
Esperanza, Fernández Juncos,
cnr Valdés; tel: (787) 722-2370

Schenectady, NY 12305: Evangeline Booth

Home and Women's Shelter, 168 Lafayette St;
tel: (518) 370-0276 (acc 17)

Syracuse, NY 13202:
Parenting Center, 667 S Salina St;
tel: (315) 479-1330 (acc 30)
Emergency Lodge, 749 S Warren St;
tel: (315) 479-1332

Trenton, NJ 08601: Homeless Drop-in Center,
575 E State St; tel: (609) 599-9373

Waterbury, CT 06720: 74 Central Ave;
tel: (203) 756-1718

Wilmington, DE 19899: Booth Social Service
Center, 104 W 5th St; tel: (302) 472-0764
(acc 52)

Wooster, OH 44691: 24-Hour Open Door
Emergency Shelter, 433 S Market St;
tel: (330) 264-4704 (acc 44)

Zanesville, OH 43701: 515 Putnam Ave;
tel: (740) 452-8350 (acc 35)

HIV Services

Bronx, NY 10458: 601 Crescent Ave;
tel: (718) 329-5410

Newark, NJ 07102: 45 Central Ave;
tel: (973) 623-5959

New York, NY 10003: 30 East 20th St
tel: (718) 329-5410

Homeless Youth and Runaways

Rochester, NY 14611: Genesis House,
35 Ardmore St, PO Box 41210;
tel: (585) 235-2600 (acc 14)

Syracuse, NY 13205: Barnabas House,
1912 S Salina St; tel: (315) 475-9774
(acc 11)
Booth House and Host Home, 3624 Midland
Ave; tel: (315) 471-7628 (acc 8)

Transitional Housing Programme

Allentown, PA 18101; Fleming Permanent
Housing, 344 N 7th St; tel: (610) 432-0128

Arlington, MA 02474-6597: Wellington House,
6510, 8 Wellington St (Single Resident
Occupancy); tel: (781) 643-8120 (acc 20)

Carlisle, PA 17013; Stuart House, 20 E Pomfret St;
tel: (717) 249-1411 (acc 41)

Cleveland, OH 44103: Railton House, 6000
Woodland; tel: (216) 361-6778 (acc 56)

Cleveland, OH 44115: Pass Programme, 1710
Prospect Ave; tel: (216) 619-4722 (acc 75)
Project Share, 2501 E 22nd St;
tel: (216) 623-7492 (acc 29)

Lancaster, PA 17603: 131 South Queen St;
tel: (717) 397-7565 (acc 21)

Norristown, PA 19404; Faith and Bridge Programs,

533 Swede St; tel: (610) 275-4183

Perth Amboy, NJ 08862-0613: Care House Transitional Residence, 433 State St; tel: (732) 293-1400 (acc veterans 11, homeless men 7)

Philadelphia, PA 19147: Reed House Permanent Housing, 1320 S 32nd St; tel: (215) 755-6789 (acc 66)

Philadelphia, PA 19123: Shelter Plus Care Program Permanent Housing, tel: (215) 787-2978 (acc 60)

Pottstown, PA 19464: Transitional Housing, 137 King St; tel: (610) 326-1621

Syracuse, NY 13205:
Transitional Family Apartments, 1482 S State St; tel: (315) 475-7663 (acc 10)
Transitional Living Project Apartments (youth), 1941 S Salina St; tel: (315) 475-9744 (acc 10)

Women's Shelter, 1704 S Salina St; tel: (315) 472-0947

West Chester, PA 19380: William Booth Initiative, 101 E Market St; tel: (610) 696-8746 (acc 7)

Wilkes Barre, PA 18703: Kirby House; 17 S Pennsylvania Ave; tel: (570) 824-8741

Senior Citizens' Residences

Cincinnati, OH 45224: Booth Residence for the Elderly and Handicapped, 6000 Townvista Dr; tel: (513) 242-4482 (acc 150)

New York, NY 10025: Williams Residence, 720 West End Ave; tel: (212) 316-6000

Philadelphia, PA 19139: Booth Manor, 5522 Arch St; tel: (215) 471-0500 (acc 105)

Philadelphia, PA 19131: Ivy Residence, 4051 Ford Rd; tel: (215) 871-3303 (acc 140)

USA EASTERN: A young boy enjoys a one-on-one game of basketball at the local Salvation Army

USA SOUTHERN TERRITORY

Territorial leaders:
Commissioners Donald C and Debora K. Bell

Territorial Commander:
Commissioner Donald C. Bell (1 Nov2013)

Chief Secretary:
Colonel F. Bradford Bailey (1 Sept 2012)

Territorial Headquarters: 1424 Northeast Expressway, Atlanta, GA 30329-2088, USA

Tel: [1] (404) 728 1300; website: www.salvationarmysouth.org

The Salvation Army was incorporated as a religious and charitable corporation in the State of Georgia in 1927 as 'The Salvation Army' and is qualified to conduct all its affairs in all of the states of the territory.

Zone: Americas and Caribbean
USA states included in the territory: Alabama, Arkansas, Florida, Georgia, Kentucky, Louisiana, Maryland, Mississippi, North Carolina, Oklahoma, South Carolina, Tennessee, Texas, Virginia, West Virginia, District of Columbia
Languages in which the gospel is preached: English, Haitian-Creole, Korean, Laotian, Spanish, Vietnamese
Periodical: *Southern Spirit*

THE USA Southern Territory Emergency Disaster Services personnel responded immediately by providing food, water and emotional and spiritual care to survivors when deadly tornadoes ravaged central Oklahoma. Thanks to generous support from the American public, corporate donors and philanthropic organisations, The Salvation Army raised over US$18 million for response and long-term recovery efforts.

In June 2013 the commissioning and ordination of the Proclaimers of the Resurrection Session of cadets took place under the leadership of the then National Commander, Commissioner William Roberts and Commissioner Nancy Roberts (NPWM).

Three Salvationist service corps teams, with a combined total of 19 members, proclaimed the gospel and met human needs during their deployments to Ukraine, Haiti, and the US southern states for a six-week period in June and July. The annual territorial music and youth institutes impacted Salvationist youth and young adults during late July and early August with special guest Staff Bandmaster Olaf Ritman of the Amsterdam Staff Band (The Netherlands and Czech Republic Territory).

The 2013 Territorial Bible Conference had as its theme 'Knowing Jesus from the Beginning', with guest speakers Commissioners Israel L. and Eva Gaither, Commissioners Kenneth and Jolene Hodder (TC/TPWM, Kenya West Territory), Dr Victor Hamilton (Asbury University), Mr Oscar Roan and Christian artist Joe Castillo.

In early September the territory publically welcomed 60 cadets into the Heralds of Grace Session at Evangeline Booth College and in the same meeting farewell tributes were shared with the then territorial leaders, Commissioners David and Barbara Jeffrey. The new territorial leaders, Commissioners Donald and Debora Bell, were welcomed in January 2014.

In January harsh winter storms crippled much of central and north Georgia and neighbouring states with ice-impacted roads. The Emergency Disaster Services team made an effort to assist stranded drivers with hot drinks, snacks and a welcoming smile at freeway exits and an extensive response was carried out in east Georgia where long-term power outages occurred.

In February, The Salvation Army's first regular news service *Salvation Army Today* increased its output following growth in worldwide viewing, an increased demand for Army news, and the availability of news items for broadcast.

Florida became the host division for the National Social Services and Disaster Services Management Conference in March, where more than 700 delegates and staff attended including more than 200 international guests who participated in a Global Conversation coordinated by IHQ. During the opening plenary session, Mr Eric Holm (a member of the National Advisory Board) was presented with the William Booth Award for his voluntary work of 21 years with The Salvation Army. General André Cox and Commissioner Silvia Cox (WPWM) and Commissioner Nancy Roberts (WSWM) were present.

Divisional youth councils weekends were held in March and April with the themes 'Live Right' and 'Holiness'. Teens and young adults gathered all across the territory in praise and thanks to God, with many making life-changing decisions including those who answered the call of God to become Salvation Army officers.

STATISTICS

Officers 1,454 (active 947 retired 507) **Cadets** (1st Yr) 60 (2nd Yr) 31 **Employees** 20,563 **Corps** 342 **Societies/Outposts** 19 **Institutions** 284 **Senior Soldiers** 29,048 **Adherent Members** 2,326 **Junior Soldiers** 6,686 **Personnel serving outside territory** Officers 28

STAFF

Women's Ministries: Comr Debora K. Bell (TPWM) Col Heidi Bailey (TSWM) Maj Susan Ellis (CCMS/Outreach)
Personnel: Lt-Col John Needham
Programme: Lt-Col Kelly Igleheart
Business: Lt-Col Samuel A. Henry
Adult Rehabilitation Centres Command: Lt-Col Mark Bell
Audit: Maj Beatrice Boalt
Community Relations and Development: Maj John Carter
Evangelism and Adult Ministries: Maj Otis Childs
Employee Relations: Maj Annette Dodd
Finance: Maj Stephen Ellis
Information Technology: Mr Clarence White
Legal: Maj Larry Broome
Multicultural Ministries: Maj Vivian Childs
Music: Mr Nicholas Simmons-Smith

Officers' Health Services: Maj Jeanne Johnson
Property: Mr Robert L. Taylor
Retired Officers: Maj Karen Carter
Risk Management: Maj James Rickard
Social Services: Maj Bruce Smith
Supplies and Purchasing: Mr Jeremy Rowland
Training: Maj Dean Hinson
Youth: Maj Bobby Westmoreland
Candidates: Capt Dan Nelson

DIVISIONS

Alabama-Louisiana-Mississippi: 1450 Riverside Dr, PO Box 4857, 39296-4857, Jackson, MS 39202; tel: (601) 969 7560; Majs Ronnie L. and Sharon L. Raymer

Arkansas and Oklahoma: Broadway Executive Park 5, 6601 N Broadway Ext, Suite 300, PO Box 12600, 73157, Oklahoma City, OK 73116 tel: (405) 840 0735; Majs Stephen P. and Wendy J. Morris

Florida: 5631 Van Dyke Rd, Lutz, FL 33558, PO Box 270848, 33688-0848, Tampa, FL; tel: (813) 962 6611; Cols Kenneth O. and Paula J. Johnson

Georgia: 1000 Center Pl, NW, 30093, PO Box 930188, 30003 Norcross, GA 30003; tel: (770) 441-6200; Majs James E. and Linda Arrowood

Kentucky and Tennessee: 214-216 W Chestnut St, Box 2229, 40201-2229, Lt-Cols Mark and Carolee Israel

Maryland and West Virginia: 814 Light St, Baltimore, MD 21230; tel: (410) 347 9944; Majs Charles and Paula Powell

National Capital and Virginia: 2626 Pennsylvania Ave NW, PO Box 18658, Washington, DC 20037; tel: (202) 756 2600; Lt-Cols John R. and Arduth Jones

North and South Carolina: 501 Archdale Dr, PO Box 241808, 28224-1808, Charlotte, NC 28217-4237; tel: (704) 522 4970; Lt-Cols James K. and Karol J. Seiler

Texas: 6500 Harry Hines Blvd, PO Box 36607, 75235, Dallas, TX 75235; tel: (214) 956 6000; Lt-Cols Kenneth and Dawn Luyk

SCHOOL FOR OFFICER TRAINING

1032 Metropolitan Pkwy, SW Atlanta, GA 30310; tel: (404) 753 4166

ATTACHED TO DIVISIONS

Alcohol and Drug Addiction Rehabilitation

Fort Worth, TX 76103: 1855 E Lancaster (women only, acc 13)
Greenville, SC 29609: 417 Rutherford St (acc 40)
Mobile, AL 36604: 1009 Dauphin St (acc 30)

Child Care Centres

Austin, TX 78767: 4523 Tannehill Hill (acc 26)
Freeport, TX 77541-2620: 1618 Ave J (acc 85)
Jacksonville, FL 32202: 318 N Ocean St (acc 125)
Lakeland, FL 33801: 835 N Kentucky (acc 45)
Naples, FL 34104: 3180 Estey Ave (acc 124)
Nashville, TN 37207: 631 Dickerson Rd (acc 37)

Children's Residential Care

Birmingham, AL 35212: Youth Emergency Services, 6001 Crestwood Blvd (acc 33)
St Petersburg, FL 33733: Children's Village, PO Drawer 10909 (acc 24)
St Petersburg, FL 33733: Sallie House Group Home, PO Drawer 10909 (acc 18)

Family Resident Programme

Aiken, SC 29801: 604 Park Ave (acc 32)
Albany, GA 31721: 304 W 2nd Ave (acc 41)
Amarillo, TX 79101: 400 S Harrison (acc 40)
Anderson, SC 29624: 106 Tolly St (acc 30)
Arlington, TX 76013: 711 W Border (acc 30)
Asheville, NC 28801: 204 Haywood St (acc 59)
Athens, GA 30606: 484 Hawthorne Ave (acc 52)
Atlanta, GA 30313: 469 Marietta Street (acc 328: men 156 women 44 Harbor Light 22)
Augusta, GA 30901: 138 Greene Street St (acc 118)
Austin, TX 78701: 501 E 8th St (acc 60)
Austin, TX 78767: 4523 Tannehill Ln (Women and Children Shelter) (acc 26)
Baltimore, MD 21030: 1114 N Calvert St (acc 75)
Beaumont, TX 77701: 1078 McFaddin (acc 10)
Bradenton, FL 34205: 1204 14th St W (acc 102)
Brunswick, GA 31520: 1620 Reynolds St (acc 22)
Cambridge, MD 21613: 200 Washington St (acc 10)
Charleston, WV 25302: 308, 308A, 310, 312 Ohio St (acc 16)
Charlotte, NC 28206: 534 Spratt St (acc 350)
Charlottesville, VA: 207 Ridge St NW (acc 36)
Chattanooga, TN 37403: 800 McCallie Ave (acc 72)
Clearwater, FL 33756: 1527 E Druid Rd (acc 64)
Columbus, GA 31909: 1718 2nd Ave (acc 39)
Corpus Christi, TX 78401: 513 Josephine (acc 28)
Dalton, GA 30720: 1101A North Thorton Ave (acc 24)
El Paso, TX: 79905: 4300 Paisano Drive (acc 106)
El Paso, TX: 79903: 3926 Bliss Avenue (acc 11 families)
Enid, OK 73701: 223 W Oak (acc 8)
Fayetteville, NC 28301: 245 Alexander St (acc 75)
Florence, SC 29501: 2210 Hoffmeyer Rd (acc 12)
Ft Lauderdale, FL 33312: 1445 W Broward Blvd (acc 251)
Ft Myers, FL 33901: 2163 Stella St (acc 134)
Fort Worth, TX 76103: 1855 E Lancaster Ave (acc 62)
Gainesville, FL 32601: 639 E University Ave (acc 24)
Gainesville, GA: 711 Dorsey St (acc 52)
Galveston, TX 77552: 601 51st St (acc 6 families)

USA Southern Territory

Gastonia, NC 28052: 107 S. Broad St (acc 65)
Greensboro, NC 27406: 1311 S. Eugene St (acc 86)
Greenville, SC 27609: 417 Rutherford St (acc 91)
Griffin, GA 30224: 329 N 13th St (acc 32)
Hagerstown, MD 21740: 534 W Franklin St (acc 30)
Harrisonburg, VA 22801: 895 Jefferson St (acc 72)
Hickory, NC 28602: 780 Third Ave Place SE (acc 85)
High Point, NC 27262: 301 W Green Dr (acc 65)
Hollywood, FL 33020: 1960 Sherman St (acc 140)
Houston, TX 77004: 1603 McGowen (acc 42)
Jacksonville, FL 32201: PO Box 52508 (acc 123)
Lakeland, FL 33801: 835 N Kentucky Ave
  (acc 166)
Louisville, KY 40203: 831 S Brook St (acc 18)
Lynchburg, VA 24501: 2215 Park Ave (acc 22)
Macon, GA 31206: 2312 Houston Ave (acc 131)
Melbourne, FL 32901: 1080 S Hickory St (acc 48)
Memphis, TN 38105: 696 Jackson Ave (acc 120)
Miami, FL 33142: 1907 NW 38th St (acc 266)
Nashville, TN 37207-5608: 631 Dickerson Rd
  (acc 53)
N Central Brevard, Cocoa, FL 32922:
  919 Peachtree St (acc 17)
Norfolk, VA 23502: Hope Village,
  5525 Raby Rd (acc 65)
Ocala, FL 34475: 320 NW 1st Ave (acc 121)
Orlando, FL 32804: 400 W Colonial Dr (acc 190)
Palm Beach, FL 33402: PO Box 789 (acc 95)
Panama City, FL 32401: 1824 W 15th St (acc 48)
Parkersburg, WV 24740: 534-570 Fifth St (acc 56)
Raleigh, NC 27604: 1863 Capital Blvd (acc 90)
Petersburg,VA 23803: 835 Commerce St (acc 40)
Richmond, VA 23220: 2 W Grace St (acc 52)
Rock Hill, SC 29730: 125 S Charlotte Ave (acc 34)
Rome, GA 30161: 317 E First Ave (acc 26)
San Antonio, TX 78212: 515 W Elmira 78212
  (acc 300)
Sarasota, FL 34236: 1400 10th St (acc 226)
Savannah, GA 31405: 3100 Montgomery St
  (acc 120)
St Petersburg, FL 33733: PO Drawer 10909 (acc 112)
Tampa, FL 33602: 1603 N Florida (acc 192)
Texarkana, TX 71854: 316 Hazel (acc 46)
Thomasville, GA 31792: 208 South St (acc 9)
Titusville, FL 32796: 1212 W Main (acc 16)
Tulsa, OK 74103: 102 N Denver (acc 100)
Tyler, TX 75701: 633 N Broadway 7570 (15 rooms)
Valdosta, GA 31601: 317 Virginia Ave (acc 10)
Washington, DC 20009: 1434 Harvard St NW
  (acc 60)
Waycross, GA 31501: 977 Tebeau St (acc 11)
Wheeling, WV 26003: 140 16th St (acc 32)
Williamsburg, VA 7131: Merrimac Trail
  (acc 17/scattered sites)
Wilmington, NC 28401: 820 N Second St (acc 52)
Winchester, VA 22603: 300 Ft Collier Rd (acc 48)

Winston-Salem, NC 27101: 1255 N Trade St (acc 82)
Winter Haven, FL 33882: PO Box 1069 (acc 40)

Harbour Light Centres
Atlanta, GA 30313: 400 Luckie St (acc 324)
Dallas, TX 75235: 5302 Harry Hines Blvd (acc 309)
Houston, TX 77009: 2407 N Main St (acc 308)
Washington, DC 20002: 2100 New York Ave,
  NE (acc 207)

Homeless Shelters
Abilene, TX 79602: 1726 Butternut Dr
Amarillo, TX 79105: 400 Harrison
Austin, TX 78701: 501 E 8th St
Beaumont, TX 77703: 2350 IH-10 East
Big Spring, TX 79721: 811 W Fifth St
Bradenton, FL 34205: 1204 14th St W
Conroe, TX 77301: 304 Avenue E
Corpus Christi, TX 78401: 1507 Mestina
Dallas, TX 75235: 5302 Harry Hines Blvd
Daytona Beach, FL 32114: 560 Ballough Rd (acc 84)
Denton, TX 76202: 2801 N Elm
Fort Lauderdale, FL 33312: 1445 W Broward Blvd
Fort Myers, FL 33901: 2400 Edison Ave
Freeport, TX 77541: 1618 N Avenue J
Gainesville, FL 32601: 639 E University Ave
  (acc 14)
Galveston, TX 77552: 601 51st St
Goldsboro, NC 27530: 610 N William St (acc 16)
Jacksonville, FL 32204: 900 W Adams St
Kerrville, TX 78028: 855 Hayes St
Laredo, TX 78040: 408 Matamoras St
Longview, TX 75601: 519 E Cotton St
Lubbock, TX 79401: 1120 17th St (acc 21 men)
  and Transitional acc 6 men
Lubbock, TX 79401: 1614 Ave J (acc 9 female)
  and Transitional acc 3 female and 7 families
Lufkin, TX 75901: 412 S Third St
Miami, FL 33142: 1907 NW 38th St
McAllen, TX 78501: 1600 N 23rd St
Midland, TX 79701: 300 S Baird
Ocala, FL 34475: 320 NW 1st Ave
Odessa, TX 79761: 810 E 11th St
Orlando, FL 32804: 624 Lexington
Palm Beach, FL 33402: PO Box 789 (acc 95)
Pensacola, FL 32505: 1310 North S St (acc 28)
San Angelo, TX 79602: 215 Gillis
San Antonio, TX 78202: 26 Nolan St (acc 76 men)
Sarasota, FL 34236: 1400 10th St
Sherman, TX 75090: 5700 Texoma Pkwy
St Petersburg, FL 33701: 310 14th Ave
Tampa, FL 33602: 1514 N Florida Ave
Texarkana, TX 75502: 400 E 4th St
Titusville, FL 32796: 1212 W Main (acc 17)
Tyler, TX 75702: 717 N Spring St
Victoria, TX 77901: 1302 N Louis St
Waco, TX 76708: 500 S 4th St

(acc 20 men and 3 women and 1 family)
Wichita Falls, TX 76301: 403 7th St

Senior Citizens' Centres
Arlington, TX 76013: 712 W Abrams
Dallas Cedar Crest, TX 75203:
1007 Hutchins Rd
Dallas Oak Cliff, TX 75208: 1617 W Jefferson Blvd
Dallas Pleasant Grove, TX 75217-0728: 8341
Elam Rd
Ft Worth, TX 76106: 3023 NW 24th St
Ft Worth, TX 76119-5813: 1909 E Seminary Dr
(acc 121)
Houston Aldine/Westfield, TX 77093:
2600 Aldine Westfield
Houston Pasadena, TX 77506:
4516 Irvington Blvd
Houston Temple, TX 77502: 2627 Cherrybrook Ln
Jacksonville, FL 32202: 17 E Church St
Lufkin, TX 75904: 305 Shands
Oklahoma City, OK 73109: 311 SW 5th St.
(includes 5 drop in centres)
San Antonio Citadel, TX 78201: 2810 W Ashby Pl
San Antonio Dave Coy Center, TX 78202:
226 Nolan St
San Antonio Hope Center, TX 78212: 521 W Elmira
St Petersburg, FL 33713: 3800 9th Ave N

Senior Citizens' Residences
Atlanta, GA 30306: William Booth Towers,
1125 Ponce de Leon Ave NE (acc 99)
Charlotte, NC 28202-1727: William Booth
Gardens Apts, 421 North Poplar St (acc 130)
El Paso, TX: 79903-2840: Pleasant View Lodge,
3918 Bliss Ave (acc 22)
Fort Worth, TX 76119-5813: Catherine Booth
Friendship House, 1901 E Seminary Dr
(acc 157)
Gastonia, NC 28054: Catherine Booth Gardens
Apts, 1436 Union Rd (acc 82)
High Point, NC 27263: William Booth Gardens
Apts, 123 SW Cloverleaf Place (acc 77)
Houston, TX 77009: William Booth Gardens
Apts, 808 Frawley (acc 62)
Ocala, FL 34470: Evangeline Booth Gardens
Apts, 2921 NE 14th St (acc 64)
Orlando, FL 32801: William Booth Towers,
633 Lake Dot Circle (acc 168)
Orlando, FL 32801: Catherine Booth Towers,
625 Lake Dot Circle (acc 125)
Pasadena, TX 77502: Evangeline Booth,
2627 Cherrybrook Ln (acc 62)
San Antonio, TX 78201-5397: William Booth
Gardens Apts, 2710 W Ashby Pl (acc 95)
San Antonio, TX 78201: Catherine Booth Apts,
2810 W Ashby Pl (acc 62)

Tyler, TX 75701: William Booth Gardens Apts,
601 Golden Rd (acc 132)
Tyler, TX 75701: Catherine Booth Apts,
602 Golden Rd (acc 75)
Waco, TX 76708-1141: William Booth Gardens
Apts, 4200 N 19th (acc 120)
Waco, TX 76708-1141: Catherine Booth Appts,
2005 Steward Dr (acc 75)

Service Centres
Ada, OK 74820: 805 N. Broadway Ave.
Alexander City, AL 35010: 1725 Hghwy 22 West
Americus, GA 31709: 204 N Prince St
Auburn, AL 36830-4026; 1038 Opelika Rd
Bainbridge, GA 39818: 600 Scott St
Bay City, TX 77414: 1911 7th St
Borger, TX 79007-2502: 1090 Coronado Circle
Center Cir 79008-1046, P.O. Box 1046
Brownwood, TX 76801: 403 Lakeway
Buckhannon, WV 26201: 21 N. Spring Street
(Upshur County)
Bushnell, FL 33513: PO Box 25 (Sumter County)
Canton, GA 30114: 121 Waleska Street
Carrollton, GA 30117: 115 Lake Carroll Blvd
Carthage, MS 39051: 610 Hwy 16 West, Suite A
Cleburne, TX 76031: 111 S Anglin St
Columbia, MD 21045: PO Box 2877 (Howard Cty)
Corinth, MS 38834: 2200 Lackey St
Covington, GA 30014: 5193 Washington St
Culpeper, VA 22701: 62 Waterloo St (operates
from Warenton, VA)
Douglas, GA 31533: 110 S Gaskin Ave
Dublin, GA 31021: 1617 Telfair St
Easley, SC 29640: 501 Old Liberty Highway
East Pasco, Dade City, FL 33523: 14445 7th St
Elberton, GA 30635: 262 N McIntosh St
Elizabethtown, KY 42701: 1006 N Mulberry
Enterprise, AL 366331: 1919-C E Park Ave
(Coffee County)
Fernandina Beach, FL 32034: 410 S 9th St
(Nassau County -TSA Hope House)
Fort Payne, AL 35967: 450 Gault Ave N
(Dekalb County)
Franklin, VA, 23851: Western Tidewater Svc Ctr,
501 N Main St
Fulton, MS 38843: 414 E Main St
Glen Burnie, MD 21061: 511 S Crain Hwy
Gloucester, VA 23072: 7057 Linda Circle, Hayes, VA
Granite Falls, NC 28630: 4370 Hickory Blvd
(Lenoir)
Guntersville, AL 35976: 1336 Gunter Ave
(Marshall County)
Houma, LA 70363: 5539 West Main Street
Houston, MS 38851: 114 Washington St
Immokalee, FL 34142: 2050 Commerce Ave,
Unit 3A

257

Jackson, GA 30233: 178 N Benton St (Jackson/
Butts County)

Jasper, AL 35502: 207 20th St E (Walker County)

Kaufman, TX 75142: 5 Oak Creek Dr
(mail PO Box 217)

LaBelle, FL 33935: 180 N Main St

Lake City, FL 32055: 303 NW Quinten Street

Lebanon, TN, 37087: 215 University Ave

Lewisburg, WV 24901: 148 Maplewood Ave
(Greenbriar Valley)

Lewisville, TX 75067: 207 Elm St 75057

McDonough, GA 30253: 401 Race Track Rd

McGehee, AR 71654: 102 E Oak St (Desha Cty)

Milledgeville, GA 31061: 461 E Hancock St

Mocksville, NC 27028: 622 N Main St (Davie Cty)

Morganton, NC 28655: 420-B W Fleming Dr

Nacogdoches, TX 75963: 118 E Hospital Ste 101

Newnan, GA 30264: 670 Jefferson St

Okmulgee, OK 74447-0123: 105-111 E 8th St

Oneonta, AL 35121: 333 Valley Rd (Blount Cty)

Oxford, MS 38655: 2649 W Oxford Loop,

Ozark, AL 36360: 1177 Andrews Ave (Dale Cty)

Pleasanton, TX 78064: 2132A 2nd St

Pontotoc, MS 38863: 303 W Reynolds St

Putnam County, WV 25177: 720 N Winfield Rd,
St Albans, WV

Sallisaw, OK: PO Box 292, Fort Smith, AR 72902

Sanford, NC 27330: 507 N Steele St

San Marcos, TX 78667: 300 CM Allen Pkwy,
Suite 200A

Scottsboro, AL 35768: 1501 E Willow St
(Jackson County)

Spencer, WV 25276: 145 Main St (Roane County)

Starkville, MS 39759:39759: 407 A Industrial
Park Rd, Industrial Parkway Road

St Mary's, GA 31558: 1909 Osborne Rd

Tarpon Springs, FL 34689: 209 S Pinellas Ave

Thomasville, AL 36784: 122 W Wilson Ave

Tifton, GA 31793: 1203 E Highway 82

Troy, AL 36081: 509 S Brundidge St

Union, SC 29379: PO Box 201

Vidalia, GA 30475: 204 Jackson St

Warrenton, VA 20186: 62 Waterloo St

Wellsburg, WV 26070: 491 Commerce St

Westminster, MD 21157: 300 Hahn Rd

Yadkinville, NC 27055: 111 E Main St
(Yadkin County)

Spouse House Shelters

Cocoa, FL: 919 Peachtree St 32922
(PO Box 1540, 32923) (acc 20)

Panama City, FL 32401: 1824 W 15th St
(PO Box 540, 32412) (acc 46)

Port Richey, FL 34673: PO Box 5517 Hudson,
FL 34674-5517 (acc 32)

Roanoke, VA 24016 815 Salem Ave, SW (acc 60)

Warner Robins, GA 31093: 96 Thomas Blvd
(acc 18)

Washington, DC 20036: PO Box 18658 (acc 26)

SOCIAL SERVICES

Adult Rehabilitation Centres (including industrial stores)

Alexandria, VA 22312: Northern Virginia Center,
6528 Little River Turnpike (acc 120)

Atlanta, GA 30318-5726: 740 Marietta St, NW
(acc 132)

Austin, TX 78745: 4216 S Congress (acc 118)

Baltimore, MD 21230: 2700 W Patapsco Ave
(acc 115)

Birmingham, AL 35234:
1401 F. L. Shuttlesworth Dr (acc 107)

Charlotte, NC 28204: 1023 Central Ave (acc 117)

Dallas, TX 75235-7213: 5554 Harry Hines Blvd
(acc 137)

Fort Lauderdale, FL 33312-1597:
1901 W Broward Blvd (acc 99)

Fort Worth, TX 76111-2996: 2901 NE 28th St
(acc 109)

Houston, TX 77007-6113: 1015 Hemphill St
(acc 167)

Hyattsville, MD 20781: (Washington, DC, and
Suburban Maryland Center) 3304 Kenilworth
Ave (acc 151)

Jacksonville, FL 32246: 10900 Beach Blvd
(acc 121)

Memphis, TN 38133-4734: 2649 Kirby Whitten
Rd, 38133-4734 (acc 86)

Miami, FL 33127-4981: 2236 NW Miami Court
(acc 134)

New Orleans, LA 70121-2596: 200 Jefferson
Highway (acc 50)

Oklahoma City, OK 73106-2409: 2041 NW
7th St (acc 81)

Orlando, FL 32808-7927: 3955 W Colonial Dr
(acc 105)

Richmond, VA 23220-1199: 2601 Hermitage Rd
(acc 81)

San Antonio, TX 78204: 1324 S Flores St
(acc 110)

St Petersburg, FL 33709-1597: Suncoast Area
Center, 5885 66th St N (acc 119)

Tampa, FL 33613-2205: 13815 Salvation Army
Lane (acc 131)

Tulsa, OK 74106-5163: 601-611 N Main St (acc 86)

Virginia Beach, VA 23462: Hampton Roads
Center, 5560 Virginia Beach Blvd (acc 123)

*In addition, 9 fresh-air camps, 29 community
centres and 94 boys'/girls' clubs are attached
to the division*

USA WESTERN TERRITORY

Territorial leaders:
**Commissioners James M. and
Carolyn R. Knaggs**

Territorial Commander:
Commissioner James M. Knaggs
(1 Jul 2010)

Chief Secretary:
Colonel David E. Hudson (1 Aug 2011)

**Territorial Headquarters: 180 E Ocean Boulevard,
PO Box 22646 (90801-5646), Long Beach, California 90802-4709, USA**

Tel: [1] (562) 436-7000; website: www.usw.salvationarmy.org

The Salvation Army was incorporated as a religious and charitable corporation in the State of California in 1914 as 'The Salvation Army' and is qualified, along with its several affiliated separate corporations, to conduct its affairs in all of the states of the territory.

Zone: Americas and Caribbean
USA states included in the territory: Alaska, Arizona, California, Colorado, Hawaii, Idaho, Montana, Nevada, New Mexico, Oregon, Utah, Washington, Wyoming, Guam (US Territory)
Other countries included in territory: Commonwealth of Northern Marianas, Federated States of Micronesia, Republic of the Marshall Islands,
'The Salvation Army' in Cantonese: Kau Shai Kwan; in Japanese: Kyu-sei-gun; in Mandarin (Kuoyo): Chiu Shi Chuen; in Spanish: Ejército de Salvación
Languages in which the gospel is preached: Cantonese, Chamarro, Chuukese, English, Hmong, Korean, Laotian, Mandarin, Marshallese, Filipino, Pohnpeian, Portuguese, Spanish, Tlingit
Periodicals: *Caring*, *New Frontier Chronicle*, *Vida* (Spanish)

THE USA Western Territory continued to emphasise its vision of winning the world for God and growing its programmes in order to share the gospel with people of all culture**s.**

In May 2013, more than 700 Spanish-speaking Salvationists attended the first Territorial Latino Bible Conference (Conferencia Bíblica del Territorio Oeste) led by the territory's multicultural secretaries, Lieut-Colonels

Zoilo and Magali Pardo. The guest speakers were Commissioners Torben and Deise Eliasen (IS and ISWM).

Territorial leaders Commissioners James and Carolyn Knaggs and Secretary for Programme Lieut-Colonel Edward Hill, led the annual Western Bible Conference held in July. More than 500 delegates joined together to hear guest speakers, Lieut-Colonels Eddie and Kathy Hobgood

(IHQ) and Colonel Janet Munn (Training Principal, Australia Eastern Territory).

In June 2013, the Proclaimers of the Resurrection Session – including 58 cadets and 15 auxiliary-captains – were ordained, commissioned and appointed at meetings held in Pasadena. During the weekend of cele-bration an Army of Stars Banquet – which honoured one soldier from each division – was held and the new lieutenants received their first appoint-ments from Commissioners James and Carolyn Knaggs (TC and TPWM). Dr Robert Docter OF charged the new lieutenants to 'Be anywhere in your town where people find themselves immersed in a world of hurt. Be there. Empathise. Emulate Christ'.

The Territorial Staff Band and Staff Songsters ministered in various locations throughout the territory and in June the Staff Songsters, led by Territorial Music Secretary Neil Smith, conducted a 10-day tour of the United Kingdom Territory with the Republic of Ireland.

In September 44 new cadets to the Heralds of Grace Session were welcomed, joining the 60 cadets of the Disciples of the Cross Session.

The Tournament of Roses Band marched for the 94th consecutive year in the world-famous Tournament of Roses Parade in Pasadena on 1 January 2014, led by Bandmaster Kevin Larsson (Southern California Divisional Music Director). The 180-member band included participants from Southern California, two young musicians from every division in the USA and the Canada and Bermuda Territories, and the Australia Southern Territory Youth Band.

Also in January more than 500 officers and youth leaders gathered at Mt Hermon Conference Center, for an intensive week of training and worship. At the end of 'boot camp' there was a strong sense that God's Holy Spirit had moved among the group and that many corps represented would benefit from the ongoing ministry of those who had attended.

In February a Worship Arts Retreat was held for more than 100 Salvationists to develop skills in corps ministry and leadership. In addition to excellent worship opportunities, there were a variety of workshops including dance, praise and worship, drama, video and film making, and leadership development.

A SAVN.tv team travelled to Zimbabwe in April to film the visit of General André Cox and Commissioner Silvia Cox (WPWM).

Responding to the change in how people receive breaking news, and to address results of surveys and focus groups, New Frontier publications changed to *New Frontier Chronicle* with an aim to empower readers to communicate the Army's mission through actionable and applicable content. Daily news is offered at newfrontierchronicle.org.

The territory has also emphasised its multimedia presence. The Online

Corps Facebook page (Facebook.com/OnlineCorps) and website (OnlineCorps.net) offers gospel stories and a weekly Bible discussion video series. LifeStories is a weekly video series of one-on-one interviews, and the OnlineCorps HangOut is where participants can chat and develop relationships with each other. With MissionBridge, the territory promoted a mission-focused approach of linking social services recipients with corps.

The Youth Department's follow-up programme for young people who have attended camps throughout the territory has continued to gain traction in 2014.

STATISTICS

Officers 1,105 (active 700 retired 405)
Cadets 121 **Employees** 8,373
Corps 258 **Outposts** 5 **Institutions** 307
Senior Soldiers 16,749 **Adherent Members** 3,853
Junior Soldiers 4,802
Personnel serving outside territory Officers 33
Lay Personnel 3

STAFF

Women's Ministries: Comr Carolyn R. Knaggs (TPWM) Col Sharron Hudson (TSWM)
Personnel: Lt-Col Douglas G. O'Brien
　Asst Sec for Personnel: Maj Eloisa Martin
Business: Lt-Col Victor R. Doughty
Programme: Lt-Col Edward Hill
　Asst Programme Sec for Corps Ministries: Maj Ronda Gilger
　Asst Sec for Programme: Mr Martin Hunt
ARC Command: Maj Man-Hee Chang
Audit: Maj Joe Frank Chavez
Candidates and Recruitment: Maj Bob Louangamath
Community Care Ministries: Lt-Col Diane O'Brien
Community Relations/Development: Mr Chaz Watson
Education: Maj Jeffrey A. Martin
Finance: Mr Tom Melott
Gift Services: Ms Kathleen Devine

Human Resources: Mr Howard Yamaguchi
Information Technology: Tim Schaal
Legal: Terrence O. Hughes
Multicultural Ministries: Lt-Col Zoilo Pardo
Music: Mr Neil Smith
Officer Care and Development: Dr Jack Andersen
Property: Maj Evelyn Chavez
Risk Management: Maj James Boyd
Senior Housing Management: Mrs Susan Lawrence
Social Services: Maj Lawrence Shiroma
Spiritual Life Development Sec: Maj Steven D. Bradley
Assoc Sec for Spiritual Life Development: Maj Patricia Bradley
Supplies and Purchasing: Mr Piers Fairclough
Training: Maj Timothy Foley
Youth: Maj Roy S. Wild

DIVISIONS

Alaska: 143 E 9th Ave, Anchorage, AK 99501-3618 (Box 101459, 99510-1459); tel: (907) 276-2515; Majs George L. and Jeanne L. Baker
Cascade: 8495 SE Monterey Ave, Happy Valley, OR 97086; tel: (503) 794-3200; Lt-Col Judith E. Smith
Del Oro: 3755 N Freeway Blvd, Sacramento, CA 95834-1926 (Box 348000, 95834-8000); tel: (916) 563-3700; Majs Bill A, Jr. and Lisa A. Dickinson
Golden State: 832 Folsom St, San Francisco, CA 94107-1123 (Box 193465, 94119-3465) tel: (415) 553-3500; Lt-Cols Stephen C. and Marcia C. Smith
Hawaiian and Pacific Islands: 2950 Manoa Rd, Honolulu, HI 96822-1798 (Box 620, 96809-0620); tel: (808) 988-2136; Majs John and Lani Chamness
Intermountain: 1370 Pennsylvania St, Denver, CO 80203-2475 (Box 2369, 80201-2369); tel: (303) 861-4833; Lt-Cols Daniel L. and Helen Starrett
Northwest: 111 Queen Anne Ave N, Suite 300, Seattle, WA 98109-4955 (Box 9219, 98109-0200); tel: (206) 281-4600; Majs Douglas and Sheryl Tollerud
Sierra Del Mar: 2320 5th Ave, San Diego, CA 92101-1679; tel: (619) 231-6000; Majs Lee R. and Michele Lescano
Southern California: 180 E Ocean Blvd Ste 500, Long Beach, CA 90802-4709 (Box 93002, 90809-9355); tel: (562) 264-3600; Lt-Cols Douglas F. and Colleen R. Riley
Southwest: 2707 E Van Buren St, Phoenix, AZ 85008-6039 (Box 52177, 85072-2177); tel: (602) 267-4100; Lt-Cols Joseph E. and Shawn L. Posillico

COLLEGE FOR OFFICER TRAINING
30840 Hawthorne Blvd, Rancho Palos Verdes,
CA 90275-5301; tel: (310) 377-0481;

SOCIAL SERVICES
Adult Rehabilitation Centres (Men)
Anaheim, CA 92805: 1300 S Lewis St;
tel: (714) 758-0414 (acc 145)
Anchorage, AK 99503: 660 E. 48th Ave;
tel: (907) 562-5408 (acc 58)
Bakersfield, CA 93301: 200 19th St;
tel: (661) 325-8626 (acc 57)
Canoga Park, CA 91304: 21375 Roscoe Blvd; tel:
(818) 883-6321 (acc 56)
Denver, CO 80216: 4751 Broadway;
tel: (303) 294-0827 (acc 98)
Fresno, CA 93721: 804 S Parallel Ave;
tel: (559) 490-7020 (acc 111)
Honolulu, HI 96817: 322 Sumner St;
tel: (808) 522-8400 (acc 77)
Long Beach, CA 90813: 1370 Alamitos Ave;
tel: (562) 218-2351 (acc 94)
Lytton, CA 95448: 200 Lytton Springs Rd,
Healdsburg, PO Box 668, Healdsburg, 95448;
tel: (707) 433-3334 (acc 75)
North Las Vegas, NV 89030: 211 Judson St,
Box 30096; tel: (702) 399-2769 (acc 115)
2035 Yale St: tel: (702) 649-2374
Oakland, CA 94607: 601 Webster St, PO Box
24054, 94623; tel: (510) 451-4514 (acc 131)
Pasadena, CA 91105: 56 W Del Mar Blvd;
tel: (626) 795-8075 (acc 107)
Phoenix, AZ 85004: 1625 S Central Ave;
tel: (602) 256-4500 (acc 142)
Portland, OR 97220: 6655 NE 82nd Ave (acc 76)
Riverside County, CA 92570: 24201 Orange Ave,
Perris, PO Box 278, Perris 92572;
tel: (951) 940-5790 (acc 125)
Sacramento, CA 95814: 1615 D St, PO Box 2948,
95812; tel: (916) 441-5267 (acc 91)
San Bernardino, CA 92408: 363 S Doolittle Rd;
tel: (909) 889-9605 (acc 122)
San Diego, CA 92101: 1335 Broadway;
tel: (619) 239-4037 (acc 132)
San Francisco, CA 94110: 1500 Valencia St;
tel: (415) 643-8000 (acc 112)
San Jose, CA 95126: 702 W Taylor St;
tel: (408) 298-7600 (acc 96)
Santa Monica, CA 90404: 1665 10th St;
tel: (310) 450-7235 (acc 56)
Seattle, WA 98134: 1000 4th Ave S;
tel: (206) 587-0503 (acc 117)
Stockton, CA 95205: 1247 S Wilson Way;
tel: (209) 466-3871 (acc 80)
Tucson, AZ 85713: 2717 S 6th Ave;
tel: (520) 624-1741 (acc 85)

Adult Rehabilitation Centres (Women)
Anaheim, CA 92805: 909 Salvation Pl;
tel: (714) 758-0414 (acc 30)
Arvada, CO 80002: Cottonwood,
13455 W 58th Ave; tel: (303) 456-0520
(acc 30)
Fresno, CA 93704: Rosecrest, 745 E Andrews St;
tel: (559) 490-7080 (acc 18)
North Las Vegas, NV 89030: 39 W Owens:
tel; (702) 649-1469
Pasadena, CA 91107: Oakcrest Women's
Program, 180 W Huntington Dr;
tel: (626) 447-4264 (acc 14)
Phoenix, AZ 85003: Lyncrest Manor,
344 W Lynwood St; tel: (602) 254-0883 (acc 14)
San Diego, CA 92123: 2799 Health Center Dr;
tel: (858) 279-1755 (acc 30)
San Francisco, CA 94116: Pinehurst Lodge, 2685
30th Ave; tel: (415) 681-1262 (acc 27)
Shoreline, WA 98155: The Marion-Farrell House,
17925 2nd Ave NE;
tel: (206) 367-0697 (acc 15)

UNDER DIVISIONS
Anti-Human Trafficking Centres
Anaheim, CA 92801: tel: (714) 783-2338
Las Vegas, NV 89030: tel: (702) 639-0277 (acc 22)
Phoenix, AZ 85008: tel: (602) 267-4122
San Diego, CA 92123: Door of Hope – Betty's
House; tel: (858) 279-1100

Clinics
Oakland, CA 94601: Kerry's Kids,
2794 Garden Street; tel: (510) 437-9437
Oxnard/Port Hueneme, CA: Medical and Dental
Clinic, 622 W Wooley Rd; tel: (805) 483-9235
Prescott, AZ 86303; 237 S Montezuma St;
tel (928) 778-0150

Family Services
Anacortes, WA 98221: 3001 'R' Ave Ste #100,
tel: (360) 293-6682
Anaheim, CA 92801-4333; 1515 W North St;
tel: (714) 491-1020
Anchorage, AK 99501: 1712 'A' St; tel: (907)
277-2593
Baker City, OR 97814-330: Service Ext,
2505 Broadway Ave; tel: (503) 523-5853
Bellingham, WA 98225: 2912 Northwest Ave;
tel: (360) 733-1410
Bremerton, WA 98337: 832 6th St;
tel: (360) 373-5550
Centralia, WA 98531: 303 N Gold;
tel: (360) 736-4339
Eastside (Bellevue), WA 98008:
911-164th Ave NE; tel: (425) 452-7300

El Cajon, CA 92021: 1011 E Main St;
tel: (619) 440-4686Everett, WA 98201: 2525
Rucker Ave; tel: (425) 259-8129

Federal Way, WA 98198: 26419 16th Ave:
S, Des Moines; tel: (253) 946-7933

Fresno, CA 93721: 1752 Fulton St;
tel (559) 233-0138

Garden Grove, CA 92841-4216; West Orange
County, 7245 Garden Grove Blvd #A;
tel: (714) 901-1480

Globe, AZ 85501-1944; Service Ctr, 161 E Cedar
St; tel: (928) 425-4011

Grandview, WA 98930; 246 Division St;
tel: (509) 882-2584

Grays Harbor (Aberdeen) WA 98520:
118 W Wishkah; tel: (360) 533-1062

Great Falls, MT 59405: 527 9th Ave S;
tel: (406) 761-5660

Green Valley, AZ 85614-1944: Service Ctr,
660 W Camino Casa Verde: tel (520) 625-3888

Havre, MT 59501: Service Ext, Social Service
Center, PO Box 418; tel: (406) 265-6411

Helena, MT 59601: 1905 Henderson;
tel: (406) 442-8244

Honokaa, HI 96727: Prevention Program, 45-511
Rickard Pl; tel: (808) 959-5855

Honolulu, HI 96819: 296 N Vineyard Blvd;
tel: (808) 841-5565

Honolulu, HI 96816: Family Treatment Services,
845 22nd Ave; tel: (808) 732-2802

Huntington Beach, CA 92647-5896; Coastal
Area, 17261 Oak Ln; tel: (714) 841-0150

Kalispell, MT 59901: 110 Bountiful Dr;
tel: (406) 257-4357

Kent, WA 98032: S King County Service Center,
1209 Central Ave #145;
tel (253) 852-4983

Kingman, AZ 86401-5835; Service Ctr, 309 E
Beale St; tel: (928) 718-2600 Lewiston, ID
83501; 1835 "G" St; tel: (208) 746-9653

Klamath Falls, OR 97603-4567: Service Ext,
2960 Maywood Dr, Units 12 & 13;
PO Box 1649

Klamath Falls, OR 97601-0248 (mail);
tel: (541) 882-5280

La Grande, OR 97850-2751: Service Ext,
1114 'Y' Ave; PO Box 897 La Grande, OR
97850-0897 (mail); tel: (541) 963-4829

Lakeside, AZ 85929; Outpost,
4367 W White Mt Rd #8A;
tel: (928)368-9953

Lewiston, ID 83501-2034; 1220 21st St;
tel: (208) 746-9653

Longview, WA 98632: 1639 10th Ave;
tel: (360) 423-3992

Los Angeles, CA 90001-2945: Siemon Family

Youth & Community Center, 7651 S. Central
Ave; tel: (323) 586-0288 ext 221

Mesquite, NV 89027: Mesquite Service Center,
355 W Mesquite Blvd #B-50;
tel: (702) 346-5116

Missoula, MT 59802; 339 W Broadway St;
tel: (406) 549-0710

Modesto, CA 95354: 625 'I' St;
tel (209) 523-7577

Monterey, CA 93942: 1491 Contra Costa:
tel 831-899-4911

Moses Lake, WA 98837: Service Ext, Social
Service Center, 212 Alder St, PO Box 1000;
tel: (509) 766-5875

Oakland, CA 94607: 2794 Garden St;
tel: (510) 437-9437

Olympia, WA 98501: Social Services,
824 5th Ave SE; tel: (360) 352-8596

Pasco, WA 99301: Tri-Cities Social Services,
310 N 4th Ave; tel: (509) 547-2138

Phoenix, AZ 85008: 2707 E Van Buren Bldg 2;
tel: (602) 267-4122

Pocatello, ID 83201-6311: Service Ext,
400 N 4th Ave; tel: (208) 232-5318

Port Angeles, WA 98362: 206 S Peabody St;
tel: (360) 452-7679

Puyallup, WA 98373: 4009 9th St SW;
tel: (253) 841-1491

Renton, WA 98055: Food Bank and
Multi-Service Center, 206 S Tobin St;
tel: (425) 255-5969

Riverside, CA 92501: 3695 1st; tel:
(951) 784-3571

Sacramento, CA 95838: 4350 Raley Blvd;
tel: (916) 678-4010

San Clemente, CA 92672-4272; South Orange
County, 616 S El Camino Real B2;
tel: (949) 366-6652

San Diego, CA 92101: Social Services;
tel: (619) 231-6000

San Diego, CA 92115: Kroc Family Service
Center, Kroc Pre-School, 6845 University Ave;
tel: (619) 269-1428

San Francisco, CA 94103: 520 Jesse St;
tel: (415) 575-4848

San Jose, CA 95112: 359 N 4th St;
tel (408) 282-1165

Santa Ana, CA 92704; 1710 W Edinger Ave;
tel: (714) 384-0481

Seattle, WA 98101-1923: Emergency Family
Assistance, 1101 Pike St;
tel: (206) 447-9944

Seattle Temple, WA 98103: 9501 Greenwood
Ave N; tel: (206) 783-1225

Seattle White Center, WA 98106:
9050 16th Ave SW; tel: (206) 767-3150

Spokane, WA 99207: 204 E Indiana;
  tel: (509) 325-6821
Tacoma, WA 98405; 1501 6th Ave;
  tel: (253) 572-8452
Tiyan, Guam: 613-615 E Sunset Blvd;
  tel: (671) 477-3528
Tucson, AZ 85716: 3525 E 2nd St #1;
  tel: (520) 546-5969
Vancouver, WA 98684: 7509 NE 47th Ave;
  tel: (360) 448-2890
Walla Walla, WA 99362: Service Ext, Social
  Service Center, 827 W Alder St;
  tel: (509) 529-9470
Washougal, WA 98671; 1612 "I" St;
  tel: (360) 835-3171
Wenatchee, WA 98801: 1205 Columbia St S;
  tel: (509) 662-8864
Yakima, WA 98907: Social Services, 9 S 6th
  Ave; tel: (509) 453-3139
Yuba City, CA 95991: 401 Del Norte Ave;
  tel: (530) 216-4530
Yucca Valley, CA 92284: Service Ext, 56659
  Twenty-nine Palms Hwy;
  tel: (760) 228-0114

Adult Care Centres

Anchorage, AK 99508: Serendipity Adult
  Day Services, 3550 E 20th Ave;
  tel: (907) 279-0501 (acc 35)
Henderson, NV 89015: 830 E Lake Mead Dr;
  tel: (702) 565-9578 (acc 49)
Honolulu, HI 96817: 296 N Vineyard Blvd;
  tel: (808) 521-6551 (acc 57)
San Pedro, CA 90731-2351:
  Sage House Adult Day Center, 138 S Bandini;
  tel: (310) 832-6031 (acc 30)

**Alcoholic and Drug Rehabilitation
Services**

Bell, CA 90201-6418: Bell Shelter, 5600
  Rickenbaker Rd 2a/b; tel: (323) 263-1206
Honolulu, HI 96816-4500: Women's Way/Family
  Treatment Services, 845 22nd Ave;
  tel: (808) 732-2802 (ext. 4938) (acc 41)
Honolulu, HI 96817: Addiction Treatment
  Services, 3624 Waokanaka St;
  tel: (808) 595-6371 (acc 80)
Honolulu, HI 96816: Therapeutic Living,
  845 22nd Ave; tel: (808) 732-2802
Los Angeles, CA 90007: Hope Harbor,
  3107 S Grand Ave; tel: (213) 744-8186
Los Angeles, CA 90073: The Haven-Victory
  Place, 11301 Wilshire Blvd, Bldg 212;
  tel: (310) 478-3711 ext 48761 (acc 200)
Marysville, CA 95901: The Depot Family Crisis
  Center, 408 J St; tel: (530) 216-4530

San Francisco, CA 94103-4405; Detox Center,
  1275 Harrison St; tel: (415) 503-3000
Tiyan, GU 96921: Lighthouse Recovery Center,
  155003 Corsair Ave, PO Box 23038, GMF GU
  96921, E Agana; tel: (671) 477-7671

Child Day Care Centres

Boise, ID Booth, 83702: 1617 N 24th, Box 1216
  83701; tel: (208) 343-3571 (acc 15)
Broomfield, CO 80020: Broomfield After-School
  Program, PO Box 1058, 1080 Birch St;
  tel: (303) 635-3018
Denver, CO 80205-4547: Denver Red Shield
  Tutor Program, 2915 High St;
  tel: (303) 295-2108 (acc 250)
Denver, CO 80219-1859: Denver Citadel Tutor
  Program, PO Box 280750, 80228-0750,
  4505 W Alameda Ave; tel: (303) 922-4540
Ewa Beach, HI 96706: Honolulu Kroc Keiki
  Learning Center, 91-3257 Kualaka'i Pkwy;
  tel: (808)-693-8337
Globe, AZ 85501: Box 1743, 85502,
  161 E Cedar St; tel: (928) 425-4011 (acc 59)
Honolulu 96816: (FTS-Therapeutic Nursery), 845
  22nd Ave; tel: (808) 739-2802 (acc 24, 12)
Kailua-Kona, HI 96740: (Ohana Keiki)
  75-223 Kalani St, Box 1358 96745;
  tel: (808) 326-7780 (acc 326)
Los Angeles, CA 90026: Alegria After-School
  Care, 2737 Sunset Blvd; tel: (323) 454-4200
  (acc 90)
Los Angeles, CA 90021: LA Day Care, 836
  Stanford Ave; tel: (213) 623-9022 (acc 144)
Los Angeles, CA 90025: Bessie Pregerson
  Childcare, Westwood Transitional Village,
  1401 S Sepulveda Blvd; tel: (310) 477-9539
  (acc 64)
Los Angeles, CA 90001: Seimon Family
  Center, 7651 South Central Ave;
  tel: (323) 277-0759 (acc 62)
Modesto, CA 95354: 625 'I' St, PO Box 1663,
  95353 (mail); tel: (209) 342-5220 (acc 60)
Monterey, CA 93942: 1491 Contra Costa St,
  Seaside, PO Box 1884, 93955 (mail);
  tel: (831) 899-4911 (acc 114)
Oakland, CA 94601: Box 510, Booth Memorial
  CDC, 2794 Garden St; tel: (510) 535-5088
  (acc 62)
Pomona, CA 91767: 490 E Laverne Ave;
  tel: (909) 623-1579 (acc 66)
Portland, OR 97296: 2640 NW Alexandra Ave;
  tel: (503) 239-1248 (acc 18)
Sacramento, CA 95817: 2550 Alhambra Blvd;
  tel: (916) 451-4230 (acc 48)
San Francisco, CA 94103: Harbor House,
  407 9th St; tel: (415) 503-3000 (acc 31)
Santa Barbara, CA 93111: Santa Barbara After-

School Program, 4849 Hollister Ave;
Box 6190, 93160; tel: (805) 964-8738

Santa Fe Springs, CA 90606: Infant/Pre-School
and After-School Care, 12000 E Washington
Blvd; tel: (310) 696-7175 (acc 57)

Tustin, CA 92680: Creator's Corner Pre-School,
10200 Pioneer Rd; tel: (714) 918-0659 (acc 90)

Tustin, CA 92680: Henley Youth Center and
After-school Care, 10200 Pioneer Rd; tel:
(714) 918-0659

Emergency Shelters, Hospitality Houses

Anchorage, AK 99501: Eagle Crest Transitional
Housing, 438 E 9th Ave; tel: (907) 276-5913
(acc 70)

Anchorage, AK 99508: McKinnell House, 1712
'A' St; tel: (907) 276-1609 (acc 110)

Bell, CA 90201: 5600 Rickenbacker;
tel: (323) 263-1206 (acc 350)

Boise, ID 83702: 1617 N 24th St;
tel: (208) 343-3571 (acc 24)

Cheyenne, WY 82001: Sally's House,
1920 Seymour St, PO Box 385, 82003 (mail);
tel: (307) 634-2769 (acc 6)

Colorado Springs, CO 80909: Hope House, 2641
E Yampa St; tel: (719) 635-1287 (acc 7)

Colorado Springs, CO 80909-4037:
2649 E Yampa St, Freshstart Transitional
Family Housing; tel: (719) 227-8773 (acc 61)

Colorado Springs, CO 80903-4023:
R.J. Montgomery Center, 709 S Sierra Madre;
tel: (719) 578-9190 (acc 210)

Colorado Springs, CO 80909: Freshstart
Transitional Family Housing, 918 Yuma St;
tel: (719) 635-1287

Denver, CO 80221-4115: Denver New Hope
(Lambuth) Family Center, 2741 N Federal
Blvd; tel: (303) 477-3758 (acc 84)

El Centro, CA 92244: 375 N 5th St;
tel: (760) 352-8462

Fresno, CA 93711-3705: Gabelcrest Women's
Transitional Home, 1107 W Shaw;
tel: (559) 226-6110 (acc 35)

Glendale, CA 91204-2053: Nancy Painter House,
320 W Windsor Rd; tel: (818) 246-5586
(acc 18)

Grand Junction, CO 81502: Women's and Family
Shelter, 915 Grand Ave, PO Box 578, 0578
81501 (mail); tel: (907) 242-3343 (acc 10)

Grass Valley, CA 95945: Booth Family Center,
12390 Rough and Ready Hwy;
tel: (530) 272-2669 (acc 45)

Helena, MT 59601: Transitional Housing,
1905 Henderson; tel: (406) 442-8244 (acc 8)

Hilo, HI 96720: Interim Home for Youth,
1786 Kinoole St, Box 5085;
tel: (808) 959-5855 (acc 18)

Honokaa, HI 96727: Residential Group Home,

45-350 Ohelo St, PO Box 5085, Hilo,
HI 96720; tel: (808) 775-0241

Honolulu, HI 96816: FTS-Supportive Living, 845
22nd Ave; tel: (808) 732-2802 (acc 24)

Kahului, HI 96732-2256: Safe Haven Drop-in
Center, 45 Kamehameha St;
tel: (808) 877-3042

Kodiak, AK 99615-6511: Kodiak, Beachcombers
Transitional Housing, 1855 Mission Rd;
tel: (907) 486-8740 (acc 10)

Lodi, CA 95240-2128: Hope Harbor Family
Service Center, 622 N Sacramento St;
tel: (209) 367-9560 (acc 99)

Lodi, CA 95240: Transitional Living Program,
331 N Stockton Ave (acc 16)

Los Angeles, CA 90015: Alegria (HIV/AIDS
housing) Aids Project, Transitional Housing,
2737 Sunset Blvd 90015; tel: (323) 454-4200
(acc 195); Zahn Family Shelter, 832 W James
M Woods Blvd; tel (213) 438-1617

Los Angeles, CA 90025-3477: Westwood
Transitional Village, 1401 S Sepulveda Blvd;
tel: (310) 477-9539 (acc 40)

Marysville, CA 95901-5629: The Depot Family
Crisis Center, 408 'J' St; tel: (530) 216-4530
(acc 64)

Marysville, CA 95901: Transitional Living
Program, 5906 B Riverside Dr;
tel: (530) 216-4530 (acc 35)

Medford, OR 97501-4630: 1065 Crews Rd;
tel: (541) 773-7005 (acc 43)

Modesto, CA 95354: Berberian Shelter,
320 9th St; tel: (209) 525-8954 (acc 110)

Nampa, ID 83651: 1412 4th St South;
tel: (208) 461-3733 (acc 54)

N Las Vegas, NV 89030: Lied Transitional
Housing, 45 W Owens Ave;
tel: (702) 642-7252 (acc 71)

N Las Vegas, NV 89030: Emergency Lodge,
47 W Owens Ave; tel: (702) 639-0277 (acc 167)

N Las Vegas, NV 89030: Horizon Crest Apts,
13 W Owens Ave; tel: (702) 639-0277 (acc 78)

Oakland, CA 94601: Family Emergency Shelter,
2794 Garden St, Box 510, 94604 (mail);
tel: (510) 437-9437 (acc 62)

Olympia, WA 98501: Hans K Lemcke Lodge,
808 5th Ave SE; tel: (360) 352-8596 (acc 58)

Phoenix, AZ 85008: Hope for a Home – Kaiser
Family Emergency Program,
2707 E Van Buren, PO Box 52177, 85072;
tel: (602) 267-4122

Phoenix, AZ 85008: Hope for A Home – Elim
Domestic Violence Program,
2707 E Van Buren, PO Box 52177, 85072;
tel: (602) 267-4122 (acc 50)

Portland, OR 97209: SAFES, Female Emergency
Shelter, 30 NW 2nd Ave; tel: (503) 227-0810

Portland, OR 97210: 2640 NW Alexandra Ave;
tel: (503) 239-1248 (acc 10)

Portland, OR 97208: Women and Children's
Family Violence Center, PO Box 2398;
tel: (503) 239-1254 (acc 53)

Redlands, CA 92374: Cold Weather Shelter
838 Alta Street; tel: 909-792-8818

Sacramento, CA 95814-0603: Emergency
Shelter, 1200 N 'B' St; tel: (916) 442-0331
(acc 134)

Salem, OR 97303:
1901 Front St NE; tel: (503) 585-6688 (acc 83)
105 River St NE; tel: (503) 391-1523 (acc 6)
1960 Water St NE; tel: (503) 566-7267 (acc 10)

San Bernardino, CA 92411: Hospitality
House, 925 W 10th St; tel: (909) 888-4880
(acc 78)

San Diego, CA 92101: STEPS, 825 7th Ave;
tel: (619) 669-2200 (acc 30)

San Francisco, CA 94103: SF Harbor House, 407
9th St; tel: (415) 503-3000 (acc 89)

San Francisco, CA 94102: Railton Place
(Permanent and Transitional Housing),
242 Turk St; tel: (415) 345-3142 (acc 110)

San Jose, CA 95112: Hospitality House,
405 N 4th St; tel: (408) 282-1175 (acc 78)

Santa Ana, CA 92701 (Orange County): 818 E
3rd St; tel: (714) 542-9576 (acc 52)

Santa Barbara, CA 93101: 423 Chapala St;
tel: (805) 962-6281 (acc 40)

Santa Fe Springs, CA 90606: Transitional
Living Center, 12000 E Washington Blvd,
Box 2009, 90610; tel: (562) 696-9562 (acc 116)

Santa Rosa, CA 95404: Transitional Living
Program; tel (707) 535-4271 (acc 12)

Seaside, CA 93955:
Casa De Las Palmas Transitional Housing,
535 Palm Ave; tel: (831) 392-1762 (acc 24)
Phase II Elm Transitional Housing, Elm Street;
tel: (831) 899-4911 (acc 30)
The Frederiksen House, 1430 Imperial St;
tel: (831) 899-1071 (acc 16)

Seattle, WA 90101: Women's Shelter (Emergency
Financial Assistance), 1101 Pike St, PO Box
20128; tel: (206) 447-9944 (acc 22)

Seattle, WA: Catherine Booth House (Shelter for
Abused Women), Box 20128, 98102;
tel: (206) 324-4943 (acc 37)

Seattle, WA 98134: William Booth Center –
Emergency Shelter and Transitional
Shelter/Living, 811 Maynard Ave S;
tel: (206) 621-0145 (acc 171)

Seattle, WA 98136: Hickman House (Women),
Box 20128, 98102; tel: (206) 932-5341 (acc 35)

Spokane, WA 99201:
Family Shelter, 204 E Indiana Ave, Box 9108
99209-9108; tel: (509) 325-6814 (acc 90)

Sally's House (Foster Care Home), Box 9108,
99209-9108, 222 E Indiana;
tel: (509) 329-2784 (acc 20)

Spokane, WA 99207-2335: Transitional Housing,
127 E Nora Ave; tel: (509) 326-7290 (acc 96)

Tacoma, WA 98405: The Jarvie Emergency
Shelter, 1521 6th Ave, Box 1254, 98401-
1254; tel: (253) 627-3962 (acc 76)

Tucson, AZ 85705: Hospitality House 1021 N
11th Ave; tel: (520) 622-5411 (acc 91)

Tucson, AZ 85716: SAFE Housing, 3525 E 2nd
St #1; tel: (520) 622-5411 (acc 117)

Ventura, CA 93001-2703: 155 S Oak St;
tel: (805) 648-5032 (acc 51)

Watsonville, CA 95076-5048: Supportive
Housing Program for Women, 232 Union St;
tel: (831) 763-2701 (acc 28)

Harbour Light Centres

Denver, CO 80205: Denver Harbor Light,
2136 Champa St; tel: (303) 296-2456 (acc 80)

San Francisco, CA 94103-4405: 1275 Harrison St;
tel: (415) 503-3000 (acc 85)

Homeless Centres

Denver, Co 80216: Crossroads Center,
1901- 29th Street; tel: (303) 298-1734

Modesto, CA 95351 320-9th St;
tel: (209) 529-7507 (acc 150)

Residential Youth Care and Family
Service Centres

Boise, ID 83702: Family Day Care Center,
1617 N 24th St, Box 1216, 83701;
tel: (208) 343-3571 (acc 15)

Los Angeles, CA 90028: The Way In Transitional
Housing (ages 18-21), 5941
Hollywood Blvd, Box 38668, 90038-0668; tel:
(323) 469-2646 (acc 24)

Portland, OR 97210: 2640 NW Alexandra Ave,
Box 10027; tel: (503) 239-1248 (acc 33)

San Diego, CA 92123: Door of Hope Haven,
Transitional Living Center, 2799 Health Center
Dr; tel: (858) 279-1100

San Francisco, CA 94102: Railton Place
Foster Youth Housing, 242 Turk St;
tel (415) 345-3400 (acc 19)

Adult Rehabilitation Programmes (Men)

Albuquerque, NM 87102: 400 John St SE, Box
27690, 87125-7690; tel: (505) 242-3112
(acc 36)

Chico, CA 95973: 13404 Browns Valley Dr;
tel: (530) 342-2199 (acc 30)

Grand Junction, CO 81502: 903 Grand Ave,
Box 578, 81502; tel: (970) 242-8632 (acc 32)

Reno, NV 89512-1605: 2300 Valley Rd;
tel: (775) 688-4570 (acc 70)

San Bernardino, CA 92410: Path to Prosperity,
730 W Spruce; tel: (909) 884-2364

San Diego, CA 92101-6304: STEPS, 825 7th
Ave; tel: (619) 669-2200

Adult Rehabilitation Programmes (Women)

Chico, CA 95973: 13404 Browns Valley Dr;
tel: (530) 342-2199 (acc 20)

Grand Junction, CO 81502: Adult Rehabilitation
Program – Women's Residence, 915 Grand Ave,
PO Box 578, 0578-81501 (mail);
tel: (907) 242-8632 (acc 10)

Senior Citizens' Housing

Albuquerque, NM: Silvercrest, 4400 Pan Am
Fwy NE, 87107; tel: (505) 883-1068 (acc 56)

Broomfield, CO 80020-1876: Silvercrest,
1110 E 10th Ave; tel: (303) 464-1994 (acc 86)

Chula Vista, CA 91910: Silvercrest, 636 3rd Ave;
tel: (619) 427-4991 (acc 75)

Colorado Springs, CO 80909-7507: Silvercrest I,
904 Yuma St; tel: (719) 475-2045 (acc 50)

Colorado Springs, CO 80909-5097: Silvercrest II,
824 Yuma St; tel: (719) 389-0329 (acc 50)

Denver, CO 80219-1859: Silvercrest, 4595 W
Alameda Ave; tel: (303) 922-2924 (acc 64)

El Cajon, CA 92020: Silvercrest, 175 S Anza St;
tel: (619) 593-1077 (acc 75)

El Sobrante, CA 94803-1859: Silvercrest,
4630 Appian Way #100; tel: (510) 758-1518
(acc 50)

Escondido, CA 92026: Silvercrest, 1303 Las
Villas Way; tel: (760) 741-4106 (acc 75)

Eureka, CA 95501-1264: Silvercrest,
2141 Tydd St; tel: (707) 445-3141 (acc 150)

Fresno, CA 93721-1041: Silvercrest,
1824 Fulton St; tel: (559) 237-9111 (acc 158)

Glendale, CA 92104: Silvercrest, 323 W Garfield;
tel: (818) 543-0211 (acc 74)

Hollywood, CA 90028: Silvercrest, 5940 Carlos
Ave; tel: (323) 460-4335 (acc 98)

Lake View Terrace, CA 91354: Silvercrest,
11850 Foothill Blvd; tel: (818) 896-7580 (acc 73)

Los Angeles, CA 90006: Silvercrest,
947 S Hoover St; tel: (213) 387-7278 (acc 92)

Mesa, AZ 85201: Silvercrest, 255 E 6th St;
tel: (480) 649-9117 (acc 82)

Missoula, MT 59801: Silvercrest, 1550 S 2nd
St W #125; tel: (406) 541-0464 (acc 51)

N Las Vegas, NV 89030: Silvercrest, 2801 E
Equador Ct; tel: (702) 643-0293 (acc 60)

Oceanside, CA 92056: Silvercrest, 3839 Lake
Blvd; tel: (760) 940-0166 (acc 69)

Pasadena, CA 91106: Silvercrest, 975 E Union St;
tel: (626) 432-6678 (acc 75)

Phoenix, AZ 85003: Silvercrest, 613 N 4th Ave;
tel: (602) 251-2000 (acc 126)

Portland, OR 97232: Silvercrest, 1865 NE Davis;
tel: (503) 236-2320 (acc 76)

Puyallup, WA 98373: Silvercrest, 4103 9th St SW;
tel: (253) 841-0785 (acc 40)

Redondo Beach, CA 90277: Mindeman Senior
Residence, 125 W Beryl St;
tel: (310) 318-2827/0582 (acc 49)

Reno, NV 89512-2448: Silvercrest,
1690 Wedekind Rd; tel: (775) 322-2050 (acc 57)

Riverside, CA 92501: Silvercrest, 3003 N Orange;
tel: (951) 276-0173 (acc 75)

San Diego, CA 92101: Silvercrest, 727 E St;
tel: (619) 699-7272 (acc 125)

San Francisco, CA 94133-3844: SF Chinatown
Senior Citizens' Residence, 1450 Powell St; tel:
(415) 781-8545 (acc 9)

San Francisco, CA 94107-1132: Silvercrest,
133 Shipley St; tel: (415) 543-5381 (acc 257)

Santa Fe Springs, CA 90670: Silvercrest, 12015
Lakeland Rd; tel: (562) 946-7717 (acc 22)

Santa Monica, CA 90401: Silvercrest,
1530 5th St; tel: (310) 393-5336 (acc 125)

Santa Rosa, CA 95404-6601: Silvercrest,
1050 3rd St; tel: (707) 544-6766 (acc 186)

Seattle, WA 98103, Silvercrest,
9543 Greenwood Ave N #105;
tel: (206) 706-0855 (acc 51)

Stockton, CA 95202-2645: Silvercrest,
123 N Stanislaus St; tel: (209) 463-4960 (acc 83)

Tulare, CA 93274: 350 North 'L' St;
tel: (559) 688-0704 (acc 60)

Turlock, CA 95380: Silvercrest, 865 Lander Ave;
tel: (209) 669-8863 (acc 80)

Ventura, CA 93004: Silvercrest, 750 South Petit
Ave; tel: (805) 647-0110 (acc 75)

Wahiawa, HI 96786: Silvercrest Residence, 520
Pine St #116; tel: (808) 622-2785 (acc 79)

Senior Citizens' Nutrition Centres

Anchorage, AK 99501: Older Alaskans' Program
(OAP), 1712 'A' Street; tel: (907) 349-0613

Denver, CO 80205-4547: Denver Red Shield,
2915 High St; (tel): (303) 295-2107

Fresno, CA 93712-1041: 1824 Fulton St;
tel: (559) 233-0139

Glendale, CA 91204-2053; Home-Delivered Meals,
320 W Windsor Rd; tel: (818) 2246-5586

Phoenix, AZ: Laura Danieli Senior Activity
Center, 613 N 4th Ave; tel: (602) 251-2005

Portland, OR 97232-2822: Rose Centre – Senior
Citizens' Program, 211 NE 18th Ave;
tel: (503) 239-1221

Redondo Beach, CA 90277-2056:
  Home-delivered meals, 125 W Beryl St;
  tel: (310) 318-2827
Salinas, CA 93906-1519: 2460 N Main St;
  tel: (831) 443-9655
San Diego, CA 92101-1679: Senior Citizens'
  Program (6 Locations), 2320 5th Ave;
  tel: (619) 446-0212 (main office)
San Francisco, CA 94107-1125: Senior Meals
  Program, 850 Harrison St; tel: (415) 777-5350
San Jose, CA 95112: 359 N 4th St;
  tel: (408) 282-1165
Seattle, WA 98106: 9050 16th Ave SW;
  tel: (206) 767-3150 Ext 115
Tulare, CA 93274-4131: 314 E San Joaquin Ave;
  tel: (559) 687-2520
Turlock, CA 95380-5815: 893 Lander Ave;
  tel: (209) 667-6091

Veterans' Centres
Beaverton, OR 97007: 14825 SW Farmington Rd;
  tel: (503) 239-1259 (acc 143)
Casper, WY 8260: 625 So. Jefferson Street:
  tel: (307) 234-1368
El Paso County, CO 80909: 910 Yuma Street;
  tel: (719) 884-1060
Fort Collins, CO 80525: 3901 South Mason
  Street; tel: (970) 207-4472
Los Angeles, CA 90073: The Haven:
  Victory Place-Drug and Alcohol Rehab;
  Naomi House For Women (Transitional
  Housing); Exodus for Mentally Ill (Emergency
  Shelter); 11301 Wilshire Blvd, Bldg 212;
  tel: (310) 478-3711 ext 44353 (acc 265)
Pueblo, CO 81003: 520 W 13th Street;
  tel: 719-543-3656

*In addition there are 14 fresh-air camps and
34 youth community centres attached to divisions,
as well as 501 service units in the territory*

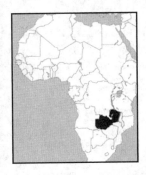

ZAMBIA TERRITORY

Territorial Commander:
Colonel Margaret Siamoya (1 Aug 2014)

Chief Secretary:
Lieut-Colonel Christopher Mabuto
(1 Jul 2011)

Territorial Headquarters: 685A Cairo Road, Lusaka

Postal address: PO Box 34352, Lusaka 10101, Zambia

Tel: [260] 1 238291/228327; email: zamleadership@zam.salvationarmy.org

In 1922 emigrants from villages on the north bank of the Zambezi river working in a mica mine near Hurungwe were converted. They carried home the message of salvation to their chief and established meeting places in their villages. Two years later, Commandant Kunzwi Shava and Lieutenant Paul Shumba were appointed to command the new opening. The Zambia Division in the Rhodesia Territory became the Zambia Command in 1966. In 1988, the Malawi Division was transferred from the Zimbabwe Territory to form the new Zambia and Malawi Territory. The Zambia and Malawi Territory became the Zambia Territory on 1 October 2002 when Malawi became an independent region.

Zone: Africa
Country included in the territory: Zambia
Languages in which the gospel is preached: Chibemba, Chinyanja, Chitonga, English, Lozi

TERRITORIAL congresses were held in various locations throughout the territory in September 2013 with the theme *Serving the Community*. At the congress held at Mazabuka and Southern Divisions, more than 2,500 Salvationists joined together under the leadership of Commissioner James Knaggs (TC, USA Western Territory).

In October, 27 cadets from the Disciples of the Cross Session were commissioned and ordained during a solemn occasion when the commitment of the cadets was acknowledged. However, the appointments meeting was filled with exuberant worship as the new officers received their first appointments.

Later in the year, the territorial League of Mercy team visited the University Teaching Hospital, distributing more than 400 parcels to patients and spreading Christmas cheer.

General André Cox and Commissioner Silvia Cox (WPWM) were given a lively welcome at Lusaka Airport by the territorial leaders Colonels Stephen and Grace Chepkurui (TC and TPWM)

accompanied by officers, soldiers and the territory's musical sections.

The General conducted an inspiring officers councils that resulted in more than 60 officers kneeling in rededication to the Lord. Commissioner Silvia Cox was the special guest at the women's rally and on the Sunday the cadets from the Messengers of Light Session were welcomed. In addressing the cadets, Commissioner Cox encouraged them to live up to their sessional name, showing the light of God to everyone. Following the General's Bible message, many Salvationists knelt in rededication.

We thank the Lord for all he has been doing in the Zambia Territory.

STATISTICS

Officers 252 (active 226 retired 26) **Cadets** 29 **Employees** 422
Corps 137 **Societies** 44 **Outposts** 156 **New Openings** 13 **Hospital** 1 **High School** 1 **Old People's Home** 1 **Farm** 1
Senior Soldiers 24,610 **Adherent Members** 3,157 **Junior Soldiers** 7,683
Personnel serving outside territory Officers 8

STAFF

Women's Ministries: Col Margaret Siamoya (TPWM) Lt-Col Annah Mabuto (TSWM) Maj Christine Chenda (THLS) Capt Esther Munkombwe (TJHLS) Maj Patricia Hangoma (TLOMS)
Sec for Personnel: Lt-Col Metson Chilyabanyama
Extension Training: Maj Mary Mizinga
Human Resources: Maj Joster Chenda
Sec for Programme: tba
Community Development, Faith-Based Facilitation and HIV/Aids Services: Maj Angela Hachitapika
Education: Maj Brighton Hachitapika
Men's Fellowships: Capt Ebbinish Kabulo
Projects: Capt Eron Zebedee
Public Relations Sec: Maj Kennedy Mizinga
Social Secretary/ Microcredit: Maj Ireen Hacamba

Child Sponsorship: Elijah Hazemba
Territorial B/M: Mweene Hambai
Youth and Candidates: Capt Ebbinish Kabulo
Sec for Business Administration: Lt-Col Shamu Meitei
Finance and Audit: tba
Property: Maj Kennedy Mizinga
Spiritual Life Centre Manager: Maj Mary Mizinga
Trade: Lt-Col Hoihnian Meitei
Training Principal: Maj Kenneth Hawkins

DIVISIONS

Lusaka North West: PO Box 33934, Lusaka; Majs Clifford D. and Moudy Chikoondo
Lusaka South East: PO Box 34352, Lusaka; tel: (01) 221960; Majs Casson and Mary Sichilomba
Mapangazya: P Bag S2, Mazabuka; Capts Aubey and Jane Hatukupa
Mazabuka: PO Box 670017, Mazabuka; tel: (032) 30420;
Southern: PO Box 630537, Choma; Majs Elisha and Alice Mankomba

DISTRICTS

Central North: PO Box 810336 Lt-Cols Frazer and Rodinah Chalwe
Copperbelt: PO Box 70075, Ndola; tel: (02) 680302; Capts John and Ackless Mweene
Siavonga: PO Box 59, Siavonga; tel: (01) 511362; Capt Victor Hamalala

SECTION (reporting to THQ)

Eastern: PO Box 510199, Chipata; tel: (097) 881828; Majs Myron and Kasamba Hamanenga

TRAINING COLLEGE

PO Box 34352, Lusaka, 10101; tel: (260) 211 261 755; email: zsaotc@gmail.com

CHIKANKATA MISSION

P Bag S2, Mazabuka
Mission Director: Maj Bernard Chisengele

CHIKANKATA HEALTH SERVICES

P Bag S2, Mazabuka; tel: (01) 222060; email: administration@chikankata.com
Administration: Capt Carl Wardley
Business Manager: Maj Isaac Kauseni
Manager/Community Health and Development: Mr Charles Mang'ombe
Manager/Nursing Education: Mrs Z. Ngalande

Hospital Chaplain: Maj Doris Namachila
Senior Medical Officer: Dr Felix Mitchelo
School of Nursing Matron: Maj Ruth Kauseni
Bio Medic School Matron: Maj Prudence
  Chisengele

Medical Clinics (under Chikankata)
Chaanga, Chikombola, Nadezwe, Nameembo,
  Syanyolo

Youth Project (under Chikankata)
Chikombola

CHIKANKATA HIGH SCHOOL
P Bag S1, Mazabuka; tel: (01) 220820;
  email: administration@chikankata.sch.zm
Headmaster: Mr Oscar Mwanza

OLD PEOPLE'S HOME AND VOCATIONAL TRAINING CENTRE
Mitanda Home for the Aged: PO Box 250096,
  Kansenshi, Ndola; tel: (02) 680460;
  email: mitanda@zamtel.zm:
  Centre Manager: Maj Joyce B. Pierce

PRE-SCHOOL GROUPS
Chikankata, Chikanzaya, Chipapa, Chipata,
  Chitumbi, Choma, Dundu, George, Hapwaya,
Ibbwe Munyama, John Laing, Kakole,
Kalomo, Kanyama, Kawama, Kazungula,
Lusaka Citadel, Maamba, Magoye, Mitchel,
Mumbwa, Ngangula, Njomona, Nkonkola,
Petauke, Peters, Siavonga, Sikoongo,
Sinazongwe, Situmbeko

COMMUNITY SCHOOLS
Chelstone, Chipata (Lusaka), Choma, George,
  John Laing, Kanyama, Kasiwe, Kawama,
  Luanshya, Maamba, Petauke

COMMUNITY WORK
Agriculture Projects: Chikankata, Chitumbi,
  Dundu, Hamabuya, Malala, Ngamgula
Health Centres: George, John Laing
HIV/Aids Training, Counselling: Chikankata, THQ
Microcredit Projects:
  Eastern: Chipata
  Lusaka North West: Mumbwa
  Mapangazya: Chikankata
  Mazabuka: Magoye, Monze, Nakambala,
    Njomona

FARM (income-generating)
PO Box 250096, Kansenshi, Ndola;
  tel: (02) 680460

ZAMBIA: The General with one of the residents at an Army facility

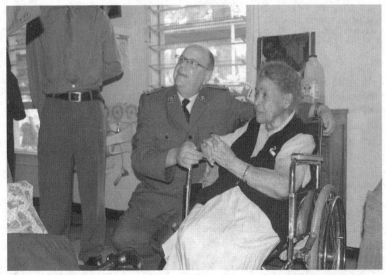

ZIMBABWE TERRITORY

Territorial leaders:
**Commissioners Henry and
Catherine Nyagah**

Territorial Commander:
Commissioner Henry Nyagah
(1 Jan 2013)

Chief Secretary:
Colonel Peter Kwenda
(1 Dec 2013)

Territorial Headquarters: 45 Josiah Chinamano Avenue, Harare

Postal address: PO Box 14, Harare, Zimbabwe

Tel: [263] (4) 736666/7/8, 250107/8; email: ZIMTHQ@zim.salvationarmy.org;

website: www.salvationarmy.org/Zimbabwe

A pioneer party led by Major and Mrs Pascoe set out from Kimberley, South Africa, on 5 May 1891 in a wagon drawn by 18 oxen, arriving in Fort Salisbury on 18 November. The then Rhodesia became a separate territory on 1 May 1931. Work spread to Botswana where The Salvation Army was officially recognised in 1997.

Zone: Africa
Countries included in the territory: Botswana, Zimbabwe
'The Salvation Army' in Ndebele: Impi yo Sindiso; in Shona: Hondo yo Ruponiso
Languages in which the gospel is preached: Chitonga, English, Ndebele, Shona, Tswana
Periodicals: *Zimbabwe Salvationist, ZEST* (women's magazine)

THE ZIMBABWE Territory has encouraged both spiritual and numerical growth during the year in review.

The visit by General André Cox and Commissioner Silvia Cox (WPWM) to celebrate Palm Sunday in Matabeleland Division and Easter with the territory as a whole was a great event. During Holy Week the world leaders visited Masiye Training Camp, Howard High School (where the General officially opened a classroom block and two staff quarters),

Howard Hospital and Bumhudzo Hospital Home. The General inspired and encouraged all who gathered together for the events.

In April 2014, the victims of the Tokwe-Mukosi floods who resided at Chingwizi Transitional Camp received medical kits, food hampers, blankets and clothing.

The Women's Ministries Department conducted local officers' seminars throughout the territory to assist the women in developing leadership skills. They also taught practical skills to enhance the women's domestic projects and increase fellowship funds. Through the efforts of the Helping Hand Project, women's ministries purchased a new bus for outreach programmes and to assist people who suffer because of HIV/Aids.

Annual youth and corps cadet councils were successfully held throughout the territory and were marked by good attendance and high participation.

It has been encouraging to witness the growth within the Christian student fellowship groups at Midlands State University, Bindura University of Science Education and the University of Zimbabwe, with members becoming involved in prayer and spiritual meetings. Students from the Bindura University of Science Education visited Bumhudzo Hospital Home, conducting a worship meeting and providing fellowship as well as donating blankets, clothing and food for the elderly.

The roof, windows, solar panels and solar water heaters of Tshelanyemba Hospital were destroyed by a severe hailstorm, but thankfully have been replaced.

The Salvation Army Schools Association (SASA) successfully held athletics competitions at Bradley High School in February 2014. The Information Technology Department set up all divisional headquarters and institutions with the Lotus Notes messaging system and installed wireless access around the territorial headquarters compound.

The territorial Self-Denial appeal ingathering services held in Kadoma and Semukwe Divisions have raised more than Z$1.2 million.

STATISTICS

Officers 646 (active 534 retired 112) **Cadets** 29
  Employees 1,300
Corps 431 **Societies** 368 **Outposts** 200
  Institutions/Social Centres 5 **Hospitals** 4
  Schools: Pre-Schools 51 **Primary** 33
  Secondary 15 **Boarding** 4
  Vocational Training 3
Senior Soldiers 124,869 **Adherent Members**
  5,828 **Junior Soldiers** 17,252
Personnel serving outside territory Officers 15

STAFF

Women's Ministries: Comr Catherine Nyagah
  (TPWM) Col Norma Kwenda (TSWM)
  Maj Mimmie Payne (TLOMS)
  Lt-Col Rumbidzayi Mambo (THLS)
Business Sec: Lt-Col Francis Nyakusamwa
Personnel Sec: Lt-Col Tineyi Mambo
Programme Sec: Lt-Col Trustmore Muzorori
Audit: Maj Laston Mbewe
Development Services: Capt Farai Jarai
Education/Human Resources Development:
  Maj Florence Pamacheche
Finance: Maj Patrick Sithole
Information Technology: Capt Jonathan Payne
Medical and Social: Maj Angeline Kapere
Property: Capt Laison Govati
Public Relations: Capt Godfrey Booramuponda
Sponsorship: Lt-Colonel Juliet Nyakusamwa
Statistics: Capt Jesline Sithole
Territorial BM: B/M M. Mtombeni
Territorial S/Ldr: S/L K.E. Mushababiri
Trade: Capt Tsaurai Mukwamuri
Training: Lt-Col Eritha Chiutsi
Youth and Candidates: Capt Duvai
  Maguranyanga

DIVISIONS

Bindura: PO Box 197, Bindura; tel: (071) 6689;
  Majs Yohana and Jesinala Msongwe
Chiweshe: PO Box 98, Glendale;
  tel: (077) 214524; Majs Onai and Deliwe Jera
Greater Harare: PO Box 1496, Harare;
  tel: (04) 747359;
  Majs Effort and Annette Paswera

Zimbabwe Territory

Guruve: c/o Box 150, Guruve; tel: (058) 505;
Lt-Cols Sammy and Ellen Nkhoma
Harare Central: c/o Highfield Temple;
Stand # 3300, Old Highfield; tel: 663 159;
Majs Casman and Martha Chinyemba
Harare Eastern: PO Box 26, Zengeza;
tel: (070) 22639;
Majs Frederick and Rosemary Masango
Harare West: c/o Dzivarasekwa Corps,
PO Box 37, Dzivarasekwa;
tel: (04) 216 293;
Majs Final and Pfumisai Mubayiwa
Hurungwe: PO Box 269, Karoi;
tel: (064) 629229;
Capts Josphat and Sisita Nyerere
Kadoma: PO Box 271, Kadoma;
tel: (068) 23338;
Majs Washington and Susan Marere
Makonde: PO Box 33, Chinhoyi;
tel: (067) 2107;
Lt-Cols Samuel and Theresa Baah
Masvingo: PO Box 314, Masvingo;
tel: (039) 63308;
Majs Isaac and Charity Mhembere
Matabeleland: PO Box 227 FM, Famona,
Bulawayo; tel: (09) 46934;
Majs Itai and Celiwe Mutizwa
Midlands: PO Box 624, Kwekwe;
tel: (055) 3992;
Majs Bigboy and Winnet Nkomo
Mupfure: PO Box 39, Mt Darwin;
tel: (076) 529;
Maj Netsai Matura
Semukwe: PO Box Maphisa Township,
Maphisa; tel: (082) 396;
Majs Joseph and Molly Madyanenzara

DISTRICTS
Manicaland: PO Box DV8, Dangamvura,
Mutare; tel: (020) 30014;
Maj Lovemore Chidhakwa
Murehwa: PO Box 268, Murehwa;
tel: (078) 2455; Maj Henry Chitanda

AREAS
Hwange: PO Box 130, Dete; tel: 018 237;
Area Coordinator: Maj Martin Chitsiko

TRAINING COLLEGE
PO Box CR95, Cranborne; tel: (04) 742298;

MASIYE TRAINING CAMP
PO Box AC800 Bulawayo; tel: (09) 60727;
Camp: tel: (0838) 222/261; tel: (0838) 228;
emails: info@masiye.com (camp),
info@byo.masiye.com (town office)

EDUCATION
Boarding Schools
Bradley Secondary School (acc 516)
Howard High School (acc 908)
Mazowe High School (acc 670)
Usher Secondary School (acc 560)

MEDICAL
Bumhudzo Hospital Home: St Mary's Township,
PO Box ZG 48, Zengeza, Harare;
tel: (070) 24911; 'C' scheme hospital home
(acc 55); 'B' scheme residential (acc 55)
Howard Hospital: PO Box 190, Glendale;
tel: (0758) 2433; emails:
howard.hospital@africaonline.co.zw (acc 144)
Tshelanyemba Hospital: PO Tshelanyemba,
Maphisa; tel: (082) 254; email:
tshelanyemba.hosp@healthnet.zw (acc 103)

SOCIAL SERVICES
Bulawayo
Enterprise House (acc men 65)
Ralstein Home (acc mixed 30)
Harare
Braeside Social Complex (acc women 20,
men 64)
Arcadia Girls' Hostel (acc 28)
Howard
Weaving and Dressmaking School: PO Howard;
tel: (0758) 45921

Words of Life
writer - Beverly Ivany

Join a worldwide readership:

• *Take time with the Father daily as you meditate upon his Word.*

• *Ask Jesus to interpret his Word and speak to your heart.*

• *Open yourself to the Spirit as he brings inspiration.*

A series of daily devotional readings inspired by Scripture, including psalms, proverbs and Christian hymns. Published three times a year, each edition features a mini-series by a guest writer, reflecting the cultural diversity of the international Salvation Army.

144pp (paperback)

Can be purchased on subscription or as individual copies from any Salvation Army trade or supplies department.

Also available online as print and ebook editions at www.amazon.co.uk

GLOSSARY OF SALVATION ARMY TERMS

Adherent Member: A member of The Salvation Army who has not made a commitment to soldiership.

Advisory Board: A group of influential citizens who, believing in the Army's programme of spiritual, moral and physical rehabilitation and amelioration, assist in promoting and supporting Army projects.

'Blood and Fire': The Army's motto; refers to the blood of Jesus Christ and the fire of the Holy Spirit.

Cadet: A Salvationist who is in training for officership.

Candidate: A soldier who has been accepted for officer training.

Chief of the Staff: The officer second in command of the Army throughout the world.

Chief Secretary: The officer second in command of the Army in a territory.

Citadel: A building used for worship and community service.

Colours: The tricolour flag of the Army. Its colours symbolise the blood of Jesus Christ (red), the fire of the Holy Spirit (yellow) and the purity of God (blue).

Command: A type of small territory.

Command leaders: A married officer couple appointed to a joint role of spiritual leadership, ministry, administration and pastoral care.

Commission: A document presented publicly, authorising an officer, or local officer to fulfil a specified ministry.

Congress: Central gatherings often held annually and attended by most officers and many soldiers of a territory, command, region or division.

Corps: A Salvation Army unit established for the preaching of the gospel, worship, teaching and fellowship and to provide Christian-motivated service in the community.

Corps Cadet: A young Salvationist who undertakes a course of study and practical training in a corps, with a view to becoming effective in Salvation Army service.

Corps Sergeant-Major: The chief local officer for public work who assists the corps officer with meetings and usually takes command in his/her absence.

Dedication Service: A public presentation of infants to the Lord. This differs from christening or infant baptism in that the main emphasis is upon specific vows made by the parents concerning the child's upbringing.

Division: A number of corps grouped together under the direction of a divisional commander (may also include social service centres and programmes), operating within a territory or command.

Divisional Commander: The officer in charge of the Army in a division.

Envoy: A Salvationist whose duty it is to visit corps, societies and outposts, for the purpose of conducting meetings. An envoy may be appointed in charge of any such unit.

General: The officer elected to the supreme command of the Army throughout the world. All appointments are made, and all regulations issued, under the General's authority (see under High Council – p 12).

General Secretary: The officer second in charge of the Army in a command (or, in some territories, a large division).

Halfway House: A centre for the rehabilitation of alcoholics or parolees (USA).

Harbour Light Centre: A rehabilitation centre, usually located in inner city areas.

High Council: See p 12.

Home League: See p 25.

International Headquarters (IHQ): The offices in which the business connected with the command of the worldwide Army is transacted (see p 29).

International Secretary: A position at IHQ with responsibility for the oversight and coordination of the work in a specific geographical zone or functional category, and for advising the General on zonal and worldwide issues and policies.

Junior Soldier: A boy or girl who, having accepted Jesus as their Saviour, has signed the junior soldier's promise and become a Salvationist.

League of Mercy: A ministry programme undertaken by Salvationists who visit prisons, hospitals and residential homes, in their own time, bringing the gospel and rendering practical aid (see p 26).

Local Officer: A soldier appointed to a position of responsibility and authority in the corps; carries out the duties of the appointment without being separated from regular employment or receiving remuneration from the Army.

Medical Fellowship: See p 26.

Mercy Seat or Penitent Form: A bench provided as a place where people can kneel to pray, seeking salvation or sanctification, or making a special consecration to God's will and service. The mercy seat is usually situated between the platform and main area of Army halls as a focal point to remind all of God's reconciling and redeeming presence.

Officer: A Salvationist who has been trained, commissioned and ordained to service and leadership, in response to God's call. An officer is a recognised minister of religion.

Officer Commanding: The officer in charge of the Army in a command.

Order of Distinguished Auxiliary Service: See p 28.

Order of the Founder: See p 27.

Outpost: A locality in which Army work is carried out and where it is hoped a society or corps will develop.

Pastoral Care Council: Established in each corps for the care of soldiers, etc, and maintenance of the membership rolls.

Promotion to Glory: The Army's description of the death of Salvationists.

Ranks of Officers: Lieutenant, captain, major, lieut-colonel, colonel, commissioner, General.

Red Shield: A symbol saying 'The Salvation Army' in the local language, identifying personnel, buildings, equipment, mobile units and emergency services.

Red Shield Appeal: A financial appeal to the general public; also known as the Annual Appeal in some countries.

Red Shield Centre: A Salvation Army facility on military premises serving the physical and spiritual needs of military personnel and their families.

Salvation: The work of grace which God accomplishes in a repentant person whose trust is in Christ as Saviour, forgiving sin, giving new direction to life, and strength to live as God desires.

Self-Denial Appeal: An annual effort by Salvationists and friends to raise funds for the Army's worldwide operations.

Sergeant: A local officer appointed for specific duty, usually in a corps.

Silver Star, Fellowship of the: This comprises parents or other significant life mentors of Salvation Army officers.

Society: A company of soldiers who work together regularly in a district, without an officer.

Soldier: A converted person at least 14 years of age who has, with the approval of the pastoral care council, been enrolled as a member of The Salvation Army after signing the Soldier's Covenant.

Soldier's Covenant: The statement of beliefs and promises which every intending soldier is required to sign before enrolment. Previously called 'Articles of War'.

Territorial Commander: The officer in command of the Army in a territory.

Territorial leaders: A territorial commander and spouse in their joint role of sharing spiritual leadership and ministry, providing pastoral care and exemplifying the working partnership of officer couples. The chief secretary is the second-in-command of the territory.

Territory: A country, part of a country or several countries combined, in which Salvation Army work is organised under a territorial commander.

Young People's Sergeant-Major: A local officer responsible for young people's work in a corps, under the commanding officer.

CHRONOLOGICAL TABLE OF IMPORTANT EVENTS IN SALVATION ARMY HISTORY 1829-2013

1829 Catherine Mumford (later Mrs Booth, 'the Army Mother') born at Ashbourne, Derbyshire (17 Jan); William Booth born at Nottingham (10 Apr).

1844 William Booth converted.

1846 Catherine Mumford converted.

1855 Marriage of William Booth and Catherine Mumford at Stockwell New Chapel, London (16 Jun).

1856 William Bramwell Booth (the Founder's eldest son and second General of the Army) born in Halifax (8 Mar).

1858 William Booth ordained as Methodist minister (27 May). (Accepted on probation 1854.)

1859 *Female Teaching*, Mrs Booth's first pamphlet, published (Dec).

1860 Mrs Booth's first public address (27 May, Whit Sunday).

1865 **Rev William Booth began work in East London** (2 Jul); The Christian Mission, founded; Eveline (Evangeline) Cory Booth (fourth General) born in London (25 Dec).

1867 First Headquarters (Eastern Star) opened in Whitechapel Road, London.

1868 *The East London Evangelist* – later (1870) *The Christian Mission Magazine* and (1879) *The Salvationist* – published (Oct).

1874 Christian Mission work commenced in **Wales** (15 Nov).

1875 *Rules and Doctrines of The Christian Mission* published.

1876 *Revival Music* published (Jan).

1878 First use of the term 'Salvation Army' – in small appeal folder (May); 'The Christian Mission' became **'The Salvation Army'**, and the Rev William Booth became known as the General; deed poll executed, thus establishing the doctrines and principles of The Salvation Army (Aug); first corps flag presented by Mrs Booth at Coventry (28-30 Sep); *Orders and Regulations for The Salvation Army* issued (Oct); brass instruments first used.

1879 First corps in **Scotland** opened (24 Mar) and **Channel Islands** (14 Aug); cadets first trained; introduction of uniform; first

278

corps band formed in Consett; issue No 1 of *The War Cry* published (27 Dec).

1880 First training home opened, at Hackney, London; first contingent of SA officers landed in the **United States of America** (10 Mar); SA work commenced in **Ireland** (7 May); children's meetings commenced at Blyth (30 Jul); SA work extended to **Australia** (5 Sep).

1881 Work began in **France** (13 Mar); *The Little Soldier* (subsequently *The Young Soldier*) issued (27 Aug); *The Doctrines and Disciplines of The Salvation Army* prepared for use at training homes for Salvation Army officers; Headquarters removed to Queen Victoria Street, London (8 Sep).

1882 The Founder's first visit to France (Mar); former London Orphan Asylum opened as Clapton Congress Hall and National Training Barracks (13 May); work began in **Canada** (21 May), **India** (19 Sep), **Switzerland** (22 Dec) and **Sweden** (28 Dec).

1883 Work begun in **Sri Lanka** (26 Jan), **South Africa** (4 Mar), **New Zealand** (1 Apr), **Isle of Man** (17 Jun) and **Pakistan** (then a part of India); first prison-gate home opened in Melbourne, Australia (8 Dec); *The Doctrines and Disciplines of The Salvation Army* published in a public edition.

1884 Women's Social Work inaugurated; *The Soldier's Guide* published (Apr); work began in **St Helena** (5 May); *The Salvation Army Band Journal* issued (Aug); *All the World* issued (Nov).

1885 Commencement of the Family Tracing Service, known as Mrs Booth's Enquiry Bureau; *Orders and Regulations for Divisional Officers* published (10 Jun); *The Doctrines of The Salvation Army* published; Purity Agitation launched; Criminal Law Amendment Act became law on 14 Aug; trial (began 23 Oct) and acquittal of Bramwell Booth – charged, with W. T. Stead, in connection with the 'Maiden Tribute' campaign.

1886 Work begun in **Newfoundland** (1 Feb); first International Congress in London (28 May-4 Jun); *The Musical Salvationist* issued (Jul); first Self-Denial Week (4-11 Sep); first slum corps opened at Walworth, London, by 'Mother' Webb (20 Sep); work began in **Germany** (14 Nov); *Orders and Regulations for Field Officers* published; the Founder first visited the United States and Canada.

1887 Work began in **Italy** (20 Feb), **Denmark** (8 May), **Netherlands** (8 May) and **Jamaica** (16 Dec); the Founder's first visit to Denmark, Sweden and Norway.

1888 Young people's work organised throughout Great Britain; first food depot opened, in Limehouse, London (Jan); work began in **Norway** (22 Jan); first junior soldiers' brass band (Clapton); the Army Mother's last public address at City Temple, London (21 Jun).

1889 Work begun in **Belgium** (5 May) and **Finland** (8 Nov); First edition of *The Deliverer* published (Jul).

1890 Work began in **Argentina** (1 Jan); *Orders and Regulations for Soldiers of The Salvation Army* issued (Aug); the Army Mother promoted to Glory (4 Oct); *In Darkest England and the Way Out*, by the Founder, published (Oct); work began in **Uruguay** (16 Nov); banking department opened (registered as The Salvation Army Bank, 1891; Reliance Bank Ltd, 28 Dec 1900).

1891 The Founder publicly signed 'Darkest England' (now The Salvation Army Social Work) Trust Deed (30 Jan); £108,000 subscribed for 'Darkest England' scheme (Feb); Land and Industrial Colony, Hadleigh, Essex, established (2 May); International Staff Band inaugurated (Oct); work began in **Zimbabwe** (21 Nov) and **Zululand** (22 Nov); the Founder's first visit to South Africa, Australia, New Zealand and India; the charter of The Methodist and General Assurance Society acquired.

1892 Eastbourne (UK) verdict against Salvationists quashed in the High Court of Justice (27 Jan); Band of Love inaugurated; League of Mercy begun in Canada (Dec).

1893 Grace-Before-Meat scheme instituted; *The Officer* issued (Jan).

1894 Second International Congress (Jul); work began in **Hawaiian Islands** (13 Sep) and **Java** (now part of **Indonesia**) (24 Nov); naval and military league (later red shield services) established (Nov); Swiss Supreme Court granted religious rights to SA (Dec).

1895 Work began in **British Guiana** (now **Guyana**) (24 Apr), **Iceland** (12 May), **Japan** (4 Sep) and **Gibraltar** (until 1968).

1896 Young people's legion (Feb) and corps cadet brigades (Feb) inaugurated; work began in **Bermuda** (12 Jan) and **Malta**

(25 Jul until 1972); first SA exhibition, Agricultural Hall, London (Aug).

1897 First united young people's meetings (later termed 'councils') (14 Mar); first International Social Council in London (Sep); first SA hospital founded at Nagercoil, India (Dec).

1898 *Orders and Regulations for Social Officers* published; work began in **Barbados** (30 Apr) and **Alaska**; first united corps cadet camp at Hadleigh (Whitsun).

1899 First bandsmen's councils, Clapton (10 Dec).

1901 Work began in **Trinidad** (7 Aug).

1902 Work begun in **St Lucia** (Sep) and **Grenada**.

1903 Migration Department inaugurated (became Reliance World Travel Ltd, 1981; closed 31 May 2001); work began in **Antigua**.

1904 Third International Congress (Jun-Jul); Founder received by King Edward VII at Buckingham Palace (24 Jun); Founder's first motor campaign (Aug); work began in **Panama** (Dec).

1905 The Founder campaigned in the Holy Land, Australia and New Zealand (Mar-Jun); first emigrant ship chartered by SA sailed for Canada (26 Apr); opening of International Staff Lodge (later College, now International College for Officers) (11 May); work began in **St Vincent** (Aug). Freedom of London conferred on the Founder (26 Oct); Freedom of Nottingham conferred on the Founder (6 Nov).

1906 *The YP* (later *The Warrior*, then *Vanguard*) and *The Salvation Army Year Book* issued; Freedom of Kirkcaldy conferred on the Founder (16 Apr).

1907 Anti-Suicide Bureau established (Jan); Home League inaugurated (28 Jan); *The Bandsman and Songster* (later *The Musician*) issued (6 Apr); honorary degree of DCL, Oxford, conferred on the Founder (26 Jun); work began in **Costa Rica** (5 Jul).

1908 Work began in **Korea** (Oct).

1909 Leprosy work commenced in **Java** (now part of **Indonesia**) (15 Jan); SA work began in **Chile** (Oct).

1910 Work began in **Peru**, **Paraguay** and **Sumatra** (now part of **Indonesia**).

1912 Founder's last public appearance, in Royal Albert Hall, London (9 May); **General William Booth promoted to Glory** (20 Aug); **William Bramwell Booth appointed General** (21 Aug).

1913 Inauguration of life-saving scouts (21 Jul); work began in **Celebes** (now part of **Indonesia**) (15 Sep) and **Russia** (until 1923).

1914 Fourth International Congress (Jun).

1915 Work began in **British Honduras** (now **Belize**) (Jun) and **Burma** (now **Myanmar**); life-saving guards inaugurated (17 Nov).

1916 Work began in **China** (Jan until 1951), in **St Kitts** and in **Portuguese East Africa** (now **Mozambique**) (officially recognised 1923).

1917 Work began in **Virgin Islands** (USA) (Apr); chums inaugurated (23 Jun); Order of the Founder instituted (20 Aug).

1918 Work commenced in **Cuba** (Jul).

1919 Work began in **Czechoslovakia** (19 Sep until 1950).

1920 Work began in **Nigeria** (15 Nov) and **Bolivia** (Dec).

1921 Work began in **Kenya** (Apr); sunbeams inaugurated (3 Nov).

1922 Work began in **Zambia** (1 Feb), **Brazil** (1 Aug) and **Ghana** (Aug); publication of a second *Handbook of Salvation Army Doctrine*.

1923 Work began in **Latvia** (until 1939).

1924 Work began in **Hungary** (24 Apr until 1950), in **Surinam** (10 Oct) and **The Færoes** (23 Oct).

1927 Work began in **Austria** (27 May), **Estonia** (31 Dec until 1940) and **Curacao** (until 1980); first International Young People's Staff Councils (May-Jun).

1928 General Bramwell Booth's last public appearance – the stonelaying of the International (William Booth Memorial) Training College (now William Booth College), Denmark Hill, London (10 May).

1929 First High Council (8 Jan-13 Feb); **Comr Edward J. Higgins elected General**; General Bramwell Booth promoted to Glory (16 Jun); Army work began in **Colombia** (until 1965).

1930 Inception of goodwill league; Order of the Silver Star (now Fellowship of the Silver Star) inaugurated (in USA, extended to other lands in 1936); work began in **Hong Kong**; Commissioners' Conference held in London (Nov).

1931 Work began in **Uganda** and the **Bahamas** (May); The Salvation Army Act 1931 received royal assent (Jul).

1932	Work began in **Namibia** (until 1939).
1933	Work began in **Yugoslavia** (15 Feb until 1948), Devil's Island, **French Guiana** (1 Aug until closing of the penal settlement in 1952) and **Tanzania** (29 Oct).
1934	Work began in **Algeria** (10 Jun until 1970); second High Council elected Commander Evangeline Booth General (3 Sep); work began in **Congo (Kinshasa)** (14 Oct); **General Evangeline Booth took command of The Salvation Army** (11 Nov).
1935	Work began in **Singapore** (28 May).
1936	Work began in **Egypt** (until 1949).
1937	Work began in **Congo (Brazzaville)** (Mar), **The Philippines** (6 Jun) and **Mexico** (Oct).
1938	Torchbearer group movement inaugurated (Jan); *All the World* re-issued (Jan); work spread from Singapore to **Malaysia**.
1939	Third High Council elected Comr George Lyndon Carpenter General (24 Aug); **General George Lyndon Carpenter took command of The Salvation Army** (1 Nov).
1941	Order of Distinguished Auxiliary Service instituted (24 Feb); International Headquarters destroyed in London Blitz (10 May).
1943	Inauguration of The Salvation Army Medical Fellowship (16 Feb) (SA Nurses' Fellowship until 1987).
1944	Service of thanksgiving to mark centenary of conversion of William Booth (in 1844) held in St Paul's Cathedral, London (2 Jun).
1946	Fourth High Council elected Comr Albert Orsborn General (9 May); **General Albert Orsborn took command of The Salvation Army** (21 Jun).
1948	First Army worldwide broadcast (28 Apr).
1950	Work began in **Haiti** (5 Feb); first TV broadcast by a General of The Salvation Army; official constitution of students' fellowship; first International Youth Congress held in London (10-23 Aug); reopening of Staff College (later International College for Officers) (10 Oct).
1954	Fifth High Council elected Comr Wilfred Kitching General (11 May); **General Wilfred Kitching took command of The Salvation Army** (1 Jul).
1956	Work began in Port Moresby, **Papua New Guinea** (31 Aug); first International Corps Cadet Congress (19-31 Jul).
1959	Over-60 clubs inaugurated (Oct).
1962	Work began in **Puerto Rico** (Feb).
1963	Sixth High Council elected Comr Frederick Coutts General (1 Oct); Queen Elizabeth the Queen Mother declared International Headquarters open (13 Nov); **General Frederick Coutts took command of The Salvation Army** (23 Nov).
1965	Queen Elizabeth II attended the International Centenary commencement (24 Jun); Founders' Day Service held in Westminster Abbey, London (2 Jul); work re-established in **Taiwan** (pioneered 1928) (Oct).
1967	Work began in **Malawi** (13 Nov).
1969	Seventh High Council elected Comr Erik Wickberg General (23 Jul); *The Salvation Army Handbook of Doctrine* new edition published (Aug); **General Erik Wickberg took command of The Salvation Army** (21 Sep); work began in **Lesotho.**
1970	Cyclone relief operations in East Pakistan (later **Bangladesh**) (25 Nov) lead to start of work in 1971.
1971	Work began in **Spain** (23 Jul) and **Portugal** (25 Jul).
1972	Work began in **Venezuela** (30 Jun).
1973	Work began in **Fiji** (14 Nov).
1974	Eighth High Council elected Comr Clarence Wiseman General (13 May); **General Clarence Wiseman took command of The Salvation Army** (6 Jul).
1976	Work began in **Guatemala** (Jun); **Mexico and Central America Territory** (now **Latin America North Territory** and **Mexico Territory**) formed (1 Oct).
1977	The ninth High Council elected Comr Arnold Brown General (5 May); **General Arnold Brown took command of The Salvation Army** (5 Jul).
1978	Fifth International Congress (Jun-Jul), with opening ceremony attended by HRH the Prince of Wales.
1979	The Salvation Army Boys' Adventure Corps (SABAC) launched (21 Jan).
1980	Inauguration of International Staff Songsters (8 Mar); The Salvation Army Act 1980 received royal assent (1 Aug); work began in **French Guiana** (1 Oct).
1981	Tenth High Council elected Comr Jarl Wahlström General (23 Oct); **General Jarl Wahlström took command of The Salvation Army** (14 Dec).

1984 International Conference of Leaders held in Berlin, West Germany (May).

1985 Work began in **Colombia** (21 Apr) and **Marshall Islands** (1 Jun); second International Youth Congress (Jul) held in Macomb, Illinois, USA; work began in **Angola** (4 Oct) and **Ecuador** (30 Oct).

1986 Work began in **Tonga** (9 Jan); *Salvationist* first issued (15 Mar); 11th High Council elected Comr Eva Burrows General (2 May); **General Eva Burrows took command of The Salvation Army** (9 Jul); International Development Conference held at Sunbury Court, London (Sep).

1988 Work began in **Liberia** (1 May); International Conference of Leaders held in Lake Arrowhead, California, USA (Sep).

1989 Work began in **El Salvador** (1 Apr).

1990 Work began in **East Germany** (Mar), **Czechoslovakia** (May), **Hungary** (Jun) and re-established in **Latvia** (Nov); sixth International Congress held in London (Jun-Jul); **United Kingdom Territory** established (1 Nov).

1991 Restructuring of **International Headquarters** as an entity separate from UK Territory (1 Feb); work reopened in **Russia** (6 Jul); International Conference of Leaders held in London (Jul-Aug).

1992 Opening of new **USA National Headquarters** building in Alexandria, Virginia (3 May).

1993 The 12th High Council elected Comr Bramwell H. Tillsley General (28 Apr); **General Bramwell H. Tillsley took command of The Salvation Army** (9 Jul); work began in **Micronesia**.

1994 First International Literary and Publications Conference held at Alexandria, Virginia, USA (Apr); General Bramwell H. Tillsley resigned from office (18 May); 13th High Council elected Comr Paul A. Rader General (23 Jul); **General Paul A. Rader took command of The Salvation Army immediately**; work began in **Guam**.

1995 International Conference of Leaders held in Hong Kong (Apr); all married women officers granted rank in their own right (1 May); work began in **Dominican Republic** (1 Jul); work reopened in **Estonia** (14 Aug); following relief and development programmes, work began in **Rwanda** (5 Nov).

1996 Work began in **Sabah (East Malaysia)** (Mar); first meeting of International Spiritual Life Commission (Jul).

1997 International Youth Forum held in Cape Town, South Africa (Jan); first ever congress held in Russia/CIS; Salvation Army leaders in Southern Africa signed commitment to reconciliation for past stand on apartheid; work began in **Botswana** (20 Nov).

1998 International Conference of Leaders held in Melbourne, Australia (Mar), receives report of International Spiritual Life Commission; publication of a fourth Handbook of Doctrine entitled *Salvation Story* (Mar); International Commission on Officership opened in London (Oct).

1999 International Education Symposium held in London (Mar); work began in **Romania** (May); 14th High Council elected Comr John Gowans General (15 May); **General John Gowans took command of The Salvation Army** (23 Jul).

2000 International Commission on Officership closed and subsequent Officership Survey carried out (Mar-May); work began in **Macau** (25 Mar); The Salvation Army registered as a denomination in **Sweden** (10 Mar); International Conference of Leaders held in Atlanta, Georgia, USA (Jun); seventh International Congress held in Atlanta, Georgia, USA (28 Jun-2 Jul) (first held outside UK); work began in **Honduras** (23 Nov)

2001 International Conference for Training Principals held in London (Mar); International Theology and Ethics Symposium held in Winnipeg, Canada (Jun); International Music Ministries Forum held in London (Jul); International Poverty Summit held on the Internet and Lotus Notes Intranet (Nov 2001-Feb 2002)

2002 The 15th High Council elected Comr John Larsson General (6 Sep); **General John Larsson took command of The Salvation Army** (13 Nov)

2004 International Conference of Leaders held in New Jersey, USA (29 Apr-7 May); International Music and Other Creative Ministries Forum (MOSAIC) held in Toronto, Canada (Jun); New International Headquarters building at 101 Queen Victoria Street, London, opened by Her

Royal Highness, The Princess Royal (9 Nov); IHQ Emergency Services coordinates disaster relief work after Indian Ocean tsunami struck (26 Dec)

2005 Eastern Europe Command redesignated Eastern Europe Territory; Singapore, Malaysia and Myanmar Command redesignated Singapore, Malaysia and Myanmar Territory (both 1 Mar); International Literary and Publications Conference held at Alexandria, Virginia, USA (Apr); European Youth Congress held in Prague, Czech Republic (4-8 Aug); All-Africa Congress held in Harare, Zimbabwe (24-28 Aug); work in **Lithuania** officially recognised by IHQ, and Germany Territory redesignated Germany and Lithuania Territory (Sep); 'Project Warsaw' launched to begin Army's work in **Poland** (23-25 Sep); East Africa Territory redesignated Kenya Territory, with Uganda Region given command status (1 Nov)

2006 The 16th High Council elected Comr Shaw Clifton General (28 Jan); **General Shaw Clifton took command of The Salvation Army** (2 Apr); Salvation Army Scouts and Guides World Jamboree held in Almere, Netherlands (Aug); 2nd International Theology and Ethics Symposium held in Johannesburg, South Africa (Aug)

2007 Website for Office of the General launched (Feb); first of General's pastoral letters to soldiers dispatched electronically (15 Mar); first International Conference of Personnel Secretaries held in London (27 May-3 Jun); International Social Justice Commission established (1 Jul), headed by an International Director for Social Justice; work began in **Burundi** (5 Aug) and **Greece** (1 Oct)

2008 Work recommenced in **Namibia** (3 Jan); new opening began in **Mali** (7 Feb); ICO renamed International College for Officers and Centre for Spiritual Life Development (Jul); first officers appointed to **Kuwait** (1 Aug); work began in **Mongolia** (13 Oct); first International Women Leader Development Programme held at Sunbury Court, UK (18 Nov-6 Dec)

2009 Official opening of work in **Nepal** (15 Apr); largest-ever assembly of SA

leaders at International Conference of Leaders held in London, UK (7-13 Jul); first International Prayer Leaders Gathering held at CSLD, London (11-18 Sep)

2010 Work began in **Sierra Leone** (1 Jan); **Nicaragua** (1 Mar); **United Arab Emirates** (1 Jun); Sweden hosted 'Raised Up' World Youth Convention (15-18 Jul); first Salvation Army building opened in **Mongolia** (9 Sep)

2011 Work began in the **Turks and Caicos Islands** (1 Jan); 17th High Council elected Comr Linda Bond 19th General (31 Jan); Work began in the **Solomon Islands** (1 Feb); **Greece** was recognised as part of Italy and Greece Command (2 Feb); Malawi, Mozambique and Uganda became territories (1 Mar); International Doctrine Council held in North Carolina, USA (23-26 Mar); Work began in **Togo**, Mali and Middle East were given regional status (all 1 Apr); **General Linda Bond took command of The Salvation Army** (2 Apr); ISB 120 celebrations in London (3-5 Jun); launch of weekly Worldwide Prayer Meeting (1 Sep); the International Vision: One Army, One Mission, One Message launched (1 Oct)

2012 *Words of Life* made available as an e-book for Kindle (Jan); The Salvation Army was granted legal recognition as a church in **Hungary** (Feb); 'I'll Fight' Congress at Royal Albert Hall, London, UK (Jun); International Conference of Leaders held in Canada, (7-14 Jul); work commenced in **Greenland** (8 Aug); first International College for Soldiers held at ICO, UK (10-24 Sep); work commenced in **Cambodia** (22 Nov); The Salvation Army officially at work in **126** countries.

2013 The united **Spain and Portugal** Command was inaugurated on 1 Feb; 'Called and Commissioned' Conference of training leaders held in London (Apr); the 18th High Council elected Commissioner André Cox General (3 Aug); **General André Cox took command of The Salvation Army immediately;** 100 years of Salvation Army Scouting celebrated at a jamboree at Gilwell Park, UK (Aug).

Biographical Information

1. The following list contains the names of all active officers with the rank of lieut-colonel and above, and other officers holding certain designated appointments.

2(a) The place and date in parenthesis immediately following the name denote the place from which the officer entered Army service and the year of service commencement. Officers commissioned prior to 1 January 1973 have their active service dated from the conclusion of the first year of training. After 1 January 1973 active service begins at the date of commissioning.

(b) Details of married women officers' entry to active service are shown separately, including maiden name. If a wife was trained separately from her husband the word *and* joins the two entries, but if trained together the word *with* joins them.

(c) At the end of each entry of married officers a joint record of their service in other countries is given. Where applicable this includes countries each served in individually before marriage.

3. Where an officer is serving in a territory/command other than his/her own this is indicated by including the territory/command of origin after the corps from which he/she entered training. In all other instances the information given implies that the officer is serving in his/her home territory.

4. Details of appointments (where not given in this section) may be ascertained under the territorial or departmental headings.

5. A key to abbreviations is given on pages 39-40.

A

ABAYOMI, Ebenezer (Ife Ife, 1988); Maj, Nig. b 4 Apr 60; and
ABAYOMI, Comfort (Ife Ife, 1990) m 1990; Maj, Nig. b 12 Dec 63.
ABIA, Edmund (Somanya, 1993); Maj, Gha, b 14 Mar 62; with
ABIA, Grace (née Awo) m 1991; Maj, Gha. b 15 Feb 69.
ADAMS, Clive (Claremont, S Afr, 1983); Comr, TC, UK. b 5 Jan 57; and
ADAMS, Marianne (née Jokobsen) (Oslo 3, Nor, 1985) m 1990; Comr, TPWM, UK. b 10 Feb 60. Served in S Afr, UK, at IHQ and in Nor (CS/TSWM, TC/TPWM).
ADDISON, Edward (Swedru, 1981); Maj, Gha. b 24 Jan 54. Ww Lt Margaret, pG 1983; and
ADDISON, Mercy (née Simpson) (Swedru, 1985) m 1985; Maj, Gha. b 4 Nov 60.
ADEPOJU, Gabriel (Ibadan, 1986); Maj, Nig. b 17 Jul 61. MSc, MA, BEd; and
ADEPOJU, Comfort (Ibadan, 1994) m 1994; Maj, Nig. b 15 Aug 70.
AHN, Guhn-shik (Oh Ka, 1985); Maj, Kor. b 23 Dec 57; and
YANG, Shin-kyong (Sudaemun, 1984) m 1985; Maj, Kor. b 5 Jul 54.
AKPAN, Joseph (Calabar, 1980); Lt-Col, Nig. b 30 Sep 58; with
AKPAN, Patience m 1978; Lt-Col, Nig. b 15 May 62.
ALARCÓN, David (Punta Arenas, 1980); Lt-Col, CS, L Am N. b 24 Jun 56; and
ALARCÓN, María (née Arredondo) (Rancagua, 1980) m 1982; Lt-Col, TSWM, L Am N. b 3 Mar 55. Served in S Am W.

ALFRED, Tharmar (Arumanai, 1977); Lt-Col, Ind SE. b 23 May 54. MA, BTh; and
RAJABAI, Alfred (Pottetty, 1975) m 1977; Lt-Col, Ind SE. b 16 Apr 53.
ALÍ, Sixto (El Tejar, 1990); Maj, S Am W. b 28 Mar 63; with
ALÍ, Aída (née Cáceres) m 1988; Maj, S Am W. b 8 Mar 68.
ALLAN, Graham (Kokomo, IN, 1975); Maj, USA C. b 24 Feb 49. BA (Counselling/Bus Adm), AA (Bus); with
ALLAN, Vickie (née Hardebeck) m 1969; Maj, USA C. b 26 Jan 50.
ALLEMAND, Carolyn (née Olckers) (Cape Town Citadel, S Afr, 1980); Lt-Col, UK. b 4 Oct 55. Served in S Afr, at IHQ and in S Am E. m 1989; Lt-Col Gustave, ret 2006.
ALLEY, Kelvin (Belconnen, Aus E, 1987); Maj, Aus Nat and Aus E. b 3 Apr 54. BA (Admin), BDiv, DMin; with
ALLEY, Julie (née Stewart) m 1975; Maj, Aus E. b 19 Jun 56. Dip Min. Served in PNG.
ALMENDARES, Saraí (Tegucugalpa, Honduras 2011) Lt. L Am N. b 4 Feb 80.
AMAKYE, Francis (Achiase, 1995); Maj, Tanz. b 25 Jul 65; with
AMAKYE, Jemima (née Agyei Yeboah) m 1992; Maj, Tanz. b 3 May 65. Served in Gha.
AMBITAN, Harold (Manado 1, 1973); Lt-Col, Indon. b 9 May 49; and
AMBITAN, Deetje (née Malawau) (Bandung, 1972) m 1975; Lt-Col, Indon. b 8 Jun 49.
AMICK, Richard (Hutchinson, KS, 1978); Lt-Col, USA C. b 24 Nov 54. BA (Bus Adm); and
AMICK, Vicki (née Anderson) (Grand

284

Haven, MI, 1978) m 1979; Lt-Col, USA C. b 29 Jun 55.

AMPOFO, Jonas (Asiakwa, 1981); Maj, Gha. b 6 Oct 1950; W w Maj Agnes pG 2000 and **AMPOFO, Constance** (née Nyamekye) m 2004; Capt, Gha. b 14 Apr 57.

AMPONSAH, Samuel (Wamfie, Gha, 1987); Maj, GS, Lib. b 30 Sep 1959, Dip BRS, Bth, MICA; FCCA, MBA, MSc; with **AMPONSAH, Hagar** (née Afia Kisiwaa) m 1985; Maj, CSWM, Lib. b 9 Jul 63. Served in Gha and at IHQ.

ANDERSEN, Henrik (Lyngby, Den, 1986); Col, CS, Neth. b 30 Aug 61; MA (Missional Leadership; with **ANDERSEN, Lisbeth** (née Bjarkam) m 1984; Col, TSWM, Neth. b 17 Apr 64. BA (Pastoral Psychology). Served in Latvia, UK and Den (CS/TSWM).

APPEATENG, Seth (Manso, 1989); Lt-Col, OC, Rwa. b 19 Oct 62; with **APPEATENG, Janet** (née Nkansah) m 1987; Lt-Col, CPWM, Rwa. b 12 Dec 67. Served in Gha and Tanz (CS/TSWM).

ARGUEDAS, Antonio (Callao, Peru, 1974); Maj, S Am W. b 9 Sep 53; and **ARGUEDAS, Lilian** (née Sánchez) (Lima Central, 1981) m 1981; Maj, S Am W. b 24 Nov 58.

ARNAL, Sylvie (Alès, 1977); Lt-Col, CS, Free and Belg. b 13 Apr 53. Served in Zaï and Con (Braz).

ARROWOOD, James (Winston-Salem Central, NC, 1983); Maj, USA S. b 23 Jan 56; with **ARROWOOD, Linda** (née Portis) m 1975; Maj, USA S. b 16 Feb 57.

ARULDHAS, Retnam (Alady, Nagercoil, 1988); Maj, Ind SE. b 17 Apr 66 and **SARADHA, Aruldhas** (Layam, Azagiapandipuram, 1988) m 1988; Maj, Ind SE. b 7 May 65.

ASHCRAFT, Larry (Lorain, OH, 1980) Maj, USA E. b 12 Nov 58. BS (Org Mgmt); with **ASHCRAFT, Jane**t (née Berkhoudt) m 1981; Maj, USA E. b 11 Mar 58. BS (Org Mgmt), MA (Counselling)

AYANAM, Friday S. (Akai, 1988); Lt-Col, CS, Nig. b 2 Oct 64; with **AYANAM, Glory** m 1986; Lt-Col, TSWM, Nig. b 28 Apr 64. Served in Zimb.

B

BAAH, Samuel (Duakwa, Gha, 1987); Lt-Col, Zimb. b 13 Mar 63; with

BAAH, Theresa (née Kumi) m 1984; Lt-Col, Zimb. b 10 Sep 64. Served in Nig and Gha.

BÅÅTH, Henrik; (Templet, Oslo, Nor, 1994); Maj, Swdn. b 23 Jun 68. Served in Nor.

BAHAMONDE, Cecilia (Lo Vial, 1983); Maj, S Am W. b 23 Mar 63.

BAIGORRIA, Eduardo A. (Córdoba, 1991); Maj, S Am E. b 2 Mar 65; with **BAIGORRIA, Andrea** (née Racellis) m 1989; Maj, S Am E, b 6 Sep 69.

BAILEY, Carol (Greenock, 1977); Lt-Col, UK. b 13 May 57.

BAILEY, F. Bradford (Kansas City Westport Temple, MO, USA S, 1982); Col, CS, USA S. b 4 May 58. BS (Soc Work); with **BAILEY, Heidi J.** (née Chandler) m 1978; Col, TSWM, USA S. b 17 Jul 54. Served in USA C, Sp (OC/CPWM) S Am W (CS/TSWM) and at IHQ.

BAKER, George L. (El Cajon, CA, 1983); Maj, USA W. b 9 Oct 59; with **BAKER, Jeanne L.** (née Chewning) m 1980; Maj, USA W. b 20 July 60.

BAKKEN, Solfrid (née Kristensen) (Tromsø 1971) Maj Nor b 11 May 52

BAMANABIO, Eugene (Mfilou, 1990); Lt-Col, CS, Con (Braz). b 10 Jul 62; with **BAMANABIO, Brigitte** (née Locko-Oumba) m 1988; Lt-Col, TSWM, Con (Braz). b 13 Dec 1963. Served in Rwa and Uga (CS/TPWM).

BAMFORD, William A. III (Quincy, MA, 1989); Col, CS, USA E. b 11 Jun 57. BS (Pharm), MS (Org Ldrshp); with **BAMFORD, G. Lorraine** (née Brown) m 1980; Col, TSWM, USA E . b 25 Jul 53. BA (Mod Langs). Served in S Am W (CS/TSWM).

BANDA, Alfred (Kaning'a, Mal, 1997); Maj, Uga. b 10 Aug 71; with **BANDA, Pamela,** (Mtendere, Zamb, 1999) m.1999; Capt, Uga. b 24 Sep 72. Served in Zamb and Mal.

BANFIELD, Stephen (Quincy, MA, 1978); Lt-Col, USA E. b 17 Mar 53. BA (Psych); with **BANFIELD, Janet** (née Anderson) m 1976; Lt-Col, USA E. b 27 Apr 55. Served in USA E and USA Nat.

BARKAT, Samuel (Thal, 1973); Maj, Pak. b 7 Aug 51; with **SAMUEL, Margaret** m 1971; Maj, Pak. b 7 Aug 52.

BARNARD, Jennifer (née Rowe) (Norwood, 1982) m 1970; Lt-Col, Aus S. b 5 Nov 50. Served in UK; m 1970; Lt-Col Rodney ret 2014.

BATE, Carole J. (née Voisey) (Hempstead Citadel, NY, 1989) Lt-Col, USA E b. 12 Mar 67. Served in EET (TSWM).

BATEMAN, David (Lower Hutt, 1988); Maj, NZ. b 17 Dec 60. Dip Bus, Cert Mgmt (NZIM); with
BATEMAN, Margaret (née Allott) m 1983; Maj, NZ. b 19 Nov 58. BN, RGON.

BECKMAN, Elisabeth (Stockholm Temple, 2006); Capt, Swdn, b 18 Jan 65.

BELL, Donald C. (Spokane, WA, USA W, 1978); Comr, TC, USA S. b 12 Oct 49. BA (Econ & Hist), JD (Law); and
BELL, Debora K. (née Perry) (Hobbs, NM, 1977) m 1979; Comr, TPWM, USA S. b 6 Feb 56. Served at USA Nat, in USA W (CS/TSWM) and NZ (CS/TSWM) (TC/TPWM).

BELL, Mark (Hagerstown, MD, 1977); Lt-Col, USA S. b 27 Mar 51; with
BELL, Alice (née Armendariz) m 1975; Lt-Col, USA S. b 26 Sep 54.

BENNYMON, C.J. (Pazhayaviduthy, Peermade, 1989); Maj, Ind SW. b 29 Oct 67. BA, ADHA; with
BENNYMON, K. Saramma (Mangalackal, Kattakada, 1990) m 1991; Maj, Ind SW. b 19 Feb 67.

BERG, Gro (née Egeland) (Stavanger, 1985); Maj, Nor. b 11 Oct 62.

BERG, Odd (Harstad, 1969); Lt-Col, Nor. b 4 Mar 47; and
BERG, Grethe (née Knetten) (Ski, 1969) m 1971; Lt-Col, Nor. b 12 May 48. Served in Nor, UK, Den and Ger (CS/TSWM).

BERNAO, Raul (Trelew,1983); Maj, S Am E. b 11 Oct 61; and
BERNAO, Lidia (née Lopez) (Santiago del Estero, 1981) m 1984; Maj, S Am E. b 20 Feb 59.

BERRY, Donald E. (Kearny, NJ, 1976); Maj, USA E. b 9 Jun 49; with
BERRY, Vicki (née Van Nort) m 1970; Maj, USA E. b 15 Jan 50. BA (Engl), MA (Strategic Comms & Ldrshp).

BEZZANT, Ivan (Wellington South, 1981); Maj, NZ. b 3 Sep 58; and
BEZZANT, Glenda (nee Mills) (Wellington South, 1982) m 1982; Maj, NZ. b 9 Jan 59.

BIAKLIANA, Sailo (Hnahthial, 1981); Maj, Ind E. b 15 Feb 56; and
BIAKMAWII Hrangkhawl (Dolchera, 1982) m 1982; Maj, Ind E. b 10 Aug 62.

BLOMBERG, Sonja (née Waern) (Kristinehamn 1994); Maj, Swdn. b 1 May 56; and
BLOMBERG, Christer (Kristinehamn 1994) Maj, Swdn. b 16 Jul 54.

BLOOMFIELD, Glenn C. (Philadelphia NE, PA, 1971); Maj, USA E. b 25 Feb 50; with
BLOOMFIELD, Carol (née Thompson) (Cleveland Temple, OH, 1971) m 1972; Maj, USA E. b 1 Jun 48.

BOADU, Stephen (Topremang 1985); Maj, Gha. b 17 Jul 61; with
BOADU, Cecilia (née Ofori) m 1983; Maj, Gha. b 4 Apr 63.

BODDU GNANA, Prakash Rao (Bhogapuram, 1987); Maj, Ind C. b 24 May 66, with
BODDU, Annamani m 1985; Maj, Ind C. b 20 July 68.

BODE, William H. (Alliance, OH, 1970); Maj, USA E. b 6 Sep 49, with
BODE, Joan I. (née Burke) (Brooklyn 8th Ave, NY, 1969) m 1971; Maj, USA E. b 30 Aug 48.

BONAZEBI, Philippe (Makaka, 1994); Maj, Con (Braz). b 14 Sep 63; with
BONAZEBI, Julie Rose (née Kouba) m 1988; Maj, Con (Braz). b 15 Jul 70.

BOOTH, Patrick (Paris-Central, Frce, 1989); Maj, IHQ. b 12 Jan 55; with
BOOTH, Margaret (née Miaglia) m 1983; Maj, IHQ. b 31 Jul 61. Served in Frce UK and S Afr.

BOUZIGUES, Ricardo (Colegiales, 1976); Col, TC, Mex. b 12 Sep 52. BA (Pract Theol), MA (Theol); and
BOUZIGUES, Sonia (née Alvez) (Cordoba, 1979) m 1979; Col, TPWM, Mex. b 12 Nov 54. Served in S Am E (CS/TSWM).

BOWERS, Thomas M. (Moline, IL, 1978); Maj, USA C. b 19 Sep 55; with
BOWERS, Jacalyn G. (née Thorson) m 1975; Maj, USA C. b 20 Mar 55. AA (Soc).

BOWLES, Marsha-Jean (née Wortley) (Woodstock, ON, Can, 1990); Lt-Col, CS, Ger. b 2 Mar 62; with
BOWLES, David m 1981; Lt-Col, Ger. b 20 Jul 60. Served in Can.

BRAUND, James (Peterborough Temple, ON, 1987); Lt-Col, Can. b 12 Nov 60. B Sc; MAL and
BRAUND, Ann (née Hennessey) (Picton, ON, 1983) m 1987; Lt-Col, Can. b 12 Apr 61. BA (Theol).

BREKKE-CLIFTON, Birgitte (née Nielsen) (Copenhagen Temple, 1980); Comr, IHQ (IS, Eur). b 17 Sep 54. SRN. Served in Nor, Sri Lan, Ban (CPWO), UK, E Eur, Pak (TPWM) and Den (TC, TPWM). Ww Col Bo Brekke, pG 2007; m 2013 General Shaw Clifton, ret 2011.

BROWN, Rosemarie (Kingston Central, Jamaica, 1978); Maj, Carib. b 17 Oct 57.

BA (Theol) Served at ICO.

BUCKINGHAM, Lyndon (Whangarei, NZ, 1988); Col, TC, Sing. b 13 Feb 62; with
BUCKINGHAM, Bronwyn (née Robertson) m 1986; Col, TPWM, Sing. b 21 Jun 65. Served in Can and NZ.

BUDGELL, Wade (St Anthony, NL, 1980); Maj, Can. b 19 Feb 1959; with
BUDGELL, Linda (née Boyd) m 1987; Maj, Can. b 3 Sep 60.

BUKIEWICZ, Ralph (Milwaukee West, WI, 1980); Lt-Col, USA C. b 3 Mar 60; and
BUKIEWICZ, Susan (née Cunard) (Dearborn Heights, MI, 1981) m 1981; Lt-Col, USA C. b 9 May 58.

BUNGAY, Wayne (Fortune, NL, 1984); Maj, UK. b 16 Oct 1960 BA, BRS with
BUNGAY, Deborah (Née Loveless) m 1981; Maj, UK b 4 May 1963. Served in Carib. Can

BURAVA, Vari (Lebogoro, 1987); Maj, PNG. b 1 Jan 62. Ww Capt Kila pG 2002; and
BURAVA, Nellie (Niuruka Opening, 2008) m 2004; Capt, PNG. b 6 Jun 76.

BURN, Margaret (née Cain) (Lincoln Citadel, 1966); Lt-Col, UK. b 12 Nov 46.

BURNS, Alan (Harlow, 1976); Lt-Col, UK. b 1 May 54. BSc (Hons), MA (Evan); and
BURNS, Alison (née Hitchin) (Regent Hall, 1979) m 1981; Lt-Col, UK. b 8 Oct 52. Served at IHQ.

BURTON, Joan (Goole, UK, 1978); Maj, Brz. b 5 Jul 55, MA (Philosophy).

BUSROE, Ronald (Danville, KY, USA S, 1978); Lt-Col, USA Nat. b 6 Dec 51. BA (Hist); with
BUSROE, Carol (née Jay) m 1974; Lt-Col, USA Nat. b 9 Jan 53. BA (Math). Served in USA S and Carib.

C

CACHELIN, Hervé (Biel, Switz, 1979); Lt-Col, IHQ. b 16 Feb 57; and
CACHELIN, Deborah (née Cullingworth) (Catford, UK, 1981) m 1983; Lt-Col, IHQ. b 2 Jul 57. Served in Aus E, UK and Switz.

CAFFULL, Michael (Worthing, 1978) Lt-Col, UK. b 20 Dec 55. MA (Miss Ldrshp); and
CAFFULL, Wendy (née Hart) (Southend Citadel, 1977) m 1978; Lt-Col, UK. b 24 Mar 57. BA (Pastoral Care with Psych). Served at IHQ.

CAIRNS, Janice (née Manson) m 1972; Lt-Col, Aus E. b 7 Oct 48. ATCL, LTCL, Grad Dip Chrstn Counselling.Ww Lt-Col Philip, pG 2014.

CALLANDER, Ian (Fairfield, Aus S, 1977); Lt-Col, Aus S. b 7 Aug 55. BTh; and
CALLANDER, Vivien (née Wiseman) (Adelaide Congress Hall, Aus S, 1977) m 1978; Lt-Col, Aus S. b 7 May 53. Dip Tech Physio, Grad Cert HR Mgmt. Served in E Eur.

CALVO, Esteban (Concepcion de Rios, 1987); Maj, L Am N. b 23 Jan 63; and
CALVO, Ileana (née Jimenez) (Concepcion de Rios, 1986) m 1989; Maj, L Am N. b 5 Jun 66.

CAMPBELL, Mark T. (Wollongong, 1986); Maj, Aus E. b 4 May 60. MA; with
CAMPBELL, Julie A. (née Woodbury) m 1983; Maj, Aus E. b 17 Sep 59.

CAMPOS Manuel (Mexicali, 1980); Maj, Mex. b 14 Jun 58; with
CAMPOS Ana (née Flores) m 1978; Maj,Mex. b 26 Jul 57.

CAÑAS, Quelvín (Central, El Salvador 2003) Capt, L Am N. b 13 Sep 65; with
CAÑAS, Ana (née López) (Central, El Salvador 2003) m 1993 Capt, L Am N. b 22 March 65.

CANNING, Joan (Moncton, NB, Can, 1983); Lt-Col, b 27 Sep 62. BA (Bib and Theol) MA (Theol). Served in USA National and at IHQ.

CANTO, Flor (Cuerpo Central Panama 1999) Capt, L Am N. b 20 May 1971

CAPSEY, Mary (Leeds Central, 1984); Lt-Col, UK. b 10 Mar 59. SRN, SCM, MSc (Health Ed & Prom). Served in Gha, Belg, Con (Braz), Zimb and at IHQ.

CAREY, Graham (Southend Citadel, 1972) Maj, E Eur. b 28 Nov 50 and
CAREY, Hélène (née Paulus) (Liege, Belg, 1972) m 1975; Maj, E Eur. b 24 Dec 50. Served in Belg, Frce and UK.

CAREY, Roderick (Dunedin Fortress, 1984); Lt-Col, NZ. b 19 Mar 58. Dip BRS, BTh; with
CAREY, Jennifer (née Cross) m 1980; Lt-Col, NZ. b 5 Feb 61. Served Aust E.

CARTMELL, Ronald (Chilliwack BC, 1983); Maj, Can. b 31 Oct 57. BRE, and
CARTMELL, Tonilea (née Crashley) (Regina Citadel, SK 1982) m 1983; Maj, Can. b 26 Nov 1955. MAL

CASEY, Barry (Unley, Aus S, 1979); Maj, IHQ. b 9 Jan 55; with
CASEY, Rosslyn (née Heaven) m 1975; Maj, IHQ. b 5 Jun 55. Served in Aus S.

CASTOR, Onal (Aquin, Haiti, 1979); Comr, TC, Con (Braz). b 20 Jul 55; and
CASTOR, Edmane (née Montoban) (Duverger, Haiti, 1980) m 1980; Comr, TPWM, Con (Braz). b 1 Oct 57. Served in

USA S, Con (Kin) and Carib (CS/TSWM, TC/TPWM).

CAVANAGH, David (Catania, It, 1992); Maj, GS, It. b 15 Jan 65; and
CAVANAGH, Elaine (née Piercy) (Southport, UK, 1992) m 1992; Maj, CSWM, It. b 28 Sep 62. Served in UK.

CENECIRO, Joel (Manila, 1989); Maj, Phil. b 23 May 66. BA (Biblical Studies), MA (Chrstn Studies); and
CENECIRO, Susan (née Pudpud) (Tondo, 1989); Maj, Phil. b 31 Oct 66. B Min.

CEREZO, Josué (Monterrey, Mex, 1985); Lt-Col, Mex N. b 16 May 57; with
CEREZO, Ruth (née Garcia) m 1983; Lt-Col, Mex. b 22 Oct 60.
Served in Mex (CS/TSWM) and L Am N (CS/TSWM).

CESAR, Danièle (née Polrot) (La Villette, 1983) m 1979. Maj, TSWM, Frce and Belg. b 26 Aug 58

CHAGAS, Edgar (São Paulo Central, 1988); Lt-Col, CS, Mex. b 24 Feb 58. BA (Phys), MSc; with
CHAGAS, Sara (née Parker) m 1982; Lt-Col, TSWM, Mex. b 26 Aug 60. BA (Psych). Served in Brz.

CHALWE, Frazer (Chikumbi, 1989); Lt-Col, Zam. b 25 Jan 65; with
CHALWE, Rodinah (née Mukunkami) m 1986; Lt-Col, Zam. b 8 May 68.

CHAMNESS, John M. (Seattle Temple, WA, 1989); Maj, USA W. b 7 Jan 63; and
CHAMNESS, Martie (Lani) L. (née Abella) (Pasadena Tabernacle, CA, 1989) m 1990; Maj USA W. b 5 Feb 60.

CHAMP, James (Chatham, ON, 1975); Lt-Col, Can. b 29 Mar 52. BRE, MBA. Served in UK. m 1976, Maj Barbara, ret 2012.

CHAMPLIN, David A. (Oneonta, NY, 1981); Maj, USA E. b 22 Dec 50. BA (Mgmt), CERT (Finance); with
CHAMPLIN, Eunice (née Schmidt) m 1972; Maj, USA E. b 11 Nov 52. BA (Christian Edu), MA (Ldrshp & Min).

CHANG, Man-Hee (San Francisco Korean, CA, 1993); Maj, USA W. b 31 Mar 58. BA (Bus Adm), MBA (Bus Adm); with
CHANG, Stephanie (née Shim) m 1983; Maj, USA W. b 1 Jun 59. BA (Math).

CHANGALWA, Henry (Lukhuna, Ken, 1996); Maj, Ken W. b 30 Apr 62; with
CHANGALWA, Grace (née Dodo) m 1988; Maj, Ken W. b 9 Dec 67

CHARAN, Samuel (Rampur, Ind N, 1978); Comr, TC, Ind SW. b 1 Apr 53; with

CHARAN, Bimla Wati m 1974; Comr, TPWM, Ind SW. Served in Ind N, Ind SW (CS/TSWM) and Ind E (CS/TSWM, TC/TPWM).

CHARLES, V. John (Oottukuzhy, Kattakada, 1990); Maj, Ind SW. b 2 Nov 59; with
CHARLES, Florance 1988; Maj, Ind SW. b 30 May 64.

CHAUHAN, Jashwant Soma (Tarapur, 1979); Maj, Ind W. b 20 Feb 52; with
CHAUHAN, Indiraben m 1976; Maj, Ind W. b 8 Jun 56.

CHAWNGHLUNA Chhangte, (Sawleng 1983); Maj, Ind E. b 13 Apr 59. BA, BTh; and
LALCHHUANMAWII Khawlhring (Bethlehem 1986); m 1986; Maj, Ind E. b 14 Jun 65.

CHAWNGHLUT Vanlalfela (Kolasib, Ind E, 1986); Lt-Col, CS, Ind SW. b 16 Dec 62; with
KHUPCHAWNG Ropari m 1984; Lt-Col, TSWM, Ind SW. b 8 Sept 65. Served in Ind E.

CHELLA Wycliff (Murukondapadu, Ind C, 1994); Maj, Ind C. b 6 Jan 65; with
CHELLA Chinnammaye m 1990; Maj, Ind C. b 5 Jan 71.

CHELLIAH, Mony (Osaravillai, Ind SE, 1976); Col, TC, Ind C. b 18 May 55. MA; and
MALLIKA, Mony (Alady, Ind SE, 1978) m 1978; Col, TPWM, Ind C. b 6 Mar 57. Served in Ind SE and Ind SW (CS/TSWM).

CHEPKURUI, Stephen (Cheptais, Ken, 1982); Col, CS, Ken W. b 22 Feb 58; and
CHEPKURUI, Grace (née Madolio) (Vigeze, Ken, 1980) m 1985; Col, TSWM, Ken W. b 15 May 55. Served in E Afr, Tanz (GS/CSWM), Rwa (RC/RPWM, OC/CPWM) and Zam (TC/TPWM).

CHEPSIRI, Harun (Toroso, 1996) Maj, Ken W. b 20 Sep 65; with
CHEPSIRI, Beatrice (née Cherop) m 1992; Maj, Ken W. b 6 Jul 68.

CHHAREL, Ranmal Bhuralal (Kharsana, 1984); Maj, Ind W. b 13 May 53; and
CHHAREL, Ambaben Maj, Ind W. b 25 Aug 60

CHIDHAKWA, Lovemore (Mabvuku, 1988); Maj, Zimb, b 3 Jan 66, with
CHIDHAKWA, Spiwe (née Dube) (Braeside 1995) m 1995; Maj, Zimb. b 10 Jun 70.

CHIGARIRO, Vinece (Gunguwe, 1975); Comr, TC, TPWM, Ken E. b 7 Mar 54. Served in Tanz (GS) Zam (TC) and Zimb (TC,TPWM).

CHIKONDO, Clifford (Nangogwe, 1995); Maj, Zam. b 12 Jul 62; with
CHIKONDO, Moudy (Mweemba 1991) m 1986; Major, Zam. b 11 Mar 68.

CHILYABANYAMA, Metson (Chitumbi, 1987); Lt-Col, Zam. b 30 Oct 55; with
CHILYABANYAMA, Rosemary (née

Biographical Information

Mboozi) m 1982; Lt-Col, Zam. b 8 Aug 61.

CHIMIMBA, Gerald (Migowi, 1986); Maj,
Mal. b 31 Jul 56; with
    CHIMIMBA, Ellen m 1983; Maj, Mal. b 4 Apr 60.

CHINYEMBA, Casman (Chimbumu, 1989);
Maj, Zimb. b 7 Jan 62; with
    CHINYEMBA, Martha (née Gomo) m
1988; Maj, Zimb. b 16 Oct 63. Served in Tanz.

CHITANDA, Henry (Chinhoyi, 1991); Maj,
Zimb. b 6 April 66, with
    CHITANDA, Sheila (née Mvere) (Kwekwe,
1992) m 1992; Maj, Zimb, b 15 Oct 1972

CHITSIKO, Martin (Bamhala, 1979); Maj,
Zimb, b 5 Jan 55, with
    CHITSIKO, Renah (née Mudimu) (Howard
Inst, 1988) m 1986; Maj, Zimb, b 11 Jun 66

CHOO, Seung-chan (Yung Deung Po, 1980);
Lt-Col, Kor. b 15 Jun 50; with
    LEE, Ok-hee m 1978; Lt-Col, Kor. b 2 Aug 54.

CHRISTIAN, Gabriel Ibrahim (Muktipur,
Ind W, 1983); Lt-Col, CS, Ind SE. b 24 Dec
59. BA (Eng) BD and
    CHRISTIAN, Indumati (née Samual Macwan)
(Petlad Central, 1985) m 1986; Lt-Col, TSWM,
Ind SE. b 30 Aug 62; BD. Served in Ind W.

CHRISTIAN, Prabhudas Jetha (Sihunj,
1978); Maj, Ind W. b 23 Jan 52 and
    CHRISTIAN, Persis (née Zumal) (Jholod,
1978) m 1978 Maj, Ind W. b 5 Apr 48.

CHRISTIAN, Rasik Paul (Chunel, 1988); Maj,
Ind W. b 7 Sep 65; and
    CHRISTIAN Ramilaben (Piplag, 1990)
m 1990; Maj, Ind W. b 17 Apr 68.

CHRISTURAJ, Rajamani (Elappara, 1983);
Maj, Ind SW. b 27 Dec 61; and
    CHRISTURAJ, Mary (née Mathew) (Elam-
pally, 1983) m 1983; Maj, Ind SW. b 11 May 59.

CHUNG, Edmund L. (Manhattan Citadel,
USA E, 1976); Lt-Col, IHQ. b 8 Aug 48.
BS (Chem), MS (Management); and
    CHUNG, Carolynne J. (née Wiseman)
(Lexington, KY, USA E, 1976) m 1977. BA,
MA (Org Ldrshp); Lt-Col, IHQ. b 28 Jul 46.
Served in USA E, USA Nat and UK.

CLÉNAT, Jean Aurore (Aquin, Haiti, Carib,
2001); Maj, GS, Rwa. b 8 Oct 73; and
    CLÉNAT, Elianese (née Pierre) (Gros Morne,
Haiti, Carib, 1998) m 2002; Maj, CSWM,
Rwa. b 22 May 68. Served in Carib.

CLINCH, Ronald (Launceston, Aus S, 1986);
Lt-Col, Aus S. b 6 Sep 54. BEd; with
    CLINCH, Robyn (née Mole) m 1982; Lt-Col,
Aus S. b 8 Nov 60. Served in Phil (CS/TSWM).

COCHRANE, William (Barrhead, Scot, 1975);
Comr, IHQ (IS to CoS). b 7 Sep 54.
Served in UK (CS).

COLA, Iliesa (Raiwai, 1995); Maj, NZ.
b 7 Nov 55; with
    COLA, Litiana (née Vuidreketi) m 1982;
Maj, NZ. b 8 Mar 62.

COLEMAN, Michael T. (Kwinana, 1986);
Maj, Aus S. b 4 Nov 54; with
    COLEMAN, Annette (née Willey) m 1976;
Maj, Aus S. b 23 Oct 55. BSc. Served in Tai
(RC/RPWM).

CONDON, James (Shoalhaven, Aus E, 1971);
Comr, TC, Aus E. b 29 Nov 49; and
    CONDON, Jan (née Vickery) (Uralla,
Aus E, 1971) m 1972; Comr, TPWM,
Aus E. b 25 Jan 47. Served in UK, PNG
(CS/TSWM) Aus E (CS/TWSM) and at
IHQ (IS/ZSWM).

CONRAD, Keith (Matroosfontein, 1988);
Lt-Col, CS, S Afr. b 31 Mar 62; with
    CONRAD, Yvonne (née Jansen) m 1984;
Lt-Col, TSWM, S Afr. b 13 Mar 63.
Served in NZ and at IHQ.

COOPER, Raymond, III (Garland, TX,
USA S, 1984); Maj, USA Nat. b 12 Jun 61.
Served in USA S.

COTTERILL, Anthony (Regent Hall, UK,
1984); Lt-Col, CS, Den. b 9 Dec 57. BA
(Hons); with
    COTTERILL, Gillian (née Rushforth)
m 1979; Lt-Col, TSWM, Den. b 15 Sep 57.
SRN. Seved in UK.

COWLING, Alison (Maclean, Aus E, 1978);
Maj, Can. b 10 Feb 50. Served in
Aus E and at IHQ.

COX, André General (Geneva 1, Switz, 1979)
(see page 17) with
    COX, Silvia (née Volet) m 1976; Comr, IHQ
(WPWM). b 18 Nov 55. Served in Switz,
Zimb, Fin (TC/TPWM), S Afr (TC/TPWM)
and UK (TC/TPWM).

CRAIG, Heather (née Mackay) (Parramatta,
Aus E, 1986); Maj, Gha. b 31 Dec 57; and
    CRAIG, Graeme (Rockhampton, Aus E,
1984) m 1986; Maj, Gha. b 10 Feb 56. Served
in Aus E.

CRITCH, Shawn (La Scie, NL, 1990); Maj,
Can. b 26 Jun 67. CGA; and
    CRITCH, Brenda (née Cooper) (St John's
Temple, NL, 1990) m 1991; Maj, Can.
b 25 Jul 63. BSc (Nursing).

CUMBERBATCH, Emmerson (Speightstown,
Barbados, 1988); Maj, Carib. b 5 Jan 54; and
    CUMBERBATCH, Carolinda (née White)
(San Fernando, Trinidad, 1987) m 1988; Maj,
Carib. b 19 Nov 62.

D

DALI, Peter (Ebushibungo, Ken, 1978);
Lt-Col, Ken W. b 2 Mar 52; and
DALI, Jessica (née Kavere) (Masigolo,
Ken, 1978) m 1979; Lt-Col, Ken W.
b 25 Dec 55. Served in Ken, Tanz, at IHQ,
in Gha (CS/TSWM), Zim (CS/TSWM) and
Lib (OC/CPWM).

DALVI, Vijay Ramchandar (Kudgaon, 1978);
Maj, Ind W. b 13 Aug 54; and
DALVI, Rajani (Kherdi, 1982); m 1981;
Maj, Ind W. b 30 Sep 62.

DALY, Gordon (Wellington South, NZ, 1977);
Lt-Col, OC, Spa. b 5 Mar 54; and
DALY, Susan (née Crump) (Te Aroha, NZ,
1976) m 1977; Lt-Col, CPWM, Spa. b 22 Oct
54. L Th. Served in NZ, Carib, S Am W, Sing
and Port (OC/CPWM).

DAMOR, Nicolas Maganlal (Jalpa, 1979);
Maj, Ind W. b 1 Jun 55; and
DAMOR, Flora (née David) (Dilsar, 1980)
m 1980; Maj, Ind W. b 26 Apr 58.

DANIEL JEBASINGH RAJ, Jeyaraj (Booth
Tucker Hall, Nagercoil, 1987); Maj, Ind SE.
b 10 Jun 61. BA (Eng), MA (Social), BTh,
BD, MTh D Min and
RAJAM, Daniel Jebasingh Raj (Kuzhikalai,
1992) m 1992; Maj, Ind SE. b 12 Mar 64.
BA (Eng), MA (History), BTh PM, MTh PM.
Served in Ind SE and at Ind Nat.

DANIEL, Washington (Gohawa, 1997);
Lt-Col, CS, Pak. b 25 Nov 56; and
WASHINGTON, Azra (née Zakar) m 1990;
Lt-Col, TSWM, Pak b 2 Feb 62.

DANIELSON, Douglas (El Paso, TX, USA W,
1987); Lt-Col, CS, Braz. b 19 Aug 58. BSc
(Cmptr Sci), MA (Missiology). Served in
USA W, S Am E, L Am N (CS), Mex (CS) and
at IHQ. Ww LtCol Rhode, pG 2010; with
DANIELSON, Verônica (née Jung)
(Cachoeira Paulista, 1984); Lt-Col, TSWM, Braz.
b 15 Sep 59. BA (Trans and Interp); m. 2013.

DANSO, Isaac (Asene, 1991); Lt-Col, Gha.
b 22 Feb 1960; with
DANSO, Eva (née Amoah) m 1988; Lt-Col,
Gha. b 1 Jul 61.

DASARI, Daniel Raju (Arul Nagar, 1991);
Major, Ind C. b 24 Feb 65; with
DASARI, Baby Sarojini m 1989; Maj, Ind C.
b 26 Jan 63.

DASARI, John Kumar (Pathamupparru, Ind C,
1991); Maj, Ken E. b 7 Jan 61; with
DASARI, Mani Kumari m 1986; Maj, Ken
E. b 3 May 66. BTh, MA. Served in Ind C.

DAVIDSON, Daniel (Trivandrum Central, 1985);
Maj, Ind SW. b 6 May 53. BA; with

DAVIDSON, M.V. Estherbai (Trivandrum
Central) m 1984; Maj, Ind SW. b 1 Jun 61.

DAVIS, David B. (Dallas Pleasant Grove, TX,
1983); Maj, USA E. b 8 Dec 62; with
DAVIS, Margaret (née Wiltshire) m 1986;
Maj, USA E. b 13 May 61. BM (Music).

DEL BELLO, Alfredo Miguel (Montevideo,
Uru, 1979); Maj, S. Am E. b 21 Jul 53;
m 1998; Maj Maria del Carmen, ret 2013.

DENGI, Michael (Tent City, 1996); Capt, PNG.
b 8 May 65; with
DENGI, Giam (née Benjain); Capt, PNG.
b 13 Jun 69.

DEN HOLLANDER, Johannes A. (Treebeek,
1992); Lt-Col, Neth. b 21 Nov 56, with
DEN HOLLANDER, Annetje C. (née
Poppema) m 1978; Lt-Col, Neth. b 4 May 57.

DIAKANWA, Wante Emmanuel (Kintambo,
1985); Maj, DR Con. b 23 Dec 50; with
DIAKANWA, Madeleine (née Sitwakemba
Luzizila) m 1974; Maj, DR Con. b 11 Nov 55.

DIAZ, Evelyn (Oakbrook Terrace, IL, 1981);
Maj, USA C. b 1 Jun 60. AA (Pract Min).
Served in Swdn.

DICKINSON, Bill A. (Seattle Temple, WA
1993); Maj, USA W. b 10 Nov 63. BS (Bus
Admin); with
DICKINSON, Lisa A. (née Schmidt) m 1984;
Maj, USA W. b 25 Sep 63.

DIKALEMBOLOVANGA, Eugene (Kinshasa,
DR Con,1981); Lt-Col, Gha, b 30 Apr 52; with
DIKALEMBOLOVANGA, Odile (née
Luasu); m 1980; Lt-Col, Gha, b 2 Mar 58.
Served in Congo (Kin), Mali and at IHQ.

DLAMINI, Thomas (Mbabane, Swaz 1992);
Maj, Swaz. b 23 Feb 65; and
DLAMINI, Doris (née Mvelase) (Mathunjwa
1992) m 1992; Maj, S Afr. b 14 Dec 68.

DONALDSON, Robert (Dunedin South,
1987); Comr, CT, NZ. b 8 Jul 61. BSc, LTh.
PG Dip Bus Admin; with
DONALDSON, Janine (née Hamilton)
m 1983, Comr, TPWM, NZ. b 23 Sep 62.
Served in Zamb and S Afr (CS/TSWM).

DOUGHTY, Victor (Seattle Temple, WA, 1984);
Lt-Col, USA W. b 25 Mar 54. BA (Soc Anthr),
MSSW (Soc Wk), CERT (Soc Wk); with
DOUGHTY, Joan (née Ritchie) m 1980;
Lt-Col, USA W. b 7 May 55.

DOUNIAMA, Jean Pierre (Gamboma, 1990);
Maj, Con (Braz). b 25 Dec 67; and
DOUNIAMA, Odile (née Ando)
(Gamboma, 1988) m 1988; Maj, Con (Braz).
b 8 Jun 69.

DOWNER, Gillian (Great Yarmouth, UK,
1977); Comr, IHQ (IS, SPEA). b 18 Mar 54.

Served in UK, Phil, Vietnam, HK, Tai, Sing (GS and CS), (TC and TPWM).

DUHU, Imanuel (Surabaya 2, 1992); Maj, Indon. b 1 Aug 63; and
DUHU, Henny (Tumpaan, 1990) m 1995; Maj, Indon. b 2 Jul 67.

E

EDUNG, Samuel (Ikot Ubo, 1988); Maj, Nig. b 4 Nov 65; with
EDUNG, Grace; Maj, Nig. b 7 Aug 67.

EDWIN SATHYADHAS, Nallathambi (Kolvey, 1981); Maj, Ind SE. b 10 Aug 55; with
GNANA, Jessibell Edwin Sathyadhas m 1980; Maj, Ind SE. b 15 Jun 57.

EIDE, Gunnar (Molde, 1979); Maj, Nor. b 20 Dec 51; and
EIDE, Ida Karin (née Folkvord) (Sandnes, 1979) m 1979; Maj, Nor. b 27 Oct 57. Served in Sri Lan.

EKPENDU, Simon (Umuogu, 1988); Maj, Nig. b 15 Apr 1958; with
EKPENDU, Evangeline (Umuahia, 1988); Maj, Nig. b 9 Jan 1962.

ELIASEN, Torben (Bosque, Brz, 1983); Comr, TC, S Am W. b 28 Nov 60; and
ELIASEN, Deise Calor (née de Souza) (Rio Comprido, Brz, 1985) m 1985; Comr, TPWM, S Am W. b 22 Feb 66. BA (Jrnlsm). Served in Brz (CS), Moz (TC/TPWM) and at IHQ (IS/ZSWM Am & Carib).

ELLIS, Stephen R. (Atlanta Temple, GA, 1989); Maj, USA S. b 25 Oct 62. BA (Eng), MA (Div), MBA; with
ELLIS, Susan (née Kennedy) m 1984; Maj, USA S. b 27 Apr 62. ABJ (PR). Served in Ger.

EVANS, Stuart (Dubbo, AUE, 1995); Maj, SBA, Neth. b 24 Nov 58, with
EVANS, Donna C. (née Hutchinson) m 1979; Maj, Neth. b 2 Feb 58.

EXANTUS, Vilo (Arcahaie, Haiti, 1984); Maj. Carib. b 12 May 57 and
EXANTUS, Yvrose (née Benjamin) (Arcahaie, Haiti, 1985) m 1986; Maj. Carib. b 17 Jan 58. Served in L Am N.

F

FARTHING, Peter (Parramatta, 1976) Maj, Aus E. b 8 Mar 51. MSocStud, DMin; with
FARTHING, Kerrie (née Gale) (Wollongong 1976) Maj, Aus E. b 31 Aug 52.

FERGUSON, Lester (Nassau, Bahamas, 1988); Maj, Carib. b 1 Sep 65. BA (Bible and Theol), MA (Chrstn Ed), MDiv; and
FERGUSON, Beverely (née Armstrong)

(Bridgetown Central, Barbados, 1999) m 1999; Maj, Carib. b 12 Dec 64.

FERNÁNDEZ, Ricardo J. (Caparra Temple, PR, 1996); Lt-Col, CS, S Am E. b 3 Jun 60; with
FERNANDEZ, Mirtha N. (née Benitez) m 1979; Lt-Col, TSWM, S Am E. b 4 Jan 57. Served in USA E.

FERNANDO, Newton (Handugala, 1981); Maj, Sri Lan. b 30 Aug 60; and
FERNANDO, Ajantha (née Marasinghalage) (Talampitiya, 1984) m 1984; Maj, Sri Lan. b 8 Jun 61.

FERREIRA, Jorge Alberto (Cordoba, 1972); Comr, TC, S Am E. b 24 Jun 53; and
FERREIRA, Adelina (née Solorza) (Lauis, 1974) m 1979; Comr, TPWM, S Am E. b 19 Sep 55. Served in S Am E (CS/ TSWM), L Am N (TC/TPWM) and S Am W (TC/TPWM).

FINCHAM, Melvin (Croydon Citadel, 1981); Lt-Col, UK. b 20 May 56; and
FINCHAM, Suzanne (née Kenny) (Stockport Citadel, 1981) m 1981; Lt-Col, UK. b 19 Jan 59.

FINGER, Aylene (née Rinaldi) (Maylands, 1976); Comr, Aus S. b 17 Apr 53. Served in Aus S (TSWM, TPWM) m 1976; Comr Raymond ret 2014.

FLEEMAN, W. Paul (Royal Oak, MI, 1976); Maj, USA C. b 23 Dec 48. BA (Psychol), MA (Relig), MDiv (Counselling/Ed); with
FLEEMAN, Paula (née Cloyd) m 1973; Maj, USA C. b 14 Jun 54.

FLORES, Eliseo (Cochabamba, 1977); Maj, S Am W. b 28 Jul 56; and
FLORES, Remedios (née Gutiérrez) (Oruro, 1977) m 1978; Maj, S Am W. b 6 Apr 55.

FLÜCKIGER, Jean-Marc (Vevey, 1994); Maj, Switz. b 13 Dec 1963; with
FLÜCKIGER, Nathalie (née Pellaton) m 1987; Maj, Switz. b 13 Mar 1967.

FOLEY, James (Pottsville, PA, 1978); Maj, USA E. b 12 Apr 54. BS (Com Min), MDiv (Theology); with
FOLEY, D. Sue (née Jones) m 1975; Maj, USA E. b 2 Nov 55. BS (Bus Admin).

FOLEY, Timothy (Concord, CA 1982); Maj, USA W. b 7 May 59. MA (Theology); and
FOLEY, Cynthia (née Hill) (Pendleton, OR, 1985) m 1985; Maj USA W. b 23 May 63.

FOREMAN, Ronald R. (Concord, NH, 1978); Maj, USA E. b 17 Sep 1952. BA (Socio), MSW (Soc Wk), EJD (Gen Law); with
FOREMAN, Dorine (née Long); m 1972; Maj, USA E. b 6 Apr 1955. BSW (Soc Wk), MSW (Soc Wk). Served at USA Nat.

FORREST, Peter (Blackpool Citadel, 1984); Maj, UK. b 24 Jun 1960; MA; Dip HRM; and
FORREST, Julie (née Raine) (Chester-le-Street, 1987); m 1987; Maj, UK. b 26 Feb 1965. MSc. Served at IHQ.

FORSTER, Malcolm (St Helier, UK, 1971); Lt-Col, S Afr. b 26 Mar 51; and
FORSTER, Valerie (née Jupp) (Croydon Citadel, UK, 1978) m 1979; Lt-Col, S Afr. b 5 Jun 55. Served in UK, at ITC, in Zam and Mal, Gha and Lib, Mal (OC/CPWM) and Tanz (OC/CPWM).

FOSEN, Jan Peder (Haugesund, 1976); Col, CS, Nor. b 18 Nov 55; and
FOSEN, Birgit (née Taarnesvik) (Trondheim, 1981) m 1979; Col, TSWM, Nor. b 27 Aug 49.

FOURNEL, Bernard (Lyon, 1980); Maj, b 4 Oct 56; and
FOURNEL, Claire-Lise (née Naud) (Paris-Montparnasse, 1979) m 1981; Maj, Frce and Belg. b 27 Nov 52.

FREIND, John (Floreat Park, 1981); Maj, Aus S. b 11 Dec 55; with
FREIND, Wendy (née Morris) m 1977; Maj, Aus S. b 5 Aug 53.

FUGE, Walter J. (Anacortes, WA, USA W, 1972); Lt-Col, USA Nat. b 18 Aug 52. MBA (Bus Adm), BS (Bus & Mngmnt), CERT (Data Analyst) (Internal Audit); and
FUGE, Ardis (née Muus) (Monterey, CA, USA W, 1974) m 1974; Lt-Col, USA Nat. b 31 Jan 53. Served in USA W and at IHQ.

FUJII, Kenji (Kyobashi, 1982); Lt-Col, CS, Jpn. b 25 Feb 60; and
FUJII, Chiaki (née Inoue) (Kiyose, 1981) m 1987; Lt-Col, TSWM, Jpn. b 17 Nov 59.

G

GABRIEL, K.M. (Kaithaparambu, 1981); Lt-Col, Ind SW. b 15 Nov 55; and
GABRIEL, Molamma (Vappala, 1986) m 1986; Lt-Col, Ind SW. b 10 May 67.

GABRIEL, Michael (Sangla Hill, 1995); Maj, Pak. b 14 Aug 61; and
MICHAEL, Shamim (née Riaz) m 1981; Maj, Pak. b 26 Dec 62.

GAINSFORD, Ian (Wellington South, NZ, 2002); Capt, Tanz. b 9 Feb 67. B Theol, PGrad Dip Theol; with
GAINSFORD Elisabeth (née King) (Launceston, Aus S, 2000) m 2001; Capt, Tanz. b 11 Jul 74. Served in NZ and Aus S.

GARRAD, Rob, (Skegness, UK, 1971); Lt-Col, IHQ. b 16 Jan 52. Served in UK and Rus.

GENABE, Alexander (Cebu, 1981); Lt-Col, Phil. b 27 Mar 58; and

GENABE, Jocelyn (née Willy) (Baguio, 1993) m 1993; Lt-Col, Phil. b 10 Feb 60. BSN, BSSW.

GEORGE, N.J. (Moncotta, 1978); Maj, Ind SW. b 24 Dec 51; and
RUTH, M.C. (Moncotta, 1977) m 1979, Maj, Ind SW. b 23 Apr 48.

GERA, Thomas (EBLH, Bapatla, Ind C. 1988); Lt-Col, Ind C. b 12 Jul 65; with
GERA, Sion Kumari m 1984; Lt-Col, Ind C. b 9 Oct 67. Served in Ind N.

GHULAM, Haroon (Bahawalpur, 1989); Maj, Pak. b 25 July 63; with
HAROON, Jennifer (née John) m 1992; Maj, Pak. b 25 Feb 69.

GHULAM, Yousaf (Lahore, Pak, 1975); Lt-Col, NZ. b 4 Jan 55; and
YOUSAF, Rebecca (née Charn Masih) (Shantinagar, Pak, 1976) m 1976; Lt-Col, NZ. b 6 May 56. Served in Pak (CS/TSWM).

GILL, Daniel (Alidullapur, 1980); Maj, Ind N. b 5 Apr 57; and
GILL, Parveen Daniel (Mukerian, 1981) m 1981; Maj, Ind N. b 3 Apr 62.

GILL, Raj Kumar (Rania, 1994); Maj, Ind N. b 6 Sept 68. BA, BD; with
FLOWRENCE m 1999; Maj, Ind N. b 19 Dec 68.

GITANG'ITA, James (Kitagutiti, 1994); Maj, Tanz. b 8 Oct 68; with
GITANG'ITA, Yustina m 1990; Maj, Tanz. b 8 May 74.

GITONGA, Isaac (Kangoro, Embu, 1992); Maj, Tanz. b 27 May 1966; with
GITONGA, Enacy M. m 1988; Maj, Tanz. b 27 Mar 69. Served in Ken E.

GLUYAS, Miriam (Wauchope, 1981); Lt-Col, CS/TSWM, PNG. b 3 Jun 59. Dip Min. Dip Bus. Served in Aus E.

GNANADASAN, Daniel (Anakotoor, Kot-tarakara 1981); Maj, Ind SW. b 10 Sep 55; and
D.I. SOSAMMA, Gnanadasan (Kottoor, Nedumangadu 1980) m 1982; Maj, Ind SW. b 24 Oct 52.

GOA, Tilitah (née Shong); Maj, PNG. b 6 Apr 69; with
GOA, Christian (Lae, 1994); Maj, PNG. b 9 Feb 69.

GOCHEZ, Agripina (née Angeles) (Reynosa, Mexico 1992) m 1993; Maj, L Am N. b 8 Nov 71.

GODKIN, David J. (Parramatta, 1986); Lt-Col, Aus E. b 14 Aug 59. Dip Min; with
GODKIN, Sandra F. (née Press) m 1982; Lt-Col, Aus E. b 20 Apr 62. Dip Min.

GONÇALVES, Adão (Pelotas, 1997); Maj, Brz. b 3 Sep 65; and

GONÇALVES, Vilma (née Rosa) (Bosque, 1983) m 1986; Maj, Brz. b 8 Nov 51. BA (SocS).

GOWER, Ross R. (Christchurch City, 1980); Col, NZ. b 15 Dec 50; with
GOWER, Annette (née Knight) m 1972; Col, NZ. Served in NZ, UK, Indon (CS/TSWM) and at IHQ.

GRAVES, Lee (Tillsonburg, ON, 1983); Lt-Col, Can. b 8 Aug 61. MBA; with
GRAVES, Deborah (née Smith) m 1984; Lt-Col, Can. b 24 Feb 1960. BA.

GREENIDGE, Brenda (Sea View, Barbados, 1980): Maj, Carib. b 25 Dec 57.

GRIFFIN, Stanley (St John's, Antigua, 1979); Maj, Carib. b 20 Feb 54; and
GRIFFIN, Hazel (née Whyte) (St John's, Antigua, 1980) m 1981; Maj, Carib. b 23 Sep 57. Served in L Am N.

GRINSTED, Stewart (West Norwood, UK, 1993); Maj, RC, MDE. b 3 Sep 53. BA (Hons); Dip Youth and Com work; with
GRINSTED, Heather (née Durman) m 1981; Maj, RPWM, MDE. b 9 Aug 58. BSc (Hons); PGCE; MA Theol. Served in UK.

GROVES, Jennifer (Wellington South, NZ, 1990); Lt-Col, RC, Tai. b 25 Sep 64. LTh. Served in NZ, Port and at IHQ.

GUIAMBA, João (Conguiana, Moz, 1997); Capt, Moz. b 2 Apr 66; and
GUIAMBA, Graça (née Rozicene) m 1992; Capt, Moz. b 17 Apr 74.

GUNADASA, Vitharamalage (Beligodapitiya, 1991); Maj, Sri Lan. b 20 Mar 59; and
GUNADASA, Nalani (née Ilandarage) (Udupitiya, 1985) m 1989; Maj, Sri Lan. b 15 Aug 62.

GUNDERSEN, Strømner Bente (Hamar, Nor, 1994); Maj, Rwa. b 26 Apr 68. MA Theol. Served in Nor, Zamb and DRC.

GUTIÉRREZ, Martín (Mexico City Corps #1, 1996); Maj, Mex. b 9 Sep 71; and
GUTIÉRREZ, Janet (née Ochoa) (Mexico City Corps #1, 1995) m 1996; Maj, Mex. b 10 Jan 73.

GUTIERREZ, Walter (Bolivia); Maj, L Am N. b 16 May 55; with
GUTIERREZ, Lidia (Bolivia) Maj, L Am N. b 29 May 58.

H

HADDICK, Eleanor (Edinburgh City, UK); Maj, Ken W. b 19 Dec 63.

HAGEN, Eli (née Nodland); Maj, Nor. b 25 Mar 57; with
HAGEN, Jan Harald m 1976 (Templet, Oslo, 1980); Maj, Nor. b 12 Feb 54.

HAGGAR, Kerry (née Geers) (Rockdale, 1982) m 1983, Lt-Col, Aus E, b 30 Nov 59. BComm, MAL.

HAN, Sea-jong (Kwachun, 1996); Maj, Kor. b 22 Sep 65; with
KIM, Ok-young; m 1991; Maj, Kor. b 1 Jul 68.

HANGOMA, Donald (Munali, 1995); Capt, Zam. b 15 Jan 70; and
HANGOMA, Patricia (née Michelo) (1993); Maj, Zam. b 19 Mar 70.

HARRIES, Elwyn (Swindon Citadel, 1982); Maj, UK. b 8 Mar 59; and
HARRIES, Carole (née Holdstock) (Northampton Central, 1979) m 1982; Maj, UK. b 15 Feb 57.

HARRIS, Ian W. (Penge, 1989); Maj, UK. b 1 Sep 56. MA, Dip Soc Wk; with
HARRIS, Jean (née Foster) m 1979; Maj, UK. b 31 Jul 56.

HARRY, Kervin Codric (Kingstown, St Vincent and the Grenadines 1985); Major, S Afr. b 14 Sep 64. BEd, MTh Served in Carib.

HAUGHTON, Devon (Port Antonio, Jamaica, 1981); Lt-Col, CS Carib. b 22 Jul 59; and
HAUGHTON, Verona Beverly (née Henry) (Havendale, Jamaica, 1976) m 1982; Lt-Col, TSWM Carib. b 15 Apr 54. BA (Guidance and Counselling), MA (Pastoral Counselling and Psych).

HAUPT, Gary W. (New Orleans, LA, USA S, 1982); Lt-Col, E Eur. b 27 Nov 53. BS (Bus Adm); with
HAUPT, Suzanne H. (née Hogan) m 1979; Lt-Col, E Eur. b 3 May 56. BS (Ed). Served in USA S and at USA Nat.

HAWKINS, Kenneth (Maidenhead, 1985); Maj, Zam. b 28 Mar 58; B Div, M Th; and
HAWKINS, Ann (née Tupling) (Maltby, 1984) m 1985; Maj, Zam. b 24 Jan 60. Served in UK.

HEATWOLE, Merle (Milwaukee Citadel, WI, USA C, 1984); Col, Nat CS, USA Nat. b 7 Jan 60. BS (Maths); with
HEATWOLE, Dawn (née Lewis) m 1981; Col, NSWM, USA Nat. b 26 Nov 62. AA (Pract Min). Served in USA C (CS/TSWM).

HEDGREN, R. Steven (Chicago Mont Clare, IL, USA C, 1978); Comr, USA S. b 7 Mar 50. BS (Bus Adm); with
HEDGREN, Judith Ann (née White) m 1975; Comr, USA S. b 14 Feb 49. AS (Bus). Served in USA C and USA E (CS/TSWM, TC/TPWM).

HEFFORD, Douglas (Buchans, NL, 1972); Lt-Col, Can. b 13 Feb 51. BRe, MDiv; with
HEFFORD, Jean (née Bowering) m 1973;

293

Biographical Information

Lt-Col, Can b 11 Aug 51.

HENNE, Ingrid Elisabeth (Bergen 1, 1982); Lt-Col, Nor. b 6 Sep 52.

HENRY, Samuel A. (Atlanta Temple, GA, 1983); Lt-Col, USA S. b 28 Nov 48; with **HENRY, Nancy** (née Southwood) m 1969; Lt-Col, USA S. b 13 Apr 47.

HERRING, Alistair Chapman (Wellington City, 1975); Comr, NZ. b 4 Mar 51. DipSW; with **HERRING, Verna Astrid** (née Weggery) m 1971; Comr, NZ. b 29 Oct 51. Served in E Eur (CS/TSWM), at IHQ (IS/ZSWM, SPEA) and in Pak (TC/TPWM).

HETTIARACHCHI, Nihal (Colombo, 1985); Lt-Col, CS, Sri Lan. b 20 Jun 64; and **HETTIARACHCHI, Rohini Swarnalatha** (née Wettamuni) (Colombo, 1994) m 1994; Lt-Col, TSWM, Sri Lan. b 18 Oct 64.

HICKMAN, Evan P. (Lexington, KY, 1993); Maj, USA E. b 4 Jan 65. BA; with **HICKMAN, Suzanne R.** (née Senak) m 1989; Maj, USA E. b 26 Mar 61.

HIGHTON, Michael (Hinckley, 1985); Lt-Col, UK. b 27 May 53; with **HIGHTON, Lynn** (née Edwards) m 1975; Lt-Col, UK. b 10 Mar 53.

HIGUCHI, Kazumitsu (Nagoya, 1976); Maj, Jpn. b 9 Apr 51; and **HIGUCHI, Aiko** (née Kutomi) (Shibuya, 1979) m 1982; Maj, Jpn. b 25 Sep 53. BA (Eng Lit).

HILL, Edward (Pasadena Tabernacle, CA, 1993); Maj, USA W. b 7 Nov 59. BA (History), MA (Chrstn Ed), M Div (Chrstn Ed); with **HILL, Shelley** (née Chandler) m 1985; Maj, USA W. b 11 Jul 63.

HILL, Martin (Northampton Central, 1984); Maj, UK. b 3 Jul 55. BA (Hons) (Soc Sci), MTh (Ap Theol).

HILLS, Cedric (Harpenden, 1986) Maj, Fin. b 1 Dec 59; with **HILLS, Lyn** (née Brown) m 1981; Maj, Fin. b 23 Dec 59. Served in UK.

HINSON, Harold Dean, Jr (Dallas Pleasant Grove, TX, 1984); Maj, USA S. b 15 Aug 58. BA (Bible), MA (Theol), MTS; with **HINSON, Pamela Gay** (née Hairston) m 1980; Maj, USA S. b 28 Jul 58.

HINTON, David (Blackheath, 1975); Col, CS, UK. b 28 Oct 53; and **HINTON, Sylvia** (née Brooks) (Bedlington, 1975) m 1977; Col, TSWM, UK. b 2 Dec 53.

HOBBINS, Charmaine (Marion, IN, 1982); Maj, USA C. b 15 Sep 57. BA (Bible Chrstn Ed), MA (Spiritual Frm and Ldrshp).

HOBGOOD, W. Edward (Greenville, NC, 1983); Lt-Col, IHQ. b 6 Apr 58; with **HOBGOOD, M. Kathryn** (née Hathaway) m 1978; Lt-Col, IHQ. b 12 Jun 54. Served in USA S.

HODDER, Kenneth G. (Pasadena Tabernacle, CA, USA W, 1988); Comr, TC, Ken W. b 16 Jun 58. BA (Hist), JD (Law); with **HODDER, Jolene** (née Lloyd) m 1982; Comr, TPWM, Ken W. b 30 Jul 61. BA (Home Econ). Served in USA W, USA S, Ken (CS/TPWM) Ken E (CS/TPWM) and at IHQ (IS Int Pers, Legal & Constitutional Advisor to the General/Assoc IS Int Pers).

HOFER, Allan (Sissach Basel, 1986); Lt-Col, CS, Switz. b 30 Mar 61; and **HOFER, Fiona** (née Pressland) (Barking, UK, 1987) m 1987; Lt-Col, TSWM, Switz. b 15 Apr 64. Served in Port, UK, Brz, USA S and at IHQ.

HORWOOD, S. Edward (Ted) (Monterey, CA, USA W, 1992); Col, TC, Tanz. b 1 Feb 61. BA (Eng), MA (Intercultural Studies); with **HORWOOD, Deborah** (née Haynes) m 1987; Col, TPWM, Tanz. b 22 Mar 66. Served in USA W, Zamb and Mal, at IHQ and in Ang (GS/CSWM).

HOSTETLER, Donald D. (Cincinnati Citadel, OH, 1972); Maj, USA E. b 2 Jan 49. BA (Socio), MA (Public Admin); with **HOSTETLER, Arvilla J.** (née Marcum) m 1969; Maj, USA E. b 14 Aug 50. BA (Org Psych). Served in USA W.

HOWARD, Steven (Hamilton, OH, 1983); Col, USA E. b 21 May 57. BS, MSc; with **HOWARD, Janice** (née Collopy) m 1979; Col, USA E. b 18 Mar 59. BS (Bus Ed), MA (Spir Form and Ldr). Served at ICO and in Ken E (CS/TLWM).

HOWELL, Willis (Hyattsville, MD, USA S, 1985); Col, CS, NZ. b 3 Mar 56; with **HOWELL, Barbara** (née Leidy) m 1978; Col, TSWM, NZ. b 3 Apr 57. Served in USA S.

HUDSON, David E. (Portland Tabernacle, OR, 1975); Col, CS, USA W. b 28 Jun 54. BS (Bus Mgmt); and **HUDSON, Sharron** (née Smith) (Santa Ana, CA, 1975) m 1976; Col, TSWM, USA W. b 14 Jun 52.

HUGUENIN, Sylvette (Payerne, 1991); Maj, Switz. b 14 June 63.

HUTSON, Ian (Spreydon, 1984); Lt-Col, NZ. b 26 Nov 54; Grad Dip Soc Work, Cert Bus; with **HUTSON, Lynette** (née Collett) m 1974; Lt-Col, NZ. b 20 Jul 54; Grad Dip Soc Work,

MA (Soc Work). Served in Can.

HWANG, Kyu-hong (Chun An, 2000); Capt, Kor. b 15 Jan 68; with
MA, Jin-young; m 1995, Capt, Kor. b 6 Jul 71.

HWANG, Sun-yup (Ah Hyun, 1985); Lt-Col, Kor. b 28 Dec 55; with
CHOI, Myung-soon m 1982; Lt-Col, Kor. b 9 Sep 59. Served in USA S and UK.

HYNES, Junior (Happy Valley, NL, 1971); Lt-Col, Can. b 6 Jan 51; MTS and
HYNES, Verna (née Downton) (Windsor, NL, 1971) m 1973; Lt-Col, Can. b 27 Aug 50. Served in UK.

I

IGHOTY, Christopher (Kamenge, 1996); Maj, Tanz. b 10 Nov 70; with
IGHOTY, Mary (née Elinazi) m 1993; Maj, Tanz. b 1 Jan 73.

IGLEHEART, Kelly (Owensboro, KY, 1992); Lt-Col, USA S. b 29 Oct 61; with
IGLEHEART, Donna (née Vincent) m 1981; Lt-Col, USA S. b 30 Apr 62.

ILUNGA, Bidwaya Clément (Salle Centrale, 1987); Maj, DR Con. b 16 Nov 62; with
ILUNGA, Béatrice (née Kalenga Monga) m 1988; Maj, DR Con. b 12 Sep 60.

IMBIAKHA, Daniel (Musingu, Ken W, 1992); Maj, Uga. b 14 Aug 60; with
IMBIAKHA, Nolega (née Clera) m 1988; Maj, Uga. b 21 Mar 69. Served in Ken W.

IMMANUEL, Sam (Thulickal, 1984); Maj, Ind SW. b 27 May 59; with
IMMANUEL, Rachel P. C. m 1982; Maj, Ind SW. b 15 Jun 57.

INDURUWAGE, Malcolm (Colombo Central, 1977); Comr, TC, Sri. b 24 Sep 50; and
INDURUWAGE, Irene (née Horathalge) (Colombo Central, 1977) m 1977; Comr, TPWM, Sri. b 29 Nov 55. Served in Phil (CS/TSWM, TC/TPWM).

IP KAN, Ming-chun Connie (Kwai Chung, 1985); Maj, CSWM, HK. b 16 Jul 62.

IQBAL, Safdar (Youhanabad, 1996); Maj, Pak. b 25 Dec 69; and
SAFDAR, Asia (née Kala) m 1993; Maj, Pak. b 22 Nov 72.

IRVING, Ray (Shiremoor, 1989) m 1989; Lt-Col, UK. b 20 Apr 51. MVA, MCMI; and
IRVING, Angela (née Richards) (Torquay, 1972) m 1989; Lt-Col, UK. b 12 Feb 51. Served at ITC.

ISHIKAWA, Kazuyuki (Suginami, 1998); Maj, Jpn. b 8 Mar 61. MA (Agriculture); and

ISHIKAWA, Yoshiko (née Sugai) (Kyobashi, 2005) m 1996; Maj, Jpn. b 1 Jun 63.

ISMAEL, Dina Dorothy (Bandung 1, 1988); Lt-Col, Indon. b 19 Jan 60.

ISRAEL, Mark H. (Warner Robbins, GA, USA S, 1982); Lt-Col, USA S. b 8 May 58. BA (Bible), MA (Theol Studies); and
ISRAEL, Carolee J. (née Zarfas) (Des Moines Citadel, IA, USA C, 1981); m 1982; Lt-Col, USA S. b 30 Mar 58. BS (Pract Min). Served at USA Nat.

IUNG, Ricardo (São Paulo Central, 1999); Capt, Brz. b 29 Nov 70. BA (Admin); with
IUNG, Cindy (née Meylan) m 1995; Capt, Brz. b 13 Feb 77. Served in Switz.

IVERS, Earle (Rockhampton Temple, 1991); Maj, Aus E. b 22 Jul 63; MA(SF), BTh, BAL.with
IVERS, Christine (née Markham) m 1983; Maj, Aus E. b 2 Nov 56. BSocSci (Counselling).

J

JACKSON, David (Romford, 1976); Maj, UK. b 10 Nov 52. Served at IHQ.

JAYARATNASINGHAM, Packianathan (Jaffna, 1973); Maj, Sri Lan. b 4 Nov 52; and
JAYARATNASINGHAM, Delankage Chandralatha (née Delankage) (Siyambalangamua, 1979) m 1980; Maj, Sri Lan. b 28 Oct 59. Served at IHQ.

JAYASEELAN, Jebamony (Maharajaduram 1982); Maj, Ind SE. b 20 May 57; and
GNANASELVI, Jayaseelan m 1980; Maj, Ind SE. b 30 Dec 57.

JEFFREY, David E. (Morgantown, WV, USA S, 1973); Comr, NC, USA Nat. b 2 Aug 51. BS, MA (Relig); and
JEFFREY, Barbara (née Garris) (Morgantown, WV, USA S, 1966) m 1969; Comr NPWM, USA Nat. b 1 Jul 46. Served in USA S (CS/TSWM, TC/TPWM) and at USA Nat (Nat CS/NSWM).

JENNINGS, Dan (Topeka, KS, 1994); Maj, USA C. b 15 Aug 65. BS (Pract Min); and
JENNINGS, Dorene A. (née Haak) (Topeka, KS, 1984) m 1988; Maj, USA C. b 12 Oct 55. BS (Pract Min).

JERA, Onai (Marowa, 1992); Maj, Zimb. b 10 Sep 67; and
JERA, Deliwe (née Gasa) (Gunguhwe, 1992) m 1994; Maj, Zimb. b 18 Jun 68.

JEWETT, Vernon Wayne (Atlanta Temple, GA, 1980); Lt-Col, USA S. b 11 Dec 47. BA, MA; with

JEWETT, Martha Gaye (née Brewer)
m 1975; Lt-Col, USA S. b 22 Oct 52. BA.
JOHN, Rajan K. (Parayankerry, 1979); Maj,
Ind SW. b 26 Mar 52; with
RAJAN, Susamma m 1977; Maj, Ind SW.
b 17 Oct 52.
JOHN, Samuel (Lahore, 1997); Maj, Pak.
b 5 Jul 69; and
SAMUEL, Rebecca (née William) m 1993;
Maj, Pak. b 11 Mar 72.
JOHNSON, Kenneth (Charlotte Temple, NC,
1984); Col, USA S. b 10 Aug 56. BS (Bus
Mgmt); with
JOHNSON, Paula (née Salmon) m 1981;
Col, USA S. b 23 Nov 62. Served in E Eur
(TC/TPWM).
JONAS, Dewhurst (St John's, Antigua, 1982);
Lt-Col, Carib. b 20 May 56; and
JONAS, Vevene (née Gordon) (Rae Town,
Jamaica, 1980) m 1983; Lt-Col, Carib. b 1 Jun 57.
JONES, Derek (Hereford 1982); Maj, UK.
b 27 Feb 55; and
JONES, Susan (née White) (Oldham, 1975)
m 1984; Maj, UK. b 14 Jan 55. Served at IHQ.
JONES, John Roy, Jr (Gastonia, NC, 1971);
Lt-Col, USA S. b 2 Feb 49; and
JONES, Arduth Eleanor (née Johnson)
(Charlotte Temple, NC, 1971) m 1973;
Lt-Col, USA S. b 1 Jan 50.
JOSHI, Devadasi (Musunuru, 1981); Maj,
Ind C. b 1 Oct 54; with
JOSHI, Leelamani m 1977; Maj, Ind C.
b 1 Jun 53.
JWILI, Lenah (Galeshewe, Kimberley, 1978);
Major, S Afr. b 5 Mar 1956. Served in Namibia.

K

KAKI, Sundara Rao (Denduluru, 1978); Maj,
Ind C. b 9 May 55; with
KAKI, Dasaratna Kumari m 1974; Maj,
Ind C. b 12 Sep 55.
KALE, Ratnakar Dinkar (Ahmednagar Central,
1977); Lt-Col, Ind W. b 1 Jul 53; and
KALE, Leela (née Magar) (Byculla, 1981)
m 1981; Lt-Col, Ind W. b 1 Mar 60.
KAMAMBO, Clever (Chrome Mine, Zimb,
1979); Lt-Col, Nig. b 28 Dec 57; and
KAMAMBO, Daphne (née Mhlanga)
(Mufakose, Zimb, 1981) m 1984;
Lt-Col, Nig. b 16 Dec 59. Served in Zimb.
KAPERE, Angeline (Chegutu, 1991); Maj,
Zim. b 1 Jun 66; and
KAPERE, Fashion (Zimbara, 1996);
Maj, Zimb. b 16 Jun 56.
KAROGO, George (Boregaina, 1997); Maj,

PNG. b 24 Dec 66; with
KAROGO, Georgina (née Borana) m 1988;
Maj, PNG. b 12 Nov 72.
KASAEDJA, Jones (Kulawi, 1982); Lt-Col, CS,
Indon. b 22 Jun 58; and
KASAEDJA, Mariyam (née Barani)
(Salupone, 1982) m 1989; Lt-Col, TSWM,
Indon. b 10 Oct 55.
KASUSO, Daniel (Pearson, Zimb, 1986); Maj,
IHQ. b 15 May 62. BTh; and
KASUSO, Tracey (née Mashiri) (Torwood,
Zimb, 1986) m 1987; Maj, IHQ. b 19 Oct 64.
Served in Zimb and S Afr.
KATHURI, Gabriel (Mombasa, Ken E, 1982);
Col, OC, Lib. b 13 Jan 51; with
KATHURI, Monica (née Minoo) m 1977;
Col, CPWM, Lib. b 22 Feb 54. Served in
Ken E (CS/TSWM) and at IHQ (Principal,
SALT, Afr).
KATSUCHI, Jiro (Hamamatsu, 1984);
Comr, TC, Jpn. b 3 May 49; and
KATSUCHI, Keiko (née Munemori)
(Nagoya, 1969) m 1986; Comr, TPWM, Jpn.
b 30 Jun 47.
KEIJZER, Benjamin (Hengelo, 1988); Major,
b 19 Apr 53 with
KEIJZER, Ingeborg M. (née Niewöhner)
(Almelo, 1988) m 1989; Major,
b 3 Nov 58.
KELLY, David E. (Cincinnati, OH, 1980);
Lt-Col, USA N. b 30 Nov 59.
AS (Bus Adm), MA (Ldrshp & Min); and
KELLY, Naomi R. (née Foster) (Tonawanda,
NY, 1977) m 1981; Lt-Col, USA N. b 14 Sep
56. BA (Org Mgmt). Served in USA E
KHAMALISHI, Fredrick (Masera, Ken,
1989); Maj, Ken W. b 22 Feb 63; with
KHAMALISHI, Jesca (née Masera)
m 1988; Maj, Ken W. b 12 Apr 65.
KHARKOV, Alexander (Moscow Central,
1993); Lt-Col, CS, E Eur. b 31 Jan 58.
KHAYUMBI, Luka (Musudzuu, Ken, 1994);
Maj, S Afr. b 5 Nov 66 Dip Ldr & Mngt, BA
Ldr & Mngt; with
KHAYUMBI, Rasoa (née Inyangala) m
1990; Maj. S Afr. b 3 Oct 70. Served in Ken E.
KHOLOWA, Paul, (Migowi, 1997); Capt, Mal.
b 1 Jan 70; and
KHOLOWA, Doreen (née Mwaitanda)
m 2003; Lt, Mal. b 5 Jan 82.
KHOZA, Jabulani (Mbabane, 1985); Lt-Col,
S Afr. b 8 Jun 62; and
KHOZA, Fikile (née Mkhize) (Ezakheni,
1986) m 1986; Lt-Col, S Afr. b 28 Aug 66.
KIBOTI, Ndombasi Théophile (Kavwaya,

1987); Lt-Col, Dem Rep Con. b 2 Apr 58; with
KIBOTI, Simone (née Kodi Kisala)
m 1985; Lt-Col, Dem Rep Con. b 12 Feb 66.

KIM, Jong-koo (Chin Chook, 1980); Maj, Kor.
b 22 Nov 51; with
KIM, Kye-suk (Chun Yun, 1980); m 1978;
Maj, Kor. b 10 May 56.

KIM, Nam-sun (Ah Hyun, 1983); Lt-Col, Kor.
b 11 Sep 54.

KIM, Pill-soo (Yung Deung Po, 1985); Col, CS,
Kor. b 2 Jan 55; with
CHOI, Sun-hee m 1982; Col, TSWM, Kor.
b 28 Sep 57.

KIM, Un-ho (Eum Am, 1979); Lt-Col, Kor.
b 31 Jan 52; with
LEE, Ok-kyung (Duk Am, 1979) m 1977;
Lt-Col, Kor. b 9 Jun 53.

KIM, Young-tae (Chin Chook, 1986); Lt-Col,
Kor. b 23 Mar 56. BAdm, MBA; with
PYO, Choon-yun m 1977; Lt-Col, Kor.
b 30 Aug 53.

KIMASWOCH, Patrick (Kaptel, Ken 1998);
Capt, Mal. b 4 Apr 70; with
KIMASWOCH, Frida (née Indusa)
m 1996; Capt, Mal. b 11 Sep 70. Served in
Ken W.

KITHOME, Lucas (Mwala, 1986); Maj, Ken E.
b 10 Feb 59; with
KITHOME, Agnes (née Nduku) m 1984;
Maj, Ken E. b 15 Jan 63.

KIVINDYO, Isaac (Kanzalu, 1982); Lt-Col,
Ken E. b 1 Aug 56; with
KIVINDYO, Naomi (née Loko) m 1978;
Lt-Col, Ken E. b 1 May 60. Served in Ken W.

KLEMAN, Johnny (Boras, Swdn, 1982);
Col, TC, Fin. b 29 Jul 59. BTh; and
KLEMAN, Eva (née Hedberg) (Motala,
Swdn, 1981) m 1982; Col, TPWM, Fin. b 6
Sep 1960. Served in Swdn (CS/TSWM).

KLEMANSKI, Guy (Lewiston-Auburn, ME,
1971); Lt-Col, USA E. b 21 Nov 50; and
KLEMANSKI, Henrietta (née Wallace)
(Cleveland, West Side, OH, 1970) m 1972;
Lt-Col, USA E. b 27 Jul 47.

KNAGGS, James (Philadelphia Roxborough,
PA, USA E, 1976); Comr, TC, USA W.
b 5 Dec 50. MPS (Urban Min); with
KNAGGS, Carolyn (née Lance) m 1972;
Comr, TPWM, USA W. b 19 Sep 51. Served
in USA E (CS/TSWM) and Aus S (TC/TPWM).

KNEDAL, Jan Øystein (Templet, Oslo, 1974);
Lt-Col, Nor. b 25 Aug 52; and
KNEDAL, Brit (née Kolloen) (Templet, Oslo,
1976) m 1978; Lt-Col, Nor. b 27 Apr 58.

KOMBO, Blaise (Makelekele, 1998); Maj,

Con (Braz). b 15 Oct 68. MA Psych; with
KOMBO, Evelynne (née Missamon)
(Sangolo, 1996) m 1992; Maj, Con (Braz).
b 6 Jan 75.

KORNILOW, Petter (Parkano, 1981);
Lt-Col, CS, Fin. b 21 Aug 53; and
KORNILOW, Eija Hellevi
(née Astikainen) (Tampere Kaleva, 1981)
m 1981; Lt-Col, TSWM, Fin. b 28 Jun 56.

KROMMENHOEK, Dick (Amsterdam
Congress Hall, Neth, 1983); Comr, TC,
Nor. b 18 Jun 52. MA (Music); with
KROMMENHOEK, Vibeke (née Schou
Larsen) m 1978; Comr, TPWM, Nor.
b 27 Nov 56. MA (Theol). Served in Neth,
Den (TC/TPWM), Frce (TC/TPWM),
Fin (TC/TPWM) and at IHQ.

KUMAR, Raj (Nawanpind, Mukerian, 1989);
Maj, Ind N. b 7 Aug 64. BA, BD: with
RAJKUMAR, Mohinder m 1987; Maj,
Ind N. b 5 May 64.

KUMARADHAS, Geevanantham
(Josephpuram 1978) Maj, Ind SE,
b 5 Aug 57; with
KALA SIROMONY (Seethapal, 1981);
Maj, India SE, b 5 May 55.
Served in Ind W.

KUMARAVEL, Felix, (Colombo 2003);
Capt, Sri Lan. b 18 Jan 80.

KWENDA, Peter (Mutondo, 1976);
Col, CS, Zimb. b 10 Apr 57; and
KWENDA, Norma (née Nyawo)
(Dombwe-Makonde, 1977) m 1977; Col,
TSWM, Zimb. b 10 Jul 55. Served in Nig.

KYEI, Edward (Fomena, 1979); Maj, Gha.
b 2 Jun 60; with
KYEI, Catherine (née Adjeiwah);
m 1979; Maj, Gha. b 23 Nov 1963.

L

LABOSSIERE, James P. (Cambridge Citadel,
MA, 1985); Maj, USA E. b 21 Feb 60.
BS (Comm Min), MS (Org Ldrshp); with
LABOSSIERE, Patricia (née Levesque)
m 1982; Maj, USA E. b 28 Nov 60. BS
(Church Mgmt).

LAITHANMAWIA, Ralte (Darlawn, 1981);
Maj, Ind E. b 15 Mar 56 with
LALBIALTLUANGI, Tochhawng
(Darlawn, 1982); Maj, Ind E. b 20 Aug 60.

LAL, Piara (Behrampur,1984); Maj,
Ind N. b 15 May 57; and
LAL, Madhu m 1981; Maj, Ind N.
b 10 May 62.

LAL, Samuel Ram (Rajpura, 1981); Maj, Ind

N. b 31 Oct 62; and
LAL, Sunila (Moradabad, 1983) m 1984;
Maj, Ind N. b 10 Jun 64.
LALAC, Valery (Dubossary, Moldova, 1999);
Maj, E Eur. b 10 May 59; with
LALAC, Victoria (née Pocotilo) m1986;
Maj, E Eur, b 9 May 67.
LALBULLIANA Tlau (Gilgal, 1987);
Lt-Col, Ind E. b 20 Sep 64; and
LALNUNHLUI Khawlhring
(Thingsulthliah, Ind E, 1990) m 1990;
Lt-Col, Ind E. b 7 Dec 66. Served in Ken E.
LALHMINGLIANA Ngurte (Chaltlang,
1994); Lt-Col, Ind E. b 29 Sep 71.
BA (Hons) (Hist); and
LALHLIMPUII Chawngthu (Bethel, 1994)
m 1994; Lt-Col, Ind E. b 28 Oct 71.
Served at IHQ.
LALLIANKUNGA Ralte (Bilkhawthlir 1992);
Maj, Ind E. b 3 Jan 69. BA, BD; with
ZONUNSANGI Pautu (Khatla 1994) m
1994; Maj, Ind E. b 5 Feb 64.
LALNGAIHAWMI, Naomi (Aizawl Central,
1978); Comr, TC, TPWM, Ind E. b 1 Jan 54.
MA. Served at Ind Nat.
LALRAMLIANA, Hnamte (Govt Complex,
Aizawl, Ind E, 1996); Maj, Ind Nat.
b 3 Jan 67. BA, BD; and
C. LALHRIATPUII m 1994; Maj, Ind Nat.
b 15 Sep 69. Served in Ind E.
LALZAMLOVA (Tuinu, Ind E, 1986);
Comr, IHQ (IS, S Asia). b 1 Feb 62. BA; with
NEMKHANCHING (Nu-i) m 1984;
Comr, IHQ (ZSWM, S Asia). b 23 Feb 63.
Served in Ind E, Ind N, Sri (TC/TPWM)
and Phil (TC/TPWM).
LAMARTINIERE, Lucien (Petit Goave,
Haiti, 1992); Lt-Col, CS, DR Con. b 13 Jun
57; with
LAMARTINIERE, Marie (née Bonhomme)
m 1980; Lt-Col, TSWM, DR Con. b 26 May
57. Served in Can and Carib.
LANCE, Donald W. (Philadelphia Roxborough,
PA, 1980); Lt-Col, USA E. b 7 Feb 53.
BA (Bus), MPA (Non-Profit Mgmt); and
LANCE, Renee (née Hewlett) (Scranton, PA,
2002) m 2003; Lt-Col, USA E. b 3 Jun 53.
RN (Nursing).
LANGA, William (Witbank, 1977); Comr, TC,
S Afr. b 15 Jul 49; with
LANGA, Thalitha (née Themba) m 1973;
Comr, TPWM, S Afr. b 1 Sep 50. Served as
CS/TSWM.
LASUT, Ernie (Bandung 1, 1986); Maj,
Indon. b 4 Sep 61.

LAWS, Peter (Wauchope, 1973); Lt-Col, Aus E.
b 23 Oct 1950. BAL, MBA; with
LAWS, Jan (née Cook) m 1970; Lt-Col,
Aus E. b 18 Jun 50.
LEAVEY, Wendy (Street, UK, 1980); Lt-Col,
IHQ. b 17 Feb 53. SRN, SCM. Served in
UK and Gha.
LEE, Chong-ho (Sang Kei, 1983); Maj, Kor.
b 20 Nov 56; with
KIM, Sook-ja m 1980; Maj. Kor. b 6 Nov 59.
LEE, Ki-yong (Chun Yun, Seoul 1982); Maj,
Kor. b 9 Aug 52; and
KIM, Sun-ho (Eum Am, 1985) m 1985;
Maj, Kor. b 19 Jan 54.
LEE, Kong Chew (Bob) (Balestier, 1983);
Lt-Col, CS, Phil. b 8 Oct 57.
Cert Mgmt, Dip Min, BDiv; and
LEE, Teoh Gim Leng (Wendy)
(Penang, 1983) m 1982; Lt-Col, TSWM, Phil.
b 24 Aug 57. Dip Min; Served in Sing
LEMPID, I. Sadia (Polonia, 1989);
Maj, Indon. b 13 Dec 64; and
LEMPID, Syastiel (née Haku)
(Semarang 3, 1996) m 1996; Maj, Indon. b 9
Oct 72.
LePINE, Darrell (Kilbirnie, 1980); Maj, NZ
b 20 Jul 51; Dip. Counselling; with
LePINE, Lorraine (née Rodgers)
(New Plymouth 1980); Maj, NZ. b 6 Jan 53;
B. Ed., Dip. Teaching., PG Dip. Ed. (Adult Ed.)
LESCANO, Lee R. (San Diego Citadel, CA,
1988); Maj, USA W. b 14 Jul 52. MA, BA,
Cert (Elementary Ed); with
LESCANO, Michele (née Meyer) m 1985;
Maj, USA W. b 3 Oct 55. BA (Bib and Theol).
LESLIE, Victor A. (Port-of-Spain, 1980);
Col,TC, Nig. b 5 Nov 56. BA (Mgmt),
MA (Relig Studies), CERT (Chem Dpndnce),
JD (Law), MBA (Mgmt); and
LESLIE, Rose-Marie (née Campbell)
(Lucea, 1977) m 1980; Col, TPWM, Nig.
b 15 Aug 57. BS (Soc Wk), AS (Nursing),
RN (Nursing), BS (Nursing), CERT (Public
Health Nurse). Served in USA W and Carib
(CS/TSWM).
LIGT, de Cornelis (Nieuwegein, Neth, 1990);
Maj, Ban. b 23 Sep 61; and
LIGT, de Jacoba (née Oosterheerd)
(Nieuwegein, Neth, 1987) m 1988;
Maj, Ban. b 24 Apr 58. Served in Neth, E Afr,
Ken E and Ken W.
LIM, Hun-taek (Kunsan, 1979); Lt-Col, Kor.
b 24 Aug 50; with
CHUN, Soon-ja m 1977; Lt-Col, Kor.
b 9 Mar 50. Served in Aus S.

LIM, Young-sik (Shin An, 1975); Lt-Col, Kor.
b 26 Jun 49; with
YEO, Keum-soo (Mokpo, 1975) m 1972;
Lt-Col, Kor. b 14 Dec 50.

LIVIALA, Isaack (Londiana, Ken, 1985);
Maj, Ken W. b 15 Jan 59 with
LIVIALA, Rose (née Kagena) m 1984;
Maj, Ken W. b 12 Dec 1963.

LÖFGREN, Edith (née Sjöström)
(Borlänge, 1974); Col, Swdn. b 2 Mar 51.
Served in UK and Nor (TSWO) m 1977;
Col Kehs David, ret 2012.

LOMAX, Denis (Prescot, 1974); Maj, UK.
b 26 Jan 53. Dip RS; and
LOMAX, Olive (née Baird) (Prescot, 1974)
m 1974; Maj, UK. b 15 Jan 55.

LOPEZ, Gerardo (Dagupan,1991); Maj, Phil.
b 6 Jan 62. BA; and
LOPEZ, Cristina (née Gonzaga)
(Orani, 1991) m 1991; Maj, Phil. b 25 Dec 66.

LOROT, Ibrahim (Lokitaung, 1994), Maj,
Ken W. b 4 Dec 61; with
LOROT, Anne (née Edung) m 1984;
Maj, Ken W. b 13 Mar 65. Served in Ken E.

LOUBACKY, Urbain (Bakongo, 1994);
Maj, Con (Braz), b 20 Dec 64; with
LOUBACKY, Judith (née Bikouta) m 1989;
Maj, Con (Braz). b 16 Apr 68.

LOUZOLO, Dieudonné (Nzoko, 1992); Maj,
Con (Braz). b 20 Apr 67. BA Lang; with
LOUZOLO, Edith (née Boudzoumou) m 1990;
Maj, Con (Braz). b 25 Jul 69. Served in Belg.

LUFUMBU, Enock (Londiani, Nakuru, 1982);
Lt-Col, Ken W. b 10 Feb 52; with
LUFUMBU, Beatrice (née Kageha) m 1978;
Lt-Col, Ken W. b 22 Feb 57. Served in Ken E.

LUKAU, Joseph (Kimbanseke 1, Con (Kin),
1977); Col, TC, Gha. b 18 Sep 53; with
LUKAU, Angélique (née Makiese) m 1975;
Col, TPWM, Gha. b 1 Sep 54. Served in
Con (Kin), Frce (CS/TPWM), Con (Braz)
(TC/TPWM) and at IHQ.

LUTHER, Lise (Harstad, 1992); Maj, Nor.
b 20 May 65.

LUYK, Kenneth E. (Columbus, GA, 1985);
Lt-Col, USA S. b 2 Oct 55. MA (Relig); with
LUYK, Dawn M. (née Busby) m 1981; Lt-
Col, USA S. b 5 Jun 60. BA (Chrstn Min).

LYONS, Edward (Savanna-la-mar, Jamaica,
1997): Maj, Carib. b 15 Dec 1966. (BA)
Theology; and
LYONS, Jennifer (nee Gibbon) (Savanna-la-
mar, Jamaica, 1997) m 1988: Maj, Carib.
b 18 Apr 1966,

M

MABASO, Zakithi (née Zulu) m 1983;
Lt-Col, S Afr. b 16 Dec 57. Served in S Afr
and Ken W and at IHQ.

MABUTO, Christopher (Chaanga, Zam, 1979);
Lt-Col, CS, Zam. b 2 Jan 54; with
MABUTO, Anne (née Hamayobe) m 1974;
Lt-Col, TSWM, Zam. b 25 Feb 58. Served in
Zam and Mal, Ken W and Tanz.

MABWIDI, Malonga Philippe (Salle Centrale,
1985); Maj, DR Con. b 25 Jan 53; with
MABWIDI Marie-Thérèse (née Biyela
Lukimwena) m 1986; Maj, DR Con. b 13 Mar 63.

MACWAN, Yakub Gala (Dabhan 1983); Maj,
Ind W. b 3 Jul 59; and
MACWAN, Sophia (Vaso 1983); m 1981,
Maj, Ind W. b 7 Sep 62.

McCOMBE, Andrew (Burton-on-Trent, 1981);
Maj, UK. b 22 Nov 58. MA (Evan); and
McCOMBE, Beverley (née Hughes)
(Burton-on-Trent, 1981) m 1983; Maj, UK.
b 30 Aug 59. BSc (Hons) (Genetics and Cell Biol).

McMILLAN, Susan (Montreal Citadel, 1979);
Comr, TC, TPWM, Can. b 20 Oct 54. BAS,
MBA, CGA. Served in Mex and Cent Am,
S Am W (CS), at IHQ and in S Am (TC,TPWM).

MADOKI, Japhael (Ilembo, 1982); Maj, Tanz.
b 7 Jan 61; with
MADOKI, Aliyinza m 1981; Maj, Tanz.
b 1 Jan 61.

MADYANENZARA, Joseph (Alaska Mine,
1986); Maj, Zimb. b 25 Dec 56; with
MADYANENZARA, Molly; Maj, Zimb.
b 25 May 58.

MAFUTA, Mavana Denis (Kamina, 1993);
Capt, DR Con. b 18 Oct 54; with
MAFUTA Modestine (née Lumwanga
Ngoy); Maj, DR Con. b 18 Oct 1962.

MAGAIGWA, Musa (Kitaguti, 1992); Maj,
Tanz. b 26 Sep 1965; with
MAGAIGWA, Esther m 1991; Maj, Tanz.
b 1 Jan 61.

MAGAYA, Bexter (Chitumbi, 1981);
Maj, Zam. b 29 Jan 56; with
MAGAYA, Jessie (née Milambo) m 1979;
Maj, Zam. b 20 Sep 63.

MAHLANGU, Solomon (Brits, 1983); Maj,
S Afr. b 29 Oct 60; and
MAHLANGU, Mercy (née Razwinani)
(Khubvi, 1983) m 1985; Maj, S Afr.
b 30 Jun 63. BA Soc Studies. Served at IHQ.

MAHLOBO, Themba (Vryheid, 2001); Capt,
S Afr. b 1 Nov 76; with
MAHLOBO, Nokuthula (née Mabaso)
(Estill, 2001) m 2002; Capt, S Afr. b 26 Jun 81;

MAIN, Paul (Rutherglen, 1986); Maj, UK.
b 11 Aug 64; and
MAIN, Jenine (née Hixon) (Basingstoke,
1986) m 1986; Maj, UK. b 12 Dec 60. BA.

MALABI, Joash (Mulatiwa, Ken, 1984);
Comr, IHQ (IS, Afr). b 17 May 55; and
MALABI, Florence (née Muhindi) (Webuye,
Ken, 1988) m 1988; Comr, IHQ (ZSWM, Afr).
b 26 Jun 64. Served in E Afr, Rw (RC/RPWM),
S Afr (CS/TSWM) and Ken W (TC/TLWM).

MALINS, Stephen (Johannesburg City, 1997);
Maj, S Afr. b 7 Sep 62. BTh; with
MALINS, Theresa (née Lotter) m 1985;
Maj, S Afr. b 27 May 65

MAMBO, Tineyi (Seke Materera, 1989);
Maj, Zimb. b 23 Jan 67; and
MAMBO, Rumbidzai (Mungate, 1989)
m 1991; Maj, Zimb. b 29 May 67.

MANDGULE Ashok (Nasarapur, 1982); Maj,
Ind W. b 4 May 59; and
MANDGULE Sheela (Fariabagh, 1983);
Maj, Ind W. b 14 Sep 64.

MANGELA, Ezra (Tomado, 1989) Maj, Indon.
b 11 Aug 66; and
MANGELA, Marisa (née Panjaitan)
(Yogyakarta, 1990) m 1995; Maj, Indon.
b 16 Dec 66.

MANGIWA, Indra (Bandung 2, 1976); Maj,
Indon. b 14 Mar 52; and
MANGIWA, Helly (née Salainti) (Surabaya,
1977) m 1982; Maj, Indon. b 16 Jun 56.

MANHARDT, Linda (Pasadena Tabernacle,
USA W, 1978); Maj, Phil. b 11 Apr 52. MA.

MANKOMBA, Elisha (Choma, 1989); Maj,
Zam. b 22 Mar 53; with
MANKOMBA, Alice (née Mutinta) m 1983;
Maj, Zam, b 4 Jun 64.

MANOHARAN, Yesudian (Nantikuzhy, Ind SE,
1987); Maj, Ind SE. b 14 May 64. MCom,
M Min; and
MANOHARAN, Vethamony (Ettamadai,
Ind SE, 1987) m 1987; Maj, Ind SE. b 20 Mar
64. Served in Ind N and Tanz.

MANULAT, Edward (San Jose Antique,
1983); Maj, Phil. b 1 Dec 59; and
MANULAT, Arlene (née Nicor) (Pandanan,
1984) m 1984; Maj, Phil. b. 10 Aug 59.

MARERE, Washington (Gunguhwe, 1993);
Maj, Zimb, b 16 Marc 62; with
MARERE, Susan (née Chinyoka) (Gunguhwe,
1993); m 1990; Maj, Zimb, b 1 Nov 1971.

MARQUEZ, Elicio (USA W 1978); Maj, L Am
N. b 31 July 56; and
MARQUEZ, Darlan (USA W 1977) m 1981
Maj, L Am N. b 25 May 55.

MÁRQUEZ, Manuel (La Esperanza, 1995);
Maj, S Am W. b 12 Feb 1971; and
MÁRQUEZ, Paulina (née Condori) (Viacha,
1987) m 1997; Maj, S Am W. b 2 Mar 1964.

MARSEILLE, Gerrit W. J. (Ribe, Den, 1978);
Comr, TC, Carib. b 8 Jun 51. MSc, MLP; with
MARSEILLE, Eva (née Larsen) m 1976;
Comr, TPWM Carib. b 18 Jun 52. Cand
Odont. Served in Neth, Zai, Den, S Afr, Con
(Braz) (CS/TSWM) and at IHQ (IS, Prog
Res/ZSWM, SPEA).

MARTI, Paul William (Templet, Oslo, 1980);
Maj, Ger. b 24 Jan 61; and
MARTI, Margaret Saue (née Saue) (Voss,
1980) m 1983, Maj, Ger. b 29 Aug 58. Served
in Switz and Nor.

MARTIN, Larry (Edmonton Northside, AB,
1980); Lt-Col, Can. b 31 Jul 1950. BA, MA,
MTS; with
MARTIN, Velma (née Ginn) m 1972;
Lt-Col, Can. b 4 Oct 1950. Served in UK.

MARZAN, Jorge L. (San Juan, PR, 1977);
Maj, USA E. b 3 Nov 56. Cert (Database); and
MARZAN, Limaris (née Negron) (Ponce, PR,
2002) m 2001; Capt, USA E. b 10 Sep 75.
BA (Soc Wk).

MARTINEZ Gilberto, (Coatzacoalcos, 1987);
Maj, Mex. b 4 Feb 67; with
MARTÍNEZ Lorena (née Sosa) m 1986;
Maj, Mex b 10 Aug 66.

MASANGO, Frederick (Mangula, 1971); Maj,
Zimb. b 24 Jul 49; and
MASANGO, Rosemary (née Handiria)
(Karambazungu, 1981) m 1981; Maj, Zimb.
b 13 Feb 56.

MASIH Ayoob (Rampur, Moradabad 1984);
Maj. Ind N. b 5 June 65; and
MASIH Reena (Rampur, Moradabad 1985);
m 1987; Maj. Ind N. b 17 Apr 60.

MASIH, Edwin (Bareilly, Ind N, 1979); Col ,
TC, Ind SE, b 6 Oct 57; and
MASIH, Sumita (Gurdaspur, Ind N, 1983) m
1983; Col, TPWM, Ind SE. b 9 Oct 63.
Served in Ind N , Carib and ICT.

MASIH, Emmanuel (Kahnuwan, 1998);
Maj, Ind N. b 15 Apr 77; and
MASIH E. Goldi m 1996; Maj, Ind N. b 20
Apr 77.

MASIH, Joginder (Bhoper, 1982); Lt-Col, CS,
Ind W. b 13 Jul 58; with
MASIH, Shanti m 1980; Lt-Col, TSWM,
Ind W. b 15 May 59. Served in Ban
(GS/CSWM) and Ind N.

MASIH, Makhan (Shahpur Guraya, 1990); Maj,
Ind N. b 30 Mar 68; and

MASIH, Sunila Makhan (City Corps, Amritsar, 1992) m 1992; Maj, Ind N. b 5 May 66.

MASIH, Manga (Bhandal, 1979); Maj, Ind N. b 1 May 54; and
MASIH, Roseleen (Batala Central, 1980) m 1980; Maj, Ind N. b 2 Jun 59.

MASIH, Manuel (Amritsar, 1994); Maj, Ind N. b 1 Apr 64; with
MASIH, Anita m 1991; Maj, Ind N. b 22 Apr 62.

MASIH, Parkash (Khunda, 1984); Lt-Col, Ind N. b 10 Mar 58; with
MASIH, Mariam Parkash m 1981; Lt-Col, Ind N. b 2 Apr 62.

MASIH, Piara (Kathane, 1982); Maj, Ind N. b 3 Mar 61; with
MASIH, Grace (Babri Jiwanwal, 1984) m 1985; Maj, Ind N. b 6 Feb 64.

MASIH, Salamat (Shantinagar, 1989); Maj, Pak. b 12 Aug 64; with
SALAMAT, Grace (née Sardar) m 1987; Maj, Pak. b 18 Apr 64.

MASIH, Sulakhan (Dina Nagar, 1988); Maj, Ind N. b 15 Apr 64; and
MASIH, Sheela (Hayat Nagar, 1984) m 1988; Maj, Ind N. b 5 Apr 64.

MASIH, Yaqoob (Chamroua, 1986); Lt-Col, Ind N. b 6 Jun 62; with
MASIH, Sumitra m 1980; Lt-Col, Ind N. b 6 Jan 63.

MASON, Winsome (Burnie, Aus S, 1987);Maj, Pak. b 2 Feb 1958. Served in UK and Aus S.

MASSIÉLÉ, Antoine (Yaya, 1982); Maj, Con (Braz). b 20 Feb 53; with
MASSIÉLÉ, Marianne (née Ngoli) m 1978; Maj, Con (Braz). b 2 Jan 50.

MATA, Mayisilwa Jean-Baptiste (Kisenso, 1983); Lt-Col, DR Con. b 21 Oct 51; with
MATA, Marie (née Mundele Kisokama), m 1981; Lt-Col. DR Con. b 22 Mar 58.

MATHANGI, Daniel Raju (M.R. Nagaram, Ind C, 1984); Lt-Col, CS, Ind N. b 20 Jun 54. MA (Econ); with
MATHANGI, Rachel (née Kondamudi) m 1982; Lt-Col, TSWM, Ind N. b 15 Jun 62. Served in Ind C.

MATONDO, Gracia Victor (Kimpese, 1985); Lt-Col, DR Con. b 23 May 60; with
MATONDO, Isabel (née Lydia) m 1982; Lt-Col, DR Con. b 8 Sep 1962.

MATONDO, Isidore Mayunga (Boma, 1989); Maj, DR Con. b 6 Jul 56; with
MATONDO, Marthe (née Nlandu Luzoladio) m 1987; Maj, DR Con. b 7 Dec 62.

MATSIONA, Pascal (Sangolo, 1992); Maj, Con (Braz). b 5 Jun 57; and

MATSIONA, Adèle (née Mibenzibandoki) m 1989; Maj, Con (Braz). b 21 Jul 55.

MATURA, Netsai (née Takawira) (Mucherengi, 1974) m 1974; Maj, Zimb, b 2 Feb 1954.

MAUBE, Fanuel (Shigomere, Ken 1990); Lt-Col, Ken W. b 24 Aug 59; with
MAUBE, Lucy (née Wambui) m 1983; Lt-Col, Ken W. b 28 Aug 62.

MAXAM, Byron (Savanna-la-mar, Jamaica, 1971): Maj, Carib. b 31 Aug 50; and
MAXAM, Joycelyn (nee Jonas) (St Johns, Antigua, 1970) m 1994: Maj, Carib. b 4 Sep 48.

MAXWELL, Wayne (Canberra City Temple, Aus E, 1984); Col, TC, Phil. b 31 May 58. DipMin, BMin, MAL; with
MAXWELL, Robyn (née Alley) m 1980; Col, TPWM, Phil. b 14 Feb 60. Dip Pastoral Counselling. Served in Aus E (CS/TSWM).

MAYASI, Mabasa Alphonse (Mbanza-Nzundu, 1985); Maj, DR Con. b 12 Nov 60; and
MAYASI, Bernadette (née Makwiza Nlandu) m 1992; Maj, DR Con. b 10 Jul 63.

MAYNOR, Kenneth (Cleveland South, OH,1980); Lt-Col, USA E. b 1 Feb 59. BS (Org Mgmt); with
MAYNOR, Cheryl Ann (née Staaf) m 1977; Lt-Col, USA E. b 27 Sep 58. BS (Church Mgmt).

MAYORGA, Julia (née Obando); Maj, L Am N. b 23 Oct 61; with
MAYORGA, Max (Central, Costa Rica, 1989) m 1981; Maj, L Am N. b 1 Feb 62.

MBAGWU, Joseph (Kano, 1994); Maj, Nig. b 21 Oct 64; with
MBAGWU, Ngozi m 1992; Maj, Nig. b 17 Sep 68.

MBAJA, Tiras Atulo (Kibera, 1986); Maj, Ken W. b 13 Jul 54; with
MBAJA, Mebo (née Mukiza) m 1983; Maj, Ken W. b 25 Mar 60.

MBALA, Lubaki Sébastien (Kifuma, 1987); Maj, DR Con. b 23 Jun 58; and
MBALA, Godette Mboyo (née Moseka) (Kintambo, 1987) m 1988; Maj, DR Con. b 26 Sep 62.

MBANGWA, Sipho (Bulawayo Citadel, Zim 1995); Maj, Mal. b 5 Jun 67; (BScPsych); with
MBANGWA, Nyarai (née Matambanadzo) (Tsabalala, 1997) m 1997; Capt, Mal. b 1 Nov 74.

MBIZI, Gabin (Ouenze, 1988); Maj, Con (Braz). b 30 Jan 63; with
MBIZI, Philomene (née Nkounkou) m 1986; Maj, Con (Braz). b 22 Aug 67.

MBUNGU, Joyce (Kagumo,1978); Maj, Ken E. b 4 Feb 56.

MBUTHU, Simon (Kilembwa, 1984); Maj,
Ken E. b 14 Nov 60; and
MBUTHU, Zipporah (née Mwikali)
(Makadara, 1996) m 1996; Capt, Ken E.
b 26 Jul 73.

MEITEI, Shamu (Leizhangphai Manipur, 1988);
Lt-Col, Ind E. b 1 Jan 61. BCom; with
HOIHNIANG m 1983; Lt-Col, Ind E.
b 10 Jun 59.

MEKATHOTI PRASAD, P.C. (Annavaram,
1981); Maj, Ind C. b 9 Sep 58; with
PRASAD, Krupamma m 1979; Maj,
Ind C. b 4 Jun 59.

MENDES, Marcio (Belo Horizonte, 1980);
Maj, S Am E. b 24 Feb 57. BA (Theol); and
MENDES, Jurema (née Mazzini) (Quarai,
1979) m 1981; Maj, S Am E. b 4 Aug 57.
BA (Ed). Served In Brz.

MENIA, Virgilio (Asingan, 1990); Lt-Col,
Phil. b 2 Jun 61. BSCE (Civil Engr); and
MENIA, Ma Luisa (née Araneta)
(Negros Oct, 1984) m 1990; Lt-Col, Phil.
b 7 Jan 62.

MERRETT, Kelvin (Renown Park, 1983);
Maj, Aus S. b 6 Sep 58. ADipTh; Grad Dip
Theology; and
MERRETT, Winsome (née Morris)
(Kempsey, 1987) m 1987; Maj, Aus S. b 21
Sep 58. MA, BSpTher, DipTh, AMusA.

MEYNER, Marianne (née Stettler) (Basel 2,
1983) m 1978; Maj, Switz. b 14 Apr 57; with
MEYNER, Urs; Maj, Ger. b 30 Jan 51.
Served in Switz

MGBEBUIHE, Benson (Amauzari, 1990);
Maj, Nig. b 1 Aug 64; with
MGBEBUIHE, Celine m 1988; Maj, Nig.
b 1 Aug 66.

MGBEBUIHE, Obed (Amauzari, 1988); Maj,
Nig. b 20 Dec 58; with
MGBEBUIHE, Violet m 1986; Maj, Nig.
b 6 May 69.

MHASVI, Evan (Shirichena, 1977); Lt-Col,
Zimb. b 1 Feb 55. Served in Zam and Mal.
Ww Lt-Col Henry pG 2006.

MHEMBERE, Isaac (Mukwenya 1989); Maj,
Zimb. b 5 May 69; and
MHEMBERE, Charity (née Muchapondwa)
(Muchapondwa, 1990) m 1991; Maj, Zimb.
b 2 Jan 67.

MIRANDA, Rodrigo (Helsinki, 2006); Capt,
Fin. b 3 Nov 78.

MKAMI, Samuel Chacha (Kitagutiti, 1988);
Lt-Col, CS, Tanz. b 16 Apr 65; with
MKAMI, Mary (née Kibera) m 1985; Lt-Col,
TSWM, Tanz. b 20 Jul 66. Served in Mal
(CS/TSWM).

MNYAMPI, Benjamin (Mgulani, Tanz, 1985);
Col, TC, Uga. b 1 Mar 54; with
MNYAMPI, Grace (née Sage) m 1984;
Col, TPWM, Uga. b 3 Jun 63. Served in E Afr,
Rwa, Zimb, Tanz (CS/TSWM) and Ken W
(CS/TSWM).

MOCKABEE, William (Anniston, AL, 1975);
Lt-Col, USA S. b 1 Nov 54; and
MOCKABEE, Debra (née Salmon)
(Oklahoma City, OK, 1976) m 1976; Lt-Col,
USA S. b 9 Sep 54. Served in Sri Lan
(CS/TSWM).

MOON, Soon-kyung (Yea San, 1984);
Maj, Kor. b 2 Jun 54; with
KIM, Soon-deuk m 1978; Maj, Kor. b 9 Jan 59.

MORENO, Julio (Santiago de Cuba, Cuba,
2005); Capt, L Am N. b 7 Aug 52; and
MORENO, Leyanis (née González); m
1991; Capt, L Am N. b 23 Dec 67.

MORGAN, Andrew (North York Temple, Can,
1997); Maj, Hun. b 12 Apr 65; with
MORGAN, Darlene (née Boutcher) m 1988;
Maj, Hun. b 24 May 65; Served in Can.

MORGAN, Gregory (Darwin, 1990); Maj, Aus
S. b 16 Oct 68, B.Th, Grad Dip Theology,
Grad Dip Ministry, MA Ministry, Grad Cert
Higher Ed; and
MORGAN, Priya (née Greene) (Ballarat
Central, 1990) m 1991; Maj, Aus S. b 25 Nov
66, ADipTh, Grad Dip Theology.

MORRIS, STEPHEN P. (Tampa, FL, 1993);
Maj, USA S. b 15 Oct 65. BA (Psych); with
MORRIS, WENDY J. (née Laxton) m 1990;
Maj, USA S. b 28 Aug 65. BA (Bus Mngmt).

MOUKOKO, Daniel (Bacongo, Con (Braz),
1990); Col, TC, Moz. b 2 Dec 60; with
MOUKOKO, Arschette (née Nguitoukoulou)
m 1988; Col, TPWM, Moz. b 30 Oct 62.
Served in Rwa, S Afr and Con (Braz)
(CS/TSWM).

MOYA, Danton (Lo Valledor, 1989); Maj,
S Am E. b 17 Jun 58; with
MOYA, Juana (neé Balboa) m 1979; Maj,
S Am E. b 24 Jun 60. Served in S Am W.

MPAKULA, Dickson (Nansolola,1999);
Capt, Mal. b 13 Oct 72; with
MPAKULA, Chricy (neé Lankeni Phiri)
(Gooke, 2003) m 2003; Capt, Mal. b 26 Jan 80.

MPANZU, Manu Emmanuel (Kimbanseke 1,
1979); Maj, DR Con. b 20 Jul 54; with
MPANZU, Albertine (née Luzayadio Yema)
m 1977; Maj, DR Con. b 27 Dec 58.

M'REWA, Bilhah (Chuka, Meru, 1978); Maj,
Ken E. b 13 Aug 53.

MSIKITA, Luke (Chiringa, 2003);
Capt, Mal. b 8 Aug 79; and

302

MSIKITA, Stella (née Lilulezi) (Chiringa, 2005) m 2005; Capt, Mal. b 12 Sept 82.

MSONGWE, Yohana (Ilembo, 1985); Maj, Zimb. b 1 Jan 62; with
MSONGWE, Jesinala m 1985; Maj, Zimb. b 15 Jun 64. Served in Tanz.

M'TETU, Sarah (Gichiche, 1986); Maj, Ken E. b 27 Jan 61. Served in Ken W.

MTIZWA, Itai (Mutova, 1992); Maj, Zimb, b 15 Dec 69 with
MTIZWA, Celiwe (née Gama) (Magwegwe, 1994) m 1994; Maj, Zimb, b 1 Sept 1973.

MUBAIWA, Final (Nyarukunda, 1990); Maj, Zimb. b 29 June 60; with
MUBAIWA, Pfumisai (née Ngwenya) m 1988; Maj, Zimb. b 12 May 69.

MUIKKU, Aino (Turku II, Fin, 1985); Lt-Col, Fin. b 3 May 56. Served in Den (CS).

MUKONGA, Julius (Kwa Kyambu, 1978); Lt-Col, Ken E. b 10 Mar 53; with
MUKONGA, Phyllis (née Mumbua) m 1976; Lt-Col, Ken E. b 28 Mar 57.

MUNN, Richard (Lexington, KY, USA E, 1987); Col, CS, Aus E. b 16 Jan 56. BA (Ed), MDiv (Theol), DM (Chrstn Ldrshp); with
MUNN, Janet (née White) m 1980; Col, Aus E. b 22 Oct 60. BA (Psych/Spanish), MA (Ldrshp and Min), DMin (candidate). Served in USA E and at IHQ.

MURRAY, John (Woodroffe Temple, Can, 1996); Maj, IHQ. b 21 Sep 64. BA, Grad Cert PR Mgt, MA Ldrshp; with
MURRAY, Brenda (née Brown) m 1987; Maj, IHQ. b 15 May 63. BA. Served in Can.

MUSAMALI, George (Buwambingwa, Uga, 1990); Maj, Rwa. b 20 Aug 60; with
MUSAMALI, Annet (née Kituyi) m 1988; Maj, Rwa. b 28 Aug 62. Served in Uga.

MUSYOKI, David (Mweani, 1999); Capt, Mal. b 5 Jan, 68; with
MUSYOKI, Grace, m 1996; Capt, Mal.

MUTUNE John (Ithanga 1996); Maj, Ken E b 25 May 1968 with
MUTUNE Catherine (née Munee) m 1993 Major, Ken E. b 5 Dec 72. Served in and Ken W.

MUTUNGI, William (Kawethi, Kenya, 1990); Maj, Uga. b 3 Nov 62; with
MUTUNGI, Florence (née Mbithe) m 1988; Maj, Uga. b 12 Dec 66. Served in Ken E, Ken W and Lib..

MUZORORI, Trustmore (Alaska Mine, 1987); Maj, Zimb. b 4 Mar 66; and
MUZORORI, Wendy (Mutukwa, 1989); m 1989; Maj, Zimb. b 16 Feb 68. Served in Kenya and Uga.

MWALUKANI, Wilson (Maendeleo, 1984); Maj, Tanz. b 1 Aug 59; with
MWALUKANI, Tamali (née Sanya) m 1983; Maj, Tanz. b 1 Jan 63.

MWEEMBA, Richard (Choma, Zam, 1989); Maj, Ken E. b 24 Feb 54; with
MWEEMBA, Eunice (née Chiyalamanza) m 1975; Maj, Ken E. b 15 Apr 60. Served in Zam.

N

NABISWA, Eliud (Butemulani, 1986); Lt-Col, CS, Uga. b 8 June 58; with
NABISWA, Aidah m 1982; Lt-Col, TSWM, Uga. b 4 April 60. Served in Zimb.

NANGI, Masamba Henri (Kinzadi, 1979); Lt-Col, DR Con. b 21 May 53; with
NANGI, Josephine (née Nsimba Babinga); Lt-Col, DR Con. b 30 Dec 53.

NANLABI, Priscilla (San Jose, Phil, 1980); Lt-Col, GS, Ban. b 15 Nov 58. Served in HK (GS) and Phil (GS).

NATHANIEL, Alladi (Bhogapuram, 1980); Lt-Col, Ind C. b 9 Dec 52. BA; with
NATHANIEL, Rajeswari (née Yesu) m 1971; Lt-Col, Ind C. b 6 Jul 55.

NAUD, Daniel (Paris-Montparnasse, 1979); Col, TC, Frce. b 8 Mar 54; and
NAUD Eliane (née Volet) (Strasbourg, 1980) m 1980; Col, TPWM, Frce. b 3 Apr 60. Served in It and Gr (OC/CPWM).

NAUD, Patrick (Paris Villette, Fra, 1987); Col, TC, Ger. b 15 Mar 58; with
NAUD, Anne-Dore (née Kaiser) (Hamburg, 1987) m 1987; Col, TPWM, Ger. b 26 Nov 59. Served in Frce and Belg.

NAYAK, Philip (Angul, 1986); Maj, Ind N. b 1 Aug 68; and
NAYAK, Nayami (Penagoberi Phulbani Orissa, 1989) m 1989; Maj, Ind N. b 15 Jan 66.

NEEDHAM, John (Atlanta, GA, 1977); Maj, USA S. b 11 Aug 51. BS, MTS; with
NEEDHAM, Marthalynn (née Ling) m 1973; Maj, USA S. b 5 Jun 52. Served in UK.

NESTERENKO, Alex (Vitarte, Braz, 1986); Lt-Col, CS, S Am W. b 13 Dec 63; and
NESTERENKO, Luz (née Henríquez) (Santiago Central, 1990) m 1991; Lt-Col, TSWM, S Am W. b 10 May 67. Served in Rus and Braz (CS/TSWM).

NGCOBO, Herbert (Imbali, 1981); Maj, S Afr. b 28 Jun 57; with
NGCOBO, Elizabeth (née Magali) (Nkondweni, 1978) m 1982, Maj, S Afr. b 11 Jun 55.

NGOY, Wa Mande Hubert (Kamina, 1989); Lt-Col, DR Con. b 5 Jul 60; with
NGOY, Mbayo Célestine (née Mbayokidi) m 1983; Lt-Col, DR Con. b 21 Nov 62. Served in Tanz.

NGWANGA, Kakinanatadiko Madeleine (Matadi, 1979); Comr, TC and TPWM, DR Con. b 25 Nov 55. Served in DR Con (CS).

NHACUMBA Mario Arräo Joäo (Bagamoyo 1995); Maj, GS, Ang. b 29 Jul 72; with
NHACUMBA Celeste Fernanda m 1997; Maj, CSWM, Ang. b 20 Dec 75. Served in Moz.

NHADUATE, Félix (Ndavela, 2003); Capt, Moz. b Aug 71; with
NHADUATE, Amélia m 2000; Capt, Moz. b Sep 75.

NHARUGUE, José (Chipangara, 2000); Capt, Moz. b Oct 76; and
NHARUGUE, Adélia (née Muaga) (Nhampossa, Moz, 2003) m 2003; Capt, Moz. b Jan 78.

NHELENHELE, Manuel (Mavalane, 1995); Lt-Col, CS, Moz. b 8 Sep 55; with
NHELENHELE, Irene (née Sevene) m 1981; Lt-Col, TSWM, Moz. b 27 April 60. Served in S Afr and Zimb.

NIELSEN, Jostein (Stavanger 1976); Maj, Nor. b 2 Jul 56; and
NIELSEN, Magna Våje (née Våje) m 1978; Maj, Nor. b 23 Sep 57. Served in E Eur.

NIEMAND, Garth (Kensington, Port Elizabeth, 1999); Maj, S Afr. b 22 Dec 1969. BTh; with
NIEMAND, Patricia (née Nel) m 1990; Maj, S Afr. b 8 Mar 1972. BTh.

NIETES, Allain (Murcia, 1987); Maj, Phil. b 20 Nov 65. BS (Accountancy); and
NIETES, Marialyn (née Casidsid) (Bacolod, 1990) m 1990; Maj, Phil. b 16 Feb 65.

NILES, Allie Laura (Pasadena Tabernacle, CA, 1985); Maj, USA W. b 24 Oct 56. BA (Psych), BA (Soc Wk).

NISHIMURA, Tamotsu (Azabu, 1995); Maj, Jpn. b 2 Aug 65. BA (Soc); and
NISHIMURA, Kazue (née Uchinaka) (Kyobashi, 2005) m 2006; Capt, Jpn. b 17 Apr 78.

NJIRU, Nahashon (Mombasa, 1984); Lt-Col, Ken E. b 30 Apr 53; with
NJIRU, Zippora (née Ndeleve) m 1976; Lt-Col, Ken E. b 22 Feb 56.

NKANU, Bintoma Norbert (Kavwaya, 1981); Maj, DR Con. b 29 Jun 54; with

NKANU, Hèléne (née Makuiza Lutonadio) m 1978; Maj, DR Con. b 18 Nov 61.

NKHOMA, Sammy (Zhombe, 1990); Maj, Zimb. b 7 Jul 61; with
NKHOMA, Ellen (née Mandizvidza) m 1987; Maj, Zimb. b 27 Sep 66.

NKOMO, Bigboy (Vumangwe, 1993); Maj, Zimb. b 6 Aug 70; and
NKOMO,Winnet (Mt Hampden, 1990) m 1995; Maj, Zimb. b 22 May 69.

NOAKES, David (Edendale, 1980); Maj, NZ. b 21 Sep 53. BA, DipTchg, Dip-Grad, PG DipTh; with
NOAKES, Vyvyenne (née Melhuish) m 1974; Maj, NZ. b 16 Mar 53. DipTchg (ECE).

NORDENBERG, Mattias (Vårby Gård 1998); Capt, Swdn. b 11 Dec 73.

NSUMBU, Sérgio (Luanda Central ,2002); Capt. Angola, b 11 Sept 1972; and
NSUMBU, Ana (née Kiawatuayaku)(Kimbanseke 1); Capt. Ang, b 14 Sept.1975; m 2003.

NTEMBI, Lukombo Esaïe (Mvuila, 1987); Maj, DR Con. b 15 Sep 57; and
NTEMBI, Marie-José (née Yoka Nzakimuena) m 1983; Maj, DR Con. b 6 Oct 62.

NTOYA, Kapela (Kinshasa IV, DR Con, 1985); Maj, RC, Ml. b 2 Apr 55. BA, ThA; and
NTOYA, Rose-Nicole (née Makuena) (Kinshasha IV, DR Con, 1985) m 1983; Maj, RPWM, Ml. b 21 Nov 60. Served in DR Con (Kin) and at IHQ.

NTSHANGASE, Shadrack (Peart Memorial, 1992); Maj, S Afr. b 27 Feb 61; and
NTSHANGASE, Rosannah (née Shabangu) (Emangweni, Komatipoort, 1994) m 2003; Maj, S Afr. b 16 Sept 1970.

NYAGAH, Henry Njagi (Kagaari, Ken E, 1986); Comr, TC, Zimb. b 21 Feb 54; with
NYAGAH, Catherine (née Njoki) m 1984; Comr, TPWM, Zimb. b 3 Sep 59. Served in E Afr, Ken W (CS/TSWM) and Mal (TC/TPWM).

NYAKUSAMWA, Francis (Karoi, 1986); Lt-Col, Zimb, b 31 May 59; with
NYAKUSAMWA, Juliet m 1978; Lt-Col, Zimb. b 19 March 58. BA Hons (Past Counsl and Psych). Served at IHQ.

NYARUBERU, Tomson (Murereka, 1987); Major, Zimb. b 15 Aug 67; and
NYARUBERU, Crisia (née Dube) (Rutendo, 1987) m 1990; Maj, Zimb. b 17 Feb 68.

NYBO, Thorgeir (Sandefjord, 1981); Lt-Col, Nor. b 4 Sep 59; and

NYBO, Marianne (née Østensen)
(Sandefjord, 1981) m 1981; Lt-Col, Nor.
b 19 Jul 59.
NYERERE, Josephat (Izumbwe, 1999); Capt,
Tanz. b 1 Jan 70; with
NYERERE Sisita m 1993; Capt, Tanz.
b 1 Dec 73.
NYONGESA, Leonard (Kisumu, Ken W,
2001); Capt, Rwa. b 18 June 73; with
NYONGESA Violet, (née Lukhaji)
m.1995; Capt, Rwa. b 31 Dec 1972.
Served in Ken E and Ken W.
NZILA, Luyeye Barthélemy (Lemba-Ngaba,
1987); Capt, DR Con. b 16 Mar 61; and
NZILA, Bibisky (née Ntombo Nsosa) m 1985;
Capt, DR Con. b 6 Oct 66.
NZINGOULA, Victor (Loussala, 1988); Maj,
Con (Braz). b 27 Mar 63; with
NZINGOULA, Emma (née Malonga)
m 1986; Maj, Con (Braz). b 27 Apr 68.

O

OBANDO, Javier (Sagrada Familia, Costa
Rica, 1991); Maj, L Am N. b 2 Mar 66; with
OBANDO, Maria Eugenia (née Vanegas)
m 1988; Maj, L Am N. b 21 Mar 65.
ÖBERG, Leif (Centrumkåren, 1986); Maj,
Swdn. b 17 Dec 60; and
ÖBERG, Helena (née Gezelius); Maj, Swdn.
b 25 May 61.
O'BRIEN, Douglas G. (San Francisco
Citadel, 1976); Lt-Col, USA W. b 1 Aug 49.
BA (Speech), M Div (Relig); and
O'BRIEN, Diane (née Lillicrap) (Staines, UK,
1975) m 1988; Lt-Col, USA W. b 8 Nov 50.
FTCL. Served in UK.
ODURO, Godfried (Kyekyewere, 1981); Maj,
Gha. b 17 Jul 54; with
ODURO, Felicia (née Obeng) m 1978; Maj,
Gha. b 25 Jun 60.
ODURO, James (Achiase, 1983); Lt-Col,
Gha, b 21 Jun 59; with
ODURO, Elizabeth (née Nimfah) m 1980;
Lt-Col, Gha. b 13 Jul 61. Served in Lib.
ODURO, Rockson (Kwao Nartey, 1993);
Maj, Gha. b 29 Jan 63; with
ODURO, Emelia (née Lamtei) m 1991;
Maj, Gha. b 12 Mar 64.
ODURO-AMOAH, Peter (Achiase, 1989);
Maj, Gha. b 26 Aug 58; with
ODURO-AMOAH, Grace (née Fosua)
m 1984; Maj, Gha. b 11 Feb 64.
OGUNDAHUNSI, Raphael (Ogbagi, 1986);
Maj, Nig. b 10 Jul 59; with
OGUNDAHUNSI, Esther m 1984; Maj,
Nig. b 13 Apr 64.

OHAERI, Emmanuel (Kano, 1996); Maj, Nig.
b 26 Jul 66. BA; with
OHAERI, Gloria m 1990; Maj, Nig.
b 10 Oct 62.
OKLAH, Samuel Kwao (Accra Newtown,
1983); Lt-Col, CS, Gha. b 5 Mar 58; and
OKLAH, Philomina (née Addo)
(Tema, 1985) m 1985; Lt-Col, TSWM, Gha.
b 21 Dec 62. Served in Mal and Ken.
OLEBUNNE, Silas (Umudike, 1988); Maj,
Nig. b 3 Mar 1961; and
OLEBUNNE, Ifeyinwa (Igboukwu, 2004);
Capt, Nig, b 12 Oct 1976.
OLEWA, John (Mukhombe, 1986); Maj,
Ken W. b 12 Nov 54; with
OLEWA, Mary (née Kadzo) m 1982; Maj,
Ken W. b 19 Sep 1960. Served in Ken E
OLORUNTOBA, Festus (Supare, Nig, 1976);
Lt-Col. b 7 Jul 55. Ww Lt-Col Gloria, pG
2009. Served in Nig (CS) and Lib (OC).
OLUBWAYO, Jacob (Bukura, Shigomere,
1988); Maj, Ken W. b 16 May 62; with
OLUBWAYO, Mary (née Okwambitsa)
m 1988; Maj, Ken W. b 17 Jan 66.
ON, Dieu-Quang (Altona, Aus S, 1983);
Maj, GS, HK. b 9 Apr 55. Served in Aus S.
ONYEKWERE, Paul (Umuogo, 1984);
Lt-Col, Nig. b 27 Jul 58; with
ONYEKWERE, Edinah; Lt-Col, Nig.
b 29 Oct 61.
ORASIBE, Patrick (Akokwa, 1988);
Maj, Nig. b 9 Oct 58; with
ORASIBE, Blessing (née Chituru);
Maj, Nig. b 5 Dec 58.
ORD, Norman (Peterborough Citadel, 1992);
Maj, UK. b 28 Sep 55. MA (Hons)
(French and Music), PGCE, CDRS.
Ww Capt Christine, pG 2009 and
ORD, Margaret (née Read) (Nunhead,
1975); Maj, UK. b 4 Aug 55. Ww Maj
Graham Grayston, pG 2008; m 2012.
ØRSNES, Bernt Olaf (Bergen 1, Nor, 1983);
Lt-Col, Nor. b 22 Apr 59; and
ØRSNES, Hildegard (née Anthun)
(Bergen 1, Nor, 1984) m 1986; Lt-Col,
Nor. b 29 Sep 61. Served in Carib.
OTA, Haruhisa (Hamamatsu, 1973); Maj,
Jpn. b 30 Jan 50; and
OTA, Hiromi (née Nakatsugawa)
(Hamamatsu, 1973) m 1976; Maj, Jpn.
b 21 Jun 48.
OWEN, Graham (Nuneaton, 1977); Lt-Col,
UK. b 8 Jul 53; and
OWEN, Kirsten (née Jacobsen) (Copen-
hagen Temple, Den, 1977) m 1978; Lt-Col,
UK. b 2 May 56. Served in Den (CS/THQ).

P

PALACIO, Faber (San Cristóbal, Colombia 1996); Maj, b 7 Feb 67; and
PALACIO, Taura (née Cuyan) (Limón, Guatemala,1997) m 1998; Maj, L Am N. b 24 Feb 77.

PALLANT, Dean (Bromley, UK, 1993); Lt-Col, IHQ. b 23 Nov 64. BSoc Sc, Dip LR, PG Dip (Theol), DTh; and
PALLANT, Eirwen (née Lowther) (Leeds Central, UK, 1992) m 1993; Lt-Col, IHQ. b 9 May 62. BSc (Hons), MB ChB, DTM and H, MRCGP. Served in UK and Zam.

PANDORANTE, Marthen (Surabaya 4, 1989); Maj, Indon. b 6 Oct 64; and
PANDORANTE, Yulien (née Ganna) (Bandung 2, 1984) m 1981; Maj, Indon. b 22 Jun 61.

PAONE, Massimo (Naples, It, 1977); Comr, TC, Switz. b 8 Jun 52; and
PAONE, Elizabeth Jane (née Moir) (Nunhead, UK, 1982) m 1982; Comr, TPWM, Switz. b 17 Dec 58. BA (Hons). Served in UK, It (OC/CPWM) and Frce (CS/TLWM, TC/TPWM).

PARAMADHAS, Arulappan (Elanthiady, 1972); Lt-Col, Ind SE. b 11 May 54; and
RETNAM, Paramadhas (Changaneri, 1974) m 1976; Lt-Col, Ind SE. b 30 May 51.

PARDO, Zoilo B. (Santa Ana, CA, 1989); Lt-Col, USA W. b 9 Dec 53. BA (Acct); with
PARDO, Magali (née Pacheco) m 1980; Lt-Col, USA W. b 20 Apr 53. BA (Acct) (Gen Ed). Served in Mex and L Am N (CS/ TSWM).

PAREDES, Tito E. (La Paz, S Am W, 1976); Col, TC, L Am N. b 14 Aug 54; and
PAREDES, Martha (née Nery) (Cochabamba, S Am W, 1976) m 1977; Col, TPWM, L Am N. b 3 Jun 54.
Served in S Am W, USA E and L Am N (CS/TSWM).

PARK, Chong-duk (Pupyung, 1977); Col, CS, Kor. b 22 May 50. ThM, DipMin; with
YOON, Eun-sook m 1975; Col, TSWM, Kor. b 23 Oct 50. Served in Aus S.

PARKER, Michael (Hucknall, 1977); Comr, TC, Indon. b 28 Jul 50; with
PARKER, Joan (née Brailsford) m 1971; Comr, TPWM, Indon. b 16 Jan 52. Served at ITC, in UK and Indon (CS/TSWM).

PARKINSON, Warren (Albion, 1989); Maj, Aus E. b 11 Apr 56. BA, BTh, Dip Min, BA; with
PARKINSON, Denise (née Young) m 1978; Maj, Aus E. b 25 Jun 55. Dip Min, BTh. Served in UKI.

PARMAR, Kantilal K. (Ode, 1983); Maj, Ind W. b 1 Jun 53. BA, BEd; and
PARMAR, Eunice K. (née Gaikwad) (Mohmedwadi, 1977) m 1983; Maj, Ind W. b 30 Oct 52.

PASWERA, Effort, (Gororo, Zim, 1993); Maj, Mal. b 26 Apr 70; with
PASWERA, Annet m 1998; Maj, Mal. b 17 Nov 70.

PATHARE, Gulab Yohan (Shevgaon 1982); Maj, Ind W. b 1 June 58; with
PATHARE, Meena (Kherdi 1982); m 1980; Maj, Ind W. b June 62.

PAWAR, Suresh S. (Ahmednagar Evangeline Booth Hall, Ind W, 1981); Maj, IHQ. b 10 Feb 60; and
PAWAR, Martha (née Shirsath) (Ahmednagar Central, Ind W, 1981) m 1981; Maj, IHQ. b 10 Feb 60. Served in Ind W.

PAYNE, Godfrey (Goff) (Tunbridge Wells, UK, 1980); Lt-Col. UK, b 15 Oct 51; with
PAYNE, Diane (née Harris) m 1975; Lt-Col. UK, b 28 Dec 52. Served in UK, E Afr, Zam and Mal, Uga (OC/CPWM), Mal (OC/CPWM) and Nig (CS/TSWM).

PEDDLE, Brian (Dildo/New Harbour, NL, Can, 1977); Comr, IHQ (IS Am and Carib). b 8 Aug 57; and
PEDDLE, Rosalie (née Rowe) (Carbonear, NL, Can, 1976) m 1978; Comr, IHQ, (ZSWM Am and Carib). b 17 Jan 56. Served in NZ, UK (CS/TSWM) and Can (TC/TPWM).

PEREIRA, Alberto (Cuba 2002); Capt. L Am N. b 22 April 66; with
PEREIRA, Carmen ((née Capote) (Cuba 2002) m 1994; Capt, L Am N. b 14 Jun 73.

PETHYBRIDGE, Kelvin (Campsie, 1981); Maj, Aus E. b 1 Nov 58; Th A, B Pro Std, MAL; with
PETHYBRIDGE, Cheralynne (née Pack) m 1979; Maj, Aus E. b 18 Apr 60. B Pro Std.

PETRUS, I. Made (Den Pasar, Bali, 1983); Lt-Col, Indon. b 12 Jul 60; and
PETRUS, Margaretha (née Pinontoan) (Ambon/Bandung 2, 1975) m 1984; Lt-Col, Indon. b 15 Mar 53.

PHILIP, Alister (Colombo, 1988); Lt-Col, Sri Lan. b 11 Oct 61; and
PHILIP, Nilanthi (née Fernando) (Colombo, 1987) m 1989; Lt-Col, Sri Lan. b 24 May 67.

PHILIP, P.K. (Thottamon, 1975); Maj, Ind SW. b 12 Dec 48; and
PHILIP, Rachel (Kottarakara Central, 1980) m 1979; Maj, Ind SW. b 10 Nov 54.

PHO, Samuel (Altona, Aus S, 1983); Lt-Col, Aus S. b 17 Jun 57. BTh. Served in HK (OC); Lt-Col Donni, ret 2014.

PILKINGTON, George A. (Lamberhead Green, 1972); Lt-Col, UK. b 11 Apr 50. SRN. Served at ITC. m 1974; Maj Vera, ret 2007.

PIÑA, Marcos (Dominican Republic, 2000); Capt, L Am N. b 12 May 65; with **PIÑA, Kenia** (née Ledesma) (Dominican Republic, 2000) m 1991; Capt, L Am N. b 7 Oct 72.

PITTAWAY, Wayne (Northam, 1985); Maj, Aus S. b 30 Sep 51. DipBus.

PITTMAN, Frank (Pilleys Island, NL, 1984); Maj, Can. b 4 Apr 1963; with **PITTMAN, Rita** (née Randell) (Englee NL, 1984) m 1984; Maj Can. b 13 Sep 1957.

PIZZIRUSSO, Hugo (Arroyito, 1989); Maj, S Am E. b 7 Nov 66; and **PIZZIRUSSO, Elsa** (née Coppeto) (Nueva Chicago, 1989) m 1991; Maj, S Am E. b 3 Feb 67.

POA, Selly Barak (Jakarta, 1979); Lt-Col, Indon. b 25 Sep 55; and **POA, Anastasia** (née Djoko Slamet) (Surakarta 2, 1984) m 1985; Lt-Col, Indon. b 29 Jun 62.

POLSLEY, Randall (Omaha, NE, 1993); Maj, USA C. b 22 Sep 61. BA; with **POLSLEY, Charlene** (née Sniffen) m 1989; Maj, USA C. b 7 Dec 67.

PORTELA, Guillermo (Colombia 1996); Maj, L Am N. b 11 Nov 63; with **PORTELA, Martha** (née Martínez) (Colombia 1996) m 1986; Maj, L Am N. b 5 Dec 64.

POSADAS, Leopoldo (Dagupan City, Phil, 1981); Lt-Col, CS, Sing. b 18 Aug 58. BBA Mgmnt; and **POSADAS, Evelyn** (née Felix) (Hermoza, Phil, 1982) m 1982; Lt-Col, TSWM, Sing. b 2 Aug 57. Served in Phil and Ban (GS/CSWM).

POSILLICO, Joseph E. (Los Angeles Lincoln Heights, CA, 1972); Lt-Col, USA W. b 29 Dec 50; and **POSILLICO, Shawn L.** (née Patrick) (San Francisco, CA, 1984) m 1988; Lt-Col, USA W. b 3 Aug 57. BS (Bus Econ).

POWELL, Charles (New Bern, NC, 1984); Maj, USA S. b 26 Aug 58. BA; with **POWELL, Paula V.** (née Johnson) m 1985; Maj, USA S. b 12 Jul 51. Served in UK.

PREUSS, Annette (née Klein) (Siegen, 1979) m 1981; Maj, Ger. b 11 Sept 54; with **PREUSS, Alfred** (Göppingen 1980); Maj, Ger. b 16 Dec 54.

PRITCHETT, Wayne (Deer Lake, NL, 1970); Lt-Col, Can. b 13 Aug 46. BA, BEd, MTS; and **PRITCHETT, Myra** (née Rice) (Roberts Arm, NL, 1969) m 1972; Lt-Col, Can. b 19 Jun 50. BRE, MTS. Served at IHQ.

PULULU, Célestin Pepe (Makala, DR Con, 1985); Lt-Col, OC, Ang. b 15 Oct 52; with **PULULU, Véronique Lukombo** (née Nkenge) m 1978; Lt-Col, CPWM, Ang. b 4 Dec 57. Served in Con (Kin) and Moz (CS/TSWM).

PUOTINIEMI, Tella (née Juntunen) (Helsinki IV, 1983); Maj, Fin. b 17 Oct 52; m 1983; Maj Antero, ret 2012.

R

RAJU, K. Samuel (Kakulapadu, 1980); Maj, Ind C. b 5 May 58; and **RAJU, K. Raja** (née Kumari) (Pedaparapudi, 1980) m 1981; Maj, Ind C. b 3 May 64.

RAMDINTHARI VARTE (Chaltlang 2001); Capt, Ind E. b 1 May 77.

RAMOS, Hugo (Salto Central, 1991); Maj, S Am E. b 22 Mar 64; and **RAMOS, María del Luján** (née León Gularte) m 1984; Maj, S Am E. b 21 Aug 65.

RAMOS, João Paulo (Lisbon Central, Port, 1988); Lt-Col, CS, Swe. b 15 Sep 67; and **RAMOS EKLUND, Karin** (née Eklund) (Jönköping, 1990) m 1990; Lt-Col, TSWM, Swdn. b 29 Apr 66. Served in Port and at IHQ.

RANDIVE, Benjamin B. (Shevgaon 1981); Lt-Col, Ind W. b 11 Nov 60; and **RANDIVE, Ratnamala** (née Teldhune) (Shevgaon Central, 1981) m 1981; Lt-Col, Ind W. b 17 Aug 62.

RANGI, Gidion (Kulawi, 1990); Maj, Indon. b 7 Aug 60; with **RANGI, Lidia** (née Norlan) m 1985; Maj, Indon. b 25 Nov 65.

RAO, S. Jayananda (Madras Central, 1981); Maj, Ind C. b 29 Oct 52; with **RAO, S. Christiansen** m 1976; Maj, Ind C. b 22 Dec 60.

RASELALOME, Johannes (Seshego, 1982); Maj, S Afr. b 3 May 60; and **RASELALOME, Veliswa Atalanta** (née Mehu) (Tshoxa, 1982) m 1985; Maj, S Afr. b 16 Jul 62.

RATHAN, P. Samuel (Mandavalli, 1974); Maj, Ind C. b 3 May 51; with **KUMARI, P. Ananda** m 1976; Maj, Ind C. b 1 Oct 57.

RAWALI, Lapu (Koki, 1982); Maj, PNG. b 27 Jul 54, BA; with

RAWALI, Araga (née Heroha) m 1974; Maj,
PNG. b 19 Apr 55.

RAYMER, Ronnie L. (Tampa, FL, 1982); Maj,
USA S. b 2 Jun 58; with
RAYMER, Sharon L. (née Wright) m 1979;
Maj, USA S. b 19 Jun 60.

READ, Alan (Newcastle Byker, 1980);
Lt-Col, UK. b 10 Apr 58. MSc, FCIS; and
READ, Janet (née Rumble) (Redhill, UK,
1977) m 1982; Lt-Col, UK. b 22 Mar 55. BA
(Hons), MA (Rel Stds). Served at IHQ.

RICE, Sandra (Roberts Arm, NL, 1980); Lt-Col,
Can. b 16 Feb 58. BEd, BA, MTS.

RICHARDSON, Lonneal (Bloomington, IN,
1983); Maj, USA C. b 3 Mar 59. BA (Bus
Adm); and
RICHARDSON, Patty (née Barton) (Omaha
South, NE, 1979) m 1983; Maj, USA C.
b 30 Jan 57. BA (Bus Adm), MA (Org Ldrshp).

RIEDER, Beat (Basel, Swi, 1989); Maj, E Eur.
b 8 Oct 58; with
RIEDER-PELL, Annette (née Pell)
(Cologne, Ger); m1989; Maj, E Eur. b 9 May
64. Served in Swi, Ger, Can, UK.

RIGLEY, Graeme (Norwood, 1988); Lt-Col,
Aus S. b 10 Aug 54. BMd, BS, Dip Th; with
RIGLEY, Karyn (née Whitehead) m 1981;
Lt-Col, Aus S. b 8 Apr 59. DipEd.

RILEY, Douglas F. (Pasadena Tabernacle, CA,
1995); Lt-Col, USA W. b 6 Feb 59. BS (Fin),
MBA (Bus Adm), MA (Theol); with
RILEY, Colleen R. (née Hogan) m 1991;
Lt-Col, USA W. b 14 Aug 68.

RISAN, Jan (Stavanger 1990); Maj, Nor. b 28
Mar 63; with
RISAN, Kjersti Håland (née Håland)
m 1982; Maj, Nor. b 30 May 63.

ROBERTS, Jonathan (Leicester Central, 1986);
Lt-Col, UK. b 20 Feb 62. BA (Theol),
BA (Econ), MTh; and
ROBERTS, Jayne (née Melling) (Southend
Citadel, 1985) m 1986; Lt-Col, UK. b 23
Apr 58. BA (Eng Lit), PGCE, MA (Chrstn
Spirituality). Served at IHQ.

ROBERTS, William A. (Detroit Citadel, MI,
USA C, 1971); Comr, IHQ (CoS).
b 26 Feb 46; BS, MA; with
ROBERTS, Nancy Louise (née Overly)
m 1968; Comr, IHQ (WSWM). b 27 Oct 43.
BS, MA. Served in USA C, S Am E
(TC/TPWM), at IHQ (IS Bus Adm/Sec
for Staff Dev), in Ken W (TC/TPWM)
and at USA Nat (NC/NPWM).

ROBERTSON, Laurie (Broken Hill, 1980);
Lt-Col, Aus E. b 26 Sep 55; Dip Min; and

ROBERTSON, Simone (née Riley) (Manly,
1980) m 1980; Lt-Col, Aus E. b 16 Nov 59.
Served in Aus S and at IHQ.

ROBINSON, Darryl (Port Pirie, 1986); Maj,
Aus S. b 16 Sep 52; with
ROBINSON, Kaylene (née Mansell) m
1974; Maj, Aus S. b 22 Jun 56.

ROWE, Lindsay (Chance Cove, NL, 1972); Col,
Can. b 21 Sep 51. BA, MDiv; and
ROWE, Lynette (née Hutt) (Winterton, NL,
1971) m 1974; Col, Can. b 13 Feb 52. Served
in S Afr, Carib (CS/TSWM) and Tanz
(TC/TPWM).

S

SABIR, Imran (Jallo, 1996); Maj, Pak. b 16
May 66; and
IMRAN, Nighat (née Daniel) m 1994; Maj,
Pak. b 28 Aug 69.

SÁENZ, Jannette (Chihuahua, 1993); Maj,
Mex. b 27 Nov 70.

SAHARIDHAS James (Manavoorkonam
1985); Maj, Ind SE. b 12 May 60' and
DAIZY Saharidhas (Aganad 1991) m 86;
Maj, Ind SE, b 20 Dec 64.

SALCEDO, Rodolfo (San Jose, Mindoro,
1989); Maj, Phil. b 25 Nov 64. BA (Broadcasting Comm), BA (Bib Stds); and
SALCEDO, Mary Josalie (née Pagasian)
m 1990; Maj, Phil. b 21 March 69, BA
(Broadcasting Comm). Served in UK/IHQ.

SALVE, Chhabu (Nimbodi,1989); Maj, Ind W.
b 7 June 67; and
SALVE, Sunita m 1987; Maj, Ind W. b 1 Jun 68.

SAMBA, Aristide (Ngambio, 1994); Maj, Con
(Braz). b 25 June 68; with
SAMBA, Nadège Stella (née Ntsomi
Loukombo) m 1991; Maj, Con (Braz). b 6
Mar 73. Served in Rwa.

SAMHIKA, Bishow (Chigango, Zim, 1995);
Maj, Moz. b Nov 75; and
SAMHIKA, Pamela (née Ncube) (Nanga,
Zim, 1994) m 1997; Maj, Moz. b Oct 74.

SAMPSON, Godpower (Nkoro, 1990);
Maj, Nig. b 24 Jul 61; with
SAMPSON, Christiana m 1988; Maj, Nig.
b 7 Oct 62.

SAMRAJ, Babu (Ettamadai Corps, Ind SE,
1997); Maj, Ind Nat. b 11 May 66; MA (Eng),
MA (JMC), MBA; with
BABU, Santhi m 1995; Maj, Ind Nat. b 6
May 69. Served in Ind SE.

SAMRAJ, Jeyaraj (Booth Tucker Hall,
Nagercoil, 1982); Maj, Ind SE. b 14 Aug 58.
BSc, MA (Sociol), MA (JMC), PGDHM; and

JESSI, Thayammal Samraj (Gnaniahpuram, 1986) m 1986; Maj, Ind SE. b 21 Oct 63. MusB. Served at Ind Nat.

SAMUEL, John (Trivandrum Central, 1984); Maj, Ind SW. b 22 May 53. Ww Maj Annamma, pG 2007.

SAMUEL, Raj Devasundaram (Vadasery, 1974); Maj, Ind SE. b 21 Sep 54; and **KANAGAMONY, Samuel Raj** (Brahmmapuram, 1978) m 1978; Maj, Ind SE. b 5 Feb 52.

SAMUEL, V.D. (Mundappally, Adoor, 1979); Maj, Ind SW. b 13 Sep 54; and **SAMUEL, O.T. Rachel** (Ullayam, Kangazha, 1980) m 1981; Maj, Ind SW. b 4 May 51.

SAMUELKUTTY, S. (Kanacode, Kattakada, 1979); Maj, Ind SW. b 27 May 57; and **SAMUELKUTTY, Lillybai** (Kiliyoor, Kattakada, 1982) m 1982; Maj, Ind SW. b 10 Jul 55.

SANCHEZ, Oscar (Lima Central, S Am W, 1982); Comr, TC, Brz. b 21 Nov 56; and **SANCHEZ, Ana Rosa** (née Limache) (Huayra K'assa, S Am W, 1985) m 1987; Comr, TPWM, Brz. b 12 Jun 60. Served in Sp, S Am W, USA W and L Am N (TC/TPWM).

SANGCHHUNGA Hauhnar (Ratu 1974); Maj, Ind E. b 15 Mar 52; with **VANLALAUVI Fanai** (Ngopa 1975); Maj, Ind E. b 6 Oct 55.

SANTOS, Mylka (São Miguel Paulista, 1991); Maj, Brz, b 20 Oct 65. BA (Soc Wk).

SATTERLEE, Allen (Lakeland, FL, USA S, 1975); Lt-Col, USA Nat. b 21 Apr 53. BS (Psych) MTS; and **SATTERLEE, Esther** (née Sands) (Laurel, MS, USA S, 1979); m 1982; Lt-Col, USA Nat. b 9 Mar 55. BS (Admin). Served in USA S, Sing, PNG and Carib.

SAYUTI, Yohannes (Surabaya 2, 1975); Lt-Col, Indon. b 28 Jul 51; and **SAYUTI, Asya** (née Tonta) (Bandung 3, 1974) m 1979; Lt-Col, Indon. b 5 Jan 51.

SEDLAR, Deborah (Philadelphia [Roxborough], PA, USA E, 1987); Maj, IHQ. b 6 Mar 59. Served in USA E.

SEILER, Paul R. (Hollywood Tabernacle, CA, USA W, 1981); Comr, TC, USA C. b 23 May 51. MBA, BS (Bus Adm); with **SEILER, Carol** (née Sturgess) m 1978; Comr, TPWM, USA C. b 6 Apr 52. RN, BS (Nursing), MPH, MS (Nursing). Served in USA W and USA C (CS/TSWM).

SEMENO, Thataetsile Piet (Stilfontein, 1999); Maj, S Afr. b 11 Aug 75; with **SEMENO, Noluntu** (née Mampemvini) (Ethembeni Eastern Cape, 1999) m 2000; Maj, S Afr. b 14 April 76.

SEYMOUR, Geanette (Belmore, Aus E, 1973); Col, IHQ. b 20 Feb 50. BA (Soc Wk). Served in Aus E (CS).

SHAKESPEARE, Karen (née Grainger) (Catford, UK, 1980) m 1981; Lt-Col, UK. b 2 Aug 54. BEd (Hons), MA (Pastoral Theol), MA (Adult Ed with Theol Reflection), DProf; and **SHAKESPEARE, David** (Catford, UK, 1981); Lt-Col, UK. b 8 Oct 59. Served at IHQ and in Ken E.

.**SHAROV, Alexander** m 1986; Maj, E Eur. b 6 Jul 57; with **SHAROVA, Svetlana** (née Blagodirova) (Chisinau Botannica, 1999); Maj, E Eur. b 18 Jun 65.

SHAVANGA, Moses (Musudzuu, 1984); Maj, Ken W. b 10 Jun 57; with **SHAVANGA, Gladys** (née Sharia) m 1982; Maj, Ken W. b 18 Mar 61. Served in Tanz.

SHEKWA, Albert Zondiwe (Emangweni, 1974); Maj, S Afr. b 12 Mar 51; and **SHEKWA, Peggy** (née Maimela) (Louis Trichardt, 1974) m 1974; Maj, S Afr. b 3 Jun 54.

SHIN, Jae-kook (Un Po, 1983); Maj, Kor. b 27 Dec 57; with **CHO, Hwa-soon** m 1981; Maj, Kor. b 20 Jul 58.

SHIROMA, Lawrence (San Francisco Citadel, CA, 1979); Maj, USA W. b 10 Mar 49. MA (Chrstn Aplgtcs), MSSW, BA (Sociol); with **SHIROMA, Victoria** (née Sorrano) (Salinas, CA, 1975) m 1977; Maj, USA W. b 14 Sep 52. M Ed, BA (Org Mngmt).

SIAMOYA, Margaret (Loubomba, Zam, 1991); Col, TC/TPWM), Zam. b 15 Jul 65. Ww Maj Siamoya, pG 2010. Served in Zimb.

SICHILOMBA, Casson (Nakambala, Zam, 1993); Maj, Zam. b 1 Jan 59; and **SICHILOMBA, Mary** (née Kalikenka) m 1984; Maj, Zam. b 24 Mar 65.

SIJUADE, Michael A. (Ife Ife, 1992); Maj, Nig. b 13 Jun 64; with **SIJUADE, Comfort** m 1990; Maj, Nig. b 11 Nov 67.

SIMIYU, Bramwell (Bukhayagi, 1984); Maj, Uga. b 11 Mar 53; with **SIMIYU, Margaret** m 1982; Maj, Uga. b 10 Aug 58.

SIMON, S.P. (Trivandrum Central, 1990); Maj, Ind SW. b 31 May 61. BA, MSW, ADHA; with

SIMON, Annamma (Trivandrum Central) m 1988; Maj, Ind SW. b 21 May 67. Served in Ind C and Ind SE.

SIMON, T.J. (Perumpetty, 1977); Maj, Ind SW. b 15 Nov 52; and
SIMON, Ammini (Pulickal, 1980) m 1979; Maj, Ind SW. b 1 Feb 60.

SINGH, Dilip (Simultala, 1990); Maj, Ind N. b 4 Nov 68; and
SINGH, Nivedita (née Christian) (Fatapukur, 1992) m 1992; Maj, Ind N. b 14 Sep 71.

SIO, Anthony (Kakata, Lib, 1997); Maj, Lib. b 25 Aug 63; with
SIO, Munah (née Kolenky); Maj, Lib. b 5 Apr 63.

SJÖGREN, Daniel (St Paul [Temple], MN, 1972); Lt-Col, USA C. b 12 Nov 51; and
SJÖGREN, Rebecca (née Nefzger) (Hibbing, MN, 1973) m 1973; Lt-Col, USA C. b 11 Jun 53.

SLINN, Brian, (Sheffield Citadel, 1977); Maj, UK. b 9 Nov 55. BA, MA. Ww Maj Doris Slinn, pG 2006 and
RAEGEVIK-SLINN, Liv, (Mandal, Norway, 1980); Maj, UK. b 13 July 1957. Served in Norway, Denmark.

SLOMP, Harm (Zwolle, 2010); Lt. Neth. b 18 Aug 61; with
SLOMP, Ann-Christell (née Kvern) m 2006; Lt, Neth. b 8 June 72.

SMARTT, Howard (Petersham, 1984); Maj, Aus E. b 3 Jan 57. BA Ed, MA; and
SMARTT, Robyn (née MacKay) (Parramatta, 1982) m 1986; Maj, Aus E. b 31 Dec 57. BA Ed, MA (Counselling). Served in Can.

SMITH, Bruce (Raleigh, NC, 1978); Maj, USA S. b 7 Mar 51. BS (Soc Work); with
SMITH, Sandra (née Hathaway); Maj, USA S. b 27 May 51. Served in Mex and Cent Am.

SMITH, Charles (Kansas City (Blue Valley), MO, 1978); Maj, USA C. b 22 Aug 57; with
SMITH, Sharon (née Cockrill) m 1975; Maj, USA C. b 7 Mar 54.

SMITH, Jeffrey (Flint Citadel, MI, 1986); Col, CS, USA C. b 19 Jan 54. BA (Bible), MRE; with
SMITH, Dorothy R. (née Kumpula) m 1974; Col, TSWM, USA C. b 22 Oct 54. BA (Psychol/Sociol), MSW, MPC (Pastoral Counselling).

SMITH, Judith E. (Monterey Peninsula, CA, 1988); Lt-Col, USA W. b 4 Aug 49. BS (Ed). Served at IHQ.

SMITH, Paul (Lansing Citadel, WI, 1985); Maj, USA C. b 23 Jun 56. BA (Psychol), MA (Theatre), MA (Org Ldrship); and
SMITH, Renea (née Bonifield) (Grand Rapids Centennial Temple, MI, 1984) m 1985; Maj, USA C. b 16 Nov 57. BS (Ed).

SMITH, Stephen C. (Renton, WA, 1988); Lt-Col, USA W. b 23 Jan 58. MA (Music Comp), BA (Music Perf); with
SMITH, Marcia (née Harvey) m 1981; Lt-Col, USA W. b 12 Jan 59. BS (Chrstn Ldrshp).

SOETERS, Judith (née Maxwell) (Camberwell, Aus S, 1991); Maj, E Eur. b 26 Nov 59. BTh; and
SOETERS, Mark (Goldfields, Aus S, 1990) m 1992: Maj, E Eur. b 3 Feb 66. BSc, Grad Dip Theol. Served in Aus S.

SOITA, Peter (Buteteya, 1984); Maj, Uga. b 3 Aug 56; with
SOITA, Elizabeth m 1979; Maj, Uga. b 62.

SOLOMON, K.M. (Ooramana, Alwaye, 1978); Lt-Col, Ind SW. b 3 Jun 55; and
SOLOMON, Elizabeth (Brahmapuram, Alwaye, 1982) m 1982; Lt-Col, Ind SW. b 5 Nov 56.

SON, Suk-young (Mapo, 1981); Maj, Kor. b 9 May 53; and
PARK, Chung-hee (Wonju, 1982); m 1982; Maj, Kor. b 23 Mar 56.

SONDA, Jean-Pierre (Mahita, 1990); Lt-Col, Con (Braz). b 28 Nov 56; with
SONDA, Jeannette (née Ndoudi); m 1988; Lt-Col, Con (Braz). b 25 Jan 67.

SOTELDO, Juan (Cabudare, Venezuela, 2012); Lt. L Am N. b 11 Dec 62; with
SOTELDO, Ignabel (née González) (Cabudare, Venezuela 2012) m 2000; Lt. L Am N. b 29 Nov 76.

SOUZA, Maruilson (Petrolina, 1987); Maj, Brz. b 6 May 64. BA (Acct), BA (Admin), BA (Theol), MA (Theol), PhD (Theol); with
SOUZA, Francisca (née Rodrigues) m 1982; Maj, Brz. b 15 Oct 66.

STALIN, Masilamony (Nettancode, 1997); Maj, Ind SE. b 27 May 71. BSc, BEd, MTh; with
KEZIAL, Stalin m 1995; Maj, Ind SE. b 9 Apr 70. BSc, BEd, MTh.

STANNETT, Mike (Ilford, 1982); Maj, Fra. b 25 Aug 58; with
STANNETT, Ruth m 1981; Maj, Fra. b 23 Dec 58. Served in UK, EET and Cze.

STARRETT, Daniel L. (Roswell, NM, USA W, 1973); Lt-Col, USA W. b 1 Jun 52. BS (Appl Bus & Mgmt), MBA; and
STARRETT, Helen (née Laverty) (San José, CA, USA W, 1973) m 1974; Lt-Col, USA W. b 20 Jul 48. Served at IHQ and USA Nat.

STEELE, Hubert S. III (Middletown, OH, 1981); Maj, USA E. b 24 Mar 59; with
STEELE, Kathleen (née Fleming) (Ithaca, NY, 1980) m 1981; Maj, USA E. b 19 Dec 54. BS (Music Ed).

STEVENS, Bruce (Moreland, 1992); Lt-Col, Aus S. b 24 Oct 58. BBus (Acc), DipTh, DipMin; with
STEVENS, Debra (née Booth) m 1980; Lt-Col, Aus S. b 19 Aug 61.

STEVENSON, Garth (Christchurch City, 1991); Maj, NZ. b 5 Apr 62. BAg, DipTchg, LTh; with
STEVENSON, Suzanne (née Makinson) (Christchurch City, 1988) m 1991; Maj, NZ. b 5 Dec 62.

STRASSE, Wilson S. (Rio Grande, 1988); Maj, Brz. b 20 Jul 63; BA (Theol); with
STRASSE, Nara (née Charão) m 1985; Maj, Brz. b 12 Feb 68. BA (Theol), BA (HR).

STRINGER, Beverly (née Barker) (Yiewsley, 1991); Maj, UK. b 20 Apr 64; with
STRINGER, Adrian m 1983; Maj, UK. b 7 July 61. Served in Czechoslovakia.

STRISSEL, Dennis L. (St Louis Northside, MO, USA C, 1974); Col, USA C.
b 4 Mar 52. BA (Org Mgt); and
STRISSEL, Sharon (née Olson) (Sioux City, IA, USA C, 1974) m 1975; Col, USA C.
b 7 Oct 51. Served in USA C, S Afr and Gha (TC/TPWM).

SUAVE, Jackson (Lae, 2001); Capt, PNG. b 10 Oct 65; with
SUAVE, Lenny (née Malo) m 1988; Capt, PNG. b 23 Sep 70.

SUPRE, Emmanuel (Duverger, Haiti, 1998); Maj, Carib. b 8 Jan 1965. AS (Bus Stud); and
SUPRE, Edeline (née Debe) (Duverger, Haiti, 1998) m 1996: Maj, Carib.
b 18 Sep 1970. Diploma (Medical Technology).

SUSEELKUMAR, John (Pallickal, 1978); Lt-Col, Ind SW. b 11 Oct 51, Ww Maj Aleyamma, pG 2007; and
SUSEELKUMAR, V.K. Thankamma (Pookkottumannu, Malabar, 1987) m 2010; Lt-Col, Ind SW. b 6 Jan 60.

SUTHANANTHADHAS, Perinbanayagam (Booth Tucker Hall, Nagercoil, 1986); Lt-Col, Ind SE. b 14 Oct 56. MA, HACDP; and
ESTER, Evangelin Suthananthadhas (Attoor, 1986) m 1986; Lt-Col, Ind SE. b 18 Apr 63. BSc.

SWAMIDHAS, Chelliah (Kannankulam, 1977); Maj, Ind SE. b 21 Apr 55; and

JOICEBAI, Swamidhas (Kaliancaud, 1973) m 1977; Maj, Ind SE. b 16 Feb 53.

SWAN, Ian (Victoria Citadel, Can, 1987); Lt-Col, OC, HK. b 16 Feb 58. BA, BEd, MA (Curriculum Design); and
SWAN, Wendy (née Ward) (Victoria Citadel, Can, 1983) m 1987; Lt-Col, CPWM, HK. b 4 April 57. BBS, MDiv. (Comparative Theol), PhD cand. (Systematic Theol). Served in Can, Zam, Malawi and HK.

SWANSBURY, Charles (Croydon Citadel, UK, 1983); Comr, IHQ (IS for Prog Res). b 7 Dec 52. BA, MBA; with
SWANSBURY, Denise (née Everett) m 1974; Comr, IHQ (Mission Resources Secretary and ZSWM, SPEA). b 9 Nov 53. BA. Served in UK, Zim, Lib (GS/CSWM) and Gha (TC/TPWM).

SWANSON, Barry C. (Chicago Mt Greenwood, IL, USA C, 1978);   Comr, TC, USA E. b 22 Apr 50. BS (Marketing); with
SWANSON, E. Sue (née Miller) m 1975; Comr, TPWM, USA E. b 13 Aug 50. BA (Soc Work). Served in USA C (CS/TSWM, TC/TPWM), at USA Nat (Nat CS/NSWM) and at IHQ (IS/ZSWM Am and Carib, CoS/WSWM,WPWM).

T

TADI, Patrick (Bimbouloulou, 1984); Maj, Con (Braz). b 17 Apr 59; with
TADI, Clémentine (née Bassinguinina) m 1982; Maj, Con (Braz). b 4 Apr 58.

TANAKA, Chieko (née Hirose) (Nishinari, 1977); Maj, Jpn. b 22 Apr 48. BA; and
TANAKA, Teiichi (Omori, 1983) m 1984; Maj, Jpn. b 19 Feb 52. MA (Econ).

TANDAYAG, Susana (née Organo) (Santiago Isabela, 1989); Maj, Phil. b 26 Feb 60. BSc (Home Tech), BSSW; and
TANDAYAG, Miguel (Pasig, 1980) m 1982; Maj, Phil. b 30 Sep 58. BAMC.

TATY, Daniel (Pointe-Noire, 1982); Lt-Col, Con (Braz). b 14 Feb 54; with
TATY, Angèle (née Louya) m 1980; Lt-Col, Con (Braz). b 6 Dec 56.

TELFER, Ivor (Clydebank, UK, 1984); Col, TC, Pak. b 26 May 54. MSc, FCMI; with
TELFER, Carol (née Anderson) m 1980; Col, TPWM, Pak. b 26 Aug 59. RGN, SCM. Served in Can and UK.

TEMINE, David (Lembina, 1992); Maj, PNG. b 3 Sep 73; and
TEMINE, Doreen (née A'o) (Kamila, 1999) m 2002; Capt, PNG. b 24 Feb 73.

THAMALAPAKULA, Raj Paul
(Rajahmundary, Ind C, 1996); Capt, Ind Nat.
b 4 Aug 68. BA; with
JAYA, Santha Kumari m 1993; Capt, Ind
Nat. b 28 Jan 73. MA. Served in Ind C.

THANHRANGA, Chhakchhuak (Luangmual
1988); Maj, Ind E. b 1 Mar 53; with
LALRUATSANGI, Fanai (Luangmual
1988); Maj, Ind E. b 15 Sept 68.

THEU, Chatonda (Migowi, Mal, 1987);
Lt-Col, CS, Mal. b 3 Mar 59; with
THEU, Joyce (née Banda) m 1986;
Lt-Col, TSWM Mal. b 5 Mar 65.
Served in Zimb and Lib (GS/CSWM).

THOMAS, Darrell (Southend Citadel, 1975);
Maj, UK. b 28 Jun 53. Served in Sing.
m 1976; Maj Katrina, ret 2014.

THOMSON, Robert E. (Evansville Asplan
Citadel, IN, 1971); Lt-Col, USA C. b 20 Nov
50. BS (Soc Wk), MSW; with
THOMSON, Nancy (née Philpot) m 1972;
Lt-Col, USA C. b 4 May 50.

TIDD, Floyd (Sudbury, ON, 1986);
Comr, TC, Aus S. b 11 Mar 61. BSc, MTS;
with
TIDD, Tracey (née Blacklock) m 1982;
Comr, TPWM, Aus S. b 9 Jan 61.
Served in Can (CS/TSWM).

TILLSLEY, Mark W. (East Northport, NY,
USA E, 1987); Col, CS, Can. b 20 Nov 57.
BA (Psych/Socio), MSW PhD (Ed); with
TILLSLEY, Sharon (née Lowman) m 1979;
Col, TSWM, Can. b 21 Jun 57. BS (Nursing).
Served in USA E.

TOLLERUD, Douglas (Santa Ana, CA, 1983);
Maj, USA W. b 16 Mar 57; with
TOLLERUD, Sheryl (née Smith) m 1978;
Maj, USA W. b 12 Jan 59. BS (Org Mngmnt).

TONI, Belo Kiangangu Antoine (Kinsuka,
1973); Maj, DR Con. b 30 Oct 50; and
TONI, Bernadette (née Yuta Lusakweno)
m 1977; Maj, DR Con. b 15 Jul 52.

TRIBHUVAN, Jagannath (Khopadi 1978);
Maj, Ind W. b 12 Apr 56; and
TRIBHUVAN, Kusum (Samangaon, 1977);
m 1977; Maj, Ind W. b 8 Oct 53.

TURNER, John E. (St. Louis, Maplewood,
MO 1988); Maj, USA C. b 12 Aug 55. AA
(Pract Min); with
TURNER, Theresa (née Rutter) m 1976;
Maj, USA C. b 24 Nov 58. AA (Pract Min).

TURSI, Massimo (Naples, 1983); Lt-Col,
OC, It. b 14 Nov 57; and
TURSI, Anne-Florence (née Cachelin)
(Bern 1, Switz, 1983) m 1983; Lt-Col,

CPWM, It. b 25 Mar 59. Served in Ger,
It (GS/CSWM) and Switz (CS/TSWM).

TVEDT, Hannelise (Copenhagen Temple,
1976); Col, TC, TPWM, Den. b 13 Dec 55.
MSc (Psych), MA (Psych). Served in Nor,
UK and Neth (CS).

U

UNICOMB, Kevin (Liverpool, 1982);
Maj, PNG. b 25 Jun 55; with
UNICOMB, Heather (née Hopper)
m 1977; Maj, PNG. b 27 Mar 57.
Served in Aus E.

UWAK, Udoh (Ikot Obio Inyang, 1992);
Maj, Nig. b 2 Oct 66; with
UWAK, Esther m 1990; Maj, Nig.
b 12 Dec 73.

V

VALDÉS, Victor (Piedras Negras, 1973);
Maj, Mex. b 28 Oct 53; and
VALDÉS, Maria (née Clara) (Reynosa
Temple, 1976) m 1977; Maj, Mex.
b 14 Oct 56. Served in USA S.

VALLINSALO, Pirjo (née Kettula)
(Pori, 1978); Maj, Fin. b 10 Jan 54; and
VALLINSALO, Lasse (Pori, 1983)
m 1983; Maj, Fin. b 18 Jul 52.

VAN VLIET, Johan C.J. (Baarn, 1975);
Comr, TC, Neth. b 17 Jul 52. DSocS Admin;
with
VAN VLIET, Maria E. (néé de Ruiter)
m 1971; Comr, TPWM, Neth. b 9 May 51.
Served in PNG (CS/TSWM).

VARGHESE, Davidson (Trivandrum Central,
1986); Lt-Col, CS, Ind SW. b 13 Dec 58. BA,
MA; and
DAVIDSON, Mariamma (née Chacko)
(Adoor Central, 1988) m 1988; Lt-Col,
TSWM, Ind SW. b 1 May 65. Served in Zam
and at Ind Nat.

VARUGHESE, Wilfred (Trivandrum Central,
Ind SW, 1985); Col, TC, Ind N. b 25 Mar 58.
BSc, BTS; and
WILFRED, Prema (née Prema)
(Anayara, Ind SW, 1987) m 1987; Col,
TPWM, Ind N. b 25 May 60. BA, BD.
Served in Ind SW, at Ind Nat and in Zimb
(CS/TSWM).

VENABLES, Brian (Ottawa Citadel, 1991);
Maj, Can. b 10 Feb 56; with
VENABLES, Anne (née Kelly) m 1977;
Maj, Can. b 4 Oct 57.

VENABLES, Neil (Unley, 1987); Maj, Aus S.
b 5 Dec 62; and

VENABLES, Lisa (née Willey) (Bentley, 1987) m 1989; Maj, Aus S. b 8 Dec 63. AdvDip Past Couns, Dip Past Couns.

VENTER, Alistair (Cape Town Citadel, 1981); Lt-Col, OC, Ban. b 19 Aug 58. ThA, BTh; and
VENTER, Marieke (née van Leeuwen) (Benoni, 1988) m 1987; Lt-Col, CPWM, Ban. b 31 Dec 62, BCur, MTh. Served in S Afr.

VERU, Zarena (Bhogiwal, 1973); Lt-Col, Pak. b 1 Jan 52.

VINCENT, Morris (Mount Pearl, NL, 1994); Maj, Can. b 1 Feb 63. BA; with
VINCENT, Wanda (née Peddle) m 1983; Maj, Can. b 10 Jul 63. BA.

W

WAHL, John (Svendborg, 1984); Maj, Den. b 13 May 62.

WAINWRIGHT, John (Reading Central, UK, 1979); Comr, IHQ (IS Bus Adm). b 13 Mar 51; with
WAINWRIGHT, Dorita (née Willetts) m 1976; Comr, IHQ, (ZSWM, Eur). b 19 Oct 51. Served in UK, E Afr, Zimb, Zam (TC/TPWM) and Ken E (TC/TPWM).

WALKER, Gerald (Auckland Congress Hall, 2008); Capt, NZ. b 4 Dec 1960; PG p. Mgmt.; with
WALKER, Kristine (née Brock); m 1982; Capt. NZ. b 6 Aug 63.

WALKER, Peter (Morley, 1982); Col, CS, Aus S. b 2 Mar 54. BA (Soc); with
WALKER, Jennifer (née Freind) m 1975; Col, TSWM, Aus S. b 26 Feb 56. BEd, Dip Teach, Dip RE. Served in Mlys.

WALTERS, Rodney (Bundamba, Aus E, 1985); Col, TC, E Eur. b 9 Jan 59. BAL; and
WALTERS, Wendy (née Woodbury) (Wollongong, Aus E, 1985) m 1985; Col, TPWM, E Eur. b 15 May 61. Served in Rus, Aus E and E Eur (CS/TSWM).

WALZ, Reinhold (Reutlingen, 1975); Maj, Ger. b 10 Sep 52; and
WALZ, Ruth (née Beckschulte) (Nuremberg, 1987) m 1977; Maj, Ger. b 10 Jul 56.

WANDULU, Joseph (Namicha, 1990); Maj, Uga b 9 Jan 63; with
WANDULU, Alice m 1988; Maj, Uga. b 11 Feb 66. Served in Rwa.

WANDULU, Moses (Bumbo, Uga, 1986); Col, TC, Mal. b 5 Aug 60; with
WANDULU, Sarah (née Rwolekya) m 1986; Col, TPWM, Mal. b 30 Aug 1964. Served in E Afr and Uga (TC/TPWM).

WANJARE, Sanjay (Vithalwadi, 1994); Maj, Ind W. b 10 Oct 67. Ww Capt Sunita, pG 2010; with
WANJARE, Nirmala (Shevgaon Central 2011) m 2013; Lt, Ind W. b 17 Feb 80.

WANYAUMA, Sarah (Wabukhonyi, Ken E, 1978); Lt-Col, Ken W. b 3 Mar 56. Served in Ken E.

WASILWA, Jamin (Bukhayagi, 1988); Maj, Uga. b 29 Oct 60; with
WASILWA, Topister (née Muyama) m 1985; Maj, Uga. b 3 Nov 62.

WATSON, Ritchie (Darwin, 1988); Maj, Aus S. b 6 Apr 1951. Cert App Mgmt; with
WATSON, Gail (née Hogan) m 1972; Aus S. b 20 Feb 1952. Served in PNG.

WATTERS, Alan (Cape Town Citadel, S Afr Brighton East, 1987); Maj, UK. b 2 May 53. BD; with
WATTERS, Linda (née Farrier) m 1980; Maj, UK. b 13 Nov 56. Served in S Afr.

WATTS, Gavin (Carina, 1994); Maj, Aus E. b 30 Oct 69. Dip Min, Dip Bus; with
WATTS, Wendy (née Wallis) m 1990; Maj, Aus E. b 27 Apr 68. DipTeach, DipMin. Served in NZ.

WEBB, Geoff (Ulverstone, 1984); Maj, Aus S. b 18 Jan 59. BD, BEd; PhD (Theol); and
WEBB, Kalie (née Down) (Box Hill, 1997) m 1993; Maj, Aus S. b 8 Jul 69. BTh; GradDipSysTheol. Served in Pak.

WEBB, Neil (Nottingham New Basford, UK, 1983); Col, IHQ. b 6 Sep 58; and
WEBB, Christine (née Holdstock) (Bromley, UK, 1983) m 1983; Col, IHQ. b 1 Mar 55. BA, Dip RS. Served in UK and PNG (CS/TSWM, TC/TPWM).

WEKALAO, Esau (Bumbo, Uga, 1982); Maj, Uga. b 6 June 55; with
WEKALAO, Elizabeth m 1978; Maj, Uga. b 7 Sep 60.

WELANDER, Knud David (Templet/Oslo-Copenhagen, Nor, 1984); Col, IHQ. b 20 May 61. BSc (Bus Admin); and
WELANDER, Lisbeth (née Wederhus) (Florø, 1984) m 1984; Col, IHQ. b 29 Nov 63. Served in Nor, Phil and Den (TC/TPWM).

WESTRUPP, Andrew (Dunedin South, NZ, 1980); Col, TC, PNG. b 4 Oct 54; with
WESTRUPP, Yvonne (née Medland) m 1974; Col, TPWM, PNG. b 13 Jul 54. Served in NZ.

WHITE, Charles (Owensboro, KY, 1967); Lt-Col, USA S. b 7 May 46; with
WHITE, Shirley (née Sanders) m 1962; Lt-Col, USA S. b 24 Apr 43.

Biographical Information

WICKINGS, Margaret (Welling, UK, 1976); Lt-Col, IHQ. b 15 Apr 51. BEd, MTh. Served in UK, Zam, E Afr and Gha.

WIDYANOADI, Wayan (Semarang 2, 1990); Lt-Col, Indon. b 2 Jan 68; and
WIDYANOADI, Herlina (née Ayawaila) (Bandung, 1995) m 1995; Lt-Col, Indon. b 30 Jan 65.

WILKINSON, Darrell (Long Bay, Barbados, 1985); Maj, Carib. b 1 Apr 55; and
WILKINSON, Joan (née Marshall) (Carlton, Barbados, 1985) m 1986; Maj, Carib. b 18 Sep 58.

WILLERMARK, Marie (Göteborg 1, 1980); Comr, TC, TPWM, Swdn. b 18 Jun 54. Served in Den and E Eur.

WILLIAMS, John (Murukondapadu, 1991); Maj, Ind C. b 7 May 66. Ww Capt K. Mary Rani; and
WILLIAMS, Ratna Sundari (Murukonda-padu, 2000) m 1999; Capt, Ind C. b 22 Nov 67.

WIMMERS, Anne E. (Amsterdam Zuid, 1984); Maj, Neth. b 18 April 57.

WITTWER, Bernhard (Brienz, 1988); Maj, Switz. b 1 Feb 61; with
WITTWER, Regina (née Mäder) m 1983; Maj, Switz. b 22 May 63.

WOLAYO, Johnstone (Sikata, Ken 1991); Lt-Col, Mal. b 17 Jan 64; and
WOLAYO, Linnet (nee Nabila) m 1991; Lt-Col, Mal. b 25 May 69. Served in Ken W (CS/TSWM).

WOODLAND, Beverley Jean (Heritage Park, Can, 1982); Lt.-Col, Phil. b 8 Sept 58. MA (Leadership), BA. Served at IHQ and in Sri, S Am W and Can.

WYLES, Russell (Hillingdon, UK, 1986); Maj, UK. b 14 Mar 64. MA; and
WYLES, Catherine (née Dolling) m 1986; (Hillingdon, UK, 1986); Maj, UK. b 29 Dec 63.

Y

YANDERAVE, Iveme (née John) (Lembina, 1991) m 1985; Maj, PNG. b 25 Oct 66. Ww Maj Borley, pG 2013.

YESUDAS, Kancherla (Pedapalli, 1984); Maj, Ind C. b 13 Apr 54. BA (Econ); with
YESUDAS, Hemalatha (née Devi) m 1979; Maj, Ind C. b 16 Jul 58.

YOHANNAN, C.S. (Kaithaparambu, 1975); Maj, Ind SW. b 8 Jan 54; and
YOHANNAN, L. Rachel (Pathanapuram, 1979) m 1978; Maj, Ind SW. b 31 Jul 55.

YOSHIDA, Tsukasa (Shibuya, 1982); Maj, Jpn. b 26 Nov 54; BA (Econ) and
YOSHIDA, Kyoko (née Tsuchiya) (Kiyose, 1980) m 1982; Maj, Jpn. b 13 Oct 53.

YOUSAF, Javed (Shantinagar, 1990); Maj, Pak. b 2 Nov 66; and
JAVED, Surriya (née Zafar Masih) m 1987; Maj, Pak. b 18 May 69.

Z

ZIPINGANI, Langton (Pearson, 1987); Lt-Col, Gha. b 22 Nov 61. BBA, MBA, Dip RS PhD; and
ZIPINGANI, Beauty (née Chimunda) (Mutonda, 1987) m 1989; Lt-Col, Gha. b 2 Aug 66. BEd. Served in Zimb.

ZOTHANMAWIA, Khiangte (Lamka Churachandpur 1992); Maj, Ind E. b 29 Sept 63; with
VANLALNUNGI, Thiak; Maj, Ind E. b 3 Oct 64.

ZÜND, Markus (Bern 1, 1977); Maj, Switz. b 18 Apr 54; with
ZÜND, Renée (née Cachelin) (Bern 1, 1978); m 1978; Maj, Switz. b 1 Mar 54. Served in Switz and UK.

ZURBRÜGG, Daniela (née Jäggi) (Aarau, 1990); Maj, Switz. b 4 Apr 65; and
ZURBRÜGG, Peter (Bern 1, 1990) m 1990; Maj, Switz. b 3 Mar 63.

Retired Generals and Commissioners

A

ADIWINOTO, Lilian E. (Malang, Indon, 1954); Comr b 31 Jul 27. Served in UK, Indon (TC) and at IHQ.

AKPAN, Mfon Jaktor (Igbobi, 1969); Comr, TC, Nig. b 21 Jul 49; and
AKPAN, Ime Johnnie (née Udo) (Ikot Udobia, 1974) m 1974; Comr, TPWM, Nig. b 8 Nov 53. Served in Con (Braz) (CS/TSWM, TC/TPWM) and Nig (TC/TPWM).

ANZEZE, Hezekiel (Naliava, Kenya, 1980); Comr b 15 Mar 49. Ww Comr Clerah, pG 2005. Served in Ken E, TC; m Margaret 2011.

ASANO, Hiroshi (Shizuoka, Jpn, 1950); Comr b 5 May 27. Served in Jpn (TC). Ww Mrs Comr Tomoko, pG 2013.

B

BAILLIE, Kenneth (Warren, USA E, 1966); Comr b 3 Nov 42. BA (Soc); with Comr **Joy M.** (née Gabrielsen) m 1962; b 30 May 41. BA (Biochem). Served in Can, USA E, E Eur (OC/CPWO) and USA C (TC/TPWM).

BANKS, Keith (Wokingham, UK, 1963); Comr b 5 Nov 42. Served in UK, PNG (OC), Jpn (CS) and at IHQ (IS Int Per). Ww Comr Pauline, pG 2008.

BASSETT, W. Todd (Syracuse Citadel, NY, USA E, 1965); Comr b 25 Aug 39. BEd; with Comr **Carol A.** (née Easterday) m 1960; b 10 Dec 40. BEd. Served in USA E, at IHQ (IS to CoS/Mission Res Sec) and at USA Nat (NC/NPWM).

BAXENDALE, David A. (Pittsburgh, PA, USA E, 1954); Comr b 23 Apr 30. MA (Col), BSc (Sprd); with Mrs Comr **Alice** (née Chamberlain); BMus Ed (Syra). Served in USA E, USA W (CS/THLS), Carib (TC/TPWO), S Am W (TC/TPWO), at ICO (Principal) and IHQ (IS/SWO Am and Carib).

BIMWALA, Zunga Mbanza Etienne (Kinshasa 1, Zaï, 1959); Comr b 29 Sep 32. Served in Zaï (TC) and Switz. Ww Mrs Comr Alice, pG 2004.

BIRD, Patricia (Fulham, UK, 1958); Comr b 7 Aug 35. Served in Nig, UK, Zam (TC) and at IHQ (IS Fin, IS Afr).

BOND, Linda General (2011-2013) (see page 16).

BOSCHUNG, Franz (Basle 2, 1977); Comr b 21 Feb 49; with Comr **Hanny** (née Abderhalden) m 1971; b 7 Apr 50. Served in Con (Braz) and Switz (TC?TPWM).

BOSH, Larry (Mansfield, OH, USA E, 1966); Comr b 9 Jun 46. BS (Acct), MBA; and Comr **Gillian** (née Reid) (Akron Citadel, OH, USA E, 1960) m 1967; b 4 Dec 40. Served at USA Nat (Nat CS/NSWM, NRVAVS), in USA E (CS/TSWM) and at IHQ (IS/ZSWM Am and Carib).

BOVEN van, Johannes (The Hague, Neth, 1955); Comr b 9 Jan 35; and Comr **Klazina** (née Grauwmeijer) (Rotterdam, 1959) m 1960; b 22 Sep 35. Served in Neth (TC/TPWO).

BRAUN, Françoise (née Volet) (Vevey, Frce, 1968); Comr b 8 Dec 43. Served in Frce and Switz. Ww Comr Edouard, pG 2010.

BRINGANS, David (Albion, NZ, 1970); Comr b 25 May 47; with Comr **Grace** (née Palmer) m 1968; b 21 Sep 46. Served in NZ, HK, Vietnam, Tai (RC/RPWM), Sing (GS/CSWO, TC/TPWM) and Mex (TC/TPWM).

BUCKINGHAM, Lorraine (née Smith) (Waimate, NZ, 1960); Comr. Served in Aus S, NZ and Aus E. Ww Comr Hillmon, pG 2009.

BURGER, Kurt (Los Angeles Congress Hall, CA, USA W, 1972); Comr b 26 Aug 46. BS (Bus Adm), BA (Psych), MBA (Bus Adm), Cert CPA; and Comr **Alicia** (née Pedersen) (San Bernardino, CA, USA W, 1976) m 1988; b 6 Jul 46. Served in USA W and Switz (TC/TPWM).

BURROWS, Eva Evelyn General (1986-1993) (see page 15).

BUSBY, John A. (Atlanta Temple, GA, USA S, 1963); Comr b 14 Oct 37. BA (Asbury); with Comr **Elsie Louise** (née Henderson) m 1958; b 11 Jun 36. Served in Can (CS/TSWO), USA S (TC/TPWO) and USA Nat (NC/NPWM).

C

CAIRNS, Beulah (née Harris) (Parramatta, Aus E, 1959); Mrs Comr. Served in Aus E and at IHQ. Ww Comr William, pG 2008.

CALVERT, Ruth (Port Hope, ON, 1955); Mrs Comr b 8 Feb 35. Served in Aus E. Ww Comr Roy, pG 1994.

CAMPBELL, Donald (Highgate, Aus S, 1945); Comr b 31 Oct 23. Served in NZ (TC) and Aus S (TC). Ww Comr Crystal, pG 2008.

CHANG, Peter Hei-dong (Seoul Central, Kor, 1960); Comr b 12 May 32. BD, STm (Union, NY), BTh MEd (Columbia, NY); and

Comr **Grace Eun-Shik** (née Chung) (Seoul, Kor, 1963) m 1963. BA, BMus (Seoul Nat). Served in UK, Sing, HK, USA E, Kor (CS/THLS, TC/TPWO), USA W (TC/TPWO) and at IHQ.

CHARLET, Horst (Berlin-Neukölln, 1969); Comr b 1 May 46. Dip SW, Dip Soc Pedagogue; with Comr **Helga** (née Werner); b 18 Oct 48. Served in Ger (CS/TSWM, TC/TPWM).

CHEVALLY, Simone (née Gindraux) (Lausanne 1, Switz, 1947); Mrs Comr. Served in Switz and at IHQ. Ww Comr Robert, pG 1989.

CHIANGHNUNA (Ngupa, Ind W, 1951); Comr b 10 Jun 29; and Mrs Comr **Barbara** (née Powell) (Ware, UK, 1948) m 1968. Served in Ind N (CS/THLS, Ind E (CS/THLS) and Ind W (TC/TPWO).

CHUN, Kwang-pyo (Duk Am, Kor, 1971); Comr b 15 Sep 41; with Comr **Yoo, Sung-ja** m 1969; b 11 Jan 41. Served in Kor (CS/TSWM), (TC/TPWM).

CLAUSEN, Siegfried (Catford, UK, 1958); Comr b 4 Mar 38; and Comr **Inger-Lise** (née Lydholm) (Valby, 1958) m 1961; b 1 Oct 39. Served in UK, S Am W, Sp (OC/CPWO), L Am N (TC/TPWO), Ger (TC/TPWO) and at IHQ (IS/SWM Am and Carib).

CLIFTON, Shaw General (2006-2011) (see page 16).

CLINCH, John H. (Fairfield, Aus S, 1956); Comr b 30 Nov 30; with Comr **Beth** (née Barker). Served in Aus S, Aus E (CS/THLS), at IHQ (IS/SWO SPEA) and in Aus S (TC/TPWO).

COLES, Alan C. (Harrow, UK, 1953); Comr b 2 Feb 25. ACIB. Ww Heather, pG 1978; and Mrs Comr **Brenda** (née Deeming) (Tipton, UK, 1959) m 1980. Served in Zimb (TC) and at IHQ.

COLES, Dudley (North Toronto, ON, Can, 1954); Comr b 22 Mar 26; and Mrs Comr **Evangeline** (née Oxbury) (Powell River, BC, Can, 1954) m 1956. Served in Can, Ind Audit, Ind W, Sri Lan (TC/TPWO) and at IHQ (IS/SWO S Asia).

COOPER, Raymond A. (Washington Georgetown, DC, USA S, 1956); Comr b 24 May 37; and Comr **Merlyn S.** (née Wishon) (Winston Salem Southside, NC, USA S, 1957) m 1959; b 2 Sep 36. Served in USA C and USA S (TC/TPWO).

COX, Hilda (née Chevalley) (Geneva, 1949); Mrs Comr. Served in UK, Zam, Zimb, Frce,

Neth and at IHQ (WSHL). Ww Comr Ron, pG 1995.

CUTMORE, Ian (Tamworth, Aus E, 1954); Comr b 27 Sep 33; and Comr **Nancy** (née Richardson) (Atherton, Aus E, 1957). Served in Aus E, PNG, UK (CS/TSWO), ICO (Principal) and NZ (TC/TPWO).

D

DAVIS, Douglas E. (Moreland, Aus S, 1960); Comr b 12 Feb 37; with Comr **Beverley J.** (née Roberts) m 1958; b 23 Feb 38. Served in NZ, UK (CS/TSWO) and Aus S (TC/TPWO).

DEVAVARAM, Prathipati (New Colony, Ind C, 1964); Comr b 15 Nov 46. MBBS, BSc; and Comr **P. Victoria** (Bapatla Central, Ind C, 1970) m 1974; b 25 Nov 49. BSc, BEd, BLSc. Served in Ind C, Ind Nat, Ind E and Ind SE (TC/TPWM).

DIAKANWA, Mbakanu (Poste Francais, Kin, Zaï, 1949); Comr b 1923. Officier de l'Ordre du Leopard (1981). Served in Zaï (TC). Ww Comr Situwa, pG 1998.

DITMER, Anne (née Sharp) (Dayton Central, OH, USA E, 1957); Mrs Comr. Served in USA S, USA C and USA E. Ww Comr Stanley, pG 2003.

DUNSTER, Robin (Dulwich Hill Temple, Aus E, 1970); Comr b 12 Jan 44. SRN, SCM, RPN, RMN, IPPF (Ed). Served in Aus E, Zimb (CS), Con (Kin) (TC, TPWO), Phil (TC, TPWM) and at IHQ (CoS).

DU PLESSIS, Paul (Salt River, S Afr, 1968); Comr b 3 Jul 41. MB ChB, MRCP, DTM&H; with Comr **Margaret** (née Siebrits) m 1964; b 17 Jul 42. BSoc Sc. Served in Zam, Ind C (TC/TPWO), S Afr (TC/TPWO) and at IHQ.

DURMAN, Vera (née Livick) (South Croydon, UK, 1942) Mrs Comr. Served in UK, Ind W and at IHQ. Ww Comr David, pG 2010.

DWYER, June M. (Windsor, NS, Can, 1952); Comr b 28 Aug 32. Served at USA Nat, S Afr (CS) and at IHQ (IS Admin).

E

EDWARDS, David (New Market Street, Georgetown, Guyana, Carib, 1962); Comr b 15 May 41; and Comr **Doreen** (née Bartlett) (Wellington St, Barbados, Carib, 1957) m 1966; b 4 Mar 35. Served in USA E, Carib (TC/TPWO), at IHQ (IS/SWO Am and Carib) and in USA W (TC/TPWO).

ELIASEN, Carl S. (Gartnergade, Den, 1951); Comr b 28 Mar 32. Served in Port (OC), Brz (TC), S Am W (TC) and at IHQ (IS Americas). Ww Comr Maria, pG 2003.

EMMANUEL, Muthu Yesudhason (Neduvaazhy, Ind SE, 1974); Comr b 8 May 51; and **Regina, Chandra Bai** (Valliyoor, Ind SE, 1978) m 1978; Comr. Served in Ind SE, Ind N (CS/TSWM), Ind E (TC/TPWM) and Ind C (TC/TPWM).

EVANS, Willard S. (Greenville, SC, USA S, 1949), Comr b 2 Sep 24. BA (Bob Jones Univ); with Mrs Comr **Marie** (née Fitton). Served in USA S, USA E (CS/THLS) and USA W (TC/TPWO).

F

FEENER, Maxwell (Port Leamington, NL, Can, 1966); Comr b 5 Jul 45, with Comr **Lenora** (née Tippett) m 1967. b 26 Dec 45. Served in Can, S Afr (CS/TSWM) and USA S (CS/TSWM, TC/TPWM).

FINGER, Raymond (Hawthorn, 1974); Comr, b 11 Jul 51. Dip Bus. Served in Aus S (TC).

FORSYTH, Robin W. (Edinburgh Gorgie, UK, 1968); Comr b 30 Aug 46. Served in Aus S,Mex, UK, L Am N (TC), NZ (CS) and at IHQ (IS Prog Res). Ww Comr Shona pG 2013.

FRANCIS, William (Paterson, NJ, USA E, 1973); Comr b 5 Mar 44. BA (Mus/Hist), MDiv, Hon DD; with Comr **Marilyn** (née Burroughs) m 1965. b 3 Feb 43. BA (Mus), MA. Served in USA E (CS/TSWM), Can (TC/TPWM) and at IHQ (IS/ZSWM Am and Carib).

FRANS, Roy (Surabaya 4, Indon, 1977); Comr b 30 Oct 50; and Comr **Arda** (née Haurissa) (Jakarta 1, Indon, 1978) m 1978. b 10 May 44. Served in Indon, Aus E, Sing, Ban, Sri Lan (TC/TPWM), at IHQ (IS/ZSWM SPEA, Rep to UN, SPEA) and Neth (TC/TPWM).

FREI, Werner (Rorbas, Switz, 1965); Comr b 6 Mar 40; and Comr **Paula** (née Berweger) (Heiden, Switz, 1965) m 1967; b 19 Mar 36. Served in Switz (CS/TSWO) and Ger (TC/TPWM).

FULLARTON, Frank (Bromley, UK, 1955); Comr b 3 Mar 31. BSc, DipSoc; and Comr **Rosemarie** (née Steck) (Croydon Citadel, UK, 1958) m 1959. BEd (Hons), MITD. Served at IHQ (CS to CoS, IS/SWO Eur), Soc S (GBI) (Ldr) and in Switz (TC/TPWO).

G

GAITHER, Israel L. (New Castle, PA, USA E, 1964); Comr b 27 Oct 44. Hon LHD, Hon DD; and Comr **Eva D.** (née Shue) (Sidney, OH, USA E, 1964) m 1967; b 9 Sep 43. Served in USA E (CS/TSWO) (TC/TPWM), S Afr (TC/TPWO), at IHQ (CoS/WSWM) and USA Nat (NC/NPWM).

GOODIER, William Robert (Atlanta Temple, GA, USA S, 1941); Comr b 23 May 16. Served in USA S (CS), at USA Nat (CS), in Aus S (TC) and USA E (TC). Ww Mrs Comr Renee, pG 2012.

GOWANS, Comr Gisèle (née Bonhotal) (Paris Central, Frce, 1955) m 1957. Served in USA W, Frce (TPWO), Aus E (TPWO), UK (TPWO) and at IHQ (WPWM). Ww General John, pG 2012 (see page 16).

GRIFFIN, Joy (née Button) (Tottenham Citadel, UK, 1957); Mrs Lt-Comr. Served in BT. Ww Lt-Comr Frederick, pG 1990.

GRINSTED, Dora (née Bottle) (Sittingbourne, UK, 1950); Mrs Comr. Served in UK, Zam, Zimb, Jpn and at IHQ. Ww Comr David Ramsay, pG 1992.

GULLIKSEN, Thorleif R. (Haugesund, Nor, 1967); Comr b 26 Apr 40; with Comr **Olaug** (née Henriksen) m 1962; b 25 Jan 38. Served in Nor, Neth (TC/TPWO) and at IHQ (IS/SWM Eur).

H

HANNEVIK, Anna (Bergen 2, Nor, 1947); Comr b 9 Aug 25. Served in Nor, UK (Ldr SocS), Swdn (TC) and at IHQ (IS Eur). Paul Harris Medal (1987), Commander of the Royal Order of the Northern Star (Sweden).

HANNEVIK, Edward (Oslo 3, Nor, 1954); Comr b 6 Dec 32; and Comr **Margaret** (née Moody) (Newfield, UK, 1956) m 1958. Served in UK, Den (TC/TPWO), Nor (TC/TPWO) and at IHQ (IS/SWO Eur).

HARITA, Nozomi (Shibuya, Jap, 1966); Comr b 10 May 39. BA (Mus); and Comr **Kazuko** (née Hasegawa) (Shibuya, Jap, 1966) m 1969; b 19 Dec 37. BA (Ed). Served in Aus E and Jap (TC/TPWM).

HARRIS, Bramwell Wesley (Cardiff Stuart Hall, UK, 1948); Comr b 25 Nov 28; and Mrs Comr **Margaret** (née Sansom) (Barking, UK, 1949), m 1955. Served in UK, at IHQ, in Aus S (CS/THLS), Scot (TC/THLP), NZ (TC/TPWO) and Can (TC/TPWO).

HEDBERG, Lennart (Nykoping, Swdn, 1954);

Comr b 12 Oct 32; and Comr **Ingvor** (née Fagerstedt) (Nykoping, Swdn, 1955) m 1956. Served in Den, Swdn (TC/TPWO) and at IHQ (IS/SWO Eur).

HINSON, Harold D. (High Point, NC, USA S, 1955); Comr b 7 Sep 35; and Comr **Betty M.** (née Morris) (New Orleans, LA, USA S, 1955); b 1 Jun 35. Served in USA S (CS/THLS) and USA C (TC/TPWO).

HODDER, Kenneth L. (San Francisco Citadel, CA, USA W, 1958); Comr b 30 Oct 30. BA (Richmond), DSS (Hons) (Richmond), JD (California); and Comr **Marjorie J.** (née Fitton) (San Francisco Citadel, CA, USA W, 1958). Served in USA W, USA C, Aus S (CS), USA S (TC/TPWO) and at USA Nat (NC/NPWM).

HOLLAND, Louise (née Cruickshank) (Invercairn, UK, 1958); Mrs Comr. Served in UK, E Afr, Nig, Gha, Pak and at IHQ. Ww Comr Arthur, pG 1998.

HOOD, H. Kenneth (Denver Citadel, CO, USA W, 1954); Comr b 27 Jan 33; and Comr **Barbara** (née Johnson) (Pasadena, CA, USA W, 1952) m 1957. Served in USA W (CS/THLS), at USA Nat (CS/Asst NPWO) and in USA S (TC/TPWO).

HOUGHTON, Raymond (Woodhouse, UK, 1967); Comr b 12 Apr 44. MCMI; with Comr **Judith** (née Jones) m 1965; b 15 Nov 45. Served in UK (CS/TSWO), at IHQ (IS to CoS/Mission Resources Sec) and in Carib (TC/TPWM).

HOWE, Norman (Dartford, UK, 1957); Comr b 13 Aug 36; and Comr **Marian** (née Butler) (Boscombe, UK, 1953) m 1959; b 9 Feb 30. Cert Ed. Served in UK, at ITC (Principal), in Aus S (TC/TPWO), Can (TC/TPWO) and at IHQ (IS Prog Res/SWO Eur, General's Travelling Representative).

HUGHES, Alex (Paisley West, UK, 1960); Comr b 29 Jan 42; and Comr **Ingeborg** (née Clausen) (Catford, UK, 1964) m 1971; b 2 Jan 42. Served in L Am N, S Am E (CS/THLS, TC/TPWO), S Am W (TC/TPWO), at IHQ (IS/SWO Am and Carib) and in UK (TC/TPWM).

HUGUENIN, Willy (Le Locle, Switz, 1954); Comr b 22 Sep 31; and Mrs Comr **Miriam** (née Luthi) (La Chaux-de-Fonds, Switz, 1953) m 1955. Served in Zaï (GS), Con (TC/TPWO), Switz (TC/TPWO) and at IHQ (IS/SWO Afr).

I

IRWIN, Ronald G. (Philadelphia, PA, USA E, 1957); Comr b 4 Aug 33. BS (Rutgers), MA (Columbia); and Comr **Pauline** (née Laipply) (Cincinnati, OH, USA E, 1953) m 1967. Served in USA W (CS/THLS) and USA E (TC/TPWO).

ISRAEL, Jillapegu (Peralipadu, Ind N, 1957); Comr b 31 May 32. BA, BEd; with Comr **Rachel** (née Amarthaluri). Served in Ind M and A (CS/THLS), Ind N (TC/TPWO) and Ind SW (TC/TPWO).

J

JAMES, M. C. (Monkotta, Ind SW, 1979); Comr, TC, Ind W. b 20 Oct 54. and **SUSAMMA, James** (Pothencode, Ind SW, 1983) m 1983; Comr, Ind W. b 1 Mar 61. Served in Ind SW, Ind N, Ind C (CS/TSWM, TC/TPWM) and Ind SE (TC/TPWM).

K

KALAI, Andrew (Koki, 1981); Comr b 18 Jan 56. BA (Psych). Ww Capt Napa, pG 1994; Ww Col Julie, pG 2006. Served in UK and PNG (TC).

KANG, Sung-hwan (Noh Mai Sil, Kyung Buk, Kor, 1973); Comr b 15 Dec 39; with Comr **Lee, Jung-ok** m1970; b 10 Nov 49. Served in Aus S and Kor (TC/TPWM).

KARTODARSONO, Ribut (Surakarta, 1975); Comr b 13 Dec 49. BA (Relig Ed), MA (Relig Ed & Public Societies); and Comr **Marie** (née Ticoalu) (Bandung 3, 1975) m 1979; b 30 Nov 52. Served in UK and Indon (CS/TSWM, TC/TPWM).

KELLNER, Paul S. (Miami Citadel, FL, USA S, 1963); Comr b 1 Sep 35. BMus; with Comr **Jajuan** (née Pemberton); b 23 Feb 39. Served in USA S, Carib, Con (Braz) and Zimb (TC/TPWO).

KENDREW, K. Ross (Sydenham, NZ, 1962); Comr b 7 Dec 38; and Comr **M. June** (née Robb) (Wanganui, NZ, 1961) m 1964; b 8 Oct 39. Served in NZ (TC/TPWO) and Aus S (TC/TPWM).

KERR, Donald (Vancouver Temple, BC, Can, 1955); Comr b 25 Oct 33; and Comr **Joyce** (née Knaap) (Mt Dennis, ON, 1955) m 1957; b 12 Jan 35. Served in UK (CS) and Can (TC/TPWO).

KIM, Suk-tai (Choon Chun, Kor, 1957); Comr b 23 Jan 26. ThB, BA, MSoc; and **Lim,**

Jung-sun (Sudaemun, Kor, 1969) m 1975. BMus. Served in Kor (TC/TPWO).

KJELLGREN, Hasse (Östra Kåren, Swdn, 1971); Comr b 1 Nov 45. BSc; and Comr **Christina** (née Forssell) (Hisingskaren, Swdn, 1971) m 1971; b 21 May 47. Served in S Am E (TC/TPWO), Switz (TC/TPWM), Swdn (TC/TPWM) and at IHQ (IS/ZSWM Eur).

L

LAHASE, Kashinath V. (Chapadgaon, Ind W, 1972); Comr b 1 Nov 49; and Comr **Kusum K.** m 1970; b 7 Jun 49. Served in Ind W, Ind SW and Ind N (CS/TSWM, TC/TPWM).

LALKIAMLOVA (Kahrawt, 1971); Comr b 7 Mar 49. BA; and Comr **Lalhlimpuii** (Saitual, 1973) m 1973; b 25 Sep 53. Served in Ind E, Ind SW (CS/TSWO), Ind C (TC/TPWM) and at IHQ (IS/ZSWM, S Asia).

LALTHANNGURA (Ratu, Ind E, 1963); Comr b 15 Sep 38. BA; with Comr **Kaphliri**; b 9 Sep 43. Served in Ind C (CS/THLS) and Ind E (TC/TPWM).

LANG, Ivan B. (Auburn, Aus S, 1967); Comr b 18 Jul 40. AM, Order of Australia (2007); with Comr **Heather C.** (née Luhrs) m 1961; b 8 Dec 42. Served in Sing (OC/CPWO), Aus E (CS/TSWO), at IHQ (IS/SWM SPEA) and in Aus S (TC/TPWM).

LARSSON, John General (2002-2006) (see page 16); and Comr **Freda** (née Turner) (Kingston-upon-Thames, UK, 1964) m 1969. Served in S Am W (THLS), at ITC, in UK (TPWO), NZ (TPWO), Swdn (TPWO) and at IHQ (WSWM, WPWM).

LEE, Sung-duk (Cho Kang, Kor, 1963); Comr b 10 Jun 35. Served in Kor (TC). Ww Comr Cho, In-sun, pG 2011.

LIM, Ah Ang (Balestier Rd, Sing, 1954); Comr b 30 May 32; and Comr **Fong Pui Chan** (Singapore Central, 1954) m 1958. Served in Sing, HK (OC/CPWO), Phil (TC/TPWO) and at IHQ (IS/SWO SPEA).

LINDBERG, Ingrid E. (Norrköping, Swdn, 1951); Comr b 12 Dec 25. Served in Swdn, Zimb, Phil (OC), Den (TC) and Fin (TC).

LINNETT, Merle (née Clinch) (Hindmarsh, Aus S, 1947); Mrs Comr. Served in NZ, at IHQ, ITC, ICO and in Aus S. Ww Comr Arthur, pG 1993.

LOVATT, Olive (née Chapman) (Doncaster, UK, 1949); Mrs Comr. Served in UK, Aus S, Aus E and PNG and at IHQ. Ww Comr Roy, pG 2000.

LUDIAZO, Jean Bakidi (Salle Centrale,

Kinshasa, Con (Kin), 1971); Comr b 19 Nov 45; with Comr **Véronique** (née Lusieboko Lutatabio) m 1970; b 26 Sep 53. Served in Con, Can, Con (Kin) (TC/TPWM) and Nig (TC/TPWM).

LUTTRELL, Bill (Greeley, CO, USA W, 1958); Comr b 4 Jul 38. BA Soc; and Comr **Gwendolyn** (née Shinn) (Long Beach, CA, USA W, 1961) m 1962; b 3 Sep 38. BA Soc. Served at IHQ (IS/SWO Am and Carib) and in Can (TC/TPWM) and USA W (CS/TSWO, TC/TPWM).

LYDHOLM, Carl A.S. (Gartnergade, Den, 1966); Comr b 14 Nov 45; and Comr **Gudrun** (née Arskog) (Odense, Den, 1967) m 1967; b 5 Aug 47. MTh. Served in Den, UK, Rus/CIS (GS/CSWM), Fin (TC/TPWM) and Nor (TC/TPWM).

M

MABENA, William (Bloemfontein, S Afr, 1959); Comr b 23 May 40; and Comr **Lydia** (née Lebusho) (Bloemfontein, S Afr, 1959) m 1960; b 25 Jun 39. Served in UK, S Afr (CS/THLS, TC/TPWM), Gha (TC/TPWO) and at IHQ (IS/SWO Afr).

MacMILLAN, M. Christine (North York, Can, 1975); Comr b 9 Oct 47. Served in UK, Aus E, PNG (TC, TPWM), Can (TC, TPWM) and at IHQ.

MAILLER, Georges (Neuchatel, Switz, 1961); Comr b 9 Nov 36. BTh; with Comr **Muriel** (née Aeberli) m 1959; b 15 Apr 35. Served at ESFOT, in Frce and Switz (TC/TPWM).

MAKINA, Amos (Gwelo, Zimb, 1971); Comr b 28 Jun 47; and Comr **Rosemary** (née Chinjiri) (Mutonda, Zimb, 1973) m 1973; b 8 Aug 52. Served in Gha, Zimb (TC/TPWM) and at IHQ (IS/ZSWM Afr).

MAKOUMBOU, Antoine (Bacongo, Con (Braz), 1968); Comr b 2 Mar 40; with Comr **Véronique** (née Niangui) m 1967; b 30 Aug 46. Served in Con (Braz) (TC/ TPWM).

MANNAM, Mrs Comr Ruby (née Manuel) (Leyton Citadel, UK, 1953) m 1975. Served in Ind M and A (TPWO), Ind W (TPWO), Ind SW (TPWO), Ind E (TPWO) and Ind N (TPWO). Ww Comr Samuel, pG 2011.

MASIH, Mohan (Khundi, Ind W, 1961); Comr b 29 Sep 39; with Comr **Swarni** m 1958;

b 14 Mar 42. Served in Ind N (CS/THLS), Ind C (TC/TPWO), Ind SW (TC/TPWO) and Ind W (TC/TPWM).

MATEAR, John (Whifflet, 1978); Comr b 26 Apr 47; and Comr **Elizabeth** (née Kowbus) (Greenock Citadel, 1977) m 1978; b 16 Aug 52. Dip Youth, Commun and Soc Wk, Emp Law. Served in Carib (TC/TPWM) and UK (TC/TPWM).

MAXWELL, Earle Alexander (Orange, Aus E, 1954); Comr b 8 Jul 34. FCIS, ASA, CPA; and Comr **Wilma** (née Cugley) (Camberwell, Aus S, 1956) m 1957. Served in Aus E, Sing (OC/CPWO), Phil (TC/TPWO), NZ (TC/TPWO) and at IHQ (CoS/WSWO).

McKENZIE, Garth (Wellington City, NZ, 1975); Comr b 19 Feb 44; with Comr **Merilyn** (née Probert) m 1968; b 20 Jul 46. Served in Aus S and NZ (TC/TPWM).

MILLER, Mrs Comr **Joan** (née Hackworth) (Hamilton, OH, USA E, 1945) m 1946. Hon LHD (Wesley Biblical Seminary, MS). Served in USA E, USA C (THLS), USA S (TPWO) and at USA Nat (NPWO). Ww Comr Andrew S., pG 2011.

MORETZ, Nancy A. (née Burke) (Kingston, NY, USA E, 1964) Comr b 29 Nov 44. Served in S Am W (TPWO), USA C (TPWM) and USA E (TPWM). Ww Comr Lawrence R., pG 2013.

MORGAN, K. Brian (Bairnsdale, Aus S, 1958); Comr b 5 Oct 37; and Comr **Carolyn** (née Bath) (Melville Park, Aus S, 1958) m 1961; b 5 Mar 38. Served in Rus/CIS (OC/CPWO), Aus S (CS/TSWO) and Aus E (TC/TPWM).

MORRIS, Louise (née Holmes) (Charleston, W VA, USA S, 1953); Comr. Served in USA S and Jpn. Ww Comr Ted, pG 2004.

MOYO, Selina (née Ndhlovu) (Bulawayo Central, 1951); Mrs Comr. Served in Zimb. Ww Comr David, pG 2005.

MUNGATE, Stuart (Mabvuku, Zimb, 1970); Comr b 15 Nov 46. BA, Grad Cert Ed, Dip Bus Admin; and Comr **Hope** (née Musvosvi) (Mucherengi, Zimb, 1974) m 1974; b 23 Mar 53. Dip Journ. Served in Zimb, Con (Kin) (CS/TSWM, TC/TPWM), Nig (TC/ TPWM) and DR Con (TC/TPWM).

MUTEWERA, Stanslous (Sinoia, Zimb, 1970); Comr b 25 Dec 47; and Comr **Jannet** (née Zinyemba) (Tsatse, Zimb, 1973) m 1973; b 11 Nov 52. Served in UK and Zimb (TC/TPWM).

N

NEEDHAM, Philip D. (Miami Citadel, USA S, 1969); Comr b 5 Dec 40. BA (Rel), MDiv, ThM, DMin; with Comr **Keitha** (née Holz) m 1963; b 9 Oct 41. BA (Ed). Served at ICO (Principal), in USA W and USA S (TC/TPWM).

NELSON, John (Victoria Citadel, BC, Can, 1952); Comr b 19 Aug 32; and Comr **Elizabeth** (née McLean) (Chatham, Ont, Can, 1953) m 1956. Served in Can, at IHQ (IS/SWO S Asia), in Carib and Pak (TC/TPWO).

NELTING, Juanita (née Prine) (Cincinnati Cent, OH, USA E, 1962); Mrs Comr. Served in USA E, at USA Nat, Neth (TPWO), and at IHQ (SWO Afr and Far East) and in USA C (TPWO). Ww Comr George L., pG 2013.

NILSON, Birgitta K. (Boone, IA, USA C, 1964); Comr. b 2 Oct 37. AB (Chicago), MSW (Loyola). Served in USA C, Swdn (TC) and at IHQ (IS Eur).

NILSSON, Sven (Vansbro, Swdn, 1940); Comr b 27 Jul 19. King's Medal (12th size) Sweden (1983). Served in Nor (CS), Den (TC) and Swdn (TC). Ww Mrs Comr Lisbeth, pG 2007.

NOLAND, Joseph J. (Santa Ana, CA, USA W, 1965); Comr b 17 Jul 37. BA, MS; and Comr **Doris** (née Tobin) (Los Angeles Congress Hall, CA, USA W, 1965) m 1966. RN. Served in USA W, Aus E and USA E (TC/TPWO).

NTUK, Patience (née Ekpe) (Ibadan, 1969); Comr. Served in Nig. Ww Comr Joshua, pG 2007.

O

ØDEGAARD, B. Donald (Oslo 3, Nor, 1966); Comr b 18 Dec 40. Cand Mag; and Comr **Berit** (née Gjersøe) (Tønsberg, Nor, 1964) m 1967; b 27 Sep 44. SRN. Served in Zimb, S Afr, Nig (TC/TPWO), E Afr (TC/TPWO), Nor (TC/TPWM) and at IHQ (IS Prog Res/'Sally Ann' Coordinator).

OLCKERS, Roy (Uitenhage, S Afr, 1952); Comr b 16 Jul 29; and Mrs Comr **Yvonne** (née Holdstock) (Fairview, S Afr, 1952) m 1955. Served in S Afr (TC/TPWO).

ORSBORN, Amy (née Webb) (Adelaide North, Aus S, 1951); Mrs Comr. Served in Aus S, NZ, UK, Swdn and Aus E. Ww Comr Howard, pG 2008.

OSBORNE, James (Washington 3, DC, USA S, 1947); Comr b 3 Jul 27; with Mrs Comr **Ruth** (née Campbell). Served in USA W (CS), USA S (TC) and at USA Nat (NC).

P

PARK, Man-hee (Chung Ju, 1975); Comr b 11 Aug 47; with Comr **Kim, Keum-nyeo** b 13 Jun 51. Served in Kor (CS/TSWM, TC/TPWM).

PARKINS, May (née Epplett) (Seattle Citadel, WA, USA W, 1951); Mrs Lt-Comr. Served in USA E, USA S and USA W. Ww Lt-Comr William, pG 1990.

PATRAS, Gulzar (Punjgarian, 1973); Comr b 19 Aug 47; and Comr **Sheila** (née John) (Amritnagar, Pak, 1973) m 1973; b 22 Sep 46. Served in Pak (TC/TPWM).

PATTIPEILOHY, Blanche (née Sahanaja) (Djakarta 1, Indon, 1955); Mrs Comr. Served in Indon. Ww Comr Herman G., pG 2000.

PEARCE, Lynette J. (Parkes, Aus E, 1971); Comr b 13 Jan 45. BA. Served in Aus E, at ICO and IHQ (IS Int Pers, WSWM).

PENDER, Winifred (née Dale) (Godmanchester, UK, 1954); Comr. Served in NZ, S Afr, Scot, at IHQ, in Aus S and UK. Ww Comr Dinsdale, pG 2006.

POBJIE, Barry R. (Paddington, Aus E, 1965); Comr b 25 Jan 45. Served in PNG. Ww Capt Ruth, pG 1978; and Comr **Raemor** (née Wilson) (Port Kembla, Aus E, 1971) m 1980; b 22 Sep 48. Served in NZ, Aus E, Rus (GS/CSWO), E Eur (OC/CPWM, TC/TPWM) and at IHQ (IS/ZSWM SPEA) (IS/ZSWM Eur).

POKE, Victor (Burnie, Aus S, 1968); Comr b 8 Jan 46; and Comr **Roslyn** (née Pengilly) (Maylands, Aus S, 1968) m 1970; b 20 Jun 45. Served in Aus S, UK (CS/TSWM) and Swdn (TC/TPWM).

PRATT, Mrs Comr **Kathleen** (née Lyons) (Harlesden, UK, 1948) m 1949. Served at IHQ, in BT, USA W (TPWO) and Can (TPWO). Ww Comr William, pG 2011.

R

RADER, Paul A. General (1994-1999) (see page 15); with Comr **Kay F.** (née Fuller) (Cincinnati, OH, USA E, 1960) m 1956. BA (Asbury), Hon DD (Asbury Theol Seminary), Hon LHD (Greenville), Hon DD (Roberts Wesleyan). Served in Kor (THLS), USA E (THLS), USA W (TPWO) and at IHQ (WPWO).

RAJAKUMARI, P. Mary (née Desari) (New Colony, Bapatla, Ind C, 1978); Comr. MA (Engl), MA (Hist). Served in Ind M & A, at IHQ, at Ind Cent Off, in Ind W, Ind N and Ind SE (TPWM). Ww Comr P.D. Krupa Das, pG 2007.

RANGEL, Paulo (Rio Comprido, Brz, 1968); Comr b 19 Nov 41. Hon DD; and Comr **Yoshiko** (née Namba) (São Paulo, Brz, 1967) m 1969; b 1 Sep 44. Served in Brz (TC/TPWM).

READ, Harry (Edinburgh Gorgie, UK, 1948); Comr b 17 May 24. Served in UK, at IHQ, ITC (Principal), in Can (CS), Aus E (TC) and BT (Brit Comr). Ww Mrs Comr Winifred, pG 2007.

REFSTIE, Peder R. (Mandal, Nor, 1965); Comr b 13 Jul 43; and Comr **Janet M.** (née Dex) (Bedford, UK, 1966) m 1969; b 7 Jul 43. Served in UK, S Am W, Port, Nor, Sp (OC/CPWM), at IHQ, in S Am E (TC/TPWM) and Brz (TC/TPWM).

RIGHTMIRE, Robert S. (Cincinnati, OH, USA E, 1946); Comr b 23 Jun 24; and Comr **Katherine** (née Stillwell) (Newark Citadel, USA E, 1942) m 1947. Served in USA E, S Afr (CS), Jpn (TC/TPWO), Kor (TC/TPWO) and USA C (TC/TPWO).

RIVERS, William (Hadleigh Temple, UK, 1952); Comr b 22 Dec 27; and Mrs Comr **Rose** (née Ross) (Aberdeen Torry, UK, 1956) m 1957. Served in UK and at IHQ (IS Admin).

ROBERTS, William H. (Detroit Brightmoor, MI, USA C, 1943); Comr b 27 May 22; and Mrs Comr **Ivy** (née Anderson) (Marshalltown, IA, USA C, 1943) BA (Wayne State). Served in USA C, Aus S (CS/TSWM) and at IHQ (IS/ZSWM) Am and Carib, IS for Dev).

ROOS, Rolf (Uppsala, Swdn, 1962); Comr b 13 Nov 40; and Comr **Majvor** (née Ljunggren) (Uppsala, Swdn, 1964) m 1965; b 15 Sep 38. Served in Fin (TC/TPWO) and Swdn (TC/TPWM).

RUTH, Fred L. (Shawnee, OK, 1955); Comr b 21 Aug 35. BA (Georgia State), Dip Ed, MA (Counselling and Psychol Studies) (Trinity). Served in Kor, USA W, USA S, at USA Nat and at IHQ (IS SPEA). Ww Mrs Col Sylvia, pG 1990.

S

SAUNDERS, Robert F. (Philadelphia Pioneer, PA, USA E, 1962); Comr b 16 Jan 37. C Th (Fuller); and Comr **Carol J.** (née Rudd) (Seattle Temple, WA, USA W, 1966) m 1967; b 10 Sep 43. Served in Carib, USA E, USA W, Kor (CS/TSWO), Phil (TC/TPWO) and at IHQ (IS/SWO SPEA).

SCHURINK, Reinder J. (Zutphen, Neth, 1947); Comr b 2 Dec 27. Officer Order of Orange Nassau (1987). Ww Mrs Capt Henderika (née Hazeveld), pG 1961. Served in Ger (CS), Neth (TC) and Rus (Cmndr). Ww Mrs Comr Wietske (née Kloosterman), pG 1997. Ww Lt-Col Dora Verhagen, pG 2014.

SCOTT, Albert P. (Lawrence, MA, USA E, 1941); Comr b 15 Oct 18. Ww Mrs Dorothy, pG 1970; and Mrs Comr **Frances O.** (née Clark) (Concord, NH, USA E, 1953) m 1971. Served in USA E (CS) and at IHQ (IS Am and Carib, and IS Development).

SHIPE, Tadeous (Mukakatanwa, Zimb, 1969); Comr b 13 Jul 43. Served in Zimb, Zam and Mal (TC/TPWM) and Zam (TC/TPWM). Ww Comr Nikiwe, pG 2008.

SHOULTS, Harold (St Louis Tower Grove, MO, USA C, 1949); Comr b 6 Mar 29; and Mrs Comr **Pauline** (née Cox) (St Louis Tower Grove, MO, USA C, 1951) m 1952. Served in USA E (CS/TSWO), USA N (CS/Asst NPWO) and USA C (TC/TPWO).

SKINNER, Verna E. (West End, Aus E, 1957); Comr b 5 May 36. Served in Aus E, HK, Sri Lan (TC), Aus S (CS), at IHQ (IS Resources) and in E Afr (TC).

STREET, Robert (Stotfold, UK, 1968); Comr b 24 Feb 47; with Comr **Janet** (née Adams) m 1967; b 19 Aug 45. Served in UK, Aus E (CS/TSWM) and at IHQ (IS to CoS/WSWM, IS/ZSWM SPEA, IS/ZSWM Eur).

STRONG, Leslie J. (Kalbar, Aus E, 1965); Comr b 5 Apr 43. BAL; and Comr **Coral** (née Scholz) (Kalbar, Aus E, 1966) m 1967; b 30 Mar 44. Served in Aus S (CS/TSWM) and Aus E (TC/TPWM).

SUNDARAM, Thota Gnana (Denduluru, Ind SE, 1963); Comr b 1 Oct 35; with Comr **Suseela** m 1955; b 16 Apr 36. Served in Ind C, Ind SE (TC/TPWO) and Ind W (TC/TPWO).

SUTHERLAND, Margaret (Sleaford, UK, 1968); Comr b 22 Jul 43. MA, ARCO. Served in Zam, UK, Zimb (CS), at IHQ (IS Afr) and at ICO (Principal).

SWINFEN, John M. (Penge, UK, 1955); Comr b 24 Jan 31. BA, Cert Ed, Chevalier de l'Ordre du Merite Exceptionnel (Congo); with Comr **Norma** (née Salmon). Served in Zimb, at ITC, in UK, E Afr (CS/THLS), Con (TC/TPWO) and at IHQ (IS/SWO Afr).

SWYERS, B. Gordon (Atlanta Temple, GA, USA S, 1959); Comr b 25 Jul 36. BBA (Georgia State); and Comr **Jacqueline** (née Alexander); b 25 Dec 29. Served in USA S and at IHQ (IS Admin/SWO SPEA).

SWYERS, Philip W. (Dallas Temple, TX, USA S, 1968); Comr b 22 Apr 44. BBA; and Comr **Patricia L.** (née Lowery) (Charlotte, NC, USA S, 1962); b 26 Aug 41. Served in USA C (CS/TSWM), USA S (CS/TSWM) and USA W (TC/TPWM).

T

TAYLOR, Margaret (née Overton) (Aylsham, UK, 1962); Comr b 13 Feb 40. Served in UK, E Afr (THLS), Pak (TPWO), and at IHQ (SWO SAsia, SWO Afr, IS Prog Resources). Ww Comr Brian E., pG 2004.

THOMPSON, Arthur T. (Croydon Citadel, UK, 1961); Comr b 23 Dec 32. BSc, PhD, PGCE, Freeman of City of London, Paul Harris Fellow; and Comr **Karen** (née Westergaard) (Camberwell, UK, 1961) m 1962. BA, PGCE. Served in Zimb, Zam, UK, NZ (CS/THLS) and at IHQ (IS Admin/IS Resources, SWO Eur).

THOMSON, Robert E. (Racine, WI, USA C, 1951); Comr b 21 Feb 28. BM (St Olaf); BA (St Olaf). Served at USA Nat, in USA C (CS), at IHQ (IS Am and Carib) and in USA E (TC). Ww Mrs Comr Carol, pG 2013

TILLSLEY, Bramwell Howard General (1993-1994) (see page 15).

TONDI, Roos (née Mundung) (Sonder, Indon, 1958); Comr. Served in Aus S and Indon. Ww Comr Victor, pG 2002.

TUCK, Trevor M. (Kensington Citadel, S Afr, 1969); Comr b 11 Sep 43; and Comr **Memory** (née Fortune) (Benoni, S Afr, 1965) m 1968; b 28 Apr 45. Served in PNG (TC/TPWM) and S Afr (CS/TSWM, TC/TPWM).

V

VAN DER HARST, Willem (Scheveningen, Neth, 1966); Comr b 13 Mar 44. Ww Capt Suzanne, pG 1985; and Comr **Netty** (née Kruisinga) (Amsterdam Congress Hall, Neth, 1984) m 1985; b 15 Feb 58. Served in Cze R, Neth (TC/TPWM) and E Eur (TC/TPWM).

VERWAAL, Sjoerdje (née Zoethout) (Zaandam, Neth, 1947); Mrs Comr. Served at IHQ and in Neth. Ww Comr Cornelis, pG 2002.

Retired Generals and Commissioners

W

WAGHELA, Chimanbhai Somabhai
(Ratanpura, Ind W, 1968); Comr b 1 Jun 47;
with Comr **Rahelbai** m 1972; b 1 May 52.
Served in Ind W, Ind SE (CS/TSWO), Ind E
(CS/TSWO) and Ind SW (TC/TPWM).

WAHLSTRÖM, Maire (née Nyberg)
(Helsinki 1, Fin, 1944); Mrs General. Served
in Fin (TPWO), Swdn (TPWO), Can (TPWO)
and at IHQ (WPWO). Ww General Jarl
Wahlström, pG 1999 (see page 15).

WALTER, Alison (née Harewood) (Calgary
Citadel, AB, Can, 1955); Mrs Comr.
Served in Zimb, E Afr, Can, S Afr and at
IHQ. Ww Comr Stanley, pG 2004.

WATERS, Margaret (née Eastland) (Niagara
Falls, Can, 1953); Comr b 1 Mar 34. Served in
Can and at IHQ. Ww Comr Arthur W., pG 2002.

WATILETE, Johannes G. (Bandung 3, Indon,
1963); Comr b 9 Sep 41. BA, MTh, DTh,
DMin (HC); and Comr **Augustina** (née
Sarman) (Bandung 3, Indon, 1962) m 1966;
b 16 Aug 39. Served in Sing (GS/CHLS),
Phil (CS/THLS and TC/TPWO) and Indon
(TC/TPWM).

WATSON, Robert A. (Philadelphia Pioneer,
PA, USA E, 1955); Comr b 11 Aug 34;
and Comr **Alice** (née Irwin) (Philadelphia
Pioneer, PA, USA E, 1956) m 1957.
Served in USA E (CS/THLS) and at
USA Nat (NC/ NPWO).

WICKBERG, Eivor (née Lindberg)
(Norrköping 1, Swdn, 1946); Mrs General.
Ww General Erik Wickberg, pG 1996
(see page 14).

WILLIAMS, Harry William (Wood Green,
UK, 1934); Comr b 13 Jul 13. OF, OBE,
FRCS (Edin), FICS. Served in Ind W,
Ind NE, Ind S (TC), NZ (TC), Aus E (TC)
and at IHQ (IS Am, IS Australasia,
IS Plan & Dev). Ww Mrs Comr Eileen M.,
pG 2002.

WOODALL, Ann (Croydon Citadel, UK,
1969); Comr b 3 Feb 50. MA, MSc, FCCA,
PhD. Served in Con, Zam, Zaï, UK and at
IHQ (IS Bus Admin).

Y

YOHANNAN, Paulose (Kalayapuram,
Ind SW, 1974); Comr b 1 Dec 45.
MA (Sociol), DD, PhD; with Comr
Kunjamma (née Jesaiah) m 1966;
b 15 Jun 47. Served in Ind SW, Ind E,
Ind SE (TC/TPWM) and Ind N (TC/TPWM).

YOSHIDA, Makoto (Shibuya, Jpn, 1969);
Comr b 7 Dec 45. BSc (Engin); and Comr
Kaoru (née Imamura) (Omori, Jpn, 1971)
m 1974; b 13 Jan 45. Served in Jpn
(CS/TSWM, TC/TPWM) and at IHQ
(IS/ZSWM SPEA).

Retirements from Active Service

AUSTRALIA EASTERN

Majs Peter and Ruth Dollin from Chaplains, Foster House Complex on 31 Oct 2013

Maj Winston Kardell from the Bridge Programme on 31 Oct 2013

Maj Colin Haggar from Manager, Samaritan Services on 31 Dec 2013

Capt Lenore Johnston from Maroubra on 31 Dec 2013

Majs Peter and Helen Pearson from Inverell on 31 Dec 2013

Maj Phyllis Thorley from Chaplain, RPA Hospital Sydney on 31 Dec 2013

Majs Frank and Narelle Moxon from Mission and Strategic Managers, Bethany Residential Aged Care Plus on 31 Jan 2014

Maj John Rees from Director, Salvation Army International Development Office on 31 Jan 2014

Maj Allison Wiseman from Assistant Director, Counselling Services Administration on 28 Feb 2014

Majs Gary and Judith Baker from The Greater West Division on 31 Mar 2014

Maj Heather Rose from Chaplaincy Services, Sydney East and Illawarra Division on 30 Apr 2014

Maj Narelle Rees from Mentor to Newly Commissioned Officers (NSW/ACT) on 30 Jun 2014

Lt-Cols David andChristine Rees from Retired Officers Chaplain (Qld) on 30 Jun 2014

Lt Joe Clark from Chaplain, Dooralong Transformation Centre on 31 Jul 2014

Majs Rodney and Denice Strong from Senior Fire Chaplain/Family Support Chaplain Qld Fire & Rescue on 31 Jul 2014

AUSTRALIA SOUTHERN

Maj Peter Stark from Melb Cent DHQ on 8 Jan 2014

Majs David and Fiona Bartlett from Red Cliffs Corps, Vic, on 9 Jan 2014

Maj Carolyn Ledger from Broadford Corps, Vic, on 11 Jan 2014

Maj Lorraine Hart from THQ on 1 Mar 2014

Maj Grady Bailey from Balga Corps, W Aus, on 1 April 2014

Maj Trevor Wilson from Bunbury Corps, W Aus, on 1 April 2014

Maj Jillian Denholm from Willagee Corps, W Aus, on 1 May 2014

Lt-Col Donni Pho from THQ on 1 June 2014

Majs Anne and John Farquharson from THQ on 1 Jul 2014

Maj Henry May from Red Shield Defence Services on 16 Aug 2014

BRAZIL

Maj Giani Azevedo from THQ on 30 Apr 2014

CANADA AND BERMUDA

Majs Richard and Judith Gilbert from Langley BC on 1 Jan 2014

Maj Roy Langer from Edmonton AB on 1 Mar 2014

Maj Judy Hann from St Mary's ON on 1 Apr 2014

Lt Col Susan van Duinen from Toronto ON on 1 Apr 2014

Maj (Dr) Dawn Howse from St John's NL on 1 Jun 2014

Majs Wilbert and Bertha Abbott from Guelph ON on 1 Jul 2014

Maj Louise Perry from Stephenville NL on 1 Jul 2014

Maj Sharon Wilson from Hespeler ON on 1 Jul 2014

Majs Gordon and Doris Jarvis from Winnipeg MB on 1 Jul 2014

Majs Roderick & Jane Sheasby from Kitchener ON on 1 Jul 2014

Lt-Col Neil Watt from Toronto ON on 1 Jul 2014

Majs Calvin and Beryl Collins from Botwood NL on 1 Jul 2014

Majs Larry and Lynda Farley from Chilliwack BC on 1 Jul 2014

Maj Robert MacDonald from Halifax NS on 1 Jul 2014

Majs David and Rosa Moulton from Terrace BC on 1 Jul 2014

Maj Karen Oldford from Toronto ON on 1 Jul 2014

Maj Audrey Tilley from Toronto ON on 1 Jul 2014

Majs Henry and Beatrice Bingle from Englee NL on 1 Jul 2014

Majs Stanley and Judith Folkins from Sussex NB on 1 Jul 2014

Majs Ronald and Linda Mailman from Yorkton SK on 1 Jul 2014

Capts Felipe and Phyllis Vega from Bridgewater NS on 1 Jul 2014

Maj Winifred Perrin from Halifax NS on 1 Jul 2014

Majs Leonard and Rossyln Millar from Kindersly SK on 1 Aug 2014

Maj Roy Dueck from Winnipeg MB on 1 Aug 2014

Maj Doreen Lacey from Mount Pearl NL on 1 Sep 2014

Maj Christopher Dickens from Winnipeg MB on 1 Sep 2014

CONGO (BRAZZAVILLE)

Lt-Cols Jean Alexis and Pauline Sakamesso from THQ on 26 May 2013

Capt Alexandre Mabanza from THQ on 26 Jan 2014

Majs Albert and Marie Jeanne Mbelani from Mfilou Corps on 2 Feb 2014

Majs Albertine Loumouamou from THQ on 6 Apr 2014

DEMOCRATIC REPUBLIC OF CONGO

Lt-Cols Joseph and Germaine Bueya from THQ on 7 Jul 2013

Majs Pierre and Marie José Mukoko from Mbanza-Ngungu Division on 2 Feb 2014

DENMARK

Capt Preben Kristensen on 31 Jul 2012

FINLAND AND ESTONIA

Maj Sirkka Paukku from THQ on 1 Jul 2014

Maj Anneli Franke from Hämeenlinna on 1 Jul 2014

FRANCE AND BELGIUM

Maj Christian Exbrayat from THQ on 1 Nov 2013

Maj Joëlle Exbrayat from THQ on 1 Nov 2013

Maj Geneviève Besson from Mazamet Corps on 1 Apr 2014

GERMANY AND LITHUANIA

Maj Christine Schollmeier from THQ on 1 Oct 2013

HONG KONG AND MACAU

Capt Chan Man-ping from Kowloon City Corps on 11 Apr 2014

INDIA CENTRAL

Lt-Cols Abbulu and Vimala Kumari from THQ on 31 May 2013

Maj D Samuel and Jaysree from Bapatla Corps on 1 Sep 2013

Maj B Yesuprema from Pinakadimi Corps on 1 Sep 2013

Maj P Ratna Kumari from Relangi Corps on 1 Sep 2013

Lt-Cols P Samuel Rathan and Ananda Kumari from THQ on 31 May 2014

Majs B Sugunakar Rao and Mahita Kumari from Alluru Corps on 31 May 2014

Maj M Koteswaramma from Madanuru Corps on 31 May 2014

Majs G Noah Kumar and Dharshavalli from Guntur Area on 31 May 2014

Majs G Vijaya Kumar and Vijaya Kumari from Stuartpuram Corps on 31 May 2014

Maj P Job from Ganapavaram Corps on 31 May 2014

Majs P V Prasada Rao and Prakasamma from Malakpet Corps on 31 May 2014

Cols T Vijaya Kumar and Manikyam from THQ on 30 Jun 2014

INDIA EASTERN

Majs Pachuau Lianhlira and Ralte Thanzuali on 30 Apr 2014

L-Cols Tochhawng Lalramhluna and Pachuau Kawlramthangi on 31 May 2014

INDIA NORTHERN

Majs Samuel and Shinto Masih from Amritsar on 30 Apr 2014

INDIA SOUTH EASTERN

Majs S N Manuel and D Roselet Mary from Nediyancode on 30 Apr 2013

Majs Y Dhason and Ranjitham from Catherine Booth Hospital on 30 Apr 2013

Majs P Muthuraj and Santha Elizabeth from Thuckalay on 30 Apr 2013

Majs Pushpaleela Moses from Saralvilai, Thuckalay on 30 Apr 2014

Majs Gnanaseelan and Ammini from Thuckalay on 30 May 2014

Commrs M Y Emmanuel and Regina Chandra Bai from Chennai on 31 May 2014

Lt-Cols A Sam Devaraj and Kanagaretnam from Palayamcottai on 30 Jun 2014

Majs Solomone and Kamalabai from Aramboly on 30 Jun 2014

Majs Sundaram and Sucila from Azagiapandipuram on 31 Aug 2014

INDIA SOUTH WESTERN

Majs P.J John and M. Santhamma John on 30 Jun 2013

Majs K.V Samuel and T.K Molly Samuel on 31 Dec 2013

Majs N.T John and R. Annamma John on 31 Dec 2013

Majs J. John and M. Aleyamma John on 31 Dec 2013

Majs Joseph Chacko and Leelamma Joseph on 31 Jan 2014

Majs K.G John and Mariamma John on 28 Feb 2014

Majs A.K John and K. Suseela John on 31 Mar 2014

Maj E.P Mariamma on 30 Apr 2014

Maj K.V Aleykutty on 30 Apr 2014

Majs A.J Joseph and Alekutty Joseph on 30 Apr 2014

Majs William David. K and Mary William on 30 Apr 2014

Maj Saramma Silas on 31 May 2014

Majs Sam Wicliff and Sudha Sam on 31 May 2014

Majs D. Sathiaseelan and Aleyamma Sathiaseelan on 31 May 2014

INDIA WESTERN

Lt-Cols David and Vimalabai Sevak from THQ on 30 Nov 2013

Lt-Cols Punjalal and Margaret Macwan from THQ on 30 May 2014

Majs Suleman Naran and Diwalibai S Macwan from Nadiad Division on 30 May 2014

Maj Mubarak Zumal Maste from Madhya Pradesh on 30 May 2014

Maj Anugrah Z. Master from Madhya Pradesh on 30 May 2014

Majs William Dahya and Pushpabai Macwan from Muktipur Colony on 30 May 2014

INDONESIA

Lt-Cols Harold and Deetje Ambitan from Surabaya 4 Corps on 1 Jul 2014

Maj Doris Rangi from Bobo Corps on 1 Jul 2014

Majs Jantje and Mince Kasumba from Maranatha Corps on 1 Jul 2014

Majs Simon and Meida Tahe from Lembosu Corps on 1 Jul 2014

Majs Henoch and Agustina Nore from Children's Home Palu on 1 Jul 2014

Majs Sakius and Damaris Liwetado from Lewara Corps on 1 Jul 2014

Majs Sadrakh and Patresia Lanto from Lompio Corps on 1 Jul 2014

JAPAN

Maj Kanako Adachi from Hiroshima Corps on 31 Dec 2013

Maj Mitsuo Igarashi from Sendai Corps on 26 Mar 2014

KENYA WEST

Majs Zadock and Janepher Cheshari from Lukosi Corps on 5 Dec 2013

Maj Rosebella Aboka from Nyalenda Corps on 5 Dec 2013

Majs Richard and Ann Naibei from Nyira Corps on 5 Dec 2013

Majs Benson and Florence Omeso from Boyani Corps on 5 Dec 2013

Majs John and Selina Chemwolo from Elgeyo Corps on 5 Dec 2013

Majs Levi and Margaret Lidwachi from Shigomere Corps on 1 May 2014

KOREA

Captain Han, Young-ja from An Eui Corps on 7 Nov 2013

Major Yom, Myung-dong and Major Kim, Ki-rim from Ki Sung Corps on 31 Nov 2013

Major Jeong, Ku-jung and Major Kim, Myung-hoon from Ganweoldo Corps on 25 Feb 2014

Major Kim, Hyung-gil and Major Lee, Heui-sook from Won Ju Corps on 25 Feb 2014

Major Do, Hee-ja from Kunsan Children's Home on 25 Feb 2014

LATIN AMERICA NORTH

Capts Rodrigo and Elizabeth León from Costa Rica in 2013

Maj Magalis Flores from Niquero, Cuba in 2014

MEXICO

Maj Guadalupe Galvan from DHQ on 28 Feb 2014

THE NETHERLANDS AND CZECH REP

Major Albert Muller from Oké department on 13 Dec 2013

Major Annita de Jong from W & G Midden Nederland on 17 Apr 2014

Major Hennie van Pelt from Goodwill Centre Amsterdam on 11 May 2014

Major Harmien Mollema from W and G Gelderland on 6 Jun 2014

Major Tineke van Huffelen from Amsterdam West Corps on 1 Jul 2014

NEW ZEALAND, FIJI AND TONGA

Maj Tanya Dunn from Wellington on 8 Jan 2014

Maj Ann-Maree Stone from Ashburton on 10 Jan 2014

Retirements from Active Service

Majs Graham and Christine Rattray from Aucklandon 12 Jan 2014

Maj Margaret Ousey from Wellington on 15 Jan 2014

Majs Terry and Glenys Heese from Auckland on 15 Jan 2014

Maj Barbara Sampson from Christchurch on 18 Jan 2014

Maj Shirleen Bradley from Wellington on 31 Jan 2014

Capt Moses Chan from Mosgiel on 28 Feb 2014

Capt Linda Travis from Auckland on 31 May 2014

NIGERIA
Comrs Mfon and Ime Akpan from THQ

NORWAY, ICELAND AND THE FÆROES
Maj Anne Marie Levang from THQ on 30 Sept 2013

Maj Steinar Halnes from Arendal Corps on 30 Nov 2013

Maj Åse Nystuen from THQ on 30 Nov 2013

Maj Inger Sofie Tjåland from Haugesund Corps on 31 Dec 2013

Maj Gunnar Flørnes Gundersen from Majorstua Corps on 28 Feb 2014

Lt-Col Odd Berg from Western Division on 31 Mar 2014

Maj Per Arne Pettersen from Eastern Division on 31 Mar 2014

Lt-Col Jørg Walter Hartveit from THQ on 30 Jun 2014

Maj Odd Løvdahl from Western Division on 30 Jun 2014

PAKISTAN
Majs Javed Daniel and Mussarat Javed from Chak 20 Corps on 31 Mar 2014

PAPUA NEW GUINEA
Majs Sere and Hanua Kala on 1 Sep 2013

Majs Leo and Susan Naua on 11 Nov 2013

Maj Auko Ebuo on 12 Dec 2013

Capt Ridia Misina on15 Dec 2013

Capt Gomuna Misina on 15 Dec 2013

Capt Stanley Warepan on 15 Dec 2013

THE PHILIPPINES
Maj Nolando Vejano on 30 Oct 2013

Maj Juanita Vejano on 30 Oct 2013

SOUTH AMERICA WEST
Maj Nancy D. Alarcón on 3 Mar 2014

Majs Juan E. and Rosa Espinoza on 31 Mar 2014

Capts Carlos and Rosa Donoso on 31 Mar 2014

SOUTHERN AFRICA
Capt Carl Ngcongo from Umlazi Corps on 30 Apr 2014

Aux-Capt Lionel Potgieter from Johannesburg Social Services on 30 Jun 2014

Majs David and Lynne Wright from DHQ on 30 Jun 2014

Maj Lorna Filies Lorna from Manenberg Corps on 31 Aug 2014

Majs Andrew and Audrey Moholoagae from Meadowlands Corps on 31 Aug 2014

SRI LANKA
Major Shanthi Rukunayake from The Haven on 27 Jul 2014

SWEDEN AND LATVIA
Maj Inge Wahlström from Lidköping on 15 Jun 2013

Capt Christer Eklöf from Östersund on 21 Jul 2013

Maj Juan Gallardo from Stockholm on 27 Jul 2013

Maj Karin Tourn from Ystad on 31 Jul 2013

Maj Kerstin Högberg from Huskvarna on 1 Aug 2013

Lt-Col Britt-Marie Alm from Luleå on 1 Sept 2013

Comr Hasse Kjellgren from Social Centre Eken on 1 Sept 2013

Maj Monica Johansson from Örebro Community Centre on 27 Sept 2013

Maj Mona Stockman from Stockholm on 24 Nov 2013

Col Kristina Frisk from Stockholm on 30 Nov 2013

Lt-Col Kenneth Nordenberg from Corps 393 on 3 Jan 2014

Maj Rolf Karlsson from Alingsås on 14 May 2014

Comr Christina Kjellgren from Söderkåren on 21 May 2014

Maj Ann-Cristine Holten from Akalla on 12 Aug 2014

Maj Karin Hultgren from Söderkåren on 18 Aug 2014

Lt-Col Ewa Nordenberg from Corps 393 on 31 Aug 2014

SWITZERLAND, AUSTRIA AND HUNGARY
Major Rosmarie Mettler from Kinderkrippe Zürich on 28 Feb.2014

Major Elsbeth Oberli from Bildungszentrum

Basel on 31 Mar 2014

Comr Franz Boschung from THQ on 31 Aug 2014

Comr Hanny Boschung from THQ on 31 Aug. 2014

UNITED KINGDOM

Maj Raymond Ward from Macclesfield on 1 Sep 2013

Capt Brian Chambers from sick furlough on 1 Oct 2013

Majs Peter and Dawn Disney from West Midlands DHQ on 1 Oct 2013

Maj Terence Andrews from Chaplain, Lyndon House Lifehouse Ipswich on 1 Nov 2013

Majs Keith andAgnes Wallis from South and Mid Wales DHQ and West Midlands DHQ on 1 Nov 2013

Lt-Col Ian Barr from Programme Service, THQ on 1 Jan 2014

Maj Michael Farrow from Administrator, Swan Lodge Lifehouse, Sunderland on 1 Jan 2014

Capt Ann Courdelle from Chaplain, Smallcombe House CH, Bath on 1 Feb 2014

Maj Ron Smith from East Midlands DHQ on 1 Feb 2014

Maj Noel Toner from Shaw on 1 Feb 2014

Maj Bryan Snell from Birmingham Airport Chaplaincy on 1 Apr 2014

Maj David Sterling from Employment Plus UK, THQ on 1 Apr 2014

Maj Lorna Doust from Kettering on 1 May 2014

Maj Philip Garnham from WBC on 1 May 2014

Maj Malcolm Walters from Glasgow West on 1 May 2014

Maj Margaret Bovey from Programme Service, THQ on 1 Jun 2014

Maj Lawrence Brown from Gorseinon on 1 Jun 2014

Maj William Fraser from Whittlesey on 1 Jun 2014

Majs Robert and Mary Johnson from South Shields on 1 Jun 2014

Maj Elizabeth Pritchard from Ballymena on 1 Jun 2014

Majs Paul and Linda Hoad from Northampton Central on 1 Jul 2014

Majs Geoffrey and Glenda Martin from Gainsborough on 1 Jul 2014

Majs Alan and Carolyn Read from Sheringham on 1 Jul 2014

Majs Alan and Linda Aggett from Employment Plus UK, THQ on 1 Aug 2014

Maj David Botting from WBC on 1 Aug 2014

Majs Robert and Christine Campbell from Lowestoft South on 1 Aug 2014

Majs Alan and Jacqueline Dixon from Scotland Secretariat on 1 Aug 2014

Lt-Col Marion Drew from Communications Service, THQ on 1 Aug 2014

Capt Jennifer Dibsdall from Eaton Bray on 1 Aug 2014

Maj Samuel Edgar from West Midlands DHQ on 1 Aug 2014

Maj David Lanceley from Business Administration Service, THQ on 1 Aug 2014

Maj Sharron Lanceley from West Norwood on 1 Aug 2014

Majs Robert and Muriel McClenahan from Programme Service, THQ on 1 Aug 2014

Lt-Col Sandra Moran from London South-East DHQ on 1 Aug 2014

Maj Rainer Nädler from Germany and Lithuania Territory on 1 Aug 2014

Maj Norman Piper from Family Tracing Service, THQ on 1 Aug 2014

Maj James Prescott from Kilmarnock on 1 Aug 2014

Maj David Radford from Brighouse and Yorkshire DHQ on 1 Aug 2014

Majs John and Lorna Smith from Tunbridge Wells on 1 Aug 2014

Maj Charmain Thomas from Business Administration Service, THQ on 1 Aug 2014

Maj Katrina Thomas from Northern DHQ on 1 Aug 2014

Maj Peter West from Welling on 1 Aug 2014

Maj Mary Wolfe from Southsea on 1 Aug 2014

USA CENTRAL

Majs Roger and Joy Ross from Wisconsin and Upper Michigan Division on 1 Sept 2013

Maj Barbara Shiels from Western DHQ on 1 March 2014

Majs P. Mark and B. Sue Welsh from Northern DHQ on 1 May 2014

Majs Thomas and Roseann Eagle from Logansport, IN on 1 Jul 2014

Majs Alan and LaVonne Fones from Virginia, MN on 1 Jul 2014

Majs Herbert and Yaneth Fuqua from Eastern Michigan DHQ on 1 Jul 2014

Majs Craig and Joan Stoker from Alpena, MI on 1 Jul 2014

Lt-Col Richard E. Vander Weele from THQ on 1 Jul 2014

Retirements from Active Service

Majs Robert and Kathy Edmonds from Alma, MI on 1 Aug 2014

Maj Vicky Horton from Metropolitan Chicago Social Services on 1 Aug 2014

Majs Steven and Melody Koehler from Grandview (Southland), MO on 1 Aug 2014

Maj Corliss Skepper from THQ on 1 Aug 2014

USA EASTERN

Maj Margaret Johnson from EPA on 1 Oct 2013

Lt-Cols W. Howard and Patricia Burr from THQ on 1 Dec 2013

Maj David and Karin Dickson from NNE on 1 Dec 2013

Lt-Cols Timothy A. and Lynda Raines from ARC on 1 Jan 2014

Majs Carl G. and Hollie Ruthberg from THQ on 1 Jan 2014

Majs William L. and Nancy Townsend from GNY on 1 Jan 2014

Cols William R. and Marcella Carlson from THQ on 1 Feb 2014

Maj Robert Ginter from EMP on 1 Mar 2014

Majs William D. and Joan Brewer from THQ on 1 Mar 2014

Majs John R. and Karen Cranford from ARC on 1 Jun 2014

Majs Vernon S. and Vicki Dolby from WEP on 1 Jun 2014

Majs Steven and Paula Loveless from EMP on 1 Jun 2014

Majs Ronald E. and Pamela Santmyer from EPA on 1 Jun 2014

Maj Kathleen K. Wadman from ARC on 1 Jun 2014

Majs William A. and Evelyn Augustine from SWO on 1 Jul 2014

Majs Raymond W. and Ruth Bartholomew from EPA on 1 Jul 2014

Majs Glenn C. and Carol Bloomfield from THQ on 1 Jul 2014

Majs Bernard W. and Claranne Meitrott from THQ on 1 Jul 2014

Majs Joseph F. and Marcia Pawlowski from WEP on 1 Jul 2014

Lt-Cols James W. and Blanche Reynolds from THQ on 1 Jul 2014

Majs Wilfred H. and A. Margaret Samuel from GNY on 1 Jul 2014

Majs John J. and Darlene Cramer from THQ on 1 Aug 2014

Lt-Cols Edmund L. and Carolynne Chung from THQ on 1 Sept 2014

USA SOUTHERN

Majs Clavin and Irene Clatterbuck from Suffolk, VA on 1 Sept 2013

Majs Tex and Mona Ellis, Sr from Paris, TX on 1 Sept 2013

Majs James and Creselia Parrish from Abilene, TX on 1 Sept 2013

Majs Phillip and Donna Murphy from Sarasota, FL on 1 Sept 2013

Majs John and Linda Queener from Texas DHQ on1 Oct 2013

Majs Richard and Barbara Branscum from Texas DHQ on 1 Nov 2013

Majs George and Sharyn Hoosier from THQ Atlanta, GA on 1 Dec 2013

Maj David B Atkins from Texas DHQ on 1 Dec 2013

Majs Leslie and Linda Wheeler from Texas DHQ on 1 Mar 2014

Majs Sherman and Lorraine Cundiff from ARC Fort Worth, TX on 1 Mar 2014

Maj Jeanne Miller, from MWV DHQ on 1 Apr 2014

Majs Gary and Patty Elliott from THQ Atlanta, GA on 1 Apr 2014

Majs Henry and Cheryl Hunter from Columbus, GA on 1 Jul 2014

Majs Edward and Delia Alonzo from Pasadena, TX on 1 Jul 2014

Lt-Cols Vernon and Martha Jewett from Florida DHQ on 1 Jul 2014

Majs Robert and Carol Bagley from THQ Atlanta, GA on 1 Jul 2014

Majs Fred and Capt Evelyn Thornhill from Wilson, NC on1 Jul 2014

Majs. Loyd and Alyce Kerns from Wm. Booth Towers, Atlanta, GA on 1 Aug 2014

USA WESTERN

Majs C. Patrick and Kitty Granat from Poland, Germany and Lithuania Territory on 1 Oct 2013

Majs William and Laura Heiselman from Portland, OR on 1 Jan 2014

Majs Wayne and Patricia Froderberg from San Francisco, CA on 1 Feb 2014

Majs Richard and Deborah Greene from Salt Lake City, UT on 1 Feb 2014

Maj Jeffrey S. and Capt Stephanie Dennis from Long Beach, CA on 1 Jun 2014

Majs Pedro and Elizabeth Delgado from Phoenix, AZ on 1 Jul 2014

Majs Antonio and Aide Horta from Santa Ana,
  CA on 1 Jul 2014
Majs Preston and Bonita Rider from Seattle,
  WA on 1 Jul 2014
Majs Samuel S. and Margarita Rodriguez
  from Stockton, CA on 1 July 2014
Majs Fredrick C. and Patricia L. Rasmussen
  from Honolulu, HI on 1 Aug 2014
Majs Ron and Keilah Toy from Rancho Palos
  Verdes, CA on 1 Aug 2014

ZAMBIA
Majs Peter and Lonely Kayungwa
Majs Leonard and Joyce Mweemba
Majs Governor and Lonika Hamoonga
Maj Donald Kasalala

ZIMBABWE
Capt Sebastian Muzeya from Braeside on 15
  Feb 2014

Promotions to Glory

AUSTRALIA EASTERN
Maj David Hodges on 8 Nov 2013
Comr Vida Bath on 9 Dec 2013
Maj Ruby Dalrymple on 18 Dec 2013
Div Env Jayne Wilson on 25 Dec 2013
Maj Dulcie Hopper on 5 Feb 2014
Lt-Col Roy Stiles on 28 Feb 2014
Maj Sophia (Josie) Nasveld on 17 Mar 2014
Maj Edna Gorringe on 13 Apr 2014
Ter Env Matthew Blessington on 30 Apr 2014
Brigadier Beth Drew on 26 Jun 2014

AUSTRALIA SOUTHERN
Maj Arthur Mawson on 3 Sep 2013
Capt (William) Leslie Blackburn on 11 Sep 2013
Maj Margaret Lilian Armstrong on 23 Nov 2013
Maj Hilton Morris on 11 Jan 2014
Maj Jean Kaus on 15 Jan 2014
Brig Joyce Baker on 22 Jan 2014
Maj Christopher Forward on 28 Jan 2014
Maj Ronald Cutts on 16 Feb 2014
Lt-Col Margaret Earl on 24 Feb 2014
Maj (John) Arfon Jones on 7 Mar 2014
Maj James Clark on 9 Apr 2014
Maj Elsie Roberts on 3 May 2014
Major (Elisabeth) Shirley Fletcher on 31 May 2014
Brig Rita Rawlings on 31 May 2014
Lt-Col (Charmian) Charm Craig on 14 Jun 2014
Maj Athlea How on 21 Jun 2014
Maj (Naomi) Marge Bevan on 26 Jun 2014
Maj Thelma Roberts on 26 Jun 2014
Maj John Booth on 13 Jul 2014
Maj (Lester) Daryl Rawlings on 11 Aug 2014

BRAZIL
Brig Erondina Oliveira on 28 Dec 2013
Aux Capt Adelaide Mendes on 29 Dec 2013
Maj Osvaldo Campos on 30 Jan 2014

CANADA AND BERMUDA
Maj Robert Zwicker on 7 Jun 2013
Lt-Col Boyd Goulding on 10 Jun 2013
Maj Hayward Noseworthy on 13 Jun 2013
Maj Dorothy Sharp on 21 Jun 2013

Maj Mark Cummings (A) from Barrie ON on 28 Jun 2013
Maj Harry Moore on 29 Jun 2013
Maj Ronald Walker on 1 Jul 2013
Lt-Col Bernice McNeilly on 15 Jul 2013
Maj William Merritt on 17 Jul 2013
Maj Fred Butler-Caughie on 3 Aug 2013
Maj Ray Pond on 27 Aug 2013
Maj Reed Wiseman on 3 Sep 2013
Lt-Col Elsie Fisher on 6 Sep 2013
Capt Susie Eveleigh on 1 Oct 2013
Maj Cyril Janes on 3 Oct 2013
Maj Lillian Jewer on 7 Oct 2013
Maj Roy Wombold on 11 Oct 2013
Maj David Peck on 22 Oct 2013
Maj Mary Park on 24 Nov 2013
Maj Robert Gilbert on 25 Nov 2013
Lt Col Catherine Halsey on 9 Dec 2013
Mrs. Maj Nancy Carr on 12 Dec 2013
Lt-Col Lorraine Moore on 6 Jan 2014
Lt-Col Douglas Kerr on 15 Jan 2014
Maj Tanya Payette (A) from Community Services Calgary AB on 18 Jan 2014
Maj Florence Curzon on 21 Jan 2014
Maj Joan Rich on 24 Jan 2014
Maj Michael Rich on 27 Jan 2014
Maj Dorothy Drover on 31 Jan 2014
Maj Cecil Pike on 1 Feb 2014
Maj Myrtle Abrahamse on 18 Feb 2014
Mrs General Maude Tillsley on 19 Feb 2014
Maj Wesley Wiseman on 1 Mar 2014
Lt-Col Kenneth Holbrook on 8 Mar 2014
Maj Pearce Samson on 26 Mar 2014
Maj William Clarke on 18 May 2014
Maj Ida Janes on 23 May 2014
Lt-Col Alvina Chapman on 24 May 2014
Capt Heather Cheon on 7 Jun 2014
Maj Anita (Peggy) Hendrickson on 30 Jun 2014
Maj Joseph Peterson on 6 Jul 2014

CARIBBEAN
Maj Lysius Salomon on 22 Dec.2013
Maj Franklin Sumter on 28 Mar 2014
Maj Ada Norton on 2 May 2014

CONGO (BRAZZAVILLE)
Maj Marthe Ntsikabaka (A) on 10 Nov 2013
Lt-Col Roberte Poaty on 21 Dec 2013

Promotions to Glory

Capt Rose Bibiane Nathalie Loukouayi on
31 Mar 2014

DEMOCRATIC REPUBLIC OF CONGO
Maj Honorine Ndongala (A) on 11 Jan 2013
Maj Gaston Lutumba on 9 Mar 2013
Maj François Nkodia on 24 Apr 2013
Maj Célestine Senga on 5 May 2013
Maj Thérèse Mbesi on 20 Sep 2013

FINLAND AND ESTONIA
Maj Maire Pylkkönen on 24 Oct 2013
Maj Airi Karhu on 8 Dec 2013

FRANCE AND BELGIUM
Capt Iéva Van Damme-Tavare on 25 Sept 2013
Maj Jeanne Hoefman-Calluys on 4 Oct 2013
Comr France Delcourt-Bardiaux on 11 Nov
2013
Maj Jean Cesar on 29 Dec 2013
Maj Ariane Alegre-Mollet on 11 Feb 2014
Maj Josette Ramondou on 10 Mar 2014

GERMANY AND LITHUANIA
Lt-Col Walter Alisch on 7 Jan 2013
Maj Else Boese on 10 May 2013
Maj Helga Müller on 11 Oct 2013
Maj Johanna Heiser on 22 Dec 2013

GHANA
Lt-Col William Gyimah, on 6 Apr 2014
Lt-Col Mike Jones Adu-Manu on 18 May 2014

INDIA CENTRAL
Maj R. Esther on 1 Sept 2013
Env I Lazar, Gudivada (A) on 22 Sept 2013
Maj Ch. Suguna Rao on 4 Oct 2013
Maj K. Vijayamma on 11 Nov 2013
Maj Ch. Ratna Manjari (A) on 28 Dec 2013
Maj K Yesupadam on 8 Feb 2014
Maj S. John Bushanam on 13 Feb 2014
Lt-Colonel P. Chandra Leela on 27 Mar 2014
Maj B. Jacob on 22 May 2014

INDIA EASTERN
Maj Lalnghengi on 14 Aug 2013
Maj Lalthansanga on 30 Nov 2013
Maj Kapliana on 18 Dec 2013
Maj Sapzinga on 27 Jan 2014
Maj Zawngkhaia on 23 Apr 2014

INDIA NORTHERN
Brig Zohra Khair Masih on 19 Sep 2013

Maj Daniel on 7 Oct 2013
Maj Noel Tudu on 4 Dec 2013
Maj Saradaran Inayat Masih on 3 Jan 2014
Brig Bachani Taran Das on 6 Mar 2014
Maj John J. Loyal (A) from Bajpur Extension
on 10 Mar 2014
Maj Samuel Das on 24 Apr 2014

INDIA SOUTH EASTERN
Major Pushpam from Nantikuzhy on 26 Aug 2013
Major Inbammal Appavoo from Muttacaud on
29 Jan 2014
Major Devanesam Manuel from BTMC on
7 Feb 14
Major S Jacob from Palayamcottai on 26 Feb
2014
Major V Pauliah from BTMC on 20 Mar 2014

INDIA SOUTH WESTERN
Aux-Capt Annamma David on 15 Jun 2013
Maj J. Sanuel on 25 Jul 2013
Maj Lissy Peter (A) on 26 Sep 2013
Maj C.Y Mathai on 6 Oct 2013
Maj Housikutty Yohannan on 13 Oct 2013
Maj M. Mikhayel on 9 Nov 2013
Maj Rachel Philip on 17 Nov 2013
S/Capt P.T Rachel Joshua on 29 Nov 2013
Maj N. Ruth Rajadas on 16 Dec 2013
Maj K.V Samuel on 16 Jan 2014
Maj P.J Yohannan on 22 Feb 2014

INDIA WESTERN
Maj Ramesh K. Bhabor (A) on 27 Oct 2013
Maj Sumatiibai L. Kasbe on 25 Nov 2013
Maj Malanbai S. Angarkhe on 25 Jan 2014
Col Gulab V. Kharat on 30 Jan 2014
Maj Ashabai D. Salve on 10 Mar 2014
Maj Purshottam D. Parmar on 6 May 2014
Maj Marthabai Timothy on 9 Jun 2014
Maj William Trikam on 2 Jul 2014

INDONESIA
Maj Mrs Rawi Rume on 16 Oct 2013
Maj Eknius Daniel Sango on 23 Oct 2013
Maj Dintje Tohuro on 22 Nov 2013
Maj Susi Soleiman on 4 Jan 2014
Maj Magdalena Carolina Sahertian on
11 Jan 2014
Lt-Col I Ketut Timonuli on 1 Feb 2014
Lt-Col Johanna Mona Losso on 6 Feb 2014
Maj Johannis Dijo (A) on 24 Feb 2014

ITALY AND GREECE
Major Mario Paone on 27 Aug 2013

JAPAN
Mrs Brig Masuko Furukawa on 11 Jan 2014
Mrs Brig Sada Hosogai on 9 Feb 2014
Maj Kiyoshi Namai on 1 Mar 2014

KENYA WEST
Maj Japheth Kinyosi on 23 Sep 2013
Maj Shem Muyeyeli on 7 Dec 2013
Maj Zachariah Imbali on 12 Apr 2014
Maj Christine Singili on 18 Apr 2014

KOREA
Capt Noh, Mi-hee on 17 Nov 2013
Maj Kwon, Sung-dal on 15 Mar 2014

LATIN AMERICA NORTH
Maj Alberto Flores on 26 Dec 2013

MEXICO
Maj Israel Garcia on 30 Sep 2013
Maj David Vera on 20 Feb 2014

THE NETHERLANDS AND CZECH REPUBLIC
Maj Reini van Ommeren on 12 Aug 2013
Maj Sib Eikenaar-de Boer on 17 Aug 2013
Maj Francien Johanna Maghielse on 23 Aug 2013
Brig Derk Pieters on 27 Sep 2013
Brig Cornelia Krommenhoek-Oerlemans on 31 Mar 2014

NEW ZEALAND, FIJI AND TONGA
Maj Dorothy Middleton on 11 Sept 2013
Aux-Capt Keith Tremain on 1 Oct 2013
Maj Daphne Brinsdon on 16 Nov 2013
Capt Berys Glendinning on 29 Nov 2013
Lt-Col Vera Williamson on 28 Dec 2013
Aux-Capt Syd Rubie on 10 Mar 2014
Lt Lisa Collings (A) on 20 Apr 2014

NIGERIA
Maj Margaret Adibe on 2 Mar 2014
Maj Godwin B Akpan on 24 Apr 2014

NORWAY, ICELAND AND THE FÆROES
Maj Odd Sørenbye on 30 Oct 2013
Maj Kjell Oddvar Nygård on 2 Feb 2014
Maj Ester Blomsø on 4 Mar 2014
Maj Inger Johanne Bratlie on 29 Mar 2014

Maj Betzy Eikemo on 25 May 2014
Maj Trygve Woldsund on 27 Jul 2014

PAKISTAN
Capt Columbus Younas (A) on 20 Jan 2014
Major Allah Rakhi Puran on 20 Apr 2014
Major Arthur Suleman on 27 Apr 2014

THE PHILIPPINES
Maj Florante Parayno on 29 Aug 2013

SOUTH AMERICA WEST
Maj Martha de Huanca on 28 Mar 2014
Maj Maria Cofre Elias on 17 Apr 2014

SOUTHERN AFRICA
Maj Ndlovu Aleck Major on 23 May 2013
Comm Margaret King on 14 Sept 2013
Maj Ndlovu Mali on 3 Oct 2013
Capt Holmes Keith on 30 Jan 2014
Maj Ndlovu Maggie on 16 Feb 2014
Maj Thandi Nxumalo on 27 May 2014

SRI LANKA
Lt-Co W. James Wickramage on 22 Sep 2013
Maj Karunawathie Edirisinghe on 11 Jun 2014

SWEDEN AND LATVIA
Lt-Col Inga Samuelsson on 7 Aug 2013
Maj Therese Svenson on 5 Sept 2013
Maj Inger Goodwin on 21 Sept 2013
Capt Ieva Van Damme on 24 Sept 2013
Mrs Brig Maj-Britt Nordin on 22 Oct 2013
Maj Elsa Ödman on 12 Nov 2013
Maj Elsa Svensson on 19 Nov 2013
Capt Gunbritt Carlsson on 26 Nov 2013
Maj Gunny Bengtsson on 29 Nov 2013
Maj Jenny Lindh on 5 Dec 2013
Maj Agnes Wikberg on 7 Dec 2013
Capt Per-Olof Nilsson on 7 Jan 2014
Maj Birgitta Lindström on 7 Jan 2014
Env Ingmar Eriksson on 19 Jan 2014
Maj Edith Larsson on 19 Feb 2014
Maj Maj Johnsson on 20 Feb 2014
Maj Gerd Willén on Mar 2014
Maj Stina Ericson on 30 Apr 2014

SWITZERLAND, AUSTRIA AND HUNGARY
Maj Christine Messerli-Zingg on 17 Jul 2013
Brig August Rickenbach-Schwyzer on 26 Oct 2013

Lt-Col Liliane Donzé-Jeanneret on 9 Nov 2013
Brig Adrienne Roth-Genoux on 27 Dec 2013
Lt-Col Martha Mägli-Egger on 12 Jan 2014

UNITED KINGDOM
Mrs Maj Margaret Thomas on 3 Sept 2013
Maj Doreen Eland on 9 Sept 2013
Maj Donald Mason on 17 Sept 2013
Lt-Col Robert Waddams on 8 Oct 2013
Mrs Maj Florrie West on 11 Oct 2013
Maj Wendy Burlinson on 18 Oct 2013
Mrs Maj Gladys Hook on 21 Oct 2013
Maj Margaret Baxter on 22 Oct 2013
Mrs Lt-Col Florence Drury on 2 Nov 2013
Brig Sarah Fordyce on 2 Nov 2013
Maj William Green on 2 Nov 2013
Maj Audrey Holmes on 3 Nov 2013
Maj Audrey Wilson on 25 Nov 2013
Mrs Lt-Col Florence Jeffs on 29 Nov 2013
Maj E. Doreen Jones on 2 Dec 2013
Mrs Maj Hilda Bower on 7 Dec 2013
Maj Colin Banks on 23 Dec 2013
Maj Esme King on 26 Dec 2013
Lt-Col Jane Hassard on 1 Jan 2014
Maj Patricia Bowthorpe on 11 Jan 2014
Maj Martha Carter on 18 Jan 2014
Aux-Capt Bert Gibbs on 23 Jan 2014
Lt-Col Peter Moran (A) from London South-
East DHQ on 23 Jan 2014
Maj Mrs May McLachlan on 2 Feb 2014
Brig Eva Richardson on 12 Feb 2014
Mrs Maj Pamela Honeyball on 13 Feb 2014
Maj Ewart Griffin on 25 Feb 2014
Maj Agnes McClements on 7 Mar 2014
Maj Jean Bruce on 9 Mar 2014
Mrs Maj Daphne Methven on 20 Mar 2014
Maj Doris Longley on 22 Mar 2014
Brig Dora Chandler on 25 Mar 2014
Mrs Maj Gladys Oliver on 3 Apr 2014
Maj Arthur Brown on 16 Apr 2014
Maj Jean Wilkes on 4 May 2014
Maj Marjorie Beddows on 21 May 2014
Maj Brenda Smith on 22 May 2014
Mrs Comr Marjorie Gauntlett on 30 May 2014

USA CENTRAL
Maj John Werner on 17 Jun 2013
Maj Homer Fuqua on 6 Jul 2013
Lt-Col H. Bernard Lodge on 7 Sept 2013
Maj Robert Scott on 2 Oct 2013
Maj Nan Metz on 8 Oct 2013
Brig Ethel Geer on 18 Oct 2013
Maj Shirley Younts on 25 Oct 2013

Maj Elizabeth Anderson on 7 Nov 2013
Maj David Higgins on 27 Nov 2013
Maj Ralph Ashcraft on 7 Dec 2013
Brig Cecil Dye on 7 Dec 2013
Mrs Comr Carol Thomson on 10 Dec 2013
Mrs Maj Marjorie Fuqua on 14 Dec 2013
Mrs Maj Neoma Garrington on 15 Dec 2013
Mrs Maj Vivian Kimmons on 28 Dec 2013
Maj Norman Nonnweiler on 3 Jan 2014
Maj Shirley Horn on 10 Jan 2014
Capt Donald Meyer on 9 Feb 2014
Mrs Maj Arline Sundell on 21 Feb 2014
Maj Dorothy Hopps on 12 Mar 2014
Maj Herbert Fuqua Sr on 30 Mar 2014
Maj George Curtis Jr on 4 Apr 2014
Col Edgar Overstake on 5 Apr 2014
Maj Harold Hatfield on 23 Apr 2014
Mrs Maj Irene Jewett on 24 Apr 2014
Maj Irene Rubin on 14 May 2014
Maj Robert Reasoner on 15 May 2014
Maj Marilyn Werner on 25 May 2014
Lt-Col William Hasney on 6 Jun 2014
Aux-Capt Stephen Diaz (A) from St Louis
Temple, MO Corps on 20 Jul 2014
Maj Paul Fuqua on 24 Jul 2014

USA EASTERN
Maj Bruce Douglas Fleming on 25 July 13
Maj Peter H. Stritzinger on 7 Aug 13
Maj Harris Daniel Wood on 27 Aug 13
Maj Daniel Edward Hilty on 8 Sept 13
Maj Velma Ruth McGee on 15 Sept 13
Maj Mary C. Davis on 30 Sept 13
Comr George L. Nelting on 18 Oct 13
Maj Lawrence J. Shaffer on 21 Oct 13
Maj Doris Fuller on 28 Oct 13
Maj Barbara J. Kelly on 4 Nov 13
Mrs Maj Margaret Spencer on 26 Nov 13
Maj Wesley D. Foster on 6 Dec 13
Maj Emily Foreman on 10 Dec 13
Brig Frederick McCracken on 25 Dec 13
Maj Grace W. Hibler on 8 Jan 14
Mrs Maj Martha A. Foster on 11 Jan 14
Maj Dorothy Bair on 11 Jan 14
Mrs Brig Ruth Jackson on 12 Jan 14
Maj Franklin D. Brown on 15 Jan 14
Maj Warren A. Smith on 15 Jan 14
Maj Ruth Brown on 17 Jan 14
Maj William Tucker on 17 Feb 14
Lt-Col Paul D. Seiler on 24 Feb 14
Maj Andrea See on 27 Feb 14
Lt-Col Clifford R. Hall on 12 Mar 14
Maj Mrs. Marion E. Wheatley on 10 Apr 14

Mrs Maj Anne F. Bulla on 13 Apr 14
Maj Gladys M. Brown on 14 Apr 14
Maj Raymond W. Simpson on 21 Apr 14
Maj Delores M. Shaffer on 1 May 14
Mrs Lt-Col Luella N. Poole on 5 May 14

USA SOUTHERN
Aux-Capt Dale Efaw on 3 Jun 2013
Maj William Whittle on 3 Aug 2013
Maj Virgina Satcher on 10 Aug 2013
Maj Helen Case on 30 Aug 2013
Brig Bertie Mamie Robins on 6 Sep 2013
Brig Gertrude Ferking on 26 Sep 2013
Maj Ruth Hudson on 4 Oct 2013
A/Capt Sherwood Tidman on 3 Oct 2013
Brig Diana H. Wade Willoughby on 6 Oct
  2013
Maj Albert Steinhauer on 15 Nov 2013
Maj Patricia Wyatt on 29 Nov 2013
Maj Minnie Smith on 1 Jan 2014
Maj James Lane on 23 Feb 2014
Maj David Singletary on 25 Feb 2014
Maj Catherine Hill on 26 Feb 2014
Maj W. Orville Chambless (A) McKinney, TX,
  on 8 Mar 2014
Lt-Col Harold J. Anderson on 18 Mar 2014
Maj Mae Harris on 23 Apr 2014
Aux-Capt Aida Ruth Mayol on 11 May 2014

USA WESTERN
Mrs Maj Jean Upton on 7 Nov 2013
Lt-Col Raymond Peacock on 14 Nov 2013
Maj John Pearson on 27 Nov 2013
Maj Carol Ganot on 1 Dec 2013
Maj William Ricken on 1 Dec 2013
Mrs Maj Vera Elliott on 10 Jan 2014
Lt-Col Herbert Wiseman on 14 Feb 2014
Brig Robert Yardley on 6 Mar 2014
Maj Thomas Elliott on 23 Mar 2014
Capt Leonard Johnson on 31 Mar 2014
Maj Chester Danielson on 14 Apr 2014
Aux-Capt Grace Bearchell on 29 May 2014
Maj Dorothy Sparks on 21 June 2014
Maj Robert Anderson on 15 Jul 2014
Maj Clifford Dickinson on 28 Jul 2014
Lt-Col Florence 'Bunty' Robinson on 20 Aug
  2014

ZIMBABWE
Maj J Chisuvi on 20 Sep 2013
Maj E Muringai on 4 Nov 2013
Maj J Shamuyarira 29 Mar 2014

INDEX

Index

TERRITORIES (T), COMMANDS (C) AND REGIONS (R) WITHIN EACH ZONE

AFRICA (17)
Angola (C)
Congo (Brazzaville) (T)
Democratic Republic of Congo (T)
Ghana (T)
Kenya East (T)
Kenya West (T)
Liberia (C)
Malawi (T)
Mali (R)
Mozambique (T)
Nigeria (T)
Rwanda and Burundi (C)
Southern Africa (T)
Tanzania (T)
Uganda (T)
Zambia (T)
Zimbabwe (T)

AMERICAS AND CARIBBEAN (11)
Brazil (T)
Canada and Bermuda (T)
Caribbean (T)
Latin America North (T)
Mexico (T)
South America East (T)
South America West (T)
USA Central (T)
USA Eastern (T)
USA Southern (T)
USA Western (T)

EUROPE (12)
Denmark (T)
Eastern Europe (T)
Finland and Estonia (T)
France and Belgium (T)
Germany and Lithuania (T)
Italy and Greece (C)
The Netherlands and Czech
  Republic (T)
Norway, Iceland and The Færoes (T)
Spain and Portugal (C)
Sweden and Latvia (T)
Switzerland, Austria and Hungary (T)
United Kingdom with the Republic
  of Ireland (T)

SOUTH ASIA (10)
Bangladesh (C)
India Central (T)
India Eastern (T)
India Northern (T)
India South Eastern (T)
India South Western (T)
India Western (T)
Middle East (R)
Pakistan (T)
Sri Lanka (T)

SOUTH PACIFIC AND EAST ASIA (11)
Australia Eastern (T)
Australia Southern (T)
Hong Kong and Macau (C)
Indonesia (T)
Japan (T)
Korea (T)
New Zealand, Fiji and Tonga (T)
Papua New Guinea (T)
The Philippines (T)
Singapore, Malaysia and
  Myanmar (T)
Taiwan (R)